SAVING EUROPE

Feb 2018

SAVING EUROPE

A Tale of Two 'Dark Ages' in the Twilight of the Pax Europa

HENRY VYNER-BROOKS

Pravda Media

CONTENTS

Dedication:
To the Europeans of the mid-21st century
from whom so much will be asked.

'...it seemed impossible to them [the traumatised post-war generation] that either nature or humanity could have survived so long had not some semi-divine stranger with superhuman powers, some Gilgamesh or Napoleon..., appeared from time to time to rescue both, for a brief bright moment, from their egregious destructive blunders.'

From *Lament of a Lawgiver*, 1947,
by W. H. Auden

ACKNOWLEDGEMENTS

'Some men will never forgive a favour.' So spoke old Mr Sedley in an adaptation of Thackeray's *Vanity Fair*. As a dyslexic man of very moderate means, I cannot truthfully claim the sort of solitary genius that would expose my ego to the temptation of that species of ingratitude. 'What have ye that ye did not receive?' asks the apostle Paul. The simple answer to that is 'everything'. And anyway, a book of this sort could never just be the product of many thousand hours in the study, but also of the kindness of many friends – some old, some new, some I have met and many more that are long dead. From the (nearly) 1000 footnotes and references, the reader will readily see that I have kept some very exalted company in my study over the last four years - a study which until recently was in our laundry – a room so small that even the mice are hunchbacks. They say that the gnat does not know if it stands on giants' shoulders or those of ordinary size, and I too have often been guilty of taking the best books for granted. And though my debt to these is profound, yet there are too many authors to list separately here. Neither will I enumerate here those people who led me towards this project, for there is some mention of that strange journey in appendix one.

I must, though, mention my longsuffering agents Pieter and Elria Kwant, whose friendship and wisdom I have no hope of repaying. And I will also mention my dear friend Richard Betts, the polymath who edited an early draft and translated a French biography for me. He was also over-generous with his time in a later draft when help was thin on the ground, and when his incisive wisdom rescued this book from many serious blunders.

And what about the specialist historians? Dr. Dominic Erdozain, Dr. Alan Fimister and Dr. Alex O'Hara; who all stayed with our family at different stages of writing and all shaped my thinking and this manuscript in various ways. At the pub, on the beaches and in the fells, you were all seasoned musketeers to my hapless D'Artagnan.

Professor Picard, Bangor Harbour Interview, July 2018

And then there are the historians who generously allowed us to film interviews which formed part of the documentary and this book's research - Dr O'Hara and Dr Fimister are among them. Indeed, Alex manfully endured a stormy night on a monastic island in a rickety tent, with my whole family, and Alan almost got hypothermia when we filmed a long interview in a cave. He never once complained and we only stopped the cameras because I noticed his bottom lip was blue! All will agree, this goes beyond the call of duty. I am also greatly indebted to Professor Madeleine Gray (Cardiff), Professor Jean-Michel Picard (Dublin) and Dr. Philip Boobbyer (Kent), who also freely gave their time and scholarship for filmed interviews.

Also, my thanks to the directors & curators of museums and libraries across Europe who gave me access (often exclusively) to film them and their collections. In no particular order I thank; Dr Constanz Itzel at the House of European History (Brussels), Dr. Philip Lenz at the San Gallen Library (Switzerland), Dr. Albert Winner at the monastic library at Maria Laach (Germany), Laurent Thurnherr, director of Schuman's House (Metz), Dr. Sabine Steidle at the Adenauer House (Germany), *Initiative of Change's* Andrew and Elaine Stallybrass at the Caux Palace & MRA archive (Switzerland), Recteur Padre Antoni at *Sanctuaire Notre-Dame de La Salette Fallavaux* high in the Julian Alps (France), Tom Bole and the staff of North Down Museum (Northern Ireland), and lastly Jacques Prudeau; for being our handler at Luxeuil (France).

And then there are those, from the 'smallest' to the greatest who gave me their time, or even just local knowledge to allow this book's research to be grounded.

I think of the octogenarian peace activist Charles Danguy who I interviewed at his flat near Metz and who formed a direct link for me to Schuman's Alsace. And then there were the strangers without names who came to my help when my best research (and even Google) failed me. I think of a diminutive Austrian Nun in Bregenz who pointed me to Gall's church, and a Croatian cleaner who had the keys to an ancient frescoed crypt. I remember two very patient bakers in Bourg who overturned all my research about Schuman's final hiding place in the war, and then literally drove me four miles to the right building! Time and again French, Italian and German people were visibly moved by our interest in their unsung heroes. On that note, I should also thank

President Ferrand at the French National Assembly

Paris, Sept 2018, French National Assembly

an unwitting President Ferrand of the National Assembly (Paris) who we collared for an impromptu interview in 2018, despite his schedule, staff, security and crowds on a very busy day. His words of solidarity for and thanks to the UK, were generous and poignant.

(Needless to say, any views and errors in this book are no reflection on the people named above.) But there is no one mentioned here who deserves a tenth part of the praise and thanks as my own family. A man with six children must do his research and writing when and where he can.

They have endured family holidays, days out and even wedding anniversary breaks centred on aspects of this project. Tom and Will, who were 12 and 16 at the time of our European research trip, transformed themselves admirably into an amateur film crew over, what by any stretch of the imagination, (200-plus locations in 12 countries in 7 weeks) was a gruelling marathon.

All Wrapped Up: Ruth doing the final revisions in a chilly Jan 2021

And then to my PA: my research assistant, beta reader, copy editor, brewer of coffee, bringer of biscuits, psychotherapist, encourager in many a dark hour – my best friend and the wife of 24 years - unfathomably gracious, unflappably kind, to my wise and wonderful Ruth; I give the final and lasting thanks.

The delicious irony is that she, who could read at aged 4 and had to move libraries at 16 for want of books, married someone like me, a dyslexic, who could not read until he was 12, and whose A' level English teacher wanted him off the course because his essays were unmarkable. Columban's 7th century biographer Jonas would probably add here: *'wonderful Providence!'* for surely *"There's a divinity that shapes our ends, Rough hew them how we will."* My only defence is that I have not asked her, as Tolstoy did his wife, to bare him 13 children, and to copy out *War & Peace* 6 times! But if there be a circle of paradise for the longsuffering wives of such troublesome writers, then I shall expect to find her drinking tea with Mrs. Tolstoy from an self-filling golden tea-pot.

Following Columban across the Alps into Italy, Sept 2018

Henry Vyner-Brooks, January 2021

Introduction: The Two Witnesses

CHAPTER SUMMARY: JULY 1950, FRANCE - An unlikely overlap between the two principal subjects of the book in Luxeuil, France. JULY 2016, BRITAIN - The difficulties and opportunities of Brexit. 543-1963, COLUMBAN & SCHUMAN – A summary of Columban and Schuman's lives and why they matter. 2016 –2020, THIS BOOK - The author's approach and treatment of the subject.

JULY 1950 - FRANCE

The lengthening shadows of the July afternoon, reach from a makeshift platform across to Luxeuil Abbey. The crowds hush, and the tannoy whistles momentarily as one of the leading politicians of the age rises to speak. Around him are many eminent European statesmen. He has called them to this abbey in central France for a conference – or more precisely, a piece of sacramental political theatre. This is 1950, and Robert Schuman is about to call up the spirit of a 6th century Irish monk in the fight to save Europe from an apocalyptic Third World War. Saint Columban, who founded the abbey, was eventually extradited from the region as a trouble-making immigrant. And now, thirteen centuries later, a French Foreign Secretary will use this Irish émigré as a poster child for the most daring political project since the league of Delos unified the Greek city states. Schuman clears his throat and approaches the microphone. In that pause between breaths, the politicians of Europe hear a collared dove cooing somewhere very near them in the lime trees. For the briefest of moments, they look up – as all Europe looks up. And they together discern the sound that a few years back they thought they would never hear again. It is the dove of peace.

French Foreign Minister Robert Schuman at Columban's Abbey, Luxeiul, 1950

We shall return to this moment in chapter 16. But suffice to say for now, it is the improbability of the personalities involved in this epoch-making event, that form the grist of our story. And with that said, let us now begin by fast forwarding to the same month 66 years later.

JULY 2016 - BRITAIN

In the French language, everything that is good is feminine. But even they refer to our departure from the European Union as *le Brexit* – which is rather touching when you think about it.

But for good or evil, Britain did leave the EU with a moderate trade deal at the dawn of 2021. But during the long and acrimonious divorce from 2016-2021, I decided to do what I had not time to do during the furore of the referendum. I wanted to take a look through the long telescope of history and to ask questions that I could not quite articulate during the hubbub of the referendum. Like others, I found it hard at times to differentiate between being European and being in the E.U. Nevertheless, I still wanted to understand what, if anything, was so special about this group of nations that we call Europe. Furthermore; what was the philosophical and historical consciousness that formed such a singular culture and civilisation? How many strands of memory - sociological, legal, ethnic, historical and religious - bind us together? And of course, how much of this, if anything, would be affected by our leaving? The islands of Britain have always stood in a peculiar relation to their neighbours for good or ill, and sometimes both at once. But how much have we Britons helped to make them who they are over the last 2000 years? And how much have they made us who we are?

In 2017, these questions and many others haunted me. I, like many, had felt deeply inadequate to vote on something so momentous when I was so ignorant. And even though that moment has passed, I still believe this book could go some way to help us post-*Brexit*-Brits to appreciate, not just our own unique position in the European story, but also the depth and richness of our neighbours' stories that still define us. Like the French philosopher Paul Ricoeur[1], my hope is, to achieve some level of 'self-understanding by means of understanding others.'[2] An island, like ours, on the edge of a great landmass must not only exalt in but also 'conquer a remoteness'[3] of outlook. This 'Anglo-Celtic archipelago' must overcome a dual distance; firstly, between itself and its European partners, and secondly, between itself and its own history. Whatever the next decade will be for Britain, surely it cannot be a time of geographical and historical parochialism. A regiment may move some distance without its allies, but it cannot be severed from the supply train at the same time. Some speak as if our only concern should be economic. Brexit will certainly do many things. One may be to shake us out of our present rootless amnesia and send us searching for the great supply train of our rich history. People with dementia cannot plan for the future, says philosopher Alain de Botton. Herein lies a great part of our challenge – to reverse-engineer our cultural amnesia.

543-1963 - COLUMBAN & SCHUMAN

This book makes tentative steps to address both tasks. My *modus operandi* may seem unorthodox at first glance but there is method in it. I want to follow two eye witnesses – an Irish monk and a French politician – who, to my mind at least, form key historical markers at either end of our European consciousness. This consciousness first arose after the collapse of the Roman Empire, and then finally took root in the rubble of two nigh-apocalyptic world wars. In observing these two witnesses within the crucible of two 'dark ages'[4], we catch a greater perspective of our own dilemma.

Both eye-witnesses are extraordinary, yet relatively unknown men, who by their tenacity and – and dare I say – humility, played key roles in saving the European civilisation of their own day. We talk about it, but these men literally moved the hour-hand of history. The first, as already mentioned is the 6th century Irish monk Columban who often found himself acting as a reluctant statesman. The second is the 20th century French statesman Robert Schuman who very nearly became a monk.

This book will be our Tardis and in it we will travel, chapter by chapter, up and down the time corridor like Dr. Who; back and forth between these two 'Dark Ages', two epochs, and two unsung heroes. Caught as they were, between the great hinges of history, and as we are, between amnesia and memory, maybe we shall eventually return to the 21st century with a new perspective.

The first is **Columban or Columbanus (543-615)**, patron saint of bikers, and bad boy of medieval monasticism. More dissenter than revolutionary, Columban was a poet, preacher, prophet, polemicist, scholar, saint.[5] Alongside Charlemagne, Columban has been referred to as the *greatest man of the Middle Ages.*[6] His surviving literary corpus alone places him head and

Columban on an Irish postal stamp

shoulders above his contemporaries as the first great Irishman of letters.[7] But it was as a monastic founder that we owe him the greatest debt. He undertook a voluntary exile from his homeland and, through a missionary odyssey in France, Germany, Austria and Switzerland, finally came to the valley in Italy that Hemmingway declaimed 'the loveliest in the world.'[8] The five houses he founded on the continent multiplied to perhaps as many as two hundred *Schottenkloster* (Irish Monasteries) that became critical in the preservation and transmission of scholarship, faith and literacy over the next two crucial centuries. In fact, nearly all surviving 7th and 8th century manuscripts from continental Europe are directly due to this one man's monastic legacy.[9]

He was also the first of his countrymen to express an Irish sense of identity in writing, and the first to articulate for us the concept of a united Europe – making reference to *Totius Europea flaccentis augustissimus* – 'all of decaying Europe' – in a letter to the Pope.[10] At about the same time, and using a biblical metaphor[11] in a letter to the disgruntled Frankish bishops, he even gives a Christian basis for a supranational understanding between European nations. *'We are all members of one body, whether Franks, or Britons, or Irish or whatever our race.'* So even as far back as 600AD, when Europe was still reeling from the barbarian migrations, and 50 years of plague that halved its population, we have this Irish immigrant claiming openly that we Western Europeans already owe to each other allegiance that supersedes (though not replaces) racial and national identity. The historian Norman Davies wrote that Columbanus was 'the first to conceive of Europe as a civilizational unit centred on Rome.'[12]

According to the medieval scholar Dr. Alex O'Hara, Columban was also *'a forceful advocate for unity and tolerance in the divisive and violent world of his day. As an immigrant in the heart of Europe, he pleaded for toleration and accommodation. His example had a surprising influence on Robert Schuman, the post-war French foreign minister and architect of the modern European Union.'*[13]

Robert Schuman (1886-1963), is the second 'eyewitness' whose life and times I wish to retell in this book. Schuman broke-out of Nazi incarceration after seven months in solitary confinement, evaded the Gestapo in a daring solo escape across the Vosges Mountains, and then rose precariously after the war

Schuman with Churchill, Metz 1951

to become the French Foreign Minister and a founding Father of the EEC.

His life, and that of two other co-founders[14] form – at least from a historical novelist's point of view – one of the most thrilling, moving and uplifting stories in any political history of any era.

Both Columban and Schuman were men of steely determination, neither ever married, and both came to the major work of their lives in middle age – which should give some of us hope. In some nebulous way they form the brackets, or bookends, of the European experiment; Columban at the inception of *Totius Europea*, and Schuman at the cementation of that pan-national fiction into a political and economic reality.

2016-2020 – THIS BOOK

The ancient Greek writer Lucian advises that 'the historian among his books should forget his nationality.' But frankly, this sort of position, which so characterised the enlightenment's 'prejudice against prejudices'[15] has itself been given such a thorough drubbing in the twentieth century by scholars like Gadamer[16] that one has to wonder whether the objectivity of the natural sciences is desirable, let alone possible, in the humanities. Of course, I have tried to be as open handed with the sources as any red-blooded Englishman can be. And at the end of the day, Anglo-centrism is not a sin – not in the north of England at any rate! So, I bring a personal view about the evolution of Western European civilisation, gazing intently, as I do, from the *finibus extremis* of that great landmass. I am conscious that my necessarily restricted western/Latin European focus might strike the broader scholar as too occidental – too reflective of a limited Enlightenment historiography – but where I am able, I will pay my respects to African influence (when discussing Anthony, the Desert Fathers, and Augustine in chapters 1 and 2, and the influence of the East in chapters 1 and 15.)

I must also confess up front that I have not given equal wordage to the three great stages through which European culture has passed. The early stages of Pagan Rome and the Christian formation will receive vastly more wordage than the Enlightenment, partly because the latter is so well established, but also because the former is so little understood and appreciated among popular readers. This fact was rather visually highlighted to me in

September 2018 when I was very kindly received at the House of European History in Brussels to film an interview with their director Dr Constanz Itzel. This extraordinary and brilliant museum is well worth a whole day's visit, though the display ratios embraced the glaring bias of a European consciousness grounded in the Enlightenment. Having literally just travelled to Brussels from Aachen, the former centre of the (Carolingian) European Union in the 8th century, this did strike me as strange. It is rather like me pointing to a cake that is just coming out of the oven and exclaiming, 'Look! That oven has just made a cake!' It acknowledges an important process in the cake's production but shows that I have only just entered the kitchen. The fires of that industrial age certainly produced much heat, and perhaps some light too, but in this book, I invite you to join me on a journey much further back; to sample the raw ingredients; as it were, to read the recipe books; perhaps even meeting one or two chefs.

I, as a northern Brit have come to this subject like Columban came to the continent; from *de finibus extremis*, the extreme fringe. And, like Columban, who journeyed south, east and west, so I too have struck out overland, following my literary sources, looking for clues and narratives. My sources like his monastic band, are from diverse nations; Franks, Lombards, Scotti, Alemani, etc. With them, I have crossed and re-crossed borders, heard their languages, and enjoyed their cultures. In his excellent 2015 book *Silk Roads*, Peter Frankopan sought to re-centre European readers geographically.[17] But the book you are holding attempts something comparable in the more fundamental realms of spirituality and philosophy.

And if there might be a European position from which to judge these things, or at least a Western European one, perhaps we might claim it for Robert Schuman – '*un homme de frontieres*' – born between France and Germany and who was a mix of both geographically, biologically, linguistically and culturally. In his person and his policies, Schuman became the essential bridge between both at that critical hour. But even his developed position could not be seen as the bridge between the Enlightenment and the Romantics; between Kant and Hegel; for Schuman's unassuming humanism – so extraordinarily assured and productive – was a stranger synthesis than any might guess. More medieval than modern; more rooted in Aquinas than Rousseau, more indebted to the socio-political writings of the popes than the purveyors of the new ideologies – he was an enigma to many in his day, and would probably be an anathema to ours. Stranger still, his worldview was quite independently shared by his political counterparts in Italy and Germany. And in a paradox worthy of an epigram, it was the neo-scholastic humanism of Schuman, Adenauer, and De Gasperi that made possible, what Javier Solana called, 'the most innovative and successful integration process in the history of humankind.'[18] In the midst of the modern amnesia, they reached back further and, in so doing, achieved something more progressive than the progressives ever dreamt, and more pragmatic than the pragmatists ever compromised for. Answering journalists' questions after his famous declaration on May 9th 1951, Schuman quietly admitted before them all that it was *a leap into the unknown* and yet he and others were able to lead the shattered nations through that unmarked door. This is a simplistic analysis and really one that is only intended to whet the readers' appetites for something rich and unexpected.

Admittedly, these great men (and some very notable women who made and supported them) are not known well in Britain, and certainly not as they should be. When Alexander the Great reached Achilles' tomb he said *'happy are you, young man, for you will have the benefit of a great spokesman of your achievement.'* Alexander knew he couldn't find a man of Homer's ilk to write his own epitaph, and nor have Columban or Schuman through these efforts of mine. Columban was actually the first Irishman to be the subject of biography, and fortunately for us, it was written only shortly after his death. But alas, Schuman has no biography available in English at present – nor does De Gasperi, who we will also meet.[19]

Columbans' sense of his own inadequacy sums up my own dilemma perfectly; *'Who could listen to a greenhorn? Who is this bumptious babbler that dares to write such things unbidden?'*[20] I appreciate that our age demands specialisation but it also desperately needs synthesis too. Those of us blue-collar scholars who serve falteringly in the latter capacity will always face the accusation of superficiality, arrogance, and dilettantism. To the specialist philosophers, historians[21], sociologists, economists, and others, I ask for special clemency. For I have trespassed through many areas of scholarship without so much as wiping my feet. This story – which we have either forgotten, or lost[22] – must be retold, even if retold imperfectly. This

I say with all humility for, unlike others qualified in these fields of study, I have so much more to be humble about.

To the general reader I also offer a very Columban' confession; 'talia confragosa loca' - *I come from a rough place*. Far removed from the refinements of academia and the urban intelligentsia, I live in the far northwest of our island; a place where the Roman legions once defended the very borders of civilisation, and where the shepherds still count in old Norse. In fact, I live very literally in the shadow of England's highest mountains, and in a figure, I wish to lead the reader – as I have led many other visiting friends over the years – along precipitous ridges and through upland environments unfamiliar to them. I recently took my flatlander-Norfolk nephews along the infamous Striding Edge; a kilometre-long arête that yearly claims lives and where the adventurer is usually only ever one step from death. There is an under-path to the left and the right, but those who walk them inevitably only see half of the view. And I don't mean this as merely an aesthetic choice, for each under-path has its own dangers too. I remember as a boy taking the under-path with my father during a winter white-out because the snow, ice, and violent winds made the ridge too dangerous. But even in this event, we overshot the end of the ridge and found ourselves making a hazardously steep ascent in deep snow, arriving just under the summit. But for our ropes, ice axes, and crampons, even the 'safe' under-path might have killed us.

But my main point here is that at various points, depending on your political or religious leaning, you might earnestly long for the under-path of your persuasion. And at those times you will inevitably feel the strength of the metaphorical rope pulling you off your normal centre. Let it do so in good faith, friend, even for a short time. My real sympathy on this hike is with the agnostic and non-religious reader. By virtue of the very subjects under consideration, this climb will take you on paths very seldom trodden. From you, I ask for a very special trust and patience. Where I have been unjust, obtuse, or just plain wrong, please forgive and correct me. My intention was to create a basis for further dialogue, not entrenchment.

Having said all that, I do not doubt that even Christian readers will also find certain sections a stiff scramble. We are a recalcitrant breed of mountaineer – scrupulous over our maps and hi-tech gear – but unfamiliar with the vast mountain ranges beyond our neighbourhood. Poor us! With titans like Schuman and Columban, we will be forced to breathe the thin mountain air of Catholic ascetics, and even have some cherished, Protestant myths about the Celtic church overturned. Even Catholic readers will have to suffer the interpretations and criticism of a sympathetic but non-Catholic pen. For the Christian readers of the next generation, I want this book to be a seedbed of inspiration for cultural engagement beyond the church door. Readers from other world religions will find plenty to interest them but alas nothing that speaks of their faith's contributions to Europe's richly diverse culture. Again; my apologies. This was purely for brevity's sake, and for focus. My comments regarding Islamism, demography, and migration form the very briefest survey of mainstream scholarly literature and are not intended as a basis for racism or xenophobia, but rather for further dialogue. So again, my only plea is that you all have patience with the path I have paced out. I hold out my hands left and right. Let us climb together, grumbling where necessary but nevertheless keeping in step with our fellow adventurers – for I believe that the view is amply worth the journey. I close with Columban's plea 1400 years ago:

> *'If any of my words have outwardly caused offence to pious ears, pardon me for my treatment of such rugged passages.... And for the freedom of my customs, so to speak, was in part the cause of my boldness. For among us it is not who you are but how you make your case that counts...'*

Striding Edge in winter - site of sublime beauty and frequent tragedy

INTRODUCTION:
FOOTNOTES & REFERENCES

1. "In proposing to relate symbolic language to self-understanding, I think I fulfill the deepest wish of hermeneutics. The purpose of all interpretation is to conquer a remoteness, a distance between the past cultural epoch to which the text belongs and the interpreter himself. By overcoming this distance, by making himself contemporary with the text, the exegete can appropriate its meaning to himself: foreign, he makes it familiar, that is, he makes it his own. It is thus the growth of his own understanding of himself that he pursues through his understanding of others. Every hermeneutics is thus, explicitly or implicitly." Ricœur, Paul, Charles E. Reagan, and David Stewart. "*Existence and Hermeneutics.*" In *The Philosophy of Paul Ricœur: An Anthology of His Work.* Boston: Beacon Press, 1978, pp. 101, and 106.

2. Paul Ricoeur, *Memory, History, Forgetting*

3. Ibid

4. The term 'dark ages' is controversial (see Norman Davies, *The Isles*, p.173 Macmillan Publishers Ltd, 1999) and I have taken some stick from one professor already for using it. Frankly, I dislike the term too (first coined in the Renaissance) which has been symptomatic of a humanistic hubris that this book, and my Renaissance novels, have often sought to challenge. Yet, I have used it here nonetheless and not always in inverted commas either. Indeed, I seek to subvert the content of this term in the popular imagination by twinning it with the dark age of the 20th century.

5. He was acknowledged to be a saint without reference to any posthumous miracles.

6. "St Columban is one of the very great men who have dwelt in the land of France. He is, with Charlemagne, the greatest figure of the middle ages." Leon Cathlin, poet, novelist, and dramatist

7. Perhaps only because Columba of Iona's work was all lost.

8. He founded a monastery at Bobbio and its library (one of the richest in Europe) was the setting for Umberto Eco's famous novel, *The Name of the Rose.*

9. These are now in the libraries in Turin, Milan, and St. Gall.

10. The full opening sentence of the letter is 'O the holy lord, and father in Christ, the Roman [pope], most fair ornament of the Church, a certain most august flower, as it were, of the whole of withering Europe, distinguished speculator, as enjoying a divine contemplation of purity. I, poor dove in Christ, send greeting.'

11. Columban is referring to the Apostle Paul's metaphor of the church as the body of Christ in his first letter to the church in Corinth, Greece.

12. Norman Davies, *The Isles*, p.180 (Macmillan Publishers Ltd, 1999.)

13. Article in the Irish Times by my friend Dr. Alexander O'Hara. Mar 17, 2017. 'The first poem about Ireland by a monk who inspired Heaney and the EU's architect'

14. In Italy, Alcide de Gasperi and in Germany, Konrad Adenauer

15. Following Heidegger's lead, H. G. Gadamer criticized Enlightenment thinkers for harbouring a "prejudice against prejudices". Gonzalez, Francisco J, *"Dialectic and Dialogue in the Hermeneutics of Paul Ricoeur and H.G. Gadamer,"* Continental Philosophy Review, 39 (2006), 328.

16. Hans-Georg Gadamer (1900 –2002) was a German philosopher of the continental tradition, best known for his 1960 magnum opus *Truth and Method* (Wahrheit und Methode) on hermeneutics.

17. Excellent it certainly was, I felt that some assertions regarding medieval European backwardness were overstated. Perhaps borne of a sincere desire to help us escape our Occidentalism, I personally could not read some passages without sensing the taint of a post-modernity's more general disdain of all things western in general, and Christian, in particular.

18. Javier Solana (former Secretary General of the Council of the European Union, and High Representative of the Common Foreign and Security Policy) wrote this in his forward to Victoria Martin De La Torre's wonderful book, *Europe, A Leap into the Unknown.*

19. Amongst others, I have used Robert de Rochefort's French version, who was a friend of Schuman and member of his cabinet. And those wishing to go further can easily find numerous other biographies and secondary sources mentioned in the footnotes. It is a rich trail to follow.

20. Columban's 5th Letter. But I will also add that at many times I have felt a supernatural help and leading in the creation of this book. For example, on the day it went to print, the eve of my 49th birthday, I was doing the final corrections to the typeset manuscript, and also listening to *Boswell's Life of Samuel Johnson* as I worked. Because the book is essentially dedicated to Millenials, my ears pricked up when I heard Johnson, in a letter to a 21-year-old man, write, *'Do take notice of my example and learn from the danger of delay. When I was as you are now, towering in the confidence of twenty-one, little did I suspect that I would be at forty-nine, what I am now.... You are busy in acquiring and in communicating knowledge, and while you are studying, enjoy the end of study, by making others wiser and happier.'*

21. Amongst Celtic specialists, those heirs of Gaulfidus - Geoffrey of Monmouth (1100-55) - I fear my condemnation will be the greatest; for their particular academic fields have always been hermetically sealed. (ref. Norman Davies, *The Isles*, p.87 (Macmillan Publishers Ltd, 1999.)

Filming in Piedmont, by the Arch of Augustus in Susa, Italy, Sept 2018

22. It was the Theologian Robert Jenson who wrote 'the world has lost its story.'

CHAPTER 1

In the Beginning

CHAPTER SUMMARY: PART 1. 2000-1000 BC – From the myth of Europa to the rise of Aegean civilisation. 1000 BC – 1 AD – The rise of Rome and the arrival of the Christian revolution. **PART II** - 0-400 AD - The decline of Rome, the survival of Christianity, and the arrival of the 'Barbarians.'

'Everything in life is memory,
save for the thin edge of the present'

Cognitive Neurologist Michael Gazzanigo

'Now the Keltoi (Celts) are outside the Pillars of Heracles (Gibral-
tar) and ....dwell furthest towards the sunset of all those who have
their dwelling in Europe.... as to the extremities of Europe towards
the West, I am not able to speak with certainty: for neither do I ac-
cept the tale that there is a river called in Barbarian tongue Eri-
danos, flowing into the sea which lies towards the North Wind,
whence it is said that amber comes; nor do I know of the real exis-
tence of "Tin Islands" from which tin comes to us.'

Histories, Herodotus of Halicarnassus

PART I: 2000-1000 BC – FROM THE MYTH OF EUROPA TO THE RISE OF AEGEAN CIVILISATION

Thus enters Europe, that last unexplored peninsula of the Eurasian landmass, into what many regard as the foundational document of Western Civilisation. Incidentally, the 'Tin islands' mentioned above is one of Europe's offshore islands that we now call Britain. In 325BC, one hundred years after Homer's death, Pytheas of Marseilles gave an eyewitness account of how our Celtic forebears brought tin in carts down to the beaches to trade with foreign merchants. One cannot but read Herodotus' references to us without getting that delicious feeling that 19th century American settlers must have known so well when they looked west; mystery, adventure, possibility.[23] So even as late as the 5th Century BC, and even as near as Halicarnassus (which is only in modern day Turkey), the gaze of the romantics and adventurers was not east to the silks of Persia, but north and west to the tin, amber and gold of Europe – fabled lands of the sunset. How strange it is that for the Greeks, the real hesperidin possibilities lay precisely where the Eritrean or Syrian migrants are now heading – towards us.

Herodotus is modest about what he thinks may be ascertained about our forebears. He is ambivalent as to whether Hesiod's fabled amber river really existed. The Eridanos river mentioned above is actually Hesiod's River to Hades – the world of the dead. But he is more certain, as are the African migrants, *'that towards the North of Europe, there is evidently a quantity of gold by far larger than in any other land.'* Herodotus is not sure *'how it is got,'* but he has heard that these riches *'most beautiful and the most rare'* are often *'carried off from the griffins by Arimaspians, a one-eyed race of men.'* Those with a taste for ancient apocalyptic, nay prophetic literature, might read herein a mystical allusion to our current blight of financial scandals, where a certain strain of myopia is also not unknown. But Herodotus does not credit the tale anyway, so let us leave those one-eyed, gold-stealing rascals to enjoy their ill-gotten gains and move swiftly on to what may be known. How about the name Europe, for example?

Alas, even here Herodotus can only hint. 'As to Europe however, it is neither known by any man ... whence it got this name or who he was who gave it, unless we shall say that the land received its name from Europa the Tyrian; and if so, it would appear that before this it was nameless like the rest.'

So, who is *Europa the Tyrian*, you might ask? Well, she was not a white middle-class man, which might be a relief to some, but an olive-skinned Lebanese teen girl who was sunbathing on the beach with her friends when something out of the ordinary happened. Yes, you might have guessed that we are about to stray into the world of Greek myths. Of course, there is a threshold above which we have, and need to have, respectable history. But we should not discount the great reservoir of poetic truth below that threshold – what one historian called 'subliminal history'.[24] Our first respectable mentions in history are those quoted above by Herodotus. After him, Aristotle, who differentiates the Greeks from Europeans, complements us as being 'full of spirit,' though 'being deficient in intelligence and skill.'[25] So much for the respectable record! Fortunately for us, in the subliminal record of myths and legends, our origins take on a richly suggestive texture.

The Myth of Europa goes something like this: a girl from Tyre was once seduced and carried across the sea to Crete by Zeus in the guise of a white bull. But from here on there is divergence in the records. One version of the myth claims that in order to secure Europa's willing consent to sex, Aphrodite promised that a continent would be named after her. Thereafter the legend claims that Zeus married her to King Asterion of Crete and although the royal marriage proved fruitless, the king

Europa riding Zeus (disguised as a bull)

adopted three sons, one of which was Minos. You can see where this is going, I hope. From that Minoan civilisation came the Greek and Latin Civilisations. And into that Greco-Roman world, came a further ineluctable, cultural force; Christianity, which came to us[26], as did Europa herself, riding the path of the sun, east to west. From that fusion came a civilisation that has transformed the countries of what we now call East and Western Europe. And from her colonies and trading empires, there is no continent – not even Antarctica – that has escaped her influence for good or ill.

This crude summary does no justice to the great south-north thrust of African Christian influence, nor to the complexities of the north-east influence from Byzantium. Nor does it allow us to gaze north, south and east with Europa's eyes to see the great power blocks like Egypt and Sumeria that also shaped those cultures at the dawn of respectable history. *But suffer it to be so for now.* Our aim here is simplicity, our direction; to follow the path of the setting sun.

But, before we do strike off west into the barbarous hinterland, leaving behind us known civilisation, let us examine briefly our cultural DNA in Crete. For there are many aspects of this tale that, if nothing else, have a heuristic value for our journey. In the Bronze Age, the Aegean was the 'cultural collector and distributor'[27] of the ancient world. The Minoans were wheat growers who had domesticated cattle, and perhaps were already cultivating wine and olive oil for export on their many maritime trade routes. They had created a sophisticated, domestic architecture that any modern European would recognise; three storey town houses, suburban villas, and even country mansions and palaces. They left no literature, but we know that they were much like us; artists, traders, builders, travellers, and colonisers. The tantalising glimpses revealed by Arthur Evans' excavations of athletes vaulting bulls show us that they also had some spirit. In fact, it is a sport still practiced in various guises in Spain and France even today. In his book *The Birth of Europe*, Michael Andrews makes an apt comparison between these islanders – our political ancestors – and the warrior barbarians of mainland Western Europe who, I suppose, we could call our genetic ancestors.

> *'...the first development of the city states took place not on the fertile open central European plains, but in a remote island to the south of the Aegean Sea which was completely lacking in metal resources. While the glittering mounted warrior-princes of central Europe dissipated their creative energy in warfare, a highly cultured yet peaceful society, built on trade and an agricultural surplus, emerged on Crete.* [28]

Their achievement was staggering when we set it in the context of history. How did these – what Evans called – Minoans, make such a quantum leap? This is a hard question, but certainly part of the reason that the Cyclades became the cradle of Western civilisation, is simple geography. No island could be entirely self-sufficient, and only a very few could supply the others with metals. Therefore, the Cretans, whose arable landmass was the greatest, used their agricultural surplus as the basis, and also the impetus, to form mutual trade ties with the other islands. Europa's stepson Minos was the king whose fleet helped him dominate the Cyclades and it was predominantly he, who established the trading colonies, which made the Minoan rulers the most powerful in Europe. Homer says that Crete had 90 cities. The palace of Knossos, which covers a staggering 75 hectares – the footprint of 75 sporting arenas – gives us some idea of their wealth and achievements. It was laid out by an architect called Daedalus. Four and a half thousand years later the ruins still include a staircase of engineering genius and a lavatory with a full water flush system. From their great granaries above the sea, the Minoans exported the necessaries of existence across the seas and in return reaped every luxury. And as they expanded their trading connections, so too increased the prosperity of those other islands. On the island of Lemnos, for example, the first proto-European city was built at Poliochini, which held the key location at the gates of the Dardanelles for the metals trade. In 2019 a Bronze age art expert Marie Nicole Pareja found some startling evidence that suggested that the Minoans were even trading as far as Asia.[29]

The Minoans, along with their stories, were eventually destroyed by a combination of calamities few civilisations could withstand. First was the great volcanic eruption on the Island of Thera, whose tsunami wave destroyed her navy and thus her trade. But it was not a tsunami that destroyed the palaces, nor volcanic ash as the great volcanic cloud emitting from Thera was blown north east over Turkey. The Cretan capital's fall wasn't the direct result of the eruption per se, but more likely the knock-on consequences of it. The collapse of a centralised economy must have wreaked civic havoc and sparked internal despoliation among the Cretans themselves, and their neighbours who still had ships. An economy that had drifted too far from its origins in agricultural surplus, too dependent on luxury goods, was as vulnerable to markets shocks then as it would be now – as we are only too aware.

But that was not all. On top of that tectonic catastrophe came yet another menace; the rampant despoliation by her neighbours. Nothing like being kicked when you are down! Who were these wreckers? Actually, it was the Greeks, of all people.[30] The weakening effects of volcanic eruption on Thera made the Minoans an easy prey for the Mycenaean Greeks – who represent for us the more barbarous warrior cultures of mainland Europe. In a sense, they are us. The displacement or subsuming of Minoan civilisation that took place then, would be much like the more familiar barbarian hordes moving on Europe in a later 4th-6th century AD 'Dark Age,' which we will examine later in this chapter. This idea of a proverbial dark age, or a period of regression following climatic or geopolitical upheaval is a recurring theme in European history.

By 1200 BC, even these usurping Mycenaean Greeks, along with vast swathes of the 'known' world were also suffering a nigh apocalyptic climate change event. During this time came horrific droughts, mass migrations and population collapse from Anatolia to Persia, and right across to Libya. The climatic effects manifested in mid-to-northern Europe more like a mini-ice age – enlarging glaciers and rising lake levels, drowning settlements. Aegean civilisation collapsed under the weight of the catastrophe that left few unscathed. One of the reasons why so little is known of this 'Iron Age' Dark Age is because under its burden of sorrows, Greek literacy collapsed. So, from the Iron Age to the 8th century there is no written record, only tantalising archaeological, environmental markers. By the time blind Homer writes of that former age, it was already a distant oral memory. Odysseus's Ithaca was already a second lost ideal, a fallen utopia of aristocratic virtue.

And from the ashes of that catastrophe, the Greek city states arose. The Athenian Greeks were as much slaves of their geography as their Minoan forebears had been. With only 20% cultivatable land and a rugged shoreline,[31] they, like their ancestors, were forced to look outwards for raw materials. And in so doing they inadvertently took Hellenic culture to the world. We can make too much of these geophysical factors, but even so, a strong case can be made that Western Europe has been, and still is, the great beneficiary of its geography. We have been formed every bit as much as the Greeks by the constraints of our environment, climate and natural resources.

There is almost too much we can say about the Athenian Greeks, indeed so much is written that it seems pointless to do so, other than raise a few points that throw light on our own situation in the 21st century. We are only too apt to imagine Athens was like San Francisco is now – full of liberal progressives with togas, rather than iPhones and artisan breads. But the *Demos* of that fledgling democracy, those actually able to vote, were only that certain class of men who had done military service. It was a very limited franchise. Furthermore, for every one of the 30,000 inhabitants of Athens, there was a corresponding slave working down the Laurion mines a few miles south in unimaginable misery.[32] This does not take into account the slaves living in the cities or working the land. It might have appeared idyllic, or the best possible of worlds under the circumstances, if you were one of the fortunate few, but from our standpoint, it was a dystopia on a par with anything imagined by our science fiction writers.

What is extraordinary, and rather instructive for us as we consider the geopolitical climate of the future, is that such brutal and appalling inequality in ancient Greece was ironically shared out more equally than anyone then imagined. When considered over decades and centuries of time, the inequality took its toll on those who had participated in the inequity of a previous generation. 'Few families owning property in Attica at this time can be traced for more than three generations before their fortunes fell.'[33] It is a lesson the west has been slow to learn. In their book 'Spirit Level' Professors Richard Wilkinson and Kate Picket show that countries with larger income differences experience increased social problems like violence, teen pregnancy, drug abuse, poor physical and mental health, and a decrease in child well-being, social cohesion, and social mobility decrease.[34]

The first and very limited democracy of the world was enabled and established on the inequities of its metals trade, the profits of which were shared amongst its citizens. Incidentally, what saved them – and perhaps all of Western Europe – from being subsumed into the Persian Empire was Thermistocles' law which redirected those very profits into armaments, in their case, a fleet of 200 new *trireme* ships.

In the 5th century BC, the supposedly united city states of Greece were not unlike the strained federated states of Europe, post-Maastricht. In the case of these ancient Greeks, it was an excess of 'civic pride' that was 'the midwife for a generation of destruction... Envy, fear, and greed between city and city, nurtured by a culture steeped in the honour of battle, led to a self-perpetuating struggle for wealth through conquest. Once the Persian menace had been curbed, the League of Delos had no function and began to break up.'[35] Here is a terrible lesson for us, and one which outside commentators like George Friedman observed of the current European situation. As the German menace passed from memory, a purely secular European Union had no mandate for existence beyond enabling 'prosperity and peace', i.e. for a vast majority of politicians and peoples it had purely prudential components and not moral ones. If the EU could not maintain the prosperity element – and demography is stacked against that – it is one leg of a three-legged stool gone. I am noting this now for we shall come back to this point in greater detail in later chapters. The League of Delos failed and while Greece dissipated its strength in the Peloponnesian and Syracusan Wars; Carthage and Rome arose. And this was how the mainland Greeks who had despoiled Crete were themselves eventually despoiled a thousand years later by the next upstart civilisation.

The Greek historian Polybius laments how, in 146BC, the Roman General Mummius asset stripped[36] Corinth:

> *'...the town was stripped of everything of value and the works of art, pictures, statues, and ornaments of every description were collected for transport to Italy. Much, however, was spoilt by the greedy and ignorant soldiers, and Polybius – who had recently returned from a similar spectacle in Carthage – saw some of the finest pictures thrown to the ground and used as dice boards. ...Corinth was then dismantled and burnt, and remained a mere village until its restoration in 46 by Caesar.'*

So poor Greece, who had held the baton so long and carried it so far, became a prey to the cultural appropriation of others. This was the vigorous yet sadder infancy of our civilisation, where the weakness of your neighbour was regarded as your strength. The mature age of solidarity between nations – the *European Spirit* as we now call it, or at least used to call it – is still two millennia away. But let us momentarily return to that Lebanese girl on Crete, for it was Europa's brother Cadmus, who had been sent to look for her, who founded Thebes and very thoughtfully brought the alphabet with him. Greek literature; drama, ethics, metaphysics and philosophy are still studied today. Their quest for the *Eudaemonia* – the good life – is still our unmet quest to the same extent.[37] Their civic architecture, perhaps part inheritance from the Minoans, is one of our great debts to them, for it expresses in durable terms the social cohesion necessary, not just for the *douceur de vivre* of community life, but also for the arts and sciences to flourish. As Kenneth

Clarke reminds us in his book and landmark 1969 TV series,[38] civilisation requires *confidence and permanence*. The roots of these two go
down deeply. A civilisation is an amalgam of shared cultures over a significant period of time. Clarke wrote that we often mistake the by-prod-
ucts of civilisation – liberal democracy and fine art – for the substance
of it, we confuse the icing for the cake – or in Marxian terms, the base
for the superstructure.[39]

1000 BC – 1 AD – FROM THE RISE OF ROME TO THE DAWN OF THE CHRISTIAN REVOLUTION

The Romans soon began to display a confidence that was hard to at-
tribute to any singular cause. Cicero thought it an accidental empire,
and that Rome had merely been defending her borders. But the Greek
Polybius, mentioned above, devoted 40 volumes to this and, in the end,
decided that there was a manifest destiny about it all. We tend not to at-
tribute such superstitious causes to the rise of empires of nations anymore, but perhaps at some level – even when Roman military drive, and
their prodigious ability to organise have been taken into account – the
rise of Rome will always be a few parts mystery. They felt a collective
inferiority to the Greeks but, as Virgil expresses below, they also knew
where they surpassed them,

> *"The Greeks shape bronze statues so real they seem to breathe,*
> *And carve cold marble until it almost comes to life.*
> *The Greeks compose great orations, and measure*
> *The heavens so well they can predict the rising of the stars.*
> *But you, Romans, remember your great arts;*
> *To govern the peoples with authority,*
> *To establish peace under the rule of law,*
> *To conquer the mighty, and show them mercy once they are*
> *conquered, and overthrow the haughty by means of war."*[40]

That reference, in the final line, of showing mercy to the conquered was something that historian Ronald Syme thought lacking in the British empire. Syme would have had George Washington in the House of Lords, and Patrick Henry as the colonial governor of Virginia. It is a fairly made point; and hindsight is a marvellous thing. The British policy resembled more often that of Alexander the Great; but even the Roman advance was hardly strewn with the garlands of peace and civility.

For example, one of the less known, rather depressing, but quite extraordinarily effective transmitters of Roman culture into Europe was wine. The Etruscans, who we always think of as bacchanalian sorts – probably from all those carousing pictures on the earthenware – were actually taught the darker arts of viniculture by Mycenaean Greek traders and colonisers.[41] It seems amazing now, but wine cultivation and grape fermentation did not seem to exist in early Etruscan society. From Italy, the Etruscans traded the new wonder drink as far around the coast to Marseille and even up the Rhone. Incidentally, Western European rivers formed a geographical kick-starter to the peninsula's trading wealth. The mighty Danube provided low-cost transport to the Black Sea, the Rhine to the North Sea, and the Rhone to the Mediterranean. (Russian rivers are not so advantageously placed and its reliance on costly land transport was a weakness.)[42]

But back to the wine imports travelling up the Rhone, which increased over the centuries. These, started with the Etruscans who eventually became the Romans with whom we are more familiar. By the 1st century BC Diodorus tells us that the demand for Roman wine among the northern barbarians was so great that 'for one amphora of wine [traders] receive in return a slave, a servant in exchange for a drink.'[43] So great was the demand that a new destructive economic cycle began. The northern chieftains engaged in more wars to get more slaves, in order to trade for more wine. In return, the Romans used the slaves on their estates around the Rhone to increase wine production. And so, in a macabre dance of befuddled misery, wine, war and Roman culture advanced hand in hand up the Rhone into north-Western Europe even before the legions marched there. But before we get side-tracked drawing comparisons with later European colonial history, let us pull back in all sobriety and redirect our gaze from the amphora to the altars of our cultural forebears.

The Greeks and Romans were a very religious and, we would say, superstitious people. The poet and essayist T.S. Elliot observed that,

> *'no culture has appeared or developed except together with a religion, according to the point of view of the observer, the culture will appear to be the product of the religion, or the religion the product of the culture.'*

In his writing, the theologian Walter Wink puts great store by our projections onto the sacred and then, by extension, back into the secular. As Voltaire put it *'Si Dieu nous a faits à son image, nous le lui avons bien rendu,'* which roughly translates as 'If God created us in his image, we certainly paid him back.'

So, let us ask the question; might there be something to learn about the modern Europeans by seeing the gods they worshipped? We have spent too long talking of material considerations; geography, resources, trade; for these are not the sum total – or even the half – of the forces that birth and sustain a civilisation. 'Man does not live by bread alone.' We have spent so much time convincing ourselves that we are so like the animals, that we have forgotten how very unlike them we are. Anthropological accounts for the origins of religion are very often insightful but sometimes unconvincing. Elliot and Wink's give a good rule of thumb. And Voltaire, who after all wanted to be buried half in and half out of the churchyard, will make us cautious of rushing to conclusions either way as we examine the core spiritual commitments of our ancestors.

The first thing that would strike us, is that the Greek gods lived apart from the populace on the mountains of Olympus – the *old man upstairs* syndrome. Curiously, we find that later on in Rome, the gods lived below, in the temples of the Forum – looked down upon by the emperor's palace. Much could be read into this fact alone. But either way, both the immortal Greek gods and Roman deities shared the same human frailties. They enjoyed an *infinite extension of existence with no corresponding projection of moral qualities.*[44] They were essentially gods unworthy of worship, deities to be avoided by the sensible or even denied by the bold. The word *'Atheistos'* originally meant someone who denied the traditional religion of the establishment.[45] In Greece it was punishable by death, as noble Socrates discovered.

The Romans, in their turn, absorbed the Greek pantheon, as they did the great legacy of Greek art. But they were pious and pragmatic in equal measure. The great tension between the Stoic and Epicurean philosophy came as part of the package, and by the 1st Century BC it would seem that Epicureanism had the upper hand. Edward Gibbon, often unreliable and perhaps with a hint of wishful thinking, says that Epicurus' type of atheistic materialism was almost universal in Rome by then. Gibbon approved, as did the proto-Darwinian, Roman poet Lucretius,[46] who said that religion was all based on fear.[47] Materialism was for Lucretius' generation, as it is for ours, not a fact of experience but a metaphysical prejudice. And it is not hard to see why an *atheistos* of late antiquity would come to that conclusion when browsing the mass of unworthy gods worshiped in Europe at that time.

The origins of the antique gods, came west with the waves of the migrants alluded to earlier. The migrants came west speaking their Indo-European languages – Celtic, Germanic, Nordic, Roman, Greek, Slavic, and more. (One cannot but think of the 19th century pioneering families who sought a similar path toward the setting sun across the prairies and plains of North America.) Amazingly, some of our most ancient forebears in the old world even come down to us with names; like Abram, Sarai and Lot mentioned in the Bible. Abram, later called Abraham, left behind the Sumerian city of Ur, almost every bit as modern and sophisticated as Boston or New York was in 1830.

Abram and Sarai turned their backs on two-storey villas with central heating and running water, and inglenook fireplaces that would not become out of place in a Cotswold cottage 4000 years later. At the call of a then unknown God, Abram journeyed away from the comforts of arithmetic, geometry, astronomy, agriculture, the wheel, the arch, the plough, irrigation; for the barbarities of the west. Familiar to him, as to us, was the lunisolar calendar, bronze sculpture, and delicate jewellery. Those Sumerians had the first legal code, writing and literature, leatherwork, saws, chisels, hammers, braces, nails, pins, rings, hoes, axes, knives, arrowheads, swords, glue, boots, sandals, harpoons, and beer. They even had a centralised tax records office. (If that does not make them identifiable enough, then consider that it was from these Sumerians in 1900BC that we have the first written joke too – which I am sorry to report was about farting.) And this was almost the exact moment Abram came west. He either left behind these innovations, or else like many others before him, brought them with him around the Fertile Crescent. In fact, he is almost symbolic of the movement I have crudely suggested throughout this chapter. And like Abram *the Hebrew* (literally; one from beyond the river) those pioneers brought not just their languages and technologies, but also their religious and philosophical worldviews.

Abram also brought news west, of a single deity; in sharp contrast to the cohorts of gods worshipped by our pagan ancestors there. Jumping forward in time, a quick survey of the gods and goddesses of Europe will give us the general flavour of our ancestors' inner geography: *AESIR, principal race of gods in Norse mythology; ANDHRIMNIR, the cook of the Aesir; ANGRBODA, goddess and wife of Loki, ASTRILD, goddess of love; ATLA, water goddess; AUDHUMLA, the primeval cow, formed from the melting ice; BALDER, fairest of the gods; BEYLA, the servant of Freyr; BORGHILD, goddess of the evening mist or moon, she slays the sun each evening; BRAGI, god of poets and the patron of all skaldi (poets) in Norse culture; BRONO, son of Balder, god of daylight; BYLGIA, water goddess; THOR, thunder-god and the protector of men and gods; TYR, the original god of war in the Germanic culture; ULL, god of justice, duelling and archery; VALI, son of Odin, and the god born to avenge the death of Balder; VALKYRIES, the battle-maidens, who choose the best warriors; VANIR, a group of fertility and nature gods; VAR, goddess of contracts and marriage agreements; VIDAR, son of Odin and the god of silence and vengeance.*[48]

Whatever happened to all these gods and goddesses? Has anyone seriously tried in the last 1500 years to build another temple to Balder – or Apollo for that matter? Gibbon, with more than a little cynicism and wish-fulfilment, wrote that the "various modes of worship which prevailed in the Roman world were all considered by the people as equally true; by the philosopher as equally false; and by the magistrate as equally useful. And thus, toleration produced not only mutual indulgence but even religious concord."[49] The extent of that indulgence and concord were shown, first in the sporadic persecution of the Christians, then in the mass conversion of the Roman world to Christianity. And so strangest of all eventualities, it was the God of Abram who prevailed, or at least outlasted the others when their claims were no longer found compelling. Yahweh – a particle of the verb to be, so something like 'the always existing one' – is a God who seems well fitted to the gaping needs of our present age; the self-proclaimed father to the fatherless, the tender defender of widows and asylum seekers, the great denouncer of social injustice, the ultimate avenger of every crime – be it violent, verbal or financial.

If I have read the Hebrew prophets aright (from Amos to Jeremiah, John the Baptist to John the Disciple) we get the picture of a God who is, if anything, more open to the charge of behaving like an indulgent parent than the divine tyrant which people often accuse him of being. Indeed, this seems to be the prophet Jonah's hidden motivation for not going to preach forgiveness to the wicked Ninevites who were the military superpower of the day. Jonah knew that God would forgive them, even for all their cruelties, and afterwards they would tread that kindness underfoot. And of course, Jonah was proved right. It confirms everything we already know about other people and about ourselves. God's concern was for people trapped in moral ignorance and for the animals....'should I not have concern for the great city of Nineveh, in which there are more than a hundred and twenty thousand people who cannot tell their right hand from their left—and also many animals?'

I don't mean here to deny there are difficult passages regarding punishments, ethnic wars, and the like, but I do want to stress that there is something very unusual about Yahweh when set alongside say Zeus, Baal, Marduk, Molech, or Apollo. Our job here is brevity and balance. And the balance of the Jewish scriptures is God's unusual tender mercy. It is summed up by Jesus' half-brother James in a letter where he writes that with God 'mercy triumphs over justice.'[50] Now, if we were looking for a metaphysical proposition that has underpinned western civilisation – a projection of a deity into secular cultural formation – then perhaps we have it here.

Jesus only confirmed and strengthened what the Old Testament revealed; a Father-God, tough on sin; but on the sinner; merciful to a fault – in fact, merciful to the point of allowing the punishment for our failure to fall on him, thus satisfying the justice we demand for others and the mercy we need ourselves.[51] The ancient deities of Europe could not adequately compete with a key that seemed to fit the human predicament so effortlessly and so completely. Zeus or Apollo might appear on earth in humbler form in order to mask their identity; but the early Christians – who were initially all Jews – understood that by truly becoming man Yahweh had come to earth, not in disguise, but to reveal himself in the truest, most incontrovertible way possible. Words can be misunderstood. Letters and ambassadors can be interpreted wrongly. But none but the most wicked could misinterpret the acts of a deity who chose to be born in a stable, grow up as an asylum seeker, to live among the poorest as a healer and teacher, and then to endure torture and execution at the hands of institutional injustice – while all the time forgiving his tormentors. No one can misinterpret that. As the New Testament says, 'In these last days God has spoken to us through his son.' This message – which quite understandably was called *the good news*, or Gospel – spread rapidly among the lower strata of society. Amidst great opposition and misunderstanding, sporadic persecutions – social and sometimes bloody – the followers of *The Way* grew and grew in number until the economic base of pagan worship itself was affected.

Quite how fast Christianity spread is still a matter of scholarly debate. Extravagant claims are often made but as Dr. George Herring reminds us, 'certain numbers, or percentages, tend to be repeated in a range of modern textbooks,'[52] including the figure of 50,000 Christians by AD 100, and the claim that 10% of the population of the Empire by AD 300.[53] Other scholars, like Robin Lane Fox, are more circumspect, estimating Christian concentration at 2% by AD 250 and under 5% by the early 5th century.[54] The lower figure may be credible when one considers that Herodian's third century histories contain no mention of Christians whatever. Of course, it might be a willful omission on his part, and we could equally argue that he wrote 100 years before Christianity was legalised and so maybe he thought the persecuted sect unworthy of note. But equally credible, to my own mind, are the computations of sociologist Rodney Stark, which are based on a very modest annual growth rate of 3.42%. Starting with an equally modest 1000 believers in AD 40, Stark's estimate would lead us to only a measly 7,530 by AD 100, but then a whopping 6,299,832 by AD 300, which would have been 10.5% of the imperial population – over double Lane Fox's figures.[55] Stark's early figures would seem too low, particularly when one considers that the New Testament's *Book of Acts* records 3000 new believers added to the church on one day in AD 33, and conversion rates were so high in the area around Ephesus 30 years later that it caused industrial rioting among those commercially invested in the cult of Diana. But taken heuristically, and considering the privations and persecutions experienced by the church in the first three centuries, it is possible that his eventual higher percentage of 10.5% by AD 300 is not so incredible after all.

And then hot on the heels of the 3rd century, which for the Latin Church culminated in the persecutions of Diocletian, came Constantine's edict to legalise Christianity – an event that Christians still cannot fully agree was good or bad, even 1700 years later. And so, the fourth century became an experiment in cultural accommodation on both sides. The Roman educational ethos, or *paideia*, prized a culture of courtesy in discourse and found it essential for the functioning of a pluralistic society. Modern historians are even unwilling now to talk of culture wars as we might when applied to our time. Fifth century historians made out the 4th century had been a war of Christian and Pagan culture but modern scholarship is less inclined to take that at face value. The extent and nature of the fusion is harder to delineate. It became very popular for 19th century German historians to see the 4th century imperium as the cynical manipulator of the church. This view, which they called *Caesaropapism*, reflected more the contemporary German experience than the reality found in the texts. A corrective, which is generally accepted by scholars today, was given in 1929 by Norman Baynes in a seminal lecture asserting Constantine's religious commitment and, more importantly, the inseparability of the political and religious spheres in the ancient world. The real battle, so little understood and talked of, was the intellectual and spiritual battle for orthodoxy within various Christian streams. 'Even by the beginning of the 4th century in some vital respects Christians were still in open and violent disagreement with each other. At the heart of early Christianity, therefore, was the search for authority.'[56] And that search for authority was not necessarily helped by the presence of a favourable imperial patron.

Clerics like Eusebius were delighted by the union of church and state but others were more nervous. By the end of the century Bishop Ambrose publicly refused Emperor Theodosius communion until he had done penance for the massacre at Thessalonica. The emperor complied because the currents of legitimation had shifted uneasily in the direction of the Church. In other words; his throne needed divine legitimation. But in becoming the official state cult, the church could not avoid terrible risks to its very essence. Even by the end of that century, when Theodosius outlawed paganism and repurposed their temples, many Christians had the foresight to see that 'the new imperial Christianity was largely a symptom of misplaced opportunism'[57] What would have seemed to someone like Eusebius as the beginning of a golden age, was in fact the reverse. It was the setting, not the rising of the sun. Constantine and Theodosius to varying degrees were like Gorbachev and Yeltsin during the Glasnost and Perestroika years. They could open things up but not dismantle the old system all at once. For example, they could take certain steps to legalise Christianity and to open up preferment for Christians, but they could not remake the old pagan world by edict.

In fact, there was still enough anti-Christian animus in 394 AD to manifest itself in an army large enough to challenge Theodosius' throne. In the event, the emperor won the battle at the River Frigidus. And going back a further 35 years, the stoic Emperor Julian did try to resuscitate the ailing pagan worship during his brief reign. But there is evidence to show that even at this early date the old gods were in terminal decline. Like the Greek gods, they were eventually found to be unworthy of worship. In all their glacial beauty and dark power, the gods had presided over, and been accessories to centuries of pitiless cruelty, cold comfort, and cosmic despair. This decline and desire for renewal had been a long time coming. Just before Christ's public ministry the historian's historian[58] Livy wrote with despair, and perhaps with deep longing; *'I would have (the reader) trace the process of our moral decline...the dark dawning of our modern day when we can neither endure our vices nor face the remedies needed to cure them.'* The Cambridge historian Herbert Butterfield said, in his 1951 Riddell lectures, that Greco-Roman 'philosophy itself had struck severe blows at the myths and legends of the ancient world, without putting anything in its place.' Much like western interest in oriental and pagan religions today, Butterfield held up the meteoric rise of Mithraism as evidence of a growing spiritual hunger. That gaping need for the 'kind of religion which would put man into relation with the whole cosmos and give him a glimpse of eternity' was eventually met in Christianity. During Rome's long decline, the Church gave the most convincing 'answer - in terms which the age could understand - to the ideals and outlook of the classical world.' It would reorder the whole consciousness of the ancient world and deal three decisive blows against the reigning worldview. Firstly, the cyclic and fatalistic view of history was superseded by the biblical view of history progressing to a divine purpose. Secondly, Fortuna was replaced with divine providence. Remember it was 'Fortune which had turned Chance into a goddess and checked any attempt to reduce the world to rationality.' And thirdly, the

Judeo-Christian view of a good creation - a physical world which was fallen, but not evil in and of itself - produced a paradigm shift with far-reaching effects.

A representative image of the people's disdain that has always stayed with me is Stilicho's wife Serene, who in 389AD defiantly took the great mother Cybele's necklace, thus defiling the temple as the last of the Vestal Virgins cursed her. More than most Cybele had provided '*divine legitimation for the practices, institutions and prejudices of a society in which the law of charity was not only an impossibility but an offense against good taste.*'[59] So, a significant minority – enough at least to excite the derision of classical historians, and the malice of official and unofficial persecution – simply chose a higher conception of reality and human dignity.[60] The polemical American philosopher and theologian David Bentley Hart puts it more strongly in *Atheist Delusions;*

> "... *my chief ambition in writing is to call attention to the particular and radical nature of the new faith... how enormous a transformation of thought, sensibility, morality, and spiritual imagination Christianity constituted in the age of pagan Rome; the liberation it offered from fatalism, cosmic despair, and terror of occult agencies; the immense dignity it conferred upon the human person; its subversion of the cruelest aspects of pagan society, its (alas, only partial) demystification of political power; its ability to create a moral community where none had existed before; and its elevation of active charity above all other virtues. ..... In comparison to the Christian revolution.... modernity is little more than an after-effect, or even a counter-revolution – a reactionary fight back toward a comfortable, but dehumanizing, mental and moral servitude to elemental nature.*"[61]

Christianity moved from the lowest in society, touching the patrician echelons only in significant numbers much later. The Roman aristocratic class did not necessarily stumble over the incarnation as the Athenian Greeks had done. 'That God would visit man was the least novel feature of Christian teaching in the eyes of the Romans.'[62] But the absolute claims of the new sect did appear seditious and other aspects of the faith did seem calculated to offend the pride of the patrician class. To worship a criminal executed under Roman law - and a non-citizen at that - seemed beyond satire. And did those illiterate fishermen imagine that the heirs and imitators of the polished style of great orators and rhetoricians would meekly imbibe divine truth written in, what has been called Cockney-Greek, as babes imbibe milk? No debate or argument? It was an insult to good taste.

From Edward Gibbon's *'Decline and Fall'* to A. H. M. Jones' *'Idle Mouths'* there have been no shortage of those who suspected Christianity to have been a contributing factor to the empire's decline by sucking the martial vigour out of it. But Sociologist Rodney Stark contends that Christianity was actually a source of urban and cultural renewal. According to Stark it 'revitalised life in Greco-Roman cities by providing new norms and new kinds of social relationships able to cope with many urgent urban problems. To cities filled with the homeless and impoverished, Christianity offered charity as well as hope. To cities filled with newcomers and strangers, Christianity offered immediate basis for attachments. To cities filled with orphans and widows, Christianity provided a new and expanded sense of family. To cities torn by violent ethnic strife, Christianity offered a new basis for social solidarity. To cities faced with endemic fires and earthquakes, Christianity offered effective nursing services.'[63]

That it was also seen as a liberation movement for women would perhaps strike modern readers as strange indeed. But the women of antiquity (like slaves) *non haben persona* – 'did not have a persona or face' – i.e., were morally irrelevant, not fully or legally human in the way that male citizens were. To get a glimpse of what this might mean today is to look at the Hindu caste system, or the diminished legal status of a human foetus. Even in its most humane form, antiquity could never have produced such a counter-cultural revolution for women. 'Classical man knew nothing of a being that was beyond this world; as a result, he was neither able to view nor shape his world from a vantage point that transcended it.'[64] But it is precisely this parochial religious worldview, that philosopher Romano Guardini contends, was irrevocably swept aside by the spread of Christianity. *'With the coming of Christ, man's existence took on an earnestness which classical antiquity never knew simply because it had no way of knowing it. This earnestness did not spring from human maturity; it sprang from the call which each person received from God through Christ.'*[65]

The Judeo-Christian concept of the *human being*, as we now understand it, where each individual and eternal being is made in the image of God (what theologians call the *Imageo Dei*), was the pebble that slew the Goliath of antiquity's indifference. In his 1951 Riddell Memorial Lectures, Professor Butterfield expanded the implications of this conceptual leap:

'This was not a theoretical valuation of personality..... For those who believed this statement, there could be nothing in the visible universe to which human beings could be regarded as subject or subordinate. Men could not be treated as mere means to some mundane purpose,.... or mere phases in an historical process... There was not a super-person - a state or a *Volk* or a social class or even mankind conceived as a corporate personality - in relation to which human beings are mere cells, mere cogs in a wheel, mere parts of a whole which is supposed to possess a more genuine identity than they have. ...Whether the Christian view on this matter is true or not, whether inferences made from it were valid or not, here is the most important single historical source of that respect for personality and for the rights of the individual man which we regard as the virtue of our western civilization.. And because God and human personalities have this absolute existence, Christianity does have ground on which to build something further - it can insist on the ultimate importance of Love as a relationship between spiritual personalities - a higher kind of Love which even presides over our natural affections, preventing them from becoming unbalanced and leading us astray, as they so often seem to do.... It is an ethic which furthermore is dynamic and creative in the sense that there is no telling what a man may or may not do for love; it is forever pressing against the frontiers of an accepted order, no matter what the regime or the state of society or the stage of development reached.'

Refering to a later development of this new view of humanity, Guardini writes, 'There is only one standard by which an epoch can be fairly judged....to what extent did it allow the development of human dignity? The medieval achievement was so magnificent that it stands with the loftiest moments in human history.'[66] Even now, we in the west are apt to take this all so much for granted that we wrongly assume that it is universally shared, when in fact it 'is not to be found in the other great oriental religions.'[67] Even in the West, not everyone has thought it obvious or even desirable. An obvious and eloquent example of course is Nietzsche, who mocked Yahweh as a *God of the Sick*. He hated Christianity precisely for this slave revolt in values, this cosmic sedition, by which the greatness and beauty of the strong were denied their ruthless mandate.

So, the old gods were displaced *en masse* by their former devotees – and the enormity of the phenomenon is easily lost on us – by the crucified Messiah of a backward nation in the back of beyond. He was a working-class builder[68] who wrote no books, led no armies, and never traveled outside an area the size of Wales? Yet his life, actions, and teaching - teachings that were often misinterpreted and misapplied - came to define the European civilisation that arose from the ashes of Rome. How this happened, and more importantly the effects of Europe's initial choice of the new religion will make a necessary focus in this book. Because without a doubt Christianity would become the most powerful and sustained influence in western civilisation. We simply cannot understand Europe apart from the religion that formed her political structures, her ethical consciousness, her scientific advances, and unprecedented affluence. Christopher Dawson wrote that 'the Christian tradition is the most fundamental element in Western culture. It lies at the base not only of Western religion, but also of Western morals and Western social idealism.' Another scholar states it more strongly still. In his introduction to, *The Story of Christianity*, David Bentley Hart writes, 'the story of Christianity is not merely the story of a religion indigenous to Western civilization; in a very real sense, it is the story of that civilization itself.' Impious though it may seem to secular ears, it was not on the battlefields but in the monasteries and churches that European civilisation was formed, consolidated, germinated, and later exported globally in so many different facets.

But it should be admitted at the outset that the new religion did not necessarily come as a friend to the empire, which was falling in any case. Christianity, initially at least, seemed entirely independent of and indifferent to 'what belonged to Caesar.' At Rome's highest point under Emperor Trajan, the reach of the *Imperium Romanum* was from the Firth of Forth to the Persian Gulf, which is all of Western Europe except Hibernia (Ireland), and the Middle East as far as the Caspian Sea. If you were not a slave, you could move – without a passport - from Chester to Athens, or York to Alexandria. You would travel on well-maintained roads, over jaw-dropping bridges, stay in well-appointed towns with sewerage systems and internal plumbing fed by aqueducts that, to later generations at least, seemed like they had been built by a race of giants. If you spoke a little Latin or Greek – and if you had enough minted coin - you could get by, in an area that stretched over 2.2 million square miles. And in every large town or city, you would expect to find theatres, stadiums, baths, guilds, procurators, law courts, and markets.

Augustine's Spanish friend Orosius, although an enthusiastic patriot, thought 'Free Movement' one of the greatest benefits of the empire. Travelling from Spain to Jerusalem, even at the time of the barbarian invasions, he could write, 'no matter where I flee, I find my native land, my law, and my religion. Wherever I go, stranger though I be, I need harbour no fear of sudden assault as would a man without protection. Among Romans, I am Roman: among Christians, as a Christian; among humans, a human.'

How it all collapsed may only be touched on below. The second part of this chapter will give only illustrative slices of information that are intended to throw further light on the principal subjects of this book.

Suffice to say at this point is that a civilisation like that of Rome does not disappear from the cultural consciousness easily. Supranational alliances – many nations at peace, cooperating rather than competing for the good of all – linger in the collective imaginations of the cultures they touched and partially transformed. But so too do the aberrations of that vision – when the ideals of civilisation and mutuality are subsumed by the hubris of Empire.

From Charlemagne to the European Commission this is a profound and unresolved tension – as unresolved as its cause, human nature. Human nature's propensity to be corrupted by power means that the noblest ambitions of culture will always succumb to the *realpolitik*. At what point, or to what extent those leading the EU institutions have confused the concepts of civilization and concepts of Empire is not easy to measure. If they have remained untainted by that power, then they will be virtually the first people in history to be so. Some of these issues will be raised in the final chapters of this book. But for now, as we come to the calamitous decline of Rome, let us recall the words of the Princeton Classical Scholar, Frank Bourne. 'In the age of Pax Americana, there is no more important lesson we can teach young Americans than the rise and decline of Pax Romana.' His words have resonance for us, as we look at what, this book's subtitle suggests and many believe, might be the twilight of the *Pax Europa*. Bourne began and ended his course with the words, *De nobis fabula narratur* - their story is our story

So, let us finish the first part of this chapter by saying that *memory* is not merely *the residue of thought*, as psychologist Daniel Willingham once claimed. It is much more. And it was much more for those who lived in the wake of Rome's slow decline. Rome was like the sinking of the Titanic, going down slowly and leaving many people on her flotsam and jetsam in the icy waters. When we come to Columban and his contemporaries, clinging to the fragments and moving forward in uncertain times, we will see that it is more as the cognitive neuroscientist Michael Gazzaniga frames it, *'everything in life is memory, save for the thin edge of the present.'*

PART II - 33-400AD - THE DECLINE OF ROME, THE SURVIVAL OF CHRISTIANITY, AND THE ARRIVAL OF THE BARBARIANS

The Historian R.H.C Davies[69] gives a neat way of weaving the elements of Rome's decline together. According to Davies, the Romans believed in and utterly relied upon, the unity of three things. These all became sundered in a corresponding trinity of ideological, legal, and strategic challenges. Rome's trinity – its recipe for stability and growth – was *firstly* the unity of their religion, the veneration of the Romano-Grecian titular deities. *Secondly* the unity of the law, the *Pax Romana*. And *thirdly* the unity of the sea, what they called *Nostrum Mare – our sea –* or in other words the security of their maritime commerce.

To these three, it was the Christians who brought the first sectarian challenge. But it was not that the new sect actively defined itself against Roman hegemony, indeed *without Roman predominance, a new religious revelation that was to be the defining influence of Europe's later character could not have taken root and prospered as it did.'* [70] But Christianity did claim to be the sole arbiter of truth, and this made compromise impossible. Jesus' teaching, at least for the present, was incapable of alloy. For them, there was but one God, who did not have a statue,[71] one Saviour and Lord who was not divine emperor, nor even a Roman citizen; and one humanity of equal dignity and value, that is; master and slave, men, and women; all equal before God.

Perhaps it does not appear so momentous to us now but, by his example and his teaching, Jesus delivered to us the fully formed concept of the human. The moral, spiritual, intellectual, and social implications of just one or two lines of Jesus' teachings were so revolutionary, so seditious even, that they threatened the fabric of the ancient world.

Celsus, a first century Richard Dawkins, thought that the flocking of women to the church was proof enough of its vulgarity and irrationality. In the 4th century, Emperor Julian chided the men of Antioch for letting their wives give so much money for the churches' aid programmes. But it is not hard to see why they found the new faith so liberating. They were accorded the same dignity and value as men. They did not have to endure forced abortions or expose their infants in jars at the side of the temples or see their female babes thrown on the rubbish heaps for wild animals to devour. And the provision of social security in old age was no small matter in days when the thought of future destitution and starvation must have haunted the middle years of many women. Under Constantine, Theodosius, and Justinian, amendments to the laws of divorce and inheritance also conferred on women (and their daughters) a new sense of value and security. For example: If a man divorced a woman, in a no-fault case, she could have her dowry and marriage gifts back. And she could also remarry, whereas the husband had to remain a bachelor. That the pursuit of this new ideal of equality was not universal is not as marvellous as the fact that such a new conception sprung up in the first place.

The Christians provided a first peremptory crack in the Roman trinity we mentioned above. The second and third came much later when the 'barbarians' arrived with laws based on the dictates of their divine ancestors and not on *reason*. Many of them joined the army under the command of their own kings who had refused Roman law, preferring Wergild – a system developed to fix the 'money-worth' of each man, woman, servant and thus curtail the rampant blood feuds. The retention of the Salian and Ripuarian laws by people groups within the empire made the law not territorial but personal, and thus the universality of the great *Pax Romana* was breached. This pattern of national or ethnic identity trumping the Roman conception the *gens humana* in Europe has a long, if not so noble lineage right down to the divergence in Hegelian nationalism and Kantian cosmopolitanism.[72] And one cannot help seeing it as analogous in some respects to the Brexit animus[73] – though of course, we must be circumspect, remembering the words of Herbert Butterfield; 'the study of the past with one eye on the present is the source of all the sins and sophistries in history.'

As Roman martial vigour weakened so too did their ability to secure the shipping lanes which grew increasingly piratical. This and other factors weakened trade, which in turn made civic life eventually untenable. Rome itself had grown from the spoils of war and lived on corn supplied by Sicily and Africa. In her long decline the city of Rome manufactured nothing, and her chief trade was money lending. It was not a sudden catastrophe for Rome but a series of events and factors working together over prolonged periods of time.

One factor was a dangerous decline in revenues through uneven taxation. This contributed to a disappearing middle class. (Forget Amazon and Facebook, the Italian elites of late antiquity made tax evasion into an art form.) Another factor was an unwieldy and self-serving bureaucracy whose survival became its ultimate goal. (Again, overtones of the Brussels' gravy train will no doubt spring to mind.) But in truth, Rome had been experiencing both economic and fertility decline for 200 years before that final collapse. As we are finding out today, demography and economy are inextricably linked. Augustus cracked down on abortions and, like the current Hungarian president, gave incentives for large families. 'In those days, a decree went out from Caesar Augustus' not just that 'all the Roman world should be taxed' but also that he could see whether his fertility policy was having any effect.[74] And with regards to the fiscal decline, we should remember that the emperors of old could not, as they do today, simply borrow against the future, but they could and did debase the *denarius* currency. This was done to the point that the purchasing power of money declined inexorably, and prudent people began to move out of the cities and invest in land. Away from the crumbling urban centres and the rampant inflation, a patrician might hope to ride out the recession in his self-sufficient villa with his family, slaves, workshops, and harvests.[75] The pinch was felt everywhere across the empire. In the mid third century, a Christian Bishop called Cyprian from Carthage in North Africa, lamented,

'... *the world has and lost its former vigour.... Winter no longer gives rain enough to swell the seed, nor summer sun enough to ripen the harvest.... The mountains are gutted and give less marble, the mines exhausted and give less silver and gold.... Fields lack farmers, the seas sailors, the encampments soldiers... there is no longer any justice in judgments, competence in trades, discipline in daily life.'*

This essentially is why the cities shrank. Bordeaux for example contracted to less than a third of its former size. Autun even more, from 500 to just 25 acres, a mere 5% of its former glory. Something else to note about this period concerns the actions of the rich because there were certainly more than faint echoes of this in the last recession. In ancient Italy the wealthy plundered the civic buildings to edify their own estates. When you see the noble ruins of Roman Italy remember that, to some extent,[76] this is what a grasping elite did to their own civilisation.[77] In the case of patricians pilfering stone the emperor's edict was simple enough; a fine of fifty pounds of gold for a magistrate found guilty, and for everyone assisting them, a flogging and loss of both hands. They were more rational times. Cutting off more than a banker's bonus might be a better way – for utilitarians such as we are – to minimise aggregate unhappiness! In the first half of the fifth century – a period when Patrick wrote his great polemic letter against slavery, there were mass enslavements of free Romans too. The patrician landlords employed special agents called *redemptores* to buy slaves back from the barbarian raiders, not to free them but to make them lifelong serfs on their own estates[78]. When the chips were down, the restless rich proved ruthlessly adaptive in their own narrow interests. They did not have to wait for Machiavelli, Mandeville, or Malthus[79] for a justification to behave without honour to their fellow man.

But let us leave the rich, a type too well known even for parody, and let us move onto another force within the European story. The so-called Barbarians really are the black sheep of history. We cannot escape the thorny issue that successive waves of immigration exposed the weakness of the Roman Empire. The current pressure of immigration into Europe will be a necessary component of the later chapters in this book, as this is an issue currently driving dangerous trends and political instability across the EU. A level of migration has always happened and has, by and large, always been mutually beneficial. Stereotypes aside, the immigrants who crossed the Rhine, at this point in our story, introduced soap to the Romans and were notable for cleaning their teeth. Some later ones were even Christians, though of an Arian persuasion – that is, they were theologically akin to the Jehovah's Witnesses, though clutching axes rather than Watchtower literature. Driven by climate change and seismic geopolitical upheavals as far east as Afghanistan, they came in wave after wave. They did not come necessarily to destroy but to enjoy the empire. It was just bad timing for Rome.

There is only so much a civilisation can do to mitigate such vast geopolitical trends. And at certain points the Romans did a surprising amount. For example, in the late 4th century, the Romans entered into dialogue with their ancient enemy, Persia. In a strategic defence alliance, (rather like the Americans and Germans within NATO as a bulwark against the USSR); the Romans helped part-fund and staff a 125-mile-long wall between the Caspian and Black Seas in order to hold back the barbarian invaders. Desperate times call for desperate measures. But, in total, it was like trying to hold back the tide on a 4,000-mile coastline. Let us first undertake a broad summary of the main invading groups and then briefly use some data to give us an idea of what it was like to be alive at that moment in our story.

At a glance, we could say that Alaric had sacked Rome but then passed down to Sicily and disappeared. The Visigoths and Vandals vanished into Spain, then North Africa, finally merging into the Arab Empire. The Lombards reached as far as Benevento but then assimilated. The Huns, led by the terrible Attila, were some of the most successful of them all. They were warriors and horsemen from their youth; heads misshapen by applying boards, faces smooth by scraping the cheek flesh of the boys when young. These merciless warriors were almost universally successful. (We can thank them for Venice, as it was desperate Romans fleeing the Huns who ended up on those marshes and began to build.) But Attila was finally defeated in central France by an alliance, not of Romans for they were gone, but of other barbarian enemies.

Who else? We have no time to speak of the Alans, the Gepids, the Sueves, the Neurians, and the Bastarnians. The Ostrogoths however must be mentioned for they too left their mark under Theodoric, whose story touches Columban. But of them all, it was the Franks, as we noted earlier, who created the largest and longest-lasting empire. That is, as I say, a very tight summary. But what of those other factors that helped to bring down the largest and most advanced civilisation the world had then known? And also, what scientific markers help us understand what it was to be alive in those momentous years?

We have seen above some of the political and financial issues that weakened Rome, but what about her political and military might? In the vital years when Emperor Honorius needed a united front against the Goths, he was instead having to deal with five usurpers, in effect five civil wars. But even before that, the political rot was manifest in a way reminiscent of the Third French Republic. Within a 70-year period of the 3rd century the Roman empire had 27 different emperors, only three of whom reigned more than five years and 23 of whom died unnatural deaths.

Little wonder he recalled his legions from Britannia, with the advice that we 'look to our own defences.' The vandal invasion of North Africa in 429 destroyed the last stable tax base from which the emperor could supply the army. Ironically, it was during this same period that the Eastern Empire was enjoying a time of prosperity. In fact, she had never had more than a third of her tax base threatened during the entire period of her twin sister's demise. (The Eastern Empire was further preserved by the happy conjunction of three other factors; the absence of civil war, over a century of relative peace with Persia, and also – as with Britain – a small strip of water separating them from some of their enemies.)

It took until 440 for Emperor Valentinian to allow citizens to arm themselves. For many Romans, perhaps most, that was too little, too late. Some were driven to suicide by the increased taxation which only went to pay tribute to invaders like Attila. Others had their cities surrendered by the Senate in acts of tragic appeasement. For example, Sidonius Apollonaris, who was Bishop of Clermont became the organiser of its resistance, and lamented bitterly, 'we have been enslaved, as the price of other people's security.' In the end, the most successful in armed resistance against invasion were those who had not been wholly subjected to Rome in the first place, the Basques, the Welsh, and the tribes of Brittany. (In fact, North Wales was not successfully subdued until 1282 by that most regal of Plantagenet barbarians, Edward I)

And following the conquest (or in Sidonius' case, the betrayal) came the colonisation. And with the colonisation came the vast exchanges of land. In 476 Odoacer, who replaced the last emperor, is said to have granted a third of the lands that we call Italy, to his army, and there is evidence to support it. (That is less radical than William of Normandy who distributed the lands of 2000 Saxons to 200 Norman barons in 1086.[80])

The man who replaced Odoacer (with a cold knife in the belly at a dinner party) was Theodoric. And his nephew Theodahad was one of those landowners who considered having 'a neighbour as a kind of misfortune,' and therefore having 'gained most of the lands of Tuscany, was eager by violent methods to wrest the remainder from its owners.' But there is also evidence of a degree of aristocratic continuity in southern Gaul and southern and central Italy, at least until the sixth century.[81]

Also, with colonisation emerged the collaborators. And the historical record is replete with the names of those who profited from their service to the new regimes. Ennodius in Ostrogothic Italy mocked a fellow Roman called Jovinianus for wearing a Roman cloak but sporting a gothic beard. Bishop Sidonius in Clermont, already mentioned, mocked Sygarius for forgetting his noble Roman lineage and education, by learning the conqueror's language, and taking service under the Burgundians. But for those who went down the route of assimilation, career possibilities could be tempting. Leo of Narbonne became a key counsellor of Euric II in 466, Cassiodorus survived as secretary of state in Lombardy (though his predecessor Boethius was executed), and Victorianus of Hadrumentum was 'as wealthy as any man in Africa' as proconsul of Carthage for the Vandals. Even one Saxon king seems to anticipate, through a law code, that there were still enough wealthy Britons, who he calls Welshmen, around to participate in the wergild (blood-price) system of justice. But even in this instance, as with their Gallic counterparts, the subjected people groups were only worth half the blood-price of their conquerors. 'If anyone kills a Frank,' reads one law around 500AD, 'let him pay .... 200 solidi. But if a Roman landowner.... Is killed, let him.... be liable for 100 solidi.'

And also, understandably with colonisation came counter-migrations. Gildas, along with many others, eventually fled to the Brittany coast after witnessing the Saxon invasion.[82] Appalled, he said there was 'no burial to be had except in the ruin of houses or in the bellies of beasts and birds...' But it wasn't as if there were any idyllic pockets waiting over the channel. Between 407-409, a poet in Gaul wrote that the whole country 'smoked on a single funeral pyre. It gives a grim view of marauding barbarians intent on pillage, but that is only a narrow view of what has been a subject of lively scholarly debate. There are even 20th century scholars who emphasise the most positive aspects of the migrations.[83]

The tragedy, and perhaps a cautionary tale against western cultural hubris, is shown in Alaric's sack of the Eternal City in 410. Rome had been almost impregnable for near 800 years. It seemed simply inconceivable. When news reached Jerusalem of the sacking of Rome, an eyewitness wrote, 'the speaker's voice failed, and sobs interrupted his speech, the city that had conquered the whole world had itself been conquered... who could believe it?' Most Romans were unwilling to see how far they had fallen; that they were so very far from what they had been. But how else could they explain their putting up with the insolence of the army, who replaced emperors with such alarming rapidity, even auctioning the empire on one occasion to the highest bidder? How else can we explain why an insipid and middling poet like Ausonius could be elevated to a position at the emperor's side? Gibbon rightly says, *'the fame of Ausonius condemns the taste of the age.'* This was a civilisation in the *rigor mortis* of cultural calcification. Tepid, vapid, rootless; rearranging the chairs while the great ship went down.

And one simply cannot read about it at this point in the West's history without real pathos, even mild dread. Far right-wing Europeans, who are now alarmingly evident even in some parliaments, might talk about racial purity; and the Hungarians might finish their wall to keep immigrants out, and their left-wing counterparts might dream of a Marxist utopia without gulags, but as far back as the 1980s the Scottish philosopher Alasdair Macintyre warned the West that our strategic threats are increasingly internal. *'This time, however, the barbarians are not waiting beyond the frontiers; they have already been governing us for quite some time. And it is our lack of consciousness of this that constitutes part of our predicament.'* [84]

Alarmist? Pessimistic? Perhaps. But could the West, hollowed out from the inside, really implode as Rome did? It is not entirely unthinkable. A civilisation depending on such ubiquitous technology, such conspicuous levels of debt, such a wafer-thin ideological base, and in such an unequal world is vulnerable at so many levels, as indeed we are beginning to see. When the lead character in Hemingway's *The Sun Also Rises* was asked how he went bankrupt, he answered, 'gradually and then suddenly.' It was ever thus. Despite the Credit Crunch of 2008, the ratio of global debt to GDP has actually risen from 179% to 217% in the last decade. In China gross public and private financial debt has doubled to a staggering 300% of GDP surpassing even Japan's 1980's debt binge.

In a 2018 interview, Bill Gates said that, just over the water from a demographically shrinking Europe, the population of Sub Saharan Africa would almost double by 2050 – that will be within most of our lifetimes. To put that in perspective, Nigeria's current population of 190 million would then be as much as 430 million. Twin that with the IPCC's[85] starkest warnings yet, forecasting a 2% increase in global temperatures and resulting catastrophes, and what optimistic impression can anyone have but that the mid-21st century will be an era of repeated financial collapse, environmental catastrophe (probably for someone else who is very poor) and sustained mass migration of millions of those poor to places of affluence, like Europe. Europe is the most prosperous area of the globe. It has a greater GDP than the USA. Europe touches the whole world through trade and cultural influence. 'Europe's geography means it cannot be united through conquest,' George Friedman wrote[86] and that 'the map of Europe in 1000 is similar to the map in

2000.' Maybe so, but internal pressures can create toxic consequences. The pressures of Europe will change the world.

Who is my neighbour? The Syrian civil war and African migration have given us only a taste of a possible future.[87] It exposed western foreign policy blindness during the Arab Spring, with a catalogue of horrors and errors thereafter. If the World Wars taught America that the front line of their enemy was Berlin, surely Syria has shown us Europeans that our neighbour is now a displaced widow in Homs or a disaffected teenager in Abuja. I'm not giving up the Scotch pessimism of Macintyre totally, but my English entrepreneurial nose is with Bill Gates; every penny we invest in places like Nigeria – to produce stable and flourishing societies will take us one second further away from a catastrophe that could otherwise ruin us both. Earlier in this chapter, we contemplated the rise and fall of the Minoans. What brought down the first expression of Western Civilisation on Crete? It was the effects of the eruption on Thera. And what caused that? Tectonic shifts over which they had no control. In their case, it was literally the pressure of the African continent pushing inexorably against Europe. And so too today; geo-tectonics and geopolitics chime together like the tolling of John Donne's bell. Ask not for whom the bell tolls, wrote Donne, *it tolls for you.*

We have been here before. Sixteen centuries ago, another philosopher as well versed in the Greek tradition as Macintyre, teased out these very things in a 'blog' that ran to over a million words. He was an African, and he called his blog, *The City of God.* He had converted to the new religion and was later made the bishop of the North African town of Hippo Regius. We know him as Augustine, but what we often forget is the tumultuous times in which he lived. He was alive to see the first wave of immigrants arriving from Italy to Africa in 410AD. Alaric had sacked Rome and now destitute Roman citizens, these proto-Europeans, were seeking asylum in Africa. And like the migrants crossing in the opposite direction today, they brought with them tales of devastation and woe. 'They brought news that could scarcely be comprehended,' wrote one historian, 'It is impossible for us today to appreciate fully the sense of psychological trauma induced by these events.'[88] The sack of Rome awakened Augustine to the hollowed-out state of the empire. Interestingly, his friend Orosius claimed that the sack of Rome in 410 was not as bad as when the pagan Gauls did the same 20 years earlier, nor indeed even the depredations of Nero. But Jerome, with typical verve, wrote in the same year from the far side of the Mediterranean ...'the whole world has died with one city.... who would have believed that Rome ...would fall, so that it would be both the mother and the tomb of all peoples?'

In 418, six years after the Goths left Italy for good, some provinces were still unable to pay taxes, even with an 80% reduction.[89] There would still be an emperor until 476, in name at least, but his passing was barely noticed. In that sense - but that sense only - what Momigliano called, 'the noiseless fall of the empire' is true.

For a philosopher, cultural commentator and pastor like Augustine, the time of writing about these things from a distance was very much over. Hot on the heels of refugees from Europe, came the Vandals across that narrow Hellespont to Africa. They are recorded by contemporaries as being particularly unrestrained in slaughter, even holding children 'by their feet, upside down, and cutting them in two.' These waves of Vandals had a sobering effect on the observant people of that generation. The pressure felt by those communities was immense. One whole convent of nuns left en masse for Egypt. But Augustine stayed, saying that he would not leave unless the whole church was able to evacuate with him. Augustine was still there twenty years later when the Arian vandals were battering at the gates of Regius Hippo. He died just before they breached the walls.

Christians of the day, like Salvian, bewailed the collapse, 'why does [God] allow us to be weaker and more miserable...and to be conquered by these barbarians?' The answer of the Christian conscience was obvious; it was a just punishment for sin. The answer of the pagan conscience for once agreed! Zosimus, blamed the unfolding catastrophe on the Christians for angering the gods, for him it was not opinion but plain fact.[90] The Christian voice was divided, and even hopeless. 'If

Rome can perish,' Jerome wrote, 'what can be safe?' To both Zosimus' charge and Jerome's question, Augustine brought the answer in his great polemic; *De Civitas Dei*. *The City of God*, he wrote, would always endure and it wasn't Rome. And neither was it, as later ages misunderstood, the papacy or the church militant, but rather the embodiment of God's justice and truth in his people past and present and future. This divine justice, this new humanity looking 'for a heavenly city whose builder and maker was God,' was the City of God, and Augustine's writings over 14 years became a powerful antidote to the Eusebian naivety that had characterised Christian thought a century before. And there is something of this far-reaching idealism in the European psyche, even if it is now clothed in secular language.

At the other 'end' of history the historian, Christopher Dawson, gives a startling application of Augustine's challenge toward the state. According to Dawson, the moment the state raises itself against 'the divine' and makes the state 'an end in itself', it becomes 'identified with Augustine's earthly city' and loses 'all claims to a higher sanction than the law of force and self-interest. Without justice, what is a great kingdom but a great robbery, *magnum latrocinium?*' Strongly stated. But in any case, this is why, for Augustine, the fall of the western empire was not as serious as the fall of justice in the earth. 'The world is dying' he wrote, 'the world is growing old, the world is overcome by weakness, it has the gasping breath of old age.' 'Do not lose heart brothers and sisters, there will be an end to every earthly kingdom.' For him, Rome might fall but, in any case, Christ had arisen. What Eusebius had externalised; Augustine now internalised. For Augustine there were two real cities that mattered, and they were the two dispositions of the human heart, of which the kingdoms of the earth are only the eventual manifestations. But unlike later Christian thinkers who drank deeply of his writing, Augustine took a generous and astute view of the fallen human nature and its capacities. 'Calvin believed that good had died in humanity with Adam's fall, whereas Augustine believed that justice was indeed wounded but capable of convalescence.'[91]

In the final book of *The City of God* (Book XIV, 28) he delineates the human who has a '*self-love reaching a point of contempt of God....* *(and the other disposition that shows) the love of God carried as far as contempt for self.*' It is a profound psychological and spiritual analysis that, along with the first chapter of Paul's Letter to the Romans, weighs heavier than all the literary criticism, philosophy, and psychoanalysis that came after it. Civil administrations could fall, but while God's grace to mankind remained there was always hope of societal renewal. That might seem like pious rhetoric and wishful thinking to 21st century, sceptical ears, but it was by such slender threads that the best of western civilisation was renewed.[92]

And it was not as if they were all jingoistic optimists. When surveying the scene two centuries later Gregory the Great wrote that there was no second way to interpret the tumultuous times other than that the end of the world had come; '*...even if the gospel should be silent about it, the world itself would proclaim. These very ruins serve as its voice. Beaten down by so many blows, the ancient kingdom has fallen from its glory and shows us another kingdom, which is coming, which is already near...(and) if then, when the world is still sinking beneath us, we still love it and cling to it, it is because we wish to perish with it.*'

We will look at Gregory's own remarkable life later, for he was Pope when Columban was building his communities in the Vosges. It is enough to say for now that the attitude, which at first might be construed as defeatist, was actually concurrent with the ideals of the movement instrumental in preserving civilisation – that of Christian monasticism. This movement also will be dealt with in more detail in a later chapter.

There were others who tried to save the West – or at least the shell of it – by strength of arms, but ironically these efforts only hastened the final collapse. In 557AD, when Columbanus and Pope Gregory were in their teens, Emperor Justinian, appalled by the Barbarian rule of Italy, sent Belisarius from Constantinople to take his western empire from them. Belisarius' list of conquests through North Africa and Italy were impressive, but his master's idealism was well behind the curve of historical processes. His supposedly pure 'Roman' army was actually propped up by Barbarian mercenaries like the Lombards who, having had a good look round Italy decided they might like a slice of the *dolce vita* themselves. And two years after Justinian's death, that is exactly what they did.[93]

> '...*the men who ushered in the Dark Ages were men like Theodoric and Cassiodorus, who were intent on restoring the cities, preserving the statues, and transcribing the classics. Their adoration of the ancient world was matched only by their inability to understand it, for by the time that they were born, the classical culture was already dead. They were the first of the great medievals and began to build a new civilisation in an attempt to restore the old.*'[94]

Justinian's attempts to unite the Roman world in one empire and one church served only to highlight that the Roman world had already disappeared. "*To the end of history, social orders will probably destroy themselves in an effort to prove they are indestructible.*"[95] Justinian spent his military energy on a fruitless conquest of the West at the expense of shoring up his eastern borders against the greater menace of the Persian Empire. This should give pause to all us modern defenders of European culture. Do we truly defend what made this culture unique, or merely a synthetic version made of aspects that are currently useful and vogue?

The irony, and perhaps the paradox, is that to a certain extent the invading barbarians became Romanised, and vice versa. Some even courted their new identity openly. Theodoric himself said, 'an able Goth wants to be like a Roman: only a poor Roman would want to be like a Goth.' His sister was lady-in-waiting to the Byzantine Empress and he, himself, had grown up there. He wrote to the emperor; 'our royalty is a copy of yours, the only empire on earth,' and he had his coins stamped with the words 'Roma Invicta' – *unvanquished Rome*. Everyone wanted it to be true. Even as late as the 570's, just before Columbanus came to the continent, the Frankish King Chilperic was building Roman-style circuses at Soissons and Paris for chariot racing. At some points, the memory of Rome held sway, and of course, still does. But gradually, and particularly on the fifth century frontiers, it became almost impossible to distinguish the Romans from the Barbarians as the years passed.[96]

And so, for better or worse, and usually both at once, we Europeans are that special blend of the secular Roman, the Christian saint and the Barbarian.[97] Or as a French historian[98] put it, European civilisation was the fertile convergence of Jerusalem, Athens, and Rome, a thing in itself that pre-existed European nations. This is, of course, to acknowledge the limited reach of an essentially voluntary religion. At least for the first three centuries, Christianity spread through every stratum of society as the obvious panacea to the human condition. And even after it was legalised under Constantine, the conservative aristocratic patricians resisted the vulgar superstitions of the populace and clung to their father's gods, as they did their hegemony in the administration of the empire. Even when Christianity was finally legalised and highly favoured by Emperor Constantine, and right up to his death in the mid-forth century; two-thirds of his top government were still non-Christian.'[99] Curiously enough, it was the successive waves of barbarian invasions in the fifth century that displaced this old order and, in its place, welded the Latin and Teutonic elements into the medieval synthesis. Butterfield, in the 1951 Riddell lectures, said that the barbarian disruption almost certainly saved the church from caesaropapism; the full unification of the sacred and secular powers. As the empire crumbled, the Church baptised the new world order, often from the top down 'as the moral principles of the religion had, so to speak, to be poured into the mould which society provided for it.'

Curiously, even in a semi-paganised form, Butterfield thought that Christianity had led to 'remarkable developments' in barbarian societies, and had strengthened 'the bond of the tribe even more effectually than would seem possible for religion in its higher or profounder manifestations.' 'In fact, the primary work of the Church was to turn the formal Christianity of mass-conversions - that christianised paganism - into a genuine faith of the profounder, New Testament kind; and this was a kind of work which in a sense could only be done in detail by the priest, preacher, missionary, and saint.' Sixty-or-so generations ago, these troubled Europeans had started their journey toward becoming us. As someone said, *the past is not history, it is not even past.*[100]

Having given snapshots of the collapsing empire, our attention must now turn to an island quite off the Roman map, an island that 'time' – or at least the Romans – had forgotten. They had a name for it, Hibernia, the Land of Winter. This cultural Galapagos had only two out of the three traits that we have observed in the first Europeans. They were barbarians, for sure; they had never been Romans – what else could they be? But they had just received the Christian religion, and this seems to have made up for it. We call them *the Irish.*

And before we visit that far offshore in *de finibus extremis*, let us be reminded by the historian J. M. Roberts, to spare a thought for those bewildered souls left to face the uncertainty of the crumbling empire.

'They could not even think of an alternative to Imperial government: it was simply The Empire, not even qualified as Roman, because no other was comparable to it. Even those who dreamed of a Judgement Day which was quickly approaching, saw it as one where earthly power would fade away and crumble – not as one that would replace one human order, one set of standards, with another. Even educated men knew hardly anything about the worlds of Persia or India, nothing of China. Rome was all they knew. It was what civilisation meant. That would continue to be true for a long time to come.'[101]

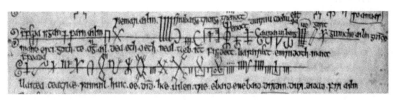

Ogham text in Leabhar Bhaile an Mhóta (The Book of Ballymote), written in 1390

CHAPTER 1:
FOOTNOTES & REFERENCES

23. Norman Davies, *Europe, a history.*

24. Bruce Allsopp, *Spirit of Europe*

25. Aristotle, *Politics*, vii, 1327b

26. The Christian faith was first brought to Europe by the apostle Paul between 51-52AD. The Bible records this in Acts chapter 17. Of course, it went south, east, and north too, until it has become in our day, at least nominally, the faith of one third of the globe. Any readers who are Coptic or Malankaran Christians, or Greek, Chaldean, and Armenian Orthodox must excuse the blinkers required by this book's task, which is to focus on how this movement, in its various institutional and cultural forms, shaped us westerners.

27. J. M. Roberts, *A History of Europe*

28. Andrew Matthews, *The Birth of Europe*, BBC books.

29. Wall paintings at Akrotiri, on Santorini, showed a grey langur monkey with its distinctive upturned tails which were only found in the Indus Valley. This suggests that the Silk Roads were operational much earlier than previously supposed.

30. 'Soon after that there is evidence.... of a remarkable new fact; the introduction of the first language from mainland Europe. This is revealed by the administrative tablets; after 1450BC or thereabouts they began to be written in a different script.... a form of Greek.' J. M. Roberts, *A History of Europe*. P.17

31. Andrew Matthews, *The Birth of Europe*, BBC books.

32. Ibid. Also, these 30,000 slaves (in Greek Antrhopoda – human cattle/tools) went down 3000 shafts (some 119m deep) and in tunnels just big enough to crouch in. They extracted 3500 tonnes of silver and 1.5 million tonnes of lead per annum

33. Ibid

34. In America for example, the share of national income going to the richest 1% has doubled from 10% to 20% since 1980, a trend repeated more or less in Britain, Canada, China, India, and even Sweden. It is a dilemma that was not given political salience during the asset bubbles and cheap credit before the 2008 Credit Crunch. For more on this subject, see my 2012 paper, John Ruskin & the Economics of Inequality, retrievable here: https://1drv.ms/b/s!Anbjq9cpZ1JDjb0zjn-RuxH8RdFEXKw?e=flB793

35. Andrew Matthews, *The Birth of Europe*, BBC books.

36. To be fair to Mummius, Polybius says that he was at least honest and kept nothing for himself.

37. As one therapist observed, after thirty years counselling couples; the rise in divorce is not that spouses are unhappy in the old sense, only that they think they might be happier.

38. I have fond memories of watching this for the first time in 1987 when studying History of Art and Architecture. I recall an aesthetic awakening of sorts at that time, something I believe the Germans call Sehnsucht, and C. S. Lewis called Joy.

39. In Marxian thought, the 'base' of necessary production determines society's superstructure, which comprises other relationships and ideas, including its culture, institutions, political power structures, roles, rituals, and state. I note here that Norman Davies, (himself trained by the great Marxist historian A. J. P. Taylor) in his book The Isles p.758, calls this aspect of Marxist theory; 'antiquated' and now 'discounted'. Although the relation of the two parts is not strictly unidirectional (the superstructure often affects the base), the influence of the base is predominant. 'The so-called superstructure is just as likely to drive the base as vice versa.'

40. Virgil, *Aeneid VI*, 847-853

41. Andrew Matthews, *The Birth of Europe,* BBC books. p.114

42. George Friedman, *Flashpoints – The Emerging Crisis in Europe*, Doubleday.

43. Andrew Matthews, *The Birth of Europe,* BBC books. p.134

44. Alastair McGrath, *The Twilight of Atheism*

45. That is why the Pagan Emperor Julian called Christians the Galilean Atheists.

46. Lucretius Flavius wrote *De Rerum Naturae*, espousing the concept of the spontaneous generation of life – a concept of Greek provenance. The sole surviving manuscript was found in the cellar of a German monastery by the garrulous, Florentine collector Poggio – who wrote the famous Poggio's Lament.

47. He cites Agamemnon's needless sacrifice of his daughter to Athena as evidence.

48. Source: Google

49. Edward Gibbon, *The Decline and Fall of the Roman Empire* 1: 180-395

50. *Bible*, James Ch.2 v13

51. This paradox is shown with pathos and wit by Dostoyevsky's most depraved character in The Brothers Karamazov. Interestingly, he gives this character his own name, Fyodor, and in a revealing passage at the end of Chapter 4, the debauched tyrant produces two straw-man arguments against 'Hell and devils with hooks' to drag sinners there. But then, in a flash of conscience, he admits that if 'there would be none to drag me down to hell, ...what justice is there in the world? Il faudrait les inventer, those hooks, on purpose for me alone, for, if you only knew, Alyosha, what a blackguard I am."

52. G.Herring, *An Introduction to the History of Christianity*. 2005, Pp 15-16

53. For examples, see Vallee, *Shaping of Christianity*, pp.106-7; and Wilkin, Christians as the Roman Saw Them, p.31

54. Lane Fox, *Pagans and Christians* pp.317, 592

55. Rodney Stark, *The Rise of Christianity* p.4-13

56. G. Herring, *An Introduction to the History of Christianity*. 2005, p22

57. Rousseau, *Early Christian Centuries*, p.247

58. The Oxford Historian John Burrows, and author of *A History of Histories*, once told me that if he could reclaim any piece of lost antique literature it would be something by Livy.

59. David Bentley Hart, *Atheist Delusions*

60. This is overly simplistic. Dr. George Herring brings a more nuanced view of the decline of pagan religion on page 18 of An *Introduction to the History of Christianity*, which is well worth seeking out.

61. David Bentley Hart, *Atheist Delusions*

62. Lane Fox, *Pagans and Christians* p.141

63. Rodney Stark, *The Rise of Christianity*, Princeton University Press, 1996, p.161.

64. Romano Guardini, *The End of the Modern World*

65. Ibid

66. Ibid

67. Christopher Dawson (2008). *"The Formation of Christendom"* Ignatius Press p.159

68. In Greek, *Teckton* refers to something more than carpentry.

69. R. H. C. Davis, *The History of Medieval Europe*

70. J. M. Roberts, *A History of Europe* p.22

71. Emperor Hadrian could not get the Jews to present a statue of Yahweh for its designated niche in his all-gods-temple; the Pantheon, in Rome. Rather poetically, the niches today are all empty and the only religious symbol in the building is a cross.

72. Further suggested reading here would be, Whose Justice? Which Rationality? It is a 1988 book of moral philosophy by the Scottish philosopher Alasdair MacIntyre. In it, he argues that there are different and incompatible accounts of rationality—notably those of Aristotle, Augustine, David Hume, and Thomas Aquinas. MacIntyre suggests that the differing accounts of justice presented by Aristotle and Hume, are due to the underlying differences in their conceptual schemes.

73. The statistics for Brexit showed that Anglicans, who made up 15% of the electorate were far more likely to vote for Brexit than Roman Catholics. One reason given by commentators is that the Anglicans are a national church, whereas Catholics find a supranational allegiance is psychologically and historically easier to accept.

74. T.R. Reid, *The Making of an Empire*, National Geographic, July 1997

75. Recent news that the Tech-elite – having stocked their Giga-mansions with cars, sweets, and modern art – are preparing themselves similar apocalypse ranches and bunkers in New Zealand, should not really come as a surprise.

76. Another reason that few large Roman buildings remain is that the concrete domes and semi-domes were made by shuttering and concrete, which has little tensile strength, and all too vulnerable to earthquakes and foundation settlement.

77. A decade after the last financial crisis Britain has only brought one banker to trial while shoring up a tragic system of greed that has little incentive not to repeat the same financial rapine again.

78. Between 410-476, in Italy, the wealthy plundered the civic buildings to edify their own estates. This led to an imperial edict which stipulated a fine of 50 pounds of gold for a magistrate found pilfering from civic buildings, and flogging and loss of both hands for any subordinate found doing so. This period saw mass enslavements of free Romans.

79. Amongst others; Machiavelli's *The Prince*; Bernard Mandeville's *Fable of the Bees*; and Thomas Malthus' essays on population, were symptoms and causes for the rise of an amoral pragmatism in public life.

80. And even today in many places in Europe the prime basis of wealth is land. For example, in the UK land is worth £5.1 Trillion about 51% of the country's net wealth. In France, it's only 42% but perhaps some of it is still owned by the descendants of those importunate immigrants who arrived at such an inopportune moment. (Source: Financial Times.)

81. These aspects of continuity give weight to the claims of historians like the Canadian Walter Goffat, who wrote in 1980 'what we call the Fall of the Western Roman Empire was an imaginative experiment that got a little out of hand.' It is a view that is thankfully not as fashionable today as it was then.

82. Brittany became Britannia Minor or New Britain. This is why the historian Norman Davies (*The Isles*, p209) says that, in a much later age, the name Great Britain was coined so as to make the distinction.

83. Lucien Musset, C. James, et al. *Germanic Invasions: The Making of Europe, AD 400-600*

84. Alasdair Macintyre, *After Virtue*

85. Intergovernmental Panel on Climate Change

86. George Friedman, *Flashpoints – The Emerging Crisis in Europe*, Doubleday

87. Another existential problem, according to Croatia's PM, and UN President Andrej Plenkovic is the depopulation of the poorer parts of Europe. A mixture of fertility decline and migration has bled 30% of the Baltic republics since 1989. Bulgaria lost 20% of its population and will cost them a further 20% by 2050. In the last 7 years, 5% of Croatians have moved to member states and Romania has lost near 14% since 2000. As the brain drain increases and the silver tsunami rolls on in the coming decades, we should not be surprised by the rise of populist governments and worse.

88. Dr. Robert Herring, *An Introduction to the History of Christianity*, from the early church to the Enlightenment. (Continuum, 2006) p.118

89. Goths in Italy by J Matthews. *History of the Goths*, Wolfram.

90. Nine centuries later Petrarch agreed. Over a hundred years later Machiavelli blamed the barbarian immigration. Two hundred years after that, Gibbon, with more than a hint of wish-fulfillment, assigned a large share of the catastrophe to enervating Christian piety.

91. Lancel, Augustine, pp.386-7

92. Bruce Allsopp makes a parallel point to this in his book *Spirit of Europe*, which I cannot wholly agree with but add here for interest's sake. 'Little has come from the privileged aristocracy, nor the poor who have largely been inhibited by their poverty. Between these extremes, it seems that what we now call the middle class has been the seedbed from which European civilisation and culture have grown.'

93. It was the second generation of these Lombard mercenaries whom Columban encountered after crossing the alps and who gave him land for his final monastery at Bobbio.

94. R.H.C. Davis, *A History of Medieval Europe*

95. Reinhold Niebuhr, *Beyond Tragedy: Essays on the Christian Interpretation of History*.

96. It was actually illegal to marry a barbarian until the sixth century, though I can't imagine that law being given much heed on the frontiers.

97. In *The End of the Modern World*, Romano Guardini described the 'mobile and nervous soul' of the Germanic immigrants as a spirit that longed 'to embrace the whole of being ...to surround the whole world in order to penetrate it completely.'

98. Denis de Rougemont, *Vingt-Huit siècles d'Europe*, Payot 1961

99. https://en.wikipedia.org/wiki/Constantine_the_Great_and_Christianity

100. I got this pithy saying from theologian James Freeman Clarke but have heard that it has an older pedigree.

101. J. M. Roberts, *A History of Europe*. p.78

**St. Cuthbert sails to the land of the Picts.
Prose Life of St. Cuthbert; extracts
from Bede's Historia Ecclesiastica**

CHAPTER 2

Columban's World

CHAPTER SUMMARY: 543-2000 AD, COLUMBAN's CAIRN. Epigrams and epitaphs, ancient and modern, for Columban. 1000 BC–543 AD, COLUMBAN'S HIBERNIA - A brief exposition of ancient Hibernian culture and how Christianity came to be expressed in that non-Roman setting. The influence of Neoplatonism in Irish Christianity via the ascetic monastic traditions of Egypt. Contrasting the lives of Patrick and his contemporary Augustine. Patrick's celebration of God as 'the Creator of Creation' and its implications for science and culture. 543-556 AD – COLUMBAN'S EXODUS: The Justinian Plague. Columban from birth to teenage runaway.

> *'St Columban, this illustrious Irishman who left his own country for voluntary exile, willed and achieved a spiritual union between the principal European countries of his time. He is the patron saint of all those who now seek to build a united Europe.'*
>
> *Robert Schuman, 1950*

The island of Ireland [is] situated at the far end of the Ocean, And there awaits the setting of Titan [the Sun], while the world is turning, And light descends into the sea in the western shadows. There the huge mountains of waves, wild in colour, With profuse snaking locks, beat everywhere on the caves, And there, in a cloak that its blue backs suddenly reveal, They strike the white foamy seashore, the final curve of the land, And do not allow the coast that we know well to release a small questing boat to the salt-swell. Above these, yellow-haired Titan descends and, with dimmed light wheeling, heads for the regions of Arcturus. Following the North Wind, he seeks his rising-place in the East, so that, revived, he may give back a pleasant light to the world, and, with fire, show himself far and wide to the shivering world. Thus, having passed through all the turning-points of day and night with completed course, he illuminates the lands filled with his brilliance, With his heat rendering the world, wet with dew, pleasant again.[102]

543-2000 AD - COLUMBAN'S CAIRN

In Ireland there existed an ancient custom called *Cloch a chur ar a leacht*, placing a stone on a chieftain's cairn as a mark of respect. It is probable that most of the noblest souls ever to walk on our earth have left no cairns, and perhaps that is as it should be. Humility, like courage, is often by its nature the quietest of the virtues. Be that as it may, it is also true that many statesmen, scholars, and saints; popes, poets, and prelates have laid their metaphorical stones on the cairn of one Irishman whose labours contributed so much to the preservation and transmission of the light of learning and faith after the collapse of Rome's western empire.

Columban does not have an Irish chieftain's tomb, for his tomb is far away in North Italy. But let us, at the outset of his story, pick up a few of these metaphorical stones to give ourselves a general impression of how

Columban has been seen by the generations that followed him. The accolades and titles given him are lavish indeed, and we will have time in the succeeding chapters to discover which ones are true and which are false.

For some, like Daniel Rops of the *Academie Francaise,* Columban was, "a sort of prophet of Israel, brought back to life in the sixth century, as blunt in his speech as Isaias or Jeremias ...for almost fifty years souls were stirred by the influence of St Columban. His passing through the country started a real contagion of holiness." Or as Sean Pere Dandin of the *Oratoire* put it, he was "a new Moses but a Moses humanised by the smile of a St Francis." Another Frenchman, this time the historian, George Goyau went further, claiming that he was the greatest of the 'magnificent apostolic personalities' that 'Celtic missionary genius' ever produced.

Yet another Frenchman went even further, the poet, novelist, and dramatist Leon Cathlin[103] outdoes them all, by saying that Columban was 'one of the very great men who have dwelt in the land of France. He is, with Charlemagne, the greatest figure of the Middle Ages." I cannot imagine any other non-Frenchman being so favourably compared. There is a Franco-Irish bond, formed at this time and consolidated in the Jacobite 'troubles' that bypassed the intermediary of England – indeed, was the later binary to it. The current loyalty of Eire to E.U (and the Brexit animus around the Irish border), have their roots not just in the Good Friday Agreement – but in the cultural exchanges extended by Columban 1400 years before.

Of course, Columban's own countrymen can also to be expected be lavish in their compatriot's praise. For Sean Mac Bride, he is 'not only a great Irishman, but also one of the greatest Europeans of his time." The devout Eamon de Valera, their 3rd President, saw Columban's spiritual zeal as a continuing inspiration among his 'modern disciples who go forth from Ireland to bring the world the true meaning of life and the blessings of Christian thought and practice.' One of Columban's twentieth century biographers, the priest Tomas O Fiaich, expands the definition by claiming that in, 'the fullest sense of the phrase, Columban is Ireland's first European. Poet, scholar, abbot, preacher, saint, co-founder of western monasticism, an associate of kings, correspondent of popes, he was the centre of controversy in his own day and has gone on generating it ever since.'

We'll come to the 'controversy' later, but while we are talking of 'popes', let us hear the words of the twentieth century Italian Pius XI, "The more light that is shed by scholars on the period known as the Middle Ages, the clearer it becomes that it was thanks to the initiative and labours of Columban that the rebirth of Christian virtue and civilisation over a great part of Gaul, Germany and Italy took place."

With the growth of 20th century European integration, Columban became an obvious poster boy for the new spirit of peace and cooperation. And little wonder, for Columban had not only practiced *free movement* with abandon but was, as we have already seen, the first to articulate the new sense of European consciousness. "If ever a man was endowed with the European Spirit,' wrote Andre Billy of the *Academie Goncourt*, 'that man was surely Saint Columban.' Even as late as 2013, Madame Christine Lagarde, then President of the International Monetary Fund, admitted that "while Europe was in the Dark Ages, Irish monks such as Columbanus... kept the flame of knowledge alive."

1000BC – 543 AD COLUMBAN'S HIBERNIA

Here are many grand claims for us to weigh in the coming chapters. We have already seen (at the end of the last chapter), that in trying to preserve Roman civilisation, Justinian's sword only hastened its end. But if these accolades are correct, Columban with his life and pen, and without the least pretence of saving it, did. This paradox, if true, might be an essential lesson for us.[104] C. S. Lewis wrote, that in the preservation of civilisation, 'mere longevity' was a 'contemptible ideal'. Our fixation with preservation might itself be a sign of stagnation, even ossification.

Where does the power of societal renewal spring from? One of Chesterton's oversized characters memorably, 'never spoke about the books he had written, for he was too much alive for that. He spoke about the books he had not yet written.' That vital spark, surely a combination of factors, is something we must tease out of these Irish. We will soon read more about the Latin pessimism and inertia that we encountered in the last chapter. Did these Irish have a corresponding ethnic optimism? Was it blarney? Hardly. Even Ireland's early ecclesiastics were bold as lions. No chinless prelates, they strode the land more like Medici princes, albeit in sackcloth rather than silk. For example, both Patrick and Declan appointed local kings.

And then where did this confidence come from that led so many Irishmen overseas? How were they so changed that they believed they could affect such wider change? Apparently, Freud once said in frustration that the Irish were the only people who could not be helped by psychoanalysis. High praise indeed! What is it with the Irish? In this chapter we will examine the Ireland into which Columban was born so that we may see him in the context of his remarkable generation.

> 'Columban, who is also called Columba, was born on the island of Ireland. This is situated in the extreme ocean and, according to common report, is charming, productive among the various nations, and free from the wars which trouble other nations. Here lives the race of the Scots, who, although they lack the laws of the other nations, flourish in the doctrine of Christian strength, and exceed in faith all the neighbouring tribes. Columban was born amid the beginnings of that race's faith, in order that the religion, which that race cherished uncompromisingly, might be increased by his own fruitful toil and the protecting care of his associates.' Jonas' Life of St Columban

The Celts, like all the other migrants of the preceding chapter, came from the east. They entered Europe, like the 'barbarians' a millennium later, by crossing the Rhine, in around 600BC. They established themselves in Gaul, and Iberia (possibly even traveling from there as far as New Hampshire) and then down to Greece and Galatia (modern day

Turkey). In the first book of his histories, Livy gives an account of the first generation of incumbent Celts (under a 6th century BC king called Ambigatus) who overran a third part of Gaul in their south and eastward expansion.[105] By 400BC they had pushed north across the channel to Britain, then to Ireland fifty years later. The historian Peter Brown even suggests[106] that if Rome had fallen in the 2nd Century most of Western Europe would now be speaking Celtic,[107] if not Arabic. They were an illiterate, seminomadic, aristocratic warrior society. But what we know of them may be deduced from their architecture and oral traditions.

In the *Táin bó Cuailnge, "The Cattle Raid of Cooley"* we find an assertive, boastful, and spirited people. They are pre-reflective, that is they do not think profoundly or ponderously *but they do act*. Here we find one possible source of later Irish confidence, to act – both men and women. In the *Táin* Queen Medb brooks no insult from her husband but recounts her noble lineage, personal wealth, and the number of soldiers that served under her. She says she outshone her six sisters in 'grace and giving and battle and warlike combat.' Helen of Troy's face might have set sail a thousand ships, but she could never, by any stretch of the Aegean imagination, have dreamt of anything like this. In fact, such is the strength and assurance of Medb's voice, that it makes someone even like Germaine Greer seem shrill and reactionary. Medb's conception of a woman is not merely a better sort of man. She does not want his trousers or his job any more than she would want his moustache. She exists as her own person, with her own property, rights, and abilities.

How different is Queen Medb of the *Táin* to Queen Dido of the *Aeneid*. Can you imagine Medb dying of grief for departing Aeneas as Dido did? Hardly! Medb boasts that she had settled only for the husband who could supply her with the best wedding gift – i.e. a husband that could prove worthy of one of the ancient Irish virtues, *generosity*. (The other two are bravery and fidelity.) Medb will fight, steal, kill and copulate with whomsoever she chooses without apology.

If we have drawn comparisons backwards to Greece, then we can also see the same gulf when we view her from our own time. We cannot imagine Medb on BBC Radio Four's *Woman Hour* bemoaning the rank patriarchy in the corporate boardroom, or doing a gender studies degree. I do not say this to be unnecessarily inflammatory or to hold this Irish woman up as a model of wholesome womanhood, but merely to highlight in the strongest possible terms how different she is and, perhaps, they all were. If you called her a proto-feminist, she would either not understand, or laugh heartily, or punch you. It is a difference of kind, not degree. In her we glimpse a people, or at least a warrior aristocracy, very much alive and confident, with an emphasis on action more than contemplation.[108] And so straight away, here is something completely different. We have no leisure to give excerpts here, but if you need convincing of the difference in temper evident in early Ireland from the Classical world just across that brief stretch of water, then do read the *Tain*.

But lest I be accused of romanticizing the past,[109] let me mention that they also sacrificed prisoners[110] to their war gods, and newborns to their fertility gods. They believed that the human head was the seat of the soul, so they displayed enemy heads hanging from their belts, or in special niches in their temples, or merely used them for sport like our footballs. They also used human skullcaps as ceremonial drinking bowls and when they had run out of uses, or heads, they also sculpted them. Modern pagans, or at least our image of them, is all rather woolly and serene; sandals, joss sticks, and dreamcatchers. Neo-pagan and pseudo-Celtic revivals have a surprisingly long lineage in modernity dating as far back to the early 18th century. The Revd. Dr William Stukeley (1687-1765) Rector of Stamford, tried to revive the cult of the Druids when, after visiting Stonehenge, he built a Druid's grove in his garden and had his friends call him 'Arch-Druid Chyndonax'.[111] As one scholar noted, 'each new generation gets the Stonehenge it deserves, or desires.'[112]

When the Revd. James Macpherson (1736-96) claimed to possess the ancient poems of a Hiberno-Christian bard called Ossian, great swathes of the European *literati* were taken in, such was the desire to recover the lost Celtic heritage.[113] Fermented by an understandable disquiet felt by many in the modern world, 'Celticity' and 'Celtomania' have reinvigorated nationalist, environmentalist, Christian, sub-Christian and neo-pagan movements from the Romantic era down to our own.[114]

But the unavoidable implications of taking your religion or philosophy from nature is that it is benign and ferocious in equal measure. And we can discern these disturbing psychological undercurrents in such people through their folklore and myth. There we find a great *cleft between conscious bravery and sub-conscious fear.*'[115] And also, in the many tales of shapeshifters the disquieting, and perhaps post-modern,[116] thought that *'reality had no predictable pattern, but was arbitrary and insubstantial. There is within this worldview a terrifying personal implication; that I myself have no fixed identity but am, like the rest of reality, essentially fluid – essentially inessential.'* [117] This 'indomitable reaction against the despotism of fact' was also high highlighted by Matthew Arnold in his 1867 *The Study of Celtic Literature.* I am tempted to say more here in relation to the blending of natural and societal boundaries in our own day – for this tendency to *developmentalism* has much in tune with post-modern sentiments – but let it suffice to hint that the fixity offered by the new religion,[118] through its doctrine of a creator, became a central theme in later Irish literature. They discovered in praxis what we in the west must rediscover; nature (in its philosophical sense) 'has nothing to teach us. It is our business to live by our own laws, not hers.'[119]

Let us also note here the doctrine of the Trinity – three persons in one god, which Patrick illustrated to them with the clover leaf. Three had always been a magical number for the Irish, they even worshipped a *three-faced god.* And this leads us onto a most singular observation from modern archeology regarding the human sacrifice of those times. Many scholars now conclude, from the evidence of the sacrificed 'bogmen', that it was not just slaves or prisoners but also high caste youths, maybe even king's sons, who were ceremonially offered. No doubt these sacrifices were for the good of the tribe, to save them from famine and the dread of occult agencies. Perhaps these young men were, even from

birth, raised for that purpose. Perhaps they even offered themselves willingly as sacrifices? This is conjecture, but parts of it might suggest how
the Irish were ripe for the Christian revolution that was already sweeping the rest of Europe and Asia. These Druid-ridden Irish may well
have found in the Christian story the resolution to their own. Namely
that the God with *the three faces* had sent his own princely son to be
sacrificed for them. That they were in fact loved by God, must have
been almost unbelievably good news. But that no other sacrifice was
thenceforth needed, might have brought relief to more than a few fathers, mothers, and sons. It is a theory, but either way, the new religion
did come to Ireland, and transform it slowly into the Island of Saints
and Scholars.[120] How and when is a subject of great and lengthy scholarly debate. There is much evidence to suggest that it was well before
Patrick[121] but for the purposes of our story let us at least use Patrick's
experience to frame what we need to know. And, to add texture, let us
also compare and contrast him with a man we have already briefly met
in the previous chapter – Augustine.

Patrick and Augustine of Hippo lived at opposite ends of the empire
(if we use the north-south axis), and were very near contemporaries.
Both their fathers were minor Roman officials (Patrick's father was a
dreaded *Curialis* – taxman) and each grew into their teens having a
good classical education and, as might be expected, hope for a good Roman career. Both, also, by their own admissions, grew up complacent
and somewhat indifferent to the Christian faith of their parents.[122] We
know this because both recorded their Christian testimonies – called
Confessions – for us to read.

And what reading they make. They are the first real autobiographies
in human history. Augustine, for example, is the first human being
recorded as using the word 'I' in the way that we mean it today – it is a
quantum leap into what we recognise as the modern self-conscious.[123]
His style and erudition would not be matched for centuries – his intellect for perhaps six centuries.[124] He is the consummate grammarian
and rhetorician, almost the last of the ancient world. 'He was, to a far
greater degree than any emperor or barbarian warlord, a maker of his-

tory and a builder of the bridge which was to lead from the old world to the new.'[125] His treatise *On Christian Doctrine* became the programme for monastic schools.[126] The German scholar Harnack goes so far as to say that 'it would seem that the miserable existence of the Roman empire was prolonged until then, only to permit Augustine's influence to be felt.'

What, compared to this, could Patrick lay claim to? Patrick is only too aware that his Latin was crude,[127] for his education had been cut short when he was kidnapped from a Romano-British coastal town at the age of sixteen. For the coming years Patrick would be schooled not in rhetoric, but 'hunger and nakedness' looking after sheep as a slave to an Irish chieftain. These are not kindly teachers but they can work in the character more than all the lessons of the grammarian. Patrick tells us in his *Confessio*, that when deprived of everything, he turned to God with his whole being. The marks of his later courage and compassion – his true greatness – are surely the fruits of this tremendous alienation and suffering.

Not so at the other end of the empire, for at about the same time Augustine was finishing his own *Confessio*. In the intervening years he had left his home in North Africa and tried his hand at teaching in Rome, then Milan. By his own admission, he seems to have indulged in a student lifestyle surpassing any modern undergraduate – even keeping a concubine from his teen years and fathering a son by her. But all the while, he writes, '*I carried inside me a cut and bleeding soul, and how to get rid of it I did not know. I sought every pleasure – the countryside, sports, fooling around, the peace of a garden, friends and good company, sex, reading. My soul floundered in a void – and came back to upon me. For where could my heart flee from my heart? Where could I escape from myself?*' [128] Even now we feel the power of what was then a completely new genre of spiritual literature. His Confession has rightly been called 'one of the most influential religious books in the Christian tradition.'[129]

And where 'did he escape' from himself? It was to hear an extraordinary Christian communicator of his day, Bishop Ambrose. Initially,

Augustine attended his sermons in Milan out of intellectual curiosity. But under Ambrose's powerful persuasion, and that of another priest called Simplicianus, Augustine came to a conclusion reached by other intellectuals, like Justyn Martyr and Marius Victorinus before him; that Jesus was the summation and answer to all Hellenistic philosophy. The shock that his mother's faith contained the ultimate answers, and that he had searched everywhere else for so long, was a fact not lost on him who wrote;

> 'too late have I loved thee, O Beauty ever ancient and ever new. Too late have I loved thee! And behold, thou wast within me, and I out of myself, and there I searched for thee.'

He became a monastic founder, bishop, and ardent polemicist. He was undoubtedly a great man, but he has not appeared to later generations with an untarnished reputation in the way that Patrick has. Some of these errors he tried to correct in his later writing, and some – we must admit – belong to the category of errors of his day. To become, as Shelley put it, an 'unacknowledged legislator of mankind' is a terrible responsibility and the particular burden of very gifted people. His attitude toward a Christian sect called the Donatists – 'error has no rights' – became the first church justification for state persecution. He also wrote that to disbelieve in forced conversion is to deny the power of God. The horror we feel with hindsight was the same horror expressed by Alcuin of York when his master Charlemagne conducted forcible baptisms in the east and extracted a compulsory church tax. But in Augustine's defense, he only advocated indirect economic sanctions against the Donatists. He never mentions torture or any physical force, even though others, like the inquisition, wrongly deduced that from his work.[130]

But for now, let us not be side-tracked. We will leave Augustine, with profound gratitude mingled with caution, as he dies nobly in Hippo Regius, the Vandals beating at the city gates, surrounded by the grateful church he had stayed to protect. Among our hedonists, I think he should be more popular. Even today he is still the patron of brewers because of his conversion out of such a life of loose living and worldly ambition. With that in mind, perhaps we could, with at least one eye to our own hearts, remember him more readily as the man who 'stressed the primacy of love in a way that almost recommends libertinism. *Dilige et quod vis fac* (Love God and do what you will) and *Cum dilectione hominum et odio vitiorum* (love the sinner and hate the sin.)[131]

While Augustine was laid to rest, Patrick – who had escaped from captivity – received a divine vision about his future life's work as he was sailing back to Ireland. It would be unlike any evangelistic mission undertaken in the Roman world; there was no *civitas*, that is, no civic centres of population. Even through the tangled mesh of later hagiography and 8th century historiography, we can assume with a degree of certainty that his *Confession* and his *Letter to Coroticus* are genuine. And in these at least, we see a courageous man, who though wounded deeply, cared profoundly for the Irish people among whom he had made himself a voluntary exile. In his life, teaching, and actions he proved himself every bit the match of any Irish chieftain in the virtues of courage, generosity, and fidelity. We laud military figures like Caesar and Alexander who sacrificed great armies and cut vast swathes of destruction across the earth in order to achieve perishable ends. Shall we not also acknowledge the greatness of a man like Patrick? A man who returned to the land of his personal nightmares to set others free from theirs.

He had seen first-hand the particular hardships of female slaves and their incredible courage. In his letter to the Christian Britons (Letter to Coroticus) and other earthly courts of tyrants, he is the first man to unequivocally denounce slavery. Who cannot be moved by such greatness of soul, such extraordinary self-sacrifice, and such humane endeavour? Adam Smith called the 'revolution' that led to the first disappearance of slavery in Europe 'one of the most obscure points in modern history.' I would suggest that he need look no further than men like Patrick (and women like Queen Clothilde, wife of Clovis I) speaking Christian 'truth to power' to an emergent European civilisation. In Smith's own day, an ethical and hermeneutic amnesia had tragically suppressed the *Imageo Dei* doctrine, with the result that Christian men and women in the Clapham sect (Wilberforce *et al*) had to raise the doctrine once more against the dehumanising forces of mammon.[132]

According to one source, Patrick lived on to a very great age at his barn-church in Saul, just south of Strangford Lough.[133] I stumbled upon the church, quite by accident, one summer's evening in 2018 and was amazed to see that the site was completely untouched by tourism. One heritage road sign, and one hand-painted-and-peeling, black wooden sign on the gate. No car park, or shop, or ticket booth – not so much as even one plastic leprechaun or clover-leaf trinket! Considering the importance of the location I was filled with amazement.

When asked about the key to Patrick's confidence and success, one historian admits that is it 'the sort of ringing, rock-solid confidence on which a civilization may be built, an unmuffled confidence not heard since the Golden Ages of Greece and Rome –such is his reliance on "the Creator of Creation," the phase with which the "Breastplate"[134] opens and closes.[135] We saw, earlier in this chapter, the reception of this new foundational concept of reality. Perhaps we might stretch the analogy now to say that the former Irish perception of the material world was similar to that of the learned Brahmins who studied the philosophy of the Upanishads. For them, the material world was a phantom, an illusion which hid and falsified our perceptions. It is not hard to see how this understanding would prohibit scientific advance. Compare it to the idea of a *Creator of Creation* who has made men and women in his image *(Imageo Dei)* and ordered those men and women to find out his ways and be custodians of his creation, and it is immediately obvious how the huge conceptual breakthroughs that we call the Scientific Revolution happened in the West.[136]

What Patrick received as God's revelation of Himself, His world, and our place in it; in the end turned out to be the formula indispensable for the breakthroughs that would come in the 16th and 17th centuries. 'Contrary to the received wisdom, religion and science are not only compatible, they are inseparable.'[137] What scholars are now finally awake to, is that it was theological assumptions unique to Judaism and Christianity alone, that gave rise to the flowering of science in Europe and nowhere else. It is a great pity that this is not understood more widely at the popular level, but there is always hope.

Another of the great errors, so often repeated by those who ought to know better, is that science was only born at the Renaissance when the church could no longer suppress it. Anyone with any reading or sympathy for the mood and genuine achievements of that time will straightway recognise this as incorrect. Far from 'recovering classical antiquity in spite of the Church,' Butterfield says, 'we ought rather... to see the Church preserving the ancient culture and then working for a thousand years (until)... the ancient classics had come to permeate the whole fabric of western civilisation.' The humanism of the Renaissance was not about advance or progress but, rather a 'homesickness for the old.'[138] If anything, it was actually a revolt against the rationalism of Aristotle and Aquinas, a reaction which the historian Preserved Smith said rendered the Renaissance merely an 'artistic, emotional reaction against reason.' What made the Renaissance important was not rediscovery, as much as Italian ethnic pride and cultural emulation. It was a movement among people of fashion; and was nostalgic and mainly aesthetic in character – not scientific.

So, the assertion that science came to Europe with the rediscovery of classical knowledge is very misleading. The main classical texts had been the subject of study since the scholastic era, as it had been in Islamic countries – though, without equivalent signs of 'revolution' taking place. This is not to decry, ignore or belittle the Muslim advancements in optics, mathematics, medicine, and astronomy (and indeed, their other technological achievements) but merely to point out that the larger conceptual breakthroughs happened among the people who were spurred on by a belief that they were made in the image of Yahweh. (As far as I can tell, the same is not claimed by Muslims for Allah. They do not make the bold claim to be made in Allah's image.) So, Science exploded in the Christian west, meaning that 'by the late 13th century Europe had (already) seized global scientific leadership.'[139]

But was this correlation or causation? Many favour the latter. Professor Eric Nelson also makes the point that the two centuries after 1550 were more biblically conscious, not less. The ubiquity of the printed word, and the imaginative leaps made by a now Bible-literate laity, would have profound effects. The old accusation that these were 'nominal Christians entering a more rational age' is also false. In *For the Glory of God*, Rodney Stark, uses all the dark arts of the sociologist to prove statistically that the most progressive and productive scientific minds of the scientific revolution were almost all fervent Christians, with barely a nominal attendee among them. He also exposes the rather shoddy efforts of the rationalists[140] to suppress Newton's religious writing in the hopes of having at least him to themselves.

Alas, it will not do. Even the Catholic Descartes, has now been set back in his proper pre-modern soil by scholars like Stephen Menn.[141] That is because scientific advance was the substantial work of a philosophical cultivation that had gone on since the early Middle Ages, and which broke the surface during the 11th century scholastic movements, and which finally flowered in the sixteenth to seventeenth centuries. It was not just Newton who stood on the shoulders of giants, they all did, and so do we all. Aquinas, Buridan or Oresme should be as well known in the classroom as other pious Christians like Kepler, Newton and Clerk Maxwell. Einstein knew he stood on Maxwell's shoulders, even as Descartes understood he was on Augustine's. That has not been the case with us. Once again, Ricoeur's references to cultural memory and amnesia arise before us. People with dementia cannot plan for the future, for they are severed from the past.

There is much more to say here, particularly about monasticism (which we cover in Ch. 4, 6, 7 & 15), literacy, and the information revolution that played such a decisive role in the Irish story, and which they embraced with such joyous zeal.[142] And there is much to say also about the decisive effects of the medieval university, which we shall touch on in chapter 15. But let us be content to travel away from all this grand talk of science, and back to the Kingdom of Meath[143] where in 543AD, a century after Patrick and in the very year of St. Benedict's death, another monastic founder was born.

543-556 AD – COLUMBAN'S EXODUS

The 540s were the dread years of a European pandemic that seems to have ended trade from the Eastern Mediterranean. It will be raging for fifty years and perhaps claiming as much as half the continental population before it finally ceases.

As is the case with Robert Schuman, Columban was born and lived out his tender years at a pivotal moment in world history. Both were the only sons of their mother, both tender shoots growing up in rocky ground. That we are all shaped by the world into which we are born, is generally accepted. But how some of us become shapers of the world thereafter, is the story we are now pursuing.

According to Jonas, Columban's[144] mother had dreamt, just before his birth, that a brilliant sun arose from her breast and illuminated the whole world. In Columban's youth, he must have sat at the feet of some learned teachers, for Jonas records that he studied grammar, rhetoric, geometry, as well as the sacred scriptures, all of which formed part of the curriculum of the Irish monastic schools. As he grew to manhood his *formae elegantia*, as Jonas calls it, appealed particularly to one young woman who tried to attract him. When Benedict, the Italian monastic founder, faced a similar temptation regarding a young woman, fifty years previously, he threw himself naked into a patch of thorns – a remedy that has fallen out of favour in more recent times! Poor Columban could not have availed himself of this prickly remedy in any case, because Gregory had not yet written up this hagiography of Benedict. But Jonas describes that, notwithstanding, Columban fought the temptation with *the gospel as his shield* and sought the advice of an anchoress who lived in a nearby cell. She told him,

> *'Fifteen years ago I abandoned my father's house to fight against temptation and sin. Christ is my leader. Since then the grace of God has kept me from turning back and if I were not a weak woman I would have crossed the seas in search of a wider battlefield. But you, burning with the fire of youth, stay at home. Whether you*

like it or not, you will find yourself in your weakness listening to the tempter's voice. Do you think you can go freely in the company of women? Don't you recall that Adam fell through the blandishments of Eve, that Samson was seduced by Delilah, that David fell through the beauty of Bethshabee, that the most wise Solomon was deceived through love of women. Away with you, young man, go away from the destruction which has ruined so many, turn from the road that leads to the gates of Hell.'

An influence immediately evident in the passage above is the asceticism which came to Ireland from Egypt via writings like Jerome's, and Athanasius' *Life of Anthony*, which were widely read. In the post Freudian world, we assume that sexual desire is the predominant driver in social relationships, but it is worth pointing out that for men like Columban, the control of *Eros* was only a litmus test, or barium-trace, of how well you were subduing the other passions. (This was more or less exactly what was written by the fifth century monastic writer John Cassian.) But when tracing the epistemic roots of this world-and-flesh-denying asceticism, we find that it is more Greek-stoic in temper than any inheritance from Christ and the apostles. It was certainly not the substance of biblical teaching – read *The Song of Solomon* if you need convincing! The Bible is unequivocal that the material world, including sexual union within proscribed relationships are not only normative, but indeed healthy, and to be enjoyed as a gift from God.

Having said that, the Bible has an almost unique remedy for sexual temptation that tallies well with the anchorite's advice. Paul admonishes his young disciple, Timothy, similarly to flee from sexual temptation. Many times Christians are told to stand, but only three times are they permitted to flee; one is from sexual temptation, another is from overt persecution whilst engaged in evangelistic endeavor, and another is from the love of money. What is conveyed in the old anchorite's words is one pole of Roman sexual culture enduring under the cover of the Gospel. With the alloy of Greek and Roman Stoicism, Latin Christianity adopted asceticism as an ideal, even if it were an ideal practiced only by the most fervent. The desert wilderness stood as antithetical to the luxury of the city; Abraham had gone there, so had John the Baptist, soon others would follow. For some, like Paul of Thebes or Malchus[145] the wilderness was a necessity for survival in times of persecution. These men, and no doubt many others, were the last generation before Constantine made Christianity a *religio licita* – a legal religion. Perhaps many in the generation which followed, looked to those hardy souls (who had emerged from the wilderness with their faith and integrity intact) and deduced that asceticism was essential to Christian piety.

Whilst there are plenty of Bible verses that, interpreted through a neo-platonic disdain for 'corrupt-matter' might spawn a social phenomenon like aestheticism; it, nevertheless, fails to adequately explain the larger movement that began around Egypt. This we will look at in more detail in Chapter 4. It is emphasized here because much of what we will see in Columban's life will make little sense if we do not see how directly the Irish were influenced by eastern asceticism; and how unnecessarily harsh their monastic rule became. But more of that later. For now though, let us enjoy this unusual glimpse of a young man fifteen centuries ago, struggling with an all-too-familiar sexual temptation[146] and going to get advice from this old wise woman. This woman comes across as a true spiritual daughter of Anthony in her renunciation of the world and her declaration of battle against the forces of darkness. She is in this respect more than a match for the great Gautama (Buddha), who sought the former without thought for the latter. But let us also notice her words, *if I were not a weak woman I would have crossed the seas in search of a wider battlefield.* Notice the aspiration already present in Irish Christianity,[147] which would one day become firmly embedded in Columban's own mind.

Also, note how different this desire is from the Romantic *Peregrini* of the eighteenth and nineteenth centuries. In his 2018 book *The Warm South*, Robert Holland suggests that these later migration of poets, painters and other culture shapers to southern Europe was due to, amongst other things, a profound cultural insecurity, which took root

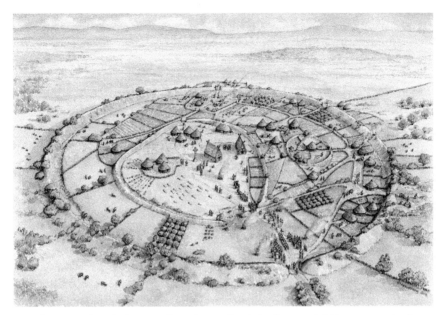

7th Century (wooden) monastic enclosure that Columbanus might have recognised.

paradoxically – or perhaps prophetically – as the British Empire was at its zenith.

Columban would one day travel across *the seas in search of a wider battlefield,* but first he had to achieve some sort of exodus from his parental home. Jonas gives us a dramatic – perhaps too dramatic – account of the final parting. It is an account worthy of a Greek tragedy but may be a true account for all that. Teenagers in any age are apt to act without thought for the feelings of others. When Columban goes home to tell his mother he is leaving, she pleads with him, bursting into tears and throwing herself across the threshold to block his exit. He tells her not to grieve, he steps across her prostrate body and sets off for the north, casting words behind him that we know first came from Jerome's pen two centuries before. *'The enemy holds the sword over me to strike me down; so what should I care for a mother's tears ....The true piety here is to be cruel.'* Was this Columban or an addition of a zealous hagiographer? He, himself, once told his disciples to *'fear bishops and women'* but, really, we will never know. What we do know is that Columban's journeys had only just begun and that he would never see her again in this world.

CHAPTER 2
FOOTNOTES & REFERENCES

102. This is a literal translation from Hiberno-Latin of the poem found in Jonas of Bobbio's *Vita Columbani* I.2. My immediate source was from the excellent: *Jonas of Bobbio: Life of Columbanus, Life of John of Réomé, and Life of Vedast*, translated with introduction and commentary by Alexander O'Hara and Ian Wood, Liverpool University Press, 2017.

103. Leon Cathlin wrote the play *La lumieres de Bebris* about Columban's monks.

104. C. S. Lewis, *First and Second Things*

105. This was in the days of Tarquin the Elder, the legendary fifth king of Rome, who died in 579, exactly 1000 years before Columban arrived on the continent.

106. Peter Brown, *The Rise of Western Christendom: Triumph and Diversity, A.D. 200-1000*: 5 (Making of Europe)

107. In his magisterial *The Isles*, p.51-59, Norman Davies gives a detailed account of the 19th-20th century philologists who established that the various Celtic languages (many now lost) had a common Sanskrit root. (Macmillan Publishers Ltd, 1999.)

108. It was not a matriarchal society by any stretch of the imagination. Nevertheless, the position of women can be seen again in Brigid of Kildare, who displayed every ounce of Medb's spirit. She ruled a double monastery (men and women) and the city that sprung up there became, according to Cogitosus, a great metropolis.

109. The idea of the 'romantic Celts from a misty past' was an 18th century wish-fulfillment dream. The authenticity of Macpherson's translation of ancient Gaelic poems on Ossian has always been a subject of scholarly debate. But whether fake or not, they caught the mood of the hour and were deeply influential across Western Europe during the Romantic movement.

110. Ibid, p.77 (Macmillan Publishers Ltd, 1999.)

111. Ibid p.91 (Macmillan Publishers Ltd, 1999.)

112. Jacquetta Hawkes, *A Guide to the Prehistoric and Roman monuments of England and Wales*. Pp.288-9

113. Norman Davies, *The Isles,* p.123 (Macmillan Publishers Ltd, 1999.)

114. Ibid p.95 & p145 (Macmillan Publishers Ltd, 1999.)

115. Thomas Cahill, *How the Irish Saved Civilisation*

116. Postmodernism is a late twentieth century philosophical and cultural movement, which someone has described ultimately as nihilism with a grin. Writers like Foucault and Derrida used their pens to communicate, with dogmatic certainty, that there was no objective truth and no possibility of communication. Butler used similar techniques to destroy the concept of gender. 'In their prejudice against prescribed data,' writes Norman Davies, these 'deconstructionists' claimed, 'that knowing something is more dangerous than knowing nothing.' They articulated the legitimation crisis for authority in post-Christian societies. But it was only a matter of time before the deconstructionists were deconstructed by their own

techniques; that Jacques Derrida, who derided so many, was himself derided. In the-meantime, the emerging orthodoxies of political correctness and identity politics, have instrumentalised all the same tools of oppression, and achieved a spectacular cultural coop. Ironically, if Derrida or Foucault were alive today, they would probably be appalled by the anarchic conformity of contemporary society.

117. Thomas Cahill, *How the Irish Saved Civilisation*

118. In Part 2 Chapter, 4 of *The Everlasting Man*, G. K. Chesterton symbolised this peculiar fixity found the Judeo-Christian worldview as a key. 'First, a key is above all things a thing with a shape. It is a thing that depends entirely upon keeping its shape. The Christian creed is above all things the philosophy of shapes and the enemy of shapelessness. That is where it differs from all that formless infinity, Manichean or Buddhist, which makes a sort of pool of night in the dark heart of Asia; the ideal of uncreating all the creatures. That is where it differs also from the analogous vagueness of mere evolutionism; the idea of creatures constantly losing their shape. A man told that his solitary latchkey had been melted down with a million others into a Buddhistic unity, would be annoyed. But a man told that his key was gradually growing and sprouting in his pocket, and branching into new wards or complications, would not be more gratified...... there was undoubtedly much about the key that seemed complex; indeed, there was only one thing about it that was simple. It opened the door.'

119. C.S. Lewis *Present Concerns* (Ethical Essays) 'Living in the Atomic Age'

120. The structures of power are naturally among the last aspects of a culture to be transformed by a non-violent revolution. Ireland's transformation was interrupted greatly by the Viking wars, but even in the 10th century, Columbkille of Iona's royal kinsmen were still expected to mate with a white mare on their coronation day.

121. Declan, for example, is one of four Munster saints who had Lives written for them claiming that they founded monasteries and preached the Gospel in Munster before Patrick ever set foot in Ireland. These bishop saints, known since the 17th century as *quattuor sanctissimi episcopi*, also included Ailbe of Emly, Ciarán of Saigir, and Abbán of Moyarney. There are others, and all found in the so-called Dublin Collection. Even here it is difficult to ascribe correct dates, though it is plain from hundreds of Ogham stones in Wales that the Irish had a close connection with Christianity from an early date through commerce, colony, and slavery. (Norman Davies, in *The Isles*, also says that Ninian's successor Crantoc was the first to bring the gospel to Ireland from Whitehorn, now in southern Galloway, Scotland.)

122. In Augustine's case, only his mother was a Christian.

123. Those wishing to glance back at the psychological canyon over which we have just leapt, might find some help in Paul Ricoeur's 1986 Gifford Lectures (published as, Oneself as Another, 1992) where the philosopher asks what it is to be 'a self' He addresses interpretations of the Cartesian cogito which made it too strong, and against which Ricoeur proposed a hermeneutic of selfhood and a "wounded cogito". 'This was a person capable of attesting to his or her own existence and acting

in the world, a self that both acted and was acted upon who could recount and take responsibility for its actions. Insofar as we can speak metaphysically of such a self it has to be in terms of act and potentiality rather than substance. Ricoeur's argument regarding selfhood proceeds through a sequence of stages. He begins from the philosophy of language and the question of an identifying reference to persons as selves, not simply things. .... this is followed by the question of the ethical aim of being such a self. This hermeneutics of selfhood culminates in the conclusion that one is a self as oneself among other selves, something that can only be attested to through personal testimony or the testimony of others. Selfhood is thus closely tied to a kind of discourse that says, "I believe-in". Its certainty is a lived conviction rather than a logical or scientific certainty. Source: https://plato.stanford.edu/entries/ricoeur/#NarrIdenTurnSelf

124. Translator F. J. Sheeds' Foreword to the *Confessions*

125. Christopher Dawson, *St. Augustine and his Age*

126. Ibid

127. This is certainly how Patrick saw himself, but this might have been a very typical and heartfelt Christian humility on his part. Other scholars have seen in his writing, limited though the canon is, a mark of literary and structural genius. For more see, *'The Book of the letters of Saint Patrick the Bishop'* by D. R Howlett, Four Courts Press ISBN I - 85182-137-6

128. A similar inner yearning is viewed in many forms across the ages; Goethe writes of our 'holy longing'; Kierkegaard, a 'sickness unto death'; the pilgrim poet Basho also referred to 'a glimpse of the under-glimmer'. Emerson spoke of 'the undersong'; Gaugin wrote on a painting; 'Why are we here, where are we going?' Jim Morison sang 'Let me tell you about heartache and the loss of god. Wandering, wandering in hopeless night.' They all, at one level or another, express our deepest earth longings (Steinbeck) to 'get back to the garden.' (Joni Mitchel)

129. St. Augustine, Albert Cook Outler, *The Confessions of St. Augustine* (Dover Thrift Editions) 05-Mar-2012

130. Henry Chadwick, *Augustine: A Very Short Introduction* (Oxford University Press, 2001) p85-6

131. Norman Davies, *Europe, a history*. P.263

132. There is not space to enlarge on this important point here, but I would suggest that those interested read the chapter on Slavery in Sociologist, Rodney Stark's book, *For the Glory of God*, or indeed William Hague's excellent biography, *William Wilberforce*.

133. Norman Davies, *The Isles*, p.176 (Macmillan Publishers Ltd, 1999.)

134. St Patrick's *Breastplate* is perhaps a 7th or 8th century reworking of Patrick's original poem, nevertheless, it is still hailed as the first expression of European vernacular poetry.

135. Thomas Cahill *How the Irish Saved Civilisation*

136. That is not to ignore or demean the work of Islamic scholars (who made contributions in some areas) but to assert the central reality that the significant conceptual breakthroughs were made not only in the West but also by those who either held personally (or inherited conceptually) the concept of biblical creation.

137. Rodney Stark, *For the Glory of God*

138. A phrase used by Johan Huizinga

139. Lynn White, Jr, *The Historical Roots of Our Ecological Crisis*

140. Christopher Dawson framed it thus: 'Faith transcends reason because divine truth is not only higher, but also wider than the human mind, and the rationalist in his haste for premature simplification always tends to shut his eyes to one aspect of the truth and to seek a false harmony of thought by the sacrifice of an essential element of reality.'

141. Stephen Menn, *Descartes and Augustine*. Cambridge University Press, 1998

142. In their *'Book of Invasions'* (woven together from earlier sources in the 11th century) the Irish, being conscious of the larger story and are zealous to have their part in it, even insert themselves into biblical (world history). Therefore, one Irishman has a peek at the Ten Commandments, another is there to garner the best idioms of language at the tower of Babel. Moreover, the Irish had the confidence to write in their native tongue. (much as Luther did during the Reformation) So much so, that their Gaelic script became the most ubiquitous script in European literature in the 7th century.

143. On the borders of the modern counties of Carlow and Wexford

144. Columban was the first Irishman to be the subject of a biography. His Vita Columbanus was written by Jonas of Susa (in northern Italy), who joined Columban's monastery at Bobbio aged eighteen, which was only three years after Columban's death. If we are to believe Sallust, that a great man was only as great as those writers who praise them, then Jonas' Vita must have been one of the most popular hagiographies of its day, because more than a hundred copies are still extant in European libraries. It is in the vein of; *Life of Martin of Tours* by Sulpicius Severus; *The Life of St Hilary of Poitiers* by Fortunatus, and *The Life of St Ambrose* by Paulinus of Milan.

145. Both of whose biographies were written up by the 'flesh-loathing' Jerome, who unfortunately transmitted his unbliblical view of sexuality into Christendom. I cannot but hear Sir Toby words to Malvolio in Twelfth Night when I think of these things; 'Dost thou think because thou art virtuous there shall be no more cakes and ale.' i.e. "Don't think that being a good (or virtuous) person means you can't have fun in life!' I confess, dissolute fellow that I am, to preferring Jerome K Jerome to Jerome, though there are many other things for which we should thank the latter.

146. "But, as his fine figure, his splendid colour, and his noble manliness made him beloved by all, the old enemy, began finally to turn his deadly weapons upon him, in order to catch in his nets this youth, whom he saw growing so rapidly in grace. And he aroused against him the lust of lascivious maidens, especially of those whose fine figure and superficial beauty are wont to enkindle mad desires in the minds of wretched men. But when that excellent soldier saw that he was surrounded on all sides by so deadly weapons, and perceived the cunning and shrewdness of the enemy who was fighting against him and that by an act of human frailty, he might quickly fall over a precipice and be destroyed,-as Livy says, "No one is rendered so sacred by religion, no one is so guarded, that lust is unable to prevail against him," - holding in his left hand the shield of the Gospel and bearing in his right hand the two-edged sword, he prepared to advance and attack the hostile lines threatening him. He feared lest, ensnared by the lusts of the world, he should in vain have spent so much labour on grammar, rhetoric, geometry, and the Holy Scriptures. And in these perils, he was strengthened by a particular aid." Columban also wrote more generally about human nature(in a manner of Paul in Romans chapter 7); 'how miserable our state! The things we ought to have loved are so remote and undiscovered and unknown to us... O

wretched man that you are! What you see you ought to hate, and what you should love you do not know.'

147. This is the 'White Martyrdom' of which we will hear more about in Ch.7

The road from war: British troops blinded by poison gas during the Battle of Estaires, 1918

CHAPTER 3

Schuman's World

CHAPTER SUMMARY- ANNO 1886 AD: EUROPEANS ON THE BRINK OF A PROTO-DARK AGE - Geopolitical and philosophical observations on the year 1886, the year of Schuman's birth. 1886-1900 AD – PEACE ON THE EDGE OF THE ABYSS - The contrast of Schuman's quiet upbringing with the tsunami of new ideologies about to tear Europe apart. Schuman's childhood influences up until the year of his father's death.

ANNO 1886 – EUROPEANS ON THE BRINK OF A PROTO-DARK AGE

We now skip forward to the year 1886, thirteen and a half centuries from Columbanus and frankly, a world away from our own times too. This was the year of Robert Schuman's birth, but before we see his childhood, let us see his world first. Let us do what we can to grasp the threads of history and get a feel for the fabric of so momentous an era in the general human story. It will not be thus in each chapter, I promise. We will come to the swifter narrative as we go on, but let us first examine the soil.

For this was the high noon of some of modernity's most influential thinkers: Darwin, Nietzsche, Marx, Huxley, Dewey, Weber. It was a far cry from Shelley's claim that the poets were the *unacknowledged legislators of mankind*. Now it would be the turn of scientists, philosophers and economists to 'legislate.' In 1886 Nietzsche published *Beyond Good and Evil*. It was also the year that Marx finally published his foundational theoretical text in materialist philosophy, economics and politics, *Das Kapital*. This he did in London while Millais was painting his 'Bubbles'; Wilde was still writing poems and fairy tales, and Gladstone was introducing the Home Rule Bill for Ireland.

Even in 1886, an unseen clock was already ticking for the greatness of Britain. Her Empire was the largest the world had ever seen. At its peak, it was six times the size of the Roman Empire, holding sway over 412 million people: a quarter of the planet's population and a quarter of its landmass.[148] Yet as the year began, Queen Victoria could scarce imagine that the first meeting of the Indian National Congress would fan such *winds of change* throughout her subcontinent. Unforeseen storms would hasten the demise of Britannia's rule of the seas, and within the lifetime of Robert Schuman most of it would be gone. Partly the hideous wars, partly the new mood of nationalism in the colonies, and perhaps also partly the publishing of those books by Nietzsche and Marx.

In the last chapter, we saw the mixed legacy of Augustine. How like a flea bite that seems now compared to the hundreds of millions who died in the twentieth century at the hands of those developing Marx and Nietzsche's[149] atheistic ideas. Nietzsche prophesied that the coming century would be the most bloody the world had ever known, and that in it, we would all go mad. He could not have been more accurate. For in the corporate madness, earnest and even well-intentioned souls – often the very ones who sincerely believed that religion was the root of all wars – became the willing accomplices of death on an industrial scale.

In *Beyond Good and Evil*, Nietzsche called on humanity to forsake *the handful of "certainty"* and take hold of '*a whole cartload of beautiful possibilities.*' Some of what he called '*the last Europeans,*' and the *'firstlings of the twentieth century'* did indeed heed him. Some in our grandparents' and great grandparents' generation did indeed seek to rise above the *'surplus of defective, diseased, degenerating, infirm, and necessarily suffering individuals'*. But it showed us anything but *beautiful possibilities*. Gulags, concentration camps, gas chambers, social eugenics, inhuman experiments, forced abortions, sterilizations, and war on a hitherto unimaginable scale.[150]

Schuman, as much as Columban was a child of the 'Dark Ages', and perhaps more so. Indeed, as one historian noted, 'there are shades of barbarism in twentieth-century Europe that would once have amazed the most barbarous of barbarians.'[151] For, if any generation might justly be seen as ushering in the *Dark Ages* by a future historian or by an unborn generation, it will surely be those being born at the time of Robert Schuman's own birth. 'No cause in history – no religion or imperial ambition or military adventure – has destroyed more lives with more confident enthusiasm than the cause of the brotherhood of man.'[152] The 20th century became exponentially the most murderous in human history; 100 million killed in war, another 100 million through political oppression and another 100 million through ethnic and sectarian violence. What dread storms were brewing as Schuman came forth from the womb.

Wherever else those storms would blow, they would certainly blow on Great Britain. Along with her Commonwealth, she would spend more than just blood and money resisting Nazism, Fascism and Communism. She would spend the prestige and strength that had bound the Commonwealth together. Furthermore, Britain's older security, that she had been the balance of power between continually warring nations, would also soon end. I have stood in wonder before that singular desk[153] (with its peculiar collapsible brass railings) where Viscount Castlereagh oversaw the signatures at the Congress of Vienna in 1815. Post-Napoleon, a coordinated international solution was needed, as it would eventually post-Hitler. Post-Napoleon, it was the British, having led the allies under Wellington, who brokered the peace and maintained the balance of power. Post-Hitler, it was the Americans to a great extent;

but it would also fall to the French, as most aggrieved party, to exert the power of forgiveness rather than the force of a victor.

The old Vienna settlement, based on national strength in correlation to the weakness of one's neighbour, brought peace to Europe for seventy years, though Castlereagh himself thought it would do well to last a mere seven. One hundered and thirty years later, in the Schuman Declaration, international solidarity would achieve the same result, thus far leading to 70 years of European peace - the *Pax Europa*.

The Allied armies won the war, but it was Schuman *et al* who would secure the peace, without which war would have become a regular fixture. The men and women of this generation were to live through two traumatic wars the like of which we can never truly know. No wonder they made it their aim to ensure that another European civil war became almost impossible. And as this dream began to become a reality, Britain, as we will note later on, found herself in unfamiliar waters. The British Empire spent its military, financial and political capital, keeping Europe free from tyranny from the time of John Churchill, 1st Duke of Marlborough, to Winston Churchill, his descendant. No doubt there was a day when Rome passed a point on the curve of rise-to-decline, but *no man knew the day nor the hour*. But perhaps Britain's was 1886.

Across the channel in 1886 (the one we in Britain call the *English Channel*) as the Orleans and Bonaparte families were being banished from France, Rodin was working on his *Kiss*, and just off to the east in Luxembourg, a French army veteran of the Prussian wars was holding his baby son for the first time. The father; Jean Pierre. The baby; Jean-Baptiste Nicolas Robert Schuman. The date: June 29th.[154] Jean Pierre might have had a double reason to smile that day, a first-born son in his old age, and the Bourbons exile. It was through Napoleon III's inept leadership that he had been captured by the Prussians at Sedan in 1870, and also that Jean Pierre Schuman's native Alsace Lorraine had been annexed by the Prussians a year later.

Jean Pierre had been a medium landowner near Evrange on the Lorraine-Luxembourg border. He was a Frenchman who had become a German citizen, but rather than stay under German rule he chose to be an *émigré voluntaire*. He moved his young wife to the leafy Clausen district of Luxembourg, where they rented[155] a new Villa called *the Hermitage*.[156] It is still there today, a handsome turreted villa, situated on a steep wooded slope, just below a memorial tower to the Crimea. That towering monument, *The Malakov Tower*, no less than the Prussian war, would cast a long and ominous shadow over the Schuman residence and the residences of Western Europe.

Some new menace was looming *beyond the borders of the shire* – and it was not just a resurgent Germany. Many sensed it, Nietzsche wrote openly about it; we have *'unchained the earth from the sun'*. It was the advent of the truly autonomous secular nation state, bringing a new 'blood and soil'[157] nationalism unfettered by religious commonalities.[158] *'How much must collapse now that this faith has been undermined,'* Nietzsche wrote. It was anyone's guess back then.

The efficiency of German compulsory secular education, its industrial advances and ruthless war machine had shaken all Europe during the Franco-Prussian war. Nietzsche could not see and could not perhaps be blamed for how history would interpret – or misinterpret – his work. But he understood that his generation were living off the fumes of the cultural capital of former generations. 'We are no longer accumulating,' he wrote in a notebook, 'we are squandering the capital of our forebears even in our way of knowing.' This alarming prognosis was picked up in the 20th century by the almost-legendary pessimism of his countrymen Oswald Spengler. The German tendency to *drang nach dem absoluten* (drive towards the absolute), to bravely and doggedly pursue ideological concepts to their natural conclusions, has meant that many of them have arrived at those conclusions before their less energetic European cousins. The very German word *Geschictsmude* – weariness of history – may be a more recognised feeling in the coming decades even as it was there then. Nietzsche's words, *how much must collapse* was not really a question but an exclamation. As highlighted by the death tolls that were to come, no one could then have imagined the trials that would so soon tear Europe, and then the world apart.

I feel we ought to linger a little longer on this sorry corner of human history and try to understand the sociological and psychological neighbourhood of Schuman. Looking back at those *firstlings of the twentieth century,* as Nietzsche' called them, we will see that when it comes to being corrupted by power, both Religion and Secular Humanism are in the dock but not equally. *'The quintessential myth of modernity is the power of the will over nature* [159].... *and that we are at liberty to remake ourselves what we wish to be.... The ambition to refashion humanity in its very essence –social, political, economic, moral, psychological was inconceivable while human beings were regarded as creatures of God.... This is why it is correct to say that the sheer ruthlessness of so much of post-Christian social idealism in some sense arises from the very concept of freedom that lies at the heart of our precious modern values.'* [160] We must admit that there was so much wrong with the old world, and the deeper the injustice, the more desperate men and women were for ever more radical and untried solutions. T. S. Eliot wrote perceptively in 1937 that the:

> *'...one reason why the lot of the secular reformer or revolutionist seems to me to be the easier is this: that for the most part he conceives of the evils of the world as something external to himself. They are thought of either as completely impersonal, so that there is nothing to alter but the machinery; or if there is evil incarnate, it is always incarnate in the other people – a class, a race, the politicians, the bankers, the armament makers, and so forth – never in oneself... for most people, to be able to simplify issues so as to see only the definite external enemy, is extremely exhilarating, and brings about the bright eye and the springy step that go so well with the political uniform. This is an exhilaration that the Christian must deny himself... It is not enough simply to see the evil and injustice and suffering of this world, and precipitate oneself into action. We must know, what only theology can tell us, why these things are wrong. Otherwise, we may right some wrongs at the cost of creating new ones.'* [161]

The brave new world order offered to Eliot's generation was a purely horizontal space to recreate the world after their liking – politically, sociologically and ethically.[162] And there was little that was to be off limits. But in denying us our old position in the realm of being, many have pointed out this was a devil's bargain.

One influential thinker, Romano Guardini (1885-1968), who was an exact contemporary of Schuman, traced a peculiar 'modern anxiety' to our loss of a 'symbolic place in reality.' The security of a purely secular man or woman, he contends, was arrested when he or she 'ceased to experience a world which guarantees him a place in the total scheme of existence.' In *The End of the Modern World*, he also wrote of a 'resentment' directed at Europe's religious past which is 'born of the realization that his own age has made revolution a perpetual institution.' We have, moreover, made the quest for independent knowledge an 'autonomous cultural process....at one with its essence.' And to this engine, he says, we have harnessed technological 'processes allowing man to posit ends in conformity to his own desires.' It is a train that makes its own rails. The foundations are threefold, and together they form a unity which needs no verification from any outside source, nor permits 'the existence of any standard above itself.'

Firstly, Guardini insisted, the modern world insisted on a natural order subsisting of itself; secondly, a human subject with an autonomous personality; and thirdly, a culture self-created out of norms intrinsic to its own essence. The constant creation and perfection of these foundations was the final goal of history. The rails would take us to glory, and if that turned out to be more a direction than a destination, then we should be grateful and patient.

Now, if we are to understand Catholics like Guardini and Schuman, we must straightaway point out the obvious. For them, there could be no truly autonomous human activity, simply because of the fact; God existed. So, for them culture rested upon the 'ability of the human spirit to both distinguish itself and to stand opposite to the natural order of things surrounding it.' And towards the idea of an autonomous human personality, they would alike scoff. For even man himself, they would say along with Guardini, 'does not belong exclusively to this world; rather he stands on its borders, at once in the world yet outside it, integrated into it yet simultaneously dealing with it because he is related directly to God.'[163] If we want one possible answer to how Columban and Schuman came to shape the world around them, then here it is.

Guardini, who along with Schuman experienced the alarming triumph of populism in his own day, saw it as much an instrument of the new politics as it was the result of it. But he was not such a pessimist as to deny that humans had been 'matured and deepened', by their 'experience of the modern world.' Even so, he finished his book with a dour challenge to the determined secularists. They must 'learn to exist honestly without Christ and without the God revealed through Him.... Nietzsche has already warned us that the non-Christian of the modern world had no realization of what it truly meant to be without Christ. The last decades have suggested what life without Christ really is. The last decades were only the beginning.'

1886-1900 AD – PEACE ON THE EDGE OF THE ABYSS

Schuman with mother

Even taking Guardini's criticism on the chin, most of his co-religionists would admit that there is more than enough blame to go around; the pursuit and misuse of power has corrupted all secular and sacred endeavour in European history. But Europe needs solutions, not scapegoats, and one solution, as we have said, was born to immigrant parents Jean Pierre Schuman and Eugenie Duren in the leafy Luxembourg suburb in 1886. His father spoke French, his mother a Germanic tongue called '*Allemansch*'. Robert was therefore, even before his *birth 'un homme de frontieres'*[164] Indeed, Jean Pierre had family lands on both sides of the border and his son was to remember ploughing one field with his uncle which lay between two national boundaries.

This to me seems poetically suggestive; permeable borders and *ploughing a straight furrow across national boundaries*. As a man Robert Schuman would never eschew patriotism *per se*, but it is easy to see his plasticity to the suggestion of supranational allegiances when you consider both this, and the Catholicism that he was raised in. In his very person, he seems to embody one of the great socio-political tensions of our times, what one writer outlines as the tensions between the patriotic *somewheres* and the globalist *anywheres*.[165]

Marcus Aurelius, the great stoic emperor of the second century wrote that 'As the emperor, Rome is my homeland; but as a man, I am a citizen of the world.... Asia and Europe are mere dots on the map, the ocean is a drop of water, mighty Mount Athos is a grain of sand...' Perhaps we could say that the emperor's internationalism was led more by the rather passive Stoic virtues of unperturbedness (*Ataraxia*, ἀταραξία) and equanimity (Apatheia, ἀπάθεια). One can expect a man of the Stoic position to give limited value to 'mere' geography – if not to outright disdain for anything as grounded and earthy as patriotism.

Might we not even go further and posit that this position perfectly reflects the position of the internationalist spirit of the Enlightenment, of men like Montesquieu, Rousseau and Voltaire? I suspect that we modern, globalist *'anywheres'* have more in common with Aurelius than someone like Justin Martyr (100-165 AD) who could say of national identity, 'how can anything so frivolous as a name outweigh the ties of nature and the bonds of Christianity?' Although there is some overlap, do we not sense the difference between a passive and an active power at work? Schuman, I would argue was of the latter stripe. Like Justin Martyr, the self-proclaimed Samaritan from Nablus, there is something wondrously providential in his beginnings and formation.

Schuman was an only child, growing up in this quiet quarter, surrounded by market gardens and brewers. Below the house was the parkland of a former Renaissance Chateau now fallen into disrepair. His house, less than a decade old would likely have been built from the palace's stones, on the site of a former hermitage (hence the name). Did he play in the ruins of that fallen arcadia as a boy? Building something new from the rubble would also be a theme in his life.

And so also was war, and particularly Prussian aggression. On his way to school the young Schuman would also walk past the German Military cemetery – a memory of when Luxembourg had been occupied by Prussia just over twenty years before. It was his mother, who was 25 years her husband's junior, who dedicated herself to her son's education.[166] He attended the local primary school, which was a short walk down the hill from his home. So too was the parish church of Saint Cunegonde, where he went every Sunday without fail. Like Augustine, Schuman's mother's piety would become his own, and not just in outward form but an essential part of his intellectual core. During these years too, came the publication of the papal encyclical *Rerum Novarum*,[167] which would one day cement Schuman's and, his later opposite numbers in Germany and Italy, Adenauer and De Gasperi's religious convictions of into political action. This letter and other's like it gave them an epistemological bulwark against the post-Christian, socialist and capitalist ideologies sweeping the continent.

Because Catholic social thought will be so important later, it is worth a brief introduction here. Like Gregory the Great, who was pope in Columban's day, there is something of the intellectual patrician in Vincenzo Pecci, called Leo XIII. He was the second son of a Roman Count who, through expansive intellectual and administrative ability, rose as a young man in service to the church. His life span (1810-1903) was comparable with Queen Victoria, and both of them lived through almost an entire century of social upheaval. His 1891, open letter called 'Revolutionary Change' (*Rerum Novarum*) addressed social inequality and social justice issues. It also focussed on the rights and duties of capital and labour. In this he was greatly influenced by Wilhelm Emmanuel von Ketteler, a German bishop who openly propagated siding with the suffering working classes in his book *Die Arbeiterfrage und das Christentum*.

Leo XIII's Papal teachings expanded on the rights and obligations of workers, the limitations of private property, the duty of social justice, with protection of individual and minority rights against the tyranny of the majority. It also warned against the politics of envy, and of socialism, laissez-faire capitalism, and a nascent Communism. Leo defined the Church as the *mother of material civilization*, because it upheld the human dignity of working people, whether collectivist or capitalist. It is not long and certainly worth a reading. The Olympian tone of the letter is often hard for a modern reader to stomach, but set in its context and with an eye on its fruit in twentieth century politics, there is no doubt that western and eastern Europe owe a tremendous debt to that energetic, roman patrician, Vincenzo Pecci.

There will be space in a later chapter to summarise this *Revolutionary Change* letter, but let us now return to the boy Schuman, whose formative years of routine and peace were more precarious than he could have guessed. These are the years of Boulanger's failed coup in Paris; when Bismarck was dismissed by Wilhelm II; when Luxembourg was separated from the Netherlands; when T.H. Huxley wrote *Agnosticism*; when Hitler, Eisenhower and de Gaulle were all born, and Van Gogh died. Across her dominions, Queen Victoria's golden jubilee was celebrated with verve.

One formative incident to recount about his home country occurred when he was only four. It was during these years that Grand Duke Adolf successfully acceded to the crown of Luxembourg, thus assuring her independence. It was a time of relief and rejoicing. Along with his friends the young Schuman was on the streets cheering the new Grand Duke as he came into his inheritance. Schuman later recalled,

'It is in Luxembourg that I acquired the first notions of patriotism. It was in 1890 under the Grand Ducal balcony. The people acclaimed Grand Duke Adolf who came to make his solemn entry into the capital. I was a little boy of four years old lost in the crowd. I was enflamed by its enthusiasm and taken up in its pride. With everyone else I sang -as best I could.... 'Wir welle ja ken Preisse sin' - before all else we didn't want to be Prussians. I only came to know the Marseillaise later. Henceforth, I knew what it is to love one's country, and the attachment to the sovereign who personifies and guarantees the unity, continuity and independence of the nation.'

A journalist who knew him reasonably well[168] posits that it was here, standing shoulder to shoulder with his friends that we can see the first patriotic stirrings of this young exile, feelings that he says would never degenerate to a chauvinistic nationalism that excluded the value of other cultures.[169] And, I suppose, how could it be otherwise when he carried in his very DNA, the transitory nature of national borders. If anything, we might expect him to despise any form of patriotism but even this was not the case. For just as *love of family* offered him the preliminary steps beyond self-love, so his fellow students and Luxembourg neighbours would lead him to see a love of one's country as a natural, earthed extension of this.

One Oxford Don who faced German imperialism head-on in the trenches[170] wrote that the ingredients of a dangerous nationalism are simple; a bias to our nation's past – real or imagined – induces a wrong superiority which then outflows in 'duties' or rights. In this demoniac form, even *love of country* itself eventually disappears and ceases to be what it was.[171] When you grow up as an exile in a tiny country, as Schuman did, with the restless German nation breathing down at you, these issues are more than academic. That the founding father of the EEC honoured patriotism must be noted here. For some ideologues today cannot mention the nationalist or patriotic impulse without confusing it with the word *populism*.[172]

The conservative philosopher Roger Scruton wrote that 'for ordinary people living in free association with their neighbours, the 'nation' means simply the historical identity and continuing allegiance that unites them in the body politic. It is the first-person plural of settlement. Sentiments of national identity may be inflamed by war, civil agitation and ideology, and this inflammation admits to many degrees. But in the normal form these sentiments are not just peaceful in themselves, but a form of peace between neighbours.'[173] In another place he extends the principal, writing that, 'when we make the laws, and make them for our purposes, we can be certain what they mean. The only question then is 'who are we?' What way of defining ourselves reconciles democratic elections with real opposition and individual rights?'[174] The natural, grounded, earthed answer at its most practical is, of course, 'the nation state.'

These first years of the 20th century were when France annexed Madagascar; when the infamous Dreyfus Case exposed military and political corruption and anti-Semitism;[175] when the first Zeppelin airship was launched; when the Boers put a £25 reward out for an escaped English journalist called Winston Churchill. These are also the years of the first peace conference at The Hague, of the Boxer Rebellion, of the assassination of King Umberto of Italy and also the Empress Elizabeth of Austria by Italian anarchists. The clock was ticking. These are the years of the Triple Alliance, signed by France, Austria and Italy, and then renewed for another 6 years. *Tick-tock, tick-tock.*

The French and English signed the *Entente Cordiale*, and even as they did so in London, the Russian social democrats split, and the new Bolshevik faction led by Lenin and Trotsky emerged. *Tick-tock, tick-tock.* In London also, which seems to have been the unnatural propagator of so much mischief, Darwin's cousin Francis Galton gives the second Huxley lecture to the Anthropological Institute entitled, *'The Possible Improvement of the Human Breed under the Existing Conditions of Law and Sentiment.'* This was October 1901, an inauspicious beginning to the sickly pseudoscience of Eugenics that would become *de rigueur* over the next decades in the UK, America and Europe. In a Hobbesian way, Galton classified the human species by civic worth; A for loafers and criminals, B for casual workers and drinkers, E for those earning 22 to 30 shillings, and so on, right up to people like him, who gave such great utility to society by their helpful observations.

The monetary worth of a child from each classification of the human species was cheerfully given also. Simply subtract the cost of raising the creature from the monetary output up until the moment of decrepitude and you are left with a reliable indicator of the creature's real worth. 'The worth of an average baby born to the wife of an Essex labourer...was found to be about five pounds' while an upper-class baby would be worth inestimably more because he might found a factory – into which, I suppose, he could stuff the spawn of any number of Essex labourers. It sticks in our throats today, but we mustn't forget that Galton was the science superstar of his day, and Eugenics was introduced to the Edwardian conscience with all the impulses and rhetoric of a new religion. The quotations above are from the October 1901 *Nature* article that printed the entire lecture with diagrams. By 1905 Galton was confident that laws must eventually be made to restrict the marriages of people whose union would jeopardize Britain from being a national laboratory where 'humanity can be represented by the fittest races.'

Liberal progressives like George Bernard Shaw 'proclaimed that nothing but a eugenic religion could save our civilisation and that we must 'never hesitate to carry out the negative side of eugenics with considerable zest, both on the scaffold and on the battlefield.'[176] Orson Welles became a co-religionist for the cause as well, particularly as it applied to others. (His own propensity to breed with anything in a skirt made his advocating prohibitions for other members of the species particularly hypocritical.) Welles' comments about race have all the chill pragmatism of darker days ahead.

> 'And the rest, those swarms of black and brown, and dirty white, and yellow people, who do not come into the new needs of efficiency? Well, the world is the world, not a charitable institute, and I take it they will have to go. The tenor and meaning of the world is, they have to go... it is their portion to die out and disappear.'

This was not some niche view. These men were the literary darlings of their generation. *Nature* was then what it is now and like good and obedient pagans, Europeans were going back to those pre-Christian roots where they took their philosophy from elemental nature. The world would soon find out what a mistake that was. Few stood against it, surely science was science, facts were facts. The British journalist G. K. Chesterton mounted a defence in a series of cutting articles that eventually became the book *'Eugenics and Other Evils.'* Like the Christian objectors to abortion and euthanasia, he saw the central issue was theological and anthropological; what is a human being: in the image of God, or an evolved ape? Two visions of humanity could lead to two different futures.

At the first International Congress of Eugenics in July 1912, the Hotel Cecil on the banks of the Thames was filled with the great and good. 'Its vice presidents included the Lord Chief Justices, the president of the College of Surgeons, the Lord Mayor of London, the Vice Chancellor of London university, the Bishops of Ripon and Birmingham, the inventor Alexander Graham Bell, the First Lord of the Admiralty... and Sir Winston Churchill. Major Leonard Darwin, the great scientist's last surviving child, gave a rousing opening speech calling for action against the genetically unfit. The purpose of the conference was 'to spread far and wide the great new creed with its glittering goal of race and class improvement through selective breeding.'[177] They need not have worried about dedicated evangelism, for by this time the news had already travelled. Germany's, soon to be, infamous Race Hygiene Department had already been established in 1905.[178] As with everything, the Germans took it all very seriously and were prepared to face the bleak reality of the new science with a clinical resolve.[179] All these disparate currents and events were taking shape around and during Schuman's formative years, many would combine and collide in the coming decades. Perhaps Welles' new book *War of the Worlds* wasn't so *avant-garde* after all.

But let us now leave the young Schuman, aged 14 at the turn of the new century. For two years he had attended the Athénée (Athenaeum) secondary school in Luxembourg where his progress gave his parents great grounds for optimism. Further afield, many, if not most, Europeans clung to a similar optimism regarding the rosy and prosperous future for Europe; whose colonies across the globe sent back the goods, and whose ancient monarchies and aristocracies remained at ease. But the clock was ticking on it all. Bold new thinkers were abroad in the earth, peeling away from the grey background to enact their own completion of modern history. Within a few short years, their ideas would be airborne and moving at startling speed. Would this be the flight of Hegel's Owl of Minerva – the big reveal of history's purpose – or another Lucifer fall? Would they be the final hand to bring shape to all that had gone before, or – again using Hegel's analogy – merely a severed hand cut off from reality and destined to a lifeless decay. Who could tell back then? In retrospect Reinhold Niebuhr noted, *"One of the most pathetic aspects of human history is that every civilization expresses itself most pretentiously, compounds its partial and universal values most convincingly, and claims immortality for its finite existence at the very moment when the decay which leads to death has already begun."*

The era of the last revolutionaries was just beginning, and the age of Europe's ancient monarchies and submissive colonies were nearly at an end. The days on earth of Jean Pierre Schuman were also numbered. In 1900, death would visit the Schuman household. The mother and son buried him at the Fetschenhof Cemetery in Luxembourg; Ground 1, Row 19, Plot 19. It is a stiff 20-minute walk up the other side of the valley from the Hermitage, to an exposed tableland, which is now also a quiet suburb. I visited, on a squally October day, and had to get some gravediggers to help find the plot. They didn't know who lay there – 'Schuman?' they repeated above the wind's howl. But with the row and plot number

The Hermitage - Schuman's childhood home with the EU Parliament brooding above

they found it. The boys and I lingered, while another family interred their loved ones and the wind and rain set the mood. On the eight-foot granite cross above the grave, each family member had a metal plaque. Jean-Pierre's plaque had a screw hanging out. If it fell off who would pick it up? His name would be lost. He would be forgotten. I screwed it back in reverently. What is a man without a name? The mourners of the other family slowly filed away. Then the gravediggers buried the deceased, leaving only love to remember.

I imagined the boy Schuman, somewhere between the ages of my older sons, Tom and Will, standing on this site a century before. Poor lad. A father doesn't have to be a saint in order to be indispensable to a teenage boy. I glanced at my own Tom, patiently waiting next to the grave; faithful, dutiful, camera in hand, face streaming with the drizzle. Even the thought of it is enough to break your heart. Robert Schuman would always visit this grave when he was passing Luxembourg. It is hard for most of us to imagine the void this would leave in a 14-year old's life, many have been crushed by lesser griefs, and still others have risen despite them. But now we must return to Ireland to see the formation of the teenage Columban fifteen centuries before. If Schuman had lost his father, Columban was about to find his.

Finding Schuman's parent's grave, (seen on left) Fetschenhof cemetery, Luxembourg

148. 13,700,000 square miles (source Wikipedia)

149. Nietzsche's own sister Elisabeth was a key adapter and transmitter of his work to suit the Nazi ideology.

150. With prophetic overtones, Dostoyevsky's character Fyodor Pavlovich in *The Brothers Karamazov* cries out to his meek, Christian son, 'Alyosha, my dear, my only son, I'm afraid of Ivan. I'm more afraid of Ivan than the other. You're the only one I'm not afraid of....' He, who I suppose to some extent represents the debauched and corrupted ancien regime. The other son referred to is Dmitri, who perhaps represents the sensate, Romantic movement. In the narrative, Dmitri has just dealt his father a savage beating, but the father, (rather like Caesar fearing the Epicurean Cassius to fat Lentulus) fears his atheist son Ivan more. And as it turned out, 40 years after this was written, it was the enlightenment-rationalist 'Ivans' of Russia - those to whom Christianity had been rendered untenable by a corrupted church – who tore down the old system in the hopes of building a socialist utopia.

151. Norman Davies, *Europe, a history* (Oxford, 1996) p.897

152. *Atheist Delusions*, David Bentley Hart p107

153. Mount Stewart House, County Down

154. His Catholic biographer De Rochefort highlights the point that the 29th is 'the feast of the holy apostles Peter and Paul'. And, says he, given Schuman's later Catholic mindset, such a date is 'not without some importance to him', even 'a happy premonition' (p.17). Robert Schuman would become a prime example of 'the apostolic laity', a major theme in Catholic circles at the time, encouraged by church leaders (p.44) and his political career a Catholic vocation (p.61).

155. They also bought a house on the Grande Rue in the upper city

156. The address is 4, Rue Jules Wilhelm, Clausen, Luxembourg. This opulent villa, dating from the 19th century, now houses the Robert Schuman Centre for European Studies and Research. Schuman's birthplace, as his biographer de Rochefort points out, was not without significance. Clausen, a suburb of the city of Luxembourg (p.18), had a name meaning 'a place of retreat', and it was built on the site of an old hermitage (p.19).

157. Norman Davies, *The Isles*, p.39 (Macmillan Publishers Ltd, 1999.)

158. Church or State Supremacy? This titanic sacred-secular European struggle, which has lasted for nearly two millennia, was essentially the attempt for the Church to baptise their societies, versus the power of the state to absorb, as David Bentley heart put it, 'every useful institution'. Doctrines like the Divine Right of Kings and Absolute Monarchy were the beginning of the sacralisation of the state. From that time on the struggle for supremacy was joined until Christianity was finally relegated to a state cult in the late modern period. At the beginning of this ghastly marriage, and I am thinking primarily about Emperor Theodosius and not Constantine, each would have to surrender something of its essence to survive. The

church may have surrendered its purity to the state, but the state also had surrendered its secular autonomy. For example, Theodosius was made to do public penance by Ambrose of Milan, something that was unthinkable a generation before.

159. We could deepen and extend Bentley Hart's critique here with that of a Dutch philosopher active in the early 20th century. Herman Dooyeweerd claimed 'to have demonstrated that theoretical thinking has always been based on presuppositions of a religious nature'; which he called ground motives. A ground motive is a spiritual driving force that impels each thinker to interpret reality under its influence. Dooyeweerd identified four major ground-motives of Western thought, three of them dualistic in nature: 1. the Form-Matter divide of Greek thought; 2. the Creation-Fall-Redemption motif of Biblical thought; 3. the Nature-Grace divide of Mediaeval, Scholastic thought; 4. the Nature-Freedom divide of Humanistic, Enlightenment thought.

160. *Atheist Delusions*, David Bentley Hart, p107

161. T.S Eliot *"Church, Community and State"* February 1937, The Listener. In this article, he also writes that 'the Church cannot be, in any political sense, either conservative, or liberal, or revolutionary. Conservatism is too often conservation of the wrong things; liberalism a relaxation of discipline; revolution a denial of the permanent things.'

162. 'The doctrine of the indefinite perfectibility of the human race,' and human civilisation was first articulated by the Marquis de Condorcet. In his *'Short History of Progress,'* Ronald Wright says that this ideology is 'a secular religion... blind to certain flaws in its credentials. Progress has become 'myth' in the anthropological sense.' The term ideology was first coined by the French educational reformer de Tracy during the years of the Revolution. Drawing on John Locke's 'Tabula Rasa' theory – that the human mind is a blank slate – de Tracy set about developing what he called 'the greatest of all arts...the regulating of society in such a way that man finds that there is most help, and the least possible annoyance of his own kind.' For him, all religion could be 'defined as an obstacle to sound logic and to sane morality.' His work was the first political attempt to regulate or manipulate people's ideas to achieve certain societal ends – in this case; freedom, equality, and brotherhood.

163. Guardini goes further at another point, writing, 'Modern man's dishonesty w͏ rooted in his refusal to recognize Christianity's affirmation of the God-ma͏ tionship. Even as the modern world acclaimed the worth of personality and o͏f an order of personal values, it did away with their guarantor, Christian Revelation.'

164. De Rochefort (p.18)

165. *The Road to Somewhere: The Populist Revolt and the Future of Politics,* David Goodhart, C. Hurst & Co. Publishers (17 Mar. 2017)

166. This puts me in remembrance of young John Ruskin, another only child, whose mother even followed him to Oxford University where she took digs. But we do not ever get any sense of such suffocation with Schuman's mother.

167. Also known as the *Rights and Duties of Capital and Labor*, is an encyclical issued by Pope Leo XIII, on 15 May 1891.

168. I found Robert Wendelin Keyserlingk's *Fathers of Europe* very helpful in weaving together the complex political picture, that is often lost to the historian who needs brevity – or who lacks sources. Keyserlingk was a war correspondent and knew the players, either as friends or interviewees. Copies can be found online but they are rare.

169. In fact, Keyserlingk says it was only later, as a student reading law at Strasbourg University, that Schuman was given a deeper appreciation of French culture by his fellow French students.

170. C. S. Lewis was wounded in action in France

171. He also warns us in *The Four Loves* that if patriotism is debunked, then each new international conflict must be spun to us on terms of solely moral grounds, 'we must do this for humanity, for democracy, for western civilisation.' By attaching a moral transcendence to words like 'democracy' we have taken a step down not up, claims Lewis; it is a step down from a grounded human love, our motives have become dehumanised with pious rhetoric and we may become easy prey to political conditioners and spin doctors. Patriotism never pretended to be more than sentiment, this meant that wars could be heroic but not religious, heroes died but not martyrs.

172. And, let us remember, that even the word Populism might only mean popular, i.e., democratic.

173. Roger Scruton, *How to be a Conservative* p33 Bloomsbury

174. Roger Scruton, *Democracy and Islamic Law*, BBC Magazine - 23.8.2013

175. The affair lasted from 1894 to 1906 and divided France deeply into two opposing camps: the pro-Army, mostly Catholic "anti-Dreyfusards" and the anticlerical, pro-republican Dreyfusards. It embittered French politics and encouraged radicalization, all of which Schuman would later have to navigate.

176. Nicolas Wight Gilliam, *A Life of Sir Francis Galton*, Oxford University Press

177. Andrew Marr, *History of Modern Britain*, p25

178. In March 2020, Germany's high court overturned previous legislation banning physicians from assisting in suicide. They still may not administer a lethal injection (as they did to 300,000 unwanted members of German society in the 1930s) but they may now advise and prescribe medication for that purpose.

179. So too were the Americans for a time. The 1924 Immigration Act stated that: 'Biological Laws show... that the Nordics deteriorate when mixed with other races.' Compulsory sterilisation for certain groups became possible in America before Germany

CHAPTER 4

Columban's Monastic Training

CHAPTER SUMMARY – HOW NOT TO SAVE CIVILISA-TION – Observations on the limits of political power. THE MOST IMPRACTICAL MEN - How the hermits' cells of Europe became the proto-universities that helped make Western Civilization. Origins of monasticism from the Far East and its evolution from Egypt, through central Europe to Ireland. Some notable Irish examples. 556-564 AD – COLUMBAN UNDER SINELL - Columban journey's north to the island monastery of Cleenish near modern Enniskillen. JULY 2018 – CLEENISH - The author's recollections of camping on the island accompanied by medieval scholar, Dr. Alex O'Hara.

"What will be lost, and what saved, of our civilization probably lies beyond our powers to decide. No human group has ever figured out how to design its future. That future may be germinating today not in a boardroom in London or an office in Washington or a bank in Tokyo, but in some antic -- outpost or other -- a kindly British orphanage in the grim foothills of Peru, a house for the dying in a back street of Calcutta run by

a fiercely single-minded Albanian nun, an easy-going French medical team at the starving edge of the Sahel... in some unheralded corner where a great-hearted human being is committed to loving outcasts in an extraordinary way."

Thomas Cahill, *How the Irish Saved Civilisation*

HOW NOT TO SAVE CIVILISATION

The theologian Karl Barth, likened Martin Luther to a man in a dark bell tower steadying himself by grabbing the rope then finding that he had grabbed the bell rope and woken up the whole countryside. And one of the constant surprises in studying those who shaped – dare I say, who helped save – Latin civilisation after the western empire's collapse, is that they were never attempting to do any such thing. If anything, their legacy to us was a by-product of them seeking to save themselves. The old adage about those who are 'so heavenly minded that they are no earthly good' is well known and often justly so. But, let us not also neglect the unusual antithesis which this book emphasises, that we owe the existence of western culture, at least in the form we experience it, to a strange assortment of characters who cared more for religion than the realpolitik.

We saw, in chapter 1, that the Irish were escaping the terror of an animist system that derived its philosophy from nature. In chapter 2, we saw Europeans, reversing that philosophical commitment, heedless of the terror which they were about to unleash. Columban was part of a new generation that were seeking to live out, 'in private and public life, the law of love and temperance.... not competition and grab,' even when it seemed necessary to survival. From now on they would accept as a 'spiritual law never to put survival first...' and also to train themselves to feel that the survival of their 'own nation or culture.... (was) not worth having unless it (could) be had on honourable and merciful terms.' These words of C. S. Lewis were written as the west dealt with its own demons after the war; but they could stand for any age of trouble and any reappraisal of first principals. Lewis continues, 'Nothing is more likely to destroy a species or a nation than a determination to preserve it at all costs. Those who care for something else more than civilisation are the only people by whom civilisation is at all likely to be preserved. Those who want heaven most have served earth best. Those who love Man less than God, do most for Man.'[180]

This might appear to be a paradoxical assertion. But, as we noted in Chapter 1 when discussing the Roman patricians, the supposedly 'practical' people of that age turned out to be of little use when the chips were down. The restless rich despoiled the material fabric of civic structures and enslaved their fellow men for private gain, while the empire's mighty 'saviours', like Justinian and Belisarius, only destroyed the thing they loved by trying to save it by force. Here is the enigma. And here also begins our profound debt to the monastic founders of the West.[181] The man Columban, typifies this principle. He once wrote, *'I want the salvation of many and seclusion for myself; the one for the progress of the Lord the other for my own desire.'*

THE MOST IMPRACTICAL MEN

Let us start by trying to grasp the threads of these movements. Monasticism was not a Christian invention but had a mixture of pagan and Jewish roots and came even from as far away as Mesopotamia. Further east and further back still, the Buddhist bhikkhus of 2500BC had already established a pattern – wandering hermits and fixed, voluntary communities – that would find its equivalent in the Christian west. It is little wonder that Christian monasticism first broke ground and flourished in Egypt, for here monastic expressions already existed with regard to the cults of Serapis, Mithras and Isis. Christian monastic communities were already established in the first half of the third century.[182] Perhaps, it was more natural in Egypt where, in reaction to the Gnostic heresy, or decadent worldliness, or secular persecution, this sort of extreme dedication would seek already well-worn tracks.

Most austere movements paradoxically attract people of societal privilege. Even Buddha's first 60 monks had 55 members from prominent families. And he himself was a prince. So likewise, 75% of ascetic Catholic saints from 500-1500 were from the nobility, indeed, 22% from royalty. But the strong tendency toward asceticism was not universal. Even before 200AD the Carthaginian Christian, Tertullian could repulse the accusation of isolationism by saying, *'we are not Brahmins or Indian fanatics who live naked in the woods or as recluses in exile from their fellow men... we mix with you, we are one people with you.'* [183]

Anthony's asceticism found expression in the desert, but it must be stressed that this was not the whole or even the earliest example of the monastic impulse within the Christian tradition. The urban and communal aspects of monasticism were reasserted and re-forged time and again before reaching their most enduring expression under Benedict. Before that, founders like Basil would preach that 'Humans are political beings, used to living together. In their common experience of public life and in their dealings with one another, they have to show generosity directed towards improving the lot of those in need.' Basil did not condemn those who withdrew but did challenge them to be ready to serve the community. He was typical of the culture shapers of his time, for these 'new religious movements such as monasticism were not the product of people on the margin of society, but of intellectuals dissatisfied with what tradition, and the current civic structures, had to offer.'[184]

Through the written rule of Antony's successor Pachomius, a pattern for monastic life was disseminated west to other founders like Basil, who modified it for what would become Byzantium; Cassian; who did the same for Gaul, where it was developed by men like Hilary of Poitiers and Martin of Tours. Augustine of Hippo was also developing a community in Africa at this time, as Benedict would later in Italy. From Gaul the monastic revolution spread to Britain by men like Ninian, who studied at Martin's monastery in Tours, and whose successor Abbot Caranoc is credited with first taking the Gospel to Hibernia.[185] If that is the case then Patrick, who studied at Auxerre after his escape from slavery, would have entered Ireland a half century after Caranoc's pioneering visit.

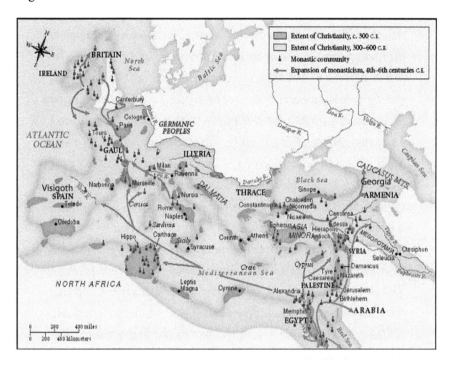

For an example of the transmission from Britain to Ireland, let us meet the Irish warrior chieftain called Enda, who was born around 450AD, i.e., a century before Columban, but contemporary with Benedict. When Enda was converted to the new religion by his sister, he travelled to Ninian's *Candida Casa* (White House) at Whithorn on the Dumfriesshire coast. It is a desolate and beautiful place on the Rhins of Galloway[186] – the very world's end. From this, one, stone-built monastery Ninian, who died in 432AD, was pioneering many other foundations further north for the first great conversion of the Picts. After serving his noviciate, Enda returned to Ireland to found a monastery on Inish Mor, the largest of the Arran Islands in Galway Bay. Here, mortification took precedence over learning but even from this barest of islands, the first motherhouse in Ireland sent out monastic pioneers; Finnian to Moville, Eugene to Ardstraw, Tighearnach to Clones.[187]

At almost the same moment at Clonard, in the heart of Ireland, another monk was doing the same. Tomas O Fiaich writes,

> *Another Finnian, this time of Clonard, who borrowed some of his ideas from the Welsh monastic founders and reformers, became 'teacher of the saints of Ireland' and sent out the next great group of pioneers who have been given the picturesque title of 'the twelve apostles of Ireland' – Columba to Derry (546), Durrow (556), and Iona (563), Ciarán to Clonmacnois (about 550), Brendan to Clonfert (554 or 559), Molaise to Devenish, Cainneach to Aghaboe, Mobhi to Glasnevin, Colman to Terryglass, Sinell to Cleenish. A third group of sixth-century foundations owed little or nothing to Clonard – Bangor, founded by Comgall (d.603), Moville on Strangford Lough founded by Finnian (d.579), Glendalough founded by Kevin (d.618), Tuam by Jarlath, Cork by Bairre. And a fourth group was founded primarily by and for women – Kildare by Brigid and Killeavy by Moninne before the end of the fifth century, Killeady in Co. Limerick by Ita, and Clonbroney in Co. Longford by Samhthann, in the sixth century.*[188]

But we must not think they were entering the genteel medieval monasteries of a later time. Rather, these young men and women of the sixth century would have found a collection of wooden huts surrounded by an embankment with a church in the centre. When the Irish took the name monastery to their tongue, it was *Muintir* and always meant for them the people, the community, and not the actual structures.[189] They were young people from a heroic warrior culture joining a revolutionary movement – this was no retreat; it was a full advance. These monasteries embodied the great Christian principle that the spiritual is more formational than the temporal, that morality is more crucial than politics, that cooperation is more efficient than competition, and that Christ's kingdom has not only come - albeit as a mustard seed – but will outlast every other. And it was not just tonsures and chanting. Nor was it just health care, agriculture and education. Each monastery was a democratic revolution in seed form, and one day those seeds would be dispersed. At certain points and places in the monastic story, even the men or women of lowliest birth might be elected abbot or abbess years later. It was quite alien to the ecclesiastical structures of their day, which themselves were the inheritance of the Roman hierarchical system. This episcopal-versus-monastic tension is well documented in the correspondence of that time, and it would be a significant factor when Columban was forcibly evicted from his Frankish monastery fifty years later.

These young Irish men and women of Columban's day were also riding the crest of a tumultuous information revolution – perhaps more profound and far reaching than anything the internet has done in the 'developed' nations. At one sweep the Irish received, along with a new religious worldview, the arts of writing; the *lingua franca* of Latin; and a certain portion of the imaginative, philosophical, theological  and scientific legacy of the classical world. By some peculiar contingent of history, all of this came fully-formed to an island that had never been subjugated to Roman rule – that is they had never known any central authority or even had the memory of one.

The authority they did know, an authority that superseded that of local kings, was that of the druids. The druids had rigidly enforced a purely oral culture, partly to cement societal cohesion but also, one suspects, to maintain their own hegemony in that society. This had been successful[190] up until the Christian message came to them.[191]

Their grandparents had used the prehistoric Ogham alphabet, a set of lines which we see cut into the corners of standing stones – laborious and painfully limited. Now, within one or two generations, they mastered Latin and even a rudimentary form of Hebrew. What is really more remarkable was the Irish delight in their own written language. They devised Irish grammars and copied out their native literature so that, by the end of the fifth century, they had even invented a new erudite Latin variation called *Hisperic Famina*. All this within a generation of gaining literacy.

And the Irish, like the Jews, enshrined literacy itself as a religious act. The Irish miniscule lettering was adopted so far afield that it became the common script of the Middle Ages. Even today, the Irish manuscripts of the early medieval period form some of the very great treasures of the libraries of England, France, Switzerland, Germany, Sweden, Italy and even Russia. If a 7th or 8th century man in Europe could speak Greek, it would be assumed that he was Irish. Even a writing tablet in Germany throughout this time, was called '*pugilares Scotorum*' – the writing tablets of the Irish. And all this was happening when the (intellectual) lights, as some academics claim, were going out in other parts of Western Europe. Lest the reader think this a fringe view, let me quote the eminently sensible Oxford historian Diarmaid MacCulloch.

> '*Perhaps most significantly, in the decades after 550, Latin culture came within a hair's breadth of extinction: the witness to that is the survival of datable manuscript copies of texts. The laborious process of copying manuscripts, the only way in which the fragile products of centuries of accumulating knowledge could be preserved, virtually came to an end, and would be not taken up again for two and a half centuries in the time of Charlemagne. In the intervening period, much of Classical literature was lost to us forever.*'[192]

Latin culture within a 'hair's breadth of extinction' sounds about as serious as it gets in terms of cultural transmission. When I was with Professor Jean Michel Picard of University College, Dublin, I put MacCulloch's point to him. We were in a cafe on the edge of Bangor marina, the very place where Columban left Ireland forever. 'But,' he said, turning down the corners of his mouth in a way only the French can really do to effect, 'of course, he is wrong.' He went on with great patience to explain how many earlier medieval manuscripts were scraped and then reused during the Carolingian period – rather like rewriting an SD card – thus only giving the effect of disappearance. I suppose that is both the blessing and curse of vellum – its longevity and flexibility. And of course, the sheer expense of vellum meant reusing it, even reluctantly, was often a dire necessity. To give an example of the sheer cost, let us consider what Abbot Coelfrid of Wearmouth and Jarrow had to do to make three new bibles.[193] He needed an extra grant of land to raise 2000 cattle for the vellum. But why go to all that trouble and expense if you already had perfectly decent books that contained the history of a previous Frankish dynasty or some antique poet whose work is either out of fashion, or maybe preserved elsewhere. You can imagine the sort of thing; out came the scraping knives and hey presto, a new book ready to record the latest and best.

But even allowing for the mature caution of Professor Picard, it does not paint the most stable picture for cultural transmission. And somewhere, into this instability, the Irish monks would busy themselves with all their verve and learning. And so, this takes us back to the provocative question. We want to ask; how did it happen? How did the hermitage cells become the proto-universities that partially saved Europe?

In order to answer this, let us use a contemporary of Finian and Enda's to illustrate what was happening all over Ireland in the mid sixth century. South of Dublin, there was a young nobleman called Kevin who was *escaping the world* to a cave above Glendalough and practicing extreme feats of asceticism. The cave was three feet high, three feet wide and seven feet long – so bijou, more like a morgue shelf. (It is still visible today). But, poor chap, he wasn't alone for long. He soon attracted a group of followers who coaxed him from the cave and into a stone beehive hut on the upper lake shore. They built wattle and daub huts nearby so that they could be near him. Eventually, even this location proved too small for the numbers of people who came from all over Ireland. And so, a prototype monastic university campus was built on a plain, east of the lower loch. And it was to here that students came from England and even Europe, and where – not forgetting the Irish virtue of generosity – noblemen and commoners received education, board, lodgings and materials free of charge.

Looking back with relish at those earlier times, Bede writes that,

> *'many of the nobility, and of the lower ranks of the English nation were there at that time, who, in the days of the Bishops Finan and Colman, forsaking their native island, retired thither, either for the sake of sacred studies or of a more ascetic life; and some of them presently devoted themselves faithfully to a monastic life, others chose rather to apply themselves to study, going about from one master's cell to another. The Scots willingly received them all, and took care to supply them with daily food without cost, as also to furnish them with books for their studies, and teaching free of charge.'*

The Irish and Britons made do with a limited number of texts which they copied in basic, functional codices. We must remember that the famous Irish illustrated manuscripts belong to the 8th century, not the sixth. We must also be careful not to fall into the exaggerations of an Irish nationalist tradition which claims that Ireland had access to the entire range of classical literature. Their access to classical texts was limited but they not only copied and saved them, but also created something new. By forming a 'Christianity of the mind' so rapidly from texts of the fourth century – think John Cassian and the heroic Egyptian monastic tradition – they also managed to skip the intervening centuries and thus escaped that gentle Roman pessimism, or perhaps realism, that we find in the lands that have been repeatedly laid waste by the 'barbarian' hordes and their erstwhile rescuers.

The Irish confidence, was undented by a dwindled heritage and an occupying barbarian army like the rest of Western Europe and north Africa. For the Irish, everything was delightfully new. In a certain way they were more like the 20th century's vibrant African churches springing up in Europe, led by ebullient pioneers who have no history with higher criticism or postmodernism. So too, these Irish came from without, untrammelled by the cultural exhaustion of their neighbours and benefactors. They had experienced no persecution, had no Irish martyrs, no apocalyptic wars, just books which they copied and studied with abandon. Classical, Christian and pagan – on and on went the scratch-scratch of the quill on parchment.

This time of 'innocence' was not uncritical either. After copying out the *Tain*, a scribe adds a gloss, *'I who have copied down this story, or more accurately fantasy, do not credit the details of the story, or fantasy. Some things are devilish lies, and some are poetical figments; some seem possible and others not; some are for the enjoyment of idiots.'* It is an extraordinary fact that the great wealth of the Celtic oral tradition was entirely lost in Gaul and Britannia. The poor scribe, mentioned above, deserves our thanks for perhaps, unbeknownst to him, it was Christian monks like him in Ireland that preserved the last repository of the Celtic oral traditions.[194] Another scribe wrote, after copying the section of Hector's death in the Iliad, *'I am greatly grieved by the above-mentioned death.'* Still another, writes on a manuscript, *'sad it is, little parti-coloured white book, for a day will come when someone will say over your page: 'The hand that wrote this is no more.'*

Columba of Iona once saved twelve hundred bards, from being suppressed at a synod in Ulster, saying – *'teach them to expand their repertoire and teach it to others'*. (Amazingly, the last bardic school was only suppressed in the time of Cromwell.)[195] There is much we cannot know of these men for their wattle and daub huts have long since gone. But we can know how they thought and laboured because of their letters, and most of all by the vast literature, copied and handed down to us. Giving attention to pagan texts was frowned on by some ecclesiastics, but it is this *'breadth and richness of Irish monastic learning derived from the classical....authors'* which eventually gave the Irish what John T. McNeill called, *'[their] unique role in the history of western culture.'*

How close did Western Europe come to losing its literary heritage – its memory of itself, and its intellectual capital? Literacy certainly had plummeted, and writing was almost certainly extinct in 5th century

Britain.[196] One way to reimagine this is to ask, what made literacy desirable or necessary? And straightaway we see that a major driver for a Roman, would have been personal advancement in a highly developed commercial and administrative culture. Taxes do not appear without a vast apparatus of bureaucracy, nor does complex trade. The fragmentation of these aspects of the empire removed an obvious necessity for literacy among a new generation of Europeans who now had more pressing needs to attend to. As one scholar argues very persuasively, it is hard to overstate the effects of continued war, rape, pillage, famine and disease that came and re-came upon Europe during this era.[197]

The archaeological record gives testament to continuity of literacy in certain places but what disappears entirely is the casual use of writing which marked the Roman age. For example, and this is not so anecdotal as it first appears, a study of graffiti between the 5th to 9th centuries shows votive and formal graffiti and not the usual level that characterised the Roman era; mentions of various body parts or that 'I love Flavia' etc. Literacy in Europe became the province of the clergy as the populace face more pressing concerns. For example, a study of 1000 subscribers on 8th century Italian charters, reveals that only 14% of lay subscribers could write their own name. The large majority (71%) that could sign their name, and label who the other scribbled marks belonged to, were clergy.[198] Considering that these were people of importance, and that it doesn't take a very high standard of literacy to sign your own name, we can deduce much about the general decline from this startling piece of research. Even decades later, Einhard tells us that Charlemagne kept writing tablets under his pillow so he could practice writing when he had time. And even this was largely a failed exercise, as he never really mastered the art.

But let us also say, that the extent of the decline is a great area of scholarly debate and we must be circumspect. In times of crisis and deep uncertainty the sources themselves may be subject to exaggeration. Ammianius Marcellinus says that by the end of the 4th century the *Bibliotecis sepulcrorum ritu in perpetuum clausis* – 'the libraries, like tombs, were closed forever.'[199] This seems like an exaggeration considering the date. The first public library was founded by Augustus in Rome and there were twenty-eight such civic establishments by the time of Constantine. One hundred and fifty years after Marcellinus, we know that King Theodoric's Chamberlain Cassiodorus – who had just returned from his fruitless embassy to Constantinople in 544 – retired from political and diplomatic service to found a monastery which he called 'Vivarium' – *place of life*. Realizing that tough times were coming, the preservation of learning and moral civility were essential.

Tangentially, and to give us a modern equivalent, when Elon Musk was interviewed about his plans for a colony on Mars, he spoke of the project exactly as people like Cassiodorus and Benedict of Nursia would have done in their day. Musk has well-founded concerns about unregulated Super-digital intelligence (AI), and the probability of a third world war at some point in the future. He sees, and speaks openly, of the Mars colony as a means for humanity to 'preserve human civilisation in seed form', against the very high probability of another 'Dark Age.' Cassiodorus' Vivarium along with other monastic foundations were aimed at the same goal. They not only modelled the ethic within an artificial, concentrated form of communal life, but they also preserved the intellectual patrimony of their civilisation. And not just Christian authors. The Vivarium, for example, copied the manuscripts of Virgil, Cicero, Ovid, Pliny, Horace, Statius, Juvenal, Terence, Persius, Lucan, Suetonius, Apuleius, Martial, Seneca and others. So, the libraries were not 'closed like tombs forever' as Marcellinus wrote. But obviously, a lot were, including, alas, Cassiodorus' Vivarium. Almost all of the books were lost, suffering the fate of other libraries either through under-endowment or more immediate ravages.

Gregory the Great (a contemporary of Columban who we shall meet later) also established a poor sort of library in Rome, but even this was almost completely destroyed by an illiterate mob during a famine. What is important to stress is that what was lost of Classical literature was *not* the result of wilful rejection by a puritanical church, but through historical accident. Literacy was certainly in decline among the upper classes[200] and, as we have noted, manuscript transmission went into serious decline. Gregory of Tours, another contemporary of Columban, lamented that *'in these times when the practice of letters declines, no, rather perishes in the cities of Gaul, there has been found no scholar trained in ordered composition to present in prose or verse a picture of the things which have befallen.'* But even then, we should not be too sensitive to individual sources. It can lead us to exaggeration or mistaking a local situation as more representative than it really was. Statements like *'The great continental libraries had vanished, even the memory of them had been erased in the minds of those who lived in the emerging feudal societies of medieval Europe'*[201] may not paint the whole picture.

Besides all this, there was always the Eastern Empire, which would hold its own for another millennium. The East had, incidentally, an emperor called Justin I who Procopius alarmingly records in 518 as entirely 'unlettered, the first such case amongst the Romans.' Yet Procopius, amongst many others, ensured that the illiteracy of the emperor did not affect the wider culture. The eastern Roman Empire survived until it fell to Mehmed II on 29th May, 1453. Hebrew, and Greek literature would survive there but let's be fair; even these Eastern survivals in part depended on there being a stable Western Europe during the Renaissance to receive it from the hands of those fleeing the fall of Constantinople. Without the preservation of the past and the unifying strength of Christendom, it seems highly probable that Europe would have become a collection of illiterate, and animist tribes, absorbed into Islam during its later expansion.

What about Latin culture? Unless the manuscripts could be preserved – and it is hard to preserve such perishable commodities without copying them – then Latin culture would disappear. Diarmaid MacCulloch's summary of Latin literary culture coming *'within a hair's breadth of vanishing forever'* may be overly bleak, but even if we crank down the overstatement a few notches, it still appears very much in a code red scenario. 'What was lost was lost forever' is a shocking and tragic lament of a contemporary source – part of our cultural patrimony would be and is now forgotten. Western civilisation would drag itself into the medieval era with severed limbs and bleeding stumps. But that it was able to crawl through those vital centuries at all is the debt we owe the monks,[202] and especially the Irish monks whose pioneer would be Columban. In this part of our story, he is a recalcitrant teen heading north. But one day the libraries of Turin, Milan, and St. Gall would bear witness that the majority of manuscript survivals from the seventh century were directly or indirectly due to his influence and that of his spiritual children. Let all parents with difficult teenagers take heart!

556-564 AD – COLUMBAN UNDER SINELL

Columban left his home in Meath as a young man fleeing the devil and as a son in search of a father. His natural father is never mentioned by Jonas. Providentially for him, sixty miles to the north at Clonard – as we have just seen – there had been an explosion of spiritual fathers under the guiding hand of Abbott Finian. At Clonard, Finian had resolved the great monastic tension of that time; whether a monk should be a *Docti* or *Sancti* – a scholar or a saint. As a younger man, Finian had been under Abbott Cadoc at LLancarfan, a monastery west of Cardiff – which incidentally is probably the earliest known educational institution in Britain during these supposed 'Dark Ages.'[203] Here Finian learned that the answer was not *'either or'* *Docti* or *Sancti* but *'both, and'*. So, he brought back to Ireland the value of study in a monk's life and calling. Indeed, Finian must have set a very high value on his mentor's system of training because, even years later, any monk who had studied at LLancarfan was also eligible for election to be abbot of Clonard.

Perhaps Columban visited Clonard for advice. Perhaps it was from here that he was deployed for training further north. Jonas does not mention it but Clonard was enroute to Columban's eventual destination – the island monastery of Cleenish. Cleenish (from *Cluan Innis* – meaning 'sloping island') on the River Erne, County Fermanagh, lies three miles south of modern-day Enniskillen.[204] It had been established only a few years before Columban arrived. Today, the monastery has long since fallen to the ravages of time. The site is marked solely by a disused rectangular graveyard with a small number of unmarked gravestones and some architectural remains, some of which were dated to the medieval period. It is a quiet and unvisited corner of Ireland but the island is still accessible by a bridge. The graveyard lies on the northwest edge of the small island, next to the water's edge and in the shadow of two small hillocks, one of which had been a ringfort.[205]

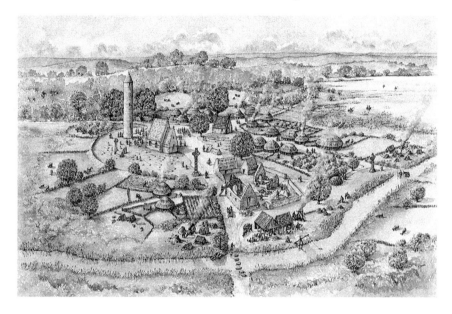

But it is not the setting that drew the lad north, but the man who dwelt there. We have talked about the transmission of culture by manuscript, and now we see the direct transmission of character, fatherhood, piety, and learning. Abbot Sinell of Cleenish was a living link to the founding fathers of Irish monasticism. Jonas puts it thus:

> 'When he left his birthplace, called by the inhabitants, Lagener-
> land, (Leinster, in Ireland) he betook himself to a holy man named
> Sinell, who at this time was distinguished among his countrymen
> for his unusual piety and knowledge of the Holy Scriptures. And
> when the holy man saw that St. Columban had great ability, he
> instructed him in the knowledge of all the Holy Scriptures. Never-
> theless, as was usual, the master attempted to draw out the pupils
> under false pretences, in order that he might learn their disposi-

tions, either the glowing excess of the senses, or the torpor induced by slothfulness. He began to inquire into Columban's disposition by difficult questions.'

Jonas goes on to tell us that Columban's answers brought him the admiration of both master and fellow pupils. It is not clear how long the young Columban stayed with Sinell but it must have been a number of years, perhaps even a decade. The Irish training in the *gráda ecnai* – grades of wisdom, show some of the different areas of learning and spiritual attainment that novices like Columban were aiming for. There was; *Desicipul* – the disciple; *Foglaintid* – the student; *Foircetlaid* – the teacher; *Druimchlí/fer léigind* – the man of reading; *Suí canóine* – the expert in canon law; *Staraige* – the historian/annalist; and *Cóectach* – the one who can recite all one hundred and fifty Psalms.[206] We will deal with the monastic rules of the time in another chapter but it is as well to have a flavour here from a contemporary school (*scola* or *schola* in their language) at Killeigh in County Laois. Here, as doubtless as in Cluan Innis, the following would have filled Columban's life:

Devotion without weariness. Humility without murmuring. Dressing without extravagance. Fasting without corruption. Exile without return. Constancy against frivolities. Blessing of the meal. Meals without wastage. Perseverance in study. Observance of the canonical hours. Constant cultivation of heaven. Strengthening of every weak one. No anxiety for the worldly life. Desiring mass. Listening to elders. Adoration of chastity. Standing by the weak. Frequent confession. Dishonour of a body. Honour of a soul. Humanity in face of need. Ministry of the sick. Cross-vigil in silence. Pity for illness. Searching Scripture. Tales for information. Honour to the old. Freedom for festival days. Brevity in chanting. Keeping friendship.

JULY 2018 – CLEENISH

These disciplines and virtues were all being cultivated in start-up monasteries throughout Ireland. And the more I read about them the more I wished to see the place for myself. In 2018, I got that opportunity. I arrived there one overcast afternoon in late July with the medieval scholar and Columban expert, Dr. Alex O'Hara. He had spent a few nights with us in a holiday cottage on the wild Atlantic coast of Donegal. A pensive and softly spoken man of Galway, mid-thirties with a thick ginger crop of hair, flecked with grey in the beard. They are a few days I shall treasure, for they were a meeting of hearts and minds. Cliff-hiking, sea-swimming, porpoise-watching, cave exploration, and beach fires with the children – Donegal is a paradise in the Emerald Isle. And when the children were bathed and fed, we then took long walks over hill and dale to the thatched Clontallagh pub in the middle of nowhere, to talk theology, philosophy, history – faith, families, and the future. We drank Guinness to the accompaniment of live Irish music and felt, certainly I did, that we were kings of the world, and that Solomon in all his glory, had scarce been as rich.

After our time there, we drove south to Cleenish via the site of that other great Irish monastic founder's birth and boyhood, Columbkille (Columba). As a teenage Columban was travelling north to Sinell, Columbkille was heading north on his epic exile to Iona. This temporary exile, which proved so fruitful, was imposed on Columbkille by the Irish church because he had incited a war that cost the lives of 2000 men. Columbanus would one day choose permanent exile of his own volition.

Alex and I left the tribal lands of the O'Neil's and crossed the border at Enniskillen at about 6pm. One off-license near the bridge offered beleaguered shoppers the simple option of everything in Euros equivalent in pounds sterling. Ten minutes' drive south along the narrow upper reaches of Lough Erne and we were crossing the metal bridge to Cleenish. When we finally arrived, the farmer, who raises cattle on the island, greeted us warmly. He had a Homeric head of white hair and the look of a poet about him – humorous, yet knowing. He was happy for us to camp, to launch the boat if needed, and showed a keen interest to understand from Alex all that was to be known about this island he loved; a place almost forgotten by everyone else.

Presently my wife arrived with the six children. They set up camp while we filmed an interview with a representative from the local history group, and then with Alex. We marvelled over the visible medieval carvings on stone fragments and also lamented that the geophysical surveys had not included the ringfort hilltop three hundred metres to the south. My twelve-year-old son William sent his drone, and a GoPro camera, up around the summit to see whether the evening light would reveal any boundaries or earthworks. There was nothing conclusive or even suggestive and by that point the rains were coming in and we had to get the equipment back under cover.

So, under the protection of the trees, coats, and umbrellas, we lit a fire on the edge of the graveyard and barbequed our food. As the night drew on and the rain eased off, and the kebabs were replaced with marshmallows and Bushmills single malt, we reclined on the grass and soaked up the moment. Neither of us had ever been here before, yet this might well have been the formational ground of a man we had both studied and written about. As the flames flickered upward and illuminated the great sycamores that enclose that historic place, our words became fewer and thoughts ranged further. We had spoken often about our own childhoods and educations, and now finally we were sharing the locus of Columban's earlier attainments and dreams. It was a night I will never forget, for it was a pause between breaths, a night when a man of even moderate means could have written poetry. Through the opening above us, the clouds gave no hint of stars that lay above. But that did not matter, for we sensed an open heaven – even when a month's rain was about to fall in the next 18 hours!

The next morning, we were sad to leave, as no doubt Columban would have been when his time finally came. For us it was the last day of a quasi-holiday and filming trip, for him it would be the end of training and time to show the world what manner of man he would become.

Columban completed his studies, obtaining good Latin – perhaps not the proficiency of Augustine – but certainly the equal of any in his own day. He was also conversant with prosody and wrote faultless hexameters and adonics. Most striking of all was his internalisation of the Christian scriptures. In just one letter, written in haste many years later, he used twenty-nine quotations taken from seventeen books of the Old and New Testaments. In years to come, Columban's monastic rule, his letter, and poems would all be suffused with Biblical references. This is undoubtedly the legacy of Sinell, who Jonas tells us was noted for his piety and scriptural knowledge: a solid foundation.

Jonas also tells us of one further effusion that surely took place at Cleenish – that of Columban's first literary work. *"So rich was the treasure of the Divine Scriptures hidden in his heart that he composed, when still a young man, a Commentary on the Psalms in a highly finished style."* Jonas says Columban also wrote hymns and treatises at this time, but they have all been lost. The commentary is undoubtedly the work mentioned in a ninth century catalogue of the library of St. Gall, and in a tenth century catalogue of Bobbio. But they were already long gone without even a trace of memory when the Irish Franciscan, Patrick Fleming, visited these monasteries in 1625. There is, however, an ancient commentary on the Psalms in the Ambrosian Library of Milan among the manuscripts which had formerly belonged to Bobbio where he died. But the original title-page and preface are missing, so the evidence is still inconclusive.

What is reasonably conclusive however is that Sinell had done his work well, in becoming a father – as the word Abbot (Abba) means – and guiding the heady youth who ran from his home with such dramatic abandon, into a methodical and sturdy scholar.[207] His novitiate was served, his first devotional literary works complete; Columban was now a man in his mid-twenties. To the east at Bangor, on the shores of Belfast Lough, another disciple of Finian had established a thriving monastery. And they were in need of a teacher.

Columban was on his way to his first academic post. It was time to spread his fledgling wings.

180. C. S. Lewis, Present Concerns (Ethical Essays) *'Living in the Atomic Age'*
181. We might compare it to the beneficial consequences of other great reformers. Some estimate that the pietistic preaching of John Wesley inadvertently lifted 20% of the UK population out of poverty. And thus, the penniless preacher wielded a greater beneficial influence than 22 other fellow Oxford graduates who became prime ministers.
182. According to Dom Hubert Van Zeller in *The Benedictine Idea* p8
183. Tertullian, *Apologeticum* , circa 197AD
184. Rubenson, *Letters of St Anthony*, p.81
185. Norman Davies, The Isles, p.141 (Macmillan Publishers Ltd, 1999.)
186. The reader might see, in these two mentions of the 'Whitehouse', that Scotland and Ireland (indeed Europe through them) owe Ninian a very great debt. I camped on the Isle of Whithorn with my family on a hot summer's night in 2018, and filmed at 6am the next day, in the remains of the stone chapel on the shore, while the sun rose above my native Cumbrian fells, 15 miles across the Solway Firth. The chapel is another forgotten place, built by largely forgotten men and women 'of whom the world was not worthy.'
187. NB: It is highly possible that the Munster saints, like Declan, Ailbe of Emly, Ciarán of Saigir, and Abbán of Moyarney, who some claim to be earlier monastic founders than Enda or Patrick, are correct. They are from the south of Ireland and thus open to influences directly from the continent.
188. *Columbanus*, Tomas O Fiaich
189. We may be tempted to scoff at the totality of the sacrifice, and the naivety of such youthful optimism, which led to the explosion of such communities; but we cannot do so from a settled position of strength. Industrialisation and many other aspects of late modernity have led to the disintegration of communities and relationships in the 'developed' world. We used to live out our lives, and form our identities, in local communities, where we observed those core values lived out before us. We grew to imitate those who embodied those core values. Belief determined values, values determined actions, and actions became culture. The political scientist Arthur Kroker laments that western societies have abandoned not only the external standards of that former age but also the intentions necessary to form authentic identities. Edward Hallowell, psychiatrist, and lecturer at Harvard Medical School says that daily personal connections are needed for longevity and happiness, but in modern society most people lack the meaningful connection with someone who will listen to them daily. Isolated people are rich pickings for media formation in what academics call an Age of Polyvocality. In just fifteen years – a millisecond in time – the number of people living alone globally has risen from about 153 million in 1996 to 277 million in 2011. That is an increase of nearly 80%. In the UK, 34% of households have one person living in them, in Sweden 47%. In some parts of

London, seven out of ten people live alone. This social fragmentation within modern societies, combined with aging populations and declining fertility are subjects of ubiquitous coverage and debate. Free market capitalism has remade and atomised human society in its own image. The overwhelming triumph of mass media has meant our social norms are changing faster than families, or legal systems can cope with. Filmmaker Andrei Tarkovsky said, 'modern mass culture aimed at the consumer, the civilisation of prosthetics, is crippling people's souls, setting up barriers between man and crucial questions of his existence, his consciousness of himself as a spiritual being.' We have such significant societal challenges ahead of us in the next thirty years that we would be foolhardy in the extreme to approach the answers given in former ages without the utmost humility.

190. Norman Davies, *The Isles*, p.50 (Macmillan Publishers Ltd, 1999.)

191. The protestant missionary William Carey achieved something similar by translating the Hindu Vedas into Guajarati.

192. Diarmaid MacCulloch, *A History of Christianity,* p.320

193. One of these Bibles, the *Codex Amiatus*, whose travels tell an amazing tale, can be seen in the Lawrentian Library, Florence.

194. Norman Davies, *The Isles*, p.80 (Macmillan Publishers Ltd, 1999.)

195. Norman Davies, *The Isles,* p.81 (Macmillan Publishers Ltd, 1999.)

196. '*The Fall of Rome and the End of Civilisation*', Bryan Ward-Perkins, Oxford University Press 2005 p.165

197. M. Canepa, *The Two Eyes of the Earth; Art and Ritual Kingship between Rome and Sassian Iran* (Berkeley 2009)

198. '*The Fall of Rome and the End of Civilisation*', Bryan Ward-Perkins, Oxford University Press 2005, p.166

199. How can we credit this so early in the history of barbarian incursions? One possible answer is that we know there were many private libraries in Rome, that were lampooned by Seneca and Petronius as being decorative rather than educative establishments. Frederick G. Kenyon suggests the disuse of private (not public) libraries by the late 4th century was actually because of the predominance of entertainment over serious reading. *Books and Reading at Rome*, (2nd Ed. (Oxford, 1951), pp. 82-83; Seneca, *De Tranquilitate Animi, IX*; Petronius, Cena Trimal. XLVIII). So too does George W. Houston, *A Revisionary Note on Ammianus Marcellinus 14.6.18: When Did the Public Libraries of Ancient Rome Close?* Library Quarterly vol. 58, No. 3 (Chicago, 1988), pp. 258-264

200. Peter Brown, *The Rise of Western Christendom*

201. Thomas Cahill, *How the Irish Saved Civilisation*

202. Perhaps monks, not usually popular in our day, should be more appreciated than they are on account of their forebears who preserved the antique and contemporary pagan literature, and not just their own preferred texts. If you can imagine modern Benedictines carefully copying out The God Delusion then you are very near what was happening. What was saved, we owe to them, and I include here the Syriac monks who acted as translators for the Muslims.

203. This is sometimes wrongly attributed to St. Illtud who, formerly an arrogant Welsh nobleman, became the founder-abbot and teacher of the divinity school known as Cor Tewdws, located in Llanilltud Fawr (Llantwit Major) in the Welsh county of Glamorgan. It is possible that later hagiographies are mistaken, but they record that Illtud was converted to a reformed life by Cadoc, who by other accounts was his senior.

204. N.B. Jonas only mentions the name Sinellis, not Cluan Innis, which has led some scholars to question the location. Another monk by this name was operating in what is now County Down and was later Abbot of Bangor.

205. 'While the fluvial geomorphology has yet to be studied, a sizeable, crescentic flood-plain, following the curve of the river Erne at this point, occurs to the north of the remains. And at the point where the ground rises, there is a bullaun stone. Bullaun stones, identified by rounded hollows on the surface, are frequently associated with early church sites where they seem to lie on the monastic boundary. They are generally dated to the 7th-10th century. This then is the only indication of the footprint of the early monastery. The geophysical survey has revealed a host of enclosing features, bringing near certainty to the hypotheses that the graveyard marks the site of the early medieval monastery'. Ref: Dr. Alexander O'Hara, writing up the 2013 Geophysical and archaeological report. After WWI, the British government gave farms to 12 ex-soldiers each a 30 – 40 acre farm on the island.

206. A significant body of Irish chants and spoken prayers, in genres such as antiphons, hymns, sequences, tropes, and spoken texts, still exists today in more than 300 manuscripts and printed books in libraries across Europe. Complete or fragmentary offices survive for Saints Brendan of Clonfert, Brigit of Kildare, Columba of Iona, Columbanus of Bobbio, Dympna of Geel, Fursa of Péronne, Findán of Rheinau, Gall of St Gallen, Kilian of Würzburg, Virgil of Salzburg, among others.

207. It is possible that Abbot Sinell later became the fifth abbot of Bangor. For there was a famed scholar called Sinlán Moccu Mín described in the list of abbots in the Antiphonary of Bangor. Indeed, this abbot was referred to as the 'famed teacher of the world.' If this is the same man, then his influence through Columban alone might have earned him the name.

A barefooted Columban monk holding a
book, pictured inside the Book of
Kells (c.800 AD)

CHAPTER 5

Schuman's Scholastic Training

CHAPTER SUMMARY – 1900-1914, THE ROAD TO HELL - Schuman and destiny. The slow descent into industrial war. Schuman's secondary and tertiary education. 1903-1914 – SCHUMAN: SCHOLASTICISM & CATHOLIC SOCIAL TEACHING – How *Rerum Novarum* and key mentors like Jacques Maritain, Thomas Aquinas, and Pope Leo XIII underpinned his intellectual formation. 1914-1919 – TRAUMA TO TRIUMPH - Schuman in the aftermath of his mother's accidental death, and how a letter diverts him from the cloister to politics. Schuman: the lawyer and politician in Metz during World War I.

"We must love them both, those whose opinions we share and those whose opinions we reject, for both have laboured in the search for truth, and both have helped us in finding it."

Thomas Aquinas,
'Summa Contra Gentiles'

*"How is it they live in such harmony, the billions of stars,
when most men can barely go a minute without declaring
war in their minds?"*

Thomas Aquinas

1900-1919 – THE ROAD TO HELL

L et us return again to Luxembourg where we can observe the life and
times of Robert Schuman. We last saw the shy and bookish 14-year-
old at the grave of his father in the cemetery above his home in the quiet
suburb of Luxembourg. Jean Pierre Schuman was survived by his much
younger wife Eugenie, a remarkable woman as we shall see later. By this
time Robert is attending the Athénée in the centre of the city. After four
years at the Athenaeum, he travelled – perhaps daily – to the Metz Lycée
Impérial where he would eventually receive a baccalaureate. From then
on it was university, and the Law. And so, for the next six years
(1904-1910) he read law at the Universities of Berlin, Munich, Bonn,
and Strasbourg. He moved freely between them, multilingual, growing
in confidence, and learning. And through these years, as in the years
leading up to this, he was increasingly aware of a call to a special destiny.[208]

Other figures who would achieve greatness have known similar calls
which are hard to explain away in the light of subsequent history. For example, when he was just 16 years old, Winston Churchill told his school
friend that he could foresee terrible and unimaginable wars, where he
would be 'in command of the defences of London' and that he would
'save London and England from disaster.' When his friend[209] asked
Winston whether that meant he would be a General, in command of the
troops? Churchill replied; *'I don't know; dreams of the future are blurred
but the main objective is clear. I repeat—London will be in danger and in
the high position I shall occupy, it will fall to me to save the Capital and
save the Empire.'*

But, back to Schuman, and before we imagine soft-focus halcyon
university days, we need to centre ourselves in the actual era. If it was a

Belle Epoque, then it was a brief one. For even as young Schuman was taking root in Europe, so were other people and other forces, less benign. The ideologies mentioned in Chapter 3 were about to break cover. It is said that the nations sleepwalked into the Great War, but there were signs to spot for those who were still awake. These were the years of rising confidence in France, which began the century by opening the Paris Metro and annexing Madagascar. Soon the French colonial possessions would amount to nearly four and a half million square miles. They were largely in North Africa; double that of Rome, but only a third the size of the mammoth British Empire at its height. It was the heyday of colonialism: the British, the Belgians, the Dutch – life was good, for now. But the winds of change were already blowing on them all. Within little over fifty years the world maps would look very different. *Tempus edax rerum*[210] – time the devourer of everything.

The same cultural forces,[211] that had given the French their mandate, were now fully at work also in a resurgent Germany. Soon the white man's burden to civilize would be matched by the Arian burden to dominate.[212] Accordingly, in 1902 the *Triple Alliance* between France, Austria, and Italy, was renewed for another 6 years. One year later the French and English would also sign their *Entente Cordiale*.

That same year, as already mentioned, the Russian Social Democrat party split in London – and the new Bolshevik faction led by Lenin and Trotsky emerged. Lenin stayed in the Hotel Imperial in Russell Square. He and Stalin met Ramsey MacDonald in white tie and tails at a drinks party in Chelsea. Stalin, already a hardened gangster, and the one who would eventually ruthlessly apply the ideology to its fullest extent, was nearly beaten up in a pub by London Dockers. These fledging revolutionaries, nevertheless, appear to have enjoyed their time among the tolerant British, though that tolerance did not appear to have rubbed off on the newly formed Bolshevik party that emerged from the split. Could anyone at the time foresee what this would mean? An old adage might well apply, *'may you never live in interesting times.'*

But another split of sorts was happening in France, which Schuman might have noted with alarm. A polarising cynicism within her politics grew in these years of the infamous *Dreyfus Case*, which exposed military and political corruption, and anti-Semitism. The affair, which dragged on for twelve years (1894 to 1906), divided France deeply and lastingly into two opposing camps: the pro-Army, mostly Catholic *anti-Dreyfusards* and the anticlerical, pro-republican *Dreyfusards*. It was a dialectic of extremes that embittered French politics and encouraged a radicalization that Schuman would have to navigate in his career.

In 1909, Norman Angell (later a Nobel winning author) published a book called *The Great Illusion* arguing that war within Europe was impossible because of the great level of integration that then existed between national economies. That was 1909. What particularly appealed to the business elites was that it seemingly positioned them at the vanguard of, not just prosperity, but also international peace. How wrong could you be?

Further back in 1860, near Schuman's childhood home, Luxembourgers had torn down the defensive walls because a treaty signed between France and some German states had, some believed, rendered them unnecessary. Twenty-eight years later, and with considerably less idealism, Bismarck prophetically remarked, 'if there is ever another war in Europe, it will come out of some damn silly thing in the Balkans.' How right could you be? Schuman was growing up in a generation sleepwalking into a 31-year apocalypse that would leave 100 million dead. But let us return to his early years, trying as hard as possible to ignore the rising darkness.

If we are to believe his French biographer de Rochefort – who is perhaps a little too unstinting with praise and light on criticism – Robert was a well behaved, honest, serious, and dutiful child.[213] An only child, extremely independent and very happy to be alone,[214] he was even a 'contemplative by vocation.'[215] At the Athenaeum he astonished peers with his memory and his prodigious intellectual ability, even when advanced to work with children two years older than him,[216] winning all the prizes at school. One teacher remarked: *'This boy will end up like an encyclopedia'.*[217]

He was the only child of his parents, raised in comparative luxury and tranquillity. And so, one might expect that the privilege would lead to selfishness, but not according to de Rochefort. Schuman was, it seems, always extremely honest from boyhood, and (remarkably) managed to retain this trait in a long political career. *'He had a horror of all deceit'* [218] as well as a passion for reconciliation of all sides when there was a dispute. Naturally, his biographer makes the connection of this boyhood trait to his later trajectory as a statesman.

But despite this independence and bookishness, he was also sociable and possessed an emotional intelligence to read other people well and to anticipate their reactions. De Rochefort particularly highlights Schuman's *'discretion, subtlety, care not to upset others.'* [219] Away from his work he was able to be a joyful and physically active companion. Among his friends, his biographer notes his preference for *'those who came from the country,'* [220] perhaps for their straightforward manners and orientation to outdoor play. He also had a love of practical jokes,[221] of which his biographer takes time to give examples. A man who can take a practical joke at his expense – one who can laugh at himself – is not a person partial to his own 'dignity'. To be aware of the ridiculous, even in – or particularly – in oneself should be a prerequisite to the human race, let alone public service.

But even if Schuman appreciated practical jokes, he was still a very private person – not effusive by temperament. There were only very few people who shared closely in his personal life.[222] But despite this reserve, his correspondence reveals that he inspired deep loyalty in those friends and colleagues with whom he grew close. Along with the surviving letters to his mother, this correspondence reveals an intimate exchange of souls and a sincere man capable of deep and genuine feeling.

This 'passion for reading'[223] never left him, and at university, his mother despaired that her son would rather invest in his library than live in a properly heated house.[224] He was, in effect, his own university research department, and it is not possible to pinpoint any single intellectual mentor, beyond his mother, who fulfilled the roles that Abbots Sinell and Comgall had for Columban. Schuman dug a deep well and

prepared broad foundations for his yet-undetermined future with assiduous study and prodigious reading. I imagine him as George MacDonald's scholar-hero Donal Grant;

> *'Give me a chair and a table, fire enough to keep me from shivering, the*
> *few books I like best and writing materials, and I am absolutely content.*
> *But beyond these things I have at the castle a fine library – useless no*
> *doubt for most purposes of modern study, but full of precious old books.*
> *There I can at any moment be in the best of company! There is more of*
> *the marvellous in an old library than ever any magic could work!"*

Anyone who has benefited from the *best sort of old books* cannot
help but be stirred with gratitude by these words. That Schuman too
was immersed in books 'useless for the purposes of modern study' was,
as it turned out, all to the good. For had he been, as Ruskin put it,
'caught in the cobwebs of German metaphysics, or sloughed in the English drainage of them,'[225] he would not have been armed in the way he
was for his later life's work. That we are free to read good books, and
not Nazi or Communist propaganda, is partly due to good men and
women like Schuman. That we even have such a wealth of classic literature, Schuman would himself credit people like Columban. As one Oxford Don eloquently put it:

> *'... in reading great literature I become a thousand men and*
> *yet remain myself. Like the night sky in the Greek poem, I see*
> *with a myriad eye, but it is still I who see. Here, as in worship,*
> *in love, in moral action, and in knowing, I transcend myself;*
> *and am never more myself than when I do.'*[226]

1903-1914 – SCHUMAN; SCHOLASTICISM AND CATHOLIC SOCIAL THOUGHT

Even as an adult, Schuman would have less than five hours sleep,[227] fill-
ing his waking hours with work, reading, meditation, correspondence,

and prayer, a constant daily diet of *'intellectual and spiritual nourish-ment'*. Starting with an inherited library of 275 volumes, he would one day finish his career with a library of 8000.[228] He knew European history in great detail, as well as possessing a coherent interpretative framework from Catholic theology and philosophy so that his eventual continental project had a firm and deep foundation. He was reading Thomas Aquinas in the shadow of the Neo-Thomist revival which started in his childhood[229] and it would be remiss of us not to 'pop the bonnet on Schuman's intellectual formation and poke about briefly among the various engine parts that he chose to assemble for it. Extending an imperfect metaphor, let us summarise in advance by saying that the engine was clearly orthodox Christianity; that the fuel was the Scholasticism of the 13th century philosopher, Thomas Aquinas, which powered the driveshaft of 19th century Pope Leo XIII's Catholic Social Teaching (CST), which itself was well-oiled by contemporary philosophers like Jacques Maritain. Of those four elements let us briefly summarise the latter three.

The thick-set Italian Dominican, Thomas Aquinas (i.e., from Aquino in Italy) was a 13th century student of Albertus Magnus of Cologne. His master was wise enough to know that the slowness of his student – the others called him the 'dumb ox' – was not for want of brains but because of an excess of excruciating methodology. Albertus prophesied that one day the ox would roar and all Christendom would hear him. He was right. Anthony Kenny considers him 'one of the dozen greatest philosophers of the western world.' Essentially as a theologian, political theorist, and jurist, he baptised Aristotle and, as Chesterton put it, 'called him up in the fight for Christ' in the areas of ethics, natural law, metaphysics, and political theory. By synthesizing Aristotelian philosophy with orthodox Christianity, in books like *The Disputed Questions on Truth* (1256–59), the *Summa contra Gentiles* (1259-1265), and the *Summa Theologiae* (1265-1274), Aquinas straddled the classical and Christian era like a Colossus.

For Schuman and his contemporaries, it was the political and legal writing that drove home the legitimacy of a Christian dedicated to the public service of governance. For Aquinas, the reconciliation between the high Stoicism of the Republic and the humility of the Church would lead to the ideal state.

> 'His analysis is precisely Aristotle + Scripture. Aristotle says the highest good in this life is to participate in government and concludes that the best form of government is a mixed polity. He prescribes friendship with one's neighbour and the virtues which render us capable and worthy of this as the recipe for natural happiness; Scripture demands that we answer the question 'who is my neighbour' in the broadest possible way as a necessary condition for the supernatural happiness of friendship with God, for which Aristotle dared not even hope. Thomas' [Aquinas] ideal political model is no more than an extrapolation from these two doctrines, one natural and one revealed. What the early Church had instinctively adopted as its own method of government, Thomas justifies by faith and reason.'[230]

The philosopher Romano Guardini,[231] a contemporary of Schuman, was also much deepened by Aquinas and wrote, 'The Summa was not only a book of science; it was a "space," vast in its ontology – deep and ordered – wherein the human spirit found its proper place and exercised that self-discipline.' But Guardini was also quick to correct the misconception that neo-Thomists like himself merely posited 'a premodern solution to modernity' or were clinging to the 'glorified Middle Ages of the Romantics,' who gave it a 'canonical status that it never possessed.' What he and others of his generation were finding in Aquinas was a large enough lever to reject the 'autonomous reason' that was drawing human society into a vortex of philosophic nihilism.

If we are looking for the source of confidence found in men like Schuman, De Gasperi, and Adenauer, then here is part of the answer. For medieval man, revelation was the absolute fulcrum – that is, the belief that the Creator himself had spoken and defined the ground rules of reality upon which humans were free to build. The tool we call reason, was for them, not sophisticated enough on its own to answer the fundamental questions of existence. Indeed, they understood that an inherited and perverse sort of independence left humanity all too open to being led astray by an autonomous reason unbridled from revelation. This essentially is where Pope Leo, Maritain, and Schuman *et al* saw Europe's great dilemma. But they believed that Aquinas gave Europe a greater lever, with a historical, religious, and philosophical pedigree. By a synthesis between 'school and tradition,' he 'achieved an intellectual synthesis completely beyond the scope of modern individualism.' And for people like Guardini, it was Aquinas and not the Renaissance scholars who were the real champion of antiquity. Renaissance fidelity to the classical literature was, he said, a blunt tool, used by the thinkers of that day knowingly or sometimes unknowingly, as they attempted 'to sever themselves from revelation and ecclesiastical authority.'

Guardini understood that even though they did not complete the break, there was a discontinuity between how people viewed their relationship to the world before and after the Renaissance. In fact, it would be, as we have seen, Schuman's father's generation that had managed to finally achieve this break, to 'unchain the earth from the sun', and 'wipe out the horizon', as Nietzsche put it. And it was exactly at this time, and in response to these currents, that Leo XIII (1810-1903), the energetic Roman Patrician we met briefly in chapter 3, wrote his letter concerning the working classes; *Rerum Novarum*, 'Revolutionary Change'. This encyclical amongst others, in our engine analogy, became the great drive shaft for Schuman and many others.

What became known generally as *Catholic Social Teaching* (CST) was essentially the Roman Church responding to five key issues: private property, the right of the Church to speak on social issues, the role of the state, the worker's right to a just wage, and the importance of worker's associations. The Industrial Revolution meant that people questioned the relationship between employers and employees, the just distribution of capital, the growing disaffection of workers, the role of worker's associations, and the decline in moral values. Leo highlighted the dire living conditions of the poor and claimed that workers were left unprotected when the old guilds were subsumed into political institutions, particularly ones that rejected the church's teaching. Leo, like the Hebrew prophets of old, steals the thunder of the Marxists by railing against the gross economic inequality (he calls it slavery,) brought about in an inhuman industrial age. He denounces both a predatory capitalism and usurious interest.

It is important to stress this because in the minds of many – and justly so – Catholicism's relationship with wealth, power and privilege has often been a tragic betrayal of Jesus' explicit commands. But you cannot mistake a man like Leo XIII. His challenge to capitalism and socialism were equally incisive and brutal. No one with a moderately sensitive conscience can sit complacently in their pew when the Pope of Rome tells them that, 'Once the demands of necessity and propriety have been met, the rest that one owns belongs to the poor.' In Leo's mind, for the rich to redistribute their wealth was as much a matter of salvation as justice. In this, he speaks very much in line with the New Testament's emphasis, where 27% of all references about money are warnings, and a further 42% exhort those who have it, to hold it as God's hand to aid the poor. Leo said that If the rich of this world wanted to 'pass through the eye of the needle' and escape Hell – yes, he did actually use the 'H' word – then they had better redistribute everything beyond 'necessity and propriety.' You might feel there is some room for manoeuvre in the word 'propriety', but even so, on the face of it, this challenge hits a lot harder compared to a socialist message, which very often merely appeals to the politics of envy.

For Leo, the socialist's proposition, that all property should be held in common, was just one more set of symptoms masquerading as a cure. He says that it is an 'obsolete' political doctrine, long disproved by natural law and history. The state may in certain circumstances have the moral right and duty to redistribute property that has become injurious to the commonweal, but it should never assume a competency (it cannot claim to have) in removing the just wages (which of course is property in miniature) from a father who has laboured to feed his family.

That, he argues, would be to usurp the primal political unit of which society comprises. The mere politics of envy, he warns, has no fruitful outcome for society. He also argues that the simplistic binary of blaming class struggle for the wretched state of modern society is to ignore other forces at work like sin and disorder, which can never be completely eradicated as some were naively claiming.

Leo also saw in socialism the same dangerous element that his contemporary Dostoyevsky observed in Russia. As soon as Dostoyevsky's character Alyosha was seriously 'convinced of the existence of God and immortality,' he at once 'instinctively said to himself: "I want to live for immortality, and I will accept no compromise." In the same way, if he had decided that God and immortality did not exist, he would at once have become an atheist and a socialist. For socialism is not merely the labour question, it is before all things the atheistic question, the question of the form taken by atheism to-day, the question of the tower of Babel built without God, not to mount to heaven from earth but to set up heaven on earth.' [232]

Leo also supplied a validation for social classes; indeed, he ascribes duties and rights to rulers and ruled. Like Ruskin, forty years before in *Unto This Last*,[233] Leo argues for a sort of chivalric or sacrificial capitalism; wealth in motion is the goal as opposed to the mere accumulation of wealth. Further, he reminded his listeners that Christ himself, and subsequently many other saintly characters, modelled the dignity of poverty in their lives. But honourable poverty aside, the decrease of poverty by those materially more secure is an important goal for Christians. In the Bible, the psalmist pleaded with God to give him neither poverty nor riches, in case he became proud and forget his maker.

Extending this principle, Leo moves onto the legitimate role of the state in social issues. In his view, the state should promote wholesome morality, safeguard the practice of religion and the security of family life, oversee the equitable distribution of burdens, and protect the weak and impoverished. That dealt with, he moves onto a subject that is still never far from the headlines, the importance of a just wage. Employers should pay a wage commensurate to the worker's personal investment and living necessity. The state's rights and duties to protect the rights of the working class should also extend from smaller worker organizations, which would pull the rug from under what he considers 'immoral' worker associations. The letter finishes with general exhortations and hopes that Christians will act according to conscience and the church's teachings.

Leo XIII wrote many other letters on related themes – Marriage, Communism, Censorship, the Bible, Americanism, and Christian Democracy – but he is mostly known now for his letter to the working class. It was updated and reiterated forty years later just before the war (Quadragesimo Anno) by Pope Pius XI and also after the war, by numerous other declarations and movements that addressed the realities of secularization and pluralism. *Opus Dei, Gaudiem et Spes*, and *Lumen Gentium* sound to the modern ear like antiquated Latin titles for some minutiae of theological window dressing, but they were in fact very solid responses to real-world issues. Thomas Rosica reminds us of what we, at our historical distance, are too apt to forget; that these Catholics 'had experienced two world wars, the horror of the Holocaust, the onset of the nuclear weaponry, the hostility of communism, the awesome and only partially understood impact of science and technology.'[234] So, this was the official Catholic intellectual response, but how was it received and developed?

Leaping forward to 1938 we can find Schuman himself citing *Quadragesimo Anno*, and insisting that the Christian church will always 'have a role not just in the sanctuary but also in the family, the workplace, the hospital and the school....' Schuman reminds his audience that the Church rejects the Liberal economic doctrine that the state should under no circumstances intervene in the economy. The church, he says, allows for this intervention, not only when some positive injustice has occurred but also when private initiative is unable to accomplish the common good. The precise boundaries of this necessary intervention, and the occasions on which the necessity exists, are not defined by the Church because they pertain to the technical order. But, citing Pius XI's encyclical against Nazism, he reminds his audience that there are boundaries beyond which the state cannot go because it would infringe the divinely-given liberty of the family and the individual, and the Church will defend these natural rights if they are called into question. 'Even the enemies of the Church,' Schuman concludes, 'have occasionally admitted that it is the Church which has historically been the principal guardian of the liberties of the individual and the family against the pretensions of the state, and it is not only for her own liberties that she fights.'[235]

But who are the intermediary conduits who deliver and expand the meanings of these encyclicals to Schuman? This brings us, in our engine analogy, to the lubricant that allowed the power of these ideas to flow freely to a new generation. Jacques Maritain was not the only philosopher bringing Aquinas and Catholic social thought into the modern world, but he was the most important one for Schuman. And so, Maritain deserves a short paragraph of biography – and not least because his life and struggles speak with volume about the philosophic tensions in Schuman's university days.

Jacques Maritain (1882–1973) was a French contemporary of Schuman and raised in an affluent and liberal Protestant family. At the Sorbonne, he studied the natural sciences: chemistry, biology, and physics. It was here that he also met and married Raïssa Oumançoff, a Russian Jewish im-

Jacques & Raissa Maritain

migrant, a gifted poet and mystic who would be become a full intellectual partner in his life and studies. What, we may well ask, turned an agnostic physical scientist into a moral philosopher who would author more than 60 books, and be so influential in the development of the Universal Declaration of Human Rights? Basically put, it was the great tension of the age, perhaps any age: truth. He famously said, 'we do not need a truth to serve us, we need a truth that we can serve.' But what set him apart was a determination to resolve it, even in the most radical way.

'At the Sorbonne, Jacques and Raïssa soon became disenchanted with scientism, which could not, in their view, address the larger existential issues of life. In 1901, in light of this disillusionment, they made a pact to commit suicide together if they could not discover some deeper meaning to life within a year.'
236

Raissa wrote that 'if it were impossible to live according to truth' then they wanted to act meaningfully – even if it meant suicide – 'before the years had accumulated their dust before youthful strength was spent.' The young couple were saved from the suicide pact by attending, the lectures of continental philosopher Henri Bergson just across the street at the *Collège de France*. His critique of scientism – scientific materialism – helped release them from existential despair and help them find an initial 'sense of the absolute.' If the world was ruled by something other than mere, pitiless force, then there was hope. This was taken a step further in 1906 when, via the influence of Léon Bloy, they converted to Roman Catholicism. A year later Raïssa introduced Jacques to the writings of Thomas Aquinas which he said came on him like a 'luminous flood.' In the following decades, he taught all over the world, and his voluminous writings covered many aspects of philosophy, including aesthetics, political theory, philosophy of science, metaphysics, the nature of education, liturgy, and ecclesiology.

Schuman devoured these works of Maritain, who came to embody the newly confident Catholic reaction against revolutionary politics. Maritain's long series of Catholic critiques of contemporary Enlightenment culture, such as *Three Reformers: Luther, Descartes, Rousseau* (1925), and *Christianity and Democracy* (1943) were particularly influential. Maritain insisted that in the last analysis, secular expressions of humanism - which neglected the spiritual aspects of human beings -

would inevitably prove to be anti-human. In his own proposition, in what he calls *Integral Humanism,*[237] he explores the prospects for a new Christendom, rooted in his philosophical pluralism, in order to find ways (that) Christianity could inform political discourse and policy in a pluralistic age'[238]

Maritain's anthropological foundations are biblical and reassuring and radically humane. 'A single human soul is of more worth than the whole universe of bodies and material goods. There is nothing above the human soul except God. In the light of the eternal value and absolute dignity of the soul, society exists for each person and is subordinate thereto. "Every individual person," writes St. Thomas Aquinas, "bears the same relationship to the whole community as the part bears to the whole." And this supremely important God-made individual for Maritain 'is not a closed whole, he is an open whole. He is not a little god without doors or windows, like Leibniz's monad, or an idol which 'sees not, hears not, speaks not.' He tends by his very nature, to social life, and to communion.'[239]

His very nature, are the all-important words for Maritain. The human being 'by reason of certain things which are in him, is in his entirety engaged as a part of political society.' The human person, by an act of creation, is anterior to the state and stands in a peculiar relation to it. He is God's creature first. 'Above the plane of civil society, the person crosses the threshold of a kingdom which is not of this world and enters a supra-national, supra-racial, supra-temporal society which is called the Church and which has to do with the things that are not Caesar's.' With such thoughts, Maritain's wartime political writing envisions a society that is, 'personalist because it considers society to be a whole composed of persons whose dignity is anterior to society and who, however indigent they may be, contain within their very being a root of independence, and aspire to ever greater degrees of independence until they achieve that perfect spiritual liberty which no human society has within its gift.'[240]

Some Aquinas' scholars criticised Maritain for being more faithful to his commentators than to the original texts, and others criticised his moral philosophy as not sufficiently distinct from moral theology. In other Catholic circles he is criticised for an underdeveloped view of culture; and his view on democratic pluralism giving too much license to the liberal philosophers like John Rawls, and his theory of the 'overlapping consensus of reasonable views.' Which means, I suppose, that you really can't please everyone. For myself, I was heartily prepared not to like him but when I read of his life, marriage, and relationships, I couldn't help being deeply thankful and moved.

When Raïssa died in 1960, he published her journal. Because of her Jewish roots, they spent the war in America, and the many personal accounts of them show a most loving and exceptional couple. When she died, he went to live with a monastic order called the *Little Brothers of Jesus* in Toulouse, eventually becoming a monk in 1970, three years before his own

Jacques and Raissa before her death in 1960

death. In a strange way, in this reversion to a monasticism born of the desert, as indeed the *Little Brothers* were, Maritain was coming full circle, chiming with many themes in this book about the spreading and evolution of culture.[241]

So that is the life of Maritain. But in order to keep pace with our narrative, and restrict the length of this chapter, I have scattered Maritain's teaching at points where they are evinced by his disciples, most notably Schuman and De Gasperi. But these vignettes have, I hope, at least given some form to the intellectual world of Schuman. Of course, it is merely a starting point. (He read the conservative Joseph de Maistre while at law school[242] as well as reading and witnessing the ultra-conservative Pope Pius X.)[243] But even so, these four major aspects, and no doubt a myriad more, were turning the cogs in Schuman's mind. And if we were to further extend the engine metaphor, we would see clearly that men like him, Adenauer, and De Gasperi were the wheels that touched the tarmac of political culture at a pivotal moment in the West's history.

1914-1919 – TRAUMA TO TRIUMPH

We return to Schuman's mother and his home – what Tertullian called *the seminary of the human race*. Mrs. Eugénie Schuman, now a widow, seems a most remarkable woman as she guides and supports her son through his teen years and into higher education. She gave him roots and wings and was as their preserved letters show: 'A woman very sweet, very pious, very devout... and also infinitely attentive, tender and loving.'[244] Like Augustine's mother

Robert Schuman, Lawyer of Metz

Monica, she had to accept that her gifted son would one day leave home,[245] but she did not, like Monica or John Ruskin's mother, follow her son to university.[246]

While Schuman was moving between the universities of Berlin, Munich, Bonn, and Strasbourg, he and his mother made up for their distance with a constant and intimate correspondence, much of which we still possess. His mother's letters at this time show an intellectually gifted woman, always suggesting new books for her son to read, mostly theology and history. Some show her thankfulness that, on medical grounds, Robert would not be drafted for active military service in the German army. She was so relieved that she took him on a pilgrimage to Lourdes in thanks. His inner life was nourished by this close companionship with his mother until her death, and then by his extremely diligent reading and Catholic piety. She became, very like Monica to Augustine, his psychic symbol for the Church.

How terrible then to Schuman when after a walking holiday in Switzerland in 1911, he received the news. In a freak accident, she had been stepping up into a carriage after four other women on the way to a cousin's wedding at Evrange. But the horse bolted and she was thrown backward from the carriage at Frisange. Her skull was cracked in the fall. A priest who knew her just happened to be passing at that moment, and he gave her the last rights as she died of internal bleeding. No one else was even hurt, it was just her. Schuman was desolate and shaken to the core. If only he had attended the wedding then this wouldn't have happened. Why her? Why now? We can get a sense of this atomising grief from what a contemporary wrote about his own mother's death just three years before this date,

> 'With my mother's death, all settled happiness ... disappeared from my life. There was to be much fun, many pleasures, many stabs of joy; but no more of the old security. It was sea and islands now; the great continent had sunk like Atlantis.' [247]

In a letter to a friend shortly before she died Mrs. Schuman wrote, "I bless God for everything he has given us up to now - that which he has in store for us later we must accept from his paternal hands, for good or ill. I ask only that it should be for our eternal salvation, this alone is of value, the rest is accidental." Schuman, now a twenty-five-year-old student, and so close to finishing his law studies began, for the first time to consider joining a monastery. If he had it would have surprised very few. He went to mass every day. 'He was like a monk,' someone said who knew him, 'he prayed all the time.'

Schuman inhabited the mystical and historical world of this Catholic culture, with constant pilgrimages and visits on occasions of the elevation of particular saints, and a constant diet of European cathedrals. He was an active member of UNITAS, the Catholic student movement, and attended the German Catholic Congress (Katholikentag) in Metz in 1913. His Catholic world was *wide as well as old*. His early life was peppered with pilgrimages, and it was a cause of much of his incessant travelling in Europe. He wrote in 1907, at the feast of St Cecilia, of *'these vast spaces, so mysteriously lighted and resonating with pious melodies.'*[248] As we have already seen he was something of a mystic and an ascetic, and so would have worn a monastic habit with ease. That he did not is perhaps partly due to his friend Henry Escbach who wrote to encourage him to continue with his studies after his mother's death:

> *"...in our society, the apostolate of the laity is an urgent neces-*
> *sity, and I cannot imagine a better apostle than you... You will*
> *remain a layman because you will succeed better at doing good,*
> *which is your unique preoccupation... it is my serious convic-*
> *tion that the saints of the future will be saints in suits" (lit. 'des*
> *saints en veston')*[249]

There is much in this statement that we must decode, not least the ecclesiastical jargon like *'apostolate of the laity.'* His friend, who will turn up again at a key moment, was referring to a movement gaining traction within Catholic thought (because of Leo XIII and Maritain, etc), even as Schuman was growing into manhood; namely that the job of a politician could be as holy as that of a priest. That the secular could be sacred and indeed should be.

This sort of conversation had been going on during that other *'dark age'* that Columban faced. As the barbarians descended on the Roman Empire, a politician and general in North Africa called Boniface exchanged many letters with Augustine. He felt embattled, bitter, and on the point of utter despair. He, like Schuman wanted nothing more than to withdraw from public life and become a monk. But Augustine's response was not what one might have expected from a monastic founder. In fact, he speaks as Henry Escbach spoke to his friend 1500 years later. 'Each person, as the apostle says, has his own gift from God, one this gift, another that.[250] Hence others fight invisible enemies by praying for you; you struggle against visible barbarians by fighting for them.' If

Boniface wanted peace, fair and good, but, says Augustine, with escha-tological caution 'we ought not to want to live ahead of time with only the saints and the righteous.' Later on, when the pressures on Boniface were mounting it was these admonitions that held him back from swap-ping them for 'holy leisure.'

At this time, Augustine reaffirms the politician in his secular career and reminds him how much benefit he has been to the church by his exercise of justice and law. 'You were acting with this intention alone, namely, that they might lead a quiet and tranquil life, as the apostle says, in all piety and chastity[251] defended from the attacks of the barbarians.' But it is not just a holy calling in the secular realm but also a debt of grat-itude he owes to society for the benefits he has received. 'If the Roman empire has given you good things,' Augustine says, 'albeit earthly and transitory ones, because it is earthly, not heavenly, and cannot give save what it has in its control—if, then it has conferred good things upon you, do not repay evil with evil.'

Schuman, similarly, was fortunate to grow up in such a new climate, where a vigorous Catholic intellectual renewal was underway and advice such as Boniface received was on hand again. In an earlier generation, where the role of the laity was conceived as essentially passive, he might easily have become a priest,[252] but now things were different – now it was possible to have 'des saints en veston' – saints in suits. Something like this was what another French philosopher would call a life of ethical intention: "aiming at a good life lived with and for others in just insti-tutions."[253] And when we step back now, we may detect at once a differ-ence between the mature Catholicism of Leo XIII, Maritain, Schuman et al and the rough-hewn faith of Columban and his heroic and guileless peers. Of course, there is continuity but also much change. It is not just the way Jonas wrote it up, Columban would really act and speak, as we shall see in succeeding chapters, as Elijah before the rebellious kings of Israel, or Moses before the magicians and idols of Egypt.

But the Old Testament settlement between 'church' and state was not at all the New Testament settlement. Perhaps Columban read the Old Testament a lot. Perhaps it was easier to forget in Columban's time, but either way, 1400 years of experience with many disastrous episodes had brought a tacit renegotiation. The Roman church had lost the Papal States during the Italian reunification in Leo XIII's own lifetime. In those days they were a denomination with an army – and I do not mean an army of volunteers but a literal army! But now, like other national churches they were finding, that in the place of a privileged state cult, fresh shoots of a more servant-hearted Christianity were springing up, more in keeping with the first phase of their master's mission. A chastened church might possibly earn the right to denounce social and economic injustice again, but only to the extent that they rid themselves of every vestige of it themselves. Jesus lambasted the religious hypocrites and whipped the money changers, but he did so while washing feet and sleeping rough.

The Enlightenment brought much tangential good to the church by raising up secular prophets against Christian compromise. In his *The Soul of Doubt: The Religious Roots of Unbelief from Luther to Marx,*[254] historian, Dominic Erdozain traces the cause of unbelief in the West to none other than the *Christian conscience* itself. And, moreover, that the universal acid of religious orthodoxy was not Darwin *et al* but the concepts of moral equity and personal freedom generated from within Christianity. His book, which examines the continuity between the radical left wing of the Reformation and philosophers like Spinoza, Bayle, and Voltaire, demonstrates that the animus of the Enlightenment, including the concept of "natural reason" was rooted in Christian ethics and spirituality. Journalists at the Treaty of Rome in 1957, who noted how strange it was to see Socialists and Christian Democrats on such good terms, and involved so intimately in such a common project, should not have been surprised. For they are twin shoots of the same stock. When we think of Marx's Hebraic parentage and the Christian pietism of Engels' early home-life, it is not so hard to find ourselves imagining that there never was a truly secular challenge to religious faith at all, but a rather series of theological insurrections against an unlived Christianity. Christian compromise against its founder's teaching has generated great waves of revolt. But we must remember that smaller waves also came; made by people like Leo XIII and Maritain, and these were large enough to be ridden by the few political actors surfing – unaware of each other – the turbulent political seas of their own nations.

One of these surfers was Schuman, who following the advice of his friend Henri Eschbach, did not become a monk but stayed on at university to complete his law studies. In 1912 he passed his final examination in Strasbourg with highest distinction and was called to the bar in Alsace Lorraine. Those studies, and extra reading, had equipped him in many fields that would be useful later (law, economics, political philosophy, theology, and statistics) but for now, he was content to open his own legal offices in 5 Kaiser Wilhelm Ring, (now Avenue Foch) near the train station in Metz, which was still in German hands at that time. He initially became involved in the Municipal Council with the view that he might be able to help French speaking people. His cousin Leon Schmidt was a priest in Metz and so naturally Schuman attended his church. Saint Martin's Catholic Church had the distinction of having mass said in both French and German. Here he found a bilingual, cross-national community, in stark contrast to the militarised atmosphere that would soon descend upon them all in the coming war.

That in itself might strike the reader as odd; to undo his father's voluntary exile at the first real opportunity, but Robert was not his father. He certainly identified as French but with an international focus. He had spent six years studying on the German side of the border[255]and although French was his heart language, he was fluent in German. And not only in language, but also in German culture, for which he always had affection and respect, 'appreciating with equal sympathy the creations of French and German genius.'[256] It is interesting to note that his lifelong favourite composer was neither French nor German but Mozart, an Austrian.[257] He loved the novels of the German, Thomas Mann, as well as the *Continental Philosophy* of Henri Bergson.

His sense of patriotism was primarily regional, to Luxembourg and Alsace-Lorraine but extended beyond these to French history and culture[258] even under the circumstance of political rule by Germany.[259] 'He always saw Germany as a sister country, belonging – like his own – to this humanist and Christian civilisation from which in his eyes came all that was best in life.' Naturally, all of this was put to the test when Germany went to war and he was left on the wrong side of the line. Wearing a German military uniform, he worked with the administrative staff at the hospital in Metz. His close friend Henri Eschbach was sent to the eastern front in Poland, and his other cousins fought in the opposing trenches. Life in Metz became very difficult. It was a vital supply hub for the German troops. For the French speakers it was particularly tense. It was not just the food shortages, the French citizens were always held in suspicion, and never more so than when the battle lines approached the city in November 1916, and the great guns at Verdun could be heard by the terrified population. Eventually, the French language was banned from being spoken in public places.

During the war, Schuman was asked to assist the administration in Boulay which was a smaller town 25km east of Metz. He went there but also continued vital work for his law firm – assisting refugees, and 'managing expropriated assets, usually for the French. For a time, he would also carry out quartermaster tasks for the population of this town in Lorraine, which was mostly German speaking but sympathised with France.'[260] By the summer of 1918, he understood that Germany could not win. He had also learned of German depredations – like the summary executions by Prussian troops in the Ardennes and Lorraine. This made him shed his 'frontiersman's indifference' toward a nation that had clearly been corrupted by the dark forces of nationalistic greed and hubris. And then, at the age of 32, he became a French citizen overnight as the border moved. And so too came reprisals and discrimination against the German speaking population. And French expats from 50 years before, now returned to the area. Many wanted to scrape back the half decade of German rule and culture. A lot of people were caught in the crossfire of a pernicious culture war.

The Germans were now in the minority and many formerly French citizens were finally able to indulge opening their deep-seated resentments toward the persons of those who may not have directly oppressed them, but were the nearest target. But resentment is very like drinking poison and waiting for the person who offended you to die – the rot inside individuals and communities will have its outworking, but it will never be beneficial. It was a time that called for cool heads and wise administration. To give us some idea of how deep this goes, one octogenarian of the region told me recently that even today many of the older generation in other parts of France do not see Alsatians and Lorrainers as true Frenchmen, but rather as a mongrel Germanic breed.

Robert Schuman, Député from Moselle (1929)

So, Schuman, at the insistence of friends, became part of the *Republican Union of Lorraine* (URL) whose aim was – even as his local church of St. Martins did – to bring together the German and French people of the area in one party, united to bring a better future. He was under no illusions about politics, writing to Eschbach he exclaimed, 'politics remains for me a great lady of dubious reputation, who often endangers her friends.' But actually, it was not such a leap for him, firstly being a lawyer, but also because two of his father's brothers were involved in politics. Ferdinand, who had been mayor of Evrange, had been close to Schuman in his university days at Strasbourg. But at this moment in time, it was his other uncle, Nicolas, who became a mentor. Nicolas was an MP who had represented Lorraine in the Independent Party but then also in the Zentrum party – of which we shall learn more when studying the life of Konrad Adenauer. Schuman's uncle had defended the rights of Lorrainers within the German empire, and now Schuman would be doing something similar with regards to France.

The fact that the culture and politics of this sister country had been temporarily usurped by an Olympian nationalism mattered less to a man like Schuman whose perspective was wider and deeper than the horrors of the present moment. Reinhold Niebuhr perhaps did not go far enough when he wrote that the, *'difference between a politician and a statesman is that the politician thinks of the next election while the statesman thinks of the next generation,'*[261] for the statesman must also have deep roots – almost like anchors – going back into the history of his civilisation. Too often we in the west have viewed tradition as so many shackles; the *'passive submission to the obsessions of former generations'*, rather than what it is; *'a living assent to a current of uninterrupted vitality.'*[262] Whatever our criticisms of Catholics, one thing we must concede; they *do tradition like pros*, and perhaps no one put it better than the Catholic journalist, G.K. Chesterton:

> *"Tradition may be defined as an extension of the franchise. Tradition means giving a vote to the most obscure of all classes – our ancestors. It is the democracy of the dead. Tradition refuses to submit to the small and arrogant oligarchy of those who merely happen to be walking about. All democrats object to men being disqualified by the accident of birth. Tradition objects to their being disqualified by the accident of their death. Democracy tells us not to neglect a good man's opinion even if he is our groom. Tradition asks us not to neglect a good man's opinion even if he is our father."*

At this point of our story, Europeans (notably in Russia, then Italy and Germany) were about to sacrifice the claims of tradition for the possibility of a higher history. But 'modernity's siren call' was and is illusory. The future has no call, and besides, we never really ever abandon any 'tradition' without stepping straight into an alternative tradition. That is the true tragedy of every progressive. Under all their bold talk and new technologies German National Socialism was, even while throwing the odd sop to the churches, essentially a self-proclaimed pagan renaissance. 'Hitler joined the Enlightenment with his hostility to

Christianity ...but with a very different focus, inequality among races.... For Hitler, the Enlightenment, just like Christianity, had sapped the will of the German people.'[263] And, as if heedless to the previous decades' catastrophe, the disqualifying of the 'dead' would soon become de riguer in the new realpolitik of Germany and Russia. Quite simply, the new breed would find that the easiest way to achieve a truly democratic majority was to scare, beat, exile, or murder their opponents.

But that is all to come. What draws our attention now is one honest man entering politics. But not just an honest man, but a border-man who could never have the *laissez faire* nationalism of a Parisian, or militarism of a De Gaulle. You simply could not when you had lived in Metz in the Great War. To be a *Homme de frontières* does not mean that you live near a border, but that the border has moved and might move around you again. And we need to account for how a Frenchman, who moved to German Metz and which then became French again; this man, whose family had faced exile under a previous German invasion, could still love German culture and people – even under such strain. One powerful reason is that he had deeper roots and was drinking from an older well.

In this respect, as in many others, Robert Schuman embodies the best of European Catholic culture. At heart, there is something of the quiet mystic about him, something that reminds us of Columban and those industrious religious orders who shaped the social structure of Europe; creating its universities, and baptising the political order of the Middle Ages. Robert Schuman and other contemporary 'saints in suits' like Gasperi and Adenauer (who we will soon meet), represent a renewal of this culture. With, what seems to us in hindsight, an almost prophetic post-war leadership, they sought to mediate Christian tradition into current concerns. Certainly, Schuman conceived of himself in the same seamless garment of this pan-European 'humanist and Christian civilisation from which,' he said, 'came all that was best in life.'[264]

Today, in an age of rising populism in Europe, even of the far-right variety, (and of polarised politics across the world) let us mark the miracle of this thirty-two-year-old Frenchman entering into politics out of disinterested service, in the broken city of his ancestors. It still is a beautiful city, ringed by rivers and canals, which had been an important city under both Rome and the Merovingian Franks. Columban would pass through here, and his nemesis Queen Brunhilda was married here and there is even a Basilica surviving from that time. *Saint Pierre aux Nonnains* on the Rue de la Citadelle is France's oldest church with sections dating back to the 4th century. This rare and wonderful survival is set in a leafy park with a view over the canal and out to the Moselle. It is a short walk to Schuman's office at that time. He must have come up to the park to stretch his legs, have his sandwiches, to see the ancient stones, and remember that he was connected to those who had walked on this particular patch of earth so many centuries before him. The boy who had since childhood felt a special calling had become the man and was now finding his feet. And, like Columban in the previous chapter, Robert Schuman was definitely on his way – not to a monastery but to the National Assembly in Paris. The day came in 1919 when he and the 22 deputies of the border region were called to move to the capital, to take their seats. It was a historic moment for France – they had waited 50 years for this.

Ad Fontes: Europeans searching for meaning amidst the rubble of two world wars

CHAPTER 5
FOOTNOTES & REFERENCES

208. *Robert Schuman* by Robert de Rochefort (Editions du Cerf, Paris 1968) p.48

209. Sir Muirland de Grasse Evans. A full transcription of the conversation can be found here: https://winstonchurchill.hillsdale.edu/shall-one-savelondon/

210. Ovid

211. In 1884, the leading proponent of colonialism, Jules Ferry, declared; "The higher races have a right over the lower races, they have a duty to civilize the inferior races."

212. Ominously, the same Zeppelin airships commercially launched in 1910 would be bombing London six years later, killing 500 people.

213. *Robert Schuman* by Robert de Rochefort (Editions du Cerf, Paris 1968) p.20

214. Ibid p.19, p.50, p.54

215. Ibid p.53

216. Ibid p.21

217. Ibid p.23

218. Ibid p.22

219. Ibid p.27

220. Ibid p.23

221. Ibid p.21, p.39

222. Ibid p.23

223. Ibid p.27

224. Ibid p.30

225. *Modern Painters*, John Ruskin, who personally credits such writers like Dr Johnston whose 'adamantine common sense' saved him from similar perils.

226. C.S. Lewis, *An Experiment in Criticism*

227. *Robert Schuman* by Robert de Rochefort (Editions du Cerf, Paris 1968) p.80

228. Ibid p.27

229. Ibid p.47

230. Alan Paul Fimister, *Robert Schuman. Neo-scholastic humanism and the reunification of Europe*. Peter Lang, 2008.

231. Romano Guardini, *The End of the Modern World*

232. Fyodor Dostoyevsky, *The Brothers Karamazov*. Chapter 5, p23

233. This is an accessible introduction the Ruskin's works on Political economy. I have also done a rough summary in my 2012 paper, *John Ruskin & the Economics of Inequality:* https://1drv.ms/b/s!Anbjq9cpZ1JDjb0zjnRuxH8Rd-FEXKw?e=flB793

234. Rosica CSB, Thomas. *"Gaudium et Spes at 50"*, Zenit, 20 July 2015

235. Alan Fimister, *Robert Schuman: Neo-Scholastic Humanism and the Reunification of Europe*

236. Source: Wikipedia. https://en.wikipedia.org/wiki/Jacques_Maritain

237. For readers wishing to go further, Dr. Alan Fimister (quoted twice earlier) has recently co-authored a book on the subject *'Integralism - A Manual of Political Philosophy.'* EDITIONES SCHOLASTICAE (30 Mar. 2020)

238. ibid

239. These exerts are from Jacques Maritain, *Christianity and Democracy and The Rights of Man and Natural Law*

240. Ibid

241. On their website this Order, that was only established in 1933, explains with words that could have come from Columbans' quill, that; 'Born in the vast Saharan desert, the brothers retain a sense of the value of living with a minimum of human supports in the simple presence of the living God. Their mission is to be "among people" (in the 'heart of the masses'), but like Jesus they retire periodically to the 'desert', to be freer to seek God, and to learn dependence on God alone. The desert is a place where one is 'stripped down' to basic essentials, a key experience on the road to contemplation.'

242. *Robert Schuman* by Robert de Rochefort (Editions du Cerf, Paris 1968) p.27 As far back as the early 19th century the French diplomat and jurist de Maistre said: 'Wherever a religion other than the Christian religion holds sway, there slavery is sanctioned, and wherever the Christian religion weakens, the nation becomes, in exact proportion, less capable of general liberty.'

243. Ibid pp.32, 39

244. Ibid p20

245. Ibid p.26

246. Helicopter parenting is nothing new: Ruskin's mother took lodgings in Oxford when her only child went up. But Monica did one better, actually following Augustine from Africa to Rome. As harshly as we may judge them, it is worth noting that both those gifted men had nothing but praise for their mother's influence.

247. C. S. Lewis, *Surprised by Joy*

248. *Robert Schuman* by Robert de Rochefort (Editions du Cerf, Paris 1968) p.32

249. Ibid p.22

250. 1 Corinthians Ch.7v7

251. 1 Timothy Ch. 2 v2

252. *Robert Schuman* by Robert de Rochefort (Editions du Cerf, Paris 1968) pp. 50-53

253. Paul Ricoeur, *Oneself as Another*, 1992, p172

254. Domonic Erdozain, *The Soul of Doubt: The Religious Roots of Unbelief from Luther to Marx*, Oxford University Press

255. *Robert Schuman* by Robert de Rochefort (Editions du Cerf, Paris 1968) p.26, p.35 record his time in Bonn, Munich, Berlin, and Strasbourg.

256. Ibid p.36

257. Ibid p.23

258. Ibid p.38

259. Ibid p.35

260. Victoria Martin De La Torre, *'Europe, A Leap into the Unknown.'*

261. James Freeman Clarke

262. *Thomas Merton: Selected Essays*, edited by Patrick F. O'Connell, 2013

263. George Friedman, *Flashpoints – The Emerging Crisis in Europe,* Doubleday

264. *Robert Schuman* by Robert de Rochefort (Editions du Cerf, Paris 1968) p.40

Police Station on the Rue Maurice Barra, Metz, where Schuman was held in solitary confinement by the Gestapo for 7 months between 1941-1942

Schuman and Churchill, Bastille Day in Metz, 1947

CHAPTER 6

Columban's Early Career (Part 1)

CHAPTER SUMMARY: 564-585 – START-UPS IN L.A. - Columbanus' first teaching post at the nascent monastic city of Bangor (called *Vallis Anglorum* by Patrick which like, Los Angeles, means the Valley of Angels). Comparing Silicon Valley to the information revolution (as well as the artistic, social and technological explosion) underway in Ireland. 556-640 AD – THE GOOD RULE OF BANGOR – Comparing Irish monastic rule to the Benedictine formula, flourishing in Italy at that time. 556 AD – FRIENDSHIP & FORGIVENESS – From Aristotle to Freud; the recovery and loss of societal glue, with reference to the Irish (Anamchara) friendships and the Irish Penitentials.

> *'At this time all Ireland was resounding with the praises of the new monastery of Bangor, of the sanctity and learning of its founder, St. Comgall, and of the severity of his discipline. Hundreds of young men were daily leaving their homes to place themselves under his guidance. Carried away by the general enthusiasm, Columban bade farewell to Lough Erne, slung his satchel of books over his shoulder, and wended his way to the Ards of Ulster.'*[265]

564-585 – START-UPS IN L.A.

W e have followed Schuman's graduation and entrance into professional life, and now we see a near equivalent for Columban.

Columban emerges from obscurity to join a thriving community on
Belfast Lough, armed with knowledge and sufficient experience to teach
the next wave of young men who were flocking to Comgall. He would
be at Bangor for the next two decades, and so I want to use this chapter
to examine the social and intellectual environment of these formational
middle years.

Firstly, the sheer scale. We must dispel the image of a few fanatical
pessimists, retreating from the world and awaiting the end. Fanatical
perhaps, but we would do better to compare them to the tech-geeks
amassing in Silicon Valley at the hottest new startup – they want to be
on the cutting edge of change. It is hard for a secular reader, or even
a religious one, to imagine so many young people being willing to give
up everything because they believed that Christianity was the only solution to the world's problems.[266] But the figures speak for themselves.
Established in 558, and perhaps a little over a decade before Columban
arrived, Bangor was already becoming a monastic city. That is all the
more staggering when we remember that Ireland had never known anything beyond the tribal village. I think the exponential urban growth of
San Francisco and Los Angeles in the mid-nineteenth century is an apt
comparison. Strangely enough, Bangor was also known as the *Vallis An-
gelorum* (Valley of the Angels), like Los Angeles, because when Patrick
passed through this area a century before, he had had a vision of a choir
of angels here.

According to an eighth-century manuscript of *The Life of St. Comgall*, there were three thousand people on the site within the lifetime
of the founder. We might find that almost unbelievable for the period,
but other sources claim Clonard was also that size. Bede also wrote that
the Welsh Bangor was so large in the early seventh century that it was
divided into seven parts not smaller than 300 monks each; i.e., more
than 2100 people. Even further back in monastic history to Egypt, the

numbers are still impressive. Serapion of Thmuis was surrounded by thousands of disciples; and we know on trustworthy authority that the monastic colony of Tabennae, in Upper Egypt, numbered nearly seven thousand members at the death of Anthony's disciple Pachomius.[267] In his *Life of Anthony*, Athanasius described how 'the desert was made a city by monks.'

Of course, Bangor in Ireland was no grand stone medieval monastery yet, but certainly a fast-expanding cultural hub with leaders like Comgall trying to keep pace with the phenomenal lateral growth. Alongside Dublin, Bangor is the only other place mentioned on the Hereford *Mappa Mundi*, which is the largest medieval world map known still to exist today. Along with Bangor in Wales, and Iona in Scotland, Comgall's monastic city was to become one of the three leading lights in what we now call 'Celtic' Christianity in the 6th century.

What did it look like? If we were to stand on the *cashel* – the surrounding rampart of stone or wood – we would have seen many small oratories of wood or dry-piled stone, and wickerwork huts. Also, guest-houses, workshops, kitchens, refectories, barns, and then slightly set apart, the abbots lodge. '*It was also of wood, but, being built on an eminence and raised from the ground on tree-stumps, it made more show than its fellows and commanded a good view of the surroundings.*'[268] All this would attract other trades to

St. Andrews, Greenstead, Ongar

establish nearby until everywhere would resound to the cutting and splitting of wood. Bernard of Clairvaux gives a description of Bangor centuries later and still mentions the construction of wooden panels.[269] From it we might imagine something like St Andrews church at Greenstead, near Ongar, Essex, whose original foundation is possibly of the same period and almost certainly the oldest wooden building in Europe. At Greenstead, we see that the split oak timbers[270] are arranged like a palisade of railway sleepers inserted on end.

Going inside the cells, which would have been shared, we might see such common-place items as a 'rude bench, a table, half a dozen waxed tablets, a few strips of vellum or parchment made from the skins of sheep, goats, or calves, a sharp-pointed style of metal, a number of goose-quills, and an ink-horn — there was nothing else at all in the room, except perhaps a satchel with a book or two suspended from the low roof. His mantle laid on a little straw or rushes was each monk's bed; if, indeed, he did not prefer to sleep on the bare ground.'[271] Here the young men studied scripture, theology, logic, geometry, arithmetic, music, and the classics in a school that became known as 'the Light of the World'.

While the physical surroundings do not make it so different from any other chieftain's settlement of the period, what is different is the manner of their communal life – the rule by which they lived. I must warn you; even by the standards of the day, it was harsh. In one of Comgall's earlier monastic attempts with friends on an island on Lough Erne, seven monks died because the ascetic life was just too austere. At Bangor, the monks ate once a day, and even then, it was only meagre – no meat or even dairy. Indeed, as we will see later, it was too harsh and would eventually be replaced across Western Europe by Benedict's Rule. Benedict, from Nursia in Italy, was only one generation before Comgall but grew up in a very different situation. His monastic revolution was one of the most powerful cultural engines in Europe during the Middle Ages – and possibly even in Western Civilisation. Indeed, one pope even called Benedict the patron saint of Europe.

In reference to what we are examining, in the life of these early Irish, we can say that Benedict's achievement was to break the cycle of extreme asceticism from Egyptian monasticism – which as we saw earlier, was more the inheritance of Greek Platonism than Hebraic Christianity. Remarkably, for the apocalyptic age he inhabited, Benedict managed to channel Roman piety into a religious community that was both ordered and productive. Henry Newman captured exactly, the movement which combined Christian spirituality with Hebraic realism;

> '*St Benedict found the world, physical and social, in ruins, and his mission was to restore it in the way, not of science, but of nature, not as if setting about to do it, not professing to do it by any set time or by any rare specific or by any series of strokes, but so quietly, patiently, gradually, that often till the work was done, it was not known to be doing. It was a restoration rather than a visitation, correction, or conversion. The new world which he helped to create was a growth rather than a structure. Silent men were observed about the country, or discovered in the forest, digging, clearing, and building; and other silent men, not seen were sitting in the cold cloister, tiring their eyes, and keeping their attention on the stretch, while they painfully copied and re-copied the manuscripts which they had saved. There was no one that 'contended, or cried out', or drew attention to what was going on; but by degrees the woody swamp became a hermitage, a religious house, a farm, an abbey, a village, a seminary, a school of learning, and a city.'*

Juxtapose the above description with the revolutionary spirit of Schuman's time, and even the Justinian response in Columban's, and we soon see how different, how practical, and eventually, how productive Christian monasticism was. It might be beneficial here to add an extra paragraph about Benedict's progress as it provides an interesting, Latin comparison to Columban's Hibernian experience. Like Columban, Benedict knew what it was like to grow up in a heroic warrior culture, but in his case, it was the Arian Christianity of the invading Ostrogoths that held sway. He was the son of a Roman patrician, but as the empire imploded, many ethnic groups and nations were dragged into a vortex of wars, famine, and carnage. Benedict was born into this tense, apocalyptic, fast-changing scenario.

He must have grown up hearing daily the news of the latest barbarian incursion and war. Maybe he saw the hordes of refugees coming down from the north. In the wake of empire, the vacuum was filled by the rise and fall of tribal kings slashing and burning their way across Europe. In the new world order of 'might is right,' Benedict at first wanted just to escape the corruption and injustice, but then later – from his wilderness – he began to reimagine it. On what basis, what sure footing, might these disparate fledgling nations learn to live in peace and cooperation? Some monks in Italy asked him to be their abbot. He developed a new way of living based on love, faith, humility, mutuality, service, and worship. They worked, they studied, they prayed.

They gave away their worldly possessions and served the poor. They ran hospitals, leper houses, and schools and gave to anyone who was in need. In short, they modelled a life absolutely counter to the prevailing spirit of the age. With the breakdown of imperial power, it would have to be social networks that saved Europe – networks like Benedict's and Columban's. It was during Columban's lifetime that Benedict's prototypical colonies of the kingdom of God, began to be exported internationally; first to England, then France, and then the rest of Europe. Benedict's idea became a lifestyle, the lifestyle became a culture, and that culture flowered falteringly into a civilisation. And it is this ability to bind together nations with diverse interests that marks out Schuman too as a modern Benedict, a saint in a suit.

As Alasdair MacIntyre wrote in the 2007 edition of *After Virtue*, 'Benedict's greatness lay in making possible a quite new kind of institution, that of a monastery of prayer, learning, and labour, in which and around which communities could not only survive, but flourish in a period of social and cultural darkness. The effects of Benedict's founding insights... were from the standpoint of his own age quite unpredictable.' Of course, we could apply this to Columban also, though perhaps to a lesser extent. For the Irish had not at this time the advantage of Benedict's influence. And so, compared to the Benedictine moderation, the almost *cart blanche*, heroic asceticism that the Irish inherited from Egyptian and Greek Christianity, became the standard at Bangor. They would boast of the 'severity of the rule' as their fathers had boasted about how many cattle they owned or how many enemies they had slain. And this asceticism is perhaps a cultural trait that endured and even resurfaced in later times too. For example, the 18th century Bishop of Cloyne, George Berkeley (whom the famous California University is named after) might be seen as a philosophical successor through his theory of 'immaterialism' or 'subjective idealism' which denied the existence of the physical world.[272]

556-640 AD – THE GOOD RULE OF BANGOR

In a previous chapter, we saw how the ethos and *modus vivendi* of Egyptian monastic traditions were passed through Gaul (modern day France) and from Britain into Ireland. Initially, it seems that each Irish monastery had its own rule which was articulated by the start-up's founder, the abbot. What was Comgall's exactly? It is hard to say because what survives is fragmentary and sometimes what is described as a 'Rule' is little more than teachings of the founder. Among the fragments of rules in old Irish verse, we have one attributed to St. Comgall. If it is authentic, even this could not be called a 'Rule of Life' for the monks of Bangor, for really it is little more than a brief collection of aphorisms and pious exhortations. We also have the Bangor Antiphonary (a church song book) which, along with the books of Durrow and Kells, is one of the greatest literary treasures of Ireland. Divine services comprising of seven hours of prayer were carried out throughout Bangor's existence. In the 11th century, the equally austere Bernard of Clairvaux spoke warmly of Comgall and Bangor; *"the solemnization of divine offices was kept up by companies, who relieved each other in succession, so that not for one moment day and night was there an intermission of their devotions."*

Choral music must have developed apace here 'which was carried to the Continent by the Bangor Missionaries in the following century."[273]

At one point the song writer of the Bangor Antiphonary, in a fit of clerical exuberance, decides he will even pen the praises of Bangor's own 'articles of incorporation'. You cannot read it without imagining that the fledgling community have just come through some constitutional crisis:

> *"The Rule of Bangor is good, correct, and divine, holy, constant, and exalted, just and admirable. It is a ship dashed by the waves, but never overturned; a bride prepared to celebrate her nuptials with the King. A house full of delights and solidly builded on a rock. ... A strong city, built on a mountain, glorious to look upon. ... A safe retreat, where the Saviour shelters His Father's flock..."* [274]

There is a reliable secondary source by which we can get more details about the Rule under which Comgall's disciples abided, but we will look at that in the next chapter. For now, let us be content to capture the spirit of the place. The mood of youthful optimism and pious fervour was white hot. One source says, *'they were like unto the angels on account of their purity; they shone like the apostles by their zeal, and were martyrs in desire, being ever ready to shed their blood for Christ.'* [275] But martyrs are not built solely on youthful idealism, it takes real grit and a lifestyle of accumulative sacrifice.

This is how one generation set about saving the world. We pride ourselves, despite evidence to the contrary, that society will be saved by free market capitalism and liberal democracy, by science and military superiority. They may be medicines but are certainly not wines. Every system we invest our hopes in, be it the round table of Arthur, or the European Union, will ultimately fail because of the fallenness of human nature. This should not discourage engagement, merely temper it with more reasonable expectations. These young Irishmen and women saw the genuine possibility of cultural and spiritual renewal and were at least prepared to have a go, and give it their all. At Bangor, this cost of discipleship was clearly understood and accepted, perhaps more so than in later generations. [276]

It is a little too easy to criticise them for their asceticism without remembering the equal and opposite errors. Dietrich Bonhoeffer, a Lutheran pastor who was jailed and eventually executed by the Nazis, saw that his countryman's capitulation to Hitler was rooted partly in a compromised and complacent Christian theology.

> *'We Lutherans have gathered like eagles around the carcass of cheap grace, and there we have drunk the poison, which has killed the life flowing from Christ. But do we also realise that this cheap grace has turned back on us like a boomerang? The price we pay today in the shape of the collapse of the organised church is only the inevitable consequence of our policy of making grace available at too low a cost.'*

People seeking *true* truth and societal change will inevitably and instinctively begin to see that the present culture is too superficial to hold it. Of course, we recognise that this is very much our challenge at this moment of history too. One of the three major crises facing Europe is that the European Union promised increasing affluence and, since the 2008 crash, has not delivered it. Perhaps we look back at these austere monks and otherworldly Christian ascetics in disgust, giving thanks to 'the hidden hand of the market' for being a more rewarding deity. The venal forces tearing Europe apart right now are directly due to the falling of an economic idol – a secondary good made absolute. Jesus had more to say about money and our attitude toward it, than almost anything else. A Christian response to acquisitiveness, contentment, and giving could be a very helpful antidote to a rampant consumerism, which inflames our basest appetites, and often destroys what we hold most dear. The great challenge for such revolutionaries is to be able to resist the prevailing culture while *simultaneously creating a richer one.*

Let us admit that Western Europe's drift from its Christian moorings is as much against the superficiality and cultural accommodation of a privileged Christian state cult, as anything else. But let us also affirm that this obvious historical corollary: that spiritual and cultural renewal can come through individuals like Comgall and Columban, who have pursued a deep path of nurturing God's presence, denying self, and rejecting conformity to the age. The secular mind, perhaps even more than the religious one, seeks eagerly for heroic rescuers and – dare one say – saints. For the *'saint is a medicine because he is an antidote. Indeed, that is why the saint is often a martyr; he is mistaken for a poison because he is an antidote. He will generally be found restoring the world to sanity by exaggerating whatever the world neglects, which is by no means always the same element in every age. Yet each generation seeks its saint by instinct; and he is not what the people want, but rather what the people need.... Therefore, it is the paradox of history that each generation is converted by the saint who contradicts it most.'*[277]

Bangor, like the other new monasteries, was founded on the three cornerstones of *Poverty, Chastity and Obedience* – complete obedience. This is what they made a public vow to do. We can read these in the collection of canons called the *Hibernensis*, and they are sufficient rebuttal to modern Protestant Christians who look to Celtic ecclesiastical practices as an ancient counterpoint to the Roman conformity. And anyone looking for a sort of egalitarian, quasi-Christian hippy commune, then 6th century Ireland is a bad place to start.

"Without the permission of the Abbot, no monk shall dare to dispose of anything he may possess, either during his lifetime or at the hour of his death."[278] For the monk, obedience itself was not holiness, but a prerequisite to holiness. As Benedict explained in his own rule, it is only when the self-will is surrendered, that egotism is undermined and the many sins that flow from pride are stemmed. That done, finally the virtue of humility can emerge. Benedict cited the sins of sloth and obedience as opposite. We see something similar at work in military Basic Training – the new recruit must surrender to the authority of his or her commanding officer if he or she is to be of any use to her comrades or the army.

One Irish synod decreed that a monk should *obey his abbot as a slave his master*; without hesitation, that he should not even express a wish in regard to the place of his burial. The true monk must have no will of his own, but must come and go as a child.[279] At this end of history, it would be dishonest not to admit how alien this seems, even to the devoutly religious. But let us also acknowledge that our cherished independence also carries its own peculiar surcharge. Happiness and fulfilment, the meaningful life, the *Eudaemonia* of Aristotle, has proved more elusive than anyone guessed. Writing of the Irish monks of Lindisfarne, the historian, scientist and monk Bede said that:

> *"They had no money, but only cattle; and if they received any money from rich persons, they immediately gave it to the poor, or used it to ransom such as had been wrongfully sold for slaves. They were so purified from all taint of avarice that none of them received lands and possessions for building monasteries, unless they were compelled to do so by the temporal authorities. The place which they governed shows how frugal and temperate they were, for there were very few houses besides the church found at their departure; indeed, no more than were barely sufficient to make civilized life possible.*[280]

And chastity? One feels many a modern Silicon Valley start-up founder would approve of these very un-Christian prescriptions passed into European Christianity from the east. How much productivity is lost, they would say, to us by maternity leave, or by employees leaving work early to take children to dentist appointments? All revolutions are unfriendly to families, just as all wars are. But we must admit, an *elite* man or woman (from the Greek '*eligo*' – chosen or plucked out) is able to accomplish much when plucked out of dealing with sinks, nappies, and dishes, etc. Whatever we think of the vow of chastity, it was of vital benefit in this epoch in protecting and disseminating much that would have been lost to us otherwise. But to transgress the boundaries of chastity was severely punished. A canon, ascribed to St. Patrick, forbids anyone consecrated to God to marry at all – punishable by excommunication if they do. Another forbids a monk and a nun to stay at the same inn, or drive in the same chariot, or even to have a prolonged conversation.

556 AD – FRIENDSHIP & FORGIVENESS

So, without the distractions of wealth and women, what did these young hot bloods do? They channelled their drive into study, work, prayer, and worship. A story about Brother Luan illustrates both the spirit of those days and the temperament of the abbot. Luan, who had originally prompted Comgall to found Bangor and helped him in the early days, was so assiduous in his studies that Comgall told him to ease off a bit. Luan said, 'If I possessed perfect knowledge of God, I should never offend him; for only those who do not know Him, disobey Him.' Abbot Comgall, an ex-soldier from Antrim, and perhaps of Pictish extraction, was pleased with the reply, 'My son, you are firmly grounded in the faith and true science will pave the way to Heaven for you.'

Columban & Gall on Lake Constance, from a 15th-century manuscript

Luan, more commonly known as Moulag, went on from Bangor to found a hundred monasteries among the Picts. In fact, he should be credited above Columba of Iona as the evangelist of the Picts, for he alone had mastered the Pictish tongue – perhaps with Comgall's help. Certainly, both had gone with Columba on the initial expedition to the Western Isles, and it seems that Luan had first been a good deputy for Comgall before striking off on his own. This has been a pattern often seen in the great founders and pioneers; they need a complementary lieutenant to augment their own skillset. Microsoft's Bill Gates had Paul Allen; Apple's Steve Jobs had Steve Wozniak, and Ronald Wayne; Google's Larry Page had Sergey Brin; Facebook's Mark Zuckerberg had Eduardo Saverin.

That these dynamic partnerships do not last forever – and sometime split acrimoniously in the latter case – is not so amazing. What is amazing is the creative multiplication of talent and vision that occurs in the years of collaboration. Comgall had been encouraged by Luan to found the monastery at Bangor, then Luan was released, no doubt a different man, to found his own. Comgall would not have been the great abbot he became without Luan, and perhaps Luan would not have been the great pioneer he became without Comgall. We make each other, it is a beautiful truth. No man is an island.

And Columban would be no exception to this rule. One of the young noblemen who joined Bangor at this time was called Cellach. Renamed Gall, this gifted linguist would one day accompany Columban to the continent as his deputy and *anamchara – soul friend*. And like Luan before him, Gall would also one day separate from his master in order to lay the foundations of his own monastery. Gall is celebrated as the Apostle of the Alamannians, and the great Abbey of St. Gall and the Swiss city of St. Gallen still bear his name. He may not be mentioned much in the succeeding chapters but Gall is one of the heroes of this story – the Samwise Gangee to Columban's Frodo, to use a Lord of the Rings analogy. And it is doubtful that Columban would have been all that Western Europe needed him to be without him.

The Irish gave the name *Anamchara* – 'soul friend' – to this type of close friendship. And they prized these friendships very highly. 'Anyone without a soul-friend is like a body without a head' was a saying in Ireland from pre-Christian times. When we hear the words, we think of affection but, as in ancient times, they primarily saw it as a particular shared recognition of and pursuit of a good. This was certainly Aristotle's understanding and Comgall's monastery was very like Aristotle's notion of a political community as a common project. Much of this is alien to the modern individualist worldview. Perhaps we think of the third sector this way or some public services like schools and libraries, but certainly, nothing concrete about the *Polis* as Aristotle meant it.

Weakened by the eighteenth-century Romantic Movement, and then again by Freud's insinuations,[281] it is little wonder that friendship has now been relegated to private life, and thus weakened from what it once was. In the time of Comgall, and before, the bond of friendship was not the description of an emotional state, as it is with us, but a type of social and political relationship. To show the difference, the philosopher Alasdair McIntyre[282] quotes E. M. Forster saying that if it came to a choice between betraying his friend and his country that he hoped he would have the courage to betray his country. But in Aristotle's view; a good man cannot be friends with a bad man because both would have to share a common allegiance to certain goals and goods. So, such a formulation as Forster's from Aristotle's point of view, shows that a man has no country, no city, no polis; that he is, as Macintyre put it, 'a citizen of nowhere.' This is why he, rather pessimistically, wrote that 'the modern liberal political society can appear only as a collection of citizens who have banded together for their common protection.'

The 'polis' of Bangor was made up of such powerful *Anamchara* friendships, and Columban would find one too. But it's important to note that the Christian conception of the polis was able to broaden the Athenian conception, with its own theology of forgiveness. This central Christian concept of loving *even sinners*, thus opened a further possibility for former offenders – both Enda and Comgall had been warriors – trained killers, and even Columba's mission to Iona was partly to atone for a war he had started in which two thousand died. Forgiveness is more than justice; it is a different species of societal adhesive. There is no word in Aristotle's age for forgiveness any more than there is for repentance, or charity as we mean them now.

For forgiveness to exist, there must first be a presupposed conception of justice, and also just punishment for the lawbreaker, or sinner. Christianity not only brought a higher standard than had yet been known, but it also brought the essential corollary; that the offended party, imitating this new God of forgiveness, should always be willing to offer forgiveness too. Furthermore, the offended party must be the proactive one! Hence the word, *fore-giving*, giving before, that is to say, sometimes even in advance of the asking. This is not the same as sweeping sin under the carpet, but rather, a debt already paid for at the cross of Christ. It is also a tacit admission that, at the deepest possible level, 'all have sinned and fallen short of the glory of God.' A post-Christian society will eventually be a post-forgiveness society. Judas was sorry for his betrayal. He even tried to make it right by returning the money. But he had ceased to believe in forgiveness and so he hung himself.

It is possible that western culture must by necessity endure several decades of woke-righteousness, with all its predestined hierarchies of grievance, before they can, at last, arrive back to where these Irish were, fifteen centuries ago. For they were experiencing a revolution that broke the cycle of blood feuding and offered real hope. In Athens, justice might be issued by a judge – the impersonal authority representing the whole community – but now in Bangor, forgiveness would be extended first by God, and then by other offended parties. (The Irish 'programmers' in these new monastic start-ups coded this revolutionary development in the Irish Penitentials – which we will examine briefly in the next chapter.)

If civilization means finding a way in which we can live well together, then here is a huge and solid building block. I write this now because when reading the Monastic Rules in the next chapter, the harshness of it might eclipse this central truth. The ability for a flawed individual to obtain forgiveness and then to forgive (the two are inextricably linked) is one of the central quests of a humane society. A third of the globe at this moment in history believes, at least nominally, that Jesus not only made this possible but as one historian put it, that the;

'...whole history since his time shows it. Quite simply, those later calling themselves Christians – the followers of Jesus – were to change the world. So far as Europe was concerned, they did more to shape its history than any other single identifiable group of men and women... What can be seen easily enough is that his (Jesus) teaching had much greater impact than that of other holy men of his age because his followers saw him crucified and yet believed he later rose again from the dead. We are what we are, and Europe is what it is today because a handful of Palestinian Jews bore witness to these things.'[283]

And this quest for forgiveness has great relevance also for our intermediate chapters about the war years and the founding of the EEC. 'Forgiveness', as one man said just after World War II, 'is the final act of love.'[284] And if not the *final act*, then it was certainly the foundational *act of love* that led to 'one of the greatest achievements in the entire record of modern statecraft; the astonishingly rapid Franco-German reconciliation after 1945.'[285] Maritain, who like Schuman had lived through the consequences of the Treaty of Versailles, understood all too well that the sheer level of devastation and suffering, 'the hell through which she has passed', had given non-German Europeans 'terrible rights over the future.' He saw that it was a watershed moment in the moral life of a civilisation. Europe could choose 'either to perpetuate the tempest...or to play her part in the advent of a better and more human common life.'[286] It was not a foregone conclusion in his time, and in many ways, it is not in our time or any time. Maritain saw dark forces at work across Europe and warned of them in words that are surely not entirely without resonance in our own day. He wrote of the;

'... danger of new forms of dictatorship, arising out of wretchedness and resentment, or out of nationalistic impulses, and the danger caused by the mental habits of those peoples not accustomed to freedom who hereditarily worship military force and whose youth has been poisoned by Nazi nihilism, these dangers will be overcome only by great political vigilance, and by a long process of education,

which will require the free peoples to look after their brothers with as much justice and charity as firmness.'[287]

So, as we continue in the next chapter to examine some of the minutiae of how the theological concept of forgiveness was worked into the Irish monastic and lay culture, let's bear in mind that the eventual outworkings of these early attempts would one day have unpredictable political ramifications. Perhaps 'to know is to forgive' but certainly *to forgive is to know,* and that is what Franco-German reconciliation enabled. Forgiveness is not obscure metaphysical speculation but the very oxygen of a viable and enduring civilisation.

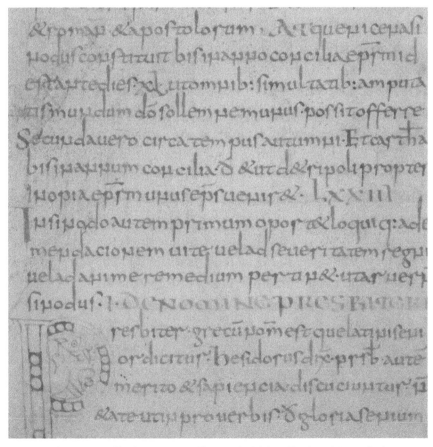

7th century Collectio Canonum Hibernensis (Irish Collection of Canon law)

CHAPTER 6
FOOTNOTES & REFERENCES

265. *The Life and Writings of Columban*, George Metlake

266. It is worth remembering many used to hold the Whiggish, *'End of History'* forecast, articulated famously by the neo-conservative Francis Fukuyama. With 25 years of hindsight, faith in the universal triumph of single markets and liberal democracy seems optimistic. Failed and failing states, increasing civil and asymmetric warfare, human trafficking, illicit trade, failed financial institutions, rising income inequality in all advanced economies and scarcity of resources, etc.) As Tomas Sedlacek says in *The Economics of Good and Evil;* in economics there was always 'more myth than maths'. The rising economic tide no longer lifts all boats. A heuristic example might serve here: the growth in US incomes in 2010 (a remarkable 93%) accrued to the top 1% of the population. (Source: http://elsa.berkeley.edu/~saez/saez-UStopincomes2010.pdf) So, when we look for the causes of the problems that bedevil our world, we must have the courage to start close to home.

267. *The Life and Writings of Columban*, George Metlake

268. ibid

269. Bernard's *Life of St Malarkey* states: 'Moreover the oratory was finished in a few days, made of smoothed planks indeed, but closely and strongly fastened together—a Scotic work, not devoid of beauty.' Also, in the Life of the Irish Saint Monenna, we read of "a church constructed of smoothed planks according to the custom of the Scottish races." The writer also adds that "the Scots are not in the habit of building walls, or causing them to be built."

270. Dendrochronologists date the timbers to 1033.

271. *The Life and Writings of Columban*, George Metlake

272. Every movement has a driving ethos that expresses and defines it. In line with the 'young and fun' image, Facebook offices had free sweets, bean bags, slides, and games. Zuckerberg wanted his platform to be cool and therefore not littered with adverts. But that part of the ethos has been quickly ditched and now Facebook is one of the biggest and fastest-growing advertisers on the planet. We observe youthful enthusiasm and idealism versus pragmatism and the lure of power. Ireland stuck by the rule of their founders. Either way, Facebook might do well to at least pay the modern Irish a more just tax on the colossal advertising revenue that it filters through Ireland's tax system. (See an article in The Irish Times by Mark Paul. Dec 12, 2017; 'Facebook will no longer use Ireland as a global tax and revenue base.')

273. Hamilton, Rector of Bangor Abbey quoted on Wikipedia

274. Antiphonary of Bangor, Ed. Warren. The Hymn is written in the same metre as Prudentius's Cathemerinon (Iambi dimeter catalect). The alternate feminine rimes are characteristic. It contains the oldest Eucharistic hymn in Europe and also contains other hymns, prayers, and poems. It is now kept in the Ambrosian Library in Milan.

275. *Acta Sanctorum*, Aug. t III, 57. Jean Bolland

276. The controversial and restless British Comedian Russell Brand has recently surprised the media (again) by deciding Jesus' teachings really are the answer for human flourishing. But, as Columbanus would tell Brand, those teachings are aimed directly at the individual – 'Anyone who chooses to do the will of God will find out whether my teaching comes from God or whether I speak on my own.' (John Ch.7.v17) People inquiring into the merits of Christianity must 'do' Jesus teachings, a priori, and then will find out whether they work, not the other way round. The natural outcome of being truly converted to Jesus' person and teaching, is a quite natural predisposition to actually do what he commanded; i.e. to be fanatically generous, merciful, humble, faithful, and loving - in short, the kind of fanaticism the world has always needed.

277. G.K. Chesterton, *The Dumb Ox*. In this excerpt Chesterton is comparing and contrasting Aquinas and Francis of Assisi.

278. Wasserschleben, *Irische Kanonensammlung*, Liber XLI, c. 8.

279. Wasserschleben, 1. c., XVIII, c. 3.

280. Bede, *Ecclesiastical History of the England* Ch.xxvi

281. The fact that we often find it hard to think of these close friendships (Pleiades and Orestes; David and Jonathan; Christ and the apostle John, Columban, and Gall, etc) in any other than sexual terms, shows firstly how conditioned our minds have become by freudian-inuendo, and, of course, how few people enjoy riches of friendship; philia, or amitas. This point is made in *The Four Loves*, C. S. Lewis.

282. *After Virtue*, Alasdair MacIntyre

283. J.M. Roberts, *A History of Europe*

284. These are the words of Reinhold Niebuhr, who also claimed that 'rationalistic egalitarianism is necessarily anti-traditional because it claims the equal right for any present decision with anything that has been decided previously. It tends to the atomisation of time and communal society.'

285. The Centre for Strategic and International Studies (CSIS) *Religion, the Missing Dimension in Statecraft*. 1994

286. Robert Schuman, *Pour L'Europe*

287. Jacques Maritain, *Christianity and Democracy and The Rights of Man and Natural Law*

The sacred & secular at work: Monnet & Schuman enjoying a joke

CHAPTER 7

Columban's Early Career (Part 2)

CHAPTER SUMMARY - 564-585 - TO LOVE IS TO SEE – Monastic models and the genius of Basil of Cappadocia, an early founder who influenced Benedict. The tension between sacred and secular service. COLUMBAN'S RULE - The harshness of the Columbanus' rule but also the spiritual and psychological revolution of the Irish Penitential. COLUMBAN'S POETRY - Early examples. PENULTIMATE SACRIFICE - The Irish concept of the 'white martyrdom' – the voluntary, lifelong exile. The future demise of Bangor under successive barbarians; Viking, English, and Irish. Columban and his band of 12 leave for a continent still reeling from mass migrations and a 50-year plague.

'Uprootedness does not mean independence. On the contrary the uprooted man can never become independent. He is predestined to become a mass-man, a particle of a collectivist mechanism, an object of the totalitarian state. The decay of tradition during the last few generations is one of the most important presuppositions of totalitarian collectivism. .... It is not the huge size of city populations which creates the mass-man, it is the lack of a common tradition.' [288]

564-585 - TO LOVE IS TO SEE

This chapter examines how certain pioneers distilled or attempted to distil the Christian principle into prototype communities. From the ancients down to the present day, everyone agrees that man is a 'political animal' but how we should then best live together is no settled matter, even now. Origins and avenues, as well as cliffs and cul de sacs appear when we read our histories and though I fear this chapter lacks pace, yet my hopes are that it will spark new thoughts in the reader. When we have got a flavour of Columban's inner intellectual and spiritual life – gained and matured through his middle years as a 'university professor' – we will then observe his calling to a voluntary and permanent exile from Ireland.

So, first let us glance briefly at the two Rules that are attributed to St Columban: the *Regula Monachorum* or Rule of the Monks and the *Regula Coenobialis* or Community Rule. These are found in a number of manuscripts dating back to the ninth and tenth centuries. Of course, these are his works of more mature years, but they are mentioned here because by seeing how Columban designed his community, we might also glimpse what life was like under Comgall at Bangor. Further to these two 'Rules', there is also his Irish Penitential – a heartily practical document that created a system of private penance available not just to the monks, but also to those Christians who lived in association with the monasteries. Because nothing earlier survives in its entirety, they are one of the most valuable documents in existence for a study of the doctrine of penance in the Irish Church.

Columban's *Rule of the Monks* differed enormously from the detailed regulations laid down in the Rule of St Benedict – which according to the historian J. M. Roberts, was the 'seminal document of western Christianity and western civilisation.'[289] Columban outlines the basic virtues of obedience, poverty, chastity, mortification and silence within the monastery, but does not give an exhaustive list of regulations concerning daily life.[290] In fact, Columban seems to have combined the two monastic traditions – that of Egypt - *seeking seclusion in the desert* - and that of Basil - *asking the question "whose feet will I wash?"* I have only mentioned Basil in passing before now but it seems a debt of justice that we add a little more here while we are talking about the formation of a viable community that could typify and express one's deeply held religious ideal.

Basil's grandfather had been martyred in that generation just before the legalisation of Christianity and so he is helpful for us when we observe a vital period of decline in the empire. He was born in 330 in Cappadocia, modern day Turkey and though both his parents were known as pious Christians, it was not inevitable that Basil would follow them. Having had a superhero Christian grandfather might have been a hindrance as much as a help in finding his own faith. Martyrdom is a hard act to follow and must have brought along with it, expectations that were not always encouraging to a baby-boomer growing up in comparative ease. In fact, during his student days in Constantinople, he attended the lectures of the resolutely pagan sophist Libanius, and in Athens he met a fellow student called Julian, who would one day be that infamous Emperor Julian *the Apostate* – and, the one who would try in vain to revive the dying Hellenic polytheism of Rome. I posited in chapter 1 that Europe was a mixture of *Pax Rom*ana and the *Pax Christi*, and in the last chapter, we saw Dr. Erdozain's claim that it was a latent Christian conscience in late modernity that worked as a solvent against orthodox Christianity. And here, with Basil and Julian, we shall see this dichotomy at work in microcosm.

Basil had already become a type well recognised; young, cosmopolitan, well-educated scholar with the world at his feet, in many ways reminiscent of his African contemporary Augustine. Basil travelled widely in Mediterranean centres, practiced law, and taught rhetoric. He was also, like Augustine, brought up short by a charismatic church leader who challenged him out of his foppish complacency. Basil reflected with regret on the affectations of his academic career:

'I had wasted much time on follies and spent nearly all of my youth in vain labours, and devotion to the teachings of a wisdom that God

had made foolish. Suddenly, I awoke as out of a deep sleep. I beheld
the wonderful light of the Gospel truth, and I recognized the noth-
ingness of the wisdom of the princes of this world.' [291]

While Basil was studying the monastic movements first hand in
Egypt, Syria, and Palestine, his university associate Julian was waging
successful military campaigns (securing a notable victory at Strasbourg)
and being elevated to Emperor of the Western Empire. Julian was the
nephew to the 'Christian' emperor Constantine, and therefore the
cousin of Constantine II with whom he co-ruled. Julian hated the free-
loading and squabbling Christian prelates, who rode the gravy-train of
the newly legalised religion, almost as much as the privileged new imperial cult. His Edict of Toleration in 362 was directly aimed at this issue.

Meanwhile, Basil, having observed the solitary hermits of the deserts
– and not much liking it – gave away his own personal fortune and
set up a monastic community on his family estates near the Black Sea,
with his brothers, mother, and sisters. His writings on this monasticism
are along the same lines as we have seen in Benedict, indeed the latter
acknowledges the debt. Basil wanted to temper the extreme asceticism
that he had witnessed. How much of his moderation reached Ireland is
unclear, but I suspect little or nothing. Nevertheless, Basil's pioneering
efforts in monasticism – most notably an emphasis on supporting the
poor – are not all he is famed for. His rhetorician's tongue and fine legal
mind were called up in the fight against the sort of synthetic doctrines
that looked so sensible and yet would have undermined the Christian
message.

And he, like Schuman, even became a politician or at least a civil
administrator in Caesarea for a number of years. A man who saw his
neighbour's need as of equal importance to his own made a humane
governor. Indeed, from the three hundred letters that remain of his, we
see an observant, kind, cheerful, and humorous man. In many ways, he
wanted what Julian wanted but he saw the solutions lay in a different
sphere altogether. Basil even preached against the gravy train mentality
of the priesthood and made very sure he selected new recruits with strin-

gent care. Julian wanted big government in the sense that all the institutions and functions of society would be guaranteed in the sacred person of the emperor. Even Basil's notable charity was, in a sense, a challenge to Julian's sacral-'socialist' worldview. Julian's political philosophy simply did not allow for a parallel institution like the church. For him, the sacral state was the ultimate provider. The echoes of such thoughts we hear and will hear again in the Schuman chapters, not just in Russia, Germany, and Italy but in England too, where the locus of social services and education moved swiftly from Canterbury to Whitehall in the early twentieth century.

COLUMBAN'S RULE

But we must not be waylaid by such considerations. We just wanted to tilt our hats at Basil before returning north to see how Columban distilled Christian doctrine in a communal form for his start-ups in Western Europe. With the exception of one long chapter on the recitation of the Divine Office and some prescriptions regarding meals, Columban's rule seems – in line with the idealist philosophy of the east – to exclusively focus on the inner landscape of the monks' souls.

> 'The food of the monks should be poor and confined to the evening; let it be such as to avoid gorging, and their drink such as to avoid drunkenness, so that it may sustain them but do them no harm: vegetables, beans, flour mixed with water, along with a small loaf of bread, lest the stomach be strained and the mind stifled.
>
> For those who seek eternal rewards should only take account of a thing's usefulness and use. Use of life must be kept under control, just as work must be kept under control. This is true discretion, so that the possibility of spiritual progress may be maintained with an abstinence that scourges the flesh.
>
> For if abstinence goes too far, it will be a vice, not a virtue. A virtue tolerates and embraces many material things. Therefore, we must fast daily, just as we must feed daily. While we must eat daily, we must re-

gale the body rather poorly and sparingly. The reason we must eat daily is because we must advance daily, pray daily, toil daily, and read daily.'

Like the Rule of the Monks, the Community Rule[292] was harsher by about a factor of three to anything penned at the beginning of the sixth century by Benedict.[293] Columban's was a rule for heroes, the SAS or Navy Seals of their day, Benedict's was for ordinary, pious men and women. Columban's rule provided a more detailed commentary on the daily life of an early Irish monk than from any other source. Unlike the typically Roman systematic approach of Benedict, this Irish rule seems to have grown more out of decisions taken as the need arose – in cases where discipline had been breached already. The severity of the 'blows', mentioned below, are open to question, but to be beaten in a Benedictine monastery for any of the below infractions would have been unheard of.

The monks of Benedict's monastery had tried to poison him, which might have something to do with his more humane approach. Benedict, with his patrician genius for ordered Roman living, allowed his monks eight hours sleep in winter and *siestas* on summer afternoons - even allocating a pint of wine as a daily ration. But these tough Irish warriors-turned-abbots weren't having any of that softly-softly approach. Even milk was considered a luxury to them. Bangor, as they said was a 'House full of delights – built on rock, a true vine – *'ex Aegypto transducta'* – transferred from Egypt.'[294]

But these considerations were not just on the agenda for the Irish and the Egyptians, for it would seem that Gildas came to Finnian in Ireland because he had fallen out with David of Wales over the severity of the Welsh Monastic Rule.[295] When a monastery is too austere for someone like Gildas, this speaks loudly! So maybe the World Series title for no-nonsense-monasticism goes to Wales after all. Regarding what was and what was not a sin, the Egyptian monks dissected sin into eight principal vices with corresponding virtues by which the vices were cured. For them, each sin was seen as an illness to which the application of virtue was the cure.

Two hundred years later and four thousand miles away the British and Irish church extended the list to cover every conceivable sin. But size and variety notwithstanding, despair was never the object. Sin, like flu was serious but manageable. And it is important to remember, as Princetown Professor Peter Brown[296] does, that it is exactly at this time that western Christianity became what it would essentially be throughout the Middle Ages and into our time. It was in the 7th century, and not before, that ancient western Christianity was replaced by what we would recognise as Christianity today. It was not so much a change in the church's teachings but in a quantum shift of corporate imagination that gave rise to a new view of the individual, of his or her sin, atonement, and the afterlife.

So, whether they knew it or not, these monastic cities were already part of a paradigm shift that has affected us to this day. That men like Comgall and Columban chose such an extreme expression, as evidenced below, is only because they saw themselves as an elite soldiery in training for great service. What might do for the Royal Engineers would not do for the SAS. They would train themselves in the spiritual disciplines that mattered to them, even as the Spartans had done in the martial disciplines that mattered in their age. No quarter, no retreat. This is borne out in what we will see below, where the rule for laity is more lenient than later English law, but the rule and punishments of the monks have almost been set in direct antithesis to it in terms of strictness.

Here is a sample of the Columban's *Regula Coenobialis*, from chapters III—V, which deal with the omission of prayers, disrespect for sacred things, and abuses of speech:

i. The monk who does not prostrate himself to ask a prayer when leaving the house, and after receiving a blessing does not bless himself, and go to the cross — it is prescribed to correct him with twelve blows.

ii. Likewise, the one who shall forget the prayer before work or after work — with twelve blows.

iii. He who on his return home does not prostrate himself within the house to ask a prayer is to be corrected with twelve blows.

iv. But the brother who confesses all these things and more, even as much as to deserve a grace penance, gets off with half penance, that is, a medium penance; and so on with these matters. Mitigate them thus for the moment.

v. The monk who through coughing goes wrong in the chant at the beginning of a psalm – it is laid down to correct him with six blows. Likewise, the one who bites the cup of salvation with his teeth – with six blows.

vi. The one who does not follow the order for the sacrifice – with six blows.

vii. The one who smiles at the synaxis, that is, at the office of prayers – with six blows; if he bursts out laughing aloud – with a grave penance unless it happens excusably.

viii. The one who receives the blessed bread with unclean hands – with twelve blows.

ix. He who forgets to make the oblation until he goes to Mass – with a hundred blows.

x. The monk who tells idle tales to another, if he censures himself at once – with a mere pardon, but if he does not censure himself – with an imposition in silence or fifty blows.

xi. He who defends himself truthfully, when questioned about something, and does not at once beg pardon and say 'It's my fault, I'm sorry' – with fifty blows.

xii. He who in all honesty sets counsel against counsel – with fifty blows.

xiii. He who strikes the altar – with fifty blows.

xiv. He who shouts loud talk without restraint, unless there is need – with an imposition of silence or fifty blows.

xv. He who makes an excuse in order to get pardon must do a like penance.

xvi. He who replies to a brother on his pointing something out 'It's not as you say,' except for seniors speaking frankly to juniors – with an imposition of silence or fifty blows. The only exception to this permitted is that he may answer a brother of equal standing if he remembers something nearer the truth than what the latter says.

The Irish Penitentials[297] contain lists of the various ways in which people are liable to commit sin, together with the penance considered appropriate for each. Scholarship is divided but at least one authority[298] believes that the Penitential of Columban[299] is a single document divided into three parts; one for monks, one for the secular clergy, and one for the laity. Columban does insist on the utmost discretion of a disciplining abbot *'so that the possibility of spiritual growth maintained with that abstinence that scourges the flesh.'* In other words, his goal was always personal development, not suffering *per se*. Again, the penances are severe and the sins listed don't beat about the bush either. For example, there is a penance listed for a man who has sex with his wife in a certain (forbidden) position. Enough said. The following excerpts, taken from the section dealing with the laity cover things like theft, perjury, wounding, and drunkenness. It is worth remembering that these penances offered real and immediate hope to an offender and certain re-admission to the community and sacraments after the period of penance was over:

a. If any layman commits theft, that is, steals an ox or a horse or a sheep or any beast of his neighbour's, if he has done it once or twice, he must first restore to his neighbour the loss which he has caused, and let him do penance for a hundred and twenty days on bread and water. But if he has made a practice of stealing often, and is unable to make a restitution, let him do penance for a year and a hundred and twenty days, and let him further promise not to do it again. He may go to Communion at Easter of the second year, that is, after two years, on condition that, out of his own labour, he first gives alms to the poor and a feast to the priest who adjudged his penance. Thus, is the guilt of his bad habit to be removed.

b. If any layman commits perjury, if he does it through greed, he is to sell all his goods and give to the poor, and dedicate himself wholly to the Lord. Let him abandon the world and be tonsured and let him serve God till death in a monastery. But if he does it, not through greed, but for fear of death, he must do penance for three years on bread and water in exile and unarmed. For two more let him abstain from wine and meats; then let him offer a life for himself, that is, let him free a slave or maidservant from the yoke of bondage, and give alms frequently for two years. During this period, he may quite lawfully use all foods except meat. Let him go to Communion after the seventh year.

c. If any of the laity sheds blood in a squabble, or wounds or maims his neighbour, he is to be forced to make good the damage he has done. If he has not the wherewith to pay, let him first carry in his neighbour's work, as long as the latter is sick, and send for the doctor. After the man's recovery, let him do penance for forty days on bread and water.

d. If any layman becomes drunk, or eats or drinks to the point of vomiting, let him do penance for a week on bread and water.

And Columban? 'He gave himself up entirely,' says Jonas with characteristic zest, 'to fasting and prayer, to abnegation of self, and to the faithful carrying of the sweet yoke of Christ; for his only aim was to follow Christ by taking up His Cross and becoming like unto Him...(and) that he who was to instruct others might first instruct himself.' Columban's learning and piety soon attracted his abbot's attention and when he had attained the canonical age, that is thirty, Comgall not only permitted him to advance to the holy priesthood — a rarity for an Irish monk in those days,[300] but also gave him a share in the direction of his great monastic school.[301]

COLUMBAN'S POETRY

Columban, amid what must have been a busy teaching schedule, was also writing verse in these years. Below is his poem *Ad Hunaldum*[302] shows many borrowings, one from Horace, one from Prudentius and one from Juvencus. He uses his own and perhaps a fellow student's name to form an acrostic device.

> C asibus innumeris decurrunt tempora vitae,
> O mnia praetereunt, menses volvuntur in annis;
> L abitur in senium momentis omnibus aetas.
> U t tibi perpetuam liceat conpraendere vitam,
> M olles inlecebras vitae nunc sperne caducae.
> B landa luxuria virtus superatur honesta.
> A rdet avaritia caecaque cupidine pectus.
> N escit habere modum vanis mens dedita curis.
> V ilius argentum est auro, virtutibus aurum.
> S umma quies, nil velle super quam postulat usus.
> H os ego versiculos misi tibi saepe legendos;
> U t mea dicta tuis admittas auribus, oro.
> N e te decipiat vana et peritura voluptas.
> A spice, quam brevis est procerum regumque potestas.
> L ubrica mortalis cito transit gloria vitae.
> D a veniam dictis, fuimus fortasse loquaces.
> O mne quod est nimium semper vitare memento.

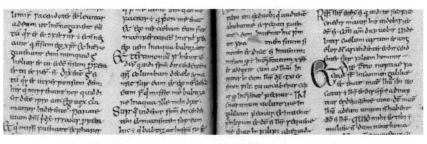

Early Irish Manuscript. The Book of Dimma, late 8th century (TCD MS 59, p. 107)

Translation of the above:

> *The seasons of life run on with numberless misfortunes.*
> *All things pass away; the months roll by year after year.*
> *Life sinks into decay with every moment.*
> *Now scorn the soft enticements of fallen life, so you can*
> *grasp eternal life.*
> *Noble virtue is overcome by the lure of luxury;*
> *the breast is aflame with avarice and blind desire.*
> *Devoted to empty cares, the mind knows no moderation.*
> *Silver is baser than gold, gold baser than the virtues.*
> *Best of all is peace: to want nothing beyond what neces-*
> *sity requires.*
> *I have sent you these little verses for you to read often.*
> *I beg you to let my words enter your ears.*
> *Do not let an empty, perishable pleasure deceive you;*
> *see how brief is the power of kings and princes.*
> *The deceitful glory of mortal life passes quickly.*
> *Forgive me my words; perhaps we have talked too much.*
> *Always remember to shun everything excessive.*

Two of his other poems *Ad Sethum* and *De Mundi Transitu* are also attributed to this period. A translation of the latter is below:

> *This world will pass away; daily it wanes.*
> *No one will stay alive; no one has stayed alive.*
> *The whole human race is born in the same manner,*
> *and having lived the same, life is subject to the same end.*
>
> *Uncertain death steals life from those who try to put it off;*
> *and death's sorrow seizes all who proudly roam*
> *What greedy men do not want to give away for Christ's sake,*
> *They all lose when least they want; others gather it up after them.*

When they are alive, they hardly venture to give God
[one] little thing; but they leave all to death.
They keep nothing they possessed.
The present life they love fades daily;
the punishment they prepare for themselves will never fail.

The slippery thing they try to amass slips away;
and they are not afraid to believe in what seduces them.
They loved the hideous darkness more than the light;
they scorned to imitate the Lord and Leader of life.

They rule as if in dreams; for one hour they are happy,
but everlasting torments are prepared for them already.
In their blindness, they do not see what awaits them after death,
and what wickedness bestows on wicked sinners.

Friend, it becomes you to think about all this;
keep aloof from loving this life's beauty.
See, all flesh is grass: although it blooms, it is burning.
All its glory is like the flowering grass.

The grass withers when the sun comes up and the flower perishes;
all youth does the same when virtue departs.
Men's beauty disappears as it grows old;
all former dignity is painfully stripped away.

You must love Christ's radiant face, lovely beyond all things,
more than the frail blossom of the flesh.
Child, beware the women's beauty,
through which death, no small disaster, enters.

Many men have suffered the fires of punishment
because they did not want to lose a wayward affection.

Never drink from a wicked woman's cup;
you often see many men, happy and laughing there.

For know, that the men you see laughing foolishly
will be weeping bitterly on the Last Day.
My dear son, realize that lust is like [Adam's]
death-bringing bite that destroys sweetness.

Do not rush forward on the road men take,
where you can see many have been shipwrecked.
Walk on tiptoe between the snares,
which have caught the rest unprepared, as we have learned.

Lift the eyes of your heart from earthly things
and love the most loving hosts of angels.
The family which dwells above is blessed;
no old man groans there, no infant wails.

There no voice is kept from praising the Lord;
no one hungers there, no one ever thirsts.
The heavenly race is fed on celestial food,
and no one dies because no one is born.

There is a royal palace . . .
in which no unharmonious voice is ever heard.
Life will be youthful and true;
neither death nor fear of sorrow will waste it away.

Having passed through death,
the joyful will see their joyful King:
they will reign with their Ruler;
they will rejoice with Him as He rejoices.

Then sorrow, weariness and labour will be abolished;

then the King of kings, the immaculate King, will be seen
by those who are themselves immaculate.

PENULTIMATE SACRIFICE

A man who could pen these words and really mean them will – depending on his temperament – either become a recluse or a legend. Columban, who I think had only the ordinary man's desire for solitude, also had a strength of personality that meant he could never have just been a hermit. The art critic Waldemar Januzczak said that the art of the Dark Ages could be summed up as *man's search for the face of Jesus.*[303] What he meant artistically we might take poetically for the era too. Christ the merciful Saviour and Friend of sinners was also the righteous King and Judge. How to frame that tension in a new movement without falling into the category of errors that belong to your age is no easy task.

We might see or think we see Columban's error easily enough but are never so sure of our own. To be fully human, fully alive is to have the plasticity in thought and responsivity of heart to enter uncertain, new paths. It is something we love in the unlikely heroes of our best-loved tales[304] but often find hard to actuate in our own lives. Ideals are never enough. By genuinely living out their ideals, Columban's generation *became the change they looked for.* And so, after many years at Bangor, Columban, now middle aged and a tenured academic in Bangor's famed *schola*, approached his abbot with the request that he might make the ultimate sacrifice; voluntary exile – for life. This was what they called the White martyrdom – not the red martyrdom of a bloody death, or the green martyrdom of local exile to a leafy or grassy wilderness, but white martyrdom – white as the wave crests that would take you either to your death or to a permanent exile among strangers. We'll let Jonas take up the story below:

After he had been many years in the cloister he longed to go into strange
lands, in obedience to the command which the Lord gave Abraham: 'Get
thee out of thy country, and from thy kindred, and from thy father's

house, into a land that I will shew thee.' Accordingly, he confessed to the venerable father, Comgall, the burning desire of his heart and the long- ing enkindled by the fire of the Lord, concerning which the Lord says: 'I am come to send fire on the earth; and what will I find, if it be already kindled.' But he did not receive the answer which he wished, for it was hard for Comgall to bear the loss of so great a comfort. At length, how- ever, the latter began to conquer himself and to think that he ought not to consider his own need more than the necessities of others. Nor was it done without the will of the Almighty, who had educated His novice for future strifes, in order that He might win glorious triumphs from his victory and secure joyful victories from the phalanxes of slaughtered ene- mies. The abbot accordingly called St. Columban and although sorrow- ful, he considered the good of others before his own good, and bestowed upon him the bond of peace, the strength of solace and companions who were known for their piety.'

So Comgall at first says, 'No.' Poor man, you can hardly blame him. He had already lost Luan (Moulag) and maybe he'd thought Columban could have been a natural successor. If Comgall had not already arrived at his three score years and ten, then he was close. The preliminary suc- cession for any start-up is one of the great keys to longevity. Columban wouldn't be going alone either, he would need eleven others. And they couldn't be saplings, they'd have to be pillars in the community – men you could build upon. Could Comgall bear this loss?

Whatever the reasoning though, and the timescale, he did eventually give his blessing. In fact, Comgall did more than that, entering heart and soul into the preparations necessary to ensure its success. He selected the twelve and ordered public prayers to be said for the safety of the expedi- tion.

Columban was now perhaps in his mid-forties, the same age that Patrick was when he had undertaken the mission to Ireland. A man in his forties is still strong and by midlife patience has had some years to forge some steel in his soul.

COLUMBANUS'S ITINERARY ON THE CONTINENT

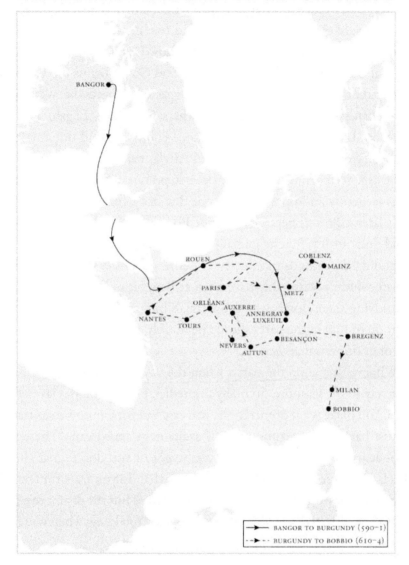

Moses was called at eighty, so was the prophet Joel, but Jeremiah was called while only a child, so perhaps we cannot be too prescriptive. But at least a man at forty can reasonably hope for another thirty years of mature work.

Who were the twelve? We have already mentioned Gall, but there was also Gall's older brother Domgall who, being in his mid-fifties was over a decade older than Columban and two decades older than Gall. History, particularly French history will know Domgall by other names, but that is for later in the story. Another was Columbanus the Younger – or junior – which someone has suggested denotes he was from Columban's home village. But of the others; Cummain, Eogain, Eunan, Gurgano, Libran, Lua, and Waldoleno, I could not find out anything else. And one, the Burgundian named Attala, who is always mentioned in the lists, seems unlikely to have been stepping on the boat at Bangor. He is evidently an important man for this story, for he shared Columban's later exile and became abbot of Bobbio after his death. But all I could find out was that he joined Columban's monastery at Luxeuil after finding the famous monastery at Lerins (opposite Cannes) too lax, and so couldn't reasonably have been at Bangor, unless he was visiting or studying there. Jonas was also Attala's biographer which means his mention of him in the party should be doubly authoritative, but on the face of it, this is not an easy fit.

Whoever made up the party, when the day finally came, they made their way to the seashore. So many unpredictable possibilities lay before them. You make what preparations you can, but for Columban as leader it must have been that moment of excitement and dread. 'There is a point at which you go with what you've got or you don't go at all.'[305] This is the 'Desert Island Discs' moment; what do you pack for eternal exile to who-knows-where? Jonas does not tell us but the distinctive get-up of the Celtic *peregrini* is well documented. You knew when you met one because they looked like nothing else in Europe.

> *'They wore a coarse outer garment, in colour as it came from the fleece, and under this a white tunic of finer stuff. They were tonsured from ear to ear across the front of the head, while the long hair behind flowed down on the back: and the eye-lids were painted or stained black. Each had a long cambutta, or curved-headed staff: and slung from the shoul-*

*der a leathern water-bottle, a wallet for food, and a satchel which con-
tained his greatest treasure — a book or two and some relics.'*[306]

They entered a boat already bound for the continent. I would imagine a large part of the community would come down to the shore to
bid them farewell. It reminds me of the Moravian missionaries who sold
themselves into slavery on the plantations of the New World. As they
were waved off from the dockside in Antwerp by friends and family who
they would never see again, one shouted 'may the Lamb, slain before the
foundation of the world, receive the price for which he died.' Similarly,
as the anchor was brought in and the boat began drifting on the tide
in Bangor that day, I wonder what was said between them, or between
them and those on the shore? Very significant partings can sometimes
happen so quickly, with so much left unsaid, and even pass in the drab
clothes of the mundane. Their last view might have been of the thin
tapers of smoke rising from the now long-established monastic 'city'.
What would become of it? They may have thought. Would they ever
achieve anything like Comgall had? The answers lay far across the grey
ocean. Bangor would thrive for a while yet. Comgall would live for another sixteen or so years. He died after a prolonged illness and in intense
pain in 601. He took communion from the herbalist Fiacre (also a later
monastic founder in Meaux on the Seine) and then died.

Columba's and Columban's example would inspire hundreds of
other Irish to take their knowledge and spiritual practices to the continent. One of the last great Irish exports to Europe was John Scotus –
philosopher and theologian. But even as he was leaving his native shore
the Vikings were already arriving in the north. A new age was born. In
793, *'on the sixth of the ides of June,'* the Anglo-Saxon Chronicle says,
*'the ravaging of heathen men lamentably destroyed God's church on Lin-
dusfarne.' 'What can I say,'* wrote fellow northerner Alcuin, with due
sympathy from the Frankish courts, *'except to weep with you in our hearts
before the altar of Christ.'*[307]

In southern and central England, under the mighty king Offa in the
late 8th century, things were not so grim. Indeed, to read Offa's corre-

spondence with Charlemagne's court, which after all was the European Union of its day, is rather heartening. The letters are the first in English diplomatic history. They concern marriage alliances, the free movement of English pilgrims on the continent, diplomatic gifts, the trade in black stones and the exact length of cloth or cloaks that England was exporting to the Franks.

We were fortunate in those days to have the Northumbrian scholar Alcuin present at Aachen – the equivalent of Brussels. Particularly when a diplomatic hiccup quite as serious as Brexit, caused Charlemagne to close all European ports to English trade. Around 789 Charlemagne proposed that his son Charles marry one of Offa's daughters. And so, Offa, quite the political chancer, countered with a proposal that his son should also marry Charlemagne's daughter Bertha instead. Charlemagne, who by now ruled an empire from the Atlantic Ocean to the Great Hungarian Plain was flabbergasted by the English cheek and so broke off diplomatic relations. Alcuin's surviving correspondence shows that even a decade later the dispute was still not resolved. Soon afterwards diplomatic relations and trade were restored, but it happened without England having to grovel. Indeed, Charlemagne calls Offa *his brother*.

But there was little to parley with the Vikings about in those days. They came to repeat their grisly work at Lindisfarne in 801, then 806, 867, and finally, in 875, the monks abandoned the site. On Iona, it was a similar tale with repeated raids. Inis Murray fell forever in 802, even Skellig Michael fell; their Abbot Etgal dying at the hands of his kidnappers. Similarly, those great houses that had witnessed the golden age of Irish monasticism and had sent the flame of learning back to Europe, fell one by one to the heathen raids; Glendalough pillaged nine times over a three-hundred-year period until it could endure no more. The ruins of Moville, Clonfert, Clonmaccnois, Kildare tell a similar story. By 840 even Patrick's Armagh was burned to its foundations.

Dublin became the centre of a Norse slave trading empire – the pattern of Christian lands falling to predatory capitalism is no new theme. Nor was it better in the east for Christian civilisation, for the Norse menace was only the latter half of a great pincer movement that had already begun in the deserts of Arabia. Islam, like Communism, was a simple binary force against, and a derivative of, the Judeo-Christian heritage. Like a whirlwind from the desert, the armies of Islam destroyed the great African, Palestinian, Syrian and Greek centres of Christianity. Constantinople would resist for another 750 years but suddenly the old certainties – those places Basil knew so well – were now under Muslim rule.[308] By 750 the armies of Islam, in a blitzkrieg advance, were only three days ride from the Brittainy coast. The battles of Poitiers and Tours, won by Charlemagne's grandfather were, as Leopold von Ranke wrote 'the turning point of one of the most important epochs in the history of the world.'[309]

Meanwhile back at Bangor, 78 years after the Battle of Poitiers, Comgall's bones were being scattered by the Danes. In fact, the whole monastic complex at Bangor was being destroyed. This was the period when Charlemagne was establishing a proto-European Union under him. But even here, and perhaps foreshadowing our own dilemma, the heirs of Charlemagne were too weak to maintain the bonds of that union against a triage of strategic threats – the Muslims, the Magyars and the Vikings. Being on a shipping lane in those days was a terrible thing.

In 1121 Bishop Malachy tried to recover – what Bernard of Clairvaux called – *the lost paradise* of Bangor, but a lawless local chieftain called Niall O'Loughlin destroyed the monastery again. It seemed that, even with the conversion of the Vikings, the barbarians were now within. The Franciscans were given the site in 1469 but the despoliation of the monasteries a century later would finish the place off for good. The child that has no ability to build with wooden bricks yet still has power to knock them down. What was happening all over the British Isles was what had happened at the collapse of Rome. Cynical opportunism and avarice among the wealthy were unleashed. Just like the Roman patricians, who destroyed the civic buildings for the stone, and enslaved their countrymen, so too now the 16th century restless-rich consolidated their holdings to the detriment of the poor. In this instance, the Earl of Kildare got himself Bangor and her lands for a knock down price. Columban, in a later sermon[310] spoke across time to all those who traded their souls for riches to the exclusion of their fellow man; *'Some are really so careless on their journey, that they seem to be not enroute as at home. They travel reluctantly rather than willingly toward their homeland that is surely already lost. They have used up their home here on the road and a brief life have bought eternal death. Unhappy men, they enjoy their disappointed trading: they have loved the perishable goods of others, and neglected their own eternal good.'*

All that can be seen today is one wall of Saint Malachy's refectory. It is little visited now in a town of sixty thousand that has grown up around it; a grim reminder that not even the most influential start-ups will outlast the ravages of time. Bangor's legacy endured in her scholars and missionaries, not in her lime mortar. For all their oddities and foibles, to our eyes at least, those great souls left the world a much better place. Perhaps that is as much as any of us can ask as a legacy. Looking at that one remaining wall; that last and now ignored relic of, what had been in its day, one of Europe's premier culture-shaping engines, we can only say as Byron did of his Newstead Abbey:

> *Hail to thy pile! more honour'd in thy fall,*
> *Than modern mansions, in their pillar'd state,*
> *Proudly majestic frowns thy vaulted hall,*
> *Scowling defiance on the blasts of fate.*

But Columban, Gall and the others could see none of these future catastrophes. For them, it was the grey waters and the horizon of Belfast Lough that beckoned. The creak of the pulleys, the sloshing waters in the bilge, the smell of brine and salt, fish and leather, sacking, mildew, and sweat. Columban and Gall might well have looked down to their sandals, the sand still between their toes, the sands of Erin, the Emerald Isle, the isle of Saints and Scholars.

They may, or may not have known it, but they were heading to the continent after fifty years of plague that had halved its population. It is impossible to overstate the devastation. No one could have been spared the pain of bereavement. And even as the plague was arriving in Europe a generation before, one contemporary, the sole survivor in his family, reported that out of an entire city there were only seven men and one ten-year-old boy who had survived.[311] Doors hung open; valuables were left unprotected, whole cities like ghost towns. In Justinian's Constantinople, they were burying 10,000 a day – 10,000 every day! [312]

Within a short time, from Bangor to Beijing, a hundred million untimely deaths must have brought unimaginable trauma – orphans, widows, and widowers with broken hearts and empty stomachs – and hungrier than ever for ultimate answers, and even more thirsty for a visible demonstration of God's solidarity with them in their suffering. It is understandably hard for us the grasp the size of the catastrophe. The nearest, equivalent pandemic we have is the Black Death of 1348 which, beyond the physical and emotional devastation, changed economic and political reality in England for ever.[313]

But in Columbanus' day, it was not just a pandemic that was devasting Europe. Research into pollutants in polar ice cores published by Harvard University in 2018 suggests that this was literally the *annus horribilis* of human history – the worst period ever to have been alive. On top of the collapse of Rome and the raging pandemic, the ice cores show that in 536 a massive volcanic eruption in Iceland blotted out the sun for 18 months in the northern hemisphere, thus making the decade before Columban's birth the coldest for 2,300 years. Mass crop failures and starvation ensued. A spike in lead particles in the ice around 640 also suggested that Europe didn't really recover from this for a century.

Furthermore, Geophysicist Dr. Dallas Abbot has also suggested that celestial dust in the Greenland ice sheet may have been from fragments from Halle's comet. Comparing her findings with the Mediterranean and Irish records, she believes that a larger fragment broke away from the comet and hit earth near the equator between 536 and 537, sending up even more dust into the atmosphere. Chronicles speak of a pale sun with no strength and stars that seemed to dance in the sky.

All these devastations were in and around the timeframe of Columban's life. And all around him suffering people must have wanted to know, perhaps even more than we do in our comparative ease, that they were not alone. Time, technology, and every supposed sophistication evaporate in the presence of death and suffering. And once more we stand shoulder to shoulder with every other human being who has ever lived on this planet – with the same questions, and same ultimate needs. Columban goes with what he believes are the answers. He goes with a confidence that we today would find staggering. He had no idea then what trials awaited him but, as Herbert Butterfield observed (in his 1951 Riddell Memorial Lectures) about such events, *'It seems equally clear in history, however, that spiritual forces have an extraordinary spontaneity and originality so that we can never tell what a man may not do when he says to himself 'How shall I worship God?', and we can never tell what he may not do just for love.'*

As the ship pulled further from the shore and the faces of good friends' faded, Columban catches Gall's eye. Gall gives a faint smile and Columban nods uncertainly. This is it. It is really happening. He can still feel the sand between his toes. The grains are drying and blowing away. It is the very last earth from Ireland he would ever see.

'So, they embarked, and began the dangerous journey across the channel and sailed quickly with a smooth sea and favourable winds to the coast of Brittany. Here they rested for a while to recover their strength and discussed their plans anxiously, until finally they decided to enter the land of Gaul.' –Jonas' Life of Columban

D-Day Armada leaving Bangor for Normandy 1944 (as Columban had done 1357 years before).

288. Emil Brunner Gifford Lectures 1947.
Source: https://www.giffordlectures.org/lectures/christianity-and-civilization

289. J. M. Roberts, *A History of Europe,* p.87

290. Laporte has suggested that these early chapters are a summary of a work composed in Bangor by Comgall.

291. Basil, Ep. 223, 2, as quoted in Quasten (1986), p. 205.

292. These were drawn up for one of Columban's monastic communities, possibly a different one from that which received the previous Rule. Walker (Jonas' translator) takes chapters I to IX of this Rule to contain the nucleus which goes back to Columban himself; he would regard the later chapters of the shorter recension, and the extra interpolations of the longer recension, as having been added by Columban's successors in Luxeuil.

293. The Rule of Saint Columbanus was approved of by the Synod of Mâcon in 627, but it was superseded at the close of the century by the Rule of Saint Benedict

294. Even the red dots in Irish manuscripts are probably derived from the Egyptian Coptic church

295. Columban first mentions it in a letter to Pope Gregory. Next, the *Life of St Finnian of Clonard* mentions a similar dispute between Gildas and David, probably about a particular form of monastic life. Gildas criticises those 'who flee to a stricter discipline', which is very like the subject of his advice to Finnian. Gildas, expressing an intention to enter the monastic life himself, nevertheless later thought David's rule too severe and strict. In any case, later tradition seems to indicate that Gildas lost the dispute, and went to Ireland.

296. *The Rise of Western Christendom*, Peter Brown, p220

297. The earliest Irish one which has survived is the *Penitential of Vinnian*, usually identified with either Finnian of Clonard (d.549) or Finnian of Moville (d.579). The Penitential of Columban shows considerable dependence on that of Vinnian.

298. Dom Jean Laporte

299. Apart from a few paragraphs at the back, there is no reason to question Columban's authorship of the document as a whole. It probably dates from his early period on the continent in Annegray or Luxeuil.

300. Of the many thousands of Celtic monks, only a small number were priests. Cf. Irische Kanonensammlung , XI, 3.

301. *The Life and Writings of Columban*, George Metlake

302. Translation from *The Field Day, anthology of Irish writing* vol. 4 ed. Angela Bourke (Hunaldas was, in Walker's opinion, a pupil from the Bangor days.)

303. BBC documentary: *The Dark Ages: An Age of Light* - Waldemar Januzczak

304. It is in exactly in this regard that Gandalf says to Bilbo Baggins, 'Hobbits really are amazing creatures.'

305. Joan Didion

306. This is from George Metlake, who gives Montalembert's *Monks of the West* as his source, though it must be noted that this is not settled scholarship. Even the style of the tonsure is disputed.

307. A tangential point, though not unconnected to the themes in this book, Norman Davies comments (*The Isles*, p.256) that it was the final expulsion of the Norse from the Hebrides (which in turn severed Ireland from Argyl, lit. East Ireland) that led to the consolidation of 'the kingdom of the Scots'.

308. It is important to point out that Christianity survived (though it did not thrive) in these places within the initial period of Islam's expansion when the Muslims did not insist on mass conversions.

309. Ranke, Leopold von. *"History of the Reformation"*, vol. 1, 5

310. *Sermon 5; 'On Human Life'*

311. Pseudo-Dionysius of Tel Mahre, *Chronicle* (also known as the *Chronicle of Zuqnin*) Part III, tr. W. Witaksowski (Liverpool, 1996), p.77

312. Procopius, *Hyper to Polemon*, 2.22-3, in *History of the Wars, Secret History, Buildings*, ed. and tr. H. Dewing, 7 vols (Cambridge, MA), 1, pp. 450-72

313. A 2020 study undertaken by Warwick University suggests that our gross national product was reduced to 26% and that it remained so for a century after the 1348 plague. The 2020 Covid-19 pandemic is obviously nearer time, but not equivalent in scale and devastation.

British troops passing through the ruined city of Ypres, September 29th 1918, the ruined tower of the famous cloth hall haunts the skyline.

CHAPTER 8

Schuman – Early Career

CHAPTER SUMMARY – 1919-1930 - NO ONE WINS A CIVIL WAR - Schuman entering Parisian politics. Europe in the aftermath of World War I and the rise of Communism, Fascism and Nazism. 1919-1930 - THE MAN FROM THE MOUNTAINS - The rise of Fascism in Italy and heroic suffering of Mussolini's nemesis and Italy's political saviour; Alcide de Gasperi. Philosophical reflections from Sophocles, Maritain, Bergson and Kuyper. 1930-1939 - THE FRIGHTENING THIRTIES - Overview of Schuman's political rise set against the tumultuous political events of that decade.

> *"War.... puts nations to the test. Just as mummies fall to pieces the moment they are exposed to the air, so, war pronounces its sentence of death on those social institutions which have become ossified."*
>
> *Karl Marx*

1919-1930 - NO ONE WINS A CIVIL WAR

In this chapter, we find Schuman arriving in Paris from the provinces. He admitted to feeling out of his depth in a city where he had no friends and among governing elites with whom he shared little in common. We all have an idea of the sort of politician we think the system needs. When I interviewed President Ferrand at the French National Assembly in 2018, the palace was given over to celebrating George Clemenceau – a great French wartime leader. He is a secular French-man's ideal leader; ebullient, unrelenting, and atheistic. I wondered at the choice. Was it not Clemenceau's short-sightedness with regards to reparations at Versailles that led to the inevitability of a second war?[314] Would the French ever dedicate rooms to the monkish Schuman?

Robert Schuman, by temperament and by religious outlook, was a polar opposite to Clemenceau. Many saw that the full-stop on the treaty under such terms was only really a comma. Lloyd George said that it would mean repeating the folly 25 years later at three times the cost. But it was not in the Third Republic, who incidentally voted Clemenceau out of office a year later for being too lenient,[315] but in the Fourth Republic, that Schuman quietly emerged as an antidote. He was the anti-venom that France needed to break the poisoned cycle started by Germany, but perpetuated by politicians like Clemenceau.

As we have previously noted, but for his ill health, Robert Schuman might well have been fighting in World War I in the trenches alongside Adolf Hitler, and against those whom he considered his own country-men. He might also have been finding himself on the wrong side of the bayonet of – or pulling the trigger at – Sassoon, Owen, Churchill, Tolkien, C. S. Lewis, or Harold Macmillan. It had been a war different from others, not just in scale but also in form. Churchill wrote in *My Early Life,* that British soldiers in his own time (1890's onwards) went into war expecting to survive. The reverse, he said, was true in 1914. The collective trauma on the European psyche is hard to overstate. After the armistice, Schuman was not the only one politicised by the horror of the previous 5 years, Adolf Hitler was too. So, in the beginning of this chapter, I want to sketch how the yeast of the new ideologies worked through the dough of geopolitical forces to create the maelstrom of the second great European civil war.

Adolf Hitler, three years Schuman's junior, had been wounded at the Somme, and in 1919 was receiving the prestigious Iron Cross – ironically, on a recommendation by his Jewish superior, Lieutenant Hugo Gutmann.[316] Like other German nationalists, Hitler believed the *Dolchstoßlegende,* the so-called 'stab-in-the-back' conspiracy theory which claimed that the German army, "undefeated in the field", had been betrayed by their civilian leaders, Jews, and Marxists. The war concluded with an armistice, not a surrender. One historian gives a view here, namely, that the treaty itself was not the problem – its terms were far less punitive than anything the Germans would have enforced if they had won. The problem was that the Allies should have occupied Germany straight away and thus circumvented the problems that followed.[317] Germany had not been invaded, but they managed to take great swathes of Europe by military manoeuvres. Most German units marched home with their banners flying and their military integrity intact. Chancellor Ebert greeted many of those troops at the Brandenburg Gate as unconquered heroes. So, we begin to see the problem.

Even in Britain, there wasn't a universal sense of jubilation. When Vera Brittain wrote about this in *Testament of Youth,* she said that when the great bells finally wrung out that the, '...men and women who looked incredulously into each other's faces did not cry jubilantly: "We've won the War!" They only said, "The War is over."

In many ways, these European wars were one civil war. And, as the saying goes, no one ever really wins a civil war. It is just that some nations lose less than others. Even on the 11th day of the 11th month – on that very last day of the war – before the 11th hour 2,738 men were killed and 8,200 were wounded before the guns fell silent. The last man to die was US Sergeant Henry Gunther, whose name suggests a German immigrant family. He charged a German machine gun position at 11.59 am with a fixed bayonet. The Germans shouted for him to go back. Is it too wild a thing to say one of them might have been his distant cousin, if not genetically then symbolically? But he would not stop or could not hear or understand. He was shot with only seconds to go and thus stands for every soldier's tragedy. In my own hometown, a small place; over a hundred young men left our Main Street waved on by mothers, fathers, sisters, neighbours. Not one returned home. Not one. No one really wins a civil war.

Germany had to give up the new territories and the older ones, like Alsace Lorraine, that she had ruled for half a century. Foreign troops now occupied her, and though she had to release the allied prisoners of war, her own remained in prison. Naturally, the German generals were only too keen that the new government should take the blame, rather than admit that their own demoniacal, imperial militarism had led to a catastrophe, that had touched every continent except Antarctica, and had brought a voluntary *econocide* on their own people. This, and the continued allied naval blockade until 1919, combined with the unenforceable terms of the Versailles treaty was to push Germany into a long and bitter poverty that cemented a road for the rise of National Socialism.

This backdrop set the scene for Hitler; a decorated war hero and impassioned rhetorician, who rose to be the leader of the party within three years. He was a soldier speaking to a generation of soldiers – a whole generation of men hardened and immured to the realities of industrial-scale killing. Without the tragedy of the war, Hitler might have become an able artist or architect. It is hard to overestimate the disjuncture that the Great War was to European civilisation. Its effects reached into every area of life.

Writing about 'the men of 1914' the novelist and artist Percy Wyndham Lewis said that the war had been 'a black solid mass cutting off all that went before it.' All the radicalism and idealism of pre-war Europe had been drowned in mud, blood, and mortar shells. 'We are the first men of a future that has not materialized. We belong to a 'great age' that has not 'come off.' In his despair over the failures in democracy he, like many of his generation, fell for the Carlylean ideal of the Great Man. Percy wrote the first book in English lauding Hitler, something he came to regret as the thirties grew darker and darker.

As we have seen in chapter 5, in the chaos of the war's aftermath, Schuman too was encouraged by friends to enter into politics. He was elected MP for Moselle in 1919 and appointed to the Consultative

Council of Alsace Lorraine in Strasbourg.[318] Two men, two different trajectories.

It was to be a momentous year for international politics; four great monarchies had fallen; the first League of Nations was convened; the peace conference opened at Versailles, and the German fleet was scuppered (by themselves) at Scapa Flow. An allied peace treaty with Austria was also signed in St. Germain.[319] As if in ominous echo from across the channel, Rutherford announced on January 3rd, that he had succeeded in penetrating the nucleus. As an omen of woe began the age of nuclear fusion.

At the same moment, the Hapsburgs were exiled; the Italians seized Rijeka from Yugoslavia; and Mussolini founded the Fascist Party. As the British observed the first two-minute silence to mark the armistice, their soldiers were still at war in Afghanistan. The Red Army was still at war with Finland, and still victorious everywhere against the White Russians. In 1919, the Soviets also entered the Crimea. Stalin and Hitler, products of WWI, began looking to the future.

Communism, Nazism, and Fascism. Three new ideologies, two only embryonic, but all three there in 1919, and all poised to drag the nations into the most disastrous war of humanity's history. The power of ideas would never be belittled again. Those pale young men in the coffee shops of Vienna or the library at the British museum were about to tear three hundred million of their fellows from the earth. Lenin, Stalin, Marx, Engels, Nietzsche would become the midwives of a nightmare. Three hundred million – the number cannot be comprehended – and all an attempt to build a utopia on the ashes of a failed Christian civilisation. In 'The Gay Science' Nietzsche's 'madman' runs into the marketplace and exclaims,

> '...we have killed God.... all of us are his murderers. ...How were we able to do this? Who gave us the sponge to wipe away the entire horizon? What were we doing when we unchained the earth from its sun? ... Is there any up or down left? ...Do we not feel the breath of the empty space.... has it not become colder?'

It is a penetrating analysis and his prose is laden with formidable imagery. In many ways, Nietzsche was also perceptive of his own century and so prophetic of ours. The phrase, is *there any up or down left?'* captures, not the inversion of *objective value*,[320] but their complete disappearance. Post-modern society became so obsessed with *Right and Left* that it did not notice the *Up and Down* of Nietzsche. They knew it had become colder, but they did not understand that the very basis of humane ethics and societal norms had been dealt a fatal blow.

But Nietzsche was also, or at least vastly, over simplistic. Modern man had not killed God, but as Seth had done to Osiris, he had done as much as was humanly possible in dismembering and scattering him abroad. In the Egyptian myth, Osiris could not, in essence, die because he was a divine being. In the myth, his widow recovers his parts and attempts to bind them back together. One of the biblical names of Satan is Diabolos, the *divider* or *scatterer* and, like Osiris' widow, the church would appear to spend considerable energy holding together the rudiments of a Judeo-Christian worldview against forces that seek to usher in, what Nietzsche called, man's 'higher history'.

It is another laden term. But as Nietzsche observed, men who had accomplished so great a murder must now create a new version of meaning, a new narrative by which to make sense of everything, a new horizon to replace the one wiped out. We must, in fairness, point out that Nietzsche was little read in his own lifetime, and often misread after it, when he was taken up by the *avant-garde* in Paris and Berlin. Thus, his *superman* became the perfect fit for the then 'settled' science of the Ayran superiority.[321]

These 19th and 20th century ideologies were only able to thrive in the vacuum left by a Christianity in retreat among the elites. But the supposedly bold, revolutionary, and original thought of the continental philosophers was nothing of the sort. For example, Shakespeare's Richard III not only uttered,*'all that Nietzsche had to say put into two lines but also in the very words of Nietzsche. "Conscience is but a word that cowards use, devised at first to keep the strong in awe."* Shakespeare had thought of Nietzsche and the Master Morality; but he weighed it at its proper value and put it in its proper place. Its proper place is the mouth of a half-insane hunchback on the eve of defeat. *This rage against the weak is only possible in a man morbidly brave but fundamentally sick; a man like Richard, a man like Nietzsche.'*[322]

And similarly, the reception of such philosophies could only be received by sections of European culture that were 'fundamentally sick' already.

In his recent book *Seven Types of Atheism*, Professor John Gray challenged modern readers to view religion and atheism not as opposites but as 'a continuation of monotheism by other means.' Hence the unending succession of God-surrogates, such as humanity and science, technology and the all-too-human visions of transhumanism.' This, if true, is a very near approximation of what the Bible would call the 'spirit of anti-Christ'[323] as the Greek word used for 'Anti' can also mean 'in place of', or a 'surrogate for' if we were to adopt Professor Gray's terminology. A form of Christianity may remain on the fringes but the designation of the penultimate *Anointed Saviour* (this is the meaning of the word 'Christ') is co-opted by an ideology in the political or economic spheres. Therefore, our ultimate salvation might be considered as coming via politics, economics, education, and the social sciences.

Writing long after the war, Schuman makes the same point:

'Christian ideas survived in the people's subconscious and influenced men who gave up practising a dogmatic religion, but were nevertheless inspired by the main principles. These principles have become the features of our civilisation, owing to which, the 18th century rationalists proclaimed and made popular human and citizen's rights, which are essentially Christian.'[324]

Christianity survived the 'Death of God' movement, as it has the necessary corollary, the Death of Man movement. No doubt it will even live to see the death of post-modernism, and its sickly spawn too. But looking back, it is little wonder that the new ideologies acted as binaries and antipodes for Christianity, conferring on their adherents' new salvations and new saviours. But there would be a terrible price to pay, for a 'people who values its privileges above its principles, soon loses both.'[325]

The three new ideologies breaking upon Europe followed the same steps. First, the redefinition of currently held norms with new ones. Then the making of the new norms and goals into absolute values. An ideology first rationalizes, then radicalises, and then instrumentalises everything in its path, starting with what Nietzsche called *die Unwertung aller Werte* – the Conversion of Values.[326] All ideologies systematically and vigorously hunt down words like justice, truth, solidarity, and love in order to annex them to serve their own ends. But they always remain, as Jacques Ellul says, 'a stolen inheritance.' We are certainly not immune from this in our own day.[327] With Nazism and Fascism,[328] the party was always right. With Communism, the truth was whatever advanced the cause of a future socialist utopia. For all three, 'Evil' was whatever stood in the way of the goal.

The decisive moment for any ideology is always reached when the opponents of it – the Aristocrats, the Bourgeoisie, the Jews, the Christians, Gays, Democrats, Republicans, Sunni, Shia, Hutu, Tutsi, Atheists, Creationists, Pro-choicers, Pro-lifers – are labelled as *de facto* 'evil'. That step taken, the final solution to 'remove the evil from among us' is only one of degree and not of kind. It is a smaller step than the ones preceding it, for, as Voltaire reminds us, 'those who can make you believe absurdities can also make you commit atrocities.'[329]

'We risk being the first people in history to have been able to make their illusions so vivid. So persuasive, so 'realistic' that we can live in them.' When the historian Daniel J. Boorstin wrote this, he was thinking of our generation, but something like this was also happening temporarily to Schuman's. It was exactly in this sort of societal illusion that Henri Bergson saw the root cause of German aggression. She had 'entrusted herself too much to certain theories' and so devoted herself to 'poetry, to art, to metaphysic. She was made, so she said, for thought and imagination; she had no feeling for the reality of things.'[330]

In his book, *The Meaning of the War: Life and Matter in Conflict,* Bergson pointed out that the seeds of the 'settled'[331] science of race were not Prussian but French. For it was the French diplomatist, Comte Joseph Arthur de Gobineau (1816-1882) whose *Essai sur l'inégalité des races humaines* in 1855 first affirmed the superiority of the Aryan race on ethnological grounds. According to Gobineau, it was the Aryans' right and destiny to rule all other races as bondsmen. Gobineau was a friend of Wagner, and also of Nietzsche.[332] Nietzsche's sister wrote of the almost reverent regard which her brother had for Gobineau, and we cannot discount that the Frenchman's ideas may well be where Nietzsche derived his doctrine of the non-morality of the superman.

With the restraints of tradition and religion weakened, the new ideologies were able to lead whole nations toward something like Nietzsche's *Higher History*. The *vivid illusions* of Nazism and Fascism were *lived in* for a few decades; the horrors of Communism, almost a century. Indeed, the other variants of Marxian analysis are still with us. At least in the west, now stripped of its ideological appeal, (which held so many western intellectuals in its grasp during the twentieth century) Marxist socialism lies in rags. Like the uber-Eurocentric Aryanism of the Nazi's, Communism was founded on illusions of philosophy, illusions of science, and illusions of history. 'If the facts are against you, argue the law. As someone said, if the law is against you, argue the facts. If the law and the facts are against you, pound the table and yell like hell.'[333] So vivid, so reasonable, but so wrong. Wrong about humanity, wrong about society, wrong about the nature of truth, of good, of evil, of almost everything.[334] Marxism posited material solutions to what were, if the Christians are right, spiritual problems.

The Christian political philosopher Nikolai Alexandrovich Berdyaev wrote in 1931 that Communism was formidable *'precisely as a religion. It is as a religion that it opposes Christianity and aims at ousting it; it gives in to the temptations Christ refused, the changing of stones into bread and the kingdom of this world.'*[335] The atheistic roots of Soviet Communism lay ultimately in Christianity itself,

> *'..and in Russian Orthodoxy in particular, though in skewed prism, with the template of creation-fall-redemption-restoration eschatology*

unmistakably intact. Bolshevism was infused with worldly asceticism, but of a graceless variety, and the heroic avenger sought to right wrongs with the methods of the modern state, and a new anthropology to create a 'New Soviet Man'. The best example of systematic and coercive state secularization in modern history had religious roots and a religious character.'[336]

Many still argue that its critique of Capitalism was useful and necessary but sober voices warn that even here, that Marxism lacks the 'ability to diagnose the fundamental phenomenological problems that such an analysis reveals.... In accepting a metaphysical dualism inherent in the idealism of Hegel, Marx failed to recognize the true nature of the conflict ....it is here that the Bible provides us with an answer that Marxism was totally unable to discover.'[337] For many the most devastating critique of Marxism was from the Polish ex-Marxist, Leszek Kolakowski, whose *Main Currents of Marxism* (1978) served 'both as a handbook and as an obituary to the movement.'[338] In his landmark 1970 book, Jean Francois Revel's framed the European dilemma succinctly 'Ni Marx, Ni Jesus' (Without Marx or Jesus), 'no one today, even in the Communist parties of the western world, seriously contends that the Soviet Union is a revolutionary model for other countries.'

But even as he was writing the obituary of Marxism, other writers like Sartre, Gramsci, Rudi Dutschke, Max Horkheimer, the Frankfurt School, and, supremely Michel Foucault were seeding the key concepts and mechanisms of Marxian and Nietzschean analysis within new generations of the academy. The impact and implications of this will be touched on again at the final chapters of this book. For now, we must move on with the story of an unassuming and pious man rising in politics at such a moment in history.

In 1920 Schuman was nominated for the Consultative Council of Alsace Lorraine in Strasbourg, and was thus in charge of general issues linked to administration, legislation, and security. In the same year, Clemenceau resigned and Mitterrand became Premiere of France. There was also a short-lived monarchist *coup d'état* in Berlin, and a conference convened in San Remo to discuss German reparations. The Hague was selected as a seat for the International Court of Human Justice. Hitler announced a twenty-five-point programme at the *Hofbrauhuas* in Munich. If the next world conflict were a jigsaw, then we can see some of the outer edges already falling into place. And further south in Italy, a whole section of corner pieces was also being assembled.

1919-1930 - THE MAN FROM THE MOUNTAINS

In 1921 Mussolini marched on Rome and formed a fascist government and dissolved all non-fascist parties. It is here that I wish to pick up the story of another young politician who will become an essential part of our story. We will briefly summarize his early biography, not just because he became one of the four founding fathers of the EEC, but also because his political survival was phenomenal. His sufferings were prolonged and his achievements profound.

Alcide de Gasperi was born in 1881, as an Austrian citizen in the Trentino region near Lake Garda. This is confusing as De Gasperi's culturally Italian hometown and area were, at the outset of our story, not Italian. In fact, they were part of the Austro-Hungarian empire, which arose after Napoleon's defeat. So, here is another *homme de frontières* like Schuman, and who also, like him, was a devout Roman Catholic. In his mid-teens he was already active in the Social Christian movement, and by seventeen the Austrian police already held a file on him as a potential separatist. But, strange as it would seem, Gasperi never questioned, even as a later politician, that the Trentino should belong to Austria–Hungary. [339]

Aged nineteen, he studied Philology at Vienna, where he helped found the Christian student movement. When he wrote home to his brother Luigi, he confided that he had to queue with the very poorest of people for hot food and that his coat was not warm enough for the wet and freezing Viennese winters. He told Luigi not to tell their parents about it. (Luigi was later ordained as a priest but died aged only twenty-three from an infection.)

Aged twenty-three himself, Alcide was arrested at a demonstration in favour of an Italian-language university and released from prison after twenty days. During the incarceration, he cemented his friendship with Pietro Romano, another native of the Trentino. Pietro's family lived in Valsugana, in the mountainous region above Lake Garda. After graduating from Vienna, De Gasperi returned home where he worked on, and soon became the editor of, the newspaper *Il Trentino*. Until September 1906 it had been called *La Voce Cattolica* (The Catholic Voice) but De Gasperi was keen for it to reach across sacred-secular boundaries. He was introduced to this line of work at the suggestion of the new prince-bishop Monsignor Celestino Endrici. Endrici, though occupying an ancient seat of privilege, was in fact a moderniser, after a fashion that agreed with De Gasperi. Both men were young Trentino frontiersmen – Endrici was only 38 – with a deep understanding of the local and international situation.

The Trentino region was unusual in that it still reflected the medieval church-state structure of the Holy Roman Empire. There was not the same separation of powers here as elsewhere, but Endrici wanted there to be. He wanted to see beneficial changes and the mobilisation of the laity in forming a political party. This was the beginnings of the *Populari* Party (PPT). Having a layman like De Gasperi as editor in chief of the paper was very much in tune with the reforms he hoped to bring across the troubled region. Endrici, like De Gasperi, was very much inspired by the *Rerum Novarum* (Revolutionary Change) encyclical issued by Pope Leo XIII in 1891.

Although fifteen years had passed since this letter had been written, it seemed ever more relevant. De Gasperi found a battleground in the north on two fronts. He learned to tread wisely in a subtle war of words and ideologies as he navigated the ambiguous geopolitical situation before him. First, as ethnically Italian, he stood up to the centralising power of Vienna, but then also to the anti-religious policies of the Liberals and Socialists of the Trentino. The socialists were *too naïve*, he wrote, *how could there be a brotherhood of man without the fatherhood of God?* In 1909 he first crossed swords with his nemesis Mussolini, who had been sent to the Trentino region to campaign for the Socialists against the *Populari*. Mussolini was then editor of the Socialist paper which launched attacks against De Gasperi's *Il Trentino* and the Christian Democrats. For Mussolini, De Gasperi was exactly the sort of slavish papist who would shackle Italy to the past and keep her from her predestined greatness among the nations.

In 1911, Gasperi was aged thirty and therefore eligible for political office. His actual name up until this point had been *de* Gasperi but the Viennese official – perhaps assuming a noble lineage – wrote him down as *De* Gasperi, which thereafter stuck. It later allowed his enemies to take cheap shots at him for elitism and some even called him Von Gasperi – casting aspersions on his loyalties even as De Gaulle would of Schuman. (De Gaulle called Schuman 'a good Bosch, but a Bosch nonetheless.')

De Gasperi won a seat in the Austrian Reichstag as a member of Parliament for the *Populari* Party,[340] a post he held for 6 years. He mainly used his time to campaign for the non-German citizens of the vast Austro-Hungarian Empire. By the start of the First World War, when the newspaper closed, the thirty-three-year-old Gasperi already had fifteen years political experience behind him. After the war, his home region was transferred to Italy, but like Schuman, he never hid his love for Austrian and German culture. Like Schuman he was a fluent German speaker, often speaking German to his family, many of whom spoke it as their first language. He never forgot his days in the Reichstag either, for here 11 different nationalities met on equal terms each allowed to speak in their own language. Here too they were not seated by ethnicity or geography but by political leaning. It was a seed for a larger future.

The Reichstag was closed after the assassination of Franz Ferdinand and the world was plunged into the first terrible conflict. De Gasperi, exempted like Schuman, by ill health worked for the 'Committee for the Relief of Southern Refugees.' Italy declared its neutrality, but 60,000 Trentino men were called on to fight for the Empire. 10,000 would never return from the Eastern Front. One of the men killed was Giuseppe Romano, the brother of his university friend Pietro.

In 1915, Alcide De Gasperi was with the Romano family in Valsugana. Pietro's sister, Francesca, whom he had known since she was 13, had recently returned from finishing school in Switzerland. She was now 21 and he was 34. 'Her cosmopolitan education had not erased her simplicity, the hearty mountain air in her lungs, and her passion for sports.'[341] He was enraptured by her friendliness and conversation and her outgoing heart – she was already a Red Cross volunteer. But she was from the opposite end of the social spectrum in many ways, and he knew he was a peasant setting his cap at a lady. She had grown up very comfortable and had been educated at privileged institutions. What could he give her? With his head in a spin, it was hard to leave the beautiful mountain town. Thinking on his feet, as only a desperate man can, he asked if they might correspond and she teach him English. Some men will try anything!

She said she would, and thus began a correspondence of hearts and minds that would lead them to the altar, seven years later, in 1922. In the letter of 1921, when he finally declared his love, he left her under no illusion that their life could ever be easy. He wanted her as an equal companion in the struggle for a more just and fraternal society.

Alcide De Gasperi and Francesca

He wanted to live an honest life, and that he confessed, probably meant they could never be rich. In exchange for the comforts she must forgo, he would offer her his undying love and a life in pursuit of worthwhile convictions. Neither knew at the time just how much they would suffer as a couple and as a family. But she agreed to be an equal partner in a marriage that made De Gasperi strong enough to hold Italy together after the war. If indeed a marriage could save a nation, this is exactly what it would look like.

But their suffering and the glory lay in the future and our story must stay with them at the beginning of their courtship in 1915. On May 24th, Italy declared war on Austria, despite De Gasperi's trips to Rome the previous year to try to prevent it. The calamity had similarities to other such border situations like Alsace and Lorraine. Soon there were Austrian and Italian men in the Trentino, who had lived side by side as neighbours for decades, but were now taking up guns against each other in a civil war. Austria evacuated 70,000 Trentini to detention camps. When the Reichstag reopened in 1917, De Gasperi denounced the deportations. How could the emperor treat his subjects in such a way? But other Trentini, who had always wanted Italian rule, saw this was the final straw and refused to acknowledge the emperor's authority. Among them were De Gasperi's political opponents like Battisti, who along with fellow Irredentists (activists for Italian unification) were executed in the courtyard of the bishop's palace. But after the armistice in 1918, Trentino became annexed to Italy. During this time De Gasperi worked, as did Schuman, for the peaceful cohabitation of the mixed populations where wounds were still raw and divisions rife.

In a simple binary, the Italians further south lauded the *Irredentists* – those who had struggled to have Trentino under Italian rule. 'Austrian imperialism bad, Italian nationalism good,' might have been their strapline. To make matters worse, a flood of poetry and literature, painting, and music had been produced to support the cause, for which Battisti and others were now the martyrs. De Gasperi and the other MPs were welcomed as heroes to the parliament in Rome. But the Romans' easy pleasure did not last long when these MPs stressed that a frontier province was not as simple a proposition as the poets had declaimed. 'Trentini.' Gasperi said, 'let's not divide ourselves. Now we come to Rome to defend our autonomy as we did in Vienna.' A centralised government was too blunt an instrument to deal with the complexities of a border territory – it must be left to the locals.

A strange link in the chain of causation occurred at this time. Up until 1919, Catholics, owing to an argument going back 50 years between the Papacy and the Italian government, had been forbidden to engage in politics. But this was lifted just after the war. Of course, there were few, if any, Catholics in Italy that had anything like the experience of the suddenly repatriated Trentini. That meant that De Gasperi's PPT was providentially experienced and ready when the change came. His friend Pietro ran with him, and in the same year that he was elected leader of the party, Francesca agreed to marry him. He hardly saw her before the wedding, but they corresponded daily. Their first home would be in the flat above the Newspaper office. After a wedding in Sella, Valsugana on July 14th, 1922, they spent a few days hiking together in the mountains of southern Italy. But this, like many things in their marriage, was interrupted when he received a telegram – there had been outbreaks of Fascist violence. He was needed straightaway in Rome.

Lifelong Nemesis: De Gasperi & Mussolini - from Newspaper activists to Political leaders

It is now that we come back to Mussolini's march on Rome.[342] This anti-parliamentary, former socialist came to power at a time when a weakened parliamentary system was all too easy to exploit. In scenes that would be repeated a decade later in Germany, the democratically elected Italian parliamentary members of 1923 abdicated their authority to an avowed anti-parliamentarian in the hopes of finding a saviour. King Victor Immanuel asked the *Populari* party's deputy Filippo Media to form a government, but he ran away from Rome without even consulting his party or the king. Prominent *Populari* were picked off individually by

Mussolini until the party all but collapsed. Others capitulated en mass behind the 'strong man.' De Gasperi, against the advice of many, attempted a coalition with the Fascists in the hopes of moderating their power. De Gasperi wrote in *Il Nuovo Trentino*:

> *'Except for the great fundamental principles on which the political programmes of the various parties are based, everything is relative in politics, and it would be absurd to reject in advance the collaboration with a particular party if doing so could somehow serve the supreme interests of the country, which is the first objective of politics.'*

It was a complicated decision, and one that presented a conundrum familiar to Schuman, who would one day vote in, (but not participate in) Vichy. And also, for Adenauer, who resisted Hitler but whose *Zentrum* party had capitulated to him. Luigi Sturzo, who had warned De Gasperi not to collaborate, was soon proved right, and De Gasperi came very soon to regret his decision to collaborate as he had. Mussolini annulled Trentino's autonomy and threw them out of the coalition in April. Sturzo, a priest, who as General Secretary of the *Populari*, and a very vocal opponent of Mussolini, was banished to England. The socialist MP, Giacomo Matteoti, was not so fortunate. He had questioned irregularities in the election that spring, which had given the Fascists 60% of the vote, and was assassinated. When Italian socialists in exile in Paris suggested an anti-Fascist coalition, Gasperi and most of the *Populari* accepted.

Beyond left and right, the existence of democracy was now at stake in Italy. Because the worst excesses of Fascism were still in the future, many disagreed with De Gasperi's level of flexibility. For some religious conservatives, it seemed quite incomprehensible, but for him, it was a zero-sum game, no democracy, no hope. *'Man's capacity for justice makes democracy possible,'* wrote Reinhold Niebuhr, *'but man's inclination to injustice makes democracy necessary.'*

On 15th July 1923, only two years after De Gasperi had been elected to the parliament, a majority in that parliament voted to abolish itself. Thus, in a pattern imitated by Hitler a decade later, Mussolini had obtained, by democratic vote and parliamentary process, the abolition of parliamentary democracy. Mussolini then immediately sequestrated opposition media, and within twelve months moved from verbal to open, physical attacks on his opponents.[343] De Gasperi was 'exposed' in the press as an Austrian enemy of the people. He resigned from the party and the newspaper, hoping to save his colleagues and Trentino Catholics from further harassment, but even that did not help.

As the terror spread, many fled abroad. But De Gasperi, wishing to stay close to his countrymen, took refuge in the far northern Valley of Sugana. Here, he was also hoping to meet the Liberal opposition leader Giovanni Amendola. But when he heard that Mussolini's *Squadristi* were nearby, he wrote to warn him to stay away.[344] But De Gasperi's warning came too late. Amendola was arrested, beaten mercilessly by the Black Shirts, and died of his injuries. Shortly after, De Gasperi and his brother were arrested in the dead of night, by two plain-clothed officers, and taken south to Vicenza for questioning. In a bizarre twist, they were rescued by a wealthy local industrialist who was also a parliamentary member of the Fascist party. He removed them for 'further questioning' to his home near Valdagno and then, a few days later, took them in his own car to the train station in Verona. They took a train to Milan and hid there for a few months.

But Alcide De Gasperi and Francesca were arrested a second time on 11th March, 1925, on a train near Orvieto. The next day, on express orders of *Il Duce*, they were taken to Rome where they were separated and interred in the Regina Coeli prison. Mussolini told the press to suppress the case, and a trial was set for 24th April, where (although no evidence of this existed) he was found guilty of attempting to flee the country. Francesca was released to return to her daughters in Valsugana; but Alcide was given a four-year jail sentence and a 20,000 Lire fine. On appeal, it was reduced to a two-year sentence and 16,000 Lire fine, but it was still a sum that would surpass the total value of all he owned.

From prison, looking over the letters from Francesca and the photos she had sent of the girls, he knew he had come as low as a man could. He was a minister without portfolio, a prophet without a voice, a husband without a wife, a father without his children, and with no way to support them. Many friends had deserted him too, but not the lively northern prelate Celestino Endrici. The Bishop of Trentino interceded with the King, and De Gasperi was eventually moved from the prison to house arrest at the Hotel Santa Chiara, near the Pantheon. Because he gained the trust of his captors, he was permitted to receive Francesca's letters. Eventually, she was also able to visit him. He inwardly wrestled with the sacrifice his career had imposed on her. 'It was my conscience that imposed it,' he wrote to her, 'my convictions, my dignity, self-respect, and loyalty to my flag and to my life.'

These years were ones of poverty, though not despair. From here he was able, even under police surveillance, to write anti-government articles under the pseudonym of "Jasper". He was still in a desert place, but now at least he was a prophet crying out in the wilderness – he had recovered his voice. He also prayed and read the Bible a lot during this period. He not only wrote much to his wife but also helped his captors write letters to their loved ones too.

After sixteen months at Santa Chiara, his loneliness eventually came to an end and he was again free. Although he would not be allowed to live in Trentino, he was granted special permission to visit there for a month on his release. On arriving, it broke his heart afresh that Lucia, his three-year-old daughter did not even recognise him. The month passed all too quickly, and as the autumn of 1928 fell, he returned to Rome once more with a heavy heart. He picked up casual work, translating, but was otherwise forced upon the charity of his friends. This increased solitude and uncertainty forced him back further on his spiritual resources. He dug deeper into his Christian faith.

On Christmas 1929, he recalled a particular moment of comfort, which in hindsight was like a beacon in the rough seas of that time. He went up onto the dome of Saint Peter's and looked out over the city. At that moment, he felt a deep sense that his life had not been in vain, that there was indeed a larger Christian story unfolding in which he – although penniless and despised – nevertheless had a central part. For him, Saint Peter's was the epicentre of the Christian community and the mainspring of a universal hope for Europe being torn apart by sin.

In 1929, after eighteen months living hand to mouth, he was eventually given a job in the Vatican archives, through the persuasions of his friend Endrici,[345] preparing a catalogue of Catholic publications. It was a menial job for a man who had been one of the key political actors in Italy, but as a husband and a father, De Gasperi had finally regained a means to support those he loved. After 18 months alone and trying to secure an income, he was now able to send north for his family. The wage allowed the family to move with him into a very small apartment. Mussolini was furious and asked the pope 'as an act of courtesy' to sack De Gasperi.

The Vatican's magnificent reply was curt:

'What you ask as an act of courtesy on our part would in fact be an act of meanness and complete incomprehension.... As far as De Gasperi is concerned, the Holy Father neither regrets nor will regret having given an honest man and good father of a family that bread which you have taken away from him.'

He stayed at the Vatican for the next fourteen years, in which time he was also able to study and write under the pseudonym of *Spectator* in an international Catholic publication. These articles were read all over the world.

The 1920s and 1930s were thus a time of great trial for De Gasperi and his young family. But they were also years where he could hone and cement his political thought. He studied the biographies and writings of those who had translated the Christian ethos into political and social action. In his difficulties, like Schuman and their German counterpart, Adenauer, he was digging a deep well ready for the time when Europe would need fresh water. After ten years, De Gasperi was appointed Secretary of the Vatican Library. Even as Hitler planned his invasion of

Poland, De Gasperi's family, now including four daughters, were able to move to a larger apartment in Via Bonifacio VIII. The following June, Mussolini declared war on France and Britain from the balcony at the Piazza Venezia while the crowds shouted, 'Duce, duce, duce.'

Two years later, after a time of nervous exhaustion, De Gasperi was made the leader of a new *Democratzia Christiana* party. It was like snowdrops breaking through the snow, with a long winter still before them. Italy, no less than France and Germany, would need brand new political parties after

Mussolini, Palazzo Venezia, Rome

the war, for the old parties had either compromised, capitulated, or been complicit in gross injustice and even genocide. Where would the mainspring for this vital resurgence come from? As the Italian government voted to abandon democracy, Hitler's *coup d'état* in Munich failed. He was sentenced to five years in prison but was released after only eight months.

In 1924, as Hitler walked free again, Schuman was enjoying his second term as MP for Moselle. In May, a leftist coalition came to power and tried to impose a secular education – which France then had – over the recovered departments of Alsace and Lorraine. Schuman saw that Conservatives held 21 of the 24 seats here and therefore it was appropriate and legitimate to resist this republican secularism. He united with different Christian and Jewish groups to successfully save religious education in his region.

This was the year that the US withdrew from the Rhineland, and the Reichsmark was established, Germany declared a policy of passive resistance against the French army, who still occupied Karlsruhe, Darmstadt, and Mannheim. It is also the year in which Lenin died and Stalin arose; when the Fascist 'elections' returned a 65% vote to Mussolini; and when the Dawes Report warned the League of Nations to scrap German War Reparations. The clock was already ticking.

Like De Gasperi, Schuman was developing and honing his political thought. The 'war' had not yet come to his door, but it was coming. Schuman was convinced that Democracy owed its,

'...existence to Christianity. It was born the day man was required to set the best example, during his life on earth (i.e., by respecting human dignity, individual rights and freedom and by exercising brotherly love towards his neighbour.) Before Christ, such ideas had never existed. [346]

This was ground zero for Christians like De Gasperi and Schuman: that the supposed *religion of man* was a rootless sham; that Europe was in the process of forsaking a living spring for a polluted pool downstream of the Christian tradition.

This will strike the secular reader as a very narrow view, but the most robust sociological analysis of the last 50 years is now firmly establishing the correlation between evangelical Christianity and democracy. Robert Woodberry's colossal research programme – he had 50 research assistants, lucky fellow – suggests that half a decade's post-war research into the rise of democracy had overlooked the most crucial and pervasive factor. It turns out now that the most despised and misrepresented of stereotypes – the 19th century protestant, conversionary missionary – was the single biggest factor in generating stable democracy overseas.

'Pull out a map,' says Woodberry in effect, and stick a pin in any place where 19th century "conversionary Protestants" had been active, and 'you will typically find more printed books and more schools per capita. You'll find, too, that in Africa, the Middle East, and parts of Asia, most of the early nationalists who led their countries to independence graduated from Protestant mission schools.' On average those areas are more economically developed, enjoy better health, lower infant mortality, less corruption, higher literacy, greater educational attainment (most notably in women) than those that only had state-funded or non-conversionary missionaries. 'One of the main stereotypes about missions is that they were closely connected to colonialism,' says Woodberry. 'But Protestant missionaries not funded by the state were regularly very critical of colonialism.' Woodberry's 14-year research programme was published in 2012 in the American Political Science Review, entitled, *The Missionary Roots of Liberal Democracy.*[347] Philip Jenkins, professor of history at Baylor University said, 'Try as I might to pick holes in it, the theory holds up.' The evidence overseas is compelling, even to the sceptic.

And according to Tom Holland's *Dominion – How Christianity made the Western Mind,* the culturally subconscious effects of Christianity was an effective solvent of colonial power.

'Repeatedly, whether crashing through the canals of Tenochtitlan, or settling the estuaries of Massachusetts, or trekking deep into the Transvaal, the confidence that had enabled Europeans to believe themselves superior to those they were displacing was derived from Christianity. Repeatedly, though . . . it was Christianity that . . . provided the colonized and the enslaved with the surest voice. The paradox was profound. No other conquerors, carving out empires for themselves, had done so as the servants of a man tortured to death on the orders of a colonial official. No other conquerors . . . had installed . . . an emblem of power so deeply ambivalent as to render problematic the very notion of power.'

But what about nearer to home? It appears now, as it ever was in post-Enlightenment Europe; we wanted the fruit without the root. In Schuman's day, they were paying a terrible price. Schuman quotes the Catholic philosopher Maritain *'nothing is easier for political counterfeiters than to deceive people with good principles and nothing is more appalling than good principles when they are put into practice the wrong way.'* Maritain had built a system, which he believed trustworthy, and which accorded with both Natural Law plus divine revelation. He wrote that 'a political philosophy based on reality must struggle against ...an optimistic pseudo-idealism, extending from Rousseau to Lenin, which feeds men with false hopes...'

Because he was so influential on Schuman and De Gasperi, and because there was no room to quote him more in chapter 5, let us hear Maritain from his books *Christianity and Democracy* and *The Rights of Man and Natural Law*. When it came to understanding Natural Law, Maritain was keen to differentiate the 'rationalism of the Encyclopaedists' from that of the Classical and Christian tradition. The Enlightenment thinkers had been too quick to discard natural law as the 'offspring of creative wisdom' in their haste to claim it as the autonomous 'revelation of reason unto itself.' Maritain's taxonomy is seen more fully below:

'The idea of natural law is a heritage of Christian and classical thought. It does not go back to the philosophy of the eighteenth century, which more or less deformed it, but rather to Grotius, and before him to Suarez and Francisco de Vitoria; and further back to St. Thomas Aquinas; and still further back to St. Augustine and the Church Fathers and St. Paul; and even further back to Cicero, to the Stoics, to the great moralists of antiquity and its great poets, particularly Sophocles. Antigone is the eternal heroine of natural law, which the Ancients called the unwritten law, and this is the name most befitting it.'

His allusion to Sophocles' play Antigone is interesting and helpful, as it shows the tension between natural law and positive (man-made) law, at a much earlier stage in our cultural evolution. This is an old quarrel, not a post-Enlightenment one, and it is one that Sophocles and Maritain believe is already won. The struggle between Creon and Antigone is, in essence, the conflict that exists between natural law and the artificial, man-made law. Maritain concludes:

'The great philosophers of antiquity knew, Christian thinkers know even better, that nature comes from God and that the unwritten law comes from the eternal law which is Creative Wisdom itself.

That is why the idea of natural law or the unwritten law was linked for them to a sentiment of natural piety, to that profound and sacred respect unforgettably expressed by Antigone. Because they understand the real principle of this law, belief in it is firmer and more unshakable in those who believe in God than in the others. Belief in human nature and in the freedom of the human being, however, is in itself sufficient to convince us that there is an unwritten law, and to assure us that natural law is something as real in the moral realm as the laws of growth and senescence [aging] in the physical.'

Following closely to Maritain, Schuman's conclusion, like Bergson's, was that *'democracy is essentially Evangelic, since love is its mainspring.'* By writing this, Schuman does not mean only Christians will necessarily be democrats, but that 'all other things being equal, if he is to be logically consistent, the Christian will be a democrat and the non-Christian democrat can never provide a coherent and adequate rational basis for his political principles.'[348] But, Maritain stressed,

'...the solution of the crisis of civilization is by no means to pretend that Christianity is linked to democracy and that Christian faith compels every believer to be a democrat; it is to affirm that democracy is linked to Christianity and that the democratic impulse has arisen in human history as a temporal manifestation of the inspiration of the Gospel.'

Not all this book's readers will find that statement compelling but let us hold the thought at least for now. Their generation were dogmatists (no less than ours) but perhaps they had come by their dogmatism honestly in the great fires of those times. Schuman wrote, much later in life when he was one of the most celebrated politicians of his generation:

'...democracy will be Christian or it will not be. An anti-Christian democracy would be a parody which would sink into tyranny or into an-

archy … Without being unjust or self-damaging the state cannot ignore
the extraordinary effectiveness of religious inspiration in the practice of
civic duty and in protecting people against the forces of social disintegra-
tion which are at work everywhere.'

How strange his certainty seems now when Christianity is almost
only ever in the public eye in connection with obscurantism and hate
speech. But how prophetic his words are too when the spectre of
tyranny and *anarchy* looms on the fringes of political life. How far away
lie Schuman's cherished hope that *'after the old quarrels* (of church and
state) *have been put to rest and mistrust dissipated, the time will come*
when relations between religion and the democratic state will be estab-
lished on new foundations which are respectful of individual freedom and
responsibilities.' Yet, he was never trying to re-establish Christendom or
any sort of Catholic Theocracy, for those lessons had been long learned.

'Although we can find deep traces of Christian ideas in today's political
life, Christianity is not and must not integrate into a political system;
it must not be identified with any form of government, however demo-
cratic it might be. Considering this point, we must distinguish between
what belongs to Caesar and what belongs to God. Each of these powers
has its own responsibilities.… However, no conflict involving these two
requirements is unsolvable, since one is an immutable doctrine of prin-
ciples and the other implies wise administration of changing situations
that have to be considered in the lives and populations of individuals.
Theocracy underrates the principle of the separation between the two do-
mains. It would have the religious principle shoulder the burden of irre-
sponsible acts for which it is absolutely not responsible.' [349]

Here is, an anti-theocratic statement to cheer the hearts of secular
readers. Here we can also see perhaps the thinking of an early 20th century Dutch Prime Minister, called Abraham Kuyper. Kuyper's Neo-
Calvinist political thought on 'Sphere Sovereignty' was formed in
response to what he called the revolutionary spirit of French secularism

in the late 19th century. He was politicized as a home-schooling father, afraid, even as far back as 1870, of overbearing, paternalistic, big-state interference in education. He reached out toward Catholics and together they formed the Anti-Revolutionary Party (ARP) which eventually came to power.

Kuyper's 'Sphere Sovereignty, 'also known as differentiated responsibility, is the concept that each sphere (or sector) of life has its own distinct responsibilities and authority or competence, and stands equal to other spheres of life. Sphere sovereignty involves the idea of an all-encompassing created order, designed and governed by God. This created order includes societal communities (such as those for purposes of education, worship, civil justice, agriculture, economy and labour, marriage and family,

Abraham Kuyper

artistic expression, etc.), their historical development, and their abiding norms. The principle of sphere sovereignty seeks to affirm and respect creational boundaries, and historical differentiation.'350

Kuyper was a pastor who fought hard for the disentangling of an interfering state and a privilege-addicted state church. He understood how divisive the unholy alliance was for both sides. The Christians of today, as much as in Kuyper's day, have every reason to acknowledge with repentance, the knock-on societal effects of an unlived Christianity. Christians found an easy analogy in that day, as they do in our day, with the Biblical record of the Jewish nation. The church, like the Old Testament Jews, had fallen into Constantinian idolatry. As the Jews had been exiled into Babylon in the 5th century, so the satiate church was being chastised for her infidelities by the overbearing 'Nebuchadnezzar' of secularism.

The Jews returned from their exile to Jerusalem after 70 years, never again to worship the idols of Baal or Ashtoreth or Molech. Here the historical analogy breaks down, as the church was only just going into her exile as the new ideologies took hold in Europe. She could not mount a significant counterpoint to the 'predominant spirit of advanced modernity'[351] before or after the wars. Many, like Bonhoeffer, felt that it was because the church had drunk too deeply of the same wine. And little wonder, he had seen the German church, much weakened by 19th century biblical 'higher criticism', going over almost wholesale to Hitler. But that does not mean there was not spirited and meaningful resistance there and elsewhere. This book hopes to highlight this in areas not normally discussed. In the age of fanatical ideology, Schuman *et al* were the vanguard of genuine change, but also moderation. Democracy would almost always involve 'finding proximate solutions to insoluble problems.'[352] It was, as Churchill said, 'the worst form of government apart from all the others' – as we have said elsewhere, a medicine, not a wine.

Nietzsche's *firstlings of the twentieth century* were trying to use politics to achieve their *Higher History* – a means of secular salvation. But politics is at best, as Otto von Bismarck said, 'the art of the possible, the attainable – the art of the next best.' Schuman saw the subtle checks and balances in the western democratic tradition as a unique and a precious thing, not least in the way that it affected the psychology of its incipients. It was most important, Schuman said that: *'Democracy cannot be improvised; it took a thousand years of Christianity to fashion it. In Africa, we have been forced to skip one or two stages. Not only did we sometimes give an illiterate population a ballot paper, but, more seriously, we left office to men who had no experience of it and who were defenceless against the temptations of arbitrary injustice.'*

1930-1939 - THE FRIGHTENING THIRTIES

But, let us return to the chronology of those pivotal years. A quick spin through the years will help us enter into the scene a bit. By 1928 Allied Military control of Germany was already a memory. Germany had been a member of the League of Nations for two years. It is the year that Schuman is elected MP for the constituency of Thionville East; that the German economy crashes on Black Friday; that Socialists riot in Vienna after fascist murderers are acquitted, and when Dr. Joseph Goebbels is named Nazi *Gauleiter* of Berlin. Ominous signs of things to come.

The question asked by successive generations has been, how could Germans have succumbed to Nazi usurpation. We have noted already the resentment over the Versailles treaty and the convenient conspiracy theory of Jewish collusion. But perhaps it is harder to give a sense of the poverty among all classes at that time. When the poor lose everything, their life and nation change little. But when the middle class loses everything, their lives and the life of the nation is drastically altered. With the Weimar Republic, 'a massive void had been created in the German nation, with the de-legitimisation of institutions. The Left held them in contempt because the institutions had plunged them into the war. The centre was exhausted... and cynical. The Right thought it could resurrect the monarchy and aristocracy.'[353] 'Blood, race, and myth filled the space left by collapsed institutions. They swept aside the exhausted centre and the impotent Weimar Republic.'[354]

In 1929 Schuman began a decade as a member, and later secretary, of the French Finance Commission. Himmler was appointed by Hitler as Reichsfuhrer S.S. A year later, just as the last allied troops were leaving the Rhineland and Saar region, the Nazis gained a further 107 seats from other parties in the national elections.

In 1932, when Schuman was re-elected MP for the constituency of Thionville East, matters over the border were coming to a head. In the German elections, Hindenburg got 18 million votes; Hitler's Nazi party, 11 million; the Communists, 5 million. But in the Reichstag elections, the Nazis won 230 seats, the Socialists, 133, the *Zentrum* 'Centre' party, a mere 97; and the Communists, 89. Hitler refused Hindenburg's offer to be vice chancellor – a year later he would get the top job anyway. Worst of all, this was the year when the Marxist experiments in collectivisation would crush the Russian peasantry. Even as Stalin rolled out his second Five Year Plan, he would be complicit in the deaths of four million Ukrainians.[355] Stalinist schemes for 'the transformation of nature' were as blind to the geographical as they were to the social realities.

And then in 1933 came news of the infamous Reichstag Fire; Goebbels was appointed minister of propaganda, Herman Goering named Prussian Prime minister; Hitler was granted dictatorial powers.

All other political parties were suppressed. German labour unions were suppressed too, and boycotts of Jews began in Germany. Even Modernist art was suppressed in favour of superficial realism. Hitler was a good painter and his hatred of modernist art was not without foundation, but once again by enforcing a solution from the political sphere, he was tackling culture against its natural flow. His preference for the veneer of superficial realism in painting could stand for much else in Germany under his iron fist. In the same year, the Nazis won the Danzig elections. As 92% of the German electorate voted for them, it marks the start of 60,000 emigrations of artists and performers from Germany.

But to read the British newspapers of 1933 and 1934, and considering the ideology and methods of the Nazis, it is absolutely astounding how little insight existed in Fleet Street and Whitehall. The exasperated George Orwell even asked, perhaps unfairly, 'what was it that made every British statesman do the wrong thing with such unnerving instinct?'[356] Even as early as this, the first concentration camps were already being built. In the next 12 years, 8-11 million people will enter them – most never to leave. How apt that this is the year that Carl. G. Jung, who himself almost became a Nazi, wrote about 'modern man in search of a soul.' In Germany, as in Italy, they were going mad in herds.

In 1935, even as the Communist show trials were beginning, the USSR was admitted to the League of Nations. A year later, in the Great Purge, somewhere between 600,000 to 1,750,000 people would die at the hands of the Stalin-led Soviet government. The fact that the numbers will never truly be known was indicative also of how insignificant human life had become. 'What is one generation?' said Stalin later to Churchill. Often mobile gas-chamber vàns were used to deliver on the spot 'justice'. And this was just a purge of fellow communists – co-seekers of a socialist utopia. The Anglo-American historian Robert Conquest suggests the number could be closer to 2 million. For an amoral atheistic religion that sought to set mankind free from the evils of religion, it was only the meagre beginning.

These initial deaths were less than one percent of the number who would have to be sacrificed before that utopia would be revealed as an illusion. Half a century before, Nietzsche had exclaimed, perhaps even with hope, 'how much must collapse now that this faith has been undermined.' He and many like his generation thought that they had been digging in a garden when all along they had been in a boat. Like Hitler, Stalin was a soldier leading a generation of soldiers who had been brutalised by industrial scale war. He was that most frightening of spectacles; the soldier turned dictator riding rails laid down by intellectuals with such a single-minded focus that even his first allies were eventually appalled – or, more usually, executed.

In 1936 the year started with Germany hosting the Winter Olympics. Schuman was elected General Councillor for the Cattenom region, just as a resurgent Germany was repudiating the Treaty of Versailles and introducing compulsory military service. Hitler's original conspiracy theories were made legal, embodied in the Nuremberg Laws against the Jews. German troops began to seize and occupy the Rhineland. With 99% of the electoral vote, Hitler published his Four-Year Plan and put Goring in charge of implementation. All 8-10-year olds were forced to join the Hitler Youth, and the summer Olympic Games were held in Berlin.

The Spanish Civil War also began in this year when a failed right-wing coup led to Republican bloodletting of between 38,000 to 172,344 people. With what horror must Schuman have received the news that among the Red Terror's victims were almost 7000 priests and nuns – their churches and monasteries looted and burned? One republican justified the action: 'these burnings were the *auto-da-fé* necessary for the progress of civilisation.' The homeland of the Inquisition ran again with blood, as the republicans proved themselves quite the equal of the loathsome 16th century Dominican Tomás de Torquemada. As Milton remarked, '*new presbyter is but old priest writ large.*'

This year was also a dark time in other parts of Europe as economies tumbled. The Franc and Lira were both devalued. Mussolini and Hitler formed what became known as the Berlin Axis. And Mussolini, not content with doing one country's worth of mischief, decided also to invade Abyssinia. In the next two years, the force of events would seem only too inevitable. Schuman watched as Germany broke its treaties and annexed its neighbours' land.

We have seen briefly in the chapter how the new ideologies led whole nations over a precipice. But under the layers of lies and inflamed hatreds, Schuman held tightly to a more certain knowledge that the Germans were not monsters. For him, the Christian doctrine of the *Imageo Dei* – that great lever which liberated the ancient world – was not just the source of solidarity between all people, but also a source of hope for the future. All the ideologies that sundered Germany, Russia, and Italy at root denied the spiritual aspect of man's nature, and so Schuman realised they would all fail. And when they did, France must be ready to lead Europe to a new future by extending that final act of love – forgiveness.[357] But that was still five exhausting years away.

Schuman's rise had been seamless. He had played such a significant role in harmonizing the French Civil and Commercial codes within the formerly German Alsace-Lorraine region, that it became known as "Lex Schuman."[358] He also became something of a champion of justice when he patiently investigated and uncovered corruption in, not only in the Lorraine steel industries but also the Alsace and Lorraine railways. Both had been purchased – the word Schuman actually used in Parliament was 'pillaged'– for a ridiculously small sum by the powerful and influential de Wendel family.[359] The quiet lawyer didn't mind stepping into the bear pit to face down the rich. He was fast becoming a people's champion. For those with eyes to see, there was a powerful focus to this young man, a tenacity and visionary thirst for justice. So far, he had not put a foot wrong.

As we have seen, the great trial of his childhood was the loss of a father; of his university days, the inexplicable loss of his mother; his early professional days, the furnace of warfare. And now in middle years, the greatest trial of his character and career lay before him. But would the years after 1939 confirm, strengthen, and reveal strength and virtue, or would he, like so many others capitulate to brute necessity? The sifting of Robert Schuman will be the subject of chapter 10, the sifting of Columban will be the subject of our next chapter.

SCHUMAN: who foresaw the Nazi collapse and planned for Franco-German reconciliation

Hitler in Paris after the French capitulation

CHAPTER 8
FOOTNOTES &REFERENCES

314. Clemenceau more than any other voice, drove the theme of fiscal vengeance. The French sought by international treaty what they could not themselves maintain by force of arms. The British, by comparison would have been happy merely to castrate Germany's naval capability.

315. One must remember the sort of terms that the Germans themselves would have forced Europe to accept if they had won. The American historian Victor Davis Hanson argues that the real mistake was the negligence of the allied powers to occupy Germany in 1918 and enforce the Weimar Republic.

316. Hitler received the Iron Cross, First Class on 4 August 1918, a decoration rarely awarded to one of his Gefreiter rank.

317. The conservative US military historian and classicist, Victor Davis Hanson, is refreshingly pro-British.

318. President of the Council for General Affairs linked to administration, legislation, and security.

319. Keynes also published 'The Economic Consequences of Peace'

320. This would be the subject of analysis in C. S. Lewis' Newcastle lectures, which eventually became the book, 'The Abolition of Man'. (See chapter 19 of this book)

321. Sue Prideaux's new 464p biography of Nietzsche called I am Dynamite! was published by Faber in 2018.

322. G.K. Chesterton, 'The Common Man.'

323. 1 John 4:3

324. *Pour L'Europe,* P. 44

325. Dwight D. Eisenhower, Inaugural Address (1953)

326. Many conservative writers feel they are living through an era when the postmodern writings of people like Sartre and Foucault are breaking forth into the mainstream; most notably in issues surrounding gender, sexuality, and race. Apart from the sheer speed with which the new orthodoxies have established themselves in the gateways of power, what strikes the observer as unusual, or at least noteworthy, is the amnesia that attends each movement. Just when post-modernism as an 'ism' is finding its cultural outworking, no one is talking about it anymore.

327. In his book 'Hope in Troubled Times,' the Dutch philosopher politician Bob Gouzwaard gives many modern examples in the East and West. There is a chapter on Islamism viewed as a thoroughly modern response to modernity (i.e., post-enlightenment, man-centered). There is also a chapter on the ideology of Wealth: of financial growth and the resulting paradoxes that arise in income inequality, care, time, environment (p87) globalisation, (p 158), commercialisation, the shifts in the financial markets, and vital interests p93, free markets, and competition p.94. I was privileged to have the then octogenarian philosopher-statesman compliment me on my 2012 Ruskin lecture at the Vrije University in Amsterdam. I repeat what I say in the first appendix; I suspect the Dutch are really too tolerant!

328. Fascism may have been constitutional, but as we will see in later chapters, it quickly moved to suppression by extra-judicial means. 329. An good modern example of 'absurdities' and 'de facto' ideals, was given by Andrew Bosworth, one of Facebook's vice presidents, when he sent an internal memo after the 2016 Cambridge Analytica data breach, in which he wrote, 'Maybe it costs a life by exposing someone to bullies. Maybe someone dies in a terrorist attack coordinated by our tools. And still, we connect people. The ugly truth is that we believe in connecting people so deeply that anything that allows us to connect more people is *de facto* good.'

330. Henri Bergson, *The Meaning of the War: Life and Matter in Conflict.* This was a lecture delivered by M. Bergson as President of the Académie des Sciences Morales et Politiques at its annual public meeting on December 12, 1914. To enlarge my point slightly I include another quote from the same lecture. 'So, too, in most cases, doctrines are the means by which nations and individuals seek to explain what they are and what they do. Germany, having finally become a predatory nation, invokes Hegel as witness; just as a Germany enamoured of moral beauty would have declared herself faithful to Kant, just as a sentimental Germany would have found her tutelary genius in Jacobi or Schopenhauer. Had she leaned in any other direction and been unable to find at home the philosophy she needed; she would have procured it from abroad. Thus, when she wished to convince herself that predestined races exist, she took from France, that she might hoist him into celebrity, a writer whom we have not read—Gobineau.'

331. I use the word 'settled' here as this is precisely how eugenic science was seen in the mid-thirties in Germany. It is a provocative word when wrongly applied to the sciences which often lack systems of external verification.

332. Nietzsche, like Hitler, was a devotee of Wagner. For a short while, Wagner used the young Nietzsche for menial tasks, like buying his silk underwear. They eventually fell out when Wagner suggested that his protégé's failing eyesight might be due to excessive masturbation.

333. Poet Carl Sandburg might have had Hitler and Mussolini in mind when he said this.

334. The study (cited below) could arguably be repulsed as a view typical of the Neo-Liberal takeover of the UN, but I add it here as a relevant and credible source. A 2018 study published in the journal Royal Society Open Science claimed that even the 'residual effect' of Communism in former eastern bloc countries was still apparent in lower life expectancies, poorer diets, levels of alcoholism, wealth and health, etc. The studies, which focus on 44 countries across Europe and Asia, examined many variables (religion, systems of governance, geography, time in education, language, etc.) through the lens of the UN Human Development Index Score and found that whether a country was or used to be Communist was the overwhelming factor in predicting national flourishing or lack thereof.

335. Nikolai Alexandrovich Berdyaev, *The Russian Revolution* (London: Sheed & Ward, 1931) p.60

336. Scott Lingenfelter, *The Dangerous God*, p.30 (Northern Illinois University Press 2017, general editor Dominic Erdozain)

337. Clifford Hill, *The Day Comes.* P.234

338. Norman Davies, *Europe, a history.* P.1076

339. We must remember that Italy had only become a nation just before his birth. Gasperi also claimed that, in the case of a referendum, 90% of the people of Trentino would nevertheless choose the popular Austrian emperor Franz Joseph I of Austria over Italy. (Wiki)

340. Popular Political Union of Trentino (Italian: Unione Politica Popolare del Trentino – UPPT)

341. Victoria Martin De La Torre, *Europe, A Leap into the Unknown.*

342. My sources for this section are Keyserlingk's *Fathers of Europe*, and Victoria Martin De La Torre, *Europe, A Leap into the Unknown.*

343. We see a similar social contract acted out today in Russia and Turkey. After this happens, a long and difficult road awaits those nations. As Stalin reportedly once said, 'It is not the vote that counts, but the one who counts the vote.'

344. Amendola had courageously exposed Mussolini's complicity in the murder of the Socialist Party leader, Giacomo Matteotti, and he was on their most wanted list.

345. The Library is located inside the Vatican Palace, and the entrance is through the Belvedere Courtyard. When Pope Sixtus V (1585-1590) commissioned the expansion and the new building of the Vatican Library, he had a three-story wing built right across Bramante's Cortile del Belvedere, thus bisecting it and changing Bramante's work significantly. At the bottom of a grand staircase, a large statue of Hippolytus decorates the La Galea entrance hall. In the first semi-basement, there is a papyrus room and a storage area for manuscripts. (Wiki)

346. Robert Schuman, *Pour L'Europe*, P. 43

347. https://www.cambridge.org/core/journals/american-political-science-review/article/the-missionary-roots-of-liberaldemocracy/3D96CF5CB2F7FEB19B1835393D084B9A

348. Alan Paul Fimister Robert Schuman. Neo-scholastic humanism and the reunification of Europe. Brussels: P.I.E. Peter Lang, 2008.

349. Robert Schuman, *Pour l'Europe*

350. 'Sphere sovereignty implies that no one area of life or societal community is sovereign over another. Each sphere has its own created integrity. Neo-Calvinists hold that since God created everything "after its own kind," diversity must be acknowledged and appreciated. For instance, the different God-given norms for family life and economic life should be recognized, such that a family does not properly function as a business. Similarly, neither faith-institutions (e.g., churches) nor an institution of civil justice (i.e., the state) should seek totalitarian control,

or any regulation of human activity outside their limited competence, respectively. The concept of sphere sovereignty became a general principle in European countries governed by Christian democratic political parties, who held it as an integral part of their ideology. The promotion of sphere sovereignty by Christian democrats led to the creation of corporatist welfare states throughout the world. (Source Wikipedia: https://en.wikipedia.org/wiki/Sphere_sovereignty)

351. This was the call of Alasdair MacIntyre in the preface to the 25th anniversary edition of *After Virtue*

352. Reinhold Niebuhr (2010). *"The Irony of American History"*, p.13, University of Chicago Press

353. George Friedman, *Flashpoints – The Emerging Crisis in Europe*, Doubleday p.74

354. Ibid

355. Like the Armenian genocide, this is still re-labelled as a natural disaster by people like Putin who want to keep Stalin as a 'great Russian figurehead.' The recent book *'Red Famine: Stalin's War on Ukraine'*, by Anne Applebaum (2017) tells a story so shocking and tragic that the pages can hardly hold the weight of it.

356. George Orwell, *The Lion and the Unicorn - Socialism and the English Genius* (London, 1941) But Churchill and Baldwin were perhaps the more obvious exceptions to Orwell's question. After Ramsay MacDonald stepped down from the National government, Stanley Baldwin purposely kept Churchill out of his cabinet. In a move of foresight and brilliance, and even as he himself was preparing for his own departure from political life (1937), the exhausted Baldwin seeded the idea to his colleagues that Churchill should be kept fresh as a wartime leader. Even Chamberlain and his small piece of paper, which he got Hitler to sign quite by surprise, are not quite what they first appear when viewed with impartial study.

357. A phrase used by the theologian Reinhold Niebuhr

358. "Conférence à l'occasion du 60e anniversaire de la Déclaration Schuman: Fondation d'une gouvernance en Europe – Europa forum Luxembourg". www.europaforum.public.lu

359. Lejeune, René (2000). *Robert Schuman, Père de l'Europe*. Paris: Fayard. p. 98. ISBN 9782213606354.

Stalin's genocide by starvation in Ukraine took 7-10 million between 1932-3

CHAPTER 9

Columban: Midlife Mission

CHAPTER SUMMARY – ASSESSING THE IRISH CONTRI-
BUTION - Brief survey of early Irish missionaries, their dispersions,
and influence. FIRST LANDING IN BRITTANY - A brief survey
of 'Dark Age' Brittany and an attempt, from the sources and personal visits, to understand where Columban landed. THE
FRANKS: OUR SORT OF BARBARIAN - The achievements and
depredations of the Frankish kings, queens, and clerics. FIRST
THREE MONASTERIES - Columban's triumphs and tragedies,
and what his movement represented then and now. Reflections on
modern entertainment culture and medical healing practices.
Columban is imprisoned and awaits extradition.

*'Be helpful in humbleness and most lowly in authority. Be simple in faith,
but well trained in manners; demanding in your own affairs, but uncon-
cerned in those of others. Be guileless in friendship, astute in the face of deceit,
tough in time of ease, tender in hard times. Keep your options open when
there is no trouble but dig in when you must choose. Be pleasant when things
are unpleasant ... disagree when necessary, but be in agreement about truth
...be strong in trials and weak in dissensions.*

Be slow to anger, quick to learn, also slow to speak. Be up and doing to make progress, slack to take revenge, careful in word, eager in work. Be friendly with men of honour, stiff with rascals, gentle with the weak. Firm with the stubborn, steadfast to the proud, humble to the lowly. Be ever sober, ever chaste, ever modest. Be patient as far as is compatible with zeal, never greedy, always generous, if not in money, then in spirit. Be timely in fasting, timely in night offices, discreet in duty, persistent in study, unshaken in turmoil, joyful in suffering, valiant in the course of truth, cautious in time of strife. Be submissive to good, unbending to evil, gentle in generosity, untiring in love and gentle in all things.

Be respectful to the worthy, merciful to the poor. Be mindful of favours, unmindful of wrongs. Be a lover of the ordinary person, and do not wish for riches, but cool down excitement and speak your mind. Obey your seniors, keep up with your juniors, equal your equals, emulate the perfect. Don't envy your betters, or grieve at those who surpass you, or censure those that fall behind, but agree with those who urge you on. Though weary, do not give up. Weep and rejoice at the one time out of zeal and hope.'

Columban's Sermon 6. *(Letter to a Young Disciple)*

FIRST LANDING IN BRITTANY

Columban's advice, reading like a forerunner of Kipling's *Desideratum*, was in a letter to a younger disciple. If applied for 'home-use,' it would serve us all well, not least Columban as he entered the bear pit - lands of the Franks.

As we saw, two chapters ago, Columban had, along with twelve others, undertaken the ultimate sacrifice: White Martyrdom, *'peregrinatio pro christo'*, (travelling abroad for Christ) upon the white tipped waves. They had forgone the comforts of the cloister and the rights of their people; firstly, for their own souls' sake, but then also to save the disadvantaged 'Europeans'. They would be as Abraham – strangers in a strange land. Landless and 'right-less' wanderers on the earth. They were not the first, for Columbkille (Columba of Iona) and Moulag had already gone north to the Picts, and they would certainly not be the last. But from humble beginnings, an unexpected stream began to flow. 'The physical scale of the beehive hermitages... may sometimes be modest, but their significance for the survival of civilisation in the Isles was vast.'[360] So, it is worth giving a few details about this stream, that eventually became a river, before moving on to consider Columban and the Franks.[361]

> *We have seen how the Irish enshrined literacy as a central religious discipline and the remarkable benefits that this later conferred on the west. And now we see a similar sacralisation of travel, of exile, of evangelism. As Columban wrote, 'Let us concern ourselves with things divine, and as pilgrims ever sigh for and desire our homeland; for the end of the road is ever the object of travellers' hopes and desires, and thus, since we are travellers and pilgrims in the world, let us ever ponder on the end of the road, that is of our life, for the end of our roadway is our home... Therefore, let this principle abide with us, that on the road we so live as travellers, as pilgrims, as guests of the world.'*

It was this call to be a pilgrim that played upon the imagination of many zealous and great-hearted souls in the Emerald Isle. Brendan, called the Navigator would go to Iceland, others – with no oars but trusting God to guide them – went wherever the tide took them. There is evidence of men and women holding bishoprics and abbacies as far south as the southern tip of Italy, and as far east as Kiev. And everywhere they went, they carried on the same work of praying, praising and teaching. These Johnny-come-latelies to civilisation, these *arrivistas* to literacy and philosophy, grew to be rightly proud of their Island of Saints and Scholars. As one 9th century Irishman would write from the Swiss monastery of St Gallen, *'caelum non animum mutant qui trans mare current'* (They change their sky but not their soul who cross the ocean.) Like Irish immigrants to America and the Navvies in England, they travelled with their own self-assured culture. So many went that Heiric of Auxerre wrote '*almost all of Ireland, despising the sea, is migrating to our shores with a herd of philosophers.*'

As alluded to elsewhere, they helped the emerging medieval European civilisation escape some of the pessimism of late antiquity and perhaps even some of the humourless uniformity of the Roman psyche. 'Wherever they went the Irish brought with them their books, many unseen in Europe for centuries, and tied to their waists as signs of triumph, just as Irish heroes had once tied to their waists their enemies' heads. .... Where they went, they brought their love of learning and their skills in bookmaking. In the bays and valleys of their exile, they re-established literacy and breathed new life into the exhausted literary culture of Europe. And that is how the Irish saved civilization.'[362]

I love the quote above, but I have been cautioned by scholars, who have made this their field of study, not to claim too much for the Irish. As we saw in a previous chapter, so we shall see in this, that there was more continuity on the continent than we might have expected after reading certain books. But neither let us be dragged away by the equal and opposite error of some modern historicism that seeks to marginalise the true and astonishing contributions of the Irish. For wherever they went, their monastic foundations garnered a reputation for learning and virtue. On our own shores: Iona, Lindisfarne, Glastonbury, Whitby are well known. And on the continent, the *Schottenkloster* (Irish Monasteries) of Peronne, Liege, Reichenau, Cologne, Luxeuil, Vienna, Salzburg, Wurzburg, Regensburg, St. Gallen, Bobbio, Fiesole, and two hundred others were established to great acclaim in succeeding centuries. And it is not surprising that the names of Columban and Gall, not to mention Kilian, Vergilius of Salzburg, Donatus of Fiesole, Wilfrid, Willibrord, Suitbert of Kaiserwerdt, Boniface, and Ursicinius of Saint-Ursanne are better known on the continent than in Britain.

As one medieval historian[363] wrote, 'the weight of the Irish influence on the continent is incalculable.' And another, slightly overstating the case, writes, 'it was due to their efforts that the west recovered from largely nihilistic and materialist pagan attitudes and began to benefit from recovered learning.'[364] Columban and the Irish' influence received little or no comment in Gibbon, or the *ancien régime* and indeed, from the entire canon of Enlightenment literature. He did receive some mild attention from Guizot[365] and Michelet[366] in the early years of the 19th century, but no one yet was calling up the ghosts of Irish saints in the fight for Christian civilisation[367] as they would a few decades later. Around 1840, continental scholars like A. F. Ozanam[368] and C. F. R de Montalembert began to assign a grander place for the Irish in the saving of Europe, indeed the latter dedicates twice as many pages to Columbanus as he does to Benedict.[369] Their enthusiasm was picked up by the Protestant Bruno Krusch who opened the fourth volume of his *Monumenta Germaniae Historica* with Jonas' Vita of Columban. From there (this is 1883, around the time of Schuman's birth) the place of the Irish as the saviours of Europe entered a world torn by ideological strife and wars that would have made even Queen Brunhilda - who we will soon meet - pale with terror. The exaggerations are only understandable when we comprehend the tumultuous times in which they took root. Every age seeks its saints according to its need. As we have already said, they look for spiritual expression that most contradicts the spirit of the age. The twentieth century needed the hope of renewal as ballast against great fear of annihilation, and the Irish gave it to them.

Where did Columban make landfall? Later legend says Columban's party may have landed somewhere near modern Saint-Malo in Brittany (known for centuries as a city of corsairs and privateers). Just around the coast, in a sheltered east-facing seaside village called Cancale, there is a granite cross bearing the saint's name to which people once came to pray for rain in times of drought. Ten miles west across the bay are the spires of the world-famous Mont San Michelle, whose first Christian structure was erected a century after Columban landed. And less than two miles west is the village of Saint-Coulomb, which also commemorates him in name. But that, as I say, are all part of a later tradition. If we take Jonas as the most reliable source – and there are no others about this first landing – then the wording 'Britannica arva' ('Breton/ British region) and *sinus Brittanicus* (Breton/British bay) are the words he uses in later to describe the region at the outflow of the Loire. Here, sheltered by the Quiberon peninsula, there is a village, a chapel, and a bay named after Columban. It is just on the coast, near the great Carnac stones, which are the largest pagan sacred space in Europe, possibly the world.

This stretch of the coast seems to have been the religious equivalent of the ex-pat communities of the Algarve and Costa del Sol. A few miles north is the island where Cadoc of LLancarfan - or someone with a similar name - retired. And a few miles down the coast Gildas[370] did the same. Just off the coast on Belle-Ille-en-Mer the 7th century monastery was even called Bangor - presumably twinned with Bangor, Ulster. In fact, a quick glance at any book on Celtic saints will amply show that there was barely a saint from the southwest of Britain who hadn't been to Brittainy and vice versa. One of my favourites is the Welshman Samson of Dol who purchased a chariot in Rome - which is I suppose equivalent to buying a Lamborghini or Ferrari - but only used it to transport his holy books around Brittany, preferring himself to walk.[371]

The *Chapelle de Saint Colomban* in the village of Saint Colomban on raised ground 500 metres from the beach of Saint Colomban would seem to fit the textual evidence better than the places nearer St Malo. The *Chapelle* is ostensibly sixteenth century with some very crude frescoes of that era, showing men in boats. It is situated in the centre of a village at the highest point – for the whole village is in almost a circular formation on a rise of ground. If some archaeologists one day found evidence here of an early monastic settlement I would not be surprised, for everywhere I have travelled from Nendrum in Ireland, Llancarfan in Wales to Annegray in the Vosges, this circular form was the tell-tale clue to an Irish monastery. It constitutes a strong association, but we won't ever know with certainty unless archaeologists dig up some new evidence.

Nor do we even know if Columban built anything in this area. Jonas is not even clear how long Columban stayed in Brittany. He makes it sound like they had just a quick rest and then moved on, but there are so many place names and associations with Columban around the peninsula that many think he might have preached here for some years. The people of this peninsula were Celts who enjoyed many trading and cultural ties to Britain and Ireland. Whatever the reason, Columban's band decided to move over the Villaine River and into Gaul where, Jonas says, they judged the Christian faith was in need of resuscitation.

> 'They wanted zealously and shrewdly to inquire into the disposition of the inhabitants in order to remain longer if they found they could sow the seeds of salvation; or in case they found the hearts of the people in darkness, go on to the nearest nations. Accordingly, they left Brittany and proceeded into the Gallic lands. At that time, either because of the numerous enemies from without, or on account of the carelessness of the bishops, the Christian faith had almost departed from that country. The creed alone remained. But the saving grace of penance and the longing to root out the lusts of the flesh were to be found only in a few. Everywhere that he went the noble man preached the Gospel. And it pleased the people, because his teaching was adorned by eloquence and enforced by examples of virtue.'

THE FRANKS: OUR SORT OF BARBARIAN

It will be hard for us to proceed with Columban further into the Gallo-Roman lands without getting our historical bearings. In chapter 1 we surveyed the reasons for and impact of Rome's collapse. How much was decline and how much fall is area specific. But as we enter that collapsed world we must ask, how quickly did Europe recover? I will give some brief examples from 'The Fall of Rome and the End of Civilisation' by the archaeologist Bryan Ward-Perkins.

Let us start close to home. In all my research, the most striking facts of catastrophic decline are those of Britain, which is apparently always the example *in extremis*. The Britons had been recalcitrant and tacitly unwilling recipients of Roman colonisation in the first place. The Romans viewed us then much as Brussels and London do now. The south they called *Britannica Superior*, the north; *Britannica inferior*[372] and beyond the wall; *Britannica Barbarrica*. Nothing has much changed. In Britannica, the Romans had to wall their towns, unlike on the continent. And here, only around a quarter of the conquered people embraced a Roman identity, which for some might suggest overtones of Brexit. Also, the island absorbed 15% of the empire's military strength for 100 years just to maintain this status quo.[373]

Unlike elsewhere on the continent, their passing left almost no lasting cultural effect except, in the words of one historian, 'a few roads, a few ruins, a few genes, and - as the sole substantial item, not itself Roman in origin - Christianity.'[374] Here, perhaps are the beginnings of that sense of British exceptionalism in relation to Europe, which was cemented further after the loss of Plantagenet continental possessions and during the Reformation. We shall examine more of that later in chapter 15. But for now, let us note the passing of the legions and what followed as we were cut loose from another fragmenting European union.

The archaeological record is stark. From that moment, the quarrying of stone, the use of mortar, the arts of glazing, pottery and metalwork, even the roofing of buildings with anything other than perishable materials, all vanished. Simply put, no-one of sense in such an uncertain time would invest money and skill in a physical structure that might be plundered and burnt any other Wednesday. Burial sites reveal the obvious: if you have wealth, make sure it is small enough to carry and keep it close.

And so, it is no surprise that when, 300 years later, a pioneer like Bishop Biscop decided to build two monasteries 'in the Roman manner' at Wearmouth and Jarrow – the sort of building he had seen on his many manuscript-borrowing-trips to the continent – he had to first bring 'craftsmen as yet unknown in Britain' to build and glaze what, to us appears, a rather modest stone barn, but which, to the people of that day, must have been a marvel.

And it was only around Biscop's time, 300 years after the departing legionaries that the wheel began to turn again to produce pottery. It also took Britain 300 years to recover an economic sophistication comparable to where they had been eight centuries before the Romans even invaded. That is the truly staggering reality and consequence of the fall of a highly specialised society. Before the Romans came, the Britons had already taken Celtic metal-work design to its zenith. They had already possessed potteries with regional distribution, silver coinage, and trading networks to the continent for wine and minerals. All of that would take three centuries to re-discover after the legions marched away. At Chedworth Roman Villa near Cirencester, we filmed a fourth-century latrine with running water. Not so marvellous you might think until you realise that such a thing (familiar to the Minoans) would not be seen again in the western world for almost another 1500 years. The Burkean assumption; that it is easier to tear down cultural gains than to discover or recover them, is written into the archaeological and historical fabric of Britain.

Over the Channel, the decline was less wholesale than in Britain and more complex. We reached our lowest point in the fifth century, but for Italy and Africa, it was still two centuries away. Further east in the portion of the empire which had not fallen, the 5th and 6th centuries were a time of prosperity and expansion.[375] At a medieval monastic site in the centre of Rome, that I visited in 2018, there is impressive evidence of continuity in trade; ten thousand potsherds, including African tableware, alongside 500 amphorae. But this site, called the Crypta Balbi, only underscores what archaeologists discovered in all other dig sites in a forty-mile area north of Rome; namely, what once had been common even amongst the most modest homeowner was now the sole preserve of the very wealthy elites.[376]

More mundane, but no less telling, was the fact that it would also be 1000 years until Europeans, except royals and ecclesiastics, floored their houses with anything but beaten earth.[377] Indeed, it is even possible that the characteristic Italian pantile was not widely available again, even in Italy, until the 14th or 15th centuries. And this meant that for a millennium, Europeans put up with perishable, inflammable, and insect infested roofs. Even in Italy, the use of terracotta pantiles, that had once been used to roof even animal hovels, did not become commonplace until the late Middle Ages.[378]

More generally, ice core samples testify that the atmospheric pollution caused by smelting lead, copper, and silver never reached Roman levels for 1000 years after the empire's collapse.[379] Copper coinage too became scarcer and scarcer throughout the fifth and sixth centuries and almost vanished in the 7th century in most of Europe, in all but Italy. Hoards show that old money could remain in circulation for centuries. This was not an economic recession or industrial abatement but 'rather the disappearance of entire industries and commercial networks.'[380]

The romantic assumption that the barter system that replaced advanced trade and currency brought a more equal society is likely to be just romantic. Coinage extended trust (our word *credit* comes from the Latin, credo – I believe) not only beyond the village border but also into the space-time continuum into the future. Without the market stability for next month or next year, life contracted to subsistence for most people. Priorities change, and lack of security means greater energy and revenue are needed at the local level. For example, consider '...it is a remarkable fact that few early empire cities (in Britannia) were walled – a state of affairs not repeated in most of Europe... until the late nineteenth century, and that only because explosives had rendered walls ineffective as a form of defence.'[381] Whatever Columbanus had read about the might of Rome, and he would have read a lot, there was precious little left of it a hundred years after its collapse.

What about primary literary sources? Fortunately for us, Columban arrived on the continent at the time when Gregory of Tours was in the final stages of writing his *Histories*. These are our major sources delineating the Frankish kingdom from its beginnings in the fifth century to 591. Gregory was the bishop who claimed that *'In these times when the practice of letters declines, no, rather perishes in the cities of Gaul, there has been found no scholar trained in ordered composition to present in prose or verse a picture of the things which have befallen.'* Also writing at this time was the Italian poet, hagiographer, and Bishop of Poitiers, Venantius Fortunatus. So the socio-political map is well chartered for us, which is a good thing because Jonas – well travelled though he might have been

– is not totally reliable either in the religious or secular politics that he gives in his *Vita*.

The Merovingian Dynasty, that is the Frankish kings of the 5th-8th century, was descended – so they claimed – from the semi-mythical Merovech. The third king was a duplicitous young thug called Clovis, and he would later be seen as the first king of the Franks. He converted to his wife's Catholic faith[382] and died a penitent, but not before dividing the kingdom between his four sons, and thus paving the way to many years of fratricidal civil war.

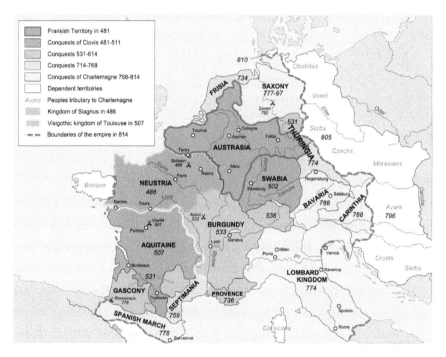

We saw the flux of national boundaries moving around Schuman and De Gasperi in a previous chapter, here we can see the same thing happening almost in a generational cycle at the time of which we are now writing. Gregory of Tours, though a bishop in a Romano-Gallic church very much under the thumb of the state, is about as pessimistic of the dynasty as Gildas had been of the rulers in Britain a generation or so before. Three of Clovis' descendants were ruling various parts of his former dominions when Columban arrived. The Franks had taken up

Latin and even added some Frankish words to it. Here perhaps we see the fresh shoots of cultural confidence as a turbulent sixth century was passing, and one of relative stability followed.

Chlothar II held the northern kingdom of Neustria, which was centered on the lower Seine. His cousin Childebert II held sway around such cities as Metz, Rheims, and Cologne in what was called the eastern kingdom of Austrasia. (He also had large fiefs in Burgundy, just to confuse us.) But by far the most imposing figure was their uncle Guntram, King of Burgundy whose territory included Chalon-sur-Saône to Orléans. (N.B. Burgundy's borders morphed like an amoeba in a petri dish over the centuries.)

But, significantly for our story; Guntram died just after Columban moved east, and the Kingdom of Burgundy passed sideways to the aforementioned Childebert II. That meant Childebert ruled pretty much all the Franks apart from a northern section between the Cotentin peninsula and the Scheldt in what is now Belgium. But alas, if you are not already totally confused, then you will be now. For three or four years later in 596, Childebert also died, and in good Frankish fashion left his kingdom to two sons: Theudebert (II), who basically got his father's original kingdom of Neustria (think Paris/Normandy), and his half-brother Theuderic (II), who took over Guntram's old territory of Burgundy. The similar names are confusing but they are important to note here because, after Guntram, both these brothers play a part in Columban's story.

At first, Columban was invited by Guntrum to stay in Burgundy. But remember, as we have just seen, after Guntram's death Burgundy would pass unexpectedly to the eight-year-old King Theuderic (II), watched over by the Queen, Grandmother Brunhilda. She was a woman of Visigoth extraction from Toledo. She and her older sister had both married into the Frankish dynasty.

Venantius Fortunatus, sometimes called the 'last Roman poet', who was present at Brunhilda's wedding in Metz, could not have been more complimentary of her stately beauty, modesty, prudence, and affability.[383] Even if this is little more than a gossip column description of a royal wedding, there would be precious little of these attributes left, except perhaps prudence, by the time Columban meets her thirty-plus years later. What had happened?

Firstly, her sister had been strangled aged just twenty four at the instigation of a legendarily wicked Queen Fredegund.[384] Then Brunhilda's heroic husband had been murdered. And then there were several attempts on her own life. Against the endless plots of the Austrasian nobles, she plied herself with superhuman energy in such a long and varied political career that one can but marvel. She met fire with fire, intrigue with intrigue, and treachery with treachery[385] until she would become almost every inch the monster she despised in Fredegund. In Chaucer's masterpiece *Troilus and Cressida*, we see the fall of a woman with pity but no fortitude, and in the life of Brunhilda we see the fall of a woman with the defect in reverse.

She would play an admirable Jezebel to Columban's Elijah. Both were born in 543, and both had wills of iron. Like Jezebel's daughter Athaliah in the Bible,[386] Brunhilda had out-survived the reign of her husband and even her son. Now, aged fifty, she would not countenance any higher power in her dominions than that of her family. The bishops knew that, the other monasteries knew that, the people certainly knew that, but no one had yet told Columban. Burgundy would not be big enough for both of them, and from the moment he entered he would be on a timed ticket of about ten years – which is just about enough time to start something.

But lest we think too ill of the Merovingian dynasty, as Jonas would have us do, we should remember that they at least among the 'barbarians' brought stability enough for the functioning of a basic society. You cannot have a monastery thrive in a constant war zone, in fact, nothing can, except anarchy, famine, and pestilence. Let us approach the dangerous edges of pragmatism and admit that *"Goodness, armed with power, is corrupted; and pure love without power is destroyed."* [387] The Franks were a brutish lot in brutish times, and the Gallic church – which always saw itself as the older sister of the daughters of Rome – was in a compromised state. But at least Columban could go to a kingdom where property title would mean something. Cassiodorus would have given his right arm to have been assured that his *Vivarium* monastic community and library would have lasted a thousand years.

Let us briefly get a snapshot of this 'Dark Age' world into which we now enter. Clovis, the first king of the Franks, had moved the capital from Tournai to Paris, which was the centre of the richest agricultural lands. So, for nearly a century before Columban arrives there had been a slow ongoing recovery. But it was the subsidiary system of feudalism and not the old imperial one. The Roman Empire's success had been achieved by harnessing the surplus of each newly conquered nation and using it to support a parasitic centre. As with the Greek city states and the Laurion mines, it was wealth unjustly got and ruinous in the end. When the Roman conquests stopped and the booty dried up, it was only a matter of time before the whole edifice crumbled.

But one of the benefits of medieval feudalism was that it provided the modicum of stability needed to exploit the wealth of the land. As the population began to recover after the fifty-year plague, the feudal system was able to tie more farmers to yet more uncultivated lands. As with Minoan civilisation two millennia before, feudalism created the agricultural surplus that formed the basis of European wealth.[388]

But what of the people? How did they view their world and each other? It may surprise us to see so many fresh shoots of green that we would recognise. It turned out, that out of all those invading tribes mentioned in chapter one, the Franks were really *our sort* of barbarian. Beyond merely plunder and rapine, they let themselves be swayed – if not by the *Pax Romana* – then the *Pax Christi*. Some of the social innovations are worth mentioning in passing. For example, the Merovingians laid the foundations for the medieval system for dealing with pauperism and beggary. The Gallic Church kept lists of *matricularii* — those entitled to receive charity. The First Council of Orleans in 511 reads like any modern set of guidelines from the Department of Social Security; those unable to work should receive food and clothing, etcetera.

The Second Council of Tours in 567 designated that every community must take care of its own poor, and see to it that their poor not wander about from place to place. There is evidence that this active charity had measurable success in limiting pauperism. Special Public buildings were raised for pilgrims and for the relief of the poor and the infirm. And special *Xenodochia* were built for the *Incurables* and prisoners – communities and appointed state officers – all highly organised. Gregory of Tours writes of a Leper Asylum in Chalon on the Saone, and we know there were others in Verdun, Metz, and Maastricht. We read of a twenty bed hospital of Colombier which had a staff of physicians.

And it wasn't that the bishops were all a terrible self-serving lot either, for many, like Bishop Desideratus greatly increased the prosperity of the people of the Verdun region. And Bishop Nicetius of Treves established Moselle as a lucrative center of viticulture. The great fourth century monastic foundations of Tours and Poitiers had sowed, by their examples, great seeds of social change and expectation. Under the Franks, the condition of the serfs was much improved.

> *"The Germans, did not employ their slaves in menial duties to minister to their personal ease; each slave had a dwelling and a home of his own; he tilled the land, paid dues to his master, but the rest of his time and labor was his own. He supported his wife and family, lived much in common with freemen, and was able in a large measure to preserve his self-respect."* [389]

So whatever we will read in Jonas about the Gallic church and *simoniacle* prelates,[390] we do know that the Frankish church was active in what we now call the 'social gospel' with regards to the slavery issue. In fact, Clovis' Catholic queen was a keen campaigner to abolish it altogether.

> *"The clergy preached, the bishops remonstrated and insisted, the annual Councils formulated their demands — which, appealing to Divine authority, were virtually decrees — in the interests of humanity. Churches, abbeys, and monasteries stood ever open as asylums for the oppressed, and at one of the Councils held at Lyons, early in the sixth century, the*

bishops were enjoined to excommunicate any master who killed his slave without giving him the opportunity of defense."[391]

If a dying slave owner loved his own soul, he was encouraged to release his slaves as an act of final penitence. The Fifth Council of Orleans was unstinting: a slave could be ordained to the priesthood, even without the consent of his owner.[392] One reason for this activity might well have been the two hundred and twenty monasteries in Gaul, compared to only about a hundred in Italy. These were the flowering of the early Gallic founders like John Cassius, Hilary, and Martin, already discussed, and not the Benedictines who were only just now ready to leave Italy for Britain in the person of Augustine of Canterbury.

But more of that later. For now let us be content to see Columban and his little band, staffs in hand and weary of foot, entering Guntram's Burgundy in the noble twilight of his reign.

FIRST THREE MONASTERIES

'When the holy man with his companions appeared before the king, the greatness of his learning caused him to stand high in the favour of the king and court. Finally, the king begged him to remain in Gallic territory, not to go to other peoples and leave him; everything that he wished should be done. Then he replied to the king that he did not wish to be enriched with the treasures of others, but as far as he was not hindered by the weakness of the flesh to follow the command of the Gospel: " Whosoever will come after me, let him deny himself and take up his cross and follow me."

Then the king answered and said: "If you wish to take the cross of Christ upon you and follow Him, seek the quiet of a hermitage. Only be careful, for the increase of your own reward and for our spiritual good, to remain in our kingdom and not to go to the neighbouring peoples." As the choice was left to him in this manner, he followed the king's advice and chose for himself a hermitage. At that time there was a great wilderness called Vogasus, in which there was a castle, which had long been in ruins, and which had been called for ages, Anagrates. When the holy man came to that place, he settled there with his followers, in spite of the entire loneliness, the wilderness and the rocks, mindful of the proverb that, "Man shall not live by bread alone,' but shall have sufficient food from the bread of life and shall never hunger.'

Jonas of Bobbio, Vita Coluambani

It is a remote place even now. Perhaps that is what Columban *thought* he wanted – a quiet place to pray away from worldly distractions. 'Anagrates', as Jonas calls it – the modern hamlet of Annegray – sits in the lea of the Vosagus (Vosges) mountains. The area reminds me of the edges of the Lincolnshire Wolds or Houseman's 'blue remembered hills' of Shropshire. To see the siting of it also reminds me of those Yorkshire abbeys like Bylands, Rievaulx, and Mount Grace Priory – perhaps remote, but with domestic possibilities. It was a forested hunting estate in Columban's time but now sits in a wide enough river valley to provide ample space for growing the necessary crops. And it was here, at the king's invitation, that Columban founded a monastery in an abandoned Roman fortress. They built in stone, they built as men with something worthy for which to build. They also restored the ruins of Diana's temple across the field to become a church dedicated to Martin of Tours.

The co-opting of pagan shrines and the rededication of this new church to Martin are also laden with significance. Benedict had done something similar to the temple of Apollo on the summit of Monte Casino – also dedicating it to Martin. Benedict had also dedicated another to John the Baptist where Apollo's altar stood. When Columban built a chapel within the monastic complex at Annegray, he too dedicated it to John the Baptist. The second dedication might be a coincidence, after all, for Columban to see himself and his mission as a second voice *'crying in the wilderness'* would have been natural. But the Martin dedication was both polite and purposive. Martin of Tours – the Hungarian soldier turned monk, who was made bishop by popular demand but against his own wishes, was the gold standard of other-worldly piety and humility. The Franks lionized him as if he were one of their own and as if they shared his vision. Of course, he wasn't and they didn't, but the point is that Columban was about to arise a century later with the same mantle, the same message. Many were hungry for it, and they flocked to Annegray, not just as a site of pilgrimage but also to join permanently.

But Jonas does not gloss over the difficulties of these early pioneers. Sometimes there was no food but the bark of trees and the roots of herbs to eat. Jonas records two miraculous deliveries of food, one from a local farmer, and another from, 'A certain abbot,' whom some scholars[393] believe to have been a Briton, 'named Caramtoc, who ruled over a monastery of which the name was Salicis, was warned by a vision, that he should bear the necessities of life to God's servant Columban, dwelling in the wilderness.' Abbott Caramtoc's cellarer Marculf was astounded to see the horses almost make their own way to Annegray to deliver the food. After each miracle, Jonas adds a characteristic literary exclamation like; 'Wonderful power!' or 'Wonderful Virtue!' It is a nice literary device and feels rather like a Marvel comic 'Pow!' or 'Wham!' One of the more moving accounts that Jonas gives is when the other Columban, the young man from the abbot's hometown, lay dying. Despite the claim to many healing miracles, Jonas does not shy away from the tenderness and grief of the abbot in a time of calamity. Jonas says that the young man felt he was at his last breath when he had a vision:

'... he saw a man clothed in light coming to him, and saying, "I am not able now to free you from your body, because I am hindered by the prayers of your father Columban." When the sick man heard this, sorrowfully as if he had been awakened from sleep, he began to call his attendant Theudegisel whom we mentioned above, and said, "Go quickly and summon our father Columban to me." The attendant went swiftly to Columban weeping in the church, asked him to hasten to the sick man. Columban came quickly and asked him what he wanted. The latter told him, saying, "Why do you detain me by your prayers in this sorrowful world? For those *are present, who would lead me away if they were not hindered by your tears and prayers. I beseech you, remove the obstacles which retain me that the celestial kingdom may open for me." Columban, struck with fear, made a signal that all should come. His joy lessened his grief at the loss of his holy companion. He gave the dying man the body of Christ as a viaticum, and after the last kiss began the death-song. For they were of the same race and name and had left Ireland in the same company.'*

Other times, Jonas tells of Columban performing miracles of food multiplication. By these and many other healing miracles, Columban's fame spread. And like Martin, who preferred his cell on the river bank a few miles from Tours, so Columbanus also sought a distant cave to pray. Jonas tells how he evicted the previous occupant:

'At another time he withdrew from his cell and entering the wilderness by a longer road he found an immense cliff with precipitous sides and rocky paths difficult for men. There he perceived a hollow side in the rock. Entering to explore its hidden recesses he found in the interior of the cave the home of a bear, and the bear itself. He ordered the beast to depart and not to return to that place again. The beast mercifully went, nor did she dare to return again. The place was distant from Anegray seven miles more or less.'

The cave, plus a small 11th century chapel, can still be visited four hundred feet above the village of Sainte-Marie-En-Chanois in the Breuchin valley. There are no immense cliffs to speak of, it's not seven miles from Annegray (more like one and a half), and it's not on *rocky paths difficult for men*, though there is an escarpment into which the cave sits. To my own mind, it is a secluded enough spot and a sensible enough distance to be away, but not too far away, from the pressures of an abbot's life. The bilberries that grow up there are still called *le brin belu de St Columban*. I camped up there with my sons on a humid evening in late September 2018. The small chapel, built hard under the escarpment, encloses the source of the spring. We signed our names in the book and then took a look around a small cave just below it, and also a small fishpond built more recently on the side of the hill. We sat out until late, playing cards and chatting by candlelight, listening to the sound of deer in the woods and the low rumble of thunder across the Vosges Mountains to the east. As the first few fingers of lightening prodded various parts of the eastern horizon I wondered whether, somewhere out there, there was another cave that folk memory had forgotten. It is possible that Jonas knew something we don't. After all, despite his penchant for stretching things into an Egyptian-desert-father mould, he did interview eyewitnesses. Columban may have had an extra-private retreat spot, perhaps this one was it, and Jonas' witness meant it was 7 miles from the second monastery at Luxeuil, which it is.

Filming in 2018 at Columban's Cave near Annegray in the Vosges

What we do know is that the monastery flourished during and after Columban's time. The 1958 excavations have uncovered the remains of a medieval stronghold as well as the foundations of a church dedicated to St. John the Baptist. Part of the find included a number of Merovingian graves – that is, stone sarcophagi of the seventh century.[394] Margaret Stokes visited the site in 1893 but found no trace of the monastery church, which was then a ploughed field. She did find the remains of a rough stone wall without mortar at the base of the knoll. The church of

St. Martin had been destroyed in the French Revolution. She recorded that numerous sarcophagi had been unearthed through ploughing, but only one had been kept intact as it had been used as a drinking trough next to the village well. Local people also told her that 'bones were found everywhere about.'[395]

But whichever site was the real one, it was soon teaming with life, despite the initial difficulties. Here the young men learned the common life of service and study. They also learned to find forgiveness every day, rather than saving up sins to be confessed at the end of their lives to a priest. The penitential, which we saw in a previous chapter, formed the user's manual for confessing and forgiveness. It became adopted by the wider church much later. To live free from the burden of guilt, that was the aim and that was one of Columban's great successes. Columban didn't need Freud to tell him of the enervating power and burden of guilt which cripples human beings. Nor did he entertain illusions that men and women laden with guilt would be any use in salting their society with hope and joy. The central Christian claim is that Christ not only forgives but also takes away the burden of sin and guilt.

I do not have sufficient training or reading to judge whether Freudian techniques have yielded the same fruit among us as Columban's penitential did among his generation. But I imagine if we were to look closer at the statistics we would find little to be complacent about. One distinction made by a scholar[396] in this regard is that while other preachers of the age offered the Gospel as a means of fulfillment for the worldly concerns of their hearers, (as had Regimus and Avitus to Clovis a century before), Columbanus, who is a 'gust of fresh air', focused more upon the attainment of 'moral perfection.' His appeal was 'personal, not institutional'. He preached not of 'saints' and 'relics' but of an individual encounter with an immanent God. His counter-intuitive marketing strategy turned out to be a more compelling fit for human needs. And we must note that when this central message of Christianity becomes alloyed with lesser emphases – the 'Muscular Christianity'[397] of Victorian Anglicanism and the Social Gospel of postwar Methodism immediately spring to mind – then that particular addition itself exerts a secularizing effect that could be seen as causing inertia within the whole.

With the increase in young men to sacrifice all to join this new monastic life, and after only two or three years, Columban was invited to open two further monasteries. In 590, King Guntram (who would still be alive another five years) gave him the Gallo-Roman castle called *Luxovium* (present-day Luxeuil-les-Bains), which was about eight miles down the Breuchin valley from Annegray. I imagine Columban rather liked the martial associations of these two former military outposts that now housed his soldiers of Christ. It had been destroyed by Attila – the epitome of barbarism – in 451, and now Columban and his trusty band – the epitome of Christian virtue – were here to restore it. The third monastery was three miles to the north through the magnificent forest of Sept-Cheveux on another Roman site called *Ad-fontanas* (present-day Fontaine-lès-Luxeuil). Of this third monastic site, there remains very little. The site of the old priory is now in private hands and the 19th century parish church gives few clues, apart from a seventh century stone sarcophagus.

Luxeuil-les-Bains is another matter. It became the premier monastery in Burgundy and much still remains, even though it was successively sacked by Muslims, Vikings, Hungarians, and revolutionary Frenchmen. Jonas says that the baths still present on the site were,

> '...constructed with unusual skill. A great number of stone idols, which in the old heathen times had been worshipped with horrible rites, stood in the forest near at hand. Here then the excellent man began to build a monastery. At the news of this people streamed in from all directions in order to consecrate themselves to the practice of religion, so that the large number of monks scarcely had sufficient room. The children of the nobles from all directions strove to come thither; despising the spurned trappings of the world and the pomp of present wealth, they sought eternal rewards.'

Two points immediately occur to me when I consider this development. Firstly, these two new monasteries were anything but isolated. They were at the crossroads of well-travelled routes. For example, within a decade Pope Gregory's emissary Augustine would pass this way on his mission to bring Roman order to the indigenous church of Britain – and perhaps even stayed here.[398] The tension within Columban himself is manifest here. Columban was one of the rare souls who were all the more fitted to lead their fellows because he did not want to. If he had ambition, it was vertical and not horizontal. As we have already said, he wrote, *'I want the salvation of many and seclusion for myself; the one for the progress of the Lord the other for my own desire.'* If Annegray had been 'seclusion', then *Luxovium* and *Ad Fontanas,* would be for 'the salvation of many.' As can be seen from even the roll call of Frankish nobles that would join, the list is numerous and illustrious. It must have felt, that Martin and Hilary once more walked among them in these stern Irish. For when the sons of the high-born elites are willing to give up their status and possessions, then we can know a profound sociological and spiritual force is at work.

The second point that strikes me as powerfully suggestive is the appropriation of the pagan healing shrine. These places rarely fall out of use,[399] and despite a resurgent Gallic church, it is not unthinkable that superstitious rural communities still visited such places in the desperation of ailment and old age.[400] Curative thermal springs draw sick people wherever they break the surface – just think of Bath, where so many English invalids bathed that attendants had to sift the warm waters of puss, flaked skin, and other detritus each morning. We may shudder, but it is too easy, with such advances in medicine, to forget the despair and desolation of an untreatable complaint.

Besides the usual rounds of sickness, Europe had been suffering for nearly fifty years with a plague that had halved the population. And ten years later, smallpox too would-be leaving India to bring more misery among the Franks. Gregory of Tours gives a pitiful description; 'and so we lost our little ones, who were dear to us and sweet, whom we cher-

ished in our bosoms and dandled in our arms, who we had fed and nurtured with such loving care. As I write I wipe away my tears...'

Columban was certainly seen as a man with the gift of healing, and
Jonas gives many examples, infertility, illness, work-related accidents,
etc. So, we would hope that such curative gifts and a compassionate hospital would prove doubly valuable to the Franks. The Roman gods were
no more, but the need for health remained. It would be a very long time
before the state would imagine that it fell to it to heal the sick, but the
church did so from the word go.

Even since the times of Constantine, there had been monastic hospitals from Syria to the western fringes of Christendom. Saint Ephrem's
plague hospitals in Edessa;[401] Basil's leper colony in Cappadocia (where
he nursed them with his own hands); John Chrysostom made sure the
hospitals of Constantinople were not only well endowed but also had
many wealthy laypersons serve there washing the sick to prove their
Christian charity. The first hospital in Western Europe was founded by
St Fabiola, a woman of high status who was moved by Jesus' example
to seek out the poor and sick in Rome and bring them to shelter and
care. Benedict did something similar at Monte Casino, the first of over
two thousand Benedictine hospitals in Europe. Two thousand! Joining
them were the Hospitalier Knights of St. John who, initially at least, did
a similar work throughout Europe and the Levant. Their hospital of the
Holy Spirit at Montpellier was a famous proto-university training hospital and is now the present-day university's faculty of medicine.

David Bentley Hart can only cite the *Valetudinaria* (Military hospital) as anything like a pagan equivalent. But I can think also of the great
Greek health centre at Epidaurus as a notable pagan one – not charita-
ble and not for the destitute I grant, but certainly an interesting combination of leisure and health that modern hospitals are only just now
replicating. At Epidaurus, the vast theatre was far and away the most
prominent building. Here were the Arts and medicine together, just like
religion and healing at the monastic foundation in Luxeuil-les-Bains.

Great culture is not a goal but a by-product, a second thing. Ideas
shape culture through leaders, or gatekeepers, and elites.[402] Columban

was such a gatekeeper, his monks were an elite of sorts. They were situated on a crossroads, offering hospitality, education, ultimate answers, and healing at a place where people had already come for generations. Soon, he was fast becoming a cultural force in Burgundy. We find this surprising, perhaps because the post-Christian West has seen the locus of cultural engines – and even genuine spiritual dialogue in the public sphere – migrate away from the church and into popular culture. Sociologist Andrew Greely argues that popular culture is not just a source of dialogue but itself a *locus theologicus*; a sociological space within which people are seeking God – engaging in ultimate questions.[403] 82% of his fellow Americans claim to be spiritual seekers, and 53% say they had talked about spiritual issues in the previous twenty-four hours.

That so few seem to find God in this new *Locus Theologicus*, is perhaps less surprising as society's acceptance that spiritual seeking should be a constant and respectable *modus vivendi*.[404] As another Irishman remarked, all our talk of *man's search for God always sounded to me like speaking of the mouse's search for the cat*.[405] Lionising a journey with no destination might be seen as a thoroughly modern phenomena, and Columban may have been *always moving from the day of birth until the day of death*[406] but he was abundantly certain of his destination – perhaps too certain for our ears. Nietzsche lived, as he said, in the *pause between the breaths* of a dying Christian consensus and the rise of the new ideologies. We live in the pause between breaths of the failure of those ideologies, and even the disappointment and boredom with what is left.

We cannot escape the strong possibility, or even conclude that, along with the new respectability of habitual, spiritual seeking, entertainment has also stepped into that void, either to soften the blow or stave off the ennui. Many on the Left and the Right fear that entertainment has even trumped reality itself. One American journalist writes that *it is not any 'ism' but entertainment that is arguably the most pervasive, powerful, and ineluctable force of our time – a force so overwhelming that it has finally metastasized into life*.[407] To the firstlings of the twenty-first century, Woody Allen's comment that 'Life doesn't imitate art (but)... bad television,' sounds more like prophecy than satire. It is all the more galling when we see the same devastating pattern in late antiquity. For it was just when the moral entropy took its greatest hold after the 'five good emperors' that the people began shouting most of *'panem et circenses'* - bread and circuses. Suddenly events that usually only took up around 7% of the year, now began to last for months, in response to popular demand. Trajan's greatest games lasted 123 consecutive days (32% of the year) and entailed the slaughter of 11,000 animals and 5,000 humans.[408]

Sociologist, Pitrim Sorokin calls ours the 'sensate culture;' the society of public image and illusion whose core values are derived from the senses, not thoughtful consideration of ideas. The ever nay-saying educationalist Neil Postman[409] part blames the switch from a literary to an image based[410] culture:

> *'...to engage in the written word means to follow a line of thought, which requires considerable powers of classifying, inference making, and reasoning....an image-based culture, on the other hand, dispenses with all these because images do not demand them.'*

Sorokin believes that such a sensate culture will eventually collapse because humans ultimately require more than junk food. This is all depressing stuff – and possibly overstated. Yet, even so, it is not wholly without reference to our study, for Luxeuil became the administrative centre of a new countercultural movement in the last days of that turbulent sixth century. Within a decade of their founding, the three monasteries contained about two hundred monks which, along with their guest houses and schools, became very famous over the years. Indeed, the motherhouse was soon acknowledged as the premier monastery in all Burgundy. But the force of new ideas rarely remained just that, and over the centuries little that has been built by such idealists can remain long. For one thing – and this must be acknowledged as a fact in both sacred and secular enterprises – every system needs constant renewal from within if it is to survive either becoming a monster, or else an irrelevance.

Luxeuil monastery[411] was first plundered by the Saracens in the 8th century, and then finally suffered, as did Annegray, under the *Liberté, égalité, fraternité* of the French Revolution.

Some manuscripts did survive but only one sheet in the Irish language, and this only because it had been used in the binding of another book. It was a great tragedy. A privileged Gallic church, which in subsequent centuries, had not been tempered by either the Re-

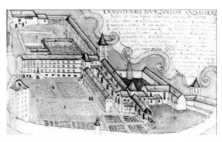

Luxeuil Abbey at the time of the Revolution

formation or the Pietist movements of the 18th century, had raised the righteous indignation of the French peasants. But later humanist philosophers like Albert Camus were in no doubt that it would take more than just strangling the last king 'with the entrails of the last priest'[412] to achieve the *Liberté* of France. So distressed that republicanism had not created a just society,[413] he wrote,

> '*the Jacobin revolution, which tried to institute the religion of virtue in order to establish unity on it, will be followed by cyclical revolutions...of right or of the left...which will try to achieve the unity of the world so as to found, at last, the religion of man. All that was God's will henceforth be rendered to Caesar.*'[414]

Camus' default position, therefore, was to rebel – to rage against the machine, without a workable alternative – which does also seem to characterize the new culture of outrage in social media and, alas, in public life. In his doctoral dissertation, Marx wrote that '*human consciousness*' alone was '*the supreme deity. There shall be none beside it.*' But in the absence of God or even natural law, man must become the sole arbitrator of value and meaning – the sole source of evil too, if indeed anything can even be called evil under those terms of reference. Curiously, Camus saw this impasse in modern secular culture, but rather than question his own presuppositions, repeatedly chose rather to blame the evil on a god who did not exist. I have a hunch that if someone like the Bible-saturated Columban could speak across history he would quote Proverbs 4:19 to Camus and us; 'The way of the corrupted ones is like deep darkness; they do not know what makes them stumble'. And I am sure he would also have tears in his eyes.

As I hinted earlier, Columban was on a timed ticket in Burgundy. His initial popularity under the patronage of Guntram would not last long when the young Theuderic II,[415] and his grandmother Brunhilda, became the new power. At first, Jonas says that Theuderic II was only too happy to have such a valuable contribution to, what we would call, his 'third sector.' Education, health care, social services, possible agricultural innovations; who would not want such powerhouses of moral and intellectual civility springing up in their kingdom? *These Irish monks were a bit odd, extreme even, but certainly value for money.* All they needed was a grant of land – and there was plenty of that going to waste – and hey presto; like the proverbial Wombles of Wimbledon; reusing the every day ruins and shrines the Romans left behind, and they make the wilderness bloom with life – a sort of Dark Ages' rural regeneration agency. These thoughts or some like them were doubtless in Theuderic's mind. The only trouble with Christian eccentrics is that they also clung to unpopular views of personal morality that they insisted on applying to everyone, even the king. I'll let Jonas take up the story that has all the later overtones of Henry II and Thomas a Beckett, or King John and Steven Langdon. It is a lengthy portion but worth putting in full.

As he very often visited Columban, the holy man began to reprove him because he sinned with concubines, and did not satisfy himself with the comfort of a lawful wife, in order to beget royal children from an honored queen, and not bastards by his concubines. After this reproof from Columban, the king promised to abstain from such sinful conduct. But the old serpent came to his grandmother Brunhilda, who was a second Jezebel, and aroused her pride against the holy man, because she saw that Theuderich was obedient to him. For she feared that her power and honor would be lessened if, after the expulsion of the concubines, a queen should rule the court. St. Columban happened one day to go to Brunhilda, who was then living in Brocariaca. As she saw him enter the court, she led to him the illegitimate sons of Theuderich. When St. Columban saw her, he asked what she wanted of him. Brunhilda answered, "These are the king's sons; give them thy blessing." He replied, "Know that these boys will never bear the royal scepter, for they were begotten in sin." Enraged, she told the boys to go. When after this Columban left the court, a loud cracking noise was heard, the whole house trembled and everyone shook with fear. But that did not avail to check the wrath of the wretched woman.

From that time she began to persecute the neighboring monasteries. She issued an order that none of the monks should be allowed to leave the lands of the monasteries, no one should receive them into other houses or give them any aid. When Columban saw that at the court all were arrayed against him, he hastened to Spissia, where the king was then staying, in order to subdue such defiance by his warnings. When he reached that place, about sunset, and it was announced to the king that Columban was there but would not enter the palace Theuderich said it would be better with due reverence to offer the needful services to the man of God, than to arouse the wrath of the Lord, by insulting His servant. Accordingly he ordered suitable food to be prepared in the royal kitchen and sent to the servant of God.

When the attendants came to Columban and, in accordance with the king's command, offered him food and drink prepared with royal magnificence, he asked what they meant by it. When they told him that it was sent by the king, he pushed it from him and said: "It is written, the most High is not pleased with the offerings of the wicked. For it is not meet that the mouth of the servant of the Lord should be defiled by the food of him who shuts out the servant of God, not only from his own dwelling, but also from the dwellings of others." At these words all of the dishes broke into pieces, so that the wine and liquor ran out on the ground and the food was scattered here and there. Terrified, the servants announced this to the king. Full of anxiety, he together with his grandmother, hastened to Columban early in the morning. Both begged him to forgive their past sins and promised, amendment. With his fears quieted by this, Columban returned to his convent. But they failed to keep their promises, and very soon the persecutions were renewed with increased bitterness by the king, who continued in his former sinful course. Then Columban sent him a letter full of reproaches, and threatened him with the ban if he did not amend his conduct.

Now Brunhilda began again to incite the king against Columban in every way; urged all the nobles and others at court to do the same, and influenced the bishops to attack Columban's faith and to abolish his monastic rule. She succeeded so fully that the holy man was obliged to answer for his faith or leave the country. The king, incited by Brunhilda, went to Luxeuil and accused Columban of violating the customs of the country and of not allowing all Christians to enter the interior of the monastery. To these accusations Columban answered, for he was unterrified and full of courage, that it was not his custom to allow laymen to enter the dwelling of the servant of God, but he had prepared a suitable place where all who came would be received.

The king replied: "If you wish to enjoy any longer the gifts of our grace and favor, everyone in the future must be allowed free entrance everywhere." Columban answered: "If you dare to violate the monastic rule in any particular, I will not accept any gift or aid from you in the future. But if you come here to destroy the monasteries of the servant of God and to undermine their discipline and regulations, I tell you that your kingdom will be destroyed together with all your royal family." This the king afterward found to be true. In his audacity, he had already stepped into the refectory; terrified by these words, he withdrew hastily.

But when Columban attacked him with bitter insults, Theuderic said: "You want me to honor you with the crown of martyrdom; do not believe that I am foolish enough to commit such a crime. But I will follow a wiser and more useful plan. Since you depart from the common customs, I will send you back to the home from which you came." At the same time the members of the court resolved unanimously that they would not put up with anyone who was unwilling to associate with every-

one. But Columban said that he would not leave his monastery unless he was dragged out by force.

Another turbulent priest! I wonder if Thomas a Becket had read any of this. I think it was G.S.M. Walker who said that 'the history of the Middle Ages is largely an attempt of the church to make the state fit for God.' That is a Sisyphean task, too great even for the Irish! At Luxeuil-les-Bains, outside the basilica[416] that stands on the site of Columbanus' church, there is a bronze of him denouncing the immoral life of King Theuderic. One gets the feeling that it would not take much to turn the other bishops against these foreign monks and their bizarre customs and appearance. Their druidic-looking tonsure and their dating of Easter seem to us like trifles, but Columban was about to stir up a hornet's nest because of his quarrel with Theuderic.

The famous, or infamous, Synod of Whitby[417] may not have been such a pressing matter if these practices had remained in *de finibus extremis*. But now, here was an Irish émigré setting the rule of his founders against those of the Roman Church. In 603 the bishops called him to give an account of himself at a special Synod.[418] Benedict had insisted that his monks should welcome diocesan control – that is, the bishop's oversight – but that was not the case with the Irish monks. Their monasteries had grown and flourished in an altogether different environment; where there were no metropolitan bishops, indeed, no cities apart from the monastic ones. In some ways, this would prove as much a strength as a weakness. From the Frankish ruling elite's point of view, these new monasteries gave them a chance to indulge in pious patronage without having to kowtow directly to local bishops and thus Rome. (One is reminded of the German princes' support of Luther.) No wonder that a hundred such monasteries sprang up in the hundred years after Columban's death. But how to walk the thin line between what is God's and what is Caesar's was as delicate then as it has ever been. When Columban left Irish waters he entered the old world of Roman order and control. Mavericks and pioneers might be welcomed as picturesque and theological curiosities, but only so long as they didn't overstep the

bounds of decorum. Columban, probably quite sensibly, sent a very polite, very humble but firm letter excusing himself, commending them on
having the meeting and encouraging them to do so more often.

A few months later, while they were digesting that, he also wrote to
the newly elected Pope Sabinian – going over their heads. It would not
be for another four hundred years that the appellation Pope (Papa, Father[419]) would be reserved solely for the Bishop of Rome. But even now
we see Columban acknowledging him as, *'the most beautiful ornament
of the Church of Christ and as the flower August of Europe languishing,
prominent guardian, to the master in Rome in the contemplation of God
and his angels, me, vile Columban, I extend my greeting...'*

He had already written some years before to Pope Gregory, giving a
positive review of his book on the Pastoral Rule, and asking for some
of Gregory's lectures and writings on various books of the Bible. I
promised in earlier chapters to introduce this exceptional bishop more
fully, and now seems the best time to do so.

A Roman patrician who voluntarily chose to be a pauper, but was
then elected pope, and yet still managed to earn the almost contradic-
tory titles of Magnus (great) and Saint, is certainly worthy of our attention. Gregory was almost the same age as Columban, perhaps three years
older. He was born into a patrician family who lived on the Caelian hill
in Rome. His family was rich but also pious. He lived through the sufferings of two Gothic sieges, the first when he was only five. The city had
become depopulated and partly ruined – he later called Rome 'a rotten
old ship.' He was called to be an urban prefect when only thirty and
would travel in a chariot drawn by four white horses. From this office
he later resigned, founding six monasteries on his Sicilian estates and another at his family villa on the Caelian Hill, in Rome which he entered
not as abbot but as a brother. This might seem like fanatical behavior
until we remember that Gregory, along with many others, imminently
expected the end of the world. He referred to his years as a monk as the
happiest of his life. But we also know that the austerities he practiced
then were to permanently damage his health.

Looking back years later with all the burdens of the papacy on his shoulders he lamented being,

> *'...splattered with the world's dust...Now I am tossed by the billows of a mighty sea, and the ship of my soul is dashed by the storms of a great tempest; and when I remember the state of my life, I sigh as one who looking back beholds the haven he has left.'*

Between 579 and 585, Gregory was sent as Papal Nuncio to Constantinople – though he never learned Greek. He is described as having a well-formed figure, with a long face, slender nose, and prominent chin. He sported a small, tawny beard, and his fine forehead was adorned with two neat curls. His fresh, dark complexion acquired an unhealthy tinge in later life.

He became the bishop of Rome at a time when its importance had sunk and where the whole world looked east to Byzantium for protection, imperial civilization, and even theological acuity. As already mentioned it is easy to forget that in the 6th century, it was inconceivable that the great Christian centers of Alexandria and Antioch in the east would soon fall into non-Christian hands. For the survival of orthodox Christian doctrine, it seems fortuitous that Rome was now placed at such a distance from the imperial centers. For at this crucial moment in history, the papacy's theology was free from compromise, with imperial power or the ecclesiastical rivalries of Alexandria. Gregory systematized a body of doctrine which was to endure for centuries, even managing to make the church a moral force for good in politics.

Deserted by the civil administration, Gregory's Rome still possessed the great Roman name and in many ways, he and other bishops were able to use this mystique to save the city from barbarian despoliation.[420] The barbarians had been taught to revere the Roman name and that fame became a most valuable currency in a rapidly disintegrating world. If Constantinople could not be relied upon, then the west must turn to what little resources she had left. Gregory was a man for the hour. He understood that this new world order had to be faced up to. The barbarians were here to stay and, in the end, it was the church rather than Justinian, that was able to become the unifying force between the Roman and barbarian invaders. If they could not be Romanised then they at least might be Christianised.

Gregory made peace with the Lombards in order to save Rome from being sacked and then set about the conversion of the heathen. He is the only pope to be elevated to sainthood or, for that matter, receive the suffix 'Magnus.' His legacy was to establish a church structure free from the empire. Gregory held the reins of the Apostolic See loosely – as much government as necessary, as much autonomy as possible. As a conservative Roman patrician, he respected the rights of other bishops and even patriarchs. He resisted the title of 'Universal Bishop', not only because that title had been usurped by the Bishop of Constantinople, but also because anyone wishing such a title, in his view, must be a forerunner of the Antichrist. He preferred the title "servant of the servants of God."

You can still visit the site of his family villa near the colosseum, and you can still stand in the sloping courtyard of the palace he turned into a monastery, and from where Augustine left on his mission to convert southern Britain. When Columban wrote to Gregory, he called him the 'fairest ornament and most honoured flower, as it were, of worn down Europe.' He said that Gregory's *Regula Pastoralis* was 'sweeter than honey to the needy.' But noble reformers like Gregory, who battled laxity and simony, seemed to wage an unwinnable war against both. As is proved in other spheres (like the abolition of slavery) movements and networks can succeed where pamphlets and papal bulls cannot. And so it was Benedict's monastic movement which achieved the piety and societal renewal that Gregory had wanted for the wider church, but could not ensure beyond his death.

The Easter dating issue[421] is mentioned in all this correspondence and one gets the feeling that Columban is defending an accusation that has already reached Gregory, three years before the bishops summon him. His letter is familiar, even presumptuous; had Gregory not studied Jerome? He says, and,

> '...how with all your learning....do you favour a dark Easter?' But he is also humble by turns; 'Don't let the sharpness of this letter keep you from explaining things, since anger explodes into error, and it is my heart's desire to pay you due honour. My part was the challenge, to question, to beg; let yours be not to deny what you have freely received, to bend your talent to the seeker, and to give the bread of doctrine according to Christ's command. Peace to you and yours.'

Columban asks Gregory to adjudicate and instruct,[422] but in so doing puts him in an impossible position. 'Let charity move you to reply,' he writes, but we know of no reply either to this earlier letter or to the later one. He writes later to Pope Boniface calling himself, with typical Irish self-deprecation, 'a bumptious babbler' and a 'slow-witted Irishman' – but then proceeds to tell the Pope what to do. There was sloth in Rome and 'I, coming from the world's end, where I have seen the Lord's leaders truly fighting the Lord's battles....am quite astounded.' Even if you know you're right, this is perhaps not the best way to make friends and influence people.

But for all his deft letter writing, and going over the heads of the bishops, Columban was about to feel the sharp edge of Brunhilda's vengeance. For Columban; the man who was willing to undergo earthly exile, willing to forgo every worldly pleasure and undergo any privation, even martyrdom, the unthinkable was about to happen – he was about to be sent back to Ireland. What a blow. I am reminded of the Irish novelist Colum McCann's words;

> 'In the end, the only things worth doing, are the things that might possibly break your heart.'

CHAPTER 9
FOOTNOTES & REFERENCES

360. Norman Davies, *The Isles*, p.222 (Macmillan Publishers Ltd, 1999.)

361. Some believe he stopped in either Galloway or Cornwall en route – the town of St. Colomb Minor is given as a possible landing point, but the evidence is not strong enough to say more.

362. Thomas Cahill, *How the Irish Saved Civilisation*

363. *European civilization; a political, social and cultural history,* by James Westfall Thompson, Franklin Charles Palm, and John J. Van Nostrand. New York: D. Van Nostrand Company, inc., 1939.

364. Sean McMahon *'Rekindling the Flame'*

365. Guizot, *Histoire de la Civilisation en France*, vol. 2, pp.18-23

366. Michelet, *Histoire de France,* vol.2 pp. 266-72

367. In The Irish in England and on the Continent in the Seventh Century, Ian Wood highlights the fact that Ozanam and de Montalembert looked to the Irish, even their contemporary Daniel O'Connell as a symbol of Catholic revival in their own time.

368. Ozanam, Etudes germaniques pour server a l'histoire des frances; Oznam *La civilisation Chretienne chez les Francs.*

369. Montalembert, *Les moines d'Occident*, vol.2 pp.3-92 (on Benedict) and pp.451-640 (on Columban).

370. Gildas, who had become a monk after the death of his wife, trained with Finian under Cadoc in Wales. He wrote his now-famous book, *'On the ruin and conquest of Britain'* between 516-547 and is the only extant history of the Celts and earliest account from the time after Caesar's invasion. It includes a violent denunciation of the kings, prelates, and people of his own time. Most will already know the famous lament addressed to the Roman consul: *"repellunt barbari ad mare, repellit mare ad barbaros; inter haec duo genera funerum aut iugulamur aut mergimur"* – "The barbarians drive us to the sea, the sea drives us back to the barbarians. So, there are two kinds of death, either killed or drowned". He spent time at LLancarfan, then on an island in the Bristol Channel, then at Clonard, and then Rhys in Brittany, dying on Haut Island off the coast. As his own life and polemical history demonstrated; beyond the posturing of the kings, tyrants, and changing frontiers, there existed among people of faith and goodwill a richer history of cooperation and cross-cultural enrichment, even in the darkest of times.

371. Samson died in Dol-de-Bretagne, a small town in north Brittany, and was among the seven founder saints of Brittany with Pol Aurelian, Tugdual or Tudwal, Brieuc, Malo, Patern (Paternus) and Corentin.

372. Norman Davies, *The Isles*, p.119, 130 (Macmillan Publishers Ltd, 1999.)

373. Norman Davies, *The Isles,* p.139 (Macmillan Publishers Ltd, 1999.)

374. Norman Davies, *The Isles,* p.140 (Macmillan Publishers Ltd, 1999.) Davies also points out on p.213 that 'perhaps the outstanding feature of the centuries following the Roman collapse lies in the fact that the Germanic and the Celtic peoples

did not mix. What is more, the political and cultural divide which came into being at that time was going to be reinforced by the emergence of the four nations.'

375. 'The Fall of Rome and the End of Civilisation', Bryan Ward-Perkins, Oxford University Press 2005 p.124

376. i.e., mass-produced tableware and household products which had been common for the middle and lower classes in the 5th century disappeared entirely from the pottery record in the 6th century. Wheel produced pottery would not reappear for 300 years.

377. 'The Fall of Rome and the End of Civilisation', Bryan Ward-Perkins, Oxford University Press 2005

378. 'The Fall of Rome and the End of Civilisation', Bryan Ward-Perkins, Oxford University Press 2005, p.96

379. A. Wilson, 'Machines, Power and the Ancient Economy', Journal of Roman Studies, 92, (2002) 1-32, at 25-7)

380. 'The Fall of Rome and the End of Civilisation', Bryan Ward-Perkins, Oxford University Press 2005, p.113

381. 'The Fall of Rome and the End of Civilisation', Bryan Ward-Perkins, Oxford University Press 2005, p.133

382. His defeat of the Arian Visigoths at Poitiers could, unfortunately, be seen at the first 'Christian' holy war

383. His words in the Carmin III are, 'pulchra, modesta, decens, sollers, pia, grata, benigna, ingenio, vultu, nobilitate potens.'

384. Fredegunde famously asked her avaricious daughter in law to choose a gift of treasure from her trunk, but then slammed the lid on her and would have killed her if not prevented by the servants.

385. Hauck, Kirchenges. Deutschlands, I

386. 2 Chronicles 22:2 and 2 Kings 11:1

387. Reinhold Niebuhr, Beyond Tragedy, 1938:185

388. And as the feudal societies settled down to the less glamorous activities of producing rather than stealing their wealth, so too came creative solutions that revolutionised production. Most of these inventions are future to Columbanus time story (like the amazing tidal mill at Nendrum Abbey on Strangford Lough which was dated to just after Columbanus' death), but let us mention a few for heuristic value. For feudalism tied human genius to the land, and so within that 'field of enquiry' – so to speak – advancement came. The creation of the solid, padded horse collar which, unbelievably, only became widespread in the 9th century doubled the plough horse's pulling power and thus its productivity. That innovation alone, combined with selective breeding for strength, meant that some horses could pull a three-tonne load – six times that of the smaller horses with the old type of harness. And that was not all, many other innovations like the nailed horseshoe, the three-year crop rotation, the iron-shod plough, and the water wheel all had widespread effects. Most notable among these was the heavy iron-shod plough which brought whole new soils under cultivation. The 'discovery' of hay meant farmers

didn't have to slaughter their cattle in the winter and could therefore expand their herds quicker. Yet with all these innovations only 20% of the land of northern Europe came under cultivation by the 10th century, the rest was still forest. Britain was an exception with only 30% woodland cover in Columbanus' day, which was reduced to 15% in 1086. In the first century following the Norman conquest, 100 new towns were established. Incidentally, the Domesday book also recorded 5624 watermills in England serving 3000 communities at the time of the Norman Conquest.

389. Sergeant, *The Franks*, p. 217.

390. Simonism is the sin of offering or purchasing ecclesiastical offices for money. Jonas' accusation may not have been totally groundless, as apart from the Bishopric of Arles, the Gallic church was administered as a branch of the state by the Frankish kings.

391. Ibid

392. 5th Council of Orleans, Can. 6. from On Slavery under the Merovingians see Gfroerer, *Geschichte deutscher Volksrechte im Mittelalter*, II, pp. 3-35.

393. Dr. Alex O'Hara, *Jonas of Bobbio*, p11

394. As we will see later, Columban says he buried 17 brothers at Annegray in his short time there.

395. There have been even more recent excavations. The ruins at Annegray are legally protected through the efforts of the Association Internationale des Amis de St Columban, which purchased the site in 1959. The association also owns and protects the site containing the cave. I should point out here, particularly if the reader is planning to visit this beautiful corner of France, that there is also a large circular area of quite a few acres directly across the field from the site that we have been describing. Because I had, before my visit, always viewed the site from a Google satellite map, I assumed that this was actually the monastic site. When I talked with the Columban Scholar, Alex O'Hara, he had a similar feeling about it. But no excavations have taken place there – though I did, in a moment of exuberance walk to the base of the rise (which might have formed a Cashel) and dug about under the roots of the trees for ten minutes looking for lost treasures! Alas, my speculations were not rewarded!

396. J. M. Wallace-Hadrill *The Frankish Church* (Oxford: Clarendon Press, 1983)

397. This is a theme in Dominic Erdozain's book, *The Problem of Pleasure*. (Oxford University Press)

398. James Bullock 'Life of the Celtic Church' (St. Andrew Press, 1963) claims that apart from Augustine's Sees in Canterbury, Rochester and London (which struggled for existence, 'all England north of the Thames was indebted to the Celtic mission for its conversion.'

399. The Latin Christian missionaries and clerics were often more accommodating than Columban would be. The co-opting of the winter solstice for the feast of Christmas is a case in point. 'In Rome, the ancient fertility rites of Cornomania were still celebrated annually, in the presence of the pope, as late as the eleventh century.' Peter Partner, *Two Thousand Years*. p.96

400. 'The 'christening' of Europe can be exaggerated or thought speedier than it was in reality. Shame and honour, rather than the Ten Commandments long provided the basic moral concepts of its rulers.' J. M. Roberts, *A History of Europe* p.89
401. After a ten-year residency in Edessa, in his sixties, Ephrem succumbed to the plague as he ministered to its victims. The most reliable date for his death is 9 June 373. Source: https://en.wikipedia.org/wiki/Ephrem_the_Syrian
402. History shines with many other intellectual and artistic giants who understood how to shape the culture of their day, like Bach, Mendelson, Dante, Milton, Bunyon, Dostoyevsky, and Rembrandt. To create an authentic folk culture, and especially a counter-culture, one must radically model better ways of living. Wilberforce laboured 47 years for the abolition of the Atlantic slave trade and saw it happen 3 days before his death.
403. One cannot write this in 2020 without observing the phenomenal success of writers and speakers like Prof Jordan Peterson, Douglas Murray, and Tom Holland; who are addressing spiritually ravenous audiences right across the West. Their post-Christian disquiet is correctly felt and often brilliantly articulated. Their prescriptions, though essentially Kantian, are a solid step in the right direction.
404. Professor Brian Cox recently told Russell Brand in an interview that he quite understood that Science might never be able to answer our penultimate curiosity, but he was happy to remain agnostic about the God that might or might not exist. For him, science's search for proximate answers was satisfying enough.
405. C. S. Lewis
406. Columban's *6th Sermon*
407. Neil Gabler, *Life: The Movie: How Entertainment Conquered Reality.*
408. The Covid pandemic gave many a taste for what some people predict will be the inevitable outcome of job losses caused by Artificial Intelligence – the universal basic income (UBI). 'Stay home, bake, break, browse Facebook, booze, and binge on box sets.' After the unrest of 2020, it would seem that there are few now so naive as to imagine that a future utopia is just around the corner.
409. 'Amusing ourselves to Death,' Neil Postman
410. PBS *'Merchants of Cool'*, presenter Douglas Rushkoff reported that teens in America come in contact with 3000 discreet adverts per day; a staggering 10 million by the age of 18.
411. Today's basilica is the 4th century built on the site, completed by Abbot Eudes de Charenton in 1330.
412. French Encyclopaedist Denis Diderot: 'Men will never be free until the last king is strangled with the entrails of the last priest.'
413. Prof W.B. Glover, *The Biblical Origins of Secular Modern Culture* p216
414. *The Rebel*, Albert Camus
415. Just to help us pin him down, he is also known as Theuderich, Theoderic, or Theodoric, and in French, Thierry. But I will spell his name thus to alleviate confusion between him and Theodoric the Ostrogoth.

416. Formally an abbey church, the basilica contains old monastic buildings, which have been used as a minor seminary since the nineteenth century. It is dedicated to Columbanus and has a bronze statue of him in its courtyard.

417. This was where the obstreperous Wilfrid of York (of the Roman party) sought to 'extirpate the rank weeds of the Irish' once and for all. Even Bede, usually so moderate, showed little charity when Aethelfrith massacred 1200 Celtic monks in Bangor-in-Coed. It was left to men like the outsider, Theodore of Tarsus, who became the archbishop of Canterbury, to do his best to heal the theological and cultural rifts within the isles - which, amongst other things included disciplining Wilfrid. Theodore also allotted Lichfield to a disciple of Aiden's called Chad. Mature actions of reconciliation like this caused a wonderful Germanic-Celtic synthesis in the arts. Norman Davies, *The Isles*, p.202 (Macmillan Publishers Ltd, 1999.)

Gregory dictating to a scribe - perhaps replying to the letter from Columban

418. *Letter to the French Bishops, 603 AD.* 'Great harm has been done and is being done to the peace of the Church by different usages and diverse traditions. But if, as I have said, we first hasten by the exercise of true humility to cure the poisons of pride and envy and vainglory, through the teaching of our Saviour who says for our example: 'Learn of me for I am meek and humble of heart,' etc., then when we have been made perfect, with no further blemish and with hatred rooted out, let us all, as the disciples of our Lord Jesus Christ, love one another with our whole hearts. If there are diverse traditions as is the case regarding Easter ... let us see which is the more true tradition – yours, or that of your (Irish) brothers in the West. For, as I have noted in the book giving my answer, which I have now sent you, though it was written three years ago, all the churches of the entire West consider that the resurrection should not take place before the passion, that is, Easter before the Equinox. They do not wait beyond the twentieth of the moon, lest they should perform a sacrament of the New Testament without the authority of the Old. But this I leave

to another time. Besides, I have informed the Holy Father in three books of their opinions about Easter, and in a short pamphlet, I have further taken the liberty of writing the same to your holy brother Arigius. One thing, therefore, I request of you, holy men: with peace and charity bear with my ignorance and, as some call it, my arrogant insolence in writing. Necessity, not pride, is the cause of it, as my own worthlessness proves. I am not the author of this variance and it is for Christ the Saviour, our common Lord, and God, that I have come to these lands as a pilgrim. I beseech you therefore by our common Lord and beg of you by him who will judge the living and the dead if you deserve to be recognised by him who will say to many: 'Amen, I say to you that I never knew you,' to allow me with your peace and charity to remain in silence in these woods and to live beside the bones of our seventeen dead brethren, just as up till now we have been allowed to live twelve years among you. This will allow us, as we have done up to the present, to pray for you as we ought. Let Gaul, I pray, contain us together, whom the kingdom of heaven shall contain if our merits are good. We have one kingdom promised and one hope for our calling in Christ. We shall reign together with him if we first suffer with him here so that with him, we may be glorified. I know that to many this long-windedness of mine will seem overdone. But I decided it was better to let you know what we are discussing and thinking here among ourselves. For our rules are the commandments of the Lord and the apostles. In them, our confidence is placed. They are our weapons, shield, and sword. These are our defence. They brought us from our native land. We strive after them here, too, though lukewarmly. We pray and hope to continue until death in them as we have seen our predecessors do. But, holy fathers, see what you are doing to poor veterans and aged pilgrims. In my opinion, it will be better for you to support them than disturb them. For the rest, fathers, pray for us as we also do for you, wretched though we be, and don't look on us as aliens from you. For we are all fellow members of one body, whether Franks or Britons or Irish or whatever our race. Thus, let all our races rejoice in knowledge of the faith and in recognising the Son of God. Let us all hasten to approach to perfect manhood, to the measure of the age of fullness of Jesus Christ. In him let us love one another, praise one another, correct one another, encourage one another, pray for one another, so that with him and one another we may reign and triumph. Pardon me, I pray, for being long-winded and presumptuous. I am labouring beyond my strength, most patient and holy fathers and brethren.'

419. It wasn't until 1073 that the term Pope or Papa could only be applied to the bishop of Rome. J. M. Roberts, *A History of Europe*. Footnote on p.87

420. Even a century earlier, in 452, Leo I was able to persuade Attila to withdraw from Italy. He also – along with Belisarius - persuaded the Vandals three years later not to plunder the three oldest basilicas or burn the city to the ground.

421. 'Columban and his monks used the Irish Easter calculation, a version of Bishop Augustulus' 84-year Computus for determining the date of Easter (Quartodecimanism), whereas the Franks had adopted the Victorian cycle of 532 years.

The bishops objected to the newcomers' continued observance of their own dating, which—among other issues—caused the end of Lent to differ.' Wikipedia

422. *The Complete Letter to Gregory:* Grace and peace to you from God our Father and from our Lord Jesus Christ. I wish, Holy Father (do not think it excessive of me), to ask about Easter, in accordance with that verse of Scripture: 'Ask your father and he will show you, your elders and they will tell you.' When an unworthy man like me writes to an illustrious one like yourself, my insignificance makes applicable to me the striking remark which a certain philosopher is said to have once made on seeing a painted harlot: 'I do not admire the art, but I

Sept 2018: Filming at Carnac, possibly the world's largest sacred space, & situated a mile inland from where Columban probably landed c.590

admire the cheek.' Nevertheless, I take the liberty of writing to you, strengthened by the assurance of your evangelical humility and I append the cause of my grief. For one has no reason to boast of writing when necessity demands it, even if the writing is to one's superiors. I have read your book containing the pastoral rule, brief in style, comprehensive in doctrine, crammed with sacred things. I acknowledge that the work is sweeter than honey to one in need. In my thirst, therefore, I beg you for Christ's sake to present me with your tracts on Ezekiel, which I heard you composed with remarkable skill. I have read six books of Jerome on him, but he did not expound even half. But, if you please, send me something from your lectures delivered in the city. I mean the last things expounded in the book. Send as well the Song of Songs from that passage in which it says: 'I will go to the Mountain of myrrh and to the hill of incense' as far as the end. Treat it, I pray, either with others' comments or with your own in brief. In order to expound all the obscurity of Zechariah, reveal his secrets, so that in these matters the blindness of the West may give you thanks. Everyone knows my demands are pressing, my inquiries wide. But your resources are also great, for you know well that from a small stock less should be lent, and 'from a large one more'. Let charity move you to reply. Don't let the sharpness of this letter keep you from explaining things, since anger explodes into error, and it is my heart's desire to pay you due honour. My part was the challenge, to question, to beg; let yours be not to deny what you have freely received, to bend your talent to the seeker, and to give the bread of doctrine according to Christ's command. Peace to you and yours. Please pardon my rashness, Holy Father, for having written so boldly. I beseech you to pray for me, a most wretched sinner, even once in your holy prayers to our common Lord.

CHAPTER 10

Schuman: Prisoner & Fugitive

CHAPTER SUMMARY - 1939-1943, FRENCH CAPITULATION - The corrupted Third Republic. Schuman as Undersecretary for Refugees as the east-west migration surges. 1942 - DARK NIGHT OF THE SOUL - Self-sacrifice, solitary confinement and torture. Plans for Dachau, last minute reprieve and house arrest with Gauleiter Burckel. YESTERDAY'S MAN: CONRAD ADENAUER - Brief mini-biography of another key politician who would play an essential part in Schuman's story. 1942-1945, THE GREAT ESCAPE - Schuman's escape with resistance dossiers about Hitler's failing military-industrial complex, and the first high-level confirmation of the holocaust. His route across Germany and occupied France to deliver the documents to Marshall Petain. His monastic hideaways in southern France and then high in the Julian Alps until liberation.

> 'How can a man die better, than facing fearful odds,
> for the ashes of his fathers and the temples of his
> gods.'

> Thomas Babington Macaulay, *The Lays of Ancient Rome*

1939-1943, FRENCH CAPITULATION

Martin Luther King Jr, requoting Ruskin – an unlikely influence – said that a 'man who does not have something for which he is willing to die is not fit to live.' There is something almost unbearably moving when acts of great devotion, piety or fidelity lead humans to make the ultimate sacrifice for another. I can never forget Edward's reply in *Children of the New Forest* when asked by King Charles what gift he would like. He replied immediately, 'to be near your majesty in the hour of danger.'

Does modern life allow us no opportunity to express this great troth in heroic sacrifice? I cannot believe it. And I doubt the words of Cleo, the muse of history, who only attributes this sort of dignity to heroic warriors. Horace asks, *Dulce et decorum est pro patria mori*; 'what could be sweeter and more decorous than to die for one's country?'[423] And I think we should answer him, 'why, to live for it, of course.' None of us can tell when the 'great necessities' of life and human history will 'call forth great virtue'[424] in us. We simply don't and can't. But we can make preparation in the present by the many smaller acts of self-forgetfulness that make their claims almost every hour. That is all that is asked of us, *sufficient unto the day is the evil thereof*. For Schuman that day of evil was now upon him, and all of Europe. The hour for the great sifting of Robert Schuman had finally come.

At the outbreak of war his political star had still been rising, though he had been passed over for ministerial office by Clemenceau. During the inter-war years, he had been teased by the press as he was such an unusual specimen in the field of politics. His baldness was depicted as a tonsure in the cartoons and he was known as 'the man in the invisible cassock.' Apart from his other specialities and attainments, this *homme de frontières* with a special knowledge of Germany, was now even more in demand as Germany initiated the second half of the World War begun in 1914, and which Clemenceau's harsh terms in the Versailles Treaty had made inevitable.

The interwar governments came in ever more rapid succession. In fact, the Third Republic, which one writer called *the reductio ad absurdum of democracy*[425] had had 103 cabinets with an average length of eight months. (We noted in Chapter 1, the similarity here between France and 3rd century Rome.)[426] At the outbreak of the war, there were 15 former prime ministers still alive and able to criticize their successors! Another writer of that era argued that the French elites had ceased to believe in French democracy after the Popular Front victory of 1936 and that they had succumbed to fascism and fatalism. Most agreed, even at this time, that the Third Republic was subject to a deep internal "rot" – Petain called it a *moral failing* – that would make their defeat by Germany, if not a punishment, then certainly inevitable.[427]

Some Catholic movements, like the far-right *Action Française* (founded in 1905 by the bombastic author Charles Maurras) were also part of the decay in political instability.[428] Like the complaints of Livy in late antiquity, the French almost universally began to recognise and call the preceding era that led to this cultural crisis, *La Decadence.*

An anecdotal example of this cultural exhaustion was given in a preface to John Ruskin's work on moral philosophy, *Sesame and the Lilies.* In it he quotes at length the letter of a French woman to an English newspaper, pleading with her British sisters not to follow French women in their decadence and general casting off of moral restraints. What the letter reveals, in a very touching way, is that English women in the mid-Victorian era were held by some French in almost beatific regard, as paragons of virtues that the French had lost. But this was a hundred years before the time in which we are writing.[429] Between then and the war, France had suffered the humiliations of a German army at the gates of Paris in the Franco Prussian War, and the trauma of the Great War.

Maurice Hankey, secretary to the British cabinet and to the Committee of Imperial Defence, could already see at the outset of the war that a France 'half rotted with discontent and Communism' was hardly good news as Britain's largest ally. In the Great War France could only mobilise 21% of their population to defend their own homeland, which is only 1% more than the British raised to defend their neighbour in the conflict.[430] But even then, as Napoleon said, 'it is not the size of the army, but the power within the army' that counts. And the French had proved themselves no heirs of Bonaparte; lambs in the camp, and then lions in the forum when pressing for the disastrous level of reparations. In a very real sense, it was the cultural rot in France - *La Decadence* - that formed a *force majeure* of European instability. No wonder there was great soul searching as the French got their 103rd cabinet (in only 70 years), and the Germans were once more on the march. But soul searching is all very well if it produces genuine change. Remorse and regret are emotions with limited motive power if real repentance is lacking. Time alone would tell. It is sufficient now to highlight that Schuman was entering into a very complex and difficult political situation. He was not riding a wave but wading into a mire. French political strength was dissolving at precisely the worst possible moment.

1942 - DARK NIGHT OF THE SOUL

He had been working late on the night of 10th May 1940 at the Matignon (the Prime-ministerial residence) when the phone rang. Here he heard that Germany had invaded Belgium. He may well have been the first member of the French government to hear the terrible news. Belgium was only the beginning of the German's lightning campaign, soon they would enter into France too. France did not fall to the Germans immediately, the Maginot Line – France's ultimate defence-answer to a repeat of 1914 – was not actually on the frontier itself but some distance inland to the west. The region between the line and the frontier, known as the 'Red Zone,' was soon evacuated, and 206,000 people moved swiftly west. For the first nine months of the War, Robert Schuman served in the near-impossible office of Under-Secretary of State for these and other Refugees,[431] trying to serve the thousands fleeing Nazi occupation in the occupied countries: Belgium, Luxembourg and the Netherlands.

This was Paul Reynaud's fated last government before French capitulation to Germany and Vichy. He had known Schuman when they had worked together in the finance committee, and now the Lorrainer must have seemed an obvious choice as German speaking Alsatians and Lorrainers streamed west into France. Here, the unbearable stress of the role took its toll on Schuman[432] but one of the advantages was that he could garner intelligence from political refugees, and also from his friend Henri Eschbach who had stayed behind in Strasbourg.

Many of these intelligence gathering interviews were carried out in the Prime Minister's building, the Hôtel Matignon. And one of them, in May 1940, is very instructive on many levels, and worth mentioning briefly. It concerns Otto and Bernard Strasser, whose brother Gregor had been shot and then left to bleed to death for over an hour during 'The Night of the Long Knives,' when Hitler had purged the left wing of the party and anyone else that stood in his way. Otto, a key political opponent of Hitler,[433] and Bernard, a Benedictine monk, both fled to France. Their interview with Schuman was recorded by an eyewitness, Count Jean de Pange, a historian of Germany and personal friend. The comments are at once instructive of Schuman's philosophy of history but also his prior vision for some form of federalisation between France and Germany. Remember, this is 1940, not 1950.

> *'Schuman and Otto Strasser were in agreement about the essential points of his programme: no dismemberment of Germany but a federalization. ... The war today was not a national war but a conflict of dictatorships against Christianity.'*[434]

While Germany was in the ascendant and planning her thousand-year Reich, Schuman had already seen her failure and was already planning her forgiveness and healing within a new cooperative political structure. Here we see the statesman, his eye on the next generation, not the next election. And not only the next generation but also with a deep sense of historical forces and tides at work around him. But even as he was gathering his information, Germany was gathering her full strength to subdue France.

As the Germans invaded France in 1940 the government was moved to Bordeaux, further from the front, and Robert moved between Poitiers, Périgueux and the new capital while the government still remained viable.[435] There were 600,000 refugees and he opened an office for the department of the Moselle. But the situation was hopeless, and on the 10th July, France surrendered with the Vichy government under Marshal Petain.[436] Along with the majority of the National Assembly, Schuman voted in the new regime. It was the best of worse alternatives. However, he did not accept a position within the new authoritarian regime aligned with Nazi Germany. And he also refused to accept the Nazi's contention that 'France no longer matters; she has no future.'[437] Instead, he chose political exile, giving up what power he had indefinitely.

This relinquishing of a 'seat at the table' of power as a matter of principle, was not as obvious to some of his contemporaries. Petain was later tried as a Nazi collaborator and would have been executed but for his heroic military leadership in the previous war. The unquestioned assumption in *Il Principe* is that Machiavelli's aspiring Prince should always maintain and increase his power, not cede it. But to wield a power unjustly gained, even for the intentions of good, was not an illusion that Schuman would countenance. But neither did he entertain the illusion that a man in his position and reputation could just walk away without repercussions. Here was the same crisis decision moment faced by De Gasperi in 1920's Italy. Whatever he did would be misunderstood.

He remained free as the Germans consolidated their regime, but soon wrote to a friend, 'I sense that I am in danger; I get the impression that the Gestapo is taking an interest in me.' Having enjoyed a wide international correspondence in the inter-war years, he knew that many of his friends could be incriminated if his letters were found unsorted. He decided to travel back into a heavily occupied zone, in the Moselle region, to sort his papers – also known as 'making a big fire.' He knew this was a serious personal risk. On 15th July 1940, Maurice Blondel[438] wrote to Schuman pleading with him not to go. 'You are exactly the kind of martyr the Gestapo are looking for at the moment.'

But three weeks later, on 6ᵗʰ August,[439] Schuman went there nonetheless; to destroy the 'compromising documents.' But not only that; he also arranged the possible safe return to occupied Lorraine of refugees. This was also an act of service. He was their elected representative after all. He must do what he could once again, to defend Lorrainers against abuse by the German occupiers. But this time he was no longer a simple local lawyer as he had been 20 years before. Now he was a respected minister of the French government. He was, to repeat Blondel's warning, *exactly the kind of martyr the Gestapo was looking for.*

But far from thinking of his own safety, he appears, in correspondence, to have an almost Christ-like preoccupation with the needs of others.

> *'I await here for the turn of events having decided to return to Metz at the same time as the refugees of the Moselle... Will I be able to stay, to act, to live? ... I feel the burden of responsibilities and the immensity of the risks. We have lived a century in six weeks. What remains to us now is our unshakeable trust in Providence, in eternal, indestructible values and the grace from on high that will not fail us at the crucial test.'* [440]

And the crucial test was about to come. Here we see, not the politician, but the real, feeling man entering his great testing point. He took three days sorting through his papers and then turned his attention and legal mind to helping those constituents who were suffering unjustly under the new regime.[441] His apartment in Metz had been seized, so he stayed with his cousin Leon Schmidt, now vicar general of the diocese. He remained in Metz for over a month before finally applying for a visa to be expelled to France, and out of the occupied zone. It was 14th September when he was interviewed at the police station, and when he refused to become part of the regime, was arrested for acts of resistance and protest against the Nazis. He was imprisoned on the Rue Maurice-Barrès in Metz; a narrow back street, no trees, no outlook, a place to be forgotten during that long winter. Perhaps to be forgotten forever.

He would be incarcerated here for the next seven months in solitary confinement. How unlike another world, that former halcyon time of his student days in Metz, when he would have walked those same streets so freely, whilst perhaps dreaming of his future as a respected lawyer. Now he was a criminal, who must either cooperate or else be executed. When asked if he needed anything, he replied that he wished for one more jumper and his 26-volume collection of the histories of the popes. He was determined that he would not be broken and therefore assumed he would be there for a considerable time, hence the 26 volumes.[442]

Firstly though, the Gestapo interrogated Schuman about his intimate knowledge of the workings of French government, some of which were now 'underground' as the French Resistance. They must have wanted to know about their other enemies who had fled to France, and whom Schuman had personally interviewed earlier that year in the Prime Minister's building, the Hôtel Matignon. He was again offered a role in the collaborative government, this time by the Nazis, more eager than ever to gain legitimacy in the eyes of local people, by recruiting a respected regional figure. His biographer, De Rochefort, claimed that Bürckel offered Schuman the post of Gauleiter of Alsace-Lorraine in exchange for his cooperation. But his 'sweet obstinacy' seemed to withstand every threat and every promise. His parents were both dead. He had no siblings, and no wife or children to protect. He did not seem hungry for wealth or power. What could they do? Did they torture him?

When asked later about this time, Schuman said, with perhaps a taciturn smile, 'I was interrogated with insistence.' But, and perhaps surprisingly to his captors, he proved a hard man to break. The man who remarked that Schuman always spoke quietly and apologetically, could never have imagined that under all that Christian humility lay a strength too strong even for the Gestapo. What do you do with a man like that? When he had no books, he prayed. When he was given books, he read them and meditated. When given paper and a pen, he read and studied. No banging or shouting or pleading, but always the slow, meticulous and methodical preparation for the future. At one time he wrote out sections of an English dictionary, on scraps of paper in a minuscule hand, and so came to improve his English. Everything was preparation.

His letters from this period show a benign tranquillity; prepared for death if necessary, but never showing fear. 'We have become a pebble tumbling in the current', he writes with equanimity. And like his contemporary Mohandas Gandhi, Schuman displayed a great tendency to asceticism. He had 'a taste for solitude, even the capacity for celibacy' and 'a profound indifference to his own material comfort... old clothes, bare rooms, lack of heating in winter, cheap hotels'[443] were always sufficient for him. How infuriating for the Gestapo to have such an unusual prisoner! And how incomprehensible to them, and perhaps even us. 'The modern era rebelled against asceticism with every fibre of itself because it saw in asceticism the quintessence of all from which it wished to be free......man...conquering and humbling himself.'[444]

The Russian novelist Alexander Solzhenitsyn, who knew about this first hand, later wrote, "You only have power over people so long as you don't take everything away from them. But when you've robbed a man of everything, he's no longer in your power – he's free again." Even when he later became prime minister of France, Schuman insisted on taking public transport – often with two cars of beleaguered security personnel following behind the bus! To visit his home of Scy Chazelles is essentially to visit a three-bed cottage. It only has heating because occupying German troops installed it during the war! In every sense of the word, he was the sort of politician we all hope for, but would probably reject if another was presented to us.

'I have not been and I am not the unfortunate victim you might think,' he wrote later when still under house arrest. 'I have found resistance easy. Grace has not failed me. I find I am never tempted under these pressures.'[445] He wrote these words under the very real threat of being moved to Dachau if he refused to cooperate, and knowing that this meant a death sentence. He was indefatigable, with a core conviction of Christian truth, which motivated a life lived with innocence and

courage. In their desperation to find some leverage against this peculiar prisoner the Gestapo sought to 'dig some dirt' on Schuman. They
'searched in his private life but wholly without success'[446] even offering
rewards for anything proving his guilt. None could be found.

If any accuse the sources of hagiography, let us remember that; *none
could be found* – even at a time when evidence was easy to manufacture.
Maybe they tried that too, thinking to attack a man proud of his reputation and eager to defend his good name. If they had, and they probably did, I expect they would have been met with that same detached
smile. We see here the fruit of all his private discipline, but the Gestapo
must have thought they had got something very strange in Schuman.
He was either the cleanest or the cleverest politician alive. And so, when
blackmail would have suited the Nazis better, they resorted to a blend
of threats, persuasion and flattery, a 'politics of seduction' but still to no
effect, discovering again only 'the sweet obstinacy of Robert Schuman.'

As the spring of 1941 came, so too came Lenten preparations to
celebrate the Crucifixion. Schuman knew that his captors would not
hold off their threats indefinitely. He knew that his time, like his Master's 1908 Easters before, was soon at hand. What he did not know for
certain, but we do now is that preparations were already afoot for his
transport to Dachau. Indeed, arrangements had been made for his transfer but his loyal friends – which of course included Germans – were
watching his case closely. One of them, Heinrich Welsch, was Attor-
ney General; when he heard of the transfer, he rushed to chide the Nazi
command. Schuman was a highly respected citizen and politician in the
area, he said. Did they want to make martyrs? Did they want to cause
civil unrest?[447] So, the stay of execution came and he stayed in prison
longer.

And so, from the dark and cold of his cell in the Rue Maurice-Barrès
in Metz, Schuman arose that Easter morning, not for a crucifixion but a
sort of resurrection. The new government had just intervened to protect
him through a local German lawyer,[448] and so, Schuman was released
into the personal custody of the regional governor. On Easter Sunday,
the 13th April 1942, Schuman was moved to Joseph Bürckel's palatial

Villa Böhm,[449] in his home town of Neustadt-an-der-Weinstrasse in the Rhineland Palatinate. Here he was placed under house arrest, which Burckel had personally sought the Fuhrer's permission to achieve.

And so, it is now that we meet Schuman's evil nemesis: Joseph Bürckel, who Schuman had first met in Metz during interrogations. We saw Brunhilda play a perfect Jezebel to Columban's Elijah, and then Mussolini play a perfect King Saul to De Gasperi's David, and now we find Schuman face to face with a perfect Rameses for his meek Moses. In his mid-forties, and ten years Schuman's junior, Bürckel was a regional governor (a *Gauleiter*) with the power of life and death over millions in the Westmark region. A fellow Austrian and confidant of Hitler,

Josef Burckel with Hitler

Bürckel was a true believer in the Nazi vision, and had been involved in the movement from the beginning. In fact, this former school teacher, and fierce anti-Semite, was even elected party leader in 1934. He had organised the referendum for *Anschluss* – that is, Germany's absorption of Austria – and also the later political and economic integration.

Burkel knew of Schuman's anti-Nazi writings, and also his earlier work in Austria obtaining international loans to help them resist *Anschluss*. Bürckel had only recently been relieved as *Gauleiter* of Vienna and *Reichsstatthalter* (governor) of that region a month before Schuman was arrested. In Vienna, he had embezzled so much confiscated wealth that it could no longer be overlooked by the party. But neither could the party deny his effectiveness as a politician – pragmatism was after all the newest of the virtues. He had established, what was euphemistically called the *Central Agency for Jewish Emigration* in Vienna, which was at first responsible for the forced emigration of Jews. But then later, he was instrumental for the subsequent deportation and murder of at least 48,767 Austrian Jews out of Vienna.[450]

This ideologue had drunk deeply of the new wine and had already exercised this new, hideous strength, when he summoned Schuman to be brought before him. He, the great Bürckel; fabulously wealthy and all powerful, prodigious collector of art (usually other peoples'), steeped in blood and avarice, would 'do for' Schuman. He had broken bishops and arch-bishops in the east, men of standing and caste. This meek mannered, softly spoken politician would be putty in his hands. Schuman could certainly, he thought, be brought to their side in time, but only once he had given them, names, places, dates, information about other enemies of the Reich. Schuman, by his history, his training, his reputation and expertise, was the man they needed to make govern-ing the essential Alsace Lorraine region easier. Joseph Bürckel was in-structed from the very top, to do at the Villa Böhm what had proved impossible with seven months solitary confinement: to break Robert Schuman.

What an extraordinary turn of events. *What strange divinity shapes our ends?*[451] It is certainly poetically suggestive and surely can't have been lost on the religious Schuman; arising on Easter Sunday morning from a dungeon to a palace, like a latter-day Joseph. Or a new Moses studying all the wisdom of the Egyptians right under their noses – right under the auspices of Pharaoh himself. One of Jonas' literary exclama-tions would work well here: *wonderful providence!* To emerge from over two hundred plus days of solitary confinement, to the sound of church bells ringing all up the Moselle and Rhine as he travelled, would have been enough to give faith to an atheist. But was there any providence in this new form of soft incarceration? Bürckel had his own plans, of course, Schuman must have known this, but might there be a higher purpose in all this? The bells were ringing, and perhaps a little bell was ringing in Schuman's mind too. If it was not for Schuman to give information, then maybe there was something Schuman could discover from Bürckel.

Over the next five months, Schuman boarded near the Villa Bohm at his own expense with Mr and Mrs Kohler. He liked her cooking and they often talked late into the night about a day when the false notion of a 'hereditary enemy' would be no more, and Europeans could live peaceably together. The Villa Bohm was actually the administrative centre for Burckel's region, while the Gauleiter himself lived with his wife and children in a lavish villa in the centre of the town, which is now (rather aptly) a carpark. As the interrogations continued, Schuman remained alert. He switched mental roles from prisoner to spy – perhaps, his 'unshakeable trust in providence' might yet yield some fruit from this present predicament. One thing Bürckel was keen to know about was Schuman's pre-war travels and contacts in Germany. And one fellow politician Bürckel wanted most to know about was Konrad Adenauer, the troublesome mayor of Cologne. Did Schuman meet the mayor when he was in Cologne in 1932? Bürckel was desperate for anything with which to incriminate Adenauer, but even though Adenauer would be so significant for Schuman's future plans, he had as yet never met him.

YESTERDAY'S MAN:[452] CONRAD ADENAUER

Having mentioned Adenauer, let us spare a moment to meet this third giant of twentieth century politics, who would become another major founder of the European Economic Community. Ten years Schuman's senior, he was born in 1876 from very modest roots. His father was a city clerk, and his mother a seamstress whose extra income helped them put bread on the table and see three sons through university. Like Schuman, Adenauer became a lawyer in a private firm for many years before entering into politics. He was elected Lord Mayor of Cologne in 1917 ,aged 41. He always said that he had not lived one life but three. His life as a lawyer finished as he became mayor and a second began. Two years before his election Adenauer had been widowed and left to raise his young family alone. It came about that his children had played in the neighbours' garden with the daughter of the house: Gussi Sinser. Though much his junior Adenauer asked for her hand and they were married in 1919.

At this time, Adenauer was also beginning to play an active role in the *Zentrum* or Catholic Centre party, which attracted every stratum of German society. This is the party in which Schuman's uncle Nicolas was an MP, and as promised in an earlier chapter, it will be useful for British readers – who have little experience of the overt continental Christian democratic movements – to get a feel for the currents in European history that gave rise to the Zentrum party.[453]

Its founder was Ludwig Windthorst who translated the Catholic social teaching of Father von Ketteler into a political programme. In the wake of the 1830 and 1848 French revolutions, von Ketteler urged Christians to unite in tackling the social problems in Germany. Revolutionary fever was spreading in Poland and Belgium, and the elites in the established parties were not seen as responsive to the new situation. A similar process was going on in the Netherlands which led neo-Calvinist and Catholic thinkers and activists to eventually unite in the Anti-Revolutionary Party (ARP). Von Ketteler challenged German Christians to establish a political order based on fairness and solidarity and the lawyer Windthorst entered parliament to defend Catholics against a militant central power. By 1871, he was successful in forming a union to defend at once the Catholic minority, but also wider individual religious freedoms. Adenauer entered the party fifty years on when

it was still forming a bulwark against the revolutionary spirit, now further energized by Marxist thought.

By advocating and demonstrating a political union of many classes at peace with each other, united in the higher service of seeking social justice as taught by the church, it proved a bulwark against Communist ideas. By 1926, through his leadership of the *Zentrum*, Adenauer was offered the position of leading a coalition of parties in the rescue of the ailing Weimar Republic. He went to Berlin but could not get the parties to work together. As early as 1933 Adenauer made himself Hitler's enemy by refusing to raise the Swastika on the city hall, and even had the police remove a Swastika from one of the Rhine bridges when the Stormtroopers put it there. It was the year that the Reichstag voted away its own power to Hitler in the Enabling Act. The Nazis were unstoppable and political dissidents had every reason to fear.

Hearing soon after that the Stormtroopers had been given orders to liquidate him, Adenauer sent his wife to the Caritas hospital at Hohenlinde to join the children, who had already been sent there for their safety. His bank account was sequestrated on trumped-up corruption charges. These were eventually dropped but not before they had done their job of rendering him destitute. Many friends shunned him, but help found him from an unexpected quarter when a German-American businessman called Heinemann came to Berlin and offered Adenauer 10,000 Marks in cash because, he said, 'you might have difficulties cashing a cheque.' Adenauer initially refused the money on the grounds that he had no certain way of repaying it, but the American would not retract the offer and slipped away. (On his first visit to America in 1953, Adenauer's first visit was to meet Heinemann.)

Now sensing his own arrest would be imminent, Adenauer escaped Berlin for the famous Benedictine Abbey of Maria Laach, where a former classmate was abbot. What had started as an intended three-month rest, turned into a twelve-month period of serious reflection and recuperation. He needed more time than he realised, to process what had happened, not just to him personally, but for his party – who had voted in Hitler with the Enabling Acts – and to his nation. We get a feel for the impact of this personal, political and national failure when he wrote in a letter that if it were not for his family and faith in God, he would have committed suicide already. For so many years, he had been too busy with politics to pay attention to the things that had really mattered, especially his family. Now, politically disgraced and virtually in hiding, the broken man began to search for the bedrock upon which to build again.

He was over fifty by now and probably wondered whether Germany could ever use one of yesterday's men ever again. In a strange coincidence Maria Laach was a place where, during Holy Week 1913, Schuman had gone on retreat on the advice of Monseigneur Benzler, and later claimed this had been formational in his 'subsequent engagement in the life of the temporal city.'[454] Adenauer took long walks, and began to notice and write about nature for the first time. He attended the monastic offices, living like a monk in what was the finest Romanesque abbey in Germany. If this were a film, you would be expecting the emotive music to start building at this point. But remember this is 1934, and this is real life. There are ten harrowing years of suffering for him and millions of others still to come. But this moment is definitely the breaking and remaking of this remarkable man – a man to whom we all owe a tremendous debt.

But he would need more than brisk walks and bird-song to armour him for any possible future work. And so, he studied *Rerum Novarum* and *Quadregesimo Anno* and the other papal encyclicals on Catholic Social Thought, that had proved so formational in Schuman and De Gasperi's thinking. Toward the end of this formational interlude, Adenauer was joined that sparklingly white Christmas by his wife and four children, who stayed in the hotel next to the abbey. He would always remember this as one of the happiest events of his life. They were all together, and despite the growing menace, each had the shelter of the other – for now. But this reconnection seems to have triggered a new wave of persecution. The abbot was immediately ordered to 'give up' the enemy of the state. Although the abbot would have refused, Adenauer felt it prudent to return to his home at the Villa Wiener in Neubabelsberg, just outside Berlin.

But in March 1934, Adenauer received a court summons to appear in Cologne on an embezzlement charge. A bank manager from Cologne gave testimony that Adenauer had received 35,000 marks as a bribe from the Deutsche Bank for putting the city's banking through them. It was obviously a Nazi ploy to discredit a political opponent with the sort of practices they themselves were only too familiar with. From morning until late afternoon, Adenauer cross-examined the bank manager before the prosecutor and judge. Again, and again, he exposed many contradictions and inconsistencies, in almost every detail of the charge, and yet the prosecutor kept repeating the charge, and every time he did so, the court clerk assiduously wrote it down. In a final moment of either inspiration or exasperation, Adenauer pointed at the crucifix on the wall and adjured the bank manager, 'In the name of all that is sacred to you – tell the truth!' His words scorched the air like gunpowder, and the witness broke down suddenly, admitting it was a frame-up. And even when the enraged prosecutor turned on the false witness and severely threatened him, the bank manager held true, 'My original statement was untrue. I withdraw my charge.'

Three months later, on June 30th, 1934, came the infamous 'Night of the Long Knives'. Hitler executed perhaps as many as 1000 rivals and former helpers. Adenauer was arrested and interrogated in Berlin. However, after a lengthy cross examination he was released to return to Neubabelsberg. But not long after, his friend the abbot warned Adenauer that an assassination was imminent. He tried moving his family to Rhöndorf near Cologne but the government forbade him to stay in that district, so he left them and moved again from place to place on his own, worn down but never in complete despair.

In 1936, the new mayor of Cologne, feeling Adenauer had been badly treated, released part of his pension and compensation for his two properties, and also allowed him to move back to the district. With this money, Adenauer bought a house in Rhöndorf, in a leafy suburb overlooking the Rhine. In the three years leading up to the war Adenauer, now over sixty was left alone by Hitler. When war was declared, his three elder sons were called up for the army, he and his twelve-year-old son were left in the house with his wife, daughters, and daughters in law – eight women in all. In 1943, he declined to take any part in the active opposition group who planned to assassinate Hitler. He was asked to be part of it but not only did he doubt the wisdom of the people involved, but he also disapproved of the underhand methods.

He was a deeply religious man. He would not fight fire with fire, he would not plough with the Devil – not with clever devils and certainly not with ones whose abilities and methods he doubted. Had he read this exert below from Jacques Maritain on the base allurements of mere pragmatism?

'Justice and moral righteousness are thus essential to the common good. That is why the common good requires the development of the virtues in the masses of citizens, and that is why every unjust and immoral political act is in itself harmful to the common good and politically bad. Thereby we see what is the root-error of Machiavellianism. We also see how, because of the very fact that the common good is the basis of authority, authority, when it is unjust, betrays its own political essence. An unjust law is not a law.'

The plot failed. The reprisals, after the July 20th assassination attempt, were shocking and far reaching, including large scale tribe-extermination of anyone implicated – wives, children, parents, cousins, on and on. Hitler's paranoia and wrath seemed unbounded. Weeks later, and without any evidence, Adenauer too was arrested and interned in a concentration camp in the Cologne Exhibition grounds. They had nothing on him, and they had certainly not got anything from Schuman to frame him. How strange and how terrible to be interred in a concentration camp in the city that you were once responsible for. The overcrowding was terrible, but it was eased by nightly transfers of political prisoners to the infamous Buchenwald prison camp – where they were never to be heard of again. Adenauer's health quickly declined in the terrible camp conditions. But there was an ardent Communist there too, called Eugen Zander, who had been interred for years and given a small administrative role. Seeing the former mayor so ill, he offered him a clean bunk in his shed. One day he saw Adenauer's name on the Buchenwald extermination list. He quickly arranged for him to be sent to hospital.

A short time later, an air force major arrived at the hospital with papers ordering the release of the prisoner, who was to be driven to Berlin for questioning. It was Adenauer's friend, Major Hans Schliesbusch. Adenauer hid in Bonn, then at a water mill at Nistermühle, Hachenburg. But under intense interrogation, in which the Gestapo threatened to arrest and abuse her daughters, Gussi Adenauer finally disclosed his whereabouts at the watermill. He was rearrested, but due to failing health was kept in the prison hospital as the war reached its climax. Daily, the allied guns became louder and nearer. The hospital guards became nervous, and so made plans to shoot the prisoners. They selected a convenient site in the yard for the executions. Surely this time, nearly approaching his three score years and ten, Adenauer must have felt that the end was imminent and his life's work was done. We shall come back to his story in chapter 12, but for now, let us remain in Germany to observe Schuman's escape from the Nazis.

1942-1945, THE GREAT ESCAPE

We left Schuman playing a dangerous cat and mouse game under the very nose of the chief Nazi official of the area, but he knew that it was not a game he could play indefinitely. Bürckel offered Schuman the prestigious, and in many ways noble position, of Counsellor at the Appeal Court of Zwei-Brücken. Clever, very clever. Could he not do good there as he had tried to do in Metz; upholding justice and the cause of the oppressed? He declined. Bürckel then pressured Schuman into writing an article for the Nazi press. Schuman declined politely in another deft side-step. He had been too out of touch in the last seven months, he said, and so any literary efforts on his part would be too amateurish and not worthy of such an important commission. Bürckel then reminded

Schuman that the decision to send him to Dachau rested now with him alone. Schuman answered politely but firmly, 'You can, of course, always send me there, but that is not an argument.' But also, it was not all one sided. Schuman argued successfully with Bürckel that he could not escape without identification papers and so was allowed less supervision and even considerable freedom of movement beyond the town. Perhaps Bürckel expected a return of favours and a building of mutual trust by such little freedoms. He was wrong. Schuman used his freedom to the maximum and explored his new locality 'very methodically, as he did everything.'[455]

> 'Ever the keen listener, Schuman gleaned all the information he could from local townsfolk and libraries. He made clandestine contact with visiting alumni and professors of the Metz seminary and with the Lorraine and German resistance. His training in statistics at the University of Munich helped him put together a picture of German casualties on the eastern front and diminishing material resources. As early as 1942, he concluded that Allied victory was a statistical certainty. Germany had lost already 1.2 million men. At least another three or four million had been immobilised through injury or disease. Defeat was a matter of time.'[456]

He also met with the Resistance movements and even acquired a copy of the *Maier Economic Report* from his friend Henri Eschbach who was able to visit him.[457] But he also learned something else, either from Bürckel[458] or from another high-ranking Nazi official who visited. It was news so horrific that he knew he had to escape into free France so that the world could know what was really happening. He would be executed if he was caught escaping, but he also knew that he would be executed in any event if he refused his captors much longer.

So, on 1st August 1942, Schuman eluded them, while officially on a journey to Fribourg. In order to buy himself time, he got a friend to send a letter on his behalf notifying them of a travel delay. Why did they fall for this? It is very simple: after each preceding walk or journey, Schuman came back a little later, always giving some excuse, but always turning up just before anyone raised the alarm. It was a way that lulled his guards into a psychological routine that he could eventually exploit in his great escape. His ruse worked, and it bought him a few precious days before the massive manhunt got underway. Bürckel[459] must have been furious; to have been outwitted by a pious 'simpleton' like Schuman! He offered a reward of 100,000 Reichsmarks for information leading to his arrest. The other prisoners were certain he had headed for Switzerland, or at least, that is what they said, or perhaps that is what Schuman seeded in their minds. Schuman's actual seven-hundred-kilometre route would be in exactly the opposite direction; west across the Vosges into Free France.

Evidence of his movements are scant in the biographies, but the towns listed are Mulhouse, where dressed as if on a walking tour, under the assumed name of Cordonnier – which is French for Schuman – and with papers forged for him by his Resistance contacts, the fifty-six-year-old headed west to Niederbruck in the Vosges mountains, and then southwest to Rougemont, Besancon, and Arc-et-Senans. Thirteen days later, he crossed the demarcation line into Free France at Montmorillon. It was here that he was welcomed by Robert de Rochefort, whose biography was one source that I have been using and who would later be a member of his Ministerial Cabinet. On seeing Schuman, Rochefort said that he must now stay and rest. Schuman replied, '*Unfortunately, it is impossible, I have a duty to inform the Government. I have a lot of very important things to tell them, things that they can't just brush aside. I must meet with the Head of State as soon as possible.*'

And so, he left for his intended destination, the abbey of St Martins at Ligugé, just south of Poitiers. What a place for a man like Schuman to seek a temporary sanctuary: Ligugé is the oldest known French monastery and the area where Charles Martel turned back the forces of Islam, thereby altering the course of European history. Such details, such poetic and historical nuance would not have been lost on the exhausted Schuman. He came to see his friend, Abbot Dom Basset, for it was to him – probably the first person in the free west who heard

it – that Schuman related that the Jews were being systematically exterminated. Dom Basset, who was later awarded the *Légion d'Honneur*
by Prime Minister Schuman for his courageous acts for the resistance,
recorded the conversation:

> *There are no more Jews in the Ukraine. Men, women and children have*
> *been separated and taken. Men and women have been transported to*
> *concentration camps. Often, they are sent with hardly any water and*
> *without food. They are left to die of starvation and cold. They are often*
> *made to dig huge trenches and they are then shot in front of them. They*
> *are set on fire with petrol, then covered in lime and earth. The Polish*
> *Jews are often destroyed by such radical methods. They are transported,*
> *separating fathers, mothers and children. When the German popula-*
> *tions are transported, the families are transferred. The same goes also for*
> *those from Alsace Lorraine. But they had to leave without taking practi-*
> *cally anything with them, leaving their country, and finding themselves*
> *in very difficult conditions.'*[460]

Fake news is not a new phenomenon, and the fact that a reliable
source like Schuman was bringing this news directly from a high-ranking Nazi source was significant. Schuman was a man the world would
listen to. After all, his training in statistics at the University of Munich
was by one of Germany's leading state statisticians, Georg von Mayr.[461]
And it was not just data on the Holocaust and losses at the Eastern
Front that Schuman had collected. Dom Basset's other notes of that
meeting showed that Schuman had amassed a detailed report on the
following aspects of the enemy: Germany's final ambition of world
domination; its ideological, political and educational structures run on
atheistic, materialist and social-Darwinian lines; free speech and critical
thinking banned from primary up to tertiary education; the systematic
corruption of the Nazi Youth *Kultur* and state education; and the warfare against minorities, religions and particularly anything more than a
nominal Christianity. He also noted Schuman's analysis of how an intolerant Nazi minority exploited the tolerance of a democratic country,

and what dangers this posed to other open societies. (Here again, is a warning and lesson for our own times.)

He stayed in Ligugé for less than forty-eight hours, departing by train, arriving in Lyon[462] on 15 August, 1942. There he stayed with Monsignor Léon Schmit, his cousin, who was Vicar General and professor at the Great Seminary of Metz. From there Schuman travelled to Vichy where he delivered the news of the Holocaust[463] to a stony-faced Marshal Petain[464], who apparently said nothing.

> 'Among the public, however, news of Schuman's escape created great excitement, especially for the refugees from Alsace-Lorraine. Schuman addressed public meetings attended by up to 1500. He had news that was 'grave, full of hope, deep and spiritual.' His message that Allied victory was just a matter of time boosted morale greatly. Germany was certain to lose the war, he told attentive crowds in Lyon and other centres. His listeners heard how that his imprisonment had enabled him to investigate Germany's enormous losses on the eastern front, and gather specific numbers and details. The war was not sustainable. Sooner or later, Germany would have to capitulate.'

It was the adept statistician's declaration of victory. For though Germany still outwardly appeared confident and successful in its programme, Schuman knew that the statistics did not lie. But the comparative freedom of Vichy France was about to end, for within weeks the Germans invaded and the SS searches continued unabated. De Gaulle invited Schuman to join the French government-in-exile in London. But he decided rather to stay among his people, moving from place to place and using his time to read and plan for the future. These subsequent journeys are still obscure for a non-Frenchman, as regional names, town names and specific religious locations are all thrown in together among the sources in Rochefort's account of Schuman's meanderings for the rest of 1942. However, the place names show a continued movement southward and then westward, to the strongholds of the Resistance. Vernon, Montmorillon, Châteauroux, Royat and Rodez in central and southern central France appear. In the winter of 1942-3, he stayed in the Ardeche region at the abbey of Notre-Dame des Neiges. Here, he had a chance to perfect his English by reading the works of Shakespeare[465] and to deepen his knowledge of Roman history, under the hospitality of the local Abbe.

In the spring of 1943, Schuman's movements are still obscure in detail, but are on an east-west axis, between Bournos in the South-West near the Pyrenees, and Grenoble in the South-East nearing the Italian border. Near the latter is the alpine valley of Isere and Sanctuaire Notre-Dame de La Salette Fallavaux, a convent that perches on a mountain at nearly six thousand feet, up the Route D212C from Corps, in the *Parc Nationale des Ecrins*. It was this most picturesque of sanctuaries that Schuman made his home in the spring of 1943. Here he read the *Summa* of Thomas Aquinas, whilst posing as a teacher and making many affectionate friends.[466]

For Schuman too, the autumn came all too soon and it was time to relocate again. He descended the mountain to the plain, like Moses, armed not with stone tablets, but a fresh vigour from his scholastic diet. As winter 1943 descended over Vichy France, he moved north again, up to Bourg-en-Bresse. Here we have a *peregrinatio pro Christo* every bit the measure of Columban. '*One afternoon in November, in heavy rain, a fugitive knocked on the door... He was a traveller without luggage, with no case or personal belongings.*' [467] Schuman had been on the run now for fifteen months and had evaded capture and betrayal. He had nothing, but his wet clothes, not even his name, for he went under the pseudonym derived from his mother's maiden name Düren. Robert Durenne went with his friend the Abbé Guerber, former Canon of Metz miles north to the secluded farm hamlet of Bevey[468] where he was hosted for one night by Monsieur and Madame Brazier. The next day he was taken or walked a further five miles north to the orphanage just north of the small village of Beaupont.[469] In a small room at the end of the corridor, Schuman spent the rest of the War. As the winter passed, news came of developments in the conflict, including the Normandy landings.

But even as the liberating allied armies moved further into France, the German occupation troops and the militia gradually strengthened their presence in the sector of Coligny. Schuman knew he must take every precaution now that the end was near. He was still in contact with the resistance and used to regularly walk the half mile to the small bridge over the River Solnan on the road to Saint-Amour with a four-year-old boy called Robert Gaillard. At a hollow willow tree next to the bridge, Schuman – whom the lad affectionately called Pépé – would deposit and retrieve secret mail from the Resistance. The mail was fixed into the child's clothing so that if Schuman was stopped en route and searched, the Gestapo would find nothing. Robert Gaillard, who claimed to have diverted German soldiers away from the orphanage several times, also said that after the war Schuman thanked him many times and sent him Red Cross food parcels.[470]

Just after two years in hiding on 5th August 1944, children from the orphanage returned from a walk babbling excitedly; 'We've met the Americans!' No-one dared believe it until they began pulling from their pockets such luxuries as chewing gum, chocolate, and even canned milk. The next day, the townsfolk of Bourg poured out into the streets jubilant at their liberation. Schuman too emerged out of his seclusion in the small room at the end of the corridor to share in the joy of the moment. For the American soldiers, and the village folk, the war was over. But Schuman understood only too well, that his real struggle was only just beginning. Many had survived the war, but few understood as he did what it would take to restore what had been destroyed.

The novel writer in me is relieved that I am not having to make this into a work of fiction, because I know most readers would never believe the details and, moreover, probably assume the melodrama was added for effect. The Easter Sunday release, the bells, the unlikely saviours and last-minute escapes. Truth really is stranger, and usually more poetic, than fiction. By the usual laws of human caprice and the balance of odds, neither Gasperi, Adenauer, nor Schuman should have survived the war. When so many millions of other good men and women, and innocent children did die, these three men specifically targeted and persecuted by the Fascists and Nazis not only survived but came out stronger for the fight that lay ahead. That they became a political phenomenon and achieved one, is a story for another chapter. But for now, let us marvel at this gossamer thread of providence that seems to have led them all through such a precarious time.

In September Schuman began to travel freely again in his country, visiting Tournus in the East on his way back North. Initially, he settled in his father's border village of Evrange in the Moselle, as Metz remained a German-occupied town. He visited Paris in November and was already gearing up for involvement in the new government, once it was elected. In 1945, the Allies gradually beat the Germans back to their homeland and sought a final victory. The occupation of France had lasted for four years: Robert Schuman had been a free man for one of them, a prisoner for the second, then a fugitive under the protection of the Resistance for the next two years, until the Liberation. He travelled until VE day, appraising the damage to his country and planning its reconstruction.

Later historians give us a glimpse of economic and infrastructure loss. 'In 1946 European steel production was only one-third of the pre-war figure, while coal managed only 60% of the 1939 output. The railway system was in ruins and agriculture was in a worse state than industry.... Coupled with the destruction of her industrial base, France, Britain and the Netherlands were also about to suffer the shock of losing their colonial possessions.'[471] The international devastation was literally brought home to Schuman when he visited his own house in Scy-Chazelles, near Metz, and found it uninhabitable and its belongings destroyed. 'The ruins are immense; one does not know where to begin,' he wrote to a friend.[472]

The construction of the Fourth Republic was only one stepping-stone in his mind. His long-cherished vision was of a united Europe in which such a war could not be repeated again. Robert understood, as the child of a historically disputed border province; that a future for both nations must involve new cooperation and fresh political thinking,[473] unlike the many squandered opportunities of the Third Republic.[474] What is striking, about his adventures during the War, is that his political identity was already formed before the conflict, and was simply deepened during his years of hiding in 1942-1945, so he emerged back into French politics barely missing a stride. His war years appear only as a delay for his broader vision, and perhaps even a chance for the rest of the world to be persuaded, by its trauma, to listen to him. More people had died in World War II than all the previous wars put together. 80% of them had been civilians. 70% had been killed by the defeated powers. This had no precedent in human history and it was time to do what was possible that such things would have no future.

But that is not to say everyone wanted to hear him or even see him. On his first visit to Paris, the Minister of War noticed Schuman on a list as a Vichy government employee and immediately ordered '*this product of Vichy to* be dismissed. Other officials encouraged him to return to the Moselle region and work there. They had him taken in an army jeep with an army officer as protection. For this was the time of the purges when many embittered communists and nationalists were busy settling political scores.

A summons for his immediate arrest followed him; Robert Schuman must be tried on charges of collaboration with the enemy while he had been in Germany during the war.

Filming in 2018 at the Bridge on the road to St Amor, where Schuman took & received messages (pinned inside a young boy's jumper) for the Resistance between 1944-1945

CHAPTER 10
FOOTNOTES & REFERENCES

423. The phrase was famously used as the title of a well-known poem by Wilfred Owen, *"Dulce et Decorum Est"*, in which he describes the experiences of soldiers in World War I.

424. The words of Abigail Adams, the remarkable wife of the second president of the United States

425. Gunther, John (1940), *Inside Europe*. New York: Harper & Brothers. p.182.

426. Within a 70-year period of the 3rd century the Roman empire had 27 different emperors, only three of whom reigned more than five years and 23 of whom died unnatural deaths.

427. Jackson, Peter (2006). *"Post-War Politics and the Historiography of French Strategy and Diplomacy Before the Second World War"*. History Compass. 4 (5): 870–905 p. 873

428. "It was intensely nationalistic, anti-Semitic and reactionary, calling for a return to the monarchy and domination of the state by the Catholic Church. In 1926, Pope Pius XI condemned Action Française because the pope decided that it was folly for the French Church to continue to tie its fortunes to the unlikely dream of a monarchist restoration and distrusted the movement's tendency to defend the Catholic religion in merely utilitarian and nationalistic terms. Action Française never fully recovered from the denunciation, but it was active in the Vichy era." Source Wikipedia: https://en.wikipedia.org/wiki/French_Third_Republic#cite_note-Jackson_page_873-108

429. And lest I am accused of nostalgia, or idealising English virtue relative to France; one family survey taken just after WWII showed that 40% of brides at British altars were already pregnant, and as much as 25% of all children born were illegitimate. (Source: *The Sceptred Isles*, BBC Audio books)

430. https://en.wikipedia.org/wiki/World_War_I

431. De Rochefort (p.141) notes that Schuman emerged into a national role alongside Charles de Gaulle, representing opposing future poles of French foreign policy, de Gaulle towards the sovereign nation state, and Schuman, the family of Europe (p.85). They both served in the cabinet of Paul Reynaud, briefly Prime Minister of the Third Republic. (Reynaud was arrested before Robert and also imprisoned until Liberation.) Robert Schuman and de Gaulle also served together in the new French governments after Liberation (as indeed did Reynaud.) De Gaulle, perhaps in defence of his behaviour and political attitudes, once said, 'patriotism is when the love of your own people comes first; nationalism is when hate of people other than your own comes first.'

432. Robert Schuman, *De Rochefort* (Editions du Cerf, Paris 1968) p.85-87

433. It is probably worth noting that Otto Strasser was a political thinker that Schuman would share much in common with. The comments recorded by de Page may be as much the sentiments of Strasser's brother Bernard, who was a monk.

434. Jean de Pange: *Mes Prisons* pp45-6.

435. De Rochefort (p.88)

436. Among many other things, the creation of Vichy averted a plan that Monnet had suggested at the time, which was the complete political union between France and Britain. It had been agreed by De Gaulle and Churchill, but is little known to-day – and no wonder! No one involved King George and by the time a minister was finally sent, the French were already surrendering to Germans, and so it became an irrelevance, just one more what-if of history.

437. Ibid (p.97)

438. Blondel's philosophy had inspired Schuman. He was twenty-five years Schuman's senior. In 1893, he published his thesis "L'Action" (Action) but was refused a teaching post at this time as would have been his due, because his philosophical conclusions were deemed to be too 'Christian' and, therefore, "compromising" of philosophical reason. In 1895, however, with the help of his former teacher Émile Boutroux, he became a Maître de Conférences at Lille, then shortly after at Aix-en-Provence, where he became a professor in 1897. He would remain in Aix-en Provence for the rest of his career. (source Wikipedia)

439. One source says the 2nd September, see Victoria Martin De La Torre, *Europe, A Leap into the Unknown.*

440. Schuman's letter from Poitiers on 6th August to his friend Henri Eschbach.

441. His biographer de Rochefort is also quick to point out this extreme 'carelessness of self, care for others' in this moment of crisis: 'The Good Shepherd is he who does not abandon the flock to the wolf's predations. And because, despite all the personal risks, he did not hesitate to take up his cross, putting his steps in those of his Master, he knew that the grace that he had found in the cruelest hours of his life, would not leave him.'

442. The fact he only got through 9 of the 26 in 7 months makes one realise how long he had been expecting to be there.

443. De Rochefort (Editions du Cerf, Paris 1968) (p.29-30)

444. *The End of the Modern World*, Romano Guardini

445. De Rochefort (Editions du Cerf, Paris 1968) (pp. 103-4).

446. Ibid (pp.19, 51, 99),

447. Schuman never knew about this imminent deportation and certain death in Dachau until after the war. When Schuman did hear about it, at no doubt a very trying time, he took it as a great encouragement from God; that he had been preserved to make sure the same mistakes made after WWI would not be repeated.

448. Welsch, Heinrich: 1888- 1976. Lawyer, barrister. In 1955-6 Welsch became Minister President of Saarland.

449. This villa had been designed by the Jewish architect Ludwig Levy and is now a museum.

450. Source: Wikipedia

451. William Shakespeare, *Hamlet*4

452. He was once referred to as 'yesterday's man' after the war when he was already

a man in his seventies with broken health. Few could have imagined then that this man who, over the next 14 years, would lead Germany out of her political abyss.

453. What I mean here is that Christian Democracy is not well understood in Britain (or even the United States). Writers like Michael Fogarty assure us in books like Christian Democracy in Western Europe 1820-1953 (London: Routledge, Kegan, and Paul, 1957) that they are some of the most important political movements of the 20th century. The Christian parties, of varying creeds and internal piety, engaged in most democratic elections in Europe from the 1890s onwards. The roots are variously Catholic, Lutheran, Reformed, and Anabaptist and mixes of each, and they have produced varied expressions in Italy, Germany, the Netherlands, Belgium, Switzerland, Sweden, Norway, Eastern Europe, and elsewhere.

454. Villaros, 2006, p. 113.

455. De Rochefort (pp.102, 104)

456. Jeff Fountain, *Deeply Rooted* (P.44)

457. This was the secret German report from a meeting of the Economic General Staff, held in Karlsruhe on 2 February 1942 by Oberregierungsrat Dr. Maier. Notizen über die Tagung des Führerstabes Wirtschaft in Karlsrue vom 2. Februar 1942 provides an overview of all the strategic goods that Germany needed and the growing problems of production and supply.

458. I tend to think it would have been Bürckel. An ideologue like him would have had no qualms in disclosing such justifications to a man like Schuman who was never leaving his custody, except as a co-conspirator, or in a box.

459. Gauleiter Bürckel died two years later 'physically and mentally worn out, spending all of his time at work because of the deteriorating situation in his Gau. He suffered an inflammation of the intestine with diarrhoea, eventually becoming too ill to continue.' (Wikipedia) At the party funeral, the eulogy was given by Reichsleiter Rosenberg (who represented the Führer.) The Gauleiter's coffin rested on the flower-strewn platform, surrounded by black pillars and the flags of the Gau. The honor guard consisted of leaders of the party and the Wehrmacht. While Beethoven's *Coriolanus Overture* was playing, the Führer's massive wreath of red roses and white chrysanthemums was carried in by two S.S. men. The family entered, greeted silently by the gathering. The Gauleiter's wife was accompanied by Reichsleiter Rosenberg. After the last chord had sounded, Reichsleiter Rosenberg, as the Führer's representative, delivered a memorial address. *Josef Bürckel was a devoted nationalist and a passionate socialist. In all of his life, he symbolized the unity that, from the standpoint of our worldview, reflects outwardly that great inner experience, that great idea, for which we fought.'* Reichsleiter Rosenberg concluded: "The Führer has authorized me, party comrade Bürckel, to express to you his thanks for your complete loyalty to him and to the movement. More than ever before, the Führer remembers the loyal support of one of his oldest fellow fighters, who never grew weary during the years of struggle, who always followed the Führer and his banner. In

particular recognition of this exemplary National Socialist life, and as a continuing reminder for coming generations,

the Führer awards you, Joseph Bürckel, the highest level of the German Order with Swords. This will be a symbol of your beloved Gau, and of your loyalty to the whole National Socialist movement. We now take leave of you. The flags of the Greater German Reich will flutter over your grave, and the soldiers of the German people will pass by you as they march west, where they will protect German territory and realize what you gave your whole life for, along with the great loyalty of your heart." After these parting words to the deceased Gauleiter, Reichsleiter Rosenberg presented, at the Führer's instruction, the German Order with Swords. Alfred Rosenberg then placed the Führer's wreath on the Gauleiter's coffin. The party ceremony ended with the moving second movement of Beethoven's Eroica. On Wednesday morning, the mortal remains of Gauleiter Bürckel were laid to rest in his native soil of the Neustadt cemetery.

460. Price, David Heilbron: *'Robert Schuman's warning of the Nazi destruction of the Jews, August 1942'*
http://users.belgacombusiness.net/schuman/Jews.htm - accessed Feb 2018

461. Mayr, Georg von: 1841-1925. Professor of Statistics, Munich. Politician. Author of Statistik und Gesellschaftslehre and other books on statistics. Responsible for statistical survey in both Bavaria and Alsace-Lorraine where he was Under Secretary of State. Member of Commission for Tariff Reform.

462. There is a rose named *"Remembrance of Robert Schuman"* designed by rose growers in Guillot de Lyon

463. Holocaust reportage: The extermination of Jews first happened as German troops advanced into Russia in July 1941. Reports of massacres leaked out of Nazi-occupied Europe. The Polish government in exile had compiled a dossier of atrocities and by the end of 1942 (i.e., 5 months after Schuman smuggled out his reports) the world knew that a genocide was underway. The UN issued a document; The Mass Extermination of Jews in Germany and Occupied Poland in late as 1942, which was referenced by Anthony Eden in the House of Commons. And yet for the reportage and eyewitness accounts from the 192 people who had escaped, it was the liberation of Bergen Belson in April 1945 that really brought the horror within reach of British public imagination. My own sister-in-law's great grandfather, Brigadier Glynn Hughes, was in charge of the liberation and a harrowing new history has just been published by Amberly called To Meet in Hell: Bergen-Belsen, the British Officer Who Liberated It, and the Jewish Girl He Saved.' by Bernice Lerner.

464. Petain's 'Statut des Juifs,' published on 3rd October 1940, excluded Jews from government, and the liberal professions such as medicine and law.

465. De Rochefort (pp.128, 129)

466. Seventy-five years later, I arrived by car at this remarkable place, enroute on the Via Francigena to Italy. It was on a cloudless and breathless autumn afternoon with thin ribbons of vapour hanging listlessly over the distant snow-capped Alps. Pilgrims, who arrived on motorbikes, in cars and coaches, were making their way

to the church, the gift shop, and the shrines. It is now also a residential centre for Catholic retreats and I found some very cheerful staff to lead me to an upper corridor where, under a large picture of Robert Schuman I was able to speak with the Polish Recteur, Padre Antoni. He was very interested in the canonisation process of Robert Schuman and wanted to use the Schuman legacy as leverage at La Salette for conferences and retreats – to encourage more Christians from their pews and into political service. The western world, we agreed, didn't need more saints in stained glass, it needed more saints in suits. The prior asked if I would be willing to come back to speak at an event if he could organise something. I, rather flattered, said yes, though on reflection thought of a handful of people who would be far more useful to him. Nevertheless, I was cheered by the encounter and when I finally went outside again to the church, I met a Guardian-reading,

French-Canadian teacher from Lyon called Matthew who seemed very interested in our project. We talked for a while about Schuman, Aquinas, Brexit, and the future. He was a Catholic who had, like many friends of mine, been touched deeply by the charismatic renewal (mentioned in a previous chapter), and had also been to Holy Trinity Brompton in London. He was a very open-hearted and tender young man and it was with difficulty that I had to end the encounter and get back to work.

467. De Rochefort p.131

468. Bévy, Marboz, Auvergne-Rhone-Alpes

469. Beaupont is in the canton of Coligny and border with the Department of Saône-et-Loire. I spent an afternoon there in September 2018. I wrongly assumed that the library (which was always featured in online pictures) was the orphanage. It was only when I went to get some bread that the middle-aged patisserie owner disabused me of my error. Apparently touched that a Brexiting Englishman would be making a documentary about a relatively unknown French hero and the part their backwater-town played in his story, she shut up the shop and drove us two miles north to the psychiatric hospital on the D56 near junction 10 of the AutoRoute. I arrived even as police were entering and I smiled politely, waited my turn to ring the buzzer, and eventually was let into the complex. In my own mind, the buildings didn't look old enough so I just entered the building with a Gopro and nothing more. In the office, I managed, through the kind interventions of various members of staff whose English was better than my French – not hard – to establish that this indeed had been an orphanage in the war. But, they said, très désolé, it would not be wise or indeed legal for me to wander any further inside with a camera. I wanted a shot in the room at the end of the corridor, but I was not to get it.

470. Gaillard, who claimed to be the youngest member of the French Resistance, was refused a Veteran's card in 1986. Some elderly ladies, whom we interviewed in Beaupont and who remembered him, said that he took Schuman as a surname later in life and had died only ten years earlier.

471. *The Birth of Europe*, Mike Andrews, BBC Books.

472. De Rochefort (p.139)

473. Ibid p.72

474. Ibid p.135

Columban – Prisoner & Fugitive

CHAPTER SUMMARY - VOSGES TO NANTES – A broken-hearted Columban on a 300-mile journey down the Loire to Nantes expecting extradition to Ireland. An unexpected sign and reversal. SOISSONS TO METZ - King Clothar II of Neustria offers Columban land on the edges of his kingdom – Bregenz on Lake Constance. Columban embarks on a 400-mile boat journey up the Rhine calling at many places whose history and culture are also discussed.

"I confess that I am broken, for while I wished to help everyone, they fought against me without cause; and while I trusted everyone, they have me driven almost mad. I wanted to write you a tearful letter, but my grief is shut up within. The tears flow, but it is better to check the fountain, for it is unbecoming for a brave soldier to lament in battle."[475]

VOSGES TO NANTES

Let us start this chapter at the end, and then jump back to the beginning. We left Columban in his thriving monastery at Luxeuil confidently denouncing the secular authorities and writing to the pope over the heads of the local bishops. We join him now a few years later, in a much-reduced state and many hundreds of miles away. We have viewed Schuman in solitary confinement in Metz, Adenauer in a concentration camp in Cologne, and De Gasperi in prison, and then hiding during his political wilderness years. Now let us observe with sympathy, the moment of Columban's great sifting. The quotation above is Columban's farewell letter to the Luxeuil monks written from Nantes as he awaited the unthinkable – the Franks are about to undo his voluntary exile, and extradite him back to Ireland.

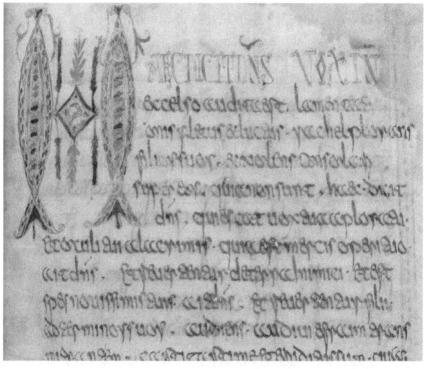

Gallican Lectionary, from Luxeuil Abbey, using Luueil minuscule script

'I confess that I am broken... they have me driven almost mad. I wanted to write you a tearful letter, but my grief is shut up within.' It is the lament of the broken-hearted dreamer on the verge of complete nervous collapse. Written in 610AD it reaches across time to us. His friend Diecole (Gall's older brother, also called Domgall), who had come with him from Ireland and was now in old age, had attempted this final exile of humiliation with his abbot, only to find that his age would not permit him to go on. These sorts of cruel partings must have piled sorrow and inward recriminations on poor Columban's head.[476]

With Schuman and Adenauer, we saw that tempered Germanic steel under tremendous pressure, yet still unyielding. If Schuman's stoic soul ever despaired or broke down, we do not hear of it. Both Adenauer and De Gasperi had, or something very like what we would call, nervous breakdowns under the titanic pressures that sought to crush them. But with Columban, we feel the full vent of his agony. He senses the abyss of self-pity and madness right before his eyes; the unanswered and unanswerable questions; the might-have-beens, the titanic forces of malice and envy always poised to crush whatever is pure and good. These are old themes to any middle-aged entrepreneur. The 'slings and arrows of outrageous fortune' are sufficient on their own to bury most of us in inertia. How people like Schuman and Columban managed to go on and on, seems almost miraculous. Churchill, who knew more than a little of this, said, 'If you are going through Hell; keep going.' Easier said than done. If you have been driven to the edge of the abyss like Columban, you will know that.

I want to linger here a moment longer, because it is on the edge of the abyss that real and lasting change can come to individuals and nations. This is the essential difference between the League of Nations and the ECSC, which became the EEC. The brink of the abyss was where remorse and regret can become repentance and true action. For Adenauer and De Gasperi, it was the catalyst for serious reappraisal and opportunity for a surer foundation. Would it be so for our Irish Elijah?

Here we find the recurrent theme in Western literature; *peripeteia*, the great and sudden reversal of circumstances. As we are here dealing with a poet in Columban, so let us compare him with one. Lord Byron, with a soul no less romantic than Columban's, was once laid low by an illness and thought himself close to death. It was in his despair of recovery, that he wrote his famous *Adieu* poem, which is full of questions and self-analysis: 'Why did my childhood wander forth, from you, ye regions of the North, with sons of pride to roam?' He sees that it was the 'hope of future fame' that led him from the simplicity of Loch na Garr's snowy slopes. 'Oh Fame!' he writes bitterly as the steel enters his soul, 'thou goddess of my heart.' His plans for stardom are undone all at once by the spectre of death, which cuts short his 'inglorious race' and 'beckons' him 'from the earth' his 'name obscure, unmark'd my birth.'

Poor Byron, he was so young and his goal such a small and vain one. Yet even he, when the world's allure had found its true place in the light of life's brevity, turned his gaze to that other world. If he was to go 'unheeded' here, then perhaps there was forgiveness in the next.

Forget this world, my restless sprite,
Turn, turn thy thoughts to Heaven:
There must thou soon direct thy flight,
If errors are forgiven.
To bigots and to sects unknown,
Bow down beneath the Almighty's Throne;
To Him address thy trembling prayer:
He, who is merciful and just,
Will not reject a child of dust,
Although his meanest care.
Father of Light, to Thee I call;
My soul is dark within:
Thou who canst mark the sparrow's fall,
Avert the death of sin.
Thou, who canst guide the wandering star,
Who calm'st the elemental war,
Whose mantle is yon boundless sky,
My thoughts, my words, my crimes forgive:
And, since I soon must cease to live,
Instruct me how to die.

Poor Byron, a remarkable man (in so many other ways unacknowledged in the West,)[477] yet he's no one's idea of a Christian saint. In fact, he probably stands antithetical to Columban and Schuman at most points, except in his courage and scholarship. Yet I cast him here as the type of a repentant and prodigal Europe, finding sanity after the madness of two, devastating wars. Also, there is something in Byron's prayer that has echoes in Columban's musing in Sermon Five, which rings with the same melancholy; "Oh, life, fragile and mortal. ... so, you are the road to life, not life itself; you are a real road, but not a level one, long for some, short for others, broad for some, narrow for others, joyful for some, sad for others."

It might be very impudent of us to pass judgment on such extraordinary people from such a different world, but might there not have been just a touch of olympian pride among these elite Irish monks? Columban's strident stance toward the secular powers and his open disapproval of the Gallic bishops has more than just a faint whiff of hubris about it. He had called the king's sons bastards, which they were, but in such a way as to meddle publicly with the dynastic succession.[478] And like a fiery John the Baptist, Columban had publicly criticised the morality of the monarch. We might not be able to agree to what extent religious belief should be reflected in secular public life, but surely this is pushing it a bit. As a self-imposed guest, an exile, a stranger and pilgrim, he could have been more circumspect. It is a controversial claim within moral psychology but surely there were those telling Columban that, for the purposes of prudence at the very least, 'more people are flattered into virtue than bullied out of vice.'[479]

Columban's tone is too self-assured and judgemental. John the Baptist was the last of the Old Testament prophets, not a pattern for the New. In his general disdain for the world, might Columban have forgotten his manners? Whatever the imperfect condition of the Gallic state and church – and I tried to give a balanced view two chapters back – it was stability in the secular realm that had enabled the monasteries to prosper in the first place. The human heart is so inventive that it can even produce pride out of genuinely achieved humility and piety. We can say this even while admitting, with Oswald Chambers, that 'conscious humility is the most Satanic form of pride.' We will never know, and perhaps these sorts of observations are better applied for home use!

Whatever the case, Columban gives full vent to his grief and heartbreak. Psychologically this was the healthiest option under the circumstances. He restates to Attala, whom he addresses very tenderly, that his real concern is for the monks left behind; that they remain united in purpose and personal development. Even staring into the abyss of an ignominious return to Ireland, his thoughts are for those he loves. We must all – parents, managers, pioneers – work towards our own redundancy. Knowing it, still doesn't make it easy. Columban gives us the tension in this letter. Not fifty percent lament and fifty percent pastoral council but a full Irish measure of both. And having done that, he will suppress further tears as unworthy of a soldier engaged in battle. He is still on a war footing, even now, he hasn't given up.

Why? How? The answer must surely be that he (and later Schuman) lived in a broader meta-narrative, a vast overarching biblical story of how good would eventually triumph over evil. This narrative structure allows, even expects, setbacks – however inexplicable, however awful. Columban is the one who wrote, 'I am always on pilgrimage, moving from the day of my birth up till the day of death, and throughout the individual days of my life I change, and what things change or how they change I do not see, and I can never see my whole life in one together, and what yesterday I was, today I am not, and thus what today I am, tomorrow I shall not be.'[480] Now he must wade forward on a path he cannot see and has not chosen. In his letter from Nantes, he goes onto remind the monks, and perhaps himself, that:

'...true disciples of Christ crucified should follow him with a cross. Blessed is the one who shares in this passion and shame, for the foolishness of God is wiser than men. Therefore, let us patiently bear all adversities for truth's sake, that we may be sharers in the Lord's passion, since none are worthy of mercy, except those who confess their unworthiness. It is through affliction of the flesh, and contrition of the heart, through Christ's grace that we enter the city of the living

*God. They come to tell me the ship is ready. The end of my parch-
ment compels me to finish my letter. Love is not orderly; it is this
which has made it confused. Farewell, dear hearts of mine; pray for
me that I may live in God.....*"

To find out whether or not he sails to Ireland, we shall have to wait to
the end of the chapter. For those with a smattering of French geography
will have noticed that Nantes is a fair way from the Vosges – about 300
miles as the crow flies. How did Columban get there? This is the story
set before us in this chapter. If you remember two chapters back, when
Theuderic II finally confronted Columbanus at Luxeuil, Columban ve-
hemently refused to cooperate. In fact, he threatened the king's whole
household with divine retribution! It was a step too far. The young king
left a nobleman called Baudulf behind who took Columban as a prisoner to Besançon. But Columban not only managed to escape them and
return to Luxeuil, but he also absolved some other condemned men of
their sins and set them free from prison too. The king and his grandmother, therefore, went a stage further: nothing but exile would now
do. But who would rid them of this turbulent priest? They sent Count
Bertarius and Baudulf with soldiers to escort him and the other Irish
monks back to Ireland by force, saying that only the Gallic monks[481]
could stay on at the three Vosges monasteries. So, a hostile takeover. A
Captain called Ragemund was left with the grisly task.

Their journey is a strange one and by no means as the crow flies. Initially south again to Besancon, then east to Autun, and then north to
Auxerre. Jonas tells us of many miracles on the way; healings and judgments. I wonder too whether the old seer had any premonition while
passing through Autun, for it was here sixty years later where a synod
ruled that all the Irish monasteries should henceforth adopt the Benedictine rule. He stayed in a Fort at Cavalo, and then also with a 'noble
and pious lady, named Theudemanda,' on the River Chord (now called
the River Cure) 'where he healed twelve demoniacs.'

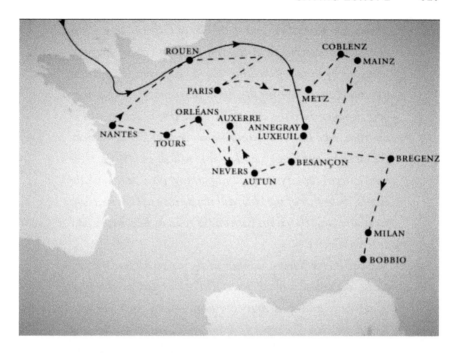

He must have passed through Vezelay en route to Auxerre; the former where Bernard preached for the second crusade, the latter where the runaway slave Patrick had trained two centuries earlier before returning to Ireland. Why they went so far north before turning sharp southwest to Nevers is not clear in the text or on the map. We know that his nemesis Brunhilda had an estate at Brocarica near Autun, so maybe they had to go there for provisions, or money, or to have Brunhilda gloat. But then why the subsequent zig-zag to Nevers is unclear. Perhaps they fell in with a crowd going that way, perhaps there was the offer of a boat from there. Whatever the reason Jonas tells us that, 'with guards preceding and following, Columban came to the city of Nevers in order to go in a boat on the Loire to the coast of Brittany.'

On the Loire, they experience abuse and persecution, though often not with the meekness of lambs. Columban, the man who courted martyrdom like a bride, could endure anything himself but was roused to indignation by the ill treatment of his friends. The journey on the Loire is so interesting and vivid that I will let Jonas tell it in full:

'From that place they went to the city of Orleans, where sorrowfully they rested for a time on the banks of the Loire in tents, for by order of the king, they were forbidden to enter the churches. When finally, their provisions gave out, they sent two men into the city, to get food. One of these was Potentinus, who later on founded a convent in Brittany, near the city of Coutances[482] and who is still alive. When these men entered the city, they found nothing, because the inhabitants, from fear of the king, did not dare to sell or give them anything, and they went back on the road by which they had entered the city.

They met a Syrian woman in the street. When she saw them, she asked who they were? They explained the state of the case, and said that they were seeking food but had found nothing. She replied, "Come, my lords, to the house of your servant and take whatever you need. "For I, too, am a stranger from the distant land of the Orient." They joyfully followed her to her house and sat down to rest until she brought what they sought. Her husband, who had long been blind, was sitting near them. When they asked him who he was, his wife replied, "My husband is from the same race of the Syrians that I am. As he is blind, I have led him about for many years."

They said, "If he should go to Columban, the servant of Christ, he would receive his sight through the holy man's prayers." The man having faith in the promised gift, regained his courage, rose and, led by his wife, followed them. They told Columban of the hospitality given to pilgrims. They had not finished their story before the blind man came and prayed the man of God to restore his sight by prayer. Columban, seeing the man's faith, asked all to pray for the blind man, and after laying for a long time prone on the ground, he rose, touched the man's eyes with his hand and made the sign of the cross. The man received his longed-for sight. He rejoiced in his recovered sight, because it was fitting that he, whose soul had been lighted internally by hospitality, should not lack the external vision.

After that a band of mad men, whom demons tortured with savage fury, hastened to the man of God to be cured. Health was granted them by the Lord; for all were healed by the man of God. The people of the city moved by these miracles supplied Columban with gifts secretly, because they did not dare to furnish anything openly on account of the guards, lest they should incur the wrath of the king. Thence Columban and his followers continued on their way.

And proceeding on the Loire, they came to the city of Tours. There, the holy man begged the guards to stop and permit him to visit the grave of St. Martin. The guards refused, strove to go on quickly, urged the oarsmen to put forth their strength and pass swiftly by the harbour, and commanded the helmsman to keep the boat in mid-stream. St. Columban seeing this, raised his eyes sadly to heaven, grieving at being subjected to great sorrow, and that he was not permitted to see the graves of the saints. In spite of all their efforts the boat stopped as if anchored, as soon as it got opposite the harbour, and turned its bow to the landing-place. The guards seeing that they could not prevail, unwillingly allowed the boat to go where it would. In a wonderful manner it sped, as if winged, from mid-stream to the harbour, and entering this accomplished the wish of the man of God.

He, truly, gave thanks to the eternal King, who does not disdain to comply with the wishes of His servants. Landing, Columban went to the grave of St. Martin and spent the whole night there in prayer. In the morning he was invited by Leoparius, the bishop of the city, to break his fast. He accepted, especially for the sake of refreshing his brethren, and spent that day with the bishop. When he sat down at table with the bishop, at the hour of refection, and was asked why he was returning to his native land, he replied, "that dog Theuderich has driven me away from the brethren."

Then one of the guests, named Chrodowald, who was married to one of Theudebert's cousins, but who was a follower of Theuderich, replied in a humble voice to the man of God, "It is pleasanter to drink milk than wormwood," and declared that he would be faithful to king Theuderich, as he had sworn, so long as it was in his power.

Columban said to him, "I know that you want to keep your oath of fidelity to king Theuderich, and you will be glad to take my message to your lord and friend if you serve king Theuderich. Announce, therefore, to Theuderich that he and his children will die within three years, and his entire family will be exterminated by the Lord."

"Why," said the man, "do you announce such tidings, O servant of God?"

"I dare not conceal what the Lord has ordered me to reveal."

All the inhabitants of Gaul saw this fulfilled later, and this confirmed what had been announced previously to Ragamund.

Joyfully then, they went in the boat to the city of Nantes and there stopped for a short time. One day a beggar cried out before the door of the cell in which the man of God was meditating. Calling an attendant, Columban said: "Give the beggar some food."

The attendant replied: "We have nothing except a very little meal."

He asked: "How much have you?" The attendant replied that he thought he did not have more than a measure of meal. *"Then give it all," he said, "and save nothing for the morrow."*

The servant obeyed and gave all to the beggar, reserving nothing for the common need. Already the third day had dawned since they had been fasting, and had had scarcely anything except the grace of hope and faith, by which to refresh their exhausted limbs. Suddenly they heard the door open; when the doorkeeper asked why the ears of the brethren were troubled by the din, he who had opened the door said he had been sent by his mistress Procula. She said she had been divinely warned to send food to the man of God, Columban, and to his companions, who were staying near the city of Nantes.

The man said the food would come immediately, and that he had been sent ahead to tell them to prepare receptacles to receive it. There were a hundred measures of wine, two hundred of grain, and a hundred of barley. The doorkeeper hastened to announce this to the father. But the latter said, very well, he knew it, and ordered that the brethren should come together to pray to the Lord in behalf of their benefactress, and at the same time to return thanks to their Creator who never fails to comfort His servants in every need; and after that they would receive the gifts.

Wonderful compassion of the Creator! He permits us to be in need, that He may show His mercy by giving to the needy. He permits us to be tempted, that by aiding us in our temptations He may turn the hearts of His servants more fully to Himself. He permits His followers to be cruelly tortured that they may delight more fully in restored health.

Another equally noble and pious woman, named Doda, sent two hundred measures of corn, and a hundred of mixed grain. This caused very great shame to the bishop of that city, named Suffronius, from whom nothing could be obtained as a gift or even by exchange. While Columban remained there, a certain woman tormented by a demon came to him, together with her daughter who was also suffering from a severe disease. When he saw them, he prayed to the Lord for them; after they had been healed, he commanded them to return home. After this Suffronius, bishop of Nantes,[483] and Count Theudebald made preparations to send St. Columban to Ireland, in accordance with the king's orders.

But the man of God said: "If there is a ship here which is returning-to Ireland, put my effects and my companions on it. In the meantime, I will go in my skiff down the Loire to the ocean."

They found a vessel which had brought Scottish (Irish) wares and embarked all Columban's effects and companions. When with a favourable wind the oarsmen were now rowing the vessel down to the ocean, a huge wave came and drove the vessel on shore. It stuck fast on the land, and the water receding, remained quietly in the channel. The bark remained high and dry for three days. Then the captain of the vessel understood that he was detained in this manner on account of the effects and companions of the man of God, that he had taken on board. He decided to disembark from the vessel all that belonged to Columban. Immediately a wave came and bore the vessel out to the ocean.

Then all, filled with amazement, understood that God did not wish Columban to return home. Accordingly, he returned to the house in which he had formerly dwelt and no one opposed him; nay, rather, all aided the man of God with gifts and food, as far as lay in their power.

SOISSONS TO METZ

And so, with such divine portents, Columban passed through his dark night of the soul and out into the glorious day of new opportunities in

Neustria, another rival Merovingian kingdom. In Jonas' narrative curve, that storm in the estuary outside Nantes was literally the turning of the tide. Columbanus was welcomed by King Clothar of Neustria and then traversed Gaul from Meaux toward Soissons and at each place had significant meetings. At Meaux[484] he blessed a nine-year-old daughter of his host, who we are told grew to be the founder of the great mixed abbey of Faremoutiers. Anyone wishing to be cheered by the freedom of women in the middle ages, or highborn women at least, couldn't do much better than to look up Abbess Fara, who like Hilda of Whitby, led this double monastery (i.e., of monks and nuns) that for centuries was subject not to the local bishops, but to the pope only.[485]

Continuing up the River Marne, Columban also blessed three sons of his wealthy host, who each went on to found similar institutions in Jouarre,[486] Rebais, and Reuil. At Soissons, King Chlothar II of Neustria made many offers of help. But Columban refused the king's offers to stay in his kingdom, asking rather for help to travel 'if possible, over the Alps to Italy.' And so, after putting the king right on a few matters of personal morality, Columban moved in 611, to the court of King Theudebert II, of Austrasia, in Metz.

It was here in Metz, that some of the monks from Luxeuil, who had stayed behind, suddenly turned up to cheer their old abbot's heart. Among them was Attala, who had been left behind as abbot. We must assume that he had resigned in favour of the Gallic nobleman Eustasius, in order to join Columban for the adventure which lay ahead. Eustasius was a highborn Gallic scholar whose uncle, Mietius, was bishop of Langres, not far from Luxeuil. Perhaps he had led the party, as the new abbot, seeking Columban's blessing? Either way, this reunion must have been a sweet moment after so much stress. Another who came to cheer the abbot's heart was Chagnoald, his faithful servant, who used to attend him when he went to his cave near Annegray, and whose father, Chagneric, had given them hospitality when they were evicted from Luxeuil.[487]

Not only that but also King Theudebert (brother and rival of Theodeuric) made similar offers of support and encouraged Columban to set up a monastery on his frontiers and offered what help was needful to him. Jonas has already told us of Columban's ultimate intention to go to Italy, but then he says that Columban and the king agreed that the ruined fort at *Brigantia* (Bregenz) would be a suitable place. It is possible that both these statements are entirely correct but I have my doubts. For one thing, Strabo tells us (in a later source) that Columban first tries to settle in Tuggen, in modern-day Switzerland. For another, I think the situation was more fluid, and I am sure there was no shortage of ruined Roman forts during the 'dark ages'. The king might have suggested the old fort on the edge of his kingdom but we never see Columban particularly attached to the place. The blessing of being so far from the seat of royal power is that you have a better chance of not being sucked again into the vortex of court politics. An attractive option for Columban who has just had his fingers burnt that way.

But the curse of such remoteness is equally obvious; in the Marches, a defenceless monastic community is at the mercy of lawless dukes and even more lawless locals. But that is for another chapter. For now, Jonas tells us that Columban travelled from the royal court in Metz north toward the Rhine. He probably went to Koblenz, and certainly downriver (i.e., north) of Mainz because at some point on their journey they arrive by boat at *Maguntiacum* (Mainz). Jonas gives us the following miracle in the city:

> The oarsmen who had been sent by the king to aid the man of God, told him they had friends in the city who would supply needful food; for already they had long been fasting. The man of God told them to go; but they did not find any. They returned, and in reply to the questions of the man of God said they had been unable to obtain anything from their friends. Then he said: "Let me go for a short time to *my* friend." They wondered how he had a friend there, where he had never been before. But he went to the church and, entering, threw himself on the pavement, and in a long prayer sought the protection of God, the source of all mercy. Immediately the bishop of the city went from his home to the church and, finding Columban asked who

he was. The latter said he was a pilgrim. The bishop answered: "If you need food, go to my house and take what you need.' After thanking him and also the Creator who had inspired him, Columban hastened to the boat and directed that all the men, except one guard, should go and bring what they wished. But lest this should seem to anyone mere chance, that bishop was accustomed to protest that he had never before given food with so little thought. And he testified that he went to the church that day by divine admonition, on account of the merit of the blessed Columban.

So here we find Columban, and his travel-weary friends, moving through those same parts of Europe that would be later torn apart in the two World Wars. These places; Koblenz, Metz, Strasbourg, etc. that were so well known to Schuman and Adenauer, had been strategic cities from the time of Rome and were now again among the Merovingian Franks. What does strike the historian as strange, is that, even though Columban only fleetingly passed through Schuman's Alsace region, the cult of the Irish saint here is strong. It leads one to think that Jonas did not tease out all the stories of that river odyssey. For example, there is no mention of Strasbourg, and yet Columban must have been here because we know, from Strabo's Life of St. Gall, that Columban later places some of Saint Aurelia's bones under the altar of a church he dedicates to her in Bregenz. Where could he have got such relics? Strabo doesn't say.

But according to a breviary of the Diocese of Strasbourg; Aurelia and Ursula had been part of a massive British women's movement that makes our modern marches look very lame indeed. The Romano-British princess, Ursula, was blown off course on the way to her fated marriage and decided instead that she would go, with 11,000 holy virgins on a pilgrimage to Rome. That such a movement could happen, or even something nearly like it, in a time when Christianity had only just been legalised, is quite extraordinary. The confident spirit of Queen Medb was still alive and well! Unfortunately, it was also the years of the Hunnish invasions[488] and, according to the records, Ursula was shot with an arrow and her maidens were all beheaded by the Huns. All that is, except Aurelia who died of a fever in Strasbourg, where, accordingly, her bones became efficacious in the cure of fevers.[489]

So Columban was certainly in Strasbourg long enough to make a good enough impression as to be entrusted with some of her relics – or at least to be sold some. And from the area's *church dedications, liturgical calendars, reliquaries, and litanies*,[490] the Irish monks may have stayed for more than a passing visit in other towns too.[491]

So much we will never know! For now, we will leave Columban, Gall, and the other brave Irishmen on their way up that vast river towards the Alps and new adventures. And I will also leave you with two poems for boatmen on these rivers. One is by Columban and the other by Wordsworth. One is pious, it is even called a hymn. The other is swarthy, manly, and full of grit. I wonder how many readers can guess who wrote which one, without peeping at the footnotes.

Jesu! bless our slender boat,
By the current swept along!
Loud its threatenings, — let them not
Drown the music of a song
Breatlied thy mercy to implore,
Where these troubled waters roar!
Saviour, for our warning, seen
Bleeding on that precious Rood!
If, while through the meadows green
Gently wound the peaceful flood,
We forgot thee, do not thou
Disregard thy suppliants now!
Hither, like yon ancient tower
Watching o'er the river's bed,
Fling the shadow of thy power,
Else we sleep among the dead;
Thou who trod'st the billowy sea.
Shield us in our jeopardy!

Guide our bark among the waves;
Through the rocks our passage smooth.
Where the whirlpool frets and raves,
Let thy love its auger soothe:
All our hope is placed in thee;
Miserere Domine!

Lo, cut in forests, the driven keel passes on the stream
Of twin-horned Rhine, and glides as if anointed on the flood.
Ho, my men! Let ringing echo sound our Ho!
The winds raise their blasts, the dread rain works its woe,
But men's ready strength conquers and routs the storm.
Ho, my men! Let ringing echo sound our Ho!
For the clouds yield to endurance, and the storm yields,
Effort tames them all, unwearied toil conquers all things.
Ho, my men! Let ringing echo sound our Ho!
Bear, and preserve yourselves for favouring fortune,
Ye that have suffered worse, to these also God shall give an end.
Ho, my men! Let ringing echo sound our Ho!
Thus, the hated foe deals as he wearies our hearts,
And by ill temptation shakes the inward hearts with rage.
Let your mind, my men, recalling Christ sound Ho! [492]

Columban's 300-mile journey up the Rhine - Filming upriver from Bonn (near Adenauer's
Rhondorf house) in 2018 with rowers visible in the distance

CHAPTER 11
FOOTNOTES & REFERENCES

475. Known as *Letter IV*

476. Deicole (or Saint Desle) gained the favour of later monarchs and founded the famous Abbey of Lure. The abbey's second Abbot was Columban the Younger, one of the original twelve who came from Ireland.

477. When visiting the Armenian monastery on an island in the Venetian lagoon, I was amazed to find that Byron is held in almost beatific regard by the Armenians. He did valuable translation work for them when he lived there for a time and even used to swim the 6km round trip back to Piazza San Marco for dinner. He died fighting for Greek independence.

478. As she saw him enter the court, she led to him the illegitimate sons of Theuderich. When St. Columban saw her, he asked what she wanted of him. Brunhilda answered, "These are the king's sons; give them thy blessing." He replied, "Know that these boys will never bear the royal sceptre, for they were begotten in sin." Enraged, she told the boys to go. When after this Columban left the court, a loud cracking noise was heard, the whole house trembled and everyone shook with fear. But that did not avail to check the wrath of the wretched woman.' Jonas, *Vitae Columbanus*

479. Robert Smith Surtees

480. *Sermon 6,*1

481. Jonas says they all wanted to go into exile with their abbot.

482. In the department of La Manches

483. There is a small village south of Nantes called St. Columban, where there was a terrible massacre during the revolution.

484. Meaux is the centre of the Brie cheese industry for which all sane Englishman give thanks. It was also the area where, sixty years after Columban's time, two other Irishman settled. One was the Fiachra, who was a hermit at Beuil and the other was Kilian who went to Aubigny. The latter, like his scholarly compatriots John Scotus Eriugena, Aldhelm, and Martin Hiberniensis, was associated with the Palace School of Charles the Bald at Laon.

485. It was the first of its kind and kept Columban's rule until forced to change in the 9th century. Like the others in France, it was suppressed during the First Republic. Faremoutiers was used first as a barracks, and thereafter as a quarry. When I visited in September 2018, apart from a later church, the site was largely abandoned. Some nuns were living in a large, run-down manse behind the church. A sister, the only person I saw on the site, kindly showed me the remains of the old abbey wall under dense undergrowth. It was all that remained of what had been a revolutionary start-up, and now it seemed there was no one even to maintain or remember it.

486. The crypt and royal tombs at Jouarre are among the great Merovingian treasures of France and well worth a visit.

487. One cannot help thinking here of Barzillai the Gileadite, who faithfully met David with supplies when the king was exiled by his son, Absalom. Bible, 2 Samuel 17:27

488. We did not discuss the vast Hunnish Empire in an earlier chapter, but it covered all of Russia, its satellites, and pretty much all Eastern Europe at this time.

489. 'The church of Sainte Aurélie in Strasbourg is supposed to have been built over the crypt in which the tomb of Saint Aurelia was situated. In 1524, Martin Bucer (a Protestant), soon after his appointment as pastor of the church, instigated members of the gardeners' guild to open the tomb and remove the bones, justifying this on the grounds that the tomb had become an object of idolatry.' Wikipedia

490. Tomas O'Fiaich, *Columbanus in his Own Words* P.155

491. The parish church at Garrebourg is dedicated to him, so is the church in Bisel in the Sundgau. And in the choir of the Cathedral at Strasbourg, he can be seen alongside the other great monastic founders in the 1878 painting by Eduard von Steinle.

492. This is Columban's 'Rowing Song', the other, by William Wordsworth, is called a Hymn - for the boatmen, as they approach the rapids under The Castle of Heidelberg

Loire 2018 - Flat bottomed boats like ones that Columban's party might have used when they passed here 1400 years ago

Finding Foundations
Beneath the Rubble

CHAPTER SUMMARY - 1945, ITALY – THE UNLIKELY RISE OF ALCIDE DE GASPERI - De Gasperi survives the war and builds a broad coalition that saves a broken and polarised nation. Reflections on his life in hiding with 800 other dissidents in St John Lateran and his genius in the secret training of a new generation of leaders untainted by collusion with Fascism. 1945, GERMANY – THE UNLIKELY RISE OF CONRAD ADENAUER - The rise of Adenauer and his new Christian Democrat Party (CDU), despite collusion by Britain in favour of the Socialist Party. 1945, THE IDEOLOGIES GO UNDERGROUND - The changing nature of the ideologies post-war. The rise of neo-secularism, Marxist & Islamic ferment, and also a theological liberalism that, while seeking to make Christianity relevant, risked rendering it obsolete.

'No civilisation, not even that of ancient Greece, has ever undergone such a continuous and profound process of change as Western Europe has done during the last 900 years. It is impossible to explain this fact in purely economic terms by a materialistic interpretation of history. The principle of change has been a spiritual one and the progress of

Western civilisation is intimately related to the dynamic ethos of Western Christianity, which has gradually made Western man conscious of his moral responsibility and his duty to change the world.'

Christopher Dawson[493]

1945, ITALY – THE UNLIKELY RISE OF ALCIDE DE GASPERI

In chapter 10, we left De Gasperi, Adenauer, and Schuman in various predicaments at the close of the war. Let us now tell their stories one by one. In this chapter, we will follow De Gasperi and Adenauer in their survival and rise to power, and then in the next part, we will join Schuman and observe the fledgling movement of European integration.

So firstly, we return to Italy where Alcide De Gasperi had been keeping a low profile throughout the 1920s and 1930s at the Vatican Library as an archivist, and just out of reach of Mussolini's wrath. He had suffered the longest of them all because Fascism in Italy arrived a decade before Nazism. But when Italy did eventually declare war on the side of Germany, De Gasperi knew the Fascists' days were truly numbered. That realisation pressed closer in 1943, when the king fled the country. De Gasperi, fearing for his family, sent them back to Valsugana whilst he went underground in Rome with nothing but his conviction that Italy must be prepared for a new government. The time for keeping his head down, and writing under an assumed name, was over. It was time to leave his job and make contact with those left who still possessed the ability and integrity to serve in a democratic government.

The problem he faced was that there were not many left whose reputations had not been sullied in the debacle that initially led to Mussolini's rise. The politicians of the 1920s had betrayed the electorate, or at least betrayed democracy, by using democratic principles to abolish democracy. In an act of what seems like almost superhuman confidence, Gasperi decided to swell the fledgling *Democrazia Cristiana's* ranks (while it was still an illegal entity) with young men from places like the Catholic Action Movements. He set them to work in study groups in order to train them for future roles in government. They met often in Archbishop Pietro Barberi's apartment, where Jews were also being shielded, and where discussions would go on late into the night.

Later, during the years of German occupation, these little groups studied subjects like the *Social Code of Malines*[494] and Catholic Social teaching.[495] At one home, he organised weekly meetings with expert speakers like Professor Vannomi, Ulpiano Lopez, and Professor Pasquale Saraceno, who could prepare the students for the problems they would face during reconstruction. Another group was established in Milan. Although these pious revolutionaries would not countenance the use of violence to achieve their ends, yet they were firm that civil disobedience toward unjust laws was an obligation.[496] You cannot stand in judgment of your laws unless you have a higher authority to draw from. They felt they had such an authority in the teachings of the Bible and the church. Set against the dark backdrop of a tyrannical state in dissolution, these Christian idealists sought to articulate the boundaries of a possible political future.

> *"The end of the state is the promotion of the common good, to which all citizens can participate in their attitudes and conditions, ...the state must not be a substitute for individuals and families... a general directive (of social justice) must always be the protection and uplift of the less well-equipped classes, ... distributive and commutative justice... As long as there are members in the society who lack the necessary, it is the fundamental duty of society to provide, both with private charity, with private charity institutions and with*

*other means, including restriction of the property of unnecessary
goods, to the extent necessary to satisfy the needy... a good economic
system must avoid the excessive enrichment (by)... fair distribution, and ...must prevent ...concentrations of wealth, overwhelming
small groups in the economy.*"[497]

This was not a narrow vision for the hegemony of Catholics, but a
bold vision for human flourishing that addressed the excesses of both
capitalism and communism. While the war raged, and Stormtroopers
marched through the towns and cities of Italy, these 'last' and most unexpected of revolutionaries crafted a manifesto that upheld the dignity
of the human person; the equality of personal and family rights; the
duty of cooperation and solidarity in economics to achieve the common
goals of society; the respect for the demands of commutative justice in
the free trade of goods and in remuneration for labour; and the need for
distributive and legal justice by the intervention of the state. In January
1943, De Gasperi published "Ideas for Reconstruction" (*Idee ricostruttive*). He became the first General Secretary of the new party in 1944
while it was still an illegal entity.

One of the more touching details of this period was that De Gasperi
lived, along with 800 other dissidents in the St John Lateran compound
in Rome. He would often meet his wife Francesca and daughter Maria
in the dark corners of the cathedral. He lived under an assumed name
with many other dissidents of opposing political stripes. It was in these
reduced conditions, and often in great hunger, that many of the future
names in Italian politics (Ivanoe Bonomi the Liberal, Pietro Nenni, the
left-wing socialist, Giuseppe Saragat the moderate socialist) learned to
live together in a climate of respect and occasional gentle ribbing.

When De Gasperi served as sacristan at Mass, they teased him that he
had missed his vocation, but they grew to respect his integrity in their
common plight. This wilderness prototype of post-war political civility
proved to be not just a refuge, but also a crucible of future possibilities.
We can never discount the way simple friendships have changed history.
De Gasperi's friendship with the moderate socialist Giuseppe Saragat,

forged in the hardships of their days together in hiding, must have been a major factor in turning the first post-war election on its head. The extraordinary reversal story which brought De Gasperi to prominence, and which constitutes one of the greatest political comebacks of the twentieth century, goes broadly as summarised below:

After the war, the communist leader Palmira Togliatti and his colleagues returned from the safety of Russia. They came back not only with a clear Communist vision for Italy but also with funds. By some extraordinary irony, the Allies supplied Togliatti with public buildings, which allowed the Communist Party to establish itself with greater strength. Worse still, the Allies hoisted him further into political prominence by offering the Communists mayoral positions key to the electoral system in Italy. It was a David versus Goliath moment.

The outcome appeared a foregone conclusion, so the moderate Socialists joined them. The results of the election initially showed that Italy would have a Communist government, but then suddenly, in the most unexpected turn of events, the Communist party split after the election, and

De Gasperi with his wife & daughters

the socialist Giuseppe Saragat decided rather to form a coalition with Gasperi's Christian Democracy party. Together they garnered just enough of a slender majority to form a new government, and thus Italy avoided a Communist landslide. But the Communists had won a third of the vote and so he had to honour the voice of the people when he formed the tripartite government which included communists and socialists. Once again, he found himself misunderstood by religious conservatives. Here, for the first time in any Italian's memory, was a Catholic holding the reins of government. Surely, they thought, he would implement church teaching and squeeze out the Reds?

This attitude went all the way to the top. The pope sent his emissary Monseigneur Pietro Pavan to express the pontiff's displeasure. But De Gasperi would not yield, even though it caused him personal anguish. For him, the separation of spheres was a matter of principle. He had a political vision grounded in Christian values, but he would not take his party further right and jeopardise the effective administration of his office and the general civic good of the Italian people. In everything that De Gasperi had seen and learned, indeed in his very person, was the embodiment of the political principle that welded a fractured nation together at an uncertain time. He would not risk a civil war as had happened in Spain. He would govern for the common good of all the Italian people, not just conservative Catholics. The pope could not understand or accept this principle, and refused to grant De Gasperi an audience on the 30th anniversary of his marriage to Francesca.

Pavan visited De Gasperi again later to discuss an audience. On this occasion, De Gasperi agreed only on the condition that if after presenting his approach the,

> 'Holy Father does not find it convincing but leaves me freedom of choice...then I will act accordingly, with the certainty that I will be doing the right thing, both for Italy and the Church. If the Holy Father decides otherwise, I will retire from political life. I am a Christian... and I will not act against the express wishes of the Holy Father.' With some emotion, this humble politician who would be dead within less than two years, concluded, 'I will retire from politics, for I would be unable to take a political course that in all conscience I saw as detrimental to the country and to the church.'

It was a final sacrifice offered by a man who had already rendered to Caesar a lifetime's worth of suffering, and who would not flinch in the final hour from rendering the same to God. He was Abraham offering

Isaac, and it was to the Pope's credit that he never let the audience go ahead.

The church too was learning to tread with greater sensitivity between the temporal and the eternal common good – the civic and the moral law. For some clerics of the day, it was new territory, for others it still is. But as we see here De Gasperi was no political lackey of the Vatican, he saw the division and necessary separation of the ecclesiastical and civic spheres. Schuman too had given this much thought and was scathing of the so-called 'Vatican Europe' conspiracy theory that was circulating in 1954.

'The "Vatican Europe" is a myth. The Europe which we envisage is as profane in the ideas which form its foundation as in the men who are establishing it. They take from the Holy See neither their inspiration nor their orders. Certainly, Christians have played, in fact, a considerable part, sometimes preponderant, in the creation of the European institutions. There is a sort of predisposition, a similarity of preoccupations that renders Christians open to European ideas. But never have they claimed any monopoly or conceived of any clericalist or theocratic conspiracy; such ideas are perfectly utopian [...] Our first initiatives were taken in cooperation with notorious unbelievers, socialists and others, anti-papist protestants and Jews.'

1945, GERMANY – THE UNLIKELY RISE OF CONRAD ADENAUER

The situation in Germany was, if anything, yet more acute than in Italy. We left Konrad Adenauer hours from execution by firing squad. Unknown to him, his son, Max Adenauer, who was then stationed on the Eastern Front, had been contacted with the news. He rushed back via Berlin where he obtained release papers from the dreaded Gestapo headquarters – not the sort of place a sensible man entered if he valued his life. Max arrived in Cologne on November 26th, the same night as the allied bombardment, and got to the prison in time to free his father. Three months later, the Americans crossed the Rhine and came looking for the former *oberburgermeister*, and asked this septuagenarian now with broken health, to resume his role and to rebuild a city reduced to rubble.

This alone could have provided a lifetime's labour for a younger man, nevertheless, the aged mayor took up the role and helped his people to rebuild the city where months before he had been in a concentration camp. Cologne had fallen only gradually to the Allies, and so the devastation was terrible, particularly to their great medieval cathedral. One wonders whether Adenauer ever drew solace from William Wordsworth's poem, written when the English poet had visited the half-completed cathedral a century and a half before. Wordsworth's request for divine help to complete what seemed beyond man's power might have been quite appropriate.

> *O for the help of angels to complete*
> *This temple, —angels governed by a plan*
> *Thus far pursued (how gloriously!) by man,*
> *Studious that he might not disdain the seat*

Who dwells in heaven! But that aspiring heat
Hath failed; and now, ye powers! whose gorgeous wings
And splendid aspect yon emblazonings
But faintly picture, 't were an office meet
For you, on these unfinished shafts to try
The midnight virtues of your harmony: —
This vast design might tempt you to repeat
Strains that call forth upon empyreal ground
Immortal fabrics, rising to the sound
Of penetrating harps and voices sweet!

A certain glimpse into Adenauer's post-war frame of mind was given a few years later, just after his wife's death from Leukaemia. 'I had lost my wife as a result of her imprisonment, which caused her fatal illness. I had experienced the results of the war. Three of my sons were at the front, causing me daily anxiety. One of them was seriously wounded. .... (I have seen) where an atheistic dictatorship can lead man.'

One month later, at seventy-two years of age, Adenauer was summoned to the State parliament in the British Zone to hear General Sir Brian Robertson, announce the division of Germany, and plead with the Germans to restore their nation. But there would be no quick political fixes for Adenauer. As Lord Mayor of Cologne, he was not sufficiently submissive to the British commander Brigadier Barraclough, whom he considered inept. Unfortunately, Adenauer was a match for Columban's stubbornness when it came to dealing with an overbearing authority. He was less than polite. In retaliation, the brigadier summoned the Lord Mayor to his headquarters. He dismissed Adenauer from his post and barred him from any political activity on pains of arrest. With tempers frayed, Adenauer refused to sign a confession and turned on his heels. But either way, he was out of a job – which at seventy-two isn't perhaps the bitterest of blows. That is what most of us would think, but not Adenauer.

Now freed from the heavy responsibilities of his mayoral post, Adenauer was able to move to another district and organise his new Christian Democrat Party (C.D.U.). Many former *Zentrum* members were bitter against Adenauer for abandoning what had been the '*old Catholic*' party, but he saw that a new start was needed. The old and ailing *Zentrum* party had been instrumental in Hitler's rise by voting him dictatorial powers in the 'Enabling Act.' He had had plenty of time to think this through during his sojourn at Maria Laach; radical change must be embraced.

A new party, on a broader consensus than a sectarian Catholicism, was a political vision he and others had been mulling over, throughout the dark years of Nazi tyranny. It was outlined, at the third and most important meeting in Neheim-Husten, near Koblenz in March 1946. It was here that Adenauer made firm that the foundations of the new party must be anti-materialist, and anti-collectivist. He secured further constitutional guarantees, safeguarding the rights of the individual and the rights of minorities from being steamrollered by a crude Hellenistic brand of democracy, a mere tyranny of the majority – which Hitler and Mussolini had so effectively exploited.[498]

The leader of the Bavarian Branch was Doctor Joseph Muller, who had been heavily involved in the resistance movement. He asserted that 'neither Germany nor Europe can ever be reconstructed on the old lines as nation states, nor can such an attempt spell anything but the end of our Western Civilisation.'

'*...our union is a group of kindred spirits and the only choice we have left, namely, whether to preserve a system of individual liberty which alone can be based on the Christian concept of man, or else accept the alternative of a degradation and disappointment – the materialist solution of the collective state of totalitarianism. Our political union is by no means just a Catholic party, but a complete partnership of Protestants and Catholics growing out of a common resistance movement against Nazi collectivism. While I am a Catholic, the Vice President of the Bavarian group is a Protestant, and while Bavaria is predominantly Catholic, similar support is given us by Protestant regions.*'[499]

Within this new party, Adenauer refused even the suggestion of having a party whip, as this could be used against the consciences of members. Solidarity was only possible to the extent that there was genuine unanimity. Only the cabinet should speak with one voice, he said.

Once again, the opposition to their rise was formidable. Clement Atlee's British Labour Party were putting their weight behind Kurt Schumacher's German Socialist party. This was at a time when the Soviets fully expected, as one Russian Colonel openly told a western journalist, *'to pluck the ripe plum'* of West Germany, because of the *'stupidity of your people leaving the field open to us.'* [500] He was referring to the Allies who had banned all western media in Germany and left Germany open to Russian propaganda. By this, and other mistakes that inadvertently played into Soviet hands, there was also gross collusion between the British Labour party and Kurt Schumacher's German Socialists. It was a brand of political double-dealing that almost crippled the C.D.U.

Adenauer & daughter with the Kennedys

On April 10th the Allied military governors gave Adenauer, as President of the Council, a set of conditions to the establishment of a 'German Basic Law.' It was not at all what Adenauer considered a just settlement, but it was a start and time was pressing for the elections – so he agreed to them. His political adversary however did not. In fact, Schumacher miraculously managed to obtain a much better deal for the German people in a very short time of negotiating. While the first post-war elections began, the public cheered his bold patriotism, and Schumacher was able to point at Adenauer and accuse him of being 'the Chancellor of the Allies' who gave in too easily. Unlike Adenauer, Schumacher and his Socialists stated they would have 'no cringing before a French General or a Roman Cardinal.'

How ironic then, just three weeks before polling, that Adenauer produced incontrovertible evidence that it was Schumacher and not, he, who was the Allied stooge. At a public meeting in Heidelberg on 22nd July, Adenauer exposed Schumacher for secretly receiving information from Clement Atlee's Labour Party, via the British Military Government's Headquarters in Frankfurt, that the Allies' conditions of April 10th could be debated and modified. They had even given him a printed ready-made set of revised negotiations dated April 10th. Collusion at such levels caused an immediate sensation. Schumacher called Adenauer an outright liar. The British denied everything. So, Adenauer revealed his source; a British officer who had witnessed everything with indignation. It was a *fait de complet*, but even so, the election was as close as it could be. I shall let Professor Norman Davies summarise:

'Adenauer took his place as the federal chancellor with a one-vote majority. The Bundersrepublik, with its capital in Bonn, took its place as Western Europe's most populous nation.... Christian Democracy, which before the war had often possessed confessional and clerical overtones, now made a fresh start free of ecclesiastical patronage, often in the hands of former left-centric Catholics. ...In Italy, the Democratzia Cristiana (DC), headed by De Gasperi was deeply riven by factions, but gradually edged its way to forming a national establishment.... In West Germany, the CDU of Dr Adenauer gradually emerged as a major political force. Adenauer was an old time conservative.... But his partnership with Ludwig Erhard, a proponent of the social-market economy, was a winning combination. Exceptionally, the Dutch 'Catholic People's Party' remained a confessional grouping.... Exceptionally, Great Britain possessed no Christian Democratic tradition.'[501]

This last sentence contains an odd assertion when one considers that early Labour's connection to Methodism was akin to Adenauer and De Gasperi's relationship to Catholic Social Teaching. A survey of the founders in 1908, showed overwhelmingly that Labour's economic thought was formed not by Marx, but by Ruskin's[502] overtly Christian political economic writings. Its founder and first MP, Kier Hardie, was a Methodist lay

Kier Hardie & the Christian roots of the British Labour Party

preacher, whose pervasive influence led the 1950s General Secretary Morgan Phillips to comment that "Socialism in Britain owed more to Methodism than Marx.'[503] Hardie's war, as was Ruskin's, was to fight against the stranglehold of a predatory capitalism and also to re-plant a flag in the industrial rubble with what we have seen throughout this book; the flag of the equality of mankind made in the image of God, or in other words, the *imageo dei* doctrine. Hardie (1856-1915) was the fatherless child miner from Midlothian who helped shift British socialism out of the orbit of Marxist and Fabian ferment. His advocacy for Christian pacifism, temperance, and women's rights made him no less an oddity in parliament than did his wearing of a scotch Tam O'Shanter in the lower chamber of the house. His biographer asserted that Hardie had 'a very generalised socialism based on a secularised Christianity, rather than Marxism. "Socialists," he proclaimed, "made war on a system, not a class."[504] The secular shift that came later with Labour, was not of the party's essence, as much as it was a general secular shift after the Great War.[505] This is worth remembering, as we come to the next chapter, where we will see Atlee the agnostic, and Ernest Bevin the Baptist lay-preacher in action after World War II.

So, in summary, here are two of the three political titans De Gasperi and Adenauer, as they emerge from the shadows having only narrowly survived their enemies. Schuman would survive too, and rise as far as a man could rise in French politics, but that is in the next chapter. For now, let us pause to briefly survey the unlikeliness of their survival and what their survival meant.

All three men were fervent Catholic Christians and, if we can believe their biographers, were also men shriven of a waspish militancy that can sometimes mark the religious bigot in that sphere. All three were patriots, but anti-nationalist. All three had been European *frontiersmen*; growing up where border disputes were common. Post war, all three men stood for individual and minority rights because they had been twenty years fighting the amoral tyrants that had led Europe to the brink of the abyss. All three emerged from hiding or prison, independently, to help rescue, not just their own nations from internal political collapse but, later, also Western Europe.

Through great privations, each emerged, having already dug a deep well from which to draw fresh water for countries so broken by war. Years later Schuman would say to Adenauer, 'I think back on my personal experiences as a student in Bonn, without realising what was awaiting all of us

De Gasperi, Adenauer & Schuman

during the last half century, I laid the foundations for a considerable spiritual and intellectual enrichment, for I was able to ascertain by myself all that can be contributed to our common welfare by our co-operation.'

From the crucible of their own trials, all three were able to perceive what so few secular leaders had; that Fascism, Communism, and Nazism shared the same bitter root – namely an atheistic dogma that reduced men and women to the functional unit of a materialist collective. Schuman, De Gasperi, and Adenauer rose to prominence, already solidly aware, as they had been for decades, of what others were only now perceiving. During the war years, writers like Theodor Adorno and

Max Horkheimer of the Frankfurt School (*Dialectic of Enlightenment*), Freidrich Hayek (*The Road to Serfdom*), and Hannah Arendt (*The Origins of Totalitarianism*), were amongst a vanguard of writers and political philosophers who sought to articulate what they and their nations had just passed through.

The rise of Schuman, Adenauer, and De Gasperi to positions of beneficial influence against extraordinary opposition is a political phenomenon that we have noted in this chapter. What can explain this trinity of political resurrections? Some, particularly Roman Catholics, might reasonably invoke the miraculous in their survival and their future work together.[506] One other, more mundane explanation, might be that for many people, damaged by the war, and indeed who had endured 10 to 30 years under totalitarian regimes, it was not the sudden offer of a free franchise that engaged them as much as the quality of the men who controlled the machinery. And even though all three placed their own lives on the line, in the cause of political freedom, they also repudiated the methodology and effectiveness of terrorist acts as a contradiction in principle to the restoration and safeguarding of freedom, law, and justice. The means must be, if nothing else, democratic and not revolutionary. As we have already noted, "Man's capacity for justice makes democracy possible, but man's inclination to injustice makes democracy necessary."[507]

1945, EUROPE: THE IDEOLOGIES GO UNDERGROUND

The three men – and most obviously De Gasperi and Adenauer – did not fight for merely a better standard of living for Europeans or anything nostalgic and vague. They bent their energies, rather, to defend the very concept of *man* itself. What saved the west after the war, to a very large extent, was their reassertion of the Christian *Imageo Dei* doctrine. It was the only other ideology strong enough to form a lever by which Western Europe could free itself from the vortex of Communism. A Canadian Journalist, who interviewed all three men, warned that the 'coming generations' will ignore this 'at their peril.' In the closing sentences of his book on the *Fathers of Europe*, Keyserlingk wrote, 'the effects will be much more exacting on their generation. My generation has already suffered so greatly by its neglect of the truth about man. It could have learned it better than it did. But it has already paid the price in suffering. History will show whether it was a fee paid in full for the lessons learned, or a down payment for a lesson taught but not accepted by the truant.'

Unfortunately, the Allies were too slow to understand how these inherently anti-Christian ideologies at the centre of Nazism, Fascism, and Communism were what bound them together. So, for both our Liberal and our Conservative elites, there was – what the historian of science Thomas Kuhn called – no 'paradigm shift' after the war. When Chesterton's articles against *Eugenics and Other Evils* were published in 1922, he lamented in the preface that the aftermath of the previous war did not bring with it a total re-examining of the reigning intellectual paradigms. C. S. Lewis did something similar after World War II, with his *The Abolition of Man* lectures.[508] But, as with the Roman elites of a previous dark age, change was resisted up until the point of collapse. The later twentieth century proved all too soon that we had been, in Keyerslingk's analogy, *truants* who have not learned the lessons and for whom the German wars were but a down payment for a future catastrophe. George MacDonald gave the necessary corollary to the *Imageo Dei* doctrine: 'he that is made in the image of God must either know him or be desolate.'

Why were the cultural elites so slow to admit this? One answer is that, in the political and philosophical spheres, they had partaken too deeply of the same bitter root the Germans had. For example, in Britain, the Christian Liberalism of Gladstone and the Christian Socialism of Kier Hardie had been permeated by the secular liberalism of Havelock Ellis, Chief Justice Hughes, H. G. Welles, and Bertrand Russell, who all espoused a liberalism devoid of spiritual content. The corollary of this urbane materialism was atheism and then, in Russia, Germany, and Italy, extremism. As one contemporary journalist remarked, to have read the memoirs of Harold Nicolson, Anthony Eden, Lord Beaverbrook and Chip Kenan *'who understood and defined their establishments (is) to realise how shallow, how callow and insensitive these men had become'* to the ideologies that drove Europe into ruin.

In this regard, they were all tip and no iceberg. An Englishman, then as now, is firm in his unquestioned view that what a citizen chooses to believe with regards to religion and philosophy, however exotic, is very much a private matter – not to be discussed at the dinner table and certainly not in parliament. The fact that one generation of European radicals did not share the reasonable Anglicanism of the English must have come as a shock. As we will see in the next chapter, the writings of a heavily bearded man in the British Museum that had inspired the Bolshevist party, itself birthed in London, and now spreading like an ineluctable force across the globe was fast becoming the focus of all new national fears.

Even if anecdotally, Schuman had established in his interviews with people around Neustadt, that most normal Germans were groaning under the Nazis, and by no means supported the ideology of the governing elite. The difficulty for the West, seventy years later, is that while it denounced the fruit of these ideologies, it never identified the root – or if it did, it was not prepared to utterly denounce it and take the necessary medicine. No doubt Schuman was assiduously reading Maritain at the time, who seemed under no illusions of the momentous and far-reaching choices Europeans were being called to make, not least those whose normative senses had been crushed by a decade (in Germany's case) and two decades (in Italy's case) of totalitarian regimes. The initiative, in his view, should start with 'those peoples acclimated to liberty,' who should trail-blaze, 'the path to a new civilization and a new democracy whose Christian inspiration will call forth not only, in the West, the living traditions of Christ's religion, but, throughout the world, the moral forces of "the naturally Christian soul." This is worth quoting at length[509] because Maritain insisted that the struggles that Columban faced in the first 'Dark Age' paled when compared to what faced the post war generation.

'...the end of the Roman Empire was a minor event compared with what we behold. We are looking on at the liquidation of what is known as the "modern world" which ceased to be modern a quarter of a century ago when the First World War marked its entry into the past... The war will not be truly won, the peace will not be won, unless during the war itself a new world takes shape which will emerge in victory—and in which the classes, races and nations today oppressed will be liberated. The war will not be truly won, the peace will not be won, unless the people understand and unless the intellectual and moral reform effected within them is equal to the suffering of their present martyrdom and equal to the breadth of social transformations alike necessary if civilization is to survive.

It also demands to know whether the free peoples will understand the meaning of the trial in which they are engaged, whether their will and intelligence will be a match for the historical event, whether they will purify their actions and their thoughts, their philosophy of life and their political philosophy, all the peoples who have decided to put an end to the enslaver's barbarism will have to choose, after victory, and are already having to choose during the war, between a common task of heroic renewal and the old selfishness and the old covetousness which would start up chaos all over again.'

But he was also keen to stress the dangers for both secular and religious-minded people. The 'catastrophe of the modern world' would not be remedied by a 'regression to a perverted aping of the *ancien régime* or of the Middle Ages.' But, that said, he did sense an epochal opportunity knocking at the doors of a generation who had been, so 'tragically awakened by the war. If the democracies are to win the peace after having won the war, it will be on condition that the Christian inspiration and the democratic inspiration recognize each other and become reconciled.' Like other Christian writers of his generation, some of whom we will examine in Chapter 18, Maritain's hope was that the secular would kiss the sacred once more, and this time neither would usurp its proper sphere. *La Decadence* of secular autonomy, which had so weakened the moral and political aspects of his own nation's public life, could only find a true remedy here.

The framer of the *Universal Declaration of Human Rights* goes on to say, 'Europe's problem is to recover the vivifying power of Christianity in temporal existence and to put an end at one stroke to the wave of anti-Christian barbarism and the wave of anti-democratic enslavement.' It was a big ask, and forty years later philosophers in Maritain's mould were far from optimistic.

Reverting to the 'Dark Ages' metaphor, philosopher Alasdair Macintyre wrote in the last lines of *After Virtue*, 'this time, however, the barbarians are not waiting beyond the frontiers; they have already been governing us for quite some time. And it is our lack of consciousness of this that constitutes part of our predicament. We are waiting not for a Godot, but for another—doubtless very different—St. Benedict.' Far from kissing each other, the decades that followed the war saw the struggles of neo-secularist materialism seeking to dominate all spheres of cultural and religious thought. Although the ideological ground was always heavily contested, it is worth our time getting the flavour of some of the tides within this area of culture.

The 'Death of God' movement hit the headlines with books like Paul Van Buren's *Secular Meaning of the Gospel* in (1963); Thomas Altizer's *Gospel of Christian Atheism*; Harvey Cox's *The Secular City* (1965); Bishop John Robinson's *Honest to God* in (1963) which was later expanded by John Shelby Spong. These writers sought to let modernity break and reshape even religion. These well-meaning liberal scholars seemed to their generation as a vanguard of something new, whereas they were in fact doing little more than repeating the road of Hegel to Marx, and Schopenhauer to Hitler – that is, the road to Totalitarianism. But within fifty years, these books now look like 'exhibits in a museum of theological curiosity.'[510] Cultural change will always erode culturally-based ideologies. 'Whoever marries the spirit of the age today would be widowed tomorrow.'[511]

Modernity's great weakness was not just that it was empirically flawed, but also that it was, and is, so pervasive as to be unquestioned.

This lack of self-analysis was a major blind spot, before and after the Great Wars. It is why, for example, one generation of Europeans could, at the Nuremberg War Crimes trials, condemn Nazis for carrying out abortions, but then, in the next generation, could legalise them.

Even acclaimed books like Paul Kennedy's magisterial *'Rise and Fall of the Great Powers'* published as late as 1987, only mentioned Islam incidentally. Religion was simply supposed to evaporate before the explanatory powers of science. But, of course, this blinkered consensus was barely even Eurocentric.[512] Realising that this unstoppable secular eclipse was never going to come, Harvey Cox revised his 1965 book, *'Secular city'* with *'Religion in the Secular City'* (1984), and then a decade later with *'Fire from heaven'* which is a complete total U-turn from his 1965 position. In this last book, Cox predicts that the 21st century will belong, not to secularism, but Pentecostal Christianity,[513] describing it as *'a spiritual hurricane that has already touched nearly half a billion people and an alternative vision of the human future whose impact may only be in its earliest stages today.'*[514]

For forty years it has been widely recognised, that the secularisation theory is not only empirically deficient but also often philosophically biased. But by a strange paradox, as the theory of secularization has grown weaker, the philosophy of secular dogmatism has grown stronger, or at least more voluble. It would seem that a neo-secular fundamentalism, in the last two decades, has achieved a binary replica to religious fundamentalism. It has certainly polarised political discourse in the US, causing historian Gertrude Himmelfarb to lament the 'collapse of ethical principles and habits, the loss of respect for authorities and institutions, the breakdown of the family, the vulgarisation of high culture and the degradation of popular culture.'

And what about Europe – called by historian Timothy Garton Ash 'the most secular continent on earth'? And here is the great shock to us all. Neo-secular ideals look almost irrelevant in the long term anyway. Without replacement level fertility from old stock Europeans, and a growing Muslim population – conservative estimates put that at 11.2-14% by 2050.[515] Even without an increase in Islamic migration or

Turkey joining the EU – it looks like the religious vote will be a crucial factor defining the next century's political landscape.[516] In countries like France, Germany and the Netherlands the figure will be more like 25%. The Council of Foreign Relations puts the general figure for Europe as high as 20%. These will form formidable voting blocs in their nations.

But if that causes secular utopians to break out in sweats, they should remember that the 25 million Muslims in Europe right now, are only half the actual number of Christians[517] who currently attend church regularly, pray often and say that their faith is of great personal importance. 'For all the secularization of Europe, Europe is still the place where Christianity is the religion to reject. To rebel against religion requires that there be a religion to rebel against.'[518] Or as Nietzsche wrote in the *Genealogy of Morals*, 'who among us would be a free thinker if it were not for the Church.' That means that Christians with a more than nominal commitment in Europe right now, enjoy the sort of political share that many fear Muslims will have by 2050. The reason Christians are not feared in the same way is that for Islam to make historical sense it must be political. That presents a problem for future Europe, but it should also be remembered that both religions possess a historical consciousness that long pre-existed the nation state, and assume will outlive it.

'With the current fertility indicator at approximately 1.5, tomorrow's Europe will have one-third fewer young active members of the labour force than today. A dip in the birth-rate for a country is like a decrease in investment for a corporation. In both cases, the bottom line looks fine for a while but only at the expense of serious problems in the future.'[519] So here we see a simplistic snapshot of the near future that many are unwilling to face. Secular liberals do not, in general, have large families, but religious people more often do.[520] It turns out that our wider social choices in the last century have been demographically suicidal in the final analysis. The aggregate choice of our individual freedoms was, it turned out, a slow-motion auto-genocide. We lionised a democratic state shriven of religious content, without realising it needed a religious birth rate to sustain it. Marxists, in all their criticisms of capitalism have never hit on this, mainly because it encompasses their own inner-commitments too. Their critique of human nature was too optimistic. Simply put, both the social spirit of Marxism and the entrepreneurial spirit of European capitalism both fail without a corresponding 'family spirit.'

After 2050, the old stock European demographic decline – which one historian called 'a self-destructive experiment unprecedented in human history'[521] – will bring the silver tsunami crashing in on all economies with unyielding force. Half the population of Europe will be over 65 by 2070. Even in June 2019, a report from the Institute of Fiscal Studies predicts that local authorities will have to cut other services, as adult social care rises from 38% (which it currently is) to 60% of their budgets in the next 15 years. But that of course is only one aspect of the issue. After 2050, a 10-15% Muslim population might double and triple over the coming decades.[522] Muslim scholar Bassam Tibi wrote 'either Islam gets Europeanized, or Europe gets Islamicized. The problem is not whether the majority of Europeans are Islamic, but rather which Islam – Sharia Islam or Euro-Islam – is to dominate Europe.'[523]

This is the stuff that makes for very uncomfortable reading in certain quarters – and adds fuel for anti-immigration movements and xenophobic parties across Europe. I only use it[524] here to highlight the impotence of purely secular solutions for what is essentially a pre-political problem. Russia offered substantial financial incentives to women to encourage childbearing, for example, but notwithstanding Russia hasn't achieved replacement level fertility (2.05) since the mid-1980s. That is nearly forty years. That is a big problem when crudely put, you need three people in work to support one retired person.[525] Of course, this is not only a European problem. But with time, this demographic trend will compound with birth rates from religious Europeans, not just Islamic but also Christians, and many of them from the global south. An interesting observation made by sociologist Rodney Stark back in 1996, was that fertility and mortality rates among early Christians relative to their pagan neighbours fuelled a 40% growth rate of Christians over several centuries.[526]

The current liberal elites, well-meaning though they may be, will not be here to face the results of this. They hope that Islam will succumb to the secularizing solvents as Christianity did. But the inherently different natures of the two religions would suggest, on balance, that this will not happen, indeed, *has* not happened. Politicians have pinned their last hopes on a Euro–reformed-moderated-Islam, but history has not offered much hope on that score either. From the Mu'tazilites of the 10th century, through to the Ali Dashti movement of Iran, reform has rarely been widespread.

Even in Europe, Islamic scholars indulging in the sort of textual criticism that the Christian scriptures received in the 19th century onwards, would not publish in their own name for fear of reprisals. Say what you want about the crude nature of a fatwa and knife – intellectually lazy, morally iniquitous, and politically cowardly – but you cannot argue that it is not an efficient and indeed an effective form of criticism.[527] Executions of journalists in Europe in the past decade, have made all but the most courageous or angry, write or film anything that would exacerbate the ongoing tensions. A teacher from a Muslim majority secondary school in Brussels was quoted in the New York Times[528] after the 2016 airport bombing. The students were quite open to their teacher about their approbation for the suicide bombers; '90% of their students, 17, 18 years old, called them heroes.' In 2015, there were more British Muslims fighting for Isis than for Britain.

This is the more worrying side of the whole picture. Europe has not been able to assimilate other cultures (as the Americans have) because Europeans have had little or no confidence in their own cultural foundations. But even if Europe had, would it have altered the outcome? Perhaps not. Even Kemal Ataturk, who influenced so many state militarists in the Middle East (the Shah of Iran, Assad of Syria, and Nasser of Egypt) was not able to secularise an Islamic country. The purely secular emphasis was not found compelling across the Middle East, and now not even in Turkey.

Chancellor Merkel speaking at Potsdam in 2010, has added to a general pessimism regarding assimilation, 'of course our approach to build a multicultural society ...has failed, has utterly failed.' A year later, David Cameron said at the Munich Security Conference, 'under the doctrine of state multiculturalism we have encouraged different cultures to live separate lives, apart from each other and apart from the mainstream... We've even tolerated these segregated communities behaving in ways that run completely contrary to our values.' A case in point is that even though there are thought to be 130,000 women who have suffered through Female genital mutilation in the UK, the first successful prosecution wasn't until February 2019.

As far back as the 1990s, Bassam Tibi, himself a Syrian émigré in Germany, used his academic writing to highlight the dilemma. If immigrants were to have any chance of integration, he said, they could not do so around something as amorphous as multiculturalism itself. There had to be a core culture or '*leitkultur*' offered them.[529] Comparing it to Jazz music he wrote that musicians can improvise and be diverse in their expression provided they know the fundamental structure of the music. Multiculturalism, as a socio-political doctrine, is an amalgam of socio-historical flotsam. Part post-colonial guilt, part political sloth, part historical contingency and geographical inevitability, it appears to be the most pervasive yet rarely debated cultural force in Europe.

Perhaps the mass of Europeans have been too close to the situation to speak with detachment. Its detractors have usually not made their case with the required sense mixed with compassion. The American political philosopher Samuel Huntington is absolute in his analysis. In *Who Are We?* he wrote that 'multiculturalism is in its essence, anti-European civilisation. It is basically an anti-Western ideology.' Even if we would shrink from such a final pronouncement, we can certainly all acknowledge the timing to be inopportune and the political management appalling.

George Friedman also points out that the post-Soviet/post-Maastricht wars occurred where Christianity and Islam formed a flashpoint, at least at an ethnic level. Paris is 10-15% Muslim.[530] Marseille, Barcelona, and Brussels are now one-third Muslim. The most popular 2017 baby name in Brussels was Mohamed. By 2016, even though

British officials had politely listed Mohammed and Mohammad separately, it was clear that the name was the most populous in England and Wales. The Vienna Institute of Demography said that by 2050 the majority of Austrians under 15 would be of a Muslim background. Europe is about to change, and the inflexible secular elites will feel this most.

Christians need fear nothing with regards to demography. Their faith was born and grew best as a minority sect. That is how it still survives and thrives in many different situations in the majority world. How easily secular progressives will handle the coming changes is another matter. One thing is for sure though, Europe will become increasingly religious in the coming decades and the effects of that will shake the current secular-liberal settlement whether they like it or not. There is more to say here, and although we shall return to this very briefly in the epilogue, most of these points must be left to more qualified thinkers and to weightier books.

So, to conclude the chapter, let us just recapture the thrust of our narrative, and let us be content to have seen Adenauer and De Gasperi survive, thrive, and rise. And in the next chapter, we will have the pleasure of seeing Schuman, and indeed Churchill and Ernest Bevin, come into their own. We will see the first green shoots of a new internationalism come forth amidst growing fears – real and imagined – of Communism. And we will also see conservatives, and socialists, Christian democrats, and secular liberals taking their seats at the Hague Congress and dreaming big dreams together.

But even with these green shoots and a renewed resolve for multilateral solutions, there was also a wistful sadness falling over the European powers. Perhaps it was the self-knowledge and renewed humility that had come with age and bitter experience. Perhaps it was really a moment of beautiful reality when Europeans came to themselves finally. Whatever it was, many understood as they took stock of a continent in ruin, that some incalculable blow had been struck.

World War I had all but destroyed the monarchies and brutalised a generation by industrial-scale killing. It had touched every continent except Antarctica and the shock of it had remade the globe. World War II had added so many nails in the coffins of empire that it would only be a matter of time before the continent that had led and had dominated the world, would finally contract once more. In the next two decades, there were flashpoints that made the elephant in the room more obvious than others. One documentary maker, looking back at the Suez Canal Crisis, which among other things exposed Britain's diminished status as a world power, was cautiously optimistic.

'It was the end of European political domination of the globe but the nature of Europe had not changed. It would retain the unique inherent advantages born of geography, that political division had squandered. The massive advantages of Europe could still be of great account, were it possible once again for political cooperation to allow Adam Smith's necessary requirements of peace, easy taxes, and justice to reign.'[531]

THE HEROIC ESCAPE OF ROBERT SCHUMAN - filming in Sept 2018 at the tomb of Schuman's Nazi nemesis Gauleiter Josef Bürkel (Neustadt)

CHAPTER 12
FOOTNOTES & REFERENCES

493. Christopher Dawson, Gerald J. Russello (1998). *Christianity and European Culture (Selections from the Work of Christopher Dawson)*, p.119, CUA Press

494. In 1943 these were consolidated in the Codice di Camaldoli (The Code of Camaldoli) which served as inspiration and guidelines for the economic policy of the De Gasperi's Christian Democrat Party.

495. Papal encyclicals *Rerum Novarum* (Pope Leo XIII, 1891) and *Quadragesimo Anno* (Pope Pius XI, 1931)

496. "If the state issues an unjust law, the subjects are not obligated to obey, but may be required to implement what the law provides for higher reasons. The object of the law is immoral, that is, it violates human dignity or is openly in conflict with the law of God, each is obliged to conscientiously not obey." *Codice di Camaldoli*

497. *Codice di Camaldoli*

498. This dilemma within our democratic traditions was dealt with extensively by J. S. Mill in *On Liberty*.

499. Montreal Star, June 18th, 1946, p.1

500. This conversation with journalist and writer R.W. Keyserlingk is recorded in his book *Father of Europe*

501. Davies, Norman. *Europe, a history*, p.1071-2 (there are more penetrating observations about post war France, Britain, and Marxism here too.)

502. An accessible introduction the Ruskin's works on Political economy can be found in *Unto This Last*. I have also done a rough summary in my 2012 paper, John Ruskin & the Economics of Inequality, retrievable here: https://1drv.ms/b/s!An-bjq9cpZ1JDjb0zjnRuxH8RdFEXKw?e=flB793

503. *The Foundations of the British Labour Party* by Matthew Worley ISBN 9780754667315 p.131

504. Morgan 2015, pp. 89–90

505. Even the text of clause IV (added after WWI) can, on a closer reading have many other possible interpretations. 'Common ownership, though later given a technical meaning by the 1976 Industrial Common Ownership Act, could mean municipal ownership, worker cooperatives or consumer cooperatives.' Source: Wikipedia

506. Schuman and de Gasperi have been muted for possible canonisation, pending proofs of the prerequisite post-mortem miracles.

507. Reinhold Niebuhr, *The Essential Reinhold Niebuhr: Selected Essays and Addresses*

508. In his first lecture, Lewis referred to the new scientifically-conditioned humanity as Men without Chests – referring to the missing part of what he considered to be essential to humanity. The Italian philosopher Romano Guardini made a similar designation in his book, The End of the Modern World. 'Non-human humanity' was the term Guardini used with reticence to describe those who are the condition and the result of the modern conditioning process.

509. Jacques Maritain, *Christianity and Democracy and The Rights of Man and Natural Law*

510. Alistair McGrath, *Protestantism's Dangerous Idea.*

511. William Ralph Inge (Quoted in *Honest to God: Forty Years on,* by Colin Slee, p.125)

512. The decline of church attendance in Europe is eclipsed immeasurably by Christianity's growth in the majority world. For example, in 1900 Africa had 10 million people and only 9% were Christian, in 2005 there 400 million and 46% were Christian, or at least nominally so.

513. The Oxford professor Alistair McGrath gives an interesting summary of this twentieth-century Christian movement in his book, *Protestantism's Dangerous Idea*. Modern Pentecostalism apparently started with Charles Parham at Bethel Bible college chapel, in Topeka, Kansas. Parnham, a Congregationalist pastor, asked his students if they felt they were experiencing the power of the Holy Spirit in a way spoken of by the New Testament. They agreed that they were not. So, in the dilapidated chapel, with plank seats, they started a prayer vigil on 31st December 1900. The next night, at 11pm when the century was less than a day old, one of Parnham's students called Agnes Ozman was filled with the Spirit. A few days later Parnham and others received this experience too. (William J Seymour heard Parnham speaking about this experience five years later. Actually, he heard through a closed door because of the Jim Crow Segregation Laws.) Seymour took the message to the Apostolic Faith Mission at 312, Azusa Street. Over the next two years a revival broke out, washing away racial lines of colour for those that received. Today at least a third of a billion people form the Pentecostal branch of Protestantism, the largest sect outside Catholicism. Parnham, a white supremacist, who spoke in glowing terms of the Klu Klux Klan, tried to seize control of the 'Asuza Street' phenomenon, being greatly alarmed by the cross-racial mixing. But he failed, dying later in disgrace. The British, black, Pentecostal scholar Robert Beckford is in no doubt that Azusa Street was, as it was for the apostle Peter, a great egalitarian leveller. Furthermore, South American Pentecostalism triumphed against Marxist ideology where Catholic Liberation Theology was not found compelling, in that it contained the answers not just for the restoration of individuals but also the transformation of the family and community by direct encounters with God. (Particularly because these encounters led people to care for the poor, marginalised and oppressed.) Pentecostalism became respectable for middle class white Americans in the post-war years and the Charismatic Renewal of the 1960s saw massive growth of this experience in most major denominations, though not really affecting the Southern Baptist convention. (This included Catholics, first happening to Catholics in Duquesne University Pittsburgh in 1967. Even in secular France, Pentecostal churches grew from just 800 in 1970 to 1800 in 2000. Pentecostalism's late arrival in modernity, and popularisation in postmodernity, means it comes without the sacral baggage of other denominations. Pentecostalism has unconsciously not had to unlearn so much that

others have with regards to Christendom and modernity. It is perfectly formed and responsive to globalism, having spread globally (like Korea and Africa) even before they were mainstream in the U.S. Its spectacular growth since the 1950s is probably unparalleled in the history of religion. (Source: Alistair McGrath, Protestantism's Dangerous Idea.)

514. Cox concedes a large measure of the movement's success to the simple fact that 'the Spirit of God needs no mediators but is available to anyone in an intense, immediate, indeed interior way.' In the 1960s the charismatic renewal, this 'spiritual hurricane' spoken of by Cox, spread across all denominations, including Roman Catholicism.

515. Pew (2017) 'Europe's Growing Muslim Population' [online] www.pewforum.org/ 2017/11/29/europes-growing-muslimpopulation [Accessed 5 January 2019].

516. Kaufmann (2010) Shall the Religious Inherit the Earth? London: Profile.

517. See article in the Guardian, Tim Radford, 'Study Refutes Faith in Silent Majority' Aug 2016. And also, Stephen Bates Decline in churchgoing hits CoE hardest, Sat 14 Apr 2001,

518. George Friedman, Flashpoints – The Emerging Crisis in Europe, Doubleday p.227

519. https://www.robert-schuman.eu/en/european-issues/0462-europe-2050-demographic-suicide

520. This aspect of demography is complex and those wishing to get more details and up to date information should see Ellison, et al in Poston (2018) Low Fertility Regimes and Demographic and Societal Change, Cham: Springer. This online Religion and Fertility Bibliography now runs to more than 700 books and articles. The societal consequences that sustained low fertility levels are having across a whole range of issues are explored at length in Poston (ed., 2018) Low Fertility Regimes and Demographic and Societal Change. The final chapter in Poston's book deals with Religion and Fertility. European Commission (2018) The 2018 Ageing Report, https://ec.europa.eu/info/ publications/economyfinance/2018ageing-report-economic-and-budgetaryprojections-eu-member-states-20162070_en . European Environmental Agency (2016) https://www.eea.europa.eu/data-andmaps/indicators/total-population-outlook -from-unstat-3/assessment-1

521. Philip Jenkins, God's Continent. p.7

522. What is perhaps curious to a demographer is that in Muslim countries like Algeria, Tunisia, Iran, and Turkey, they have had below replacement level fertility for two decades.

523. Quoted in an article by Silvia Taules, La Nueva Espana musulumana (Barcelona: Debolsillo, 2004.)

524. Pew Research Center (2017) Europe's Growing Muslim Population, www.pewforum.org/2017/11/29/europes -growing-Muslim population. Pew

Research Center (2018) *Eastern and Western Europeans Differ on Importance of Religion, Views of Minorities, and Key Social Issues*, www.pewforum.org/2018/10/ 29/ eastern-and-western-europeans-differ-on -importance-of-religion-views-ofminorities-and-keysocial-issues.

525. With a similar fertility history, and with no immigration to compensate, Hungary is another example of what the future may look like. The Hungarian government, reacting to acute labour shortages, passed a law in December 2018, allowing businesses to ask employees to do 400 hours of overtime per annum without being paid for it for three years. After holidays, that amounts to over 8 hours a week; essentially an extra day's work per week to be paid in 2022. There is an insinuation that those who refuse could be dismissed. Opponents on the Left called it the Slave Law, but the government, no doubt, argues that demographic catastrophes require radical solutions and tremendous sacrifice. Incidentally, the government has also offered substantial financial incentives for married couples having three or more children. I record it here without comment, simply to give a taste of the problems that have been growing quietly but definitely over decades, and for which we are ill-prepared. Europe is shrinking and has been shrinking for decades – a slow-motion auto-genocide. Perhaps AI will save us, perhaps it won't.

526. Stark (1996) *The Rise of Christianity*, Princeton: Princeton University Press.

527. The same point has also been made for 'membership retention.' In a 2013 interview, the cleric Sheikh Yusuf al-Qaradawi controversially suggested that if Muslims had not insisted on the death penalty for apostasy then 'Islam would not exist today.'

528. New York Times, 7th April 2016

529. Bassam Tibi, 1996 Essay *'Multukultureller Werte-Relativsmus und werte-Verlust.'*

530. In March 2020 President Macron launched a campaign against political and 'separatist' Islam in France. In language more reminiscent of his far-right foe Marie Le Pen, Macron announced new restrictions on Mosque funding and visiting Imams.

531. Mike Andrews, *The Birth of Europe*, BBC Books

532. Herodotus, *Histories*, Book IX, 100

533. Alan Paul Fimister, *Robert Schuman. Neo-scholastic humanism and the reunification of Europe*. Peter Lang, 2008.

534. Poidevin, 1986, p. 126

535. Kirby, *The Anglo-American Cold War Alliance*

536. Jacques Maritain, *Christianity and Democracy and The Rights of Man and Natural Law*

537. http://churchill-society-london.org.uk/astonish.html

538. I am very grateful to George Friedman for his 2015 book *'Flashpoints – the coming Crisis in Europe'* but the brevity of his narrative between 1945-8 was regrettable.

539. The financial debt was only finally cleared in 2006.

540. The isolationist Munroe doctrine was also cemented in American political thinking by George Washington's farewell address, where he warned future generations against 'entangling alliances' abroad.

541. *Forging the Alliance: NATO 1945-1950*, Don Cook, Arbor House, 1989

542. American officials warned that British socialism could even deter the extension of American aid. See Anstey, *'The Projection of British Socialism'*, op. cit., 428.

543. Henry Vyner-Brooks, John Ruskin & the Economics of Inequality, 2012. Retrievable here: https://1drv.ms/b/s!Anbjq9cpZ1JDjb0zjnRuxH8Rd-FEXKw?e=flB793

544. A prototypical John Prescott, Bevin once even had to be restrained by security guards from throttling a Russian diplomat during an animated exchange.

545. Kirby, *The Anglo-American Cold War Alliance*

546. Anstey, *'The Projection of British Socialism'*, op. cit., 418.

547. George Friedman, *Flashpoints – The Emerging Crisis in Europe*, Doubleday p.102

548. Alan Fimister, *Robert Schuman: Neo-Scholastic Humanism and the Reunification of Europe:* 15 (Philosophie et Politique / Philosophy and Politics)

549. This is Alan Fimister's translation of Churchill's speech as recorded in the municipality of Metz (http://www.mairiemetz.fr/METZ/HIST/CHURCHILL/HIST_CHURCHILL1.html). The speech was delivered in French. It differs in certain respects from the English version printed in (Churchill, 1948, pp. 171-175) but for our purposes, we assume this is what the French people, including Schuman, heard and understood that day.

550. Churchill to Bevin, 13 November 1945; FO 800 513.

551. Saville, *The Politics of Continuity*, op. cit., 81–111.

President Schuman

CHAPTER 13

Schuman & the New Europe

CHAPTER SUMMARY : 1948-1950, SCHUMAN & CHURCHILL - Schuman as French Foreign Minister and his meeting with Winston Churchill in 1950. Churchill and Ernest Bevin's religious framing of geopolitics and Bevin's decisive legacy in bringing America into NATO. Churchill's attitude of British exceptionalism within Europe. 1947-1948, PRIME MINISTER SCHUMAN - Schuman faces down leftist unrest and saves the 4th Republic. 1948, THE HAGUE CONGRESS - The 25-year-old pan-European movement meets in The Hague. Politicians and cultural gatekeepers, led by Churchill imagine a mechanism for European unity without the weaknesses of the League of Nations.

'...sober, lean, bald, without illusions, serious but not without a sense of humour, incorruptible, hard-working, deeply religious, a mite quirky, does not quite fit the image of a statesman of the French Republic. He does not even speak very good French. His mother tongue is German and, unlike most of his compatriots, he has absolutely no ear for music. A confirmed bachelor, Schuman admits quite openly that he is intimidated by women. In

the Third Republic, he would have been unthinkable. That he is today playing such an important role is symptomatic of the transformation that France has undergone, of how fundamentally modest it has become... Schuman is not ... corrupt like so many ministers of the Third Republic, he is not grandiloquent and unbending like de Gaulle, nor does he share the dazzle and wit of Bidault; he is straight and honest—nothing more nor less. A politician who eschews trickery and affectation is a rarity, and an agreeable one at that—and not only in French politics.'

The Swiss paper, Sie und Er (describing Robert Schuman)

1948-50, SCHUMAN & CHURCHILL

In the opening words *of A History of Europe,* J. M. Roberts wrote, 'Human beings make history and sometimes do so consciously. They can only do so, nevertheless, with the materials they find to hand, the ideas they and others have confidence in, their notions of what is possible, and what is impossible – in short, within conditions set by circumstance and the past.' Let this serve us as a guide in this chapter. Schuman, who had been aware since childhood of a peculiar destiny would now find himself linked into a network of relationships that would enable him to *'make history and ....do so consciously.'*

An earlier historian still – some say *the* earliest – would want us to expand this understanding of historical events. "Many things prove to me that the gods take part in the affairs of man.'[532] I accept that some of my readers honestly doubt this but let us hold up the point for consideration, even as Hamlet did to his Epicurean (Atheist) friend, Horatio – there really might be, he tells him, 'more things in heaven and earth than your philosophy.'

In previous chapters we left the three founding fathers of Europe in various predicaments, and then showed two of them rise to positions of prominence. Now we shall follow the progress of Schuman after the war and examine his unlikely rise to power and his battles with the communist unions. We will also see Britain battling to re-leverage its position after the war, simultaneously dealing with its past and future. After that we will have a further chapter examining the unusual forces that eventually brought these men together, first as political partners, and then as friends.

We left Schuman, who had survived eighteen months in hiding from the Gestapo, being dismissed from office by the new French Minister of War, who had wrongfully called him a 'product of Vichy.' And so, aided by an American jeep and accompanied by Henri Bayer, an officer of his general staff as protection, Schuman left for the Moselle region, staying in Evrange, because Metz was still in German hands. When an arrest warrant was issued days later, his friends reminded him that a wave of purges and terror fomented by the Communists and other groups was the root cause, and advised him to simply ignore the summons. In any case, they said, the charges were risible; Schuman had been the first French Member of Parliament to be arrested by the Nazis. He had spent seven months in solitary confinement in a Gestapo jail and had been the subject of a massive manhunt with a colossal price on his head. The charges were dropped in time for him to stand for election in October 1945.

Only the Socialists and Radicals emerged from the war with their parties intact. Schuman changed his political allegiance three times. When he first entered Parliament 26 years previously, it had been as part of the *Union Républicaine Lorraine*, and then in 1932, he joined the *Parti Democrate Populaire*. In 1936, as a justification for his party-switch, Schuman told the electorate of Thionville-campagne, that the change arose from a 'hostility to the politics of blocs and fronts, manipulated by the extremes, those who turn one section of the country against another, paralyse the work of parliament and create an atmosphere of civil war.'[533]

However, in 1939, he even resigned from the PDP because he was so appalled by the speech of the Secretary General at the party's management committee on 11th January, 1939. That was how he had found himself at the outbreak of war as an independent without a party.[534] The MRP (*Mouvement Republican Populaire*) which Schuman now joined in 1945 was an amalgam of many different groups from vastly differing ideological backgrounds. The moderate Schuman was not really trusted by the party leader George Bidault, who was a hero of the resistance. But Schuman's clear objectives, which did not include revenge, and which had been forged by years of study, prayer, and suffering 'in the wilderness' meant that he soon became a leader not only within the party but also on the international scene.

Less than a year after the arrest warrant, he was appointed as the French Minister of Finance. And a seat at the table, at least meant he was not on the menu. This was to be the beginning of a prominent career in a succession of French cabinets over the next decade, successively as minister of Finance, Foreign Affairs, and Justice.

But right at the beginning came an unexpected event of which we should speak briefly, not least because it concerns Winston Churchill, and moreover because it shows the key role the British played in the creation of the European Economic Area. In order to do so, however, we must also draw on sources that highlight the extent of Christian underpinnings in geopolitical dialogue (in rhetoric and often substance too) that will, perhaps, surprise the more secular reader.

In the spring of 1946 Winston Churchill gave his *Iron Curtain* speech in Fulton, Missouri, which was a 'direct response to papal warnings that if all truly religious people did not stand together, civilization was likely to be destroyed.'[535] In it, and quite in line with President Truman's own binary view of the situation in the old world (Christian Europe vs Atheist USSR), Churchill returned to the rhetoric of "Christian Civilisation" under threat from the forces of evil – a device he had not used since the darkest days of the War in July 1940. 'Except in the British Commonwealth and in the United States, where Communism was in its infancy, the Communist parties or fifth columns constitute a growing challenge and peril to Christian civilisation.'

Neither leader was alone in this view, and nor was this the first time this level of religious rhetoric had been employed by political leaders.

Schuman's intellectual mentor Jacques Maritain, calling for a 'reconstruction' in 'moral philosophy which the democracies must undertake
if they are to survive, referenced Roosevelt as far back as January 4th,
1939;

> *'President Roosevelt stressed the fact that democracy, respect for
> the human person, for liberty and for international good faith
> find their soundest foundation in religion and furnish reli-
> gion with its best guarantees. He recently affirmed that "we [the
> United Nations] shall seek . . . the establishment of an interna-
> tional order in which the spirit of Christ shall rule the hearts of
> men and of nations." In an important speech delivered on May
> 8, 1942, Henry A. Wallace, the Vice-President of the United
> States, declared in turn: "The idea of freedom . . . is derived
> from the Bible with its extraordinary emphasis on the dignity
> of the individual. Democracy is the only true political expres-
> sion of Christianity.'* [536]*

On 19th September, 1946 in Zurich, six months after the Missouri
speech, Churchill warmed to the same theme with an even greater
rhetorical flourish, claiming that his 'noble continent ... is the fount of
Christianity and Christian ethics and the origin of most of the culture,
arts, philosophy and science both of ancient and modern times.' Setting
aside the obvious historical error and exaggeration, let us capture the
spirit of his thrust as he laments the state of post-war Europe. He went
on to use familial language, speaking of re-establishing the sense of 'the
European Family, and then appealed to the moral imperative upstream
of politics that alone could make a 'sort of united states of Europe' possible.

'The process is simple. All that is needed is the resolve of hundreds
of millions of men and women to do right instead of wrong, and gain
as their reward, blessing instead of cursing.' Churchill acknowledged
the groundwork of the Pan-European union which owed so much to

Count Coudenhove-Kalergi and Aristide Briand. He acknowledged the lessons learned by the failure of the League of Nations – or more precisely the failure of 'those States who had brought it into being.' The League, 'failed because the Governments of those days feared to face the facts and act while time remained. This disaster must not be repeated. There is, therefore, much knowledge and material with which to build; and also, bitter dear-bought experience.' And Churchill also mentions that other vital agreement that gave him hope in 1946, and that was the help of the Americans.

> 'I was very glad to read in the newspapers two days ago that my friend President Truman had expressed his interest and sympathy with this great design. There is no reason why a regional organisation of Europe should in any way conflict with the world organisation of the United Nations. On the contrary, I believe that the larger synthesis will only survive if it is founded upon coherent natural groupings.'[537]

European integration became an essential component of American foreign policy. The Americans, quite reasonably, wanted a strong Europe as a ballast to the Communist aggression. Some very credible modern American writers, like George Friedman,[538] would lead us to believe America *made* European integration. This book has hopefully given a more nuanced, if not truer picture. That the Americans voluntarily taxed themselves an extra 1.3% to allow Marshall Aid to rebuild a broken continent is something we will never forget and can scarce repay.[539] But the pan-European movement was almost a quarter century old and already finding the expression it would take when Truman gave it added support. What we can affirm though, as Churchill rightly understood, is that the Americans were key to the future stability of the world. Soon after the Missouri speech, Truman sent the industrialist and diplomat Myron C. Taylor as his personal envoy to Pius XII. It was a tacit warning to the Soviet Union of a dramatic shift in US foreign policy.

But for us, Ernest Bevin was really the great unsung hero of the US paradigm shift, because it was he who doggedly steamrolled opposition within the US to their joining NATO. A titan indeed in physical presence and persistence, Bevin would untie the only foreign policy[540] the Americans had ever known. In his history of NATO,[541] Don Cook writes about the 'propelling, pushing and pulling' needed to pull their entire continent closer to Europe, and he leaves us in no doubt to whom Europeans owe the 70 years of peace; it is Bevin.

But at the outset, he wouldn't have been the bookies' choice for Whitehall; an illegitimate West Country lad who became an orphan while still young, Bevin was a truck driver contemplating a vocation as a Baptist preacher when a political career opened to him in the unions. Such was his negotiating abilities; Bevin became known as the Dockers' QC. This fervent, bullish Christian socialist was so effective in building up the unions, that Churchill eventually gave him the job of coordinating British labour during the war. It was an unexpected and brilliant appointment. Now the man who might have faced Churchill across the picket lines was facing him across the cabinet table.

After the war, Bevin was made foreign secretary in Atlee's Labour government. And so here comes the nuance, for the Vatican had always lumped socialism and communism together in those encyclicals we have already studied. And the Americans too were at first suspicious of a socialist Britain. This was the first time Labour had been elected – indeed by a landslide.[542] But then they had to blink, for Atlee's foreign secretary was a good Protestant with evangelical credentials. (Atlee himself was agnostic, famously saying that he preferred the 'ethics of Christianity' but not 'the mumbo-jumbo' as if it was possible in the long term to have one without the other.) In fact, the longer any foreigner looked into the British Labour party the more they might have been amazed or dismayed by turns. As we have already seen, the overwhelming majority of labour's founders were inspired by the Christian economic thought of Ruskin, not Marx.[543]

And so thus it was Bevin, a man with little idea of what a socialist foreign policy would be, who became yet another essential post-war link in our story. In fact, Bevin could be equally as bullish in diplomacy as Columban; he had a deep suspicion of Catholics, yet he hated Communists even more.[544] And as Taylor remarked to Truman in 1946, 'the cause of Communism versus Christianity and Democracy transcends minor differences in Christian creeds. It is the Great Issue of the future and thus of today.' It was Bevin's Christian convictions, more than any policy that made him the 'logical and clever Foreign Office response to Truman's anti-communist crusade.'[545]

Earnest Bevin - the Dockers' QC & the man who 'made' NATO

The Truman administration exaggerated the Soviet menace to gain public and congressional support, and their simplest weapon in the containment ideology was the rhetoric of crusade; it was the Christian civilisation of the west defending itself against the atheistic menace of Soviet communism. By 1947, American public opinion was firmly fixed about the *red menace*. All future fears were channelled or projected east of Berlin. Correspondingly Atlee's Britain used this as leverage for her status as a solid and essential ally in the great new crusade to save civilization during the Cold War.[546] In hindsight, we can detect more than a faint whiff of political cynicism, but we should not forget that this was a traumatised civilisation on tenterhooks. They were dealing with a new and then-unpredictable situation. There was political opportunism, no doubt, but equally, there was genuine ideological soul-searching among leaders. But we have rushed ahead in giving this wider background. Let us return to the immediate aftermath of the war.

In line with Truman's growing commitments, in 1947 we find William Clayton, Undersecretary for State for Economic Affairs, writing to George C. Marshall (then Secretary of State) about the seriousness of the economic and humanitarian crisis in Europe. American aid was essential but 'such a plan should be based on a European economic Federation of the Belgium-Netherlands-Luxembourg Customs Union. Europe cannot recover from this war, and again become independent, if her economy continues to be divided into many small watertight compartments as it is today.' Clayton was mindful that the USA had benefitted from a 'large domestic market with no trade barriers' and reasoned that Europe might accrue similar benefits, countries receiving Marshall Aid to 'exert common efforts... [in order to] ...speedily achieve cooperation in Europe which is essential for lasting peace and recovery.' This is how US foreign policy and American generosity coincided with, and added impetus to, the existing pan-European movement.

It was the strange conjunction of heavenly bodies in international politics. But they did not envision anything more than a limited bureaucracy within a free trade zone. Nor were they particularly thrilled in July of that year, when the Committee on European Economic Cooperation could not agree on a full-scale integrated solution for reconstruction such as they had wanted.[547]

But before we move on into the late forties, let us briefly go back to the summer of 1946, when the municipality of Metz invited Churchill to celebrate Bastille Day. And, of course, who better to receive Britain's great Wartime leader, than France's new Finance Minister and local hero Robert Schuman. And so, this is how, on the 14th July, Churchill and his daughter Mary toured the city with Robert Schuman in an open-top car to the great joy of the crowds. 'He inspected the troops on the Place de la Republique, signed the Golden Book at the Hotel de Ville, and then addressed the crowds from the balcony.'[548] Here Churchill reiterated his vision for a united Europe, but this time with France taking the lead.

Churchill & Schuman, Bastille Day, Metz 1946

'Europe must arise from the ruins. At the head of the United Nations Organisation, there is the United States with her immense power and her noble virtues. But without the support of a united Europe, the great world organisation could be destroyed, destabilised, evaporated. It is for this reason that today I give you the first word: Europe. We must be good Europeans; Europe must take the first place in our thoughts. Thus, through Europe we will win the peace [...] My second word is France. It is not possible to have a rebirth of Europe, with her charm, her culture and her power without a strong France... By this effort of yourselves you will save Europe and in saving Europe you will save yourselves.' [549]

One wonders what else the two might have spoken about on that day, and how Schuman might have interpreted Churchill's position generally. As far back as the 1920s, Churchill had given vocal support to Count Richard

Coudenhove-Kalergi's Pan-Europa Union. In the thirties, Churchill was writing about the need for a German-led United States of Europe. But and here it must be emphasised, Churchill did not see Britain as part of it. He endorsed the idea of a united Europe, but he knew Britain could never lead it, partly it was our prior commitment to the Commonwealth, but also it was because he saw Britain in a unique relationship with America. He articulated this 'special relationship' in November 1945 in a letter to Ernest Bevin. The letter was marked 'Most Secret.' Churchill wrote,

> *'Whom God has joined together, let no man put asunder... The future of the world depends upon the fraternal association of Great Britain and the Commonwealth with the United States. With that, there can be no war. Without it, there can be no peace. . . What we may be able to achieve is, in fact, Salvation for ourselves, and the means of procuring Salvation for the world.'*[550]

This concept of a 'spiritual conception of Europe,' and the West generally, was something Bevin inherited from Churchill,[551] who spoke about it openly, at events like the United Europe meeting in the Albert Hall in May 1947.

Bevin: Baptist preacher/foreign policy genius

But when Adenauer visited Churchill in London, he found the great wartime leader's position confusing. Why so in favour of European integration for the continent but not for Britain? Using a letterhead from No.10 Downing Street, Churchill sketched an info-graphic diagram of how he saw the geopolitical situation. Using a trinity of overlapping circles (Britain, Europe, and the USA) he explained;

'We have our own dreams and our own task. We are with Europe, but not of it. We are linked, but not comprised. We are interested and associated, but not absorbed."

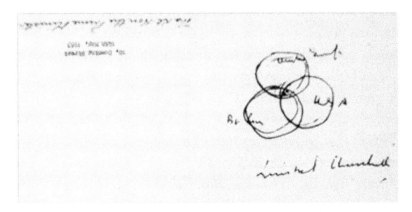

But the winds of change were soon to do for European colonialism what the Great War had done for the continental monarchies. Many already saw Churchill's estimation of Great Britain's place among the nations as hopelessly out of touch. But, as Churchill saw it, Britain still had a free trade zone throughout its empire based

Adenauer with Churchill at No.10

on the sterling. And, though financially broken, Britain was a joint victor in the war. Furthermore, the empire was still very much there. Churchill, who after all had grown up in Victorian Britain, could never see his *Sceptered Isle* on a par with defeated nations like Germany or France. In fact, like many, he was alarmed at the thought of what a united France and Germany would do to their position on the world stage. Where would Britain fit in if not to hold the balance of power between rival European factions? Where indeed.

He knew very well that by encouraging France and Germany together, Britain would need to find a new lever by which it could manoeuvre in a drastically changed geopolitical ecosystem. The special relation with America was that lever. No one knew better than Churchill that Britannia no longer ruled, and never would again rule, the waves. After all, it was he who had signed the Lend Lease programme with the Americans. The USA lent Britain destroyers to patrol the seas for U-boats in return for Britain leasing all their naval bases (except Halifax, Nova Scotia) to the United States for 100 years. 'In effect, this meant turning over their empire in the Caribbean to the Americans. Britain retained formal control but the islands were under the domination of the Americans. The United States was simultaneously aiding the British and using aid to whittle away its empire.'[552]

So, Britain, the one nation who had entered the war to defend an ally, the one nation who had fought at the beginning of the war and was still fighting on the last day, the one nation who had mobilized for war more dramatically than any other nation, would be the nation to lose the most.

Two thirds of the working population (over the age of fourteen) were employed in the breaking of Hitler. 95% of the country's spending was directly controlled by either rationing or price. 'State-set wages and government control seemed to apply to everything except poetry, sex, and dreaming.'[553] 1.7 million Britons managed to boost the production of sophisticated aircraft from 3,000 to 26,000 by 1944. Even church-pew carvers, housewives, and piano makers adapted their skills to aircraft production. If you had visited a bus or shoe factory, you would have found men and women, side by side, busily making parts for Lancaster Bombers. Retired men were sent hundreds of miles away to where labour was needed. Young men were selected by lottery to work down the mines, called Bevin's Boys. This was the difference between French capitulation and British resistance – *a nation stripped for war*. We would do everything in our power to survive, to go down fighting, even when no one was going to help us.

And even when help came – and remember that America only came into the war eventually because Hitler declared war on them – Britain, though greatly weakened and stretched, was still a force to reckon with in that hour. To see some Hollywood films, or read some histories, one would imagine that the British forces were a mere side show at the Normandy landings when actually, the invasion was conceived and developed by British General Frederick Morgan, coordinated on the ground by General Montgomery, and on the sea by Allied Naval Commander Bertram Ramsey, and in the air by Allied Air Commander in Chief Trafford Leigh Mallory, who were all British. In the largest invasion fleet in world history, 74% of active ships were British, and 75% of the landing craft. British and Canadian troops landed made up 60% of the total soldiery, more if you count the 1800 RAF personnel landed on D-Day. The Royal and Merchant Navies provided 137,824 personnel and half the 11,590 aircraft were flown by the RAF. And none of this would have been half as successful as it was if Bletchley Park had not cracked the Enigma codes and thereby fed false information to the Germans about a supposed landing in Calais.

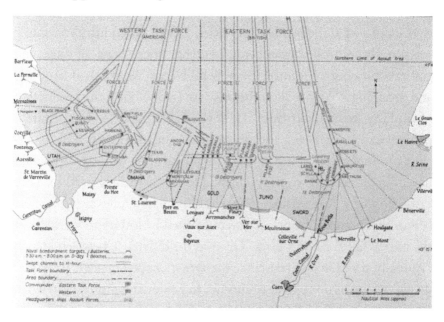

Of course, our gratitude to the Americans goes beyond words, but 'lest we forget,' let us also give credit to where credit is due.[554] And for those sceptical still, let them at least acknowledge, as is brilliantly highlighted in John Lukac's *Five Days in London: May 1940,* that Britain did not lose the war when she could have – which after all is the foundation of victory.

But although Britain survived and – with her Allies – triumphed, she would soon have to suffer the treble loss in the decades following the exhilaration of that victory. First, she would lose her long-held prestige as a global power, then her heavy industrial base, and then also her empire. She had played her best hand in her 'finest hour.' Britain was among the winners and yet she was utterly bankrupt. In 1949, Atlee was forced to devalue Sterling by a massive 33%. Rationing would continue for another decade. It was the price Britain paid and still pays for coming to the aid of her allies. The French capitulated in 6 short weeks. The British mobilised and fought on for 6 years until she was all but spent. As Maynard Keynes reflected, 'We threw good housekeeping to the winds, but we saved ourselves, and we helped save the world.'[555] If Britain could not appropriate this new relational lever with America, she knew – as certainly Churchill and Eden understood – that even Germany would come out of the ashes better - which she did.[556] The 'special relationship' lever was the best card Churchill saw Britain had. Learning how to play this new hand was difficult and not without its incongruities.

'Britain... preserves its room for manoeuvre by being useful to the United States. This means that Britain is constantly faced with the choice of playing a subsidiary role in American conflicts or losing its influence, and therefore its balance. Britain is in a unique position of needing to engage in conflict in order to indirectly retain its room for manoeuvre.'[557]

It was a bitter pill that even now, has only partially been swallowed. In Britain's case, America has been both a reluctant saviour and willing emasculator, using 'anti-imperial rhetoric whilst itself pursuing an informal variant of imperialism exercised largely by economic means.'[558]

The Yankee smile has been both that of an eleventh-hour Hollywood-hero and a eugenic doctor, approaching Britain's imperial bed, needle in hand. Britain had been successful but it 'paid for that success by losing its grip on the Empire, by accepting a position of political, economic, and military dependence on the USA, and colluding in the rise of the USSR.'[559]

In 1956, the Suez Canal debacle (when Americans refused to support France and Britain)[560] was a case in point. 'Britain's Waterloo,' as one of Eden's critics called it, was a shocking lesson about Britain's new position on the world stage. The psychological trauma observed by Sir Charles Johnson, the colonial governor of Aden, went deep into the British subconscious.

> '(O)ne of the worst things that has happened to us.... since Suez, is that in the Middle East we have lost confidence in our ability to deal with situations. The loss of confidence is a very odd thing - it is something, which has happened inside us and bears no particular relation to the facts as observed in the field. Our Suez fiasco seems, in effect, to have left a far deeper mark on ourselves than on the Arabs.'[561]

In 1960, the British impetus to create the European Free Trade Association (EFTA) was really her last major attempt to salvage a position as a global power. At the beginning of the same year, Harold MacMillan was giving his *Winds of Change* speech in Cape Town, and a decade later Britain was seeking admission to the EEC.

Fintan O'Toole mischievously highlights this in his 2019 book *'Heroic Failure: Brexit and the Politics of Pain.'* He identifies, without due sympathy, a *'strange sense of imaginary oppression'* that the British project onto Brussels, which he traces to a thwarted sense of British entitlement. Unlike love, it turns out better to have never had an empire, than to have had one and lost it. The British Empire had been the biggest in human history and her power had been the greatest. Making the climb down from that height at a speed that did not resemble a free fall, was certainly no walk in the park.

Acheson, Bevin & Schuman

The US Secretary of State, Dean Acheson, was quicker to see the pathos of our *peripeteia* (sudden reversal) than others like Churchill were ready to admit.[562] But even Acheson's overtly natural Christian empathy with the underdog[563] could achieve little but sympathy for Britain. No doubt, unhealthy pathologies of victimhood still linger like ghosts in the British psyche and its 'cenotaph culture,' yet for all that, and despite our many sins, we deserve more than just scorn. It is hard, wrote John Bunyan, 'to go down into the valley of humiliation and not catch a slip by the way.' Orwell, himself a reluctant child of the empire, wrote with a sort of prophetic, Anglo-Saxon pessimism that England must inevitably be reduced 'to a cold and unimportant little island where we should all have to work very hard and live on herrings and potatoes.'[564]

That Britain's fall did not become a free fall is to the credit and far sight of Harold Macmillian and his colonial secretary Iain Macleod, who 'set out to ride the tide, not to stop it' and so developed 'moderate leaders in the nationalist movements,' and 'sought to grant independence on terms that were favourable to Britain.'[565] But the multiple fronts of British decline could not be faced by the canniest statesmen with optimism. As the winds of change blew away the empire, so too the winds of industrial decline began to blow away the fabric of the heavy industries; 'coal mining, iron and steel, textiles, machinery and shipbuilding (which had) held their own up until 1945.'[566] The timing was coincidental, and though it was a very bitter pill in Britain's industrial heartland to swallow (and still is), yet overall, it was not totally devastating.

For one thing, the expected economic decline following decolonization - an economic axiom asserted by Lenin and believed by many[567] - never actually materialised. British GDP between 1951-73 increased and was stable at a level not known since Victorian times. The conclusion, reached by some scholars, is both striking and counterintuitive; 'the Empire was more burden than benefit.'[568] Our last colonial governor, Chris Patten, left Hong Kong on 30th June 1997. In a speech given in Oxford two years later Pattern remarked wryly that on the day after the handover, he arrived back in Heathrow carrying his own suitcases and looking for his own taxi.

But if that climb down appears complete then we should beware, for appearances are deceptive. Up until now, we have spoken of Britain as if it were a self-evident political unit, which it is not. Indeed, many academics now agree that the *British nation* as an invention is 'not much older than the United States.'[569] Brexit has accentuated and accelerated national sentiments within England's first colonies, and, for a small coterie of historians, it now seems likely that the English could 'lose' Northern Ireland, Scotland, and even Wales in the coming decades. This need not be inevitable, or indeed negative, as Historian Norman Davies observed in 1999. But if the 'United Kingdom was established to serve the interest of Empire and the loss of Empire has destroyed its *raison d'être*' [570] then the impulse to bind largely unwilling partners will be both ruinous and, in the end, futile. Atlee and Macmillan's handling of the more recent additions to the empire was not perfect but, in playing a bad hand reasonably well, it should give us some small hope for the next chapter in our island story.

A Frenchman of Schuman's vintage called Élie Halévy, who is acknowledged by the English as a perceptive outsider analyst, observed in 1913 that 'England is a free country, which means at bottom that England is a country of voluntary obedience, of an organisation freely initiated and freely accepted.'[571] It is to be hoped that this summary - if evident a century ago to a sympathetic outsider – would increasingly become a garment better-fitting as our post-imperial-post-EU years roll on. George Orwell made many caustic observations of class-ridden England and yet beyond all that did not despair. For he found something to cheer even him in the steadfastness of the ordinary people. If there was something that shone through 'English Civilisation,' for Orwell, it was its 'gentleness.' And perhaps this is why even he could end his book thus, 'I believe in England, and I believe that we shall go forward.'[572]

Our finest hour may yet still be before us, and Europe may yet depend on us for something more than our ships and guns, or our birthing of sciences and industries. Perhaps for a season, we could continue to play the part of the,

'vanquished Greeks teaching the arts of civilisation to the new Romans.'

But that should not be our preoccupation, for that would be to run merely on the fumes of a spent cultural capital. As I wrote in the introduction, our real work will be to rediscover what the 5th century Irish discovered and to let that mainspring shape our national future whether that future be small or great. Nothing is written. Britain's *lowlier* status in the latter 20th century, combined with her *lonelier* status post-Brexit in the 21st century, may yet prove the seedbed that brings forth unexpected shoots of renewal – a renewal for which her forefathers and continental cousins may one day be justly proud.

In some ways the English are better fitted than others for this ordeal, because their national myth is centred on the rise and decline of Camelot. Arthur had conquered the Romans and is advancing on the final prize of Rome, when he his betrayed and undone. The Arthurian legends are redolent with both the lofty aspirations and the frailty of human nature; of failure, loss, and the transitoriness of political endeavour. The Round Table failed from within, because the darkness was within, not just 'out there' with Morgana and Mordred in the forest. Lancelot was the 'best of us', but the best was not enough. The melancholy is palpable, and the pathos is keenly felt in English literature down the ages. But Arthur also stands for the possibility of renewal in the midst of decline, of revival in the very throws of death;

> *"Yet some men say in many parts of England that King Arthur is not dead, ... and men say that he shall come again..."*

The English *cri de coeur* within the Anglo-Saxon poem, *The Battle of Maldon* (where Earl Byrhtnoth and his thanes fell to the Vikings on 11th August, 991 AD) could serve Britain well in the coming decades.

> *'Courage must be the firmer, heart the bolder, spirit must be the greater, as our strength grows less.'*

1947-1948, PRIME MINISTER SCHUMAN

Back in the late 1940's, Schuman had more on his mind than Britain's dilemmas. One year and two governments after he had ridden through Metz with Churchill, Robert Schuman was appointed French Prime Minister. It was a role he held during the tumultuous year of 1947-1948.[573] Awed by the task ahead of him in leading a Fourth Republic every bit as unstable as the Third, Schuman wrote to Pius XII asking to receive from him an Apostolic blessing. 'The responsibilities of so heavy an office bring home to me each day the inadequacy of my own powers and my need for special graces. The blessing which I ask of Your Holiness would be for me a precious pledge and encouragement.' Schuman was voted in as Prime Minister by the National Assembly on 22nd November with only the Communists (who had just called for a general strike) casting ballots against him.

The strike soon brought the beleaguered nation to a standstill. The labour minister saw no other possibility than to capitulate, it was that serious. Many, thought there would be an actual revolution. On 27th November, Schuman secured approval for his cabinet at the National Assembly to further strengthen the position of his government. Schuman gave a frank address to the Assembly, everything that they must swiftly undertake was for the defence of the Republic. They must:

> 'affirm the authority of the state, that is to say, to maintain public order, to ensure the strict execution of governmental decisions and the rule of law.'

All were behind him as he called up 80,000 reservists to maintain order and prevent intimidation by the Communist pickets. From 29th November to 4th December, Schuman made the Assembly remain in permanent session while he secured all measures necessary to defend the republic. The Communist leader Jacques Duclos was incensed by the confident grip Schuman held over the situation. Reverting to *ad hominem* abuse, he railed across the Assembly at him for his Lorraine accent and accused Schuman of being one of the *Boche*. But gradually Duclos' power to exploit French political divisions was itself dissipated.

On 9th December 1947, the National Strike Committee called off the strike.[574]

In less confident political hands, or under a vacillating politician too prone to public opinion, the strikes could have been a national catastrophe, even to the elevation of Communism in France. Schuman's two-year premiership was not dazzling, but it brought the stability needed for the fledgling Fourth Republic to gain a sure footing after the war. Toward the end of his time as Prime Minister, on 18th April 1948, Schuman went once more to Poitiers.

What an extraordinary place this must have seemed to him. Had he been back since his troubled days as minister for refugees? Yes, he had passed that way – even as Columban had – as a fugitive and an outlaw, delivering his secret dossier to the abbot at Ligugé, just a few miles south. Now, here he is once more at the place where Charles Martel turned back the Islamic armies in 733. He must have been mindful of the menace that France had more recently escaped during, not just the war, but also the industrial unrest. In his speech entitled *La situation en France*, he said,

> 'France has forgotten none of the lessons of the past nor has she renounced any of its friendships. Our foreign policy is and remains oriented towards a single objective: peace, guided by a single ideal: the fraternity of peoples. We exclude no-one even those who were but yesterday ranged against us.'

And so, while the countries of Europe lay financially and often physically in ruins, the great new work of living together as nations was underway. Of course, Schuman was not alone for, from many quarters and ideological persuasions, people now came together to see if there might be a better way to live. Maritain gives us a good summary of who they were and what he thought they should be about:

> *'Whether they adhere to Socialist or Christian schools of thought, a great many men of goodwill, taught by our horrible ordeal, are*

in the process of ridding their minds of the prejudices and tempta-
tions of which I have just spoken. From this point new conceptions
must be worked out. I believe that such conceptions will have to sub-
ject the classical notion of State sovereignty to a rigid criticism, not
merely in the international sphere, where, in order to enter into a
federation of free peoples, States will have to give up the privileges
of absolute sovereignty, but also in the national order itself, while
pretending to hasten it, distorts the emancipation to which they as-
pire; and on the other hand, against a pessimistic pseudo-realism
that extends from Machiavelli to Hitler and that bends man un-
der violence, retaining only the animality which enslaves him.'[575]

1948, THE HAGUE CONGRESS

And thus, it was a few weeks later, in May 1948 that some of the intellectual groundwork for European integration occurred in The Hague.
The Congress of The Hague, as it became known has many striking
features, not least the post war austerity. If we were trying to slim this
drama down for a stage production, then this fledgling congress would
be a good setting at the beginning of Act II. The main heroes (except
Schuman who, still busy as prime minister, sent his foreign minister)
and notable supporting characters assemble on the rubble of a traumatised and now financially broken Europe, in order to build a new future
together.

'Europe is threatened by its own suicidal tendencies' were the words
of Salvador de Madariaga, a Spanish born professor of literature who
taught at Oxford and who attended the 1948 Congress. The *Joint Inter-*
national Committee of the Movements for European Unity was actually
the brainchild of Winston Churchill (through his son in law, Duncan
Sandys MP) and this was its moment to gather a cross-section of cul-
ture-shapers so they could solidify the pan-European vision.

The foreign governments exiled to London during the war had
gained plenty of time to bridge-build between themselves and
Churchill, and discuss European solutions. The 1948 Hague Congress,

was that first tentative step, and Churchill was their most honoured guest. 800 delegates arrived in a country still suffering food shortages, and still bearing the terrible scars of the war. They assembled in the majestic Ridderzaal (Knight's Palace), where over the monumental chimneypiece hung an impromptu and giant letter 'E' for Europe. Among them, policy-makers, captains of industry, public intellectuals – Bertrand Russel and T. S. Eliot among them – trade unionists, scientists, and artists.

Adenauer was there, but he was still grieving for the death of his wife, which had happened a few weeks earlier. She had never recovered from the trauma of the Gestapo interrogation that caused her to betray her husband's hiding place. She died of the prolonged effects of Leukaemia and a suicide, attempted on March 3rd. Adenauer had never imagined that he, over 20 years her senior, would outlive his much younger wife. While she was still able, Gussi had prepared him sandwiches and a flask. And when she was finally unable to leave her bed, he spent as many precious hours with her as he could. But this time was seriously curtailed by the travel restrictions placed on him by the occupying army. In his own heart, he had found this the hardest thing for which to forgive the British.

At the moment of the Congress, when these wounds of grief were still raw, it took every last ounce of courage to put the past behind him and work for a better future. No doubt he found solace and strength in the friends he had made through Frank Buchman (who will meet in chapter 16), and also through the Geneva Circle, which was a meeting at Victor Koutzine's apartment in Geneva, where Adenauer had already met Robert Bichet and Georges Bidault, and where Bidault used this informal forum to 'coordinate the Christian-inspired political leaders in Europe' toward a sustainable future.

At the Hague, there were not enough beds in the local hotels, so residents offered to host delegates. Food was scarce, but the local Dutch businesses gave generous donations to make the congress possible. This one element catches the modern reader off-guard; an inauspicious yet somehow apt beginning. It is profoundly moving. After a meal,

Churchill (having just been offered a cigar) proposed a toast to the future of Europe. But most delegates only toasted with water, as wine was still too scarce.[576]

Count Richard Coudenhove-Kalergi, aged only 54, was already the French grandfather of the Pan-European movement which he was instrumental in launching in 1922. The delegates listened attentively as he reminisced with great pathos,

> *'This congress marks the 25th anniversary of the Pan-European Movement, that is to say, 25 years of fighting for peace and freedom in Europe.' He looked out across the war-weary faces, perhaps remembering those who had not lived to see this day, 'in terms of history this is not much, but for the human generation it is.'*

They had made a beginning, and great goodwill existed, but all knew that goodwill alone was nothing without integrated solutions. There were serious differences to identify and articulate too, even if solutions took longer. For example, the Dutch intellectual Hendrik Brugmans and the Swiss Denis de Rougemont were very wary of the Churchillian leadership, and a possible Atlanticist view of Europe becoming a reality. They did not want Western Europe to be caught having to side between the blocs of American Capitalism and Russian Communism. Between the self-sufficient individualism of Capitalism and the mass man of Communism, they favoured a personalist view of humanity, which acknowledged the social and spiritual dimensions and was thus more tuned to the Christian conception.

This renewal of the *Imageo Dei* doctrine, which we have observed all through this book, may strike us as an irrelevant point of theology. But perhaps for their generation, it was more paramount when they had seen where other more Hobbesian and Nietzschean, conceptions had taken Europe. 'Both communism and fascism were organized on the idea of the mass. This was the vision of men not as individuals but more humanity as a mass of men, differentiated by function, but driven by appetites, illusions, and fears.'[577]

Many had come now to a place where they could see the sense of Pope Leo XIII's warning half a century before, 'that the State must not absorb the individual or the family; both should be allowed free and untrammelled action.' But naturally, many others did not have the foresight, or perhaps the leisure, to revisit these first principles. After all, the generosity of the Americans through the Marshall Plan – which offered financial aid to countries who coordinated their recoveries[578] – made the Atlanticist view appear like a foregone, and not unpleasant, conclusion.

Churchill at The Hague Congress, where delegates can only toast the future with water

A resolution was made on 10th May, that nations were being called upon to notionally transfer some of their sovereign rights to some sort of higher institution that could, by some mechanism, guarantee joint political action, and above all, peace. They would need a European Assembly, a Charter of Human Rights, and a Court of Justice to uphold them. De Rougemont, an untiring Christian political activist declared, 'Human dignity is Europe's finest achievement, freedom her true strength. Both are at stake in our struggle. The union of our continent is now needed not only for the salvation of the liberties we have won, but also the extension of their benefits to all mankind.' Many were satisfied with the progress made to those ends at The Hague. But others, like Spinelli were disappointed in the details and timings. He feared that the cautious realism of the British and Norwegians would temper and dilute the vision of the Italian, German and French federalists.

But it was a start. How the people, some of whom we have met here at The Hague, will forge together as allies and then friends is a deeply moving story, but a story nonetheless for chapter 16.

Churchill addressing The Hague Congress, 1948

Sir Anthony Eden arriving at the Hall of Knights in The Hague (May 9, 1948)

552. G. Friedman, *Flashpoints – The Emerging Crisis in Europe,* Doubleday p.95

553. Andrew Marr, *The making of Modern Britain,* p417

554. Let us also not forget the extraordinary sacrifice of the Russian people, who bled more than any of the allies in the breaking of Hitler. A 1945 survey showed that 57% of French people credited the Soviet Union for the biggest contribution, while only a fifth named the US. By 2004, these numbers were reversed. https://www.vox.com/2014/6/16/5814270/the-successful-70-year-campaign-to-convince-people-the-usa-and-not 555. Quoted by A. J. P. Taylor, *English History,* 1914-1945 (Oxford, 1965)

556. The speed with which Adenauer's Christian Democrat Party led Germany's recovery must have galled many English. Indeed, as Norman Davies records in *The Isles*; in 1967 (just after Adenauer's death aged 91), while the British were forced to devalue the Pound a second time, the Deutschmark nearly doubled against the Pound in the ensuing six years. (From 10.971 DM = £1 in 1967 to 6.540 DM = £1 in 1973) Part of Germany's recovery was aided by negligible spending on armaments and defence compared to Britain who still grasped at the last threads of her long-held naval supremacy. (The British navy was still number three in the world.) Notwithstanding, Britain's military manpower declined throughout the century; 1918: 8,500,000 1944: 5,067,000 1975: 388,000 1999: 119,000

557. George Friedman, *Flashpoints – The Emerging Crisis in Europe*, Doubleday p.248

558. Norman Davies, *The Isles,* p.907 (Macmillan Publishers Ltd, 1999.)

559. Norman Davies, *The Isles,* p.1014 (Macmillan Publishers Ltd, 1999

560. There was even talk from one US Admiral that the American fleet in the Mediterranean might actually shell British ships as they approached Egypt. That dire option was probably not too seriously considered but the fact that we even know about it shows us more than is comfortable with regards to Britain's new status in the world.

561. Wm Roger Lewis, *The Dissolution of Empire. The Oxford History of the British Empire* (Oxford 1999) Vol. IV, The Twentieth Century p.17

562. As the leader of HM Opposition during the partition of India, Churchill wrote, 'The British Empire seems to be running off almost as fast as the American Loan. The steady and remorseless process of divesting ourselves of what has been gained by so many generations of toil, administration, and sacrifice continues. In the case of Burma.... this haste is appalling. 'Scuttle' is the only word that can be applied.' Wm Roger Lewis, *The Dissolution of Empire.' The Oxford History of the British Empire* (Oxford 1999) Vol. IV, *The Twentieth Century,* p.11

563. Acheson's father was an English-born, Canadian immigrant who became an Episcopal Bishop when he moved the family to Connecticut. As a politician, his son was not above publicly quoting scripture against the mob spirit of the

McCarthy Communist witch hunts. He even defended his friend Alger Hiss who, as it turned out, unfortunately, was a Communist spy. Ref: Robert l. Beisner SHAFR Presidential Address: The Secretary, the Spy, and the Sage Dean Acheson, Alger Hiss, and George Kennan. Downloaded from https://academic.oup.com/dh/article/27/1/1/365032 on 09 November 2020

564. George Orwell, *The Road to Wigan Pier,* Penguin pp.139-140

565. Norman Davies, *The Isles,* p.910 (Macmillan Publishers Ltd, 1999.)

566. Norman Davies, *The Isles,* p.945 (Macmillan Publishers Ltd, 1999.)

567. Ibid. p.950 Here, Davies casts doubt on the usual claim that imperial wealth was solely the fruit of exploitation in the colonies. British exports to the USA helped but it was the drastically increased export to Western Europe that formed the backbone of British recovery.

568. Charles Feinstein, *The End of Empire and the Golden Age,* P. Clarke, C. Trebilcock, eds, *Understanding Decline: perceptions and realities of British economic performance.* Essays presented to Barry Supple (Cambridge, 1997) p.229

569. P. Scott, *Knowledge and Nation,* (Edinburgh, 1990)

570. Norman Davies, *The Isles,* p.1053-1054 Macmillan Publishers Ltd, 1999

571. This quote is from the last page of volume 1 of *Histoire du Peuple Anglais.* This history of Britain from 1815 to 1914 influenced British historiography. The author Élie Halévy, a French philosopher and historian who also wrote studies of the British Utilitarians, the book of essays called *Era of Tyrannies.*

572. George Orwell, *The Lion and the Unicorn - Socialism and the English Genius* (London, 1941) p.126

573. 1947-1948 - Schuman found roles in; the Finance Ministry under the Ramadier Government (January to November 1947), President of the Council (24th November to 19th July 1948); Foreign Minister in 1948. 1948 is the year when Churchill chairs The Hague Congress on European unity, when the USSR stopped road and rail links between East and West Berlin, and when the Communists staged a coup in Czechoslovakia. A year later in 1949 - the NATO treaty is signed in Washington, and the US grants $5.43 billion in loans to Europe.

574. Poidevin, 1986, pp. 141-142.

575. Jacques Maritain, *Christianity and Democracy: The Rights of Man and Natural Law*

576. One wonders what these firstlings of the European integration would make of their modern counterparts, who will not give in to mounting pressure to be transparent with their expenses but proposed rather a 1-billion-euro budget to persuade disaffected onlookers to support European values. Unfortunately, history has taught us that such lessons are caught not taught. One journalist pointed out that the cheapest and most effective lesson would be delivered by increased transparency.

577. George Friedman, *Flashpoints – The Emerging Crisis in Europe,* p.68

CHAPTER 14

Columban among the Heathen

CHAPTER SUMMARY - 611-613, SUCCESSION & STRIFE – Urscinius leaves the band for the Jura mountains. Gall and Columban confront pagans on their own turf with mixed results. A new monastery on Lake Constance. Changing geopolitics and other factors cause Columban to move on. 611-613, LOSS & LEGACY - Sigisbert and Gall leave Columban's band as he heads toward the alps. Both men found monasteries (San Gallen and Disentis) that proved very influential.

> *'At length, they arrived at the place designated, which did not wholly please Columban; but he decided to remain, in order to spread the faith among the people, who were Swabians.'*

Jonas, Life of Columban

611-613, SUCCESSION & STRIFE

We now journey deep into the Jura mountains of Switzerland. We are in search of Columbanus' Irish disciple Urscinius and also pondering two issues that have vexed every parent, mentor and leader since time began, namely transmission and succession. How can we, to borrow Ruskin's phrase, having *perfected the functions of our own lives, have the widest helpful influence... over the lives of other*s. And just as important, having given them roots, how can we give them wings as well.

Columban and his remaining compatriots had been in their self-imposed exile from Ireland for twenty years. Having incurred the wrath of one Frankish monarch, they are now travelling south, then east under the protection of another. At Basle, one of that trusty band called Urscinius left the group in order to pioneer a new monastery in the Jura Mountains – which is now the Abbey, indeed the town, of St. Ursanne.

I passed through the area in the autumn of 2018 and camped up-river a short walk from the picturesque village. We arrived at night, appearing in the steep-sided limestone valley via one of those tunnels that the Swiss are so famed for building. We set up camp in a car park, next to a paddock full of horses. Early the next morning, while the mists still hovered in the alders, I walked through the fields and across the bridge into the medieval town. I needed to buy bread but was also curious to see the abbey. What bliss to have the town and Romanesque abbey all to myself. What joy to walk around that compact cloister, and ascend high up the limestone escarpment to view the original hermitage without another soul around. Later, as the sun warmed the valley floor, the boys and I dived and swam in the golden river and washed our hair in the peaty waters, before finally tearing ourselves away from this latter-day Rivendell.

Even if Ursicinius wasn't continuing with Columban, we were. Our path led us deeper into the Jura Mountains, and new adventures. As the billiard-table smooth Swiss road took us out of the valley, I caught one last glance at the village and abbey. However well we fare in transmission and succession, I think we can assume that this was something Columban had mastered. We have seen again and again, that wherever he leaves a disciple, they seem to contain within their intellectual and spiritual formation, that very seed from which a moral civilization can grow and flourish.

After leaving their oarsmen and a 350-plus mile journey up the Rhine, Columban and the departing monks may have settled for a time at the far end of the lake at Tuggen. A Carolingian monk called Walafrid Strabo gives us an extra story that Jonas does not. He records that Gall burned two heathen temples and threw their idols into the lake. When Columban hears that the disgruntled heathen are about to assassinate Gall, he decides it is time to move on. Did Gall really do it? Strabo is writing 200 years later, so what he is handing down to us may not be accurate. Considering that they were travelling up the Rhine to Bregenz on the orders of their new benefactor, this would certainly seem like a very strange diversion. Besides, something very like it will happen in Bregenz so it is not unimaginable that the account was confused over the centuries, or even that later hagiographers (in works now lost) added these details of the then culture wars, so as to make these Irish émigrés comparable to the earlier Gallic saints like Martin of Tours who burnt down the sacred tree.

Politics and freedom of conscience aside, one would hope that a man so comparable to Elijah as Columban, would at least call down fire from heaven rather than take matters into his own hands with flint and steel – an action more in line with the pagan priests of Baal. Christianity's collusion with worldly force has invariably led it to forsake Jesus' teaching. If this story is true, then Gall would not be the first Christian, or the last, to play with fire. It was exactly this variety of militant Christianity that Schuman *et al* were keen to distance themselves from when forming or joining their post war parties.

These men were no doubt all too familiar with what their mentor Maritain wrote during the war, that, 'nothing is easier for human weakness than to merge religion with prejudices of race, family or class, collective hatreds, passions of a clan and political phantoms which compensate for the rigors of individual discipline in a pious but insufficiently purified soul.'[579] Yes, we must concede the accusation levelled at us by history, and the secular historians; a little power even goes to the heads of very holy men and women.[580] And that is why perhaps it was men shriven of that legacy that were able to lead Europe out of its darkest hour.

Unfortunately, it would not be the first such expression of religious militancy from these Irish zealots among the Suevi. For when they escaped north from the angry pagans to the majestic Lake Constance, they quickly had another altercation with the locals, who were either lapsed Christians or full-on Alemani Woden worshippers who had never been converted. Columban had journeyed north to the former Roman settlement of Brigantium[581] via boat from Arbon. Here he finds, according to Strabo, an oratory which he dedicated to Saint Aurelia, but had contained three brass images of their pagan deities.[582]

Columbanus had Gall preach to the inhabitants in their own language and many were converted. The three brass idols were destroyed, and Columbanus placed the relics of Saint Aurelia beneath the altar. Jonas omits this detail and the previous burning incident but does tell us of the occasion when Columban interrupted some pagans who,

'had a large cask that they called a cupa, and that held about twenty-six measures, filled with beer and set in their midst. On Columban's asking what they intended to do with it, they answered that they were making an offering to their God Wodan (whom others call Mercury).'

According to Jonas, when Columban breathed on the barrel, it suddenly burst. It probably was not the last clash of the two opposing cultures.

That Columban and his friends showed so little inclination to interfaith dialogue is not so marvellous when one considers that some, or perhaps all of the Irishmen, had grown up around Woden worshippers themselves. To live under the grinding oppression and abject terror of occult agencies is a terrible thing. Columban and Gall may have seen or known friends who had been sacrificed to such deities. This would go some way to explain their intolerance if these things did indeed happen. That they had come, in one sense, with royal permission and perhaps with a royal commission to re-establish Christianity might have further blurred the lines of what belonged to God and Caesar. Christianity exported with Empire has a chequered history and mixed legacy, even now. If all missionaries had gone with the spirit of William Carey (India) or James Hudson Taylor (China) then Christianity might have survived colonialism better than it has.

Brigantium, originally a Celtic settlement that ultimately became an important trading station and military fort, was a strategic location by any measure. Today, the town known as Bregenz is famous for its floating opera and is within spitting distance of Austria, Switzerland, Germany, and Liechtenstein. But even in Columban's time, it was on a major route from Italy to northern Europe. The lake is like one vast, sixty-kilometre bend in the Rhine with an abundance of fish. The surrounding lands are fertile and the climate is amazingly temperate for somewhere so close to the Alps. In fact, the area is still famous for its orchards and vineyards.

In 2018, we spent a few days in the rural Austrian village of Horbranz, a few miles from Bregenz, staying with my cousin's mother-in-law. She was old enough to remember the American soldiers occupying her home after the war. 'They were good soldiers,' she said, and then laughing 'and they had chocolate!' She also remembered vividly the conflagration of Friedrichshafen after the allied bombing, which could be seen even from her home thirty miles away. Now seventy years on, a hospitable widow and devout Catholic, she worries about the levels of immigration and the stability of the region. Austrians born during the Third Reich are not likely to forget the lessons of history; fear, hatred, populism, tyranny. One morning, as our hostess was returning from a morning service at her church, she announced she had brought someone to see us and we must come to the porch. There, as the sun was beginning to warm the apple trees after a cold night, she introduced me to her friend Heinrich, a wiry gardener and odd job man, of about Columban's age when he came here.

Heinrich, with wild white hair and a knowing eye, had lost his faith while studying for the ecclesiastical ministry. The German liberal theology and Higher Criticism, still strong in the sixties, had done for him what it had done for countless others. It was what many believed, had led to the weakening of German churches in the 1930s and made them putty for Hitler. But Heinrich had travelled the world and escaped the parochialism of the theological neighbourhood of his birth. Away from the pseudo-reality of the lecture hall, he had found God outside in the real world. He laughed like a man gasping for air, and well he might. The deep lines on his face and the love in his eyes were enough to break your heart. He kept joking about how bad his English was, as he reached up to grab words and concepts from the sharp morning air. He wouldn't leave without giving gifts to the boys from his shopping sack. With calloused hands, he retrieved – almost apologetically, as if he should have anticipated meeting new friends that morning – a gift bag of chocolate ginger biscuits for William and some salami sausage for Tom. We arranged to meet that night for a longer talk, but in the end, Heinrich could not make it. So, in the end, I suppose we passed, not as ships in the night, but as pilgrims in the bright morning of a new day.

Jonas, with his hagiographer's eye for spectacle, is keener to point out Columban's miracles than say too much about how the community functioned on the edge of 'civilisation.' Columbanus stayed only about one year, and the circumstances of his leaving, and split with Gall, are shrouded either by the mists of time, or else the discretion of the sources. Jonas doesn't even mention it, but rather gives us some wider geopolitical data that serves his larger narrative curve for Columban's story. Once again, the Merovingian family feuds are the grist of Jonas' plot. Columban's enemy, Theuderich, and evil nemesis, Brunhilda, had murdered Desiderius,[583] Bishop of Vienna and were warring with Columban's new patron Theudbert, whom they also deposed and murdered. Jonas claims Columbanus witnesses the battle in a vision, and in great distress:

At that time the man of God was staying in the wilderness, having only one attendant, Chagnoald. At the hour when the battle near Zülpich began, Columban was sitting on the trunk of a rotten oak, reading a book. Suddenly he was overcome by sleep and saw what was taking place between the two kings. Soon after he aroused, and calling his attendant, told him of the bloody battle, grieving at the loss of so much human blood. His attendant said with rash presumption: "My father, aid Theudebert with your prayers, so that he may defeat the common enemy, Theuderich." Columban answered: "Your advice is foolish and irreligious, for God, who commanded us to pray for our enemies has not so willed. The just Judge has already determined what He wills concerning them." The attendant afterwards enquired and found that the battle had taken place on that day and at that hour, just as the man of God had revealed to him. Theuderich pursued Theudebert, and the latter was captured by the treachery of his followers and sent to his grandmother, Brunhilda. She, in fury, because she was on Theuderich's side, shut him up in a monastery; but after a few days also had him murdered, mercilessly. Not long after this Theuderich, struck by the hand of the Lord, perished in a conflagration in the city of Metz. Brunhilda then placed the crown on the head of his son Sigibert.

On top of the political downturn in his fortunes, Columban also suffered a more pressing domestic situation. For around this time Strabo, in his *Vita Galli*, tells us that two monks were murdered whilst out looking for escaped cattle. This might have been a simple retaliation over hunting rights, or something more sinister. Whatever the facts of the case, they did not feel Duke Gunzo (at the other end of the lake in Uberlingen) was in their corner. According to Jonas, Columban had been planning Italy as a final destination for some time. Bregenz had proved a sore trial; they had nearly starved again in the winter, surviving on berries and wild apples, when even Gall's skills as a fisherman brought them little. Bishop Gaudentius of Constance sent them famine relief, and Columban had even considered going east to the Slavs;

Once Columban thought of going to the land of the Wends, who are also called Slavs, in order to illuminate their darkened minds with the light of the Gospel, and to open the way of truth to those who had always wandered in error. When he purposed to make his vows, the angel of the Lord appeared to him in a vision, and showed him in a little circle the structure of the world, just as the circle of the universe is usually drawn with a pen in a book. "You perceive," the angel said, "how much remains set apart of the whole world. Go to the right or the left where you will, that you may enjoy the fruits of your labours.' Therefore, Columban remained where he was, until the way to Italy opened before him.

611-613, LOSS & LEGACY

But when he did feel that the door had been opened for him, to cross the Alps to Italy, Gall could not or would not go. And so here we come to the great schism between these friends. Strabo writes that Gall pleaded an illness of the stomach, but surely Columban's response tells us that it must have been something else. As abbot, he commanded that Gall never celebrate Mass again until he gave him leave. Gall favoured the people and the area and was a skilled fisherman. Apparently, he spoke the language and perhaps felt that he could make a real impact where he was. It was time for Columban to do without him. This surely is nearer the truth. The cover-up is no doubt inspired at some level by reverent and loving memory, but it shows the weakness of the hagiographic genre. The Bible, when discussing the fallouts and failings of Christians, is very much warts-and-all. Peter is called out by Paul as 'clearly a hypocrite.'[584] The New Testament is refreshingly unsparing in its criticism of the faults of the apostles and the occasional misconduct of the early churches. In fact, this has added great weight to its authenticity in the eyes of many.

Before following Columban over the Alps, we had better cast our eyes about what he left in the area, even after so brief a sojourn. The greatest thing he left was Gall himself, his *Anamchara* – soul friend. Gall rowed back across the lake with his fishing nets and was nursed by a priest called Willimar. Later Gall set up a small hermitage at Arbon, near the outflow of the River Steinach, where he continued to attract converts from among the locals. Why here, and not at Brigantium, is not clear.[585] Some take inference that Attala, the monk who had thought the monastery of Lerins too lax and who, as abbot, had been ejected by the monks for being too strict, stayed with Gall but it is hard to be certain. It is even possible that Columban was the only Irishman in the party that crossed the Alps. Had there been a crisis of leadership? Had those bold Irishman gone as far as they could go with their pioneer leader? Perhaps there is a dusty manuscript resting even now in an even dustier monastic archive that could throw light on this.

We do know that another Irishman to leave Columban at this time was Sigisbert, who founded a hermitage at the foot of Mount Saint Gotthard, 'a desert land, a place full of horror, and of vast wilderness,' where he built a little hermitage of staves, and twigs and 'taught the half-civilised Rhaetians the truths of Christianity and the arts of peace.'[586] The first discernible abbey was founded in 720, well after Sigisbert's death, and it almost straightaway seems to have become a cultural and political centre, during the Carolingian renaissance. Its position at the foot of the Oberalp Pass to Italy allowed kings and emperors like Charles Martel, Pepin,[587] and Charlemagne to be visitors and patrons.

During the Middle Ages this, remotest of all valleys, became a place of international importance. The prince abbots of Disentis were the lords of the Rhine valley and played an important role in the founding of the Grey League in 1395 which, when allied to the Swiss Confederation in 1497, became the political nucleus of Switzerland as we know it today. It grew in prominence, and at one time housed a valuable collection of manuscripts, before being burned by the French in 1799. It was rebuilt and can still be visited today.

And what of this intriguing man Gall? It seems he became a powerful preacher among the Alemani, but refused any honours including the Bishopric of Constance, or even to follow Eustasius as abbot of Luxeuil.

He appears to have been so humble – or at least so unwilling to have any involvement with the local worthies – that he initially refused to go and pray for Duke Gunzo's daughter up the lake at Uberlingen. That he did eventually go, and that she was healed of the malady, only increased his prestige. Gunzo had been hostile to Columbanus but now, at his point of need, one of these strange Irish émigrés had saved what was precious to him. And thus, not tampering overmuch with what pertained to Caesar, Gall passed his remaining years in peace – which were surprisingly lengthy. He eventually died in his mid-to-late nineties in 646.

2018 Camping on Walansee, en route to film Irish Manuscripts at St Gallen's library

Though Gall trained under Comgall at Bangor, scholars have posited that he might have been, like Schuman, from the Alsace region – which would perhaps account for his language skills. The monastery and city of St Gallen were founded after his time, on the site where he had built a stone oratory. The Monastery became one of the great lights of medieval Europe. And its library? The UNESCO heritage listing says that as a monastery it is, 'one of the most important in Europe. Its library is one of the richest and oldest in the world, and contains precious manuscripts such as the earliest-known architectural plan drawn on parchment.' This plan is a very detailed schematic of a Benedictine monastery drawn up at the Irish abbey at nearby Reichenau.[588] One of the high points of our trip, was to have exclusive access to the library, where we filmed an interview with Dr. Philip Lenz, an expert on medieval Irish manuscripts. Imagine my sheer bliss, as the golden evening light pierced the sepulchral gloom of that magical place, and we gazed upon commentaries and Bibles and letters in the Irish minuscule hand. Time fell away, and it was as though the ancients awoke from their rest and spoke once more. I will never forget the moment as long as I live.

Filming the Irish manuscript collection with Dr. Philip Lenz, San Gallen, Sept 2018

As for the *Brigantium*, the site that Columban had occupied, it too became a notable monastery in time, though the exact link between his foundation and Mehrerau Abbey is not known, as the earliest preserved records date it to 1079. Having said that, the area south of the town centre has always had strong associations with Columban and Gall, so the current abbey may well be on the exact spot. For seven hundred years, it was the burial place of the counts of Bregenz and Montfort. The cloister used to be frescoed with scenes from the lives of Boniface and Columban, but they have gone with the ravages of time. Sketches of the frescoes remain in the 90,000-volume library, as do some later manuscripts of Columban. The original Romanesque Abbey was replaced by the Baroque equivalent. (To see what it might have looked like[589] one should visit Reichenau at the other end of the lake.)

The church and tower were pulled down in 1806, during the 'secularisation period', and the stones used for the new harbour – *o tempora o mores!* But a modern abbey church, which makes powerful use of textured concrete has been built in more recent times. This was built by the Cistercians, whom Emperor Franz Joseph allowed to occupy the site, half a century after the secularisation era. So here, back and forth, the oscillations between the sacred and secular, what is Caesar's and what is God's, the conundrum of past ages and every age – came full circle again.

Schuman's intellectual bulwark, Maritain, believed that it was exactly this 'distinction which has been unfolding throughout our history in the midst of accidents of all kinds and which freed religion from all temporal enslavement by stripping the State of all sacred pretensions; in other words, by giving the State secular standing.' This dialectic proposed by Maritain has a distinctly Catholic flavour, but I think it has value for our current situation too. The less we believe in a divine order, the more we have imbued politics and science with divine sanctions over human life and society. Against that concern Maritain bellows across the 20th century to us from his hermitage, 'Government alone cannot govern, it needs either slavery which reduces the number of active wills in the State, or divine force, which, by a kind of spiritual grafting, destroys the natural harshness of these wills and enables them to work together without harm to one another.'[590]

When we were staying in the area, I allowed the boys a day off to cycle from Horbranz to explore Bregenz, and also the mountain behind it which can be accessed by cable car. I too went to Bregenz, on my own, with the intention of finding what I could of Columban's legacy. It was a cloudless and breathless day, and though the summer had seen 30% less rain generally in Europe, the orchards and vineyards that led to the lake were still verdant with life. In Bregenz, I was pleased to see streets named after these two eminent Irishman, and a modern parish church dedicated to St Kolumban. At this church, an amiable nun showed me a reliquary of Columban, and also a rock outside associated with him.

As with the relics of Burgundafara, I tried not to let any personal disquiet show at the sight of unburied human bones. Catholics are apt to forget how strange the customs seem. I remember my wife, raised in a Pentecostal family, being astounded that the skull of one of my Elizabethan ancestors (a Lancashire yeoman called John Finch who was hung, drawn, and quartered for hiding priests) was still kept by family members. In her mind, and no doubt many more reading this book, the best way to honour a brave and pious man would be to give his remains a decent Christian burial. Nevertheless, we must admit that this has not been the sole view of the majority of Christian groups through the ages.

We have already seen Columban, who no one would describe as a superstitious or retrogressive sort, bringing Aurelia's bones from Strasbourg. For myself, I cannot imagine the apostles doing such a thing, or encouraging others to do so. But I confess, there is something of the democratic principle at work in it all, and an almost triumphant disregard of that last enemy – death. Perhaps, to disqualify someone from Christian service merely by the accident of their death seemed too limiting a principle, or too trifling an interruption, before their resurrection could tie up the loose ends of history.

With these thoughts in my heart, I followed the sister outside. Here, she very helpfully pointed me further up the hill on the *Kolumbstrasse*, up beyond the hospital, to a rise of ground, where she said I would find an older church dedicated to Gall. I had read about this church built on a crag called Saint Gall's Rock, *Gallusstein,* and so I was pleased to have found it. An information card showed the various eras of construction for the church and I quickly saw that the oldest section was a crypt-like chapel under the south part of the apse, and accessed by a stairwell on the outside of the church.

I found a Croation parishioner cleaning the sacristy, who was only too pleased to unlock the small chapel. Here, in a room perhaps three metres by four, were medieval frescoes and many variations of the conch shell symbol of pilgrims and other graffiti – but nothing older. Even so, I was rather pleased to have found it. As in life, so for the traveller; every chance meeting and every opened door is ample repayment for the others where we are shut out and left to wonder. I filmed a quick interview in the chapel, as my Croatian guide looked on approvingly, and then headed to the far end of the lake to the monastic island of Reichenau, where I feasted on yet more Romanesque treasures.

Reichenau sits like a three-mile-long market garden, where the idling Rhine finally leaves the lake. In the centre is a monastery, founded by a Celtic monk[591] called Pirmin in 724. It was originally run by a mixed Irish and Benedictine rule, and during the Carolingian renaissance was one of the great culture-shaping engines of Western Europe. Gall's biographer, Walafrid Strabo (the Squinter) produced literary works in multiple genres from the age of eighteen, including a biography of an Iona monk called Saint Blathmac. Strabo also wrote down his prophetic dreams here and published poems on botany and lengthy works of theology. His *Visio Wettini* is surely a forerunner of Dante's *Divine Comedy*.

Another monk originally taught by the Irish was Nokter *the Stammerer*, who became a prodigious historian and psalmist. Another, Herman *the Lame*, who even needed help to get dressed, became known as the Marvel of Europe. In Hitler's Germany, he would have been disposed of as a 'useless eater' but in Reichenau, he became a scientist whose renown was on a par with another physically challenged genius, the late Professor Hawkins. The Abbots of Reichenau were even sent on diplomatic missions to Constantinople by Charlemagne, and tutored the king's sons.

Walking in those basilicas, I once more marvelled at the ancient frescoes and let my mind imagine what Bregenz and St Gallen may once have looked like. Driving back east along the lake that evening the sun dyed the Austrian and Swiss Alps a wine red and cast russet shadows in the vineyards. I called into Arbon, that port where Columban had first encountered the lake. I sat on the beach there, near the site of the former Roman Castrum, and thought about Columban's arrival and rather quick departure from the area. There was a discontinuity here somehow, in the story of his mission. His breaking with Gall cast a shadow over the narrative arc, and there was an unspoken sadness in it. As evening fell with a deep stillness on the lake, the eastern horizon was indiscernible from the sky as the mists arose.

And if we were allowed to lift the veil of history, to peer back through the mists of time and past the inscrutable what-might-have-beens, could we say that heaven touched earth here? Or that a divinity shaped the rough ends, even of this abortive episode? I think we can. Gall found a better settlement, an accommodation with the secular powers – something that had been lacking in the Vosges. He did what Duke Gunzo could not do; heal the sick, give answers to ultimate questions, and laid strong foundations upon which to build an equitable way of life. There was human failure here for Columban but also an unintended success. That gives me hope. The incomprehensible sadness felt by many in advanced modernity is perhaps the realisation – the haunting fear – that the best human efforts and institutions are not enough. Perhaps this was part of late antique pessimism too. But into the despair of that realisation, the Christian message brought, and still brings, hope. There is a lot more to say here, but we must journey on.

So, let us leave Lake Constance, with this thrilling vision of the arts and sciences flourishing side by side within a theistic framework, and busy monks with self-deprecating names helping each other, out in the fields and in the scriptoriums. Not everything about the Carolingian era can be seen as a golden age, but surely this can.

Whatever Columban's regrets or disappointments on the *Swabian See* (Lake Constance), Europe at least felt the benefits of those scattered seeds. Even the seed of Columban and Gall's severed friendship – something I see as the most tragic moment of both their lives – was supremely fruitful with the benefit of hindsight. Gall's continued presence for there for nearly forty years preserved and strengthened the endeavour.

PRAYER OF ST COLUMBAN

Lord, grant me, I pray you in the name of Jesus Christ your Son, my God, that love which knows no fall, so that my lamp may feel the kindling touch and know no quenching, may burn for me and for others may give light. Do you, Christ, deign to kindle our lamps, our Saviour most sweet to us, that they may shine continually in your temple, and receive a perpetual light from you the light perpetual, so that our darkness may be enlightened, and the word's darkness may be driven from us. Thus, do you enrich my lantern with your light. I pray you, Jesus mine, so that by its light there may be disclosed to me those holy places of the holy, which hold you the eternal priest of the eternal things, entering there the courts of that great temple of yours, that constantly I may see, observe, desire you only, and loving you only may behold you, and before you my lamp ever shine and burn. I beg you, most loving Saviour, to reveal yourself to us who beseech you, so that knowing you, we may love you only, love you alone, desire you alone, contemplate you alone by day and night, and ever hold you in our thoughts; and do you deign so far to inspire us with your love, as it befits you to be loved and cherished as our God; that your charity may possess all our inward parts, and your love may own us all, and your affection may fill all our senses, so that we may know no other love apart from you who are eternal; that such affection may be in us impossible of quenching by the many waters of this air and land and sea, according to that saying 'many waters are not able to quench love', which in us also can be fulfilled even in part, by your gift, our Lord Jesus Christ, to whom is the glory unto ages of ages. Amen

578. It is perhaps worth also noting that Marshall Aid was only possible because the American economy had boomed during the war due to vastly increased export to war-torn Europe.

579. Jacques Maritain, *Christianity and Democracy and The Rights of Man and Natural Law*

580. Even the incomparable Elven Queen Galadriel (in *The Lord of the Rings*) knew that she could not be trusted with Tolkien's ring of power.

581. Jonas recorded in his *Vita* that Columbanus goes to Brigantia, but it is the later document of Strabo (*Vita Galli*) that gives the extra detail about Arbon, and of the trouble at Tuggen with the Woden worshippers.

582. There is an obvious discrepancy between Jonas and Strabo. I suspect that the place had either been an abandoned church occupied by pagans, or else a pagan temple that was appropriated by the Irish. The only way both could be right is if the king had already told Columban of the abandoned church on his frontier, and with that knowledge, Columban had made arrangements to get the relics when passing Strasbourg.

583. Desiderius fell afoul of Theuderich for the same reasons Columban had; i.e. he did not acknowledge his illegitimate progeny. Incidentally, Gregory the Great wrote to Desiderius to caution him against his devotion to the Roman pagan classics.

584. *Galatians Ch2 v11*, and see also the split between Barnabas and Paul in *Acts 15 v36-40*

585. During Roman times, Arbon was probably another Roman fort like the ones Columban was used to building on. And there is something poetical, as well as practical, in building sacred structures over the ruins of the crumbled temporal power of the Caesars. At the end of the Bible, the book of Revelation prophesied a time when the 'kingdoms of the world' would become the 'kingdoms of our Lord and his Christ' and this must have seemed a suitable foreshadowing to a biblically-minded man like Columban. The elevated situation and view over the lake would also have been strategically important, and for those moving north and south using a boat crossing, it was even more direct than Brigantium. Since 1957, regular excavations of Arbon have shown the remains of late Roman fortifications. The Latin name Arbor Felix first appears in around 280, and then again in 300 in the Itinerarium Antonini. According to the chronicles of Ammianus Marcellinus, Emperor Gratian went to Arbon in 378 and stayed there until 401. (source: Wikipedia)

586. George Metlake, *The Life and Writings of St. Columban* p.193

587. Pepin's effect on Christendom was almost as profound as that of Constantine and Theodosius. By carving out the Papal States, Pepin made the papacy an all-too-earthly power – easily distracted and compromised by earthly diplomacy and temporal concerns. It was a genius move by Pepin but devastating for the church's moral voice.

588. It is still considered a national treasure in Switzerland and is also now being used as a template for a major new visitor attraction in Germany. Campus Galli is a Carolingian monastic community under construction in Meßkirch, Baden-Württemberg, using only traditional techniques. This hopefully will open up more lines of enquiry for experimental archaeology and new insight into, and respect for, the lives and labours of these monastic pioneers.

589. The 1962 excavations also exposed some of the Romanesque building, giving clues to the architectural historians.

590. Jacques Maritain, *Christianity and Democracy and The Rights of Man and Natural Law*

591. It is unlikely he was Irish, though certainly heavily influenced by them. Saint Pirmin - Wikipedia/wiki/Saint_Pirmin

Author crossing a high mountain plateau on the Luc Magna pass, Sept 2018

2018: Filming under glacier topped alps at the church of San Columbano, Olivone

CHAPTER 15

The Europeanisation of Europe

CHAPTER SUMMARY - 380-1949 AD, EUROPEAN EXCEP-
TIONALISM - Early concepts of Christian identity, biblical nomenclature, the minting of standard coinage, the crusades, the propagation of
charters, the growth of monastic and military orders, and the flowering
of the universities. The divergence between British Common Law and
European Statute law. 1400-2016, BRITISH EXCEPTIONALISM –
From the proto-Brexits of the Hundred Years War and Reformation,
to the 2016 referendum. 800-1920, THE LONG MARCH OF EU-
ROPEAN RE-INTEGRATION - Miscellaneous Enlightenment projects and treaties that called forth an almost quasi-messianic teleology
within European society. From mercantile colonialism, and the hubris
of Eurocentric supremacy to its later manifestations in the Aryanism
of the Nazis. The defeat of Hitler, the collapse of the monarchies and
fragmentation of the colonial empires, and the rise of Soviet Russia.
A CHRISTIAN PERSPECTIVE - The perspective of 20th-century
Christian religious thinkers, and also how one of them, Jacques Maritain, became an unusual link – not just between medieval and modern
Christian thought – but also a personal link between De Gasperi and
Schuman.

'It was magnificent to behold, contradictions and all. Triumphant over the earth, and triumphant over the mind – Europe revolutionized everything and by the beginning of the twentieth century stood astride the world in seemingly absolute dominion over nations and nature.' [592]

380-1949 AD – EUROPEAN EXCEPTIONALISM

At this juncture, when we are about to see Schuman, Adenauer and De Gasperi et al, forging a new European Economic Area, it is necessary for us to fly back over the intervening centuries from Columban's time, and pinpoint the key moments in what has been called, the *Europeanisation of Europe*.[593]

Let me again offer apologies for my occidental default to the Latin or Western conception. I have imposed this artificial boundary on our study for the sake of focus and brevity. But, of course, this is not the whole of Europe, either at origin (both sides of the Empire) or at present (since parts of the Eastern bloc left the USSR and joined the EU). In many ways even the enforced simplicity of this book's limitation – using the physical geography of a peninsula as the mainframe – means we begin to see the peripherality of Britain and Russia. It is a tale that needs to be briefly told. So, let us take leave of Columban and Schuman, for one chapter, and give a more general summary of cultural development in Western Europe. We will have to be unforgivably brief, but hopefully, highlight enough to whet our appetites for further study and dialogue.

Constantine[594] and Theodosius' legacy[595] form our easiest starting point. It was a twofold legacy; firstly, a state legitimised, sometimes even sacralised, by the church; but then also a church privileged by the state, and often compromised by its association with power. In chapter 1, we read about Justinian's *Reconquista* of the fragmented western empire; militarily successful but in the final analysis, a failure. That 27-year campaign was completed by the time Columban had reached his teens. But fifty years later, he arrived in a fragmented, gothic Italy whose memory of Rome was fading beneath the weight of the new order. Civilisation cannot be held together solely by military and political solutions. When T. S. Eliot observed the post-war generation attempting a Justinian-style technocratic reconstruction, he was nervous. Civilisation is not a machine, but a tree, he wrote. You can't make a tree, you can only plant one and nurture it. In many ways, Justinian's conundrum is much like the EU's now. Sixth century Europeans had become unfitted to be good Romans. Could it be that their 21st century counterparts have become unfitted to be good Europeans?

Columbanus, Benedict, and many, many others planted the 'trees' that would do for Europe what Justinian could not do with the superstructure of politics and military power. We shall return to this at the end of the book, but for now let us remember Western Europe as it was in the 6th century; which by the measures of climate, famine, pandemic, and political instability was arguably the worst century ever to have been alive in recorded memory. And then moving on 200 years, let us also observe something of that peculiar Frankish genius which culminated in Charlemagne's spirited creation of a Holy Roman Empire, which Voltaire wittily remarked 'was neither holy, nor Roman, nor an Empire.'[596]

Charlemagne ruled a European Union from his palace in Aachen, Germany. Its centre of gravity was a Germano-French Axis; a geopolitical imprint that still exists today. Charlemagne waged 50 military campaigns, almost all successful except his Basque defeat, and the death of Roland (which is so famously remembered in the Chanson). The most revolutionary leap in the reign of Charlemagne was a new obligation not just to protect his subjects, but also to educate them.[597] This burden to lift his subjects created a renaissance in art, poetry, philosophy, and science. 'It had a spectacular effect on education and culture in Francia, ...and an unmeasurable effect on what mattered most to the Carolingians, the moral regeneration of society.'[598] But many of these gains were lost within three generations, partly because his union did not possess a comparable civil service to the Romans, or a regular army. The perception of a false dawn was voiced even by contemporary sources, like Walahfrid Strabo:

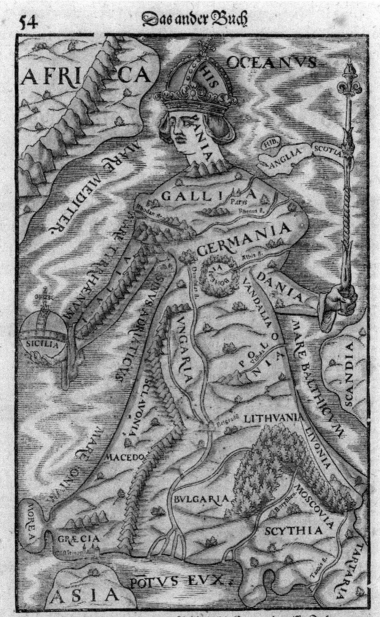

'Europa Regina' in the 1570 Cosmographia by by Sebastian Münster (1488–1552)

'Charlemagne was able to offer the cultureless and, I might say, almost completely unenlightened territory of the realm which God had entrusted to him, a new enthusiasm for all human knowledge. In its earlier state of barbarousness, his kingdom had been hardly touched at all by any such zeal, but now it opened its eyes to God's illumination. In our own time the thirst for knowledge is disappearing again: the light of wisdom is less and less sought after and is now becoming rare again in most men's minds.'[599]

But the memory of that era also haunted European chivalric culture for generations to come. Even before Charlemagne, we must remember that Columban (as we have noted in chapter 2) was the first man actually to use the word *European* and give us some understanding of what was meant by it. This presupposes an earlier acknowledgment of a shared history and cultural trajectory. The split of the Eastern and Western empires was obviously a huge geopolitical factor here, and so too was the rise of western Christendom itself.

Early medieval manuscripts are littered with 'the name Christian' which took on great international significance as the barbarian nations received that 'name' and became part of, what they called, the *populus christianus*. The Latin word '*nomen*' denotes family or stock, and along with the Roman church's zeal for order and uniformity, the name Christian led unfortunately to an almost pseudo-ethnic status.[600] In the later medieval period, around 1000, this was more obvious. Pope Gregory VII talks of a *Christian race*, and a 'holy race of Christians'.[601] A French prelate, writing of the first crusade refers to this landmark event in the Europeanisation of Europe, not as the enterprise of this or that nation in a supranational alliance, but as 'our race', *genus nostrum*. In this, we see that Western Christianity was not just militarised but also territorialised.[602]

And while we are on the subject, let us also not forget the unintended consequences of the Crusades, which firstly welded the Christian nations in a supranational alliance, but then also created a great antithesis and binary in heathendom. But the power of a holy war to unite was impressive. For example, the young warriors of Norman Sicily were so moved by the prospect of the first crusade in 1096 that they vowed not to fight against Christian lands any more until they had made war on the lands of the pagans, *paganorum fines.*[603] In the absence of a common goal, a common enemy would suffice. 'The Christendom that became aware of itself in the eleventh century was not the Christendom of Constantine but an assertively western or Latin Christendom.'[604] This was graphically illustrated when Western Crusaders sacked Christian Constantinople in 1204.

Another essential element within this was the religious orders of the Middle Ages. The larger houses of the Benedictines were the richest corporations of Europe – their influence incalculable. What the edicts and armies of Justinian could not achieve, Benedict and Columban's progeny did. We have talked already of the growth and efficacy of early medieval monasticism, but not yet mentioned the explosion of other new orders like the Cistercians, Dominicans, and Franciscans in the High Middle Ages. Bearing a common culture, they fanned out across the continent and sometimes beyond. (For example, in 1254, one Franciscan friar travelled to the Great Khan's court in Mongolia, where he debated with Muslims, Buddhists, and pagans using a theological textbook written by the Parisian, Peter Lombard.) The supranational breadth of the crusades, led Fulcher of Chartres to enthusiastically write,

> 'Who has ever heard of speakers of so many languages in one army? ....
> If a Breton or German wished to ask me something, I was completely unable to reply. But although we were divided by language, we seemed to be like brothers in the love of God and like near neighbours in one mind.'
> 605

This burst of internationalism was referred to by Odric Vitalis as 'that unanticipated transformation that took place in our times.'[606] The choosing of a leader for the second crusade was no less a thorny task than appointing a new EU Commissioner is today.

And a direct result of the first crusade was the rise of the crusading orders – which was as meteoric as it was improbable. A fusion between the diametrically opposed characteristics of the medieval knight and the medieval monk was an uneasy alloy, but a successful one, at a political level. Within a hundred years, they had formed a vast military and political network, even taking on the form of international bankers. The first Order State (*Ordenstaat*) was in Livonia, under the Sword Brothers, who were eventually absorbed into the Teutonic Knights. These warrior monks captured and ruled a vast area of the eastern Baltic, which they called Christian Prussia. The Hospitalier Knights of St John held 58 cities in the Levant, and sovereign possessions throughout Europe. They lost Rhodes to the Turks in 1520, but you can still see, in the Street of the Knights, that each *Langue* or nation had a separate convent there – Castille, Auvergne, England, Aragon, etc. These were truly international outfits, with bureaucratic systems of governance and electoral procedures. We may not like to look back upon our ancestors' exploits, but these many and varied ties between nations go some way to help us understand the sociological framework of the Western Europe within which we now live. We have a long history of working together, if not in fraternal bliss, then certainly against those we considered our enemies.

And what spectacular enemies they were. Islam formed not only the largest and most enduring Christian heresy but also the last major 'Völkerwanderung,' Muslim armies doing to Rome's Eastern empire what the barbarian invasions had done to the Western Empire. To what extent that the threat of Islam created a militarised Christendom, and vice versa is hard to guess, but one would suspect that it is quite a lot. But for Charles Martel's victory at Poitiers, all of Europe would almost certainly have been part of a vast Islamic Empire. Their lightning campaign across Africa and Asia, subsuming the oldest centres of Christian culture, left a psychological scar in the minds of generations of Europeans. To some extent, that deep divide is still with us.

The Latin language was also a major medium of cultural exchange and homogenisation, and so too was a revolution in nomenclature that spread through 'barbarian' lands as they became, at least nominally, Christianised. Studies show the speed with which indigenous names were being replaced, within two or three generations, by the names of those of powerful neighbours, popular saints, or Bible characters. It may seem like a very much smaller picture of the international ties that we are studying, but anyone can see how neighbours don't seem quite so alien when they have similar names. After the 1219 crusade, two mosques in Egypt were rededicated as churches to St Edmund and St Thomas Becket. A Suffolk saint in Egypt is a strange thought. I have yet to meet a modern Egyptian called Edmund, which I suppose means that the crusaders did not hold the country sufficiently long.

The minting of coins and the writing of charters, was also a significant factor in the Europeanisation of Europe.[607] Pennies and parchment may not look as proud and powerful as an army with banners, but a shared form of monetary and legal practice became *de rigueur* in Europe during the supposed 'Dark Ages'. Charlemagne first minted 1.7-gram silver coins. He was quickly imitated by the later Anglo-Saxon kings. A century later beyond the Rhine, the Bohemian dukes copied the English system with a 1.2-gram coin, and by 980 the Polish dukes were following suit. Five years later, Harold Bluetooth, who had won for himself all Denmark and Norway and made the Danes Christians, minted the first royal Scandinavian currency. This, among other systems of connection across the national boundaries was why a much later Dane gave Harrold's name to the modern Bluetooth connection protocol. (The Bluetooth symbol is the runes of Harold's initials.)

In 997, the Norse kings of Dublin produced a mint on the English model. Fifteen years later, the new Christian dynasty in Hungary did the same. Thereafter the new millennium saw an explosion of new mints from the Black Sea, and the middle Danube to the Baltic. Even countries slow to follow could catch up quickly once they had started. For example, Scotland didn't mint silver coins until 1100, but nevertheless had 40 million in circulation within two hundred years.[608] Because they were modelled on the coinage of England & Germany – which, incidentally, are still the economic centres of Europe today – these silver coins were of an identifiable family. Not quite the Euro, but for the travelling merchant and the international marriage dowry, it must have been a good start.

The charters followed in the pennies' wake. These formal written grants for land or rights within a certain area, were normally recorded on parchment. Again, we can largely credit their initial proliferation to the Carolingian dynasty, with the flow of use from the ecclesiastic to the secular ruler, and culminating in the establishment of native secular chancelleries. The 'shift from sacral script to practical literacy'[609] went mainstream in the twelfth century. For example, in Silesia the first indigenous document was in 1139, the first secular charter in 1175, and the first chancery in 1240. Countries such as Pomerania were transformed from non-literate, undocumented societies to the world of chancery in little over a hundred years. Dermot MacMurrough, king of Leinster, was the first to bring the continental Latin charter tradition to Ireland in 1160. English and Scottish sealed writs were so similar, that one contemporary remarked he could not even tell them apart.[610] The growth of these charters was colossal. For example, in Picardy, there were four times more written charters in the 13th than in the 12th century.[611]

In both cases, of the pennies and the parchment, we see the power of objectifying human relationships. The immaterial rights and claims were made incarnate by creating these universal mediums of exchange, whose worth was validated by the heads of state.

Universities were also soon disseminating a common intellectual culture among the elites: Paris for theology and the arts, Bologna for the law. France and Italy led the field even though the Iberian kingdoms and England had their own universities. Because the spread was uneven, students travelled widely to study, and so the universities, no less than the military orders, became places of international exchange. The student returning to his homeland took with him the same intellectual habits, technical language, and pedagogic expectations as his continental peers. Around 1200, Arnold of Lubeck wrote of the Danes, *'they are also distinguished in their knowledge of letters since the nobles send their sons to Paris, not only to secure promotion in the church, but also to instruct them in secular affairs. ...Indeed because of their natural faculty of tongue, they are not only subtle logicians but also excellent canon and civil lawyers when dealing with ecclesiastical business.'* [612]

In the first 150 years of their existence, it is estimated that European universities enrolled 750,000 students. (Paris, Bologna, Oxford, and Toulouse enrolled between 1000-1500 students each per annum, in an era when London's population was only 35,000.) These were not only places to receive past wisdom, but institutions that won renown for innovation. Students and faculty alike were granted extraordinary privileges, equal to priests. Cities vied for the most notable academic minds and bent over backward to accommodate these rapidly expanding cultural engines. And no wonder, whole faculties were free to move cities, if they felt they were not getting their way. And professors too, accrued status and money by changing universities, as footballers do today when changing clubs. The freedom of universities from overt sacred or secular interference bore rich intellectual fruit for the world but also that all-important freedom: dissent. (Remember many of medieval Europe's most revolutionary minds first held academic posts as university professors; Hus, Wycliffe, Luther etc.)

'By 1300, Europe existed as an identifiable cultural entity. It could be described in more than one way, but some common features of its cultural face are the saints, names, coins, charters, and educational practices. By the late medieval period, Europe's names and cults were more uniform than they had ever been; Europe's rulers minted coins and depended on chanceries, Europe's bureaucrats shared a common experience of higher education. This is the Europeanisation of Europe.' [613]

This new stability led to social, economic, and even territorial expansion. It was like the Roman Empire version 2.1. Germanic territories doubled between the 12th and 13th centuries. The crusades, mentioned above, led to new polities, and new settlements. The colonization of the eastern Baltic, by entrepreneurial missionaries, merchants, nobles, and military monks led to a completely new political entity, the *Ordenstaat*, or Order State. These Europeans were the product of conquest and colonization before ever they left their shores to colonise others.

How they eventually became colonisers, from the 15th to 19th centuries, is a vast and complex story; but one of the great catalysts for European expansion happened in the wake of Mehmed II's capture of Constantinople in 1453. The Ottomans 'squeezed Europeans by first blocking and then imposing extremely high tariffs on goods transiting the Silk Road.... If the Europeans could bypass the Ottomans, they could not only access India but also capture the profits now going to the Ottomans and Venetians.'[614] Poised on the southern periphery, and squeezed also by Spain, Portugal was the first to gaze south and west across the ocean.

Like the nations that would follow them, they had diverse motivations; 'containing Spain, reaching India, finding gold in Mali, making contact with Prester John, spreading the word of Christ and seizing islands in the Atlantic. The complexity of motives remained one of the hallmarks of European imperialism.'[615] It is little wonder that such a mixture of motivation produced a corresponding spectrum of explorers. These faces of Europe are perhaps seen best in two explorers, Henry the Navigator and Cortes. Henry; aristocratic, patient, methodical, conservative, pious. Cortes; low born, opportunistic, ambitious, rapacious.[616]

Columbus, if anything, was a mixture of the two, and the effects of his legacy are still debated. 'The wealth exploited by the Spaniards in the New World gave them the power to seek to unite Europe. Their failure to dominate and unite Europe freed France, Britain, and the Netherlands to pursue their own imperial strategies.'[617] That is a chronologically simplistic assessment, and yet, even in very broad terms, we begin to see in Spain that same 'Justinian impulse' at work that we noted earlier in the chapter. But the New World's gold could not, any more than the armies of Napoleon or Hitler, impose a unity on Europe by force.

1400-2016, BRITISH EXCEPTIONALISM

But, as intimated in the introduction to this book, I also wish to understand Britain's part in this vast European story. Let us, therefore, turn our gaze northwards to glimpse Shakespeare's *Sceptred Isle*, and observe how she sits within the overall drama. As we saw in a previous chapter, Churchill viewed Britain, *'with Europe, but not of it. We are linked, but not comprised. We are interested and associated, but not absorbed.'* Many saw Churchill as hopelessly out of touch with the times. It certainly is amazing to us that the man who had led a daring cavalry charge (with pistol and saber) against the Dervishes at the Battle of Omdurman could end his career as the Prime Minister of a nuclear power. He had lived almost in two separate times. And yet, like Schuman, Churchill also possessed an encyclopedic knowledge of his country's history, and so we should not be too quick to dismiss what he said to Adenauer, as recorded above. Certainly, there are some aspects of English history that explain why he thought as he did, and why Britain voted as it did in the 2016 referendum. Uncomfortable as this will be for many readers, we must now try to understand what we can of Britain's exceptionalism within Europe.

In his book *Albion, the Origins of the English Imagination*, Peter Ackroyd acknowledges (almost guiltily) that within the context of English medieval internationalism there was always a typically Anglo-Saxon insistence on 'one Rule and one country.' He cites the 'Regularis Concordia' from the 10th century Council of Winchester as an initial source but then writes that 'this disparity between England as part of European civilisation and England as the burgeoning source of native culture' is a paradox that is apparent all through later English history.

English relations with France give us points on both sides of the argument. The thought of 'our own' Edouard III swearing fealty to the King of France as his liege lord, before ever crossing the channel for his coronation at Westminster, is not something we English choose to reflect on, even if he had been the last in a long line to do so. Monarchs such as Henry II and Richard the Lionheart lived on the continent, not in England. They are buried in Fontevraud Abbey, not Westminster. For many, the very idea that we can even talk about separate histories of the 'French' and the English for the 400 years after the conquest is 'an illusion.'[618] In some very real sense, we were, even as Jerusalem became for a season, merely 'France overseas.'

Indeed, the language at the English court was French until almost the sixteenth century, and in legal circles, right up to 1600. And even as some began to think of themselves as English, those thoughts themselves were still in French. The elites of England had to be tri-lingual. They 'needed Latin to follow international trends, to address a universal audience, or participate in Church affairs. They.... needed French to communicate with the nobility, the court, and administration. They needed English to communicate with the uneducated masses.'[619] (Even in the late 14th century, an Oxford student found speaking English and not Latin would, on the second offence, be isolated in a corner and made to eat on their own. One more reminder, that long before the English became colonisers, they themselves had been subjected to colonisation.) But it wasn't just omnipresent French connections: in 1213, under 'wicked' King Jean *sans Terre*, the Kingdom of England and the Lordship of Ireland was formally accepted into the Papal fiefs.[620] In those days it was the money going to Rome, not Brussels, that exercised the English animus. And so we see, even from these two paragraphs above, that in the late medieval period our ties to the continent were more profound and more intricate than anything that has existed with the European Union.

Several factors changed this state of affairs and made the English who they are today. The Hundred Years War, fought always in France and not England, helped the English nurture their characteristic, retaliatory xenophobia. If Henry V had lived a little longer, it is possible that his great grandfather's ambition of an Anglo-French monarchy would have become reality. But it did not, and it probably would have been a poisoned chalice anyway. By ostensibly losing the Hundred Years War, the English became English and the French, by winning, became French. Professor Norman Davies argues persuasively that these English losses actually freed England from further centuries of continental war.[621] So, in the end, this Plantagenet 'failure' had a deep and lasting effect on the British psyche. Davies points out that under the Plantagenets:

> *'The English found themselves in the enviable position of being able to attack a major European power without serious threat of retaliation... As a result, the heart of England became one of the safest locations in the world. An unusual degree of security in the home base created the grounds for unusual confidence and expansiveness.'*[622]

Right up until the German bombers crossed the channel, the English would not experience an armed, foreign invasion on her own soil. The English inflicted war in Wales, Scotland, and Ireland, and they also knew the turmoil of civil war, yet never experienced a substantial invasion from overseas.[623] But from 25th July 1909, the day when Louis Bleriot landed his 25hp monoplane in the meadow outside Dover Castle, the isolation[624] of the British was ended.

When comparing Britain to France in his 1939 *Study of History*, Arnold Toynbee wrote that Britain's 'particular merit' lay in that, 'to any exceptional degree...(she) has been kept in isolation - first by her physical geography and secondly by a certain policy on the part of her statesmen in the age during which she has been most creative and most powerful.' Norman Davies also adds that: 'Two hundred years of unbroken mastery of the sea left deep traces on the British psyche. The British came to believe what the English had suspected earlier, that they were invulnerable.' But we have rushed chronologically ahead in our glimpses of British or English exceptionalism. Let us return to Tudor England.

The Tudors, who emphasised their 'Welshness as an instrument of unification'[625] capitalised on England's new isolation, mentioned above by Toynbee. Indeed, they made a most decisive break with the continent during the Reformation. No longer a mere papal fief, English payments abroad stopped, and soon after, the physical remnants of 1000 years of connectedness (the monasteries) were liquidated in a matter of years. 'The European dimension to England's internal affairs was one of the many things that the Reformation destroyed.'[626] The masterminding of this hatchet job was Thomas Cromwell. For many Catholics, the monastic ruins and reassigned ecclesiastical buildings still constitute a painful reminder.

'In a still more powerful way, the ghost of medieval monasticism remained and remains to haunt this island. The grey walls and broken cloisters, the ...bare ruin'd choirs, where late the sweet birds sang, speak more eloquently for the past than any historian would dare, and pose for every beholder questions that words cannot answer.'[627]

From that time on, it was not just the 'cloisters' and 'choirs' of the island that were being reassessed, but also English history too. Many (in Britain and America) saw the events leading on from the Reformation as one of unilineal progression to protestant or secular glory. Others did not. The battle for interpretation was joined. Davies, summing one camps position, writes with disdain that:

'Once the Whigs had triumphed in that 'glorious Revolution' of 1688-9, their view of history triumphed with them. Everything that happened post-1688 was building on the glorious achievement. The 'Whig Interpretation' did not come under serious attack for 150 years. In the eighteenth century, things medieval fell out of fashion. David Hume's monumental History of England (sic) saw... the Church as an enemy of civilisation.'[628]

But even Davies seems to overstate Whig success here. This 'Whig Interpretation', represented by historians like Stubbs, Hallam, Rapin, and Maitland, was more strongly contested – and by the best writers, and more in the early and mid-18th century than it was later.[629] Hume slated Rapin's *History of England* as 'totally worthless.' In fact, the Whig interpretation really only gained its monopoly 150 years later, with

Macauley, because historical writing only settled in properly in his day. Also, 'things medieval' never really 'went out of fashion' either. The appetite for historical and cultural tourism from 1750-1800 included the Gothic as a major component, and it had major antecedents as far back as the 1720s. The Tories, the Baroque, the Jacobites, Walpole's neo-Gothic, the Ossian hoax, all showed literary and artistic sensibilities alive to 'things medieval'. (Lord Acton saw the seeds of Whig progressivism in the medieval era itself, even calling Aquinas the first Whig.) Even, Hume's rationalism (which leant itself in the end to Whig progressivism) was only ever one side of the coin. The quest to understand the soul of Britain's past, and to project its future, was endlessly contested inside the politicised nature of British culture in the eighteenth century. In many ways, this was a positive sign of a balanced parliamentary settlement and a relatively free press.

But 200 years later, and after Britain's meteoric international ascendancy, a war-stricken British people did enter the EEC, if nervously. The 'force of events' that Schuman had envisaged, that paved the way for our joining, were financial. We had stripped naked for war, had burnt down to our last wick in the defeat of Hitler. Britain, her Icarus-wings clipped, her empire disintegrating, would need over fifty years to make good her debts.

But 500 years of history and 300 years of historiography doesn't disappear overnight. Schuman was right, the British would not stomach more than 50 years of being embroiled once more in continental responsibilities. The European Commission would not be the United Kingdom's *liege lord* any more than a French king or an Italian pope.

Our geographical and historical distance from the continent also affected our legal structures. From Justinian through to Charlemagne, our European cousins inherited Statute law, that is, rationalist, state-based law. But we Britons have, from local councils and via king Alfred,[630] inherited English Common Law, that is, empiricist, case-based law. And that is why we have been, over the last 40 years, harder to integrate into EU systems, and why we always felt ill at ease accepting laws from Brussels that superseded our own. For France and Germany is was like grafting a pear to an apple tree, for Britain it was more like attempting the same thing with an oak - it was a difference of kind, not degree. Writing in 1999 the historian Norman Davies explains,

> 'English law resembles nothing else in the world except, of course, for those legal systems such as the American or the Australian, which are descended from it. It has defied codification and systematization, and hence to the outsider appears both chaotic and obscurantist. It has developed organically over a long time, dating the central role of its royal courts to the twelfth century, the emergence of its characteristic juries of the thirteenth, and the institution of Justices of the Peace or lay magistrates to the fourteenth.'

Nor, of course, did Britain have the *Code Napoleon* imposed on it, an imposition that proved formative in the political institutions of many other European nations. Indeed, seen from certain angles, we are more like Russia – simply other. We appear to be different, or at least since the Plantagenet's loss of our continental possessions, we have told ourselves that we are, which is almost the same thing. Since that time, Whig historians have worked hard to make us forget what Trevelyan attempted to remind us; that we were once *'a mere extension of Franco-Latin Europe'*.

THE LONG MARCH OF EUROPEAN RE-INTEGRATION

Curiously enough, British public perceptions of isolation, mentioned in the last section, were greatly at variance with reality in other areas. In fact, British cooperation in supranational European organisations had already crept back since the split with Rome. For example, the Hague Tribunal, a court of internal arbitration set up in 1899, proved a great hit with the British, not least because they used it straightaway to win a case against Venezuela. The British had submitted its sovereignty to a similar process of international arbitration in the 1794 Jay Treaty (UK vs USA). This was essentially repeated when Britain joined the League of Nations in January 1920,[631] and thus, recognised its place under the Permanent Court of International Justice.

The First World War had by then demonstrated that unrestrained national sovereignty was, 'if not a myth, then an impossible ideal.'[632] Even the British people, who 'had been brought up to think of sovereignty, like virginity, as an absolute item...either intact or not'[633] came to see the sense of supranational forms of arbitration as desirable. And when it came down to business, the British always chose to be involved in the continent.[634] (Indeed, our involvement in the empire also applied an unavoidable solvent to our notions of sovereignty.)

From Cromwell, to William of Orange, John Churchill to Wellington, and from Asquith[635] to another Churchill, Britain chose to put Europe first - or at least, her interests in Europe first. This tendency in foreign policy - springing variously from genuine solidarity, dynastic ties, religious prejudice, colonial interests or just good-old-fashioned meddling as an international policeman - eventually led Britain to a sacrificial decision in 1939 that would break her wealth and diminish her status until she was only a regional power.

In the autumn of 2018, when visiting the French National Assembly in Paris, I asked Nicolas Ferrand, President of the National Assembly for a message to Britain:

'Greetings to the British and French people, who have gone through the great trials of history together. There is no reason why we cannot continue to write the history of Europe together, and, together, continue to preserve the space of prosperity and peace that our predecessors established after their trials. It affirms my desire that there be no separation between our peoples because we still have so much to do together in the work the founding fathers began. You can be sure that the French have not forgotten that, in the worst moments of our history, it was Winston Churchill who welcomed General De Gaulle (to Britain) and allowed the French to regain their freedom. So, let us continue to follow this path. There is no reason to keep away from each other.'[636]

His words were well chosen and full of solidarity, although the reference to our hosting the French government in exile and allowing the French 'to regain their freedom' doesn't quite encompass the reality of their liberation. It was not the French themselves, but very many others, not least the British (see Chapter 13), who paid the highest price (in blood, money and prestige) for their nation's freedom. But Ferrand rightly points out that the French and British 'have gone through the great trials of history together,' and often on opposing sides. Much of this conflict, often religious, at least in outward appearance, would find a welcome solvent in the Age of Reason.

> The Enlightenment came on the heels of many generations of national and religious conflict. In a supposedly rational age, it 'became an embarrassment for the divided community of nations to be reminded of their common Christian identity; and the word 'Europe' filled the need for designation with more neutral connotations.'[637]

In the West, the wars of Louis XIV inspired a number of publicists to appeal for common action in settling the divisions of their day. The much-imprisoned William Penn (1644 -1718) had the distinction of advocating both universal toleration and for a 'European dyet, or Parliament.'[638] The dissident French abbé, Charles Castel de St Pierre (1658-1743), author of Projet d'une paix perpetuelle (1713), called for a confederation of European powers to guarantee a lasting peace. In the East, the emergence of the Russian Empire under Peter the Great, required a radical rethinking of the international framework. "The Treaty of Utrecht in 1713, provided the last major occasion when public reference to the *Respublica*,[639] the 'Christian Commonwealth', was made." The term 'perpetual peace' became popular again, 70 years later, when German philosopher Immanuel Kant published his 1795 essay *Perpetual Peace: A Philosophical Sketch*. Kant's liberal internationalism, having shed its overt Christian clothing, found many new expressions in the foreign policies of actors as diverse as Canning, Palmerston, Woodrow Wilson and even the drafters of the United Nations' *Four Freedoms*.

There is a case to be made that the talk of a *new internationalism* was essentially just the continuation of the medieval international spirit in secular clothing. Standing at the crossroads between the medieval and the modern were the Renaissance humanists. "The humanists varied in the degree of their own national attachments. Erasmus[640] had the least, for seldom did he mention his native Holland, and he had nothing but scorn for the boast of Pope Julius II that he was a Ligurian Italian."[641] And certainly, after 200 years of international conflict, notions of supranational unity became more desirable as a panacea. Voltaire described his aspirations for Europe as 'a kind of great republic divided into several states, some monarchical, the others mixed... but all corresponding with one another. They all have the same religious foundation, even if divided into several confessions. And they all had the same principal of public law and politics, unknown in other parts of the world.'[642] Rousseau announced that 'there are no longer Frenchmen, Germans, and Spaniards, or even English, but only Europeans.'

The 'or *even* English' is perhaps a hint again of the slightly unique British status among the nations of Europe. Long before we even joined the European Economic Area, Schuman seemed to have had tremendous insight into our national psyche. But, even if all this is taken for granted, most modern British - even Brexiteers - would still echo Edmund Burke's words that *'no European can be a complete exile in any part of Europe.'*

Hot on the heels of these French Romantic and Enlightenment desires for international unity, came the corresponding imperial solution. Under Napoleon, Europe tasted once more the Justinian-technocratic impulse to manufacture unity through force. And as in the French case, so too in the German; Europe repulsed that imposition in great wars which brought her to her knees.

Between the Napoleonic and World Wars, Europeans saw three attempts at limited fiscal unity. The first, the German Zollerverein (1834-1871), encompassed nearly 40 states and was seen by its admirers as a model whereby economic grouping could lead to political affiliation. (At the same time, Goethe and Shiller desired to use the arts for a similar purposes.) The second, the Latin Monetary Union (1865-1926), included 18 countries (incl. Belgium, Switzerland, France, and Italy) and was tied to the French gold franc. The third, the Scandanavian Monetary Union (1873-1924), was tied to a common kronor. The Bank of England showed little interest in these innovations, something that caused Walter Bagshot, editor of the *Economist* in 1877, to write, 'Before long, all Europe, save England, will have one money.'

It was around the time of the failure of these fiscal, ideological, and military schemes (to bring European unity dawned on a broken continent), that T. S. Elliot had the privilege of broadcasting to a defeated Germany about the great dangers that were then facing Western Civilisation. For Eliot, the most pressing casualty was the weakening of the Christian heritage - a source of unity deeper than the merely fiscal, and stronger than the appeals of arms and empire. The conservative Anglican poet and literary critic, said that 'Europe's mental frontiers' had closed, and a *'kind of cultural anarchy followed inevitably on the political and economic autarchy.'* Enlightenment and Industrial man, with his obsessions for machines and social sciences, had thought that civilisation was just one such machine. It was not, contended Elliot. Hence his comments already given above, that *'culture is something that must grow. You cannot build a tree; you can only plant it, and care for it, and wait for it to mature.'* He stressed the need for cross-cultural 'trade' and the importance of the Christian tradition which in itself absorbed *'the legacy of Greece, of Rome, and of Israel.'* His analysis is striking and insightful and worth quoting at length:

> "The dominant feature in creating a common culture between people, each of which has its own distinctive culture, is religion... I am talking about the common tradition of Christianity which made Europe what it is, and about the common cultural elements which this common Christianity has brought with it... It is in Christianity that our arts have developed; it is in Christianity that the laws of Europe – until recently – have been rooted. It is against a background of Christianity that all our thought has significance. An individual European

may not believe that the Christian faith is true; and yet what he says, and does and makes will all.... depend on [the Christian heritage] for its meaning. Only a Christian culture could have produced a Voltaire or a Nietzsche. I do not believe that the culture of Europe could survive the complete disappearance of the Christian faith."[643]

If Eliot can say that *only a Christian culture could have produced a Voltaire or a Nietzsche*; then we can say by extension that only Christian civilisation could have produced a Montesquieu or a Kant, indeed only Christian civilisation could have produced Capitalism and Communism. Eliot's conservative voice was essentially repeating what Burke had said 150 years before. And if Eliot and others' minority Christian view went unheeded (see chapter 19), there were still many others seeking the unity of our civilisation in the more progressive centre at the same time, e.g. Atlee, Nehru, William Temple, who actually had more power.

Even the more utopian view of European Union, seen as far back as the Treaty of Westphalia, or even farther back to Charlemagne, had a distinctly Christian and messianic element to it. William of Orange appealed to it in raising an alliance against Louis XIV, as others did against Napoleon. 'It was the rhetoric of the Balance of Power in the eighteenth century, and of the Concert in the nineteenth. It was an essential feature of the peaceful Age of Imperialism which, until shattered by the Great War in 1914, saw Europe as the home base of worldwide dominion.'[644]

When Professor Butterfield gave his Riddell lectures a year after the 1950 Schuman Declaration, he did not mince his words about secular impulses toward internationalism:

> *'Modern Internationalism is the system of medieval Christendom with the religion evaporated out of it..... Humanism and Humanitarianism, Liberalism and Internationalism, then, emerge as the result of a tendency to translate into secular terms certain movements and aspirations that had characterised Christianity. ... From 1660, however...they begin to forget their origin, pretending entirely to stand on their own feet.... All of them lost some-*

thing by this fact - all of them are thin and attenuated when compared with the Christian version.... they are the imperfect secular substitutes which the world began to take up when it was losing the genuinely religious outlook.'

The Messianic burden on Europeans to export civilisation glowed hottest when fanned by commercial interest. The French historian and statesman François Guizot, who died just before Schuman was born, wrote, 'European civilisation has entered ...into the eternal truth, into the plan of providence.... It progresses according to intentions of God.'[645] This sacralised narrative, present also in the 'Manifest Destiny' of America and 'Absolute Spirit' of Hegel was the tip of a very large iceberg of hubris globalised by writers as diverse as Marx and Fukuyama. And few eras of history (except our own, of course!) have escaped this error.

Even the impish grandfather of British liberalism, Charles James Fox – no ones' idea of a religious extremist – along with many Whig followers, openly delighted in the triumph of *la Révolution* and even Napoleon. Why? Because the revolution was obviously God's will. Fox once boasted, though quietly, 'the triumph of the French government over the English does in fact afford me a degree of pleasure which is very difficult to disguise.' But leaving these anecdotes to one side and attempting a more distanced view – if such a thing were indeed possible – let us ask; can we see any truth in the claims of a divinely favoured west? It is a thorny issue so let us tiptoe gently!

'Western European supremacy is one of those dogmas which holds good at points in European history and not at others. It does not apply in the earlier centuries, when, for example, Byzantium was far more advanced.'[646] Some argue that it was only much later, through the effects of the Counter-Reformation, and the opening up of America and India by Columbus and Vasco da Gama, that Western Europe transformed 'from its position as a regional backwater into the fulcrum of a sprawling communication, transportation and trading system: at a stroke it became the new mid-point between east and west.'[647]

By the turn of the 20th century Europe had colonies totalling 40 million square kilometres. Britain ruled 25 of those, tiny Belgium controlled the Congo, the Netherlands governed tens of millions of people in today's Indonesia, and France had its own substantial possessions in Africa and Indochina. Then suddenly, with a speed and ferocity that left everyone stunned, the supposedly civilised Europeans at the height of their power and sophistication spent the next 31 years killing 100 million[648] of themselves.

Between 1939-1945 a total of 10% of Europeans perished in the war. For example, 10% of Germany, 16% of Poland, 14% of Russia. From it, they would never rise again to global leadership. 'Ultimately the ability of Europeans to conquer the world but their inability to conquer themselves would prove part of their fatal flaw.'[649] From the 1950s to the 1980s, geopolitics was dominated by the struggle between the Soviets and the Americans around the big issue, 'who would become the heir of the European empire. Multiple borderlands, like the Korean Peninsula or Vietnam, or Afghanistan, became flashpoints that drew the two superpowers in.'[650]

And so, with an irony that was surely not lost to Russians or Americans, the two powers founded on anti-imperial premises, were forced to act with imperial reach. During this period, and up until 2008, Europeans congratulated themselves that, without the inconvenience of Empire, they had 'pioneered a new dimension of human existence, prosperity without risk and without war.'[651] And then on August 7th, 2008, Russia invaded Georgia, which exposed the impotence of NATO. And then again, a month later on Sept 15th the Lehman Brothers went bankrupt, signalling a credit crisis that would further destroy the complacency of Europe. NATO was supposed to handle security, and the EU was supposed to deliver prosperity, but in the autumn of 2008 two legs of the three-legged stool which comprised the European project began to look very weak. For those expecting a third leg, often called 'the soul of Europe', to see Europe through, the decade that followed must have been a shock, as fears and hatred emerged. That is a simplistic analysis, and one which we shall visit again in the epilogue. But for the purposes of this chapter let us just pull back to the general curve of European world domination with a sense of detached enquiry.

There is certainly something Faustian in the European rise and fall, even a great sense of pathos. One writer compared Europe's tragedy with that of Odysseus, 'that the act of learning about the world destroyed its enchantment and made it prosaic. .... as the discovery of an enchanted world devolved into mere business devoid of magic. ...Columbus discovered the enchanted, but not the secret of knowing it without destroying it.'[652]

When Europeans look at the Americans (the inheritors of our mantle in the west) they see an incomprehensible optimism, and when Americans look back to the old world, they see an equally incomprehensible sadness. With older cultures come greater self-knowledge – and often great cynicism and world-weariness. We Europeans are to the Americans what the Greeks were to the Romans, and what the Romans were to the Irish of Columban's generation. And for this reason, we need each other.

We have, in this chapter, really only touched on material considerations in the rise of Europe. But I am never totally convinced by a view that places too great an emphasis on geography, politics and economics. They are of very great importance but never the whole story. For good or ill, and often both, Christianity had assumed, from a very early time, a cultural dominance in Western Europe that it had not done east of Byzantium. The philosophical underpinnings – the worldview – of a civilisation is surely at least as important as its trade, if not more so.

In chapter 2 we noted the signal contribution, not present in Islam, Hinduism, Buddhism, or Confucianism, of the concept of humans made in the image of God – and therefore that men and women could, as Newton said, 'think God's thoughts after him.' It was a game-changer that led to the most gargantuan conceptual leaps in the scientific revolution and social justice.

There is too much to say here, but if we note only the changes after Western Europe began reading Bibles in their own national languages, then we will see a major clue to the scientific and democratic revolutions that jettisoned us for good and ill beyond our neighbours. The rise of the West from the fifteenth century is extraordinary, so too Europe's global reach within such a short time. Of the evils that ensued from the White Man's Burden to have 'dominion over pine and palm' and denigrating 'the lesser breeds of man,' we are now well aware – painfully so. It is echoed too in Western European culture which neglects the claims and viewpoints of the majority world. When Oxford University Press last published a one volume history of Europe (in 1927), they were able to say without any hint of irony, and with typically Anglo-Saxon verve: 'Although a number of grand civilisations have existed in various ages, it is the civilisation of Europe which has made the deepest and widest impression, and which (as developed on both sides of the Atlantic) sets the standard for all peoples of the earth.'

This Western Eurocentric supremacy found its most extreme expression in the Aryanism of the Nazis. For them, the white Aryan-Europeans were responsible for all the great achievements of human history. Other racial groups were classified as Untermenschen or 'subhuman' and treated accordingly. When that ideology imploded in 1945, there came a moment of reflection that Schuman and others could seize. But into the vacuum left by the deflated Eurocentric ego stepped other claims also. In fact, the counter-claims to Western supremacy have come thick and fast; from Afro-Caribbean communities (expressed most extremely in Afrology), to the rise of the Far East in the last few decades.

What is also often forgotten is that many closer counterclaims have come from the near East. The Orthodox Church, the Russian Empire, The Pan Slav movement, and the Soviet Union have all offered theories about their own supremacy and glorious futures – uncorrupted by Western European ideological and moral canker. The European story itself has also been rethought from within, to fit the embrace of Eastern Europe since 1990. The concept of 'the West' has been so problematic for so many scholars as to become nearly meaningless. Any of the recent books on Eurasia, combined with a cautious glance at the future is enough to put most thinking Europeans, if not in their place, then certainly on their guard.

A CHRISTIAN PERSPECTIVE

We have seen, in a quotation above, that T. S. Eliot did 'not believe that the culture of Europe could survive the complete disappearance of the Christian faith.' This claim or fear, that 'religion generically is the basis of culture and that therefore the disappearance of Christianity... would be a disaster for Europe because it would mean the end of European culture, is very different from the claim that a just, natural civil order cannot actually occur without the acceptance of Christianity, and that thus any culture that fails to accept Christianity is by definition unacceptable. The former claim is made by Mauras, and Dawson and Eliot; the latter is made by Leo XIII, his successors, and Gilson.'[653] Leaving that second view to one side, as I don't think the assertion is within this book's remit or intent, let us linger with the former position for a moment, for here we come to the crucial moment that we shall observe in greater detail in the next chapter.

Christopher Dawson, mentioned above, his eye ever on Augustine's dialectic between the two cities, was more 'fearful lest the cause of Christian civilisation be tied too closely to one secular culture or temporal struggle.'[654] Writing in 1943 he explained his hesitance:

'[W]e have the hard task of carrying on simultaneously a war on two fronts. We have to oppose, by arms, the aggression of the external enemy, and at the same time to resist the enemy within - the growth in our society of the evil power we are fighting against. And this second war is the more dangerous of the two, since it may be lost by victory as well as by defeat, and the very fact that we are driven to identify the evil with that manifestation of it that threatens our national existence, tends to blind us to the more insidious tendencies in the same direction that are to be found in our own social order. The disintegration of Western culture under the moral and economic strain of war is not a danger that can be lightly dismissed. Nor can it be accepted by Christians in the same spirit in which they accepted the fall of the Roman Empire. For that was an external disaster that left the sources of spiritual vitality unimpaired, while this is a spiritual catastrophe which strikes directly at the moral foundations of our society, and destroys not the outward form of civilisation but the very soul of man which is the beginning and end of all human culture.'[655]

Dawson was not the only major Catholic thinker of the inter-war era shriven of Belloc's grand claim the generation before, that 'Europe is the Church and the Church is Europe.' Jacques Maritain was too, and so was Etienne Gilson, both men of Schuman's generation and both important figures in understanding Schuman's intellectual formation. Gilson was a philosopher who shared Maritain's views on the inadequacy of natural ethics but he was hesitant to join Maritain's optimism as seen in his 1940 *Commonweal* article, "The acceptance by all the members of the [European] federation of the reductions in the sovereignty of the State required by an authentic international organisation would lead at the end, if they are conceived under the banner of liberty, to the establishment of what we can properly call in its own right a new Christendom."

Maritain, unlike his American hosts, did not favour the concept of a European Federation as merely a vehicle against communism. His vision was larger still; indeed, no less than to see 'liberal capitalism transcended as well as Fascism and Marxism.'[656] This was a radical leap in thought and probably only one that could have been made by a man who was something of a mystic as well as a philosopher. Unencumbered by the myriad, earthed connections of daily politics, Maritain's ideas went further in the end than someone like Schuman, Adenauer or De Gasperi could ever go. His principles, evinced between the lines of his 1948 book *Man and the State* showed a writer whose gaze was 'fixed on the more ambitious goal of world government and it was in this context that [the book] was written.'[657]

That is why, just as these disciples (Schuman *et al*) were stepping into the breach of history, their intellectual master displayed 'such a reserved attitude towards Christian Democracy and European Integration.'[658] So, in a strange way, we have a political parting for Schuman and Maritain akin to the relational breakdown between Gall and Columban; as the latter headed from the plain to the mountain, the former stayed north of the Alps where there was work to be done.

Maritain became, not just an intellectual link between Aquinas and politics to Schuman and De Gasperi, but also a social link between these two 'disciples' – if we can use the word loosely. Maritain knew both men independently and was able to make the personal introductions when the time came. This meant that when they finally met in the winter of 1948 under politically tense conditions, the friendship was quickly established and misunderstandings easily cleared.

When returning home, Gasperi said to his wife about Schuman, 'we have both lived long on the border of the national thoughts, we have both reflected the same way and we understand current problems also in the same way.' Maritain, no less than geopolitical forces, had provided valu-

Adenauer, like most of Europe, was praying for a miracle in Franco-German relations

able intellectual rails upon which the two nations could meet in the persons of De Gasperi and Schuman. These men would not travel Maritain's train to the end of the line, but it took them far enough, to a station or at least a platform where they could meet to plan their cross-country journey to European Federation.

There is one link in the chain of providence on which we will leave Maritain. It occurred in the summer of 1949 in the middle of the Atlantic Ocean on board a liner. To Schuman's delight, he found that Jacques and Raissa Maritain were on the same boat that was taking him to America for diplomatic talks. The two weeks of discussions over dinner between the three of them seemed like a gift of providence and great source of encouragement. Schuman told them that he had finally met De Gasperi. Raissa had time to speak warmly of De Gasperi and encouraged Schuman to move forward with him.

Schuman, in his turn, encouraged Maritain to return to Europe permanently and to help him set up the European University in Saarbrucken. Maritain loved the idea but could not commit at that moment in time. As ever; the gap between the ideal and the reality, the mountain and the plain. Perhaps Schuman had time to explain of what he was thinking. Perhaps he helped Maritain see more clearly, we shall never know. And the two of them setting up the university? It never did happen. And so, like Columban and Gall it was a story without a conclusion, or at least not one that we can readily understand.

And as Schuman concluded his American trip, and 1949 turned into 1950, there was another very great task that he foresaw – but from which he shrank. This great task, this seemingly unassailable mountain, was to be jointly tackled by men and women too numerous to list except for the few key players we have met already and a few more we shall meet in the next chapter. The failure of the League of Nations – or more correctly the failure of the nations within the League – had led to such devastation that the political field now lay open to a more radical solution – if not a complete paradigm shift. That solution will be the subject of the next chapter.

British Foreign Secretary Ernest Bevin with Schuman at the Quai d'Orsay, 23rd July 1949.

Jan 1947 - De Gasperi with President Truman at the Cleveland Economic Forum

Resetting relations: Adenauer with the Nixon family

Adenauer and daughter at the Whitehouse with the Eisenhowers

CHAPTER 15
FOOTNOTES & REFERENCES

592. George Friedman, *Flashpoints - The Emerging Crisis in Europe*, Doubleday p.56

593. Robert Bartlett, *The Making of Europe* – for which I am indebted for much of the material beneath.

594. It is interesting that Constantine once made Trier – between Brussels and Strasbourg, the political centre of gravity for the area. Jerome studied theology here, before going east. Salvian writes that by the mid sixth century Trier, the capital of the military government, had been sacked four times. With regards to political stability, the comparison to Ireland is marked. Cogitosus tells us that this was a time when Kildare, the third most important monastic site in Ireland, was becoming a city.

595. With the founding of Constantinople as the new Roman capital (and the ensuing proliferation of new buildings) the 'Byzantine' builders entered a new phase of architecture, recovering the corbel arches and domes of the Mycenaean and Minoan ages. Hagia Sophia, with its enormous domes, was built at a time when most Christians worshiped in little more than wooden sheds.

596. Voltaire, *Oeuvres Complètes de Voltaire: Essai sur les moeurs et l'esprit des nations*, 'Ce corps qui s'appelait et qui s'appelle encore le saint empire romain n'était en aucune manière ni saint, ni romain, ni empire.'

597. Such a thought had never crossed the minds of his predecessors. The Merovingian monarchs thought little more of their subjects than they would any other chattel. Even Charlemagne's father and grandfather, who accepted the duty to protect their subjects, would have thought their education a complete waste of time.

598. Contreni, John G. (1984), *"The Carolingian Renaissance"*, Renaissances before the Renaissance: cultural revivals of late antiquity and the Middle Ages. See also, Nelson, Janet L. (1986), "On the limits of the Carolingian renaissance", Politics and Ritual in Early Medieval Europe.

599. This quote was from Strabo's introduction to *Einhard's, Life of Charlemagne*. also in, Lewis Thorpe, tr., Einhard and Notker the Stammerer, *Two Lives of Charlemagne*, 1969:49f.

600. This had Patristic precedent: the idea of a third race had been mooted as rhetoric e.g., in the Letter to Diognetus and (paraphrasing) in Athanasius' Incarnation of the Word. The key difference from usage among the Fathers was from a dynamic to a static sense of the term 'class'. Among early Patristic writers, the talk of a 'race of Christians' had the overtone of a new humanity with everyone welcome and included. The problem with it here (as in Constantinople at the same time) was the territorial, exclusive overtone. 'Fortress Europe' is born, and here lies the ultimate root of all later European racism. It was exactly the same dynamic present in ancient Israel before Jesus: from a beach-head, Israel had become an exclusive club. Their name for a non-Jew was Goyim, literally, dog. When Jesus whipped money-

changers out of the temple, he was making an important point; 'my house should be called a house of prayer for all nations'.

601. The encounters between east and west during the crusades had a deep impact. Western Europeans for a long time afterwards were simply known as Franks in Greece, and Franji in Syria, just as some Algerians and Tunisians still refer to us as Roumi after the Romans who colonised their shores.

602. Nicolaus Serarius, 1604, *Moguntiacarum Rerum ab initio usque ad, Reverendissimum et il, Libri Quinque.*

603. Robert Bartlett, *The Making of Europe* p.254

604. Robert Bartlett, *The Making of Europe: Conquest, Colonization, and Cultural Change*, 950-1350. P.261

605. Ibid

606. Ibid

607. Ibid

608. Here we can sense the great shift from the time, only a few centuries before, when none – not even the high born – except ecclesiastics could read. Charlemagne could read but could never get the hang of writing. The great autodidact King Alfred could do both, but it took him until the age of 40.

609. Earl David of Huntingdon (1152-1219)

610. Robert Bartlett, *The Making of Europe*

611. Ibid

612. Ibid p.254

613. George Friedman, Flashpoints: The Emerging Crisis in Europe, Doubleday, p.31

614. Ibid p.31

615. Ibid p.36

616. Ibid

617. Norman Davies, *The Isles*, p.330 (Macmillan Publishers Ltd, 1999.) It is still strange to imagine that before this point, both the English and Scotch nobles were conscious of Norman descent. For example, my ancestors the Melvilles were from Malleville, in Pay de Caux, the Balioll's were from Bailleul in Picardy, and the Bruces (de Brus) were from Brix in Normandy. Most still held lands in both England, Scotland, and on the continent into the 14th century. Edward III's, and through him England's, claim to be kings of France was only formally rescinded in 1801.

618. Norman Davies, *The Isles*, p.426 (Macmillan Publishers Ltd, 1999.)

619. Norman Davies, *The Isles*, p.354 (Macmillan Publishers Ltd, 1999.) The English annual tribute was 700 marks, the Irish was 300. In 1300 Pope Boniface VII also tried to stake his claim as lord paramount of England and Scotland, a move which provoked a strong reaction of independence within both nations. (Ibid p. 378)

620. Norman Davies, *The Isles* (Macmillan Publishers Ltd, 1999.)

621. Norman Davies, *The Isles*, p.439 (Macmillan Publishers Ltd, 1999.) Davies also uses the same section to show the negative effects of this impunity, in the way that the English treated their nearer neighbours, like Ireland.

622. We certainly primed ourselves for an invasion in 1756 and in the time of Napoleon; we also had coastal attacks by the Dutch and the Americans in between.

623. Speech to the House of Commons, 30th July 1934. It is worth adding that 'the Rhine' was just a temporary marker for the range of military aircraft. This frontier expanded past Moscow.

624. Norman Davies, *The Isles* (Macmillan Publishers Ltd, 1999.)

625. Norman Davies, *The Isles,* p.397 (Macmillan Publishers Ltd, 1999.)

626. Dom David Knowles, *The Religious Orders of the England*, vol. III (Cambridge, 1959) p.468

627. Norman Davies, *The Isles*, p.386 (Macmillan Publishers Ltd, 1999.)

628. For more detail and nuance on this subject, please read the famous, Cambridge historian Sir Herbert Butterfield's *The Whig Interpretation of History* (1931). Also connected to this section (on the British mindset) are Butterfield's comments in 1944, 'We are all of us exultant and unrepentant Whigs. Those who, perhaps in the misguided austerity of youth, wish to drive out that Whig interpretation, (that particular thesis which controls our abridgment of English history,) are sweeping a room which humanly speaking cannot long remain empty. They are opening the door for seven devils which, precisely because they are newcomers, are bound to be worse than the first. We, on the other hand, will not dream of wishing it away, but will rejoice in an interpretation of the past which has grown up with us, has grown up with the history itself, and has helped to make the history... we must congratulate ourselves that our 17th-century forefathers... did not resurrect and fasten upon us the authentic middle ages... in England we made peace with our middle ages by misconstruing them; and, therefore, we may say that "wrong" history was one of our assets. The Whig interpretation came at exactly the crucial moment and, whatever it may have done to our history, it had a wonderful effect on English politics... in every Englishman there is hidden something of a Whig that seems to tug at the heart-strings.' Herbert Butterfield, *The Englishman and His History* (Cambridge University Press, 1944), pp. 1–4, 73

629. While we are talking of Alfred, let me also add a counterpoint to the general thrust in this paragraph. There was a moment in the decades before WWI when the English-German axis was talked up with passion using King Alfred as a central emblem and historical icon of this; during Victoria and Albert's reign. From Coleridge to Forster, for most of the 19th century, our mainstream was not as carte blanche isolationist as I make out below.

630. Part 1 of the Treaty of Versailles came into effect on 10 January, 1920, 6 days before the first meeting of the Council of the League. Source: Wikipedia. (See also: Norman Davies, The Isles,(Macmillan Publishers Ltd, 1999.)

631. Norman Davies, *The Isles*, p.997 (Macmillan Publishers Ltd, 1999.)

632. Norman Davies, *The Isles*, p.994 (Macmillan Publishers Ltd, 1999.)

633. Norman Davies, *The Isles*, p.994 (Macmillan Publishers Ltd, 1999.)

634. Unlike Russia and France, which had a formal treaty, France and Britain had an informal Entente. Necessity and honour did not make our involvement a foregone conclusion.

635. This can be viewed at https://www.youtube.com/watch?v=eLLSBu5NmOo

636. Davies, Norman. *Europe, a history*

637. https://en.wikipedia.org/wiki/Ideas_of_European_unity_before_1945

638. Davies, Norman. *Europe, a history* p.9

639. Someone once called Erasmus 'Europe's 'free-floating brain'

640. Roland Bainton, *Christian Attitudes to War and Peace*

641. Voltaire, *Le Siècle de Louis XIV,* quoted by Denys Hay, *Europe, The Emergence of an Idea*. (Edinburgh, 1957)

642. T. S. Eliot, Die Einheit de Euroaeischen (Berlin 1946)

643. Davies, Norman. *Europe, a history*. P.9

644. F. Guizot, *The History of Civilisation in Europe*

645. Davies, Norman. *Europe, a history*. P.28

646. Peter Frankopan, *Silk Roads*, Bloomsbury 2015, p. xviii

647. https://en.wikipedia.org/wiki/List_of_wars_by_death_toll

648. George Friedman, *Flashpoints – The Emerging Crisis in Europe*, Doubleday p.35

649. Ibid

650. Ibid p.96

651. Ibid p.41

652. Alan Paul Fimister, *Robert Schuman. Neo-scholastic humanism and the reunification of Europe*. Peter Lang, 2008.

653. Ibid

654. Christopher Dawson's *The Judgment of the Nations* (1942)

655. Alan Paul Fimister, *Robert Schuman. Neo-scholastic humanism and the reunification of Europe*. Peter Lang, 2008.

656. Ibid

657. Ibid

658. Recorded vividly by Spaak in his Memoir *'Combats Inacheves'*

CHAPTER 16

Schuman: Moving Mountains

CHAPTER SUMMARY - 1949-1950, BACK TO LUXEUIL - Schuman chairs a conference at Columbanus' monastery and networks behind the scenes for European solidarity. 1949-1950, THE PRAGMATIST & THE PREACHER - Two friendships that spur Schuman to greatness. The preacher is the American Lutheran evangelist Frank Buchman, a man too practical for politics but who helped effect the 'greatest achievement of modern statecraft' – the swift Franco-German reconciliation. The pragmatist is Jean Monnet who formulated the architecture of the proposed Coal and Steel Community. May 9th, 1950, EUROPE'S 'PRIME MOVER' - Schuman Declaration and the British response to the French *'leap in the dark.'* Reflections of the EU post-Maastricht.

'Now these, Roman, will be your arts:
To teach the ways of peace to those you conquer
Spare defeated peoples, tame the proud.'

Virgil, Aeneid, Book 6, lines 1135-37

'If your dreams do not scare you, then they are not big enough.'
Liberian President Ellen Johnson Sirleaf

'A leader takes people where they want to go. A great leader takes
people where they don't want to go, but ought to be.'

Rosalynn Carter, 35th First Lady of the United States

'Adenauer, Schuman, De Gasperi and Jean Monnet were our chefs
de file. At one time following their lead, at another time urging them
on, we made progress towards that Europe of which we were all dreaming. It was exhilarating.'[659]

*The Belgian Prime Minister Henri Spaak after the first meet-
ing of the Council of Europe 1949*

1949-1950, BACK TO LUXEUIL

At the start of this chapter, I am fast forwarding a few months ahead
in our narrative so we can capture a few key moments. And then I
will rewind to capture two moments leading up to the Schuman Declaration on May 9th, 1950.

And so, we return to where this book started, that event in July 1950
which almost justifies the dual-biography approach. We have passed
back and forth between these two men that I have chosen as two bookends to our European consciousness. We have used them as a lens to observe what came before and in between their brief hour on the stage of
history, and now we come to the point where their lives intersect for a
pivotal if ephemeral, moment.

Schuman called Columban 'the patron saint of all those who seek to
construct a united Europe' and since the end of the war he, Schuman,
had been 'filled with the desire to build the new edifice of Europe
on Christian foundations.'[660] Now, on a beautiful afternoon in July

1950, he has summoned the leading European statesmen to Columban's Abbey at Luxeuil for this conference – or more precisely, a piece of sacramental political theatre.

When we last left Luxeuil, Columban was being dragged away by force, along with the other Irishmen. It was the saint's darkest hour; the dread possibility that all he had worked for would be destroyed. But sitting on a platform outside the abbey thirteen centuries later it is evident that the Irish have returned; ecclesiastics yes[661] but also Minister for Foreign Affairs Seán MacBride and Taoiseach, John A Costello.

The latter statesman, perhaps moved by the sense of occasion, remarked that 'If we remove from Europe her Christian civilization, what remains will not be very important.' Along with the other leading political figures from across Europe, who similarly have just been through their own darkest hour, these Irish delegates are sitting under the shade of the trees and variously staring at Columban's abbey or the man who has chosen this, of all places, to reiterate his daring project.

Two months prior to this moment, Schuman had made a sensational declaration in Paris that would signal the initial commitment of France to a more integrated economic solution for the Franco-German problem. And the previous summer[662] in Strasbourg he had outlined his vision thus:

> *"We are carrying out a great experiment, the fulfilment of the same recurrent dream that for ten centuries has revisited the peoples of Europe: creating between them an organisation, putting an end to war and guaranteeing an eternal peace ... Our century, that has witnessed the catastrophes resulting in the unending clash of nationalities and nationalisms, must attempt and succeed in reconciling nations in a supranational association. This would safeguard the diversities and aspirations of each nation while coordinating them in the same manner as the regions are coordinated within the unity of the nation."[663]*

And now as Schuman takes the microphone again, forgotten Luxeuil is at the very centre of international media attention. But the journalists might have had cause to complain that day or even fall asleep. For the conference was, on the surface at least, a purely academic and ecclesiastical affair to mark the 14th centenary of Columban's birth. But there was method in his madness, for behind the scenes and out of the spotlight, Schuman used the event to garner support for a European coal and steel community among key politicians and diplomats.

Cooperation rather than competition in this vital industry was one of the simplest, yet most controversial, ways to fireproof Europe against another war. Economic integration could work where mere treaties had failed. In the nuclear age it might be Europe's last chance. And so, taking the deal brokers away from the halls of power to this backwater with such a seminal backstory was a masterstroke. While the conference educated the largely secular politicians with a broader historical perspective, Schuman's quiet, winsome networking behind the scenes secured key support. A year later in April 1951 at the Treaty of Paris, the European Coal and Steel Community (ECSC) was born. It became the forerunner of what we know as the European Economic Community, which in 1992 became the European Union.

But we have rushed ahead. That nice little vignette serves as an entrée but doesn't do justice to the immense personal struggle that Schuman underwent in the previous two years; or the people who helped him overcome insuperable odds. He knew that he was the vital link for the future of a peaceful Europe. Adenauer and De Gasperi had achieved, through their integrity and great personal suffering, positions of vital political importance within their countries. But at the end of the day, they were countries still 'applying for readmission to the human race'[664] in the eyes of millions of Europeans.

For example, when De Gasperi made his first diplomatic visit to London he was met with almost total incivility.[665] And we have already seen in a previous chapter how Adenauer was treated by Sir Brian Robertson and Clement Atlee's Labour Party. So, Schuman was the key, but he also knew that he did not represent the majority view of his countrymen or his government. He was also painfully aware that, if he did not act his part well, the other two would have *no friends at court*,[666] no seat at the table.

History often hangs on slender threads. We are taught to think in terms of global financial interests, omnicompetent states, and military power blocks, but less of the soft power of simple friendships that can often transcend all these boundaries. It seems a recurrent theme and one that offers much encouragement. It was Professor Tolkien, emerging from the trenches of Ypres and Verdun who sought, through fantasy literature, to show us the simple friendship of Sam and Frodo thwarting the titanic powers of Mordor. This offers hope to every age, and not just of the sentimental kind, as we shall see.

1949-1950, THE PRAGMATIST & THE PREACHER

The next steps – or perhaps the next connections – in Schuman's story would require two new friendships: the American Lutheran Evangelist Frank Buchman and the French political economist and diplomat Jean Monnet. Even if the readers of this book have heard of Jean Monnet, I doubt many would have heard about Buchman – unless it is in connection with conspiracy theories. The truth is, as ever, far humbler and indeed, far more interesting. For without this unlikely pair (who never actually met each other as far as I know) Europe would look very different today.

But this is not just a story about friendships, but also of virtue. The hope, faith, and love that we have witnessed in the abstract must now, at this stage in our story, be made active and concrete through forgiveness. *Forgiveness is the game-changer.* The speed of Franco-German reconciliation still stands today as one of the loftiest achievements of statecraft in any age. And it is made stranger and more wonderful by the fact that it was not only in the hands of professional diplomats but also other men and women of goodwill. 'Nothing that is worth doing can be achieved in our lifetime,' wrote Reinhold Niebuhr, *"therefore, we must be saved by hope. Nothing which is true or beautiful or good makes complete sense in any immediate context of history; therefore, we must be saved by faith. Nothing we do, however virtuous, can be accomplished alone; therefore, we must be saved by love. No virtuous act is quite as virtuous from the standpoint of our friend or foe as it is from our standpoint. Therefore, we must be saved by the final form of love which is forgiveness."* [667]

Let us deal with Buchman first. And here, I think, we get a most personal and insightful glimpse of Schuman at a crucial point of his story. We see him at two private dinner parties in the spring of 1948 and the autumn of 1949. The spring party is in Paris. Among the guests are the Swiss diplomat Philippe Mottu and two others who are also associated with the Moral Rearmament Movement (MRA).

But before we come to the dinner parties, we need a little background about the MRA. This Christian holiness movement was founded and led by the preacher and spiritual entrepreneur Frank Buchman. And though initially, an international student movement called the Oxford Group, it had latterly developed into a force for post-war international reconciliation. But Buchman's involvement with Germany went right back to the first Great War where he did what he could to alleviate

Lutheran Evangelist Frank Buchman

suffering among friends, which even included members of the German nobility. For example, he helped the Kaiser's son, Prince August Wilhelm, to sell some pictures to alleviate his poverty. We must never forget the real suffering among Germans after the first war when 20 million did not have enough to eat.

Buchman's Oxford Group ran evangelistic house parties across the country and as National Socialism took firmer hold and began to compromise and cause divisions in the churches, he also sought to mediate in a way that was not always appreciated – which is a polite way of putting it. Theologians like Bonhoeffer, Barth, and Brunner were aghast as Buchman got close to those German political leaders and also those church leaders who had defiled themselves with Hitler. Two revealing letters show us the complexity of the situation and the hearts of a Swiss theologian often quoted in this book.[668] Buchman, writing to Emil Brunner in 1931 about associating with a young but influential Nazi-supporting Christian Bishop. Remember that this is the early thirties where the world was still largely open-minded about Hitler and it was really only the theological antenna that was twitching wildly. Buchman writes,

'Your danger is that you are still the professor thundering from the pulpit and want to be theologically perfect. But the German church crisis will never be solved that way. Just think of your sentence, 'unfortunately the hopeless fellow Hossenfelder has damaged the reputation of the Groups.' It sounds to me like associating with 'publicans and sinners.' Just keep your sense of humour and read the New Testament. The Groups in that sense have no reputation and for myself I have nothing to lose. ... I would be proud to have Hossenfelder be in touch with such real Christianity that someday he would say, 'Well, as a young man of thirty-two I made many mistakes, but I have seen a pattern of real Christianity.' It is not a question of this man's past but of his future. What might it mean for the future of Germany, if by the grace of God, he could see a maximum message of Christ incarnate in you? And that you might be the human instrument to effect that mighty change. Our aim is never to mediate, but to change lives and unite them by making them life changers – to build a united Christian front.'[669]

Even as things got more heated and the 1930s rolled on, Buchman, blind to people's label and past mistakes, pursued not just compromised church leaders, but also powerful politicians like Reichsfuhrer Himmler. Brunner, much to his great credit, writes to another Swiss theologian Carl Barth in 1933, with a great deal of humility,

> '...he [Buchman] is childlike enough to believe that even a Fezer and a Hossenfelder could belong to Christ. It is his habit to approach the great and the dangerous... So, I knew partly from talks with Buchman, that he saw in Fezer one of his targets. Simply because he is – like Hossenfelder – a leading man in the church. While we shout anathemas he gets moving, travels to Berlin, gets close to the people he has in mind, and then gets them to come to London, following the recipe; Come and see. (see John 1:46.) Time will tell who is right; you and I who stand on the side-line and curse, or he who dares to proclaim Christ even to these people so that they realise that they have to stop being what they have been. I have seen this approach at work in Homburg and have seen at a house party how hard-boiled German Christians have softened, and how those who began with grand words and cocky manners went away quietly at the end as people with broken hearts and sincere faith... Such things do not seem to happen, in my experience, too often around us.'[670]

By October 1934 a German Christian in the Oxford Group, was writing to Buchman about the serious changes now underway in his country. Church divisions were undermining the Third Reich, Hitler had lost legitimation in the eyes of most Christians and, they felt that satanic forces of great darkness were taking over the Nazi party. 'I never thought this state of affairs could come so soon...H. [Hitler] and his friends don't see where this trouble is leading. It is time their eyes were opened...'[671] The protestant churches had, except for the bishops of Bavaria and Wurttemberg who had resisted even police pressure, come under the control of Hitler. The Catholics had made accommodations with Hitler not to mobilise in political action against him. Groups like the Confessing church and the Oxford Group were more difficult for the Nazis to bring to heel. But great efforts were made to infiltrate them by the intelligence services, who were sure the Group was really a spy network.

Even in 1933, when Buchman had sensed the revival of militarism, remarked to Frau von Cramon, 'this smells of war.' But remember, we are still in the very early days, still 6 years before the war, still at a point where the British press are optimistic about Hitler. Two years later though, Frau Von Cramon, a high-born member of the Oxford Group was taken to Himmler's House and offered a job organising the welfare of SS families.[672]

She recalls Himmler who used to often ask her, like Pilate or Herod Agrippa asked Paul, 'Tell me, who is Christ?' But Himmler's objections were always the same. Substitutionary atonement was anathema to him, 'It is Jewish to make someone else responsible for your guilt.' 'But *Reichsfurhrer*,' she would reply, 'what do you do with your sins when nobody can relieve you of them and you cannot restore for them?' Himmler replied, 'I can manage that too without Christ.' In another place, Himmler said, 'it accords with German thinking not to be dependent on Grace but to know that what you have done here will be used against you; you will not escape. But you have a chance through your own strength to alter your destiny in a new life.'[673] In an essay on the creed of the SS, John M. Steiner wrote,

> *'The National Socialist God was not the God of Christian teaching...the God of love and mercy, to whom the strong and the weak took up equally. The National Socialist God was partisan, hard, and cruel.... The fight for survival was considered the most fundamental of all eternal laws....'*

Buchman kept up his trips to Germany until 1936. With a holy innocence, that reminds one of Dostoyevsky's Prince Lev Nikolayevich Myshkin in *The Idiot*, Buchman continued to reach out with Christ-like good faith toward even people like Himmler, who he intuited were troubled by their loss of faith. He was heedless to his own reputation but driven on, while the door remained even slightly ajar, to hope against hope.[674] Buchman knew he would be misunderstood and he was certainly misquoted by journalists, but perhaps no more than others. His last visit was the 1936 Olympic Games and his final meeting with Himmler was recorded by a Danish Journalist.

'In the afternoon he was to have a conversation with SS-Furhrer Himmler who had invited Dr Buchman to come and see him. The conversation, of course, became a complete fiasco. Himmler was unable, as he had intended, to exploit the 'absolute obedience' of the MRA [Oxford Group] people towards God for his own purpose, to make them obedient slaves of the SS and the Nazis. ...Frank Buchman was burdened by the development of Germany under Hitler, for he was deeply attached to this land and this people .... He said [later] during this meal: "Germany has come under the dominion of a terrible demoniac force. A counteraction is urgent. We must ask God for guidance and strength to start an anti-demoniac counteraction under the sign of the Cross of Christ in the democratic countries bordering Germany, especially the small neighbouring countries.'[675]

Himmler recognised one thing correctly at least, and it was the *Totalitatsanspruch* – the total claim – that Christianity placed on its true adherents. This was summarised neatly in January 1945 when a Christian nobleman was on trial for treason. The president of the court, Roland Freisler shouted at Count von Moltke, 'We and Christianity are the same in only one way; we demand the whole person!' In a scene reminiscent of Dostoyevsky's Grand Inquisitor Moltke describes the trial in a letter to his wife, 'It is a kind of dialogue – a spiritual dialogue between Freisler and me.... Of the whole gang only Freisler sees me clearly, and he is the only one of the whole gang who knows why he has to kill me... It was in deadly earnest: 'From whom do you take your orders? From the next world or from Adolf Hitler.'[676]

Security analysts within the Nazi apparatus noted these competing truth claims and reported that the Oxford Group, 'operates underground in Germany.... It fundamentally denies the concept of race by consciously blurring all racial differences by means of the liberalist idea of humanity and a pacifist delusion about the union of peoples.' The underlining is theirs, they understood that biblical anthropology (the Imageo Dei doctrine) threatened the basis of their race theory.

From as early as 1934 spies were sent to infiltrate the Group. One spy, called Arthur Demuth actually recovered his faith while at the Group meetings. Without revealing his identity, he subsequently tempered his reports to Berlin, once writing 'I have met so many individuals of integrity and spiritual quality that the national Socialists would congratulate themselves if they had people like that in their ranks.' When he was eventually requested to give up twenty names for internment in the concentration camps, he agonised about what to do. Eventually he went in person to Berlin and told his superiors flatly that he knew of no group member worthy of any punishment. Amazingly he survived this episode, and also was given only a limited sentence by the allies who saw that he had saved more lives than he had compromised. Another letter from an SD chief of the SS North-West region to officers seems to suggest an almost paranoid overestimation of the Oxford Groups size and reach. It is dated May 20th, 1937.

> 'The Reichsfuhrer-SS had ordered the strictest observation of the movement. The (Oxford) Group movement is starting to have success in spreading across Germany and is trying, also with apparent success, to gain influence in Party circles.'[677]

Another letter from the same SD chief on December 3rd, 1937 is equally fraught. The other officers should be in no doubt of the 'extremely careful and sophisticated operating tactics' of the Group. Sounding more and more like something out of *The Screwtape Letters*, he continues that, 'The Group Movement [believes it] has received from Christ an almost overwhelming task. The Church must be filled with the Group spirit so that the church struggle (*Kirchenkampf*) will cease... In the Party itself, there are sure to be people who have 'a chink in their armour' and that is where a Group member has to start the work of enlistment.' The following spring the same SS-Oberabschnitt warned his officers that they should expect that 'the movement will launch a major public offensive this year...' and reminds them that '...the fight against this Group movement is one of the primary tasks which has been entrusted to the SD...'

There are few readers who could imagine MI5 dedicating substantial resources to monitoring the Salvation Army's activities, or the Archbishop's latest initiatives in evangelism, but that is what was happening in Germany in 1938. Real or imagined, the fears that this Oxford 'Group spirit' could revitalise the compromised German churches and thus bring down the party, were apparent enough as the Nazi those records show. (Many other records were destroyed in the allied bombing.) In 1942, after laws were promulgated banning any army or party member from association with the Oxford group, Himmler's office published a 125-page report on *Die Oxford-Gruppenbewegung* which might serve as a back-handed badge of honour for any group seeking to follow Jesus of Nazareth.

> 'The Oxford Group strives for revolution in the life of every individual and the nation with the aim of a new world order under the "dictatorship of the Saviour" ... The Oxford Group provides a Christian-religious cover for the democracies' world aims... It preaches revolution against the national state and has quite evidently become its opponent in Christian-religious guise, not only in its approach but in the very goals it works for. ...The Oxford Group preaches the equality of all men ... No other Christian Group has underlined so strongly the character of Christianity as being supranational and independent of all racial barriers ... It tries fanatically to make all men into brothers.' [678]

And then came the war, and Buchman said, 'someone, someday is going to have to win the peace.' And then came the peace. And then Buchman said, with tears in his eyes to a newly-arrived team of demobbed co-workers, 'Well you are home. Now let's get on with the fight.' And so, he came back to Europe and re-established connections with the group in Germany.

And this brings us back to that dinner party mentioned earlier where the host, Louis Boucquey was listening carefully to the words of the French Foreign Minister Robert Schuman as he gave his views on the forthcoming Atlantic Pact (NATO). They wanted to know how effective this Anti-Communist treaty would really be. Schuman spoke quite openly and said that if the treaty could only touch the political and military spheres, then it would fail. They had already proved the impotence of mere force and bombs. Inner change in the West's way of life was needed.

"We need to give fresh ideological content to the life of the millions of Europe. The Germans need a lot of courage to work with the French. It is no good being sentimental about these things." he told them, and then added, "We all need to reach a deep inner change in order to find the solutions to our major problems."[679] At once, Louis Boucquey recognised how much Schuman's language resonated with that of Frank Buchman's[680] speeches and so suggested that the two of them meet at Caux Palace.

Caux Palace was Switzerland's largest and grandest hotel when it was built in 1902 but had become a run-down asylum for refugees after the war. It was then bought by ninety-five Swiss Christian families associated with MRA (Moral ReArmament), the new name for the Oxford Group. They had given family jewels, life insurance policies, and even houses, to buy the former hotel which they re-named Mountain House.

When Buchman first visited Mountain House in the summer of 1946, an excited international delegation of volunteers greeted him in its vast foyer. Some were dressed in their national costumes but Buchman merely asked in a loud voice, "Where are the Germans?" After an embarrassing silence, he continued, "Some of you think that Germany has got to change, and that is true. But you will never be able to rebuild Europe without the Germans!" Like Schuman, Buchman understood that if prodigal Germany did not receive Christian forgiveness and reconciliation, then the effects would be disastrous. But how does one forgive the unforgivable? That was the burden of the moment, and in some ways a burden that each new generation faces at different levels. In the intervening decades writers from every spectrum – from Jacques Derrida to Richard Holloway – have explored this most critical and complex of issues.

But Buchman knew, it was only not books that were needed after the war – but also many face to face meetings. So, in accordance with his vision, from 1947 onwards, thousands of leading German citizens were given special permission by the Allied authorities to travel to Caux to meet their opposite numbers from within Europe and the world. In the summer of 1948, four hundred and fifty Germans had visited Caux at one time, among them Konrad Adenauer and 11 members of his family. A total of 3113 Germans took part in the Caux meetings between 1946-50, including 83 government members, 400 trade unionists, 210 industrialists, 14 clergy (including bishops & theologians), 160 media representatives, and 35 educationalists (including university rectors and professors).[681]

Numbers and statistics perhaps do not give a sense of the spirit of the place as much as this simple exchange between two men who represented polar opposites in the Franco-German problem.

'One day Villiers sat at table beside Böckler, whose part in creating the new Germany some historians consider second only to Adenauer's. Böckler said, 'We ought to be enemies on two counts - I am a German, you are French; you are the head of the employers, I am a trade union leader.' Villiers replied, 'Yes, and there's a third count. Your countrymen condemned me to death; I was in a political concentration camp; I saw most of my comrades die around me. But that is all past. We must forget it. And personally, I would like to shake your hand.'[682]

This was a snatched fragment of conversation recorded in the Caux archives in 1946. We must imagine thousands of interactions like this were happening as the ice of cynicism was melting and the legacy of fear, hatred, and bitterness was being healed.

Buchman had wanted to finally introduce Schuman to Adenauer at Caux but the timings had not worked out for either politician.[683] But in the autumn of 1949[684] Buchman and Schuman were finally introduced by Louis Boucquey.[685] At this first meeting Schuman, usually such a private man, opened up to Frank Buchman over dinner, "If I have contributed anything to mankind, I must also admit that much of my work has been destroyed and frustrated. But Dr. Buchman, because he has concentrated his efforts on one section of human life – the most important one – has the joy of seeing them succeed and spread all over the world. Statesmen can propose far-reaching plans, but they cannot put them into effect without far-reaching changes in the hearts of people." Then speaking directly to Buchman, he continued: "That is your work, and it is the kind of work I would like to do for the rest of my life."

Later Schuman confided to Buchman that he had cherished a dream to withdraw from politics and retire to a quiet monastery library, where he could write up all he had learned. He finished by saying, "I could do my best work there. What should I do?"

Buchman simply replied, "Monsieur Schuman, what do you think in your heart you should do?"

Schuman leaned back in his chair for a moment, put his hands resignedly in the air, and laughed, "Of course! I know I must stay where I am!" But the laugh quickly vanished and the Frenchman grew serious again. He told Buchman that in his heart, he knew what he had to do, but that he was afraid. He explained about his upbringing on the borders and how he more than any understood the mind-set of both the French and the Germans and their problems. Like Moses growing up in Egypt, Schuman intuitively seemed to know that providence had placed him in a key position at a momentous time in history and that his destiny was to help bring peace between these two nations.

'There is one thing I must do. I feel it in my bones and it has led me as far as I have gone recently, but I am afraid of it. I am from Lorraine, and I was brought up as a German. Then Lorraine returned to France and I became a Frenchman and served in the French army. I know the problems and mentality of both countries. I have known for a long time that I have a big part in ending the hatred between us. I have talked about it with De Gasperi. He is in the same situation – born Austrian and served in the Austrian army, then Italian, and understanding both. We know that something can and must be done and that we are the men to do it. But I shrink from it.'[686]

Buchman quietly told him that he was sure Schuman was right to maintain his course. "Under God, that is your place."

Schuman said, "I don't know who to trust in the new Germany," adding that he had only just met the new Chancellor Conrad Adenauer.

Buchman replied, "We have some excellent men in Caux," by which he meant the Germans, like Adenauer who had attended meetings there, and offered to supply Schuman with a list of a dozen key names. Later, Schuman acknowledged with profound gratitude how Buchman had helped create a 'climate in which the new relationship between France and Germany had been rendered possible.'[687]

And a 'new climate' was really needed because the Saar region stood politically and physically be-

Buchman with Schuman at the Caux Palace

tween the two nations in a way that seemed immoveable at that time. For seventy years the industrial region had provided the raw materials for German aggression against France – war munitions. Now there was strong feeling among the French – who were already occupying it as a protectorate – that they should annex the entire area as a reparation and insurance policy against future war. Obviously, the Germans were not happy about this. It was the sticking point that threatened Schuman and Adenauer's ability to bring a better solution.

Schuman had already tasted one frosty reception from the Germans because of this. And when he went again to meet Adenauer in Bonn, January 13, 1950, he and Jean Monnet were met at the train station by the Chancellor on his own. After he got the Frenchmen in his car and away from the station, Adenauer explained that he feared that Schuman might be assassinated, 'because you French are on the way to absorbing the Saar.'[688]

A little background to this is helpful. The previous November, Adenauer had astounded the world by refusing the offer for Germany to be admitted to the Council of Europe as an associate member, with the Saar joining as an independent state. (A 1936 referendum had shown that 90% of the region wanted to be German.) After World War I the League of Nations had granted France administrative control with rights to extract minerals as war compensation. Now, again under French occupation after WWII, France's call to make the Saar independent looked like a longer game to annex it for herself. Worse was to come. As Schuman got off the train in Bonn, he learned from the German press that his own French government had, unbeknownst to him, announced that it intended to exploit the Saar mines for the next 50 years. No wonder Monnet observed an '*atmosphère glacée*'!

To show how far the situation had drifted, let us have a brief exert from Adenauer's Memoirs from two years before:

'In October 1948 I had met Robert Schuman, then French Foreign Minister, for the first time. We had a very frank and confidential conversation at Baffenheim, dealing chiefly with the Saar question. Schuman intimated that France regarded the return of the Saar to Germany as possible. France's main concern was the securing of her economic interests. Robert Schuman's views on this nerve-point of Franco-German relations had put my mind at rest. After our conversation, I observed the greatest reticence on the Saar in my speeches and was under constant attack for it from Dr. Schumacher, the chairman of the SPD.'

No wonder, two years later, Adenauer almost delivered an ultimatum to Schuman, 'in this context I cannot ask the German people to support the entry into the Council of Europe.' Schuman was momentarily stunned by the strength of the declaration, but then quietly replied, 'Is the Saar problem really more important than creating a united Europe?' Adenauer did not answer and after a further two hours of negotiations, the men parted with a deep sense of failure.

And then, on 3 March, in line with Adenauer and the German people's fears, the French Government took more formal steps to integrate the Saar into France.[689] When asked about the negotiations at one point by some of Buchman's friends, Adenauer bitterly called Schuman a 'lying Alsatian peasant.'[690] Taken aback, they

Adenauer and Buchman

asked the chancellor if there was anything he might do to help change Schuman. Having blown off steam and remembering all that he had learned at Caux, Adenauer humbly admitted, 'I also need to change.' On 7th March 1950, Adenauer astounded everyone in an interview with the American journalist Joseph Kingsbury-Smith. Using the interview to signal to the other nations his resolve to move forward despite the obstacles, he said,

> *'A union between France and Germany would give new life and vigour to a Europe that is seriously ill. It would have an immense psychological and material influence and would liberate powers that are sure to save Europe. I believe this is the only possible way of achieving the unity of Europe. It would cause the rivalry between the two countries to disappear.'*

The German undersecretary for Foreign Affairs and one-time ambassador to Britain was in no doubt who Europe had to thank for the new possibilities of peace. When Baron von Etzorf was asked by an American journalist, 'What is the most significant development in Europe since the war?' He simply replied, 'The new accord between France and Germany. For this, the work of Moral Re-Armament is largely responsible.'[691] That is a staggering admission from a man who was actually there. The mediation of this largely unacknowledged Christian group had helped Europe win the peace. The 'astonishingly rapid Franco-German reconciliation after 1945,' said a later Washington Think Tank, who also acknowledged MRA's essential role, was, 'one of the greatest achievements in the entire record of modern statecraft.'

And later Adenauer too accredited[692] the MRA's role at these times as 'an invisible but effective part in bridging differences of opinion between negotiating parties... Moral ReArmament has rendered great and lasting service.'[693] Invisible, yes, but marked by those who knew, like Professor Henri Lieben of Lausanne University, who wrote, 'I have not forgotten what Europe owes to the dialogue and co-operation developed in the decisive post-war years between Buchman on the one hand and Konrad Adenauer and Robert Schuman on the other.'[694]

But that does not mean that there would not be far reaching and complex difficulties to be overcome. Novelist Fay Weldon correctly observed that 'weakness admitted is the stuff of good friendship.' Back in his home village of Scy-Chazelles, nursing himself through a bout of flu, Schuman also had time to reflect on the apparently insurmountable problems still facing Franco-German relations, and also the utter practicality of forgiveness as the new foundation of escape from what he called 'the terrible mortgage of fate: fear.' He expressed his thoughts at this time while writing a forward to Buchman's book, 'Remaking the World.'

'To begin by creating a moral climate in which true brotherly unity can flourish, overarching all that today tears the world apart—that is the immediate goal. The acquisition of wisdom about men and affairs by bringing people together in public assemblies and public encounters—that is the means employed. To provide teams of trained people, ready for the service of the state, apostles of reconciliation, and builders of a new world– that is the beginning of a far-reaching transformation of society in which, during fifteen war-ravaged years, the first steps have already been made... It is not a question of change of policy: it is a question of changing people. Democracy and her freedoms can be saved only by the quality of the people who speak in her name. That is what Dr. Frank Buchman has articulated in such simple and moving terms. He has declared war on materialism and individualism, both generators of our egoistic divisions and social injustices.'

That last sentence of Schuman's strikes at me powerfully, its challenge never more prescient. In Buchman and Schuman's view, Jesus' teaching constituted humanity's final and most magnificent rebellion; an insurrection of one man or woman against the fallen aspects of his or her own nature. The political analyst George Friedman, says that his Hungarian-Jewish father, having fled to America after the war, gave him the bleakest possible viewpoint of the reconciliation. 'My father never forgave Europe for being monstrous, and he never forgave Europeans for how easily they forgave themselves ...Europe will never change. It will act as if nothing happened.'[695]

A dark analysis from a man traumatised by a conflict we can scarce imagine. But it is not to be brushed aside, for it presented then and even now, a dilemma for Europe. Could the reconciliation be more than skin deep? That is as relevant now as much as it ever was. Buchman's unreservedly individual and interior emphasis seems to have been the necessary corollary to the mind-set of the industrial and political elites whom he so influenced. Even for the three Catholic statesmen, we are considering, and perhaps especially for them, Buchman brought some new power or emphasis from outside their existing thought world. At a crucial moment, Buchman and his MRA network became the difference, the change, the miracle that Europe needed. Schuman sensed it and even hinted at it when recalling the message in Buchman's *Remaking the World*. 'I had a sort of intuition that came to me through that book, I saw new perspectives opening before me.'[696]

Buchman was certainly a controversial figure throughout his life and much criticized, especially by other Christian thinkers like Bonhoeffer,

Niebuhr, and Brunner, who I have also quoted liberally. Events like Buchman's failed efforts to convert the Nazi elites showed a man careless of his own reputation but often guilty of little more than, if not a deeply Christian, then at least a New-world, optimism.[697] He may have been naïve and politically unsophisticated, but there is no doubt that he played a key role for good at a vital moment in history.[698] As with many times in history, the most impractical men of the age became its prime movers.

It is therefore appropriate, before moving onto Claude Monnet, to finish this section with Buchman's own emphasis that 'we need a power strong enough to change human nature and build bridges between man and man, faction and faction.' In this sense, he was the man who became a preacher because he was too practical for politics. The very heart of the problem is, of course, the problem of the human heart, and Buchman was under no naïve illusion in this regard at least. Nor was he under any delusion about the power necessary to make *that* supreme change possible. For Buchman it was, at bottom, neither a political or military one; 'God alone can change human nature. The secret lies in that great forgotten truth, that when man listens, God speaks; when man obeys, God acts; when men change, nations change.'[699]

When making the documentary for this book I visited Caux in September 2018. After filming some interviews, the boys and I went higher up the alp to set up camp. Far below us and stretching out like a vast mirror, Lac Leman ran west toward Geneva. Freshwater from the mountains splashed gently into a hollowed-out log nearby and a soft breeze kissed the larch trees around us. As the sun dipped from orange to red, it painted the French and Swiss Alps in deepening purples and blues. And as those reds and purples grew darker, so the lights of Geneva and Lausanne revealed their true extent. It was then that I fell into a conversation with a young German couple who had their VW camper near us. He was a doctor, she a scientist, and both in their early thirties.

They were lovely people, he was in manner and appearance very like my brother-in-law, and, as we shared grapes and crackers in the waning light, I felt like I had known them for many years. We chatted and laughed about the joys and trials of parenthood. Having just one toddler themselves they held me, or at least my wife, in near beatific regard for having survived six attacks of the 'terrible-twos.' Assuming the air of an expert I let the little girl play with my LED fairy lights, while her father lamented his deep concerns for Germany's future. The alarming rising of the far right in Germany was totally incomprehensible to him. I pointed out that it was only symptomatic of a larger political pathology. In response to a raft of pressures, internal and external, Poland, Hungary, Italy, Slovakia and Austria were all succumbing to a populism farther right than most thought sane or safe. I used the word 'most' while realising that it was often the group deafness of an illiberal liberalism that exacerbated the trend.

After mutual headshaking, and assurances that at least *we* were still sane, there came a long pause in the conversation and a disquieting quietness. Is the post war settlement unravelling before our eyes and we are too blind to see it? Could, what many call, Brussel's 'imperial overreach'[700] hasten a collapse of the western bloc as happened to the Soviet one? Who really foresaw that coming, and happening so quickly too? Not one leading sovietologist did. How strange. Small internal movements, even from those we count as the allies of our progress, can turn out to be our nemeses in the end. 'It is a grim irony that it was... the union between shipbuilding and steelworkers, that destabilised the communist regime in Poland, starting the domino-like collapse of the Communist governments in the Soviet bloc.'[701]

I looked at the reflected glow in his daughter's eyes. She arranged the tangle of fairly light wires and joyed in the pool of warm light that illuminated her parent's faces, while all around them the darkness grew more certain. It was a sober moment. We all knew that the madness of the Inter-War generation was driven by great, untried ideologies and very deep suffering. If our generation refused the plea of history, and chose that same route with so little real provocation, and from such a position of ease relative to theirs, then God help us all.

The conversation naturally came to the Great Wars and as I talked about the great work of post-war reconciliation, which had in small part taken place a few hundred metres below us at the Caux Palace, they were amazed and much cheered. They were also visibly moved to hear of my great regard for their Chancellor Adenauer. But as I spoke on, perhaps with too much evangelistic zeal, about the Christianity of Schuman, De Gasperi, the MRA, and all the Christian influence that formed the bedrock of so much Franco-German reconciliation, I could see the usual shutters coming down.

And so here, my boorishness aside, is perhaps a symptomatic barrier in the secular liberal mind-set. They want the fruit without the root – what some have called a 'cut-flower civilisation'. In a mixed bouquet, some flowers last longer than others. Carnations seem almost to survive until the next bouquet is bought. My personal view is that in some great way the post war leaders and activists replenished the 'cultural bouquet' and that we are living (in the political sphere at least) among the falling petals of their great labours. In his 1951 Riddell Memorial lectures, the Cambridge historian Herbert Butterfield sensed something akin to this in his own generation:

> 'I think that people even in England are living more than they know on old capital, on an unthinking acceptance of of traditional values, on what are essentially secularized religious ideals or concealed Christian assumptions.... The whole tendency I have been describing raises questions how, when mankind has moved on this particular inclined plane, it can ever ascend again - how you can stop the rot - any more than water can rise above its own level. And this is where religion is calculated to be an essential factor in the rise of civilization, and where those who hold the Christian view have a chance to contribute to the march of history.'

That old Whig (progressivist) view, famously presented in Francis Fukuyama's *The End of History* has proved to be, if not empirically flawed, at least vastly peremptory. The irreversible path towards liberal democracy and secularism, the triumph of the rule of law and attachment to personal freedoms, has not displaced tribal and religious politics as expected. Other writers of the 1990s, like Samuel P. Huntington in *The Clash of Civilisations* and Robert D. Kaplan in *The Coming Anarchy*, did predict this and the breaking down of state authority.

To be fair to Fukuyama, he actually predicted something very like it too in an addendum to *The End of History*, entitled *The Last Man*. "It is impossible to complete our present discussion without referring to the creature who reportedly emerges at the end of history, the last man." This Nietzschean reference to the 'victorious slave,' is very telling, even chilling, for he may yet prove to be the prophet of our great undoing. The *last man* is the archetypal nihilist, only able to tear down, but unable to build or act upon a self-actualized ethos. This haunted Nietzsche and it should haunt every secular humanist.

"Left to themselves," Fukuyama asks, "can those stable, long-standing liberal democracies of Europe and America be indefinitely self-sustaining, or will they one day collapse from some kind of internal rot, much as communism has done?" With our needs largely met – or at least met to a degree unknown anywhere else in history – will secular liberalism itself be enough for us? Fukuyama perceptively asks "whether there are other deeper sources of discontent within liberal democracy" and, of course, "whether life there, is truly satisfying." The post-Cold War resurgence of Islamic cultural separatism, for one thing, has created real soul searching among western thinkers – admittedly not enough, perhaps. We are open to question many reasons for this historical reversal but few have questioned seriously whether failures within Liberal Democracy itself might be the cause.

Perhaps we dare not because that would be admitting that it is all we have – our final flag around which to rally. The right-wing populism of eastern and southern Europe may make us shake our heads in disbelief. A resurgent Islamism may make us fear. And the illiberalism of Russia, Turkey, and China, etc. may make us tremble. But deep down we know that each is, at some point, and in varying degrees, a binary of western liberal democracy, an attempt to answer its failures and inadequacies. At many points, they are not our enemies, but our critical children.

Nietzsche's *Superman* (Ubermensch) in the *Nazi Aryan Man* was a disaster and his *Last Man* (Der Letzte Mensch) is now all around us in the academy and on the streets. Lenin's *Soviet Man* (*Novy Sovetsky Chelovek)* was a sham and the Capitalist West's *Individualist Man,* a shell. When Bacon called for 'a radical purifying of the national character' and Plato for an 'utter change in constitution', they were not calling for new laws, any less than the Christian and Hebrew scriptures were; they were crying out for a new species of humanity. And in reply, Jesus Christ offers *The New Man,*[702] (Homo Novus), transformed from the inside out by his Cross and resurrection power. The Bible calls Jesus 'the bright morning star',[703] because the Morning Star is the last one shining when all the others have faded. Even those who disbelieve in Christ's words can easily understand what an attractive proposition they make for people who have failed to meet their own best expectations. This is the message Buchman preached, the last hope of humanity, the final revolution. Schuman, De Gasperi, and Adenauer knew it with joy, the Nazi SD acknowledged it with dismay. Jesus' invitation is universal and unconditional; 'let him that is thirsty come. And whosoever will let him take the water of life freely.'[704]

The Caux Palace is a remarkable edifice with an even more remarkable if forgotten, role in European history. The day we left the alp, we filmed that afternoon in the archive room in the very bowels of that vast building. Here we were introduced to what looked like a large vinyl record player by Andrew and Elaine Stallybrass. As I examined the vinyl 14-inch disc, they explained that this wartime relic was in fact a recording and replaying device. 'It's been down here for seventy years and we only switched it back on last year, so we could transcribe the speeches for the archive... amazingly it works just fine.' Elaine placed the needle on a disc that she knew I had particularly wanted to hear. It was Schuman's farewell address when leaving Caux. After a short crackle and through the ambient hum, came the clarion voice of Robert Schuman. The hairs on the back of my neck stood up as the years suddenly disappeared.

'I'm leaving, (he says) in a spirit that is noticeably different from the one that I came with. I have thirty-four years of political life; during this time, we have learned scepticism. I leave you with a lot less scepticism and, at my age, that is already progress. I have experience of meetings - in parliament, politics, international conferences, all of this usually ends with big disappointments, personally and for the community. But here, we have only satisfaction and great hope. I was moved by the words that have been said here, and especially those that have been pronounced by the representatives of Germany ... and also by the young people from my own country. Thank you for giving me this hope, we need it. And now we will not give up.'[705]

Schuman would need all the hope and determination he could get. They all would. We have seen Schuman and Adenauer struggling with these deep truths and their nations' respective positions. To translate good intentions into political reality would need the combined genius of diverse actors, both religious and secular. And so, we now turn to an essential character in the drama of European integration. Jean Monnet was a singular actor who is almost impossible to pigeonhole. He was the scion of an international Cognac business and had cultivated many contacts in Switzerland, Britain, and America over many years.

Monnet never finished school and was never elected to an official public office in France. He had actually wanted to be a boxer – the solitary fighter who can see the openings and deliver the punches, which is almost exactly what he became. A Romantic Secularist, Monnet was, in a strange and

Monnet & Schuman

complimentary way, an antithesis of Schuman. When his father sent him, aged 18, to America and Canada for the family firm, he said, 'don't take any books. No one can think for you in your place. Look out of the window, talk to people, and pay attention to what is next to you.' We could not imagine the same advice coming to the bookish Schuman from his mother. But Monnet took his father's advice and talked to many, many people, cultivating contacts around the globe. It was just the beginning.

Returning to Europe, he loved London and made good friends among the business elite as he frequented the gentlemen's clubs. He was a networker, not a rhetorician, developing his talent at a time when the world needed links to bring it closer together. During World War I, when only in his twenties, he persuaded the Minister of War to allow him to use his international contacts to streamline the supply chain for food and fuel, working in cooperation with Britain, not in isolation. In a strange foreshadowing, he set up common procurement systems with the British for coal and steel. In times of necessity, cooperation might tip the balance of success or failure.

Another great lesson came to him when he was in the USA during the 1929 stock market crash. He observed that the solutions which would have prevented the crash were obvious and known, but, as he wrote later, 'wisdom and reform come into play only after major difficulties have run their course. Would a few simple measures taken earlier have prevented the crisis? Asking that question means being unaware that men accept change only in a time of need, and they see need only in a time of crisis.' Too true, and good advice for our own financial institutions even now.

He had plenty of time to ruminate on this when, by the age of just thirty-one, he was made Deputy Secretary General of the League of Nations in 1919. He resigned three years later in disillusionment. 'The new institution was born with a defect originating in the Treaty of Versailles: discrimination against peoples. All the power was in the hands of the three victorious states, while Germany, in his view, was humiliated by punitive reparation payments and territorial concession.'[706] 20 years later Monnet was instrumental again during World War II in coordinating war supplies from the Americans, which, according to economist John Maynard Keynes, shortened the war by a year.

Like Maritain, who stayed in America because his wife Raissa was a Russian Jew, Monnet also lived in the US during the War. But unlike Maritain, Monnet took his French chef with him, much to the delight of guests like the *bon vivant* Paul Henri Spaak who loved the Gourmet food only marginally less than the delicious talk of post war peace through some acceptable common management of economic resources. The seeds of change were blowing in from different directions. The US Theologian Austin Phelps once observed that 'a great idea is usually original to more than one discoverer. Great ideas come when the world needs them. They surround the world's ignorance and press for admission.'

Thinking and working with an international perspective, between and after the wars, Monnet, no less than Schuman and others, saw the need to reframe Astride Briand's call for 'a kind of central union, a big European market without customs barriers', 'a true yielding of sovereignty' to counter the nationalism 'which is the curse of the modern world.' He had worked with Schuman on France's financial planning just after the war and the two had grown to respect each other. Indeed, so much so – and here really is a mark of the times – that on one hot day, they had even allowed themselves the unusual liberty of removing their jackets!

In *For Europe*, Schuman was keen to point out 'the exceptional merits of an exceptional man: my friend, Jean Monnet'. But their friendship was often strained; Monnet was too pushy; he was always in a rush and one thing Schuman hated was to be rushed into something without having sufficient time to think it through.

They had first met in 1946 when Schuman was finance minister, and Monnet had upbraided him for not sufficiently funding his modernisation plan. President De Gaulle had made Prime Minister George Bidault accept Monnet as the head of modernising the French economy above the authority of all other elected ministers. Schuman, like other ministers, resented this undemocratic imposition and felt the lack of co-ordination was detrimental to France.

But eventually, the two men came to have profound respect for each other's strengths. Monnet had moved across borders like Columban, whereas the borders themselves had moved around Schuman over the years. The psychological effects were probably as different in the men, as they themselves were by temperament. But their external outlook had been lifted from the parochialism of geography, or national politics, and many aspects that had blinded other politicians and generals to the changes that had come upon the modern world.

After the war, Monnet continued his thinking. But he would not be tied down to any political party or institution. The boxer must be free to move and not succumb to the inertia of institutions or the popularity-driven vacillations of politicians. His position was quite unique and the part he played quite as remarkable and miraculous as the others.[707]

He became a key alliance-maker in French politics. He insisted on answering only to the President and, although some detractors suspected him of being a CIA stooge, the people who really mattered recognised his decisive energy, and selfless sense of public duty. Others were less generous, particularly as Monnet, unlike Schuman, had the misfortune to write his own epitaph. It is a temptation from which few of us could pass unscathed. In his 1976 biography, Monnet assigns himself too comprehensive a share of the glory. As the proverb goes, 'Let another praise you, and not your own mouth— a stranger, and not your own lips.'[708]

'His idealism,' wrote Alan Fimister, 'is emphasised and other actors rated according to whether they are the witting accomplices, unwitting instruments or recalcitrant opponents of his benevolent designs. Schuman is patted on the head but he is Ney to Monnet's Bonaparte. This portrayal is unjust to Schuman, helps to obscure the true origins of the European Community, and emphasises the popular perception of the EU as the offspring of a sinister bureaucratic plot to tidy the paperclips of history.' One economic historian, Alan Milward, describes Monnet as "an assiduous self-publicist." But at least it is a forgivable foible.

After all, a truly cold egoist would not care enough to court history's favour so arduously. And remember also that his biography is the writing of old age, which brings its own trials. Let us not be harsh. We owe this energetic international networker a tremendous debt of thanks. And with that, let us now return to his brainchild over the Saar, which had become a political thorn.

Immediately after the war, it was his proposal (called the Monnet Plan) to take over the Coal and Steel production of the Saarland. This was keenly adopted by de Gaulle in 1946, becoming firmer under the French Protectorate of 1947[709] until the final annexation, already mentioned, in 1949. It was the bitter, but a necessary temporary pill that the Germans had to swallow in order to gain the Federal Republic.[710] To get an insight into how Adenauer saw this in January 16th, 1947. We can find him, in his own words, trying to balance his country's guilt with the far-reaching implications of French reprisals.

> '*I am looking ahead to 1947 with much apprehension – not only as a German but also as a European and a man deeply imbued with the importance of the Occident for the whole of humanity. I fear that the mistake made in 1918 is being repeated on a much greater scale, even though I am completely clear in my own mind about the guilt of the majority of the German nation... But I am of the view that people must be found in Allied countries who will think for the future and for future generations.*' [711]

No one knew then how the Saar issue would eventually work out. The initial plan for the Saar originated in Monnet, and so it is perhaps no surprise that it was Monnet who finally framed a more integrated solution to counter the enmity for which he was partly responsible. Monnet, the pragmatic financier without the deep historic sensibilities of his religious colleague, once remarked, 'Europe has never existed, one genuinely has to create Europe.' By 1950, the pressure from the USA for direct action was acute. The Americans could see that their Marshall Plan investment in Europe's future would be in vain if those nations merely repeated the mistakes of the last three decades. Something had to give. Marshall Aid could be withdrawn unless the recalcitrant French did more than just talk. Someone needed to produce a miracle. Monnet provided the hat, but Schuman as Foreign Minister would have to be the one to pull out the white rabbit.

In April 1950, Schuman took a train from Metz to Paris. As he was entering his compartment his private secretary handed a dossier to him, saying, *'Monsieur, could you read Monnet's paper, s'il vous plait? C'est important!'* It was about the dreaded Saarland issue; but by some miracle, Monnet had found a way to turn Schuman's thorniest problem into the possibility of a new future. Schuman later wrote, 'an area was available to start this experiment: coal and steel.... these two key industries comprised a comparatively limited number of companies...they were using the same operating systems, had a relatively small, evenly skilled workforce.... They were independent of local climate and customs, unlike agriculture.... Their coordination seemed quite easy to achieve, without excessive difficulty.'[712] In other words, if it could work in this industry, then maybe it could work elsewhere.

MAY 9TH, 1950 - EUROPE'S 'PRIME MOVER'

At a hotel on the Rue de Martignac in Paris,[713] a small team worked in utmost secrecy on the various redrafts. Monnet and Paul Reuter, along with Etienne Hirsch a young mining engineer, locked themselves away in his room for hours to draft their secret plan. A first paragraph of the first draft was typed by Mrs. Miguez,

'World peace can be safeguarded only by creative efforts commensurate with the dangers that threaten it. The contribution which an organised and vital Europe can make to civilisation is indispensable to the maintenance of peaceful relations.'[714]

Monnet took the first draft to Pierce Uri, an economist that he trusted. Uri reworked it. On a fourth draft, Uri renamed the Common High Authority as rather, a supranational one. Monnet didn't like it. 'Isn't there another word?' But Uri insisted he needed to distinguish this authority from a national or a merely international one. This, of course, from our point of view, is incredibly telling; for as Uri points out to Monnet, 'this is something totally new, above the national level, but holding sovereign powers.'

Monnet's small international team, working without translators on the ECSC wording

Schuman made sure the plan was only known by a very few people. There were two cabinet meetings remaining before Schuman was due to meet with the American Ambassador Dean Acheson and the English foreign secretary Ernest Bevin in London, one on the 3rd and one on the 9th May. Before that important meeting Schuman would have to get the French Cabinet to accept his plan. The 3rd was too soon and the 9th was cutting it fine, but that would have to do. There was just enough time to finish the final draft and check the Germans would support it. Even then Schuman was not confident his colleagues would even accept it. He was caught between two bulls, holding each by the nose ring. At the final moment, only he could lead them out of the bullring and into new pastures. He was the human link, only he could make the play. How did he do it?

Alan Fimister puts it very succinctly; 'not to put too fine a point on it, his tactic was to get them to agree to it without them really knowing what they were doing and then announce the Plan with such a fanfare that it would be impossible for them to change their minds.'[715] Schuman first wrote to Adenauer,

'You have yourself indicated, in public declarations and in conversation between the two of us, your perfect accord with such an objective. You have notably suggested the establishment of an economic union between our two countries. The moment has come for the French Government to take this path. To this end it is proposed to take action immediately on a limited but decisive point.'

Finally, on May 9th at Quai d'Orsay, home of the French Foreign Ministry, Schuman prepared to deliver a proposal regarding the Coal and Steel industries that made concrete the more general speeches he had been making for the previous four years.[716] This was the 9th May 1950 at which point he was still waiting to hear

Schuman and Monnet in the Clock Room

back from Adenauer. The tension must have been almost unbearable. Where was the response? Without it he couldn't announce what he had planned. As the morning dragged on, he asked for a recess, during which time Adenauer's note finally arrived, 'This French proposal is in every way historic: it restores my country's dignity and is the cornerstone for uniting Europe.... I approve your proposal with all of my heart.' One bull was secured, but what about the other?

As the cabinet returned to the Clock Room Schuman took his seat. Only one or two present knew that history was about to be made. When his moment came to speak, Schuman, with typical demureness, made this most revolutionary piece of political integration sound as technical and boring as possible. The resistance hero, president Georges Bidault – who had a copy in his in-tray but had not read it – asked for opinions of those gathered. 'Pleven and Mayer, on cue, simulated spontaneous approval for the proposal; the latter even rather over-did it, so that the President's suspicions were momentarily aroused. The difficult moment passed, however, and the plan was blandly adopted and lunch convened.' Schuman however got to work straight away to convene a press conference. The Plan must now be announced as explicitly and widely as possible so that the French could not turn back.

So, at 6pm a press conference was called and all European ambassadors then in Paris, plus two hundred journalists came to the same Clock Room, the *Salon de l'Horloge.* When 6pm came, Monnet 'worked the door and impressed upon the diplomats the seriousness of the occasion'[717] The famous speech can still be viewed online; no fanfare, no rhetoric. The tortoise-shelled glasses and the tortoise-like Schuman spoke from a well-crafted script. He started without looking up, *'La paix mondiale ne saurait être sauvegardée sans des efforts créateurs à la mesure des dangers qui la menacent...'*

The Schuman Declaration, 6pm May, 1950

'World peace cannot be safeguarded without the making of creative efforts proportionate to the dangers which threaten it. The contribution which an organized and living Europe can bring to civilization is indispensable to the maintenance of peaceful relations. In taking upon herself for more than 20 years the role of champion of a united Europe, France has always had as her essential aim the service of peace. A united Europe was not achieved and we had war.

Europe will not be made all at once, or according to a single plan. It will be built through concrete achievements which first create a de facto solidarity. The coming together of the nations of Europe requires the elimination of the age-old opposition of France and Germany. Any action taken must in the first-place concern these two countries.

With this aim in view, the French Government proposes that action be taken immediately on one limited but decisive point:

It proposes that Franco-German production of coal and steel as a whole be placed under a common High Authority, within the framework of an organisation open to the participation of the other countries of Europe.

The pooling of coal and steel production should immediately provide for the setting up of common foundations for economic development as a first step in the federation of Europe, and will change the destinies of those regions which have long been devoted to the manufacture of munitions of war, of which they have been the most constant victims.

The solidarity in production thus established will make it plain that any war between France and Germany becomes not merely unthinkable, but materially impossible. The setting up of this powerful productive unit, open to all countries willing to take part and bound ultimately to provide all the member countries with the basic elements of industrial production on the same terms, will lay a true foundation for their economic unification.

This production will be offered to the world as a whole without distinction or exception, with the aim of contributing to raising living standards and to promoting peaceful achievements. With increased resources Europe will be able to pursue the achievement of one of its essential tasks, namely, the development of the African continent.

In this way, there will be realised simply and speedily that fusion of interest which is indispensable to the establishment of a common economic system; it may be the leaven from which may grow a wider and deeper community between countries long opposed to one another by sanguinary divisions.

By pooling basic production and by instituting a new High Authority, whose decisions will bind France, Germany and other member countries, this proposal will lead to the realisation of the first concrete foundation of a European federation indispensable to the preservation of peace.

To promote the realisation of the objectives defined, the French Government is ready to open negotiations on the following bases:

The task with which this common High Authority will be charged will be that of securing in the shortest possible time the modernisation of production and the improvement of its quality; the supply of coal and steel on identical terms to the French and German markets, as well as to the markets of other member countries; the development in common of exports to other countries; the equalisation and improvement of the living conditions of workers in these industries.

To achieve these objectives, starting from the very different conditions in which the production of member countries is at present situated, it is proposed that certain transitional measures should be instituted, such as the application of a production and investment plan, the establishment of compensating machinery for equating prices, and the creation of a restructuring fund to facilitate the rationalisation of production. The movement of coal and steel between member countries will immediately be freed from all customs duty, and will not be affected by differential transport rates. Conditions will gradually be created which will spontaneously provide for the more rational distribution of production at the highest level of productivity.

In contrast to international cartels, which tend to impose restrictive practices on distribution and the exploitation of national markets, and to maintain high profits, the organisation will ensure the fusion of markets and the expansion of production.

The essential principles and undertakings defined above will be the subject of a treaty signed between the States and submitted for the ratification of their parliaments. The negotiations required to settle details of applications will be undertaken with the help of an arbitrator appointed by common agreement. He will be entrusted with the task of seeing that the agreements reached conform with the principles laid down, and, in the event of a deadlock, he will decide what solution is to be adopted. The common High Authority entrusted with the management of the scheme will be composed of independent persons appointed by the governments, giving equal representation. A chairman will be chosen by common agreement between the governments. The authority's decisions will be enforceable in France, Germany and other member countries. Appropriate measures will be provided for means of appeal against the decisions of the authority.

A representative of the United Nations will be accredited to the authority, and will instructed to make a public report to the United Nations twice yearly, giving an account of the working of the new organisation, particularly as concerns the safeguarding of its objectives.

The institution of the High Authority will in no way prejudice the methods of ownership of enterprises. In the exercise of its functions, the common High Authority will take into account the powers conferred upon the International Ruhr Authority and the obligations of all kinds imposed upon Germany, so long these remain are in force.'

And thus, France stated its intention to create a supranational body (which one day could include all East and West Europe) that would encourage world peace, and make war between member states impossible. Starting with coal and steel, it would create a single market across the Community and be the world's first international anti-cartel agency. It would revitalise European industries and even have beneficial effects on Third World economies.

"Europe will not be made all at once, or according to a single plan. It will be built through concrete achievements which first create a *de facto* solidarity. The coming together of the nations of Europe requires the elimination of the age-old opposition of France and Germany." It was the moment that sociologists call 'The Paradigm Shift', that moment when the old way of thinking and living are seen to be empirically flawed – when a bold and visionary alternative becomes a genuine possibility. The scale of the last World War had made this paradigm shift possible, but as we see, not inevitable. Three minutes, five hundred words are all it took. Schuman's challenge was effective to respond to the present reality, rather than cling to a romanticised past. Five hundred words are but a drop in the bucket, a mere seed in the winds of history. Yet this seed would become the Coal and Steel Community, the ground zero of any further integration.

'We do not pretend to adjust history, nor do we wish to create rationalised, controlled geography. What we want is to loosen up the borders......Poor borders! They can no longer claim to be inviolable nor can they guarantee our security and our independence. They are trampled down, they are flown over, they are disregarded by parachutists and the fifth columnists. Borders are no longer fortified, the Marginot Line is no longer, that marvellous illusion behind which we imprudently used to hide, is no more.'[718]

After he had finished, one of the more astute journalists, realising that the unprecedented aspect of the plan was its open-endedness, said, 'so it is a leap in the dark?' Monnet's jaw dropped as he heard Schuman's quiet reply, 'yes, a leap in the dark.' But it certainly was.

The 'Schuman Declaration' caused a sensation as no one was expecting such a move from the French.[719] It constituted a quantum leap in international relations; a move as bold and innovative as the situation demanded. The next day Schuman and Monnet were in London and noticed the,

'...plan had provoked coolness among our English friends.... We the French had hoped the English would fully adhere to our plan, give a few final touches' and even when the government found it too difficult to fit such a project 'to the British frame of mind,' Schuman offered Britain 'accession to the Community via a purely contractual link. Free from institutional subordination.'[720]

The Americans however were thrilled. Schuman later recalled his discussion of the plan with Dean Acheson. His and Acheson's explicitly religious understanding is instructive.

'He treated my fear almost as an irrelevance, as back he went to the central theme, the unity of Europe; the end of national rivalries in a new spacious and vastly productive Europe. As we talked, we caught his enthusiasm and the breadth of his thought, the rebirth of Europe, which, as an entity, had been in eclipse since the Reformation.'

A year before, at the second Council of Europe in 1950, Harold MacMillan[721] stated plainly that Britain was of the same mind as the Scandinavians and not prepared to bear that loss of sovereignty. In a speech recorded by Henri Spaak in his memoir, Macmillan acknowledged that the conceptual leap being attempted by Schuman *et al* was too much for the 'pragmatism' of the English, who valued the 'method of Bacon and Newton' over the 'Continental tradition which likes to reason a priori and descends from the summit to the plain, starting from a general principle in order to arrive at its political application.

'That,' he said, 'is the tradition of Thomas Aquinas, the scholastics and the great Continental thinkers.' Macmillan, who had been wounded out of the Somme, and had campaigned against northern unemployment, knew the temper of his own constituents:

'Our people will not cede to a supranational authority to close our mines or our steel mills......to reduce to unemployment a large portion of our fellow citizens of Durham, the Midlands, or South Wales or Scotland. These fears might be illusory but their existence, is in fact, a fact that no British government can ignore.'

Leaving aside the irony that it was his political successor, Margaret Thatcher, who almost entirely closed this industry, let us catch an even more valuable glimpse of ourselves reflected in the eyes of Schuman.

Chapter five of *Pour L'Europe is given* the rather long title of, 'England will only agree to integrate with Europe by the force of Events'. He understood that the giving up of 'sovereign powers for the benefit of a common authority' would be especially difficult for an island nation, with a 'chronological' as well as 'sentimental' attachment to the Common Wealth. The British were living in the twilight of the largest empire the world had ever seen. Schuman wrote that European integration for the British would be analogous to someone forcing entry into an Englishman's house which, after all, is his castle. He could not see the British being subject to such controls for even as long as 'a fifty-year period.' This has turned out to be somewhat prophetic. The deadline for any extension to the 'Future Relations' negotiations transition period can only be extended until December 31st 2022. The United Kingdom, along with Denmark and Ireland, finally ratified the Accession Treaty on 1 January 1973. If the UK-EU's final negotiations run to the wire, as they have so far, then that is exactly 50 years to the day. The ratification of the Accession treaty was so controversial that the Labour Party sought a referendum on continued membership in 1975, which returned a 67% vote in favour of continued membership. Schuman's summary of our nation proves very interesting reading:

'Insular and cosmopolitan, traditional and instinctively distrustful of any ideological innovation, but at the same time, so flexible when having to adapt its old institutions to new circumstances, and so ingenious for interpreting unwritten customs. England does not, in my opinion, appear to be a good example of the European spirit. As a matter of fact, it is thoroughly prejudiced against the accuracy and the strictness of texts which fill continental jurists with delight. In the same way it is hostile, on principle and in all circumstances, to any form of integration or federal structure.'

Schuman, writing in *Pour l'Europe* over a decade later, said that he could still vividly remember the look on his friend Ernest Bevan's face when he mentioned the project. Schuman understood at that moment, it would be unthinkable for a Briton to acknowledge any authority higher than its own parliament. Under this light, one scholar reminds us that our credentials for European integration are no less ambiguous than Russia's.[722] Unlike the medieval period, where we were deeply enmeshed in Europe for reasons already enumerated in the last chapter, the British of the modern period sought their fortunes further afield. But 'the continent next door', they looked on as through a telescope. When Victorian sculptors represented Europe on the Albert Memorial, they only showed Britain, Germany, France, and Italy. The myalgia and myopia of empire had taught us to view nations only in terms of the greatness of their powers; big ones in the west, little ones in the east.

In 1966, Rene Albrecht-Carrie referred to 'the two special cases: England and Russia'[723] but even back in the 1920s no one in the pan-European movement really thought Britain or Russia would ever join. The 'force of events' that Schuman spoke about did finally happen even as the empire on which the sun never set, finally did set. By 1961, we were feeling isolated. It didn't take long. But remember that back in 1973, Britain joined the EEC and not the EU. When the Maastricht Treaty of 1992 expanded the competences of the EEC beyond economic affairs, the writing was suddenly on the wall for Britain. Perhaps Schuman could have told us that from one look on Bevan's face seventy years earlier.

In 1992 at Maastricht (close to Aachen where Charlemagne ruled his empire, and also near Constantine's first capital at Trier) the nations of Europe were invited to move beyond the economic unity of the past forty years. It might seem the logical extension of the Treaty of Rome's intention in 1957 of 'an ever-closer union' but it was not self-evident. Neither was it axiomatic that just because Europeans had achieved stability in the economic sphere that a radical new extension of the principle into the political and social spheres would achieve similar results. Some steps are *sui generis* – of their peculiar kind – and incommensurate with the steps that have gone before. Indeed, some steps might be the threads that unravel the whole.

The Euro appears to have been one such step. The extension of the supranational authority to (practically) control the fiscal policy of sovereign states, was itself a quantum leap. It seemed fine when everything was rosy and everyone was making money, but after the 2008 Credit Crunch, the ugly side of an inflexible monetary system was made known to Cyprus, Greece, Italy, and Spain. The European Central bank quite naturally crafted policies that favoured the largest economies. As a former Greek Finance Minister described it, the design of the Eurozone was like having a car without shock absorbers. Indeed, the analogy could be extended to add, that it was fine-tuned for the smooth roads of Germany and northern Europe. In Britain, the sort of surrender of fiscal policy required by the Euro, though initially entertained, could not be borne either by John Major's or Tony Blair's governments.[724] Others joined without counting the cost.

Would the founding fathers have agreed with such a step? This is a harder question to answer. Schuman, who after all left the project open-ended, was very clear that *strong sovereign nations* were the building blocks of a peaceful Europe. I have endeavoured to more correctly term him the father of the European Economic Area so that we don't automatically associate him with what happened later. For one thing, the increased federalism in practice usually runs counter to Catholic Social Teaching on 'Subsidiarity'. The founding fathers at their best wanted *as much federalism as necessary* (for securing peace), but as much autonomy as possible. Democracy works best when the links of action are as long as they need to be for the correct effect. In *Perpetual Peace* Immanuel Kant wrote in preference of the democratic state over the 'universal monarchy', simply because the 'wider the sphere of their jurisdiction, the more laws lose in force; and soul-less despotism, when it has choked the seeds of good, it at last sinks into anarchy.'

When is *more* too much? Which thread might be the one to undo the whole? In his *Treatise on Government,* John Locke repeated what he says was a popular epigram of his day, 'that the reigns of good princes have been always most dangerous to the liberties of their people.'[725] On the back of previous successes, the Maastricht Treaty effectively created a 'European identity at least as important as.... national identity.'[726]

Of course, it was natural for the European elites to claim the moral mantel of the founding fathers. Perhaps they are, perhaps they are not – perhaps they are traitors, albeit unwittingly. One cannot escape the conclusion that Maastricht betrayed the necessary sovereignty of nations. And this might inadvertently prove to be the death blow to the level of integration necessary for peace. We are painfully aware that the developing telos of any concentration of power is the perpetuation and extension of itself. The taint of liberal imperialism may unconsciously attend the project despite the best intentions of the majority of political actors.

The ever-evolving system of governance and omnicompetent bureaucracy has done nothing to mask the EU's glaring inability to preserve sovereignty and unity at the same time.

Maastricht may yet prove to be the straw that will break the camel's back. By it, the European elite attempted to do what the Romans, Charlemagne, Napoleon, and Hitler could not – to create a united Europe. Hitler presented racial superiority plus military might. Napoleon presented national superiority, the *Code Napoleon,* and a similar military might. But Europe, led preponderantly by Britain in both cases, rejected both these solutions and when the times demanded, matched their convictions with a steely resolve to carry the hour.

The Romans, even with a coherent legal and bureaucratic system of governance, failed because their military strength was insufficient to meet the challenge from the east. Charlemagne failed because his bureaucratic system was too weak and he had no standing army. The EU has bureaucracy in plenty but no military strength (without America,) equal to its threats and no unifying ideology beyond a vague, enlightened self-interest. It is an economic-turned-political federation in search of a soul. As the economic benefits have receded for many since 2008 – and will further recede post-Covid and post Brexit, and then more so again as European demography declines – the missing soul of Europe has only become more obvious – and more necessary.

But this level of political integration was not considered back in 1950, certainly not by the Americans like Dean Acheson or the British, or Schuman. The central European nations, who had lost so much, knew they might risk losing even more without drastic action. The ceding of national sovereignty to a supra-national authority in the coal and steel industries did not seem natural, but when they considered a repeat war, many understood it was necessary. In the spring of 1951, when the European project was at its most vulnerable, and the Communist menace seemed strongest, all would be put to the vote at the Treaty of Paris.

In those excruciatingly tense months, Schuman had to face down the aggressive Communist section of the French National Assembly. And De Gaulle, whose favourite political expression was, 'Non', could always be counted on to make unhelpful appearances from his retirement at the Colombey-les-deux-Eglises to denounce Schuman's pipe dreams as a 'hodgepodge of coal and steel.' As the winter waned and spring came once more, it was time to see whether all Schuman's campaigning; all his back-room meetings; all the conferences at Luxeuil and Strasbourg, all the forces and events that had shaped his life and family history, everything that had led him to this very place; would actually come to something. The grand proposals at The Hague were one thing, so was his announcement at the Quay d'Orsay, but would the various governments ratify such an unprecedented proposal. It was time to see whether he could now achieve the seemingly impossible. Would the nations forgive each other enough, and trust each other enough to surrender part of their sovereignty for the joint good?

Just at this tense moment, Schuman remarked to a journalist, 'if things don't work out there will be nothing left for me to do but to enter a monastery so as better to pray for the world.'[727]

'We cannot deny that the integration of Europe is a huge and laborious task which has never been attempted before. It requires a complete change in relations between European states, particularly France and Germany. After experiencing her utmost suffering and hatred, we now undertake this task in common....in mutual respect and confidence. ..... France had to overcome some painful memories. It was France's responsibility to take the initiative in showing how willing it was to trust its neighbour. .... It would try to find, in the bonds of a multilateral community, the permanent guarantees that have never been found in constraint and subordination. In the place of territorial rivalry and distrust there would be solidarity of interest which would remove the reasons for seemingly irremediable antagonism.' Robert Schuman, Pour l'Europe.

CHAPTER 16
FOOTNOTES & REFERENCES

659. These words were actually addressed to Schuman in a letter from Adenauer.

660. Among them, Monsignor Roncalli, future Pope Saint John XXIII, convener of the Second Vatican Council

661. This was at the first Council of Europe on August 10th, 1949, where Schuman, Adenauer, and Gasperi stood shoulder to shoulder with high hopes for the future, but not entirely sure how the goodwill could yet be converted into solid political action.

662. On p.61 of *'Deeply Rooted'*, Jeff Fountain points out that by the time Schuman made the Strasbourg speech; 'The Marshall Plan had already been underway a year, helping European countries to modernise business and industry, lower trade barriers and promote hope and self-reliance. Yes, these were all essential factors in the rebuilding of a devastated and exhausted Europe. But, Schuman felt, two things were still missing. One was the political willpower and framework for a 'supranational union'. While to Schuman it was clear what steps had to be undertaken to build a new Europe, others were not so convinced; least of all his own successor as prime minister, Georges Bidault. He felt little support from his own government for the task ahead. The second was the personal willpower for deep, inner change, from the inside-out. All the help from America, economically and militarily, he knew, could never compel French and Germans, or Europeans in general, to 'love their neighbours as themselves'.

663. This phrase, used humorously by the cynical civil servant Humphrey in the UK comedy, *Yes, Minister*, sums up the brutal truth of the matter for millions of Europeans in that generation.

664. This is recounted by the Canadian journalist Keyserlingk in *Fathers of Europe* (p.90) but is too mortifying for an Englishman to recount. One of De Gasperi's staff present told Keyerslingk that it was a 'mortifying and humiliating reception for a foreign minister and for a man of the calibre and achievements of De Gasperi...'

665. Keyserlingk *Fathers of Europe* p106

666. Reinhold Niebuhr. *The Irony of American History*

667. Following the war, Brunner was invited to give the Gifford Lectures at the University of St Andrews in 1947-1948. His lecture series *Christianity and Civilization* was divided into two parts Foundations and Specific Problems. They form a thought-provoking book, and can also be obtained online, free of charge, at https://www.giffordlectures.org

668. Frank Buchman to Emil Brunner, quoted in Garth Lean, pp.212-213

669. Brunner to Barth, 27.12.1933

670. John Bentinck to Buchman (in English), 22.10.1934 (Vaud Cantonal Archives.)

671. She took the job warily, but soon found it compromised her integrity and so resigned.

672. F. Kersten, *Totenkopf und Treue*

673. There are overtones of Matthew 10:18-19 in Schuman's interrogations by the Nazis. But in Buchman, we sense a man who did not wait to be 'brought before governors and kings as witnesses to them and to the Gentiles,' but a man who actually went to them uninvited. I think here of the words of Fr Zosima in The Brother's Karamatoz: 'Brothers, have no fear of men's sin. Love a man even in his sin, for that is the semblance of Divine Love and is the highest love on earth.' p.355

674. Flensborg Avis, 2nd Jan 1962. See also Garth Lean, *Frank Buchman*, p.238

675. Helmuth James von Moltke (Deutsche Verlags Anstalt, Stuggart 1975) p.312

676. Letter from SS-Oberabschnit Nord-West, Hamburg. dated May 20th, 1937

677. *Die Oxford-Gruppenbewegung* (Printed in the Security Head Office, 1942.) Copies in the Document Cenyre, Berlin; Bundersarchic Loblenz; Achives Cantonales du Canton de Vaud, Lausanne.

678. This conversation was recorded by an eyewitness (Swiss Diplomat and MRA activist) Philippe Mottu, The Story of Caux (Grosvenor, 1970), p. 118.

679. Forgiveness and personal transformation (holiness) were key themes of Buchman's message, and they are deeply rooted in his own story. He left Pennsylvania under a cloud of disappointment after resigning from a Christian organisation. In a fit of depression, he came to the Keswick convention (UK) hoping to meet the key speaker of the event, F. B. Meyer. Although this never happened, he did have what he called a transformational encounter in a small chapel in Keswick. There, he says, God spoke powerfully to him. He began to see that he had been just as much in the wrong as the people he had not yet forgiven in America. It was the turning point for him. He wrote letters of apology and forgiveness to the offended parties in America. And then went on to found a spiritual revival that swept European universities.

680. *Deeply Rooted*, Jeff Fountain

681. Report of the Caux Conference, 1949 (German edition, p. 45).

682. Adenauer and Schuman first meeting: According to Adenauer it was October 1948, but not according to Schuman and various others. Schuman contradicts this in his own writings where he claims he met Adenauer for the first time in August 1949 at the residence of M. Hittier de Boislambert, the High Commissioner for the Rhine Palatinate Land at Coblenz. Actually, this is the venue to which Adenauer refers, so perhaps Schuman is incorrect. Other sources complicate the matter further by giving alternative dates and locations for their first meeting. Georgette Elgey even claims they actually first met on an NEI day-retreat at the Abby of Maria Laach long before the war.

683. A few months previously (May 5, 1949) Schuman had gathered with leaders of ten European nations in St James Palace, London, to sign The Statutes of the Council of Europe. Belgium, Denmark, France, Ireland, Italy, Luxembourg, the Netherlands, Norway, Sweden, and the United Kingdom were the founding signatories.

684. For this section of the narrative and dialogue, I am indebted to my friend Jeff Fountain for his excellent book *Deeply Rooted*. I am not certain of his sources for the dialogue but I suspect the reference to Schuman serving in the French army is an error: it was the German army. (see ch.8)

685. Spoerri, *Dynamic out of Silence*, pp. 166-7.

686. Schuman also decorated Buchman as a Chevalier of the Legion of Honour.

687. Georgette Elgey: *La Republique des Illusions* (Fayard, 1965), p.422

688. R. C. Mowat: *Creating the European Community* (Blandford, 1973), pp. 91-3.

689. Victoria Martin De La Torre, *Europe, A Leap into the Unknown*.

690. Twitchel, *Regeneration in the Ruhr*, p.60

691. This was in an article for the New York Herald Tribune, June 4, 1951

692. Adenauer awarded Buchner the German Order of Merit

693. Henri Lieben, *Des Guerres européennes à l'union de l'Europe*, 1987, p.18

694. George Friedman, *Flashpoints – The Emerging Crisis in Europe*, Doubleday p.23

695. Caux Transcripts, 12 September 1953

696. There is a comprehensive list of criticisms at https://en.wikipedia.org/wiki/Frank_Buchman

697. Considering this outcome, it could equally be argued that the naïve person is really the one who believes in militant worker strikes, and armies, and mere economics.

698. Frank Buchman *Remaking the World* p.54

699. The phrase was first used by historian Paul Kennedy about third-century Rome.

700. Mike Andrews, *The Birth of Europe*. BBC Books.

701. 'Therefore, if anyone is in Christ, he is a new creation. The old has passed away; behold, the new has come.' 2 Corinthians 5:17

702. Revelation 22:16

703. Revelation 22:17

704. This address is also recorded by Michel J Sentis, *Eveillers de Conscience*. Caux Books p.89

705. Victoria Martin De La Torre, *Europe, A Leap into the Unknown*.

706. An insight into his decisive strain of independence was seen in 1929 when he, the settled bachelor of 42, set eyes on the 22-year-old, unhappy wife of a philandering, Italian bank manager at a dinner party in Paris. They talked all night, transfixed by the other, almost ignoring everything else around them. The next day he sent her a dozen red roses and began a passionate affair that eventually led to their marriage against extraordinary odds. Decisive, determined, and dogged in pursuit of his aim – the boxer.

707. Bible, Proverbs Ch.27 v2

708. As early as August 1947, Monnet has received documents from Marjolin that prove that on current figures, Germany would need all the coal and steel from the

Rhur to meet the targets of recovery set by the Americans. He saw that too many nations competing for too few resources was a recipe for disaster.

709. The Saarland would only be politically repatriated to Germany in 1957.

710. Konrad Adenauer, *Briefe 1945-1947* (Rhondorfer Augsabe, Siedler Verlag, Munchen 1983) p.417

711. *Pour l'Europe,* Robert Schuman p.117

712. The same hotel where Monnet had worked on the 'Monnet Plan.'

713. Victoria Martin De La Torre, *Europe, A Leap into the Unknown.*

714. Alan Fimister, *Robert Schuman: Neo-Scholastic Humanism and the Reunification of Europe*: (Philosophie et Politique / Philosophy and Politics) – 18 Nov. 2008

715. 'All the key elements—a new organisation of Europe, the supranational innovations, the European Community, the High Authority, fusion of vital interests such as coal and steel, and a single European market and economy — were floated in a series of major speeches given by Schuman in the previous, preparatory years. They include his speeches at the United Nations, at St James's Palace, London at the signing of the Statutes of the Council of Europe and in Brussels, Strasbourg and in North America.' Source: Wikipedia.

716. Alan Fimister, *Robert Schuman: Neo-Scholastic Humanism and the Reunification of Europe:* 15 (Philosophie et Politique / Philosophy and Politics) – 18 Nov. 2008

717. Robert Schuman, in *Pour l'Europe,* makes this point about 'poor borders' which is doubly true in our own age of asymmetric warfare.

718. We must remember that conception of Europe held by some French – one of French hegemony – was largely the historical echo of Napoleon's republic, further warped by the genuine grievances of two world wars. De Gaulle had denounced the EDC (and then NATO) the same way that Hitler had denounced the League of Nations – it would rob his nation of her sovereignty. De Gaulle was fuelled by past enmities against enemies and allies. He came back to power when the fourth republic was crumbling and financially broken. How extraordinary, and unexpected that Adenauer's Germany was the country that offered the loan to save the French economy when Britain and America hesitated. Adenauer even accepted De Gaulle's leadership to save the European Common market, because he knew that it was not politics but economic ties that would produce the lasting peace they needed.

719. *Pour l'Europe,* Robert Schuman p.122

720. I have not been able to understand why Macmillan attended this meeting when the Torys were not in office. He definitely was there on 24th November, and a transcript of his magnificent speech (which does not include the words that Spaak remembers, and may perhaps have been spoken in private or at another meeting) can be found here: https://www.cvce.eu/en/obj/speech_by_harold_macmillan_at_the_council_of_europe_strasbourg_24_november_1950-en-dba9a6fa-1a7d-47b7-b1c8-0507a67d299d.html

721. Norman Davies, *Europe, a History* p.15

722. Rene Albrecht-Carrie, *The Unity of Europe, a historical survey* (1966) p.24

723. One of the stranger twists in the British fiscal journey came in 1992, when the John Major government suffered humiliation at the hands of a Hungarian-born US investor called George Soros. By borrowing an astronomical sum on the money market for just a couple of days, Soros managed to single-handedly cause the Bank of England to devalue the pound. He cashed in his borrowings at the new rate and made himself a tidy profit. Retrospectively, Brexiting Britain should be thankful to Soros, because it was this humiliation that drove Britain out of the ERM and made it hard for her to enter the next round of negotiations. Norman Davies, *The Isles*, p.956. Macmillan Publishers Ltd, 1999 Also, see: George Soros, Soros on Soros: staying ahead of the Curve (New York, 1995)

724. The Enhanced Edition of John Locke's *Two Treatises of Civil Government* (1689, 1764)

725. George Friedman, *Flashpoints – The Emerging Crisis in Europe*, Doubleday p.110

726. Keyserlingk's *Fathers of Europe* (p162) also records a very moving recollection from the author some years later, when the internal problems within Russia were more evident and the European Economic Area well on its way. Keyserlingk saw a very-much aged Schuman ambling with his niece in the piazza of Santa Maria Novella in Florence. 'Monsieur le President, it pleases me to see that you are not in orders and wearing a tie.' After a brief remembrance the old statesman replied, 'But, remember, there is still a need to pray.'

727. https://en.wikipedia.org/wiki/Theodelinda

Belgium's Paul Henri Spaak, Churchill and Schuman

CHAPTER 17

Columban: Crossing Mountains

CHAPTER SUMMARY – 614 AD, COLUMBAN AMONG THE LOMBARDS - Columban in Lombardy as apologist against the dominant Arian heresy. His poetry and letter admonishing the pope. A glimpse at a previous generation; Theodoric, Cassius and Boethius. 615 AD – BOBBIO: LIFE, DEATH & LEGACY - His final monastery at Bobbio, and its significant library. Repairing the breach between himself and Gall. The final act of love is forgiveness. His death in a mountain cave. His legacy in Italy and Europe.

'Since we are all travellers and pilgrims in the world, let us ponder on the world as a road, that is our life, for the end of our roadway is our death.'

Columban's 8th Sermon

'When Columban saw that Theudbert had been conquered by Theuderich, as we said above, he left Gaul and Germany and went to Italy. There he was received with honour by Agilulf, king of the Lombards. The latter granted him the privilege of

settling in Italy wherever he pleased; and he did so, by God's di-
rection. During his stay in Milan, he resolved to attack the er-
rors of the heretics, that is, the Arian perfidy, which he wanted
to cut out and exterminate with the cauterizing knife of the
Scriptures. And he composed an excellent and learned work
against them.'

Jonas of Bobbio, Vita Columbani

614 AD, COLUMBAN AMONG THE LOMBARDS

We left Columban among the Alemanni bidding farewell to Gall (and possibly Attala) at Bregenz and then Sigisbert at Disentis. The year is 612, and it is possible that Columban was now the only Irishman in the party to then ascend the Via Lucmagn over the Alps toward Lombardy. At the age of seventy, and after so many miles together one can only guess how that must have felt. Twenty-four miles up through the mountains the reduced party must have stopped at the mountain village of Olivone. It is a good day's journey. Today, surrounded by jagged peaks, the Chapel of San Columbano lies on the outskirts of the village. The current chapel is an 18th Century reconstruction of a 12th century structure, which itself is thought to have been built on top of an even earlier chapel.

Jonas is scant on detail, but another week's journey could easily have seen him at the court of King Agiluf and Queen Theodelinda in Milan. As mentioned in Chapter 1, these barbarian *arrivistas* were actually Germanic tribes, and former mercenaries under Emperor Justinian's pay. They had decided that they rather liked northern Italy after rampaging through it a generation before. Like the Ostrogoths who displaced the Lombards they had originally been Arians, that is, they did not accept the divinity of Jesus Christ. How they became Roman Christians under the influence of Queen Theodelinda[728] is an interesting tale.

Agiluf was not Theodelinda's first husband. She was the devout daughter of Duke Garibald I of Bavaria, and had originally been married to King Authari of the Lombards. She was not an Arian, and not keen that any in Italy should be either.

Theodelinda's Crown in Monza Cathedral where she was married

15th century fresco in Monza Cathedral of Agiluf & Theoldelinda's wedding

When Authari died in 589, whether by custom or some former nuptial contract, Theodelinda was allowed to pick her next husband. A kingdom to gain and a young queen without a child – the suitors cannot have been lacking. She picked her deceased husband's relative Agiluf, who was 'raised on the shield'[729] in 592, and who adopted Christianity for the Lombards, probably as a wedding gift to please his wife – though Arian Christianity, to perhaps show her who was wearing the trousers. A decade later, however, in 603, the queen had her way. Agiluf and the Lombards, just like Clovis and his Franks, adopted Roman Christianity.[730] This date happily coincides with the completion of the stunning cathedral in Monza, just north of Milan, where Agiluf had his newly born son and heir baptised.[731]

It was ten years after these happenings, that Columban appeared at court like an Elijah coming out of the wilderness. He was welcomed and quickly turned his pen toward a popular theme at court: the refutation of Arianism, still pervasive in other parts of Italy.[732] These writings were lost, but his sermons from this period of his life have survived. So does a letter to Pope Boniface IV, which he wrote at the king's request, on the 'Three Chapters' controversy.[733] In it he appeals with passion as a 'foolish scot' from the 'world's edge' for the Pope to refute the heresy and show leadership on the issue. The letter runs to five thousand words, and Columban makes full use of alliteration, idiomatic expression, assonance, prolonged metaphors, parallel phrases, proverbs (called *seanfhocail* in Irish) and puns. Columban shows sincerity, vigour, and a strength of expression which borders on pugnacity. As with the letter to Gregory,[734] no reply exists.

Another poem, the Fidolius, which was possibly drafted as a letter to another Irishman called Fiadal, is also likely a production of this sojourn in Milan. G.S.M. Walker believes this to be the case, calling these Adonic verses[735] the 'crown of Columban's achievement' in literary terms, even claiming that 'Latin verses of this quality had seldom been written for 500 years and it seemed almost that Horace sang again by the lips of an Irish exile in the valley of the Po.' The comparison with Horace bears out, not least because, along with Virgil and Ovid, Columban uses many metaphors straight from Horace's *Odes III*. While others may have strained to inherit the Roman laurels, Columban won them inadvertently while trying to warn a friend of the dangers of riches. The sparse couplets do not translate well from the Latin but I give a few of the hundred and fifty plus lines below:

> *I ask no rich gifts,*
> *That will not endure –*
> *Gold that the miser,*
> *Hoards up, yet is poor*
> *It blinds wise men's eyes*
> *And just like the dart,*
> *Of a fire, it consumes*
> *The reprobate heart*
> *Christ be your portion,*
> *Lord of Creation,*
> *God, the Almighty's*
> *One generation.*

Columban was the king and queen's guest for some months and it is therefore probable that he visited Pavia, which was only a day's journey to the southwest. If Monza was the place for Columban to see the creations of Agiluf and Theodelinda, then Pavia was definitely the nearest place for him to meet the works of their predecessors, the Ostrogoths. It was at Pavia, over a century before in 476 AD, that the last emperor[736] of the Western Roman Empire was deposed, and where Roman rule ceased in Italy. But the usurping general, Odoacer, was defeated by Theodoric on the 15th March, 493, and then assassinated by him at a banquet meant to establish concord between the two ethnic groups. Because Theodoric lavished money on the city and expanded it, Pavia has some sites from a century before, which make it a place of historical pilgrimage for lovers of architecture.

It was here that Theodoric built a Roman-style amphitheatre and bath complex, which was probably among the very few still functioning outside of the Eastern Roman Empire in Columban's day. It was in Pavia in 522 that Boethius – a sort of Thomas More of his day – became Theodoric's *magister officiorum* (head of all the government and judiciary). A feverish Hellenist, Boethius, who was always happier with his Aristotelian and Platonic texts than purely biblical study, finally got

Last of the Romans: Boethius in a 5th c. ivory diptych in Museo di Santa Giulia, Brescia.

his solitude whilst accused of treasonous correspondence with the Byzantine emperor and jailed in one of Pavia's churches. It was here, over the three-year period before his execution, where he wrote his *Consolation of* Philosophy for which he is remembered today.[737] Along with Augustine, Boethius[738] is now buried in *San Pietro in Ciel d'Oro.*[739] His replacement in office was Cassiodorus, the pliant historian and courtier whom we met in chapters 4 and 9, and who later managed to retire to his Vivarium[740] (*Living Place*) in the South of Italy, where he hoped his (as it turned out) under-endowed library would survive the ravages of such uncertain times.[741]

But it was not just the Ostrogoths that favoured Pavia. Columban was passing through the city just before the golden age of Lombard patronage too, where many great monasteries and great churches were constructed, including the 7th century monastery of *Santa Maria Teodote* which became the resting place of the Lombard Kings. But, as we have said, the length of Columban's stay among these important cultural centres is uncertain. It may have been a time of relative ease and respite or a time of frustration for a septuagenarian who may have

sensed that his time was short. Either way, the day came when it was
time for him to move to his final pasture – not a retirement home, but a
new start-up seventy miles to the south.

615 AD – BOBBIO: LIFE, DEATH & LEGACY

> 'At that time a man named Jocundus appeared before the king and
> announced that he knew of a church of the holy Apostle Peter, in a
> lonely spot in the Apennines; the place had many advantages, it was
> unusually fertile, the water was full of fishes; it had long been called
> Bobium from the brook that flowed by it. There was another river
> in the neighbourhood, by which Hannibal had once passed a win-
> ter and suffered the loss of a very great number of men, horses, and
> elephants. Thither Columban now went, and with all diligence re-
> stored to its old beauty the church which was already half in ruins.'
> 742

Other ancient sources say he journeyed south with newly arrived
monks. He went via the old Celtic town of Lodi, where Napoleon
would one day do his heroic charge over the River Adda, and, as it is a
day's journey from Milan, we can assume Columban's party stayed here
at least one night. We next find him another day's journey south at the
town called Mombrione, later called San Colombano al Lambro,[743] in
his honour. Here he preached to either Lombards or indigenous Italians, who were pagans or who had reverted to paganism. We are not told
how long he stayed, but to make disciples is not an overnight affair, so
it might have been a few days or more. When he did leave, however, his
road was the old Roman 'Via Emilia' highway which had taken many
a Roman army north in its time and would carry many northern invaders south in the next thousand plus years. On another day's journey,
Columban crossed the mighty Po River and entered Piacenza, formerly
an important Roman town at the junction of the Po and Trebbia rivers.

Piacenza is a sobering place, for here was the site of Rome's darkest hour when in 218BC Hannibal inflicted heavy losses on them during the Punic Wars. What we call civilization, appeared even more fragile at this time than it did in 1940. At least in 1940, central Europe had the Americans and the British Commonwealth to call on. The Scipios had no one. And if the saner paganism of Rome had been defeated by the brute power of the Carthaginian, Molech-worshippers, then history would have looked very different. But, under the Scipios' leadership, the Romans arose from the ashes of the Trebbia defeat. They not only repulsed Hannibal from their homeland, and then Spain, but also extinguished the vile Carthaginian Empire on its own soil. If Texans 'remember the Alamo' then we Europeans 'remember the Trebbia'.

One US Classicist[744] points out that the Scipios faced down and defeated twice the number of enemies, as the later Romans would face in the 5th century. Why were the last Romans not able to defend their empire or even their country? Perhaps it is the same calamity we observed in the Third French Republic; a failure of leadership, an exhaustion of culture (*La Decadence*), and a terrible lesson for us all.

From Piacenza, Columban's party journeyed the remaining twenty-eight miles up the valley to Bobbio, which as far as we know was his most southerly destination.[745] It was in this mountainous defile in the Apennines, under the brooding eye of *Monte Penice*, that Columban began his last monastic community. Hemingway called it 'the loveliest valley on earth' but I would suppose that very few of my readers have ever heard of it, let alone been to such a remote location. At seventy miles from Milan, it was most likely given as a strategic base for the fuller conversion of the southern Lombard people. As noted above, Columban was arriving here only about fifty years since the last of the *Völkerwanderung;* the mass migrating of barbarian tribes that had sundered the empire. In the language of Schuman, Gasperi, and Adenauer, Columban was still very much part of the 'Reconstruction' phase following that slow apocalypse.

St Peter's Church, Bobbio, restored by Columban 2 years before his death

We visited in 2018 but, unlike Columban, drove over the ancient Via Francigena. This great road, travelled by so many great armies from Italy to France and vice versa, passes over the hills behind Bobbio and wends its way down through forest and farmland to the town. It was a stiflingly muggy day, and we were glad to park up under the magnificent Roman bridge and stretch our legs. After a good night's sleep (we honestly only saw the no camping sign the next day) we swam in the river and explored the town. The basilica is what you might expect, no real surprises, and the monastic buildings are variously reused as a museum and a school. What did thrill us was to find some abandoned monastic buildings at the back, perhaps from the 17th century, maybe earlier even. A rusty wrought iron gateway – all very 'gothic' – led up some steps in an area where the roof had collapsed and masonry lay everywhere. On the right; a crumbling chapel, stucco motifs on a dusty altar, rubble and marble gravestones all around. Up some more steps and there was a corridor with great studded doors with peeping hatches and inch-thick, rusty bolts. Were these monastic cells, prison cells, or asylum cells?

The rooms down the corridor varied in sizes and would be suitable for classrooms, which they may well have been. Timbers succumbed to wet rot, lay crumbling on the floor and plants were springing from the rubble at the end of the corridor, where the views south across the cupolas and campanile were obscenely picturesque.

Crossing the Trebbia on the Roman bridge towards Columban's last monastery at Bobbio

In other parts of the town a basilica and an old convent were boarded up and derelict – forlorn apses, sagging pantile roofs, cracked walls covered in convolvulus and memories. It was like walking into a set piece for a Napoleonic classic – I almost expected to meet Byron and Shelley round the next corner. A romantic like me could not stand amongst those stones without recalling the lines of Wordsworth among a ruined convent in the Apennines, perhaps even this one. For these stones that yet remain surely speak to us of many things, no less important because they are hard for us to hear.

> Ye Trees! whose slender roots entwine
> Altars that piety neglects;
> Whose infant arms enclasp the shrine
> Which no devotion now respects;

If not a straggler from the herd
Here ruminate, nor shrouded bird,
Chanting her low-voiced hymn, take pride
In aught that ye would grace or hide—
How sadly is your love misplaced,
Fair Trees, your bounty run to waste!
Ye, too, wild Flowers! that no one heeds,
And ye—full often spurned as weeds—
In beauty clothed, or breathing sweetness
From fractured arch and mouldering wall—
Do but more touchingly recall
Man's headstrong violence and Time's fleetness,
Making the precincts ye adorn
Appear to sight still more forlorn.

Before leaving the ruins of Columban's 'altars that piety neglects', I retrieved an enormous nail from some loose rotten timber on the ground. It was handmade, 5 inches long with a 1-inch flat, square head. Even the nails here are picturesque! I keep it in my office as a prized possession – my little piece of Columban's Bobbio, my little memory of his final labours, my warning that the work of cultural renewal is a constant and essential process.

The much-amended charter still reads, 'Flavius Agilulfus cedes to the venerable Columban and his monks the basilica of the blessed Peter, the prince of the Apostles, and four miles of land, cultivated or uncultivated, on every side of it, with complete property rights over all planning thereto except one half of a well, which he had previously bestowed upon Sundarit, a Lombard nobleman. In return for the royal munificence, the monks were to pray daily to God for the stability and prosperity of the kingdom.'

In some ways, this feels like Luxeuil 2.1. For here, on this vital artery at *Ebovium* (Bobbio) were curative water springs[746] and also, the old associations with Diana, whose altar was found during local excavations and is now in the Bobbio museum. These were formerly papal lands, or as one source says 'wastelands', and at its heart stood the ruins of Saint Peter's church. Columbanus erected a monastery in 614, next to this church. We are told he laboured alongside the others, bringing wood down from the hills on his own shoulders.

It reminds us of that other great pioneer, Francis of Assisi, whose first calling was to rebuild the ruined church of St Damian. Like some of the Hebrew prophets, Francis first modelled in sacramental metaphor what he would thereafter accomplish in reality – nothing less than to renew the church from the ground up. And, while we are on the subject let me extend the application a little. Rebuilding on the compromised, or vandalised and forgotten Christian past has been a large theme of this book. Here we see Columbanus literally, and metaphorically re-building after those great migrations sundered the western Empire. In like manner, Schuman, De Gasperi, and Adenauer, were also completely conscious of doing this after 1945, even if many in the current E.U. care not to remember it.

The eighteen-year-old Jonas, who would serve his novitiate here only a few years later, gives us a glowing account of the pioneer builders:

'In this restoration the wonderful power of the Lord was visible. For, when beams of fir were cut amid the precipitous cliffs or in the dense woods, or those cut elsewhere, fell into such places by accident, so that beasts of burden could not approach, the man of God going with two or three companions, as many as the steep paths furnished footing for, placed, in a wonderful manner, on his own and his companions' shoulders beams of immense weight, which thirty or forty men could scarcely carry on level ground; and where they had hardly been able to walk before, on account of the steepness of the paths, and had moved as if weighed down with burdens, they now walked easily and joyfully, bearing their burden. The man of God, seeing that he was receiving so great aid, urged his companions to finish joyfully the work which they had begun, and to remain in

the wilderness with renewed courage, affirming that this was God's will. Therefore, he restored the roof of the church and the ruined walls, and provided whatever else was necessary for a monastery.'

And no sooner was his fledgling monastery up and running than Eustace, the then abbot of Luxeuil, arrived. He had been sent with extraordinary news and a very tempting invitation. Columban had left Bregenz when he heard that Brundhilda and Theuderich had defeated and killed his patron. But now, it seemed that the winds of political change, which blew frequently through that exposed region, had finally broken Columban's old nemeses. The prophecy against Theuderich, which he made at Tours

The cruel death of Queen Brunhilda

had come to pass. Let us hear Jonas deliver the news with his usual verve.

'But Chlothar thought of Columban's prophecy[747] and gathered together an army to reconquer the land which belonged to him. Sigibert with his troops advanced to attack him, but was captured, together with his five brothers and great-grandmother Brunhilda, by Chlothar. The latter had the boys killed, one by one, but Brunhilda he had placed first on a camel in mockery and so exhibited to all her enemies round about; then she was bound to the tails of wild horses and thus perished wretchedly. As the whole family of Theuderich was now exterminated, Chlothar ruled alone over the three kingdoms and Columban's prophecy had been literally fulfilled. For one of the kings and his whole family had been entirely exterminated within three years; the second had been made a clerk

by violence; the third was the possessor and ruler of all the king-doms.'

Eustace also brought the invitation from the victorious king; return and be Abbot of Luxeuil again. A tempting offer; a chance to escape the hardships of the pioneer life, and to spend his final years amongst the adulation of many disciples in the success which was Luxeuil. How grand the patronage of such an omnipotent monarch? And how sweet to savour the vindication over those bishops and nobles who had conspired to be rid of him? Some of the greatness of Columban's soul is revealed here, in this last of his great struggles; the struggle with ego.

At Bregenz, he showed this largeness of his soul in his refusal to pray for his own side in the battle, and now we see it as he not only declines Clothar's invitation but also chides the King for his excessive use of degradation and torture in the execution of Brunhilda. Besides all that, it was now also no time for ease. News must have reached them by the autumn of this year 614, of the loss of Jerusalem to the Persians, an event that sent the Christian east into near hysteria. The unimaginable was happening, the great Christian centres of the east were fragmenting. And into the vacuums and fissures created by the Byzantine-Persian wars, a forty-five-year-old man from Mecca was about to change the spiritual and geopolitical map forever. The southwest (of Western Europe), needed underpinning more strongly and more than ever. So perhaps with a prophet's eye on the near future, Columban stayed in Italy – the land that might soon be the new frontline of Mediterranean Christianity.

In the letter that he sends back with Eustace, he also commits his Vosges abbeys to the protection of the king. This, the king had ample opportunity to do when attacks came from within and without in later years, but they are part of another story. As for Columban, we know that he was afflicted with some unspecified illness, and so perhaps he was already sensing his time was near. In the concluding lines of his letter to Fidolius, he complains of more than just the usual agues of age.

'I dictated these verses to you all weighed down as I am with a cruel malady; my frail body feels the sad effects of old age, for, in the headlong flight of the years, I have already completed the thrice sixth Olympiad of my life. All things pass away; the days fly beyond recall. Farewell. May you be happy – and think on the sadness of old age.'

He would only survive for one more year, which means his personal presence in the area was less than two years. That is not long, but it proved enough to establish Bobbio. He chose obscurity and hard graft to the end, and it paid off – not as an Irish project, but as a Christian one. The most recent scholarship has shown the Irish influence in Bobbio was not as great as some have claimed.[748] There are church dedications[749] and town names in north Italy that honour him, but his cult south of the alps is small.[750] Even in Bobbio, where succeeding Lombard nobles lavished their gifts,[751] there are no Irish names recorded in the community after him, and his rule was not practiced long after his death. But this is perhaps to look at the legacy issue in a wrongheaded and very un-Columban way. His concerns were not ethnic, nor vainglorious. They were, as far as I can make out, purely for the survival of orthodox practice and doctrine.

If anything, he gloried in the unlikely *grace dieu* that sent the former barbarian Hibernians back into Europe as teachers. The paradox appealed to Irish humour. But I don't think he would have spilled a drop of ink defending anything so parochial as the *Irish miniscule* hand, or even his own monastic rule if someone like Gregory had corrected him with a better argument. In this regard Columban's Christianity triumphed over the narrowness of mere nationalism or ethnicity.

But that does not mean his influence was not profound further north. One later writer[752] could ask rhetorically, 'what city of the province may not boast of possessing a bishop, or abbot from the school of the blessed Columban?'[753] Following Columban's trail, the Irish embraced the martyrdom of exile on the continent with abandon. And even in Italy, the library at Bobbio Abbey[754] became one of the richest in Europe during the Middle Ages – which is probably why Umberto Eco chose it as the location for his famous novel, *The Name of the Rose*.

What is rather thrilling, is that part of the library's wealth in manuscripts was actually due to Cassiodorus' *Vivarium*, already mentioned. This monastic school and library in southern Italy, still intact in 630, was broken up sometime after.[755] Cassiodorus,[756] is one of those unacknowledged heroes in the same manner as the Irish were, for they were both engaged in the same work at opposite ends of the empire. Many of the *Vivarium*'s treasures were lost forever, but some did survive. When scholars examined the Bobbio and Verona codices they found that they had actually come from Cassiodorus' *Vivarium*. How? No one knows. One theory is that monks fleeing the Greeks brought them north to Rome, even as nearly a thousand years later, those of Constantinople would flee west from the Turks, bringing similar precious manuscripts. By some means, however, Bobbio received them and copied them – and what a good thing for us all that they did. George Metlake gives this overview:

'A glance at the oldest manuscripts of Bobbio reveals the fact that the interest of the monks centered chiefly on liturgical and patristic works. Bible texts, collections of Canons, Rufinus, Josephus, Cassiodorus, and grammatical treatises were not prescribed; while the profane authors were for the most part sacrificed to the theologians. Thus, Cicero's Orations, Fragments of Galen, Dioscorides, Lucan's Pharsalia, the Orations of Fronto and Symmachus, Gargilius Martialis, Pelagonius, the Codex Theodosianus, and various mathematical treatises had to make way for Sedulius' Carmen Paschale, St. Isidor's Etymologies, Acts of Councils; St. Cyprian's De Opere et Eleemosynis, Cassian's Conferences, the Liber Pontificalis and various treatises on Grammar and Prosody.'

Columban, as was his usual habit, retired often to desolate places to pray. In Bobbio he had two such places; one was a cave called *La Spanna*[757] which was five hundred feet above the Trebbia, and another called the Hermitage of San Michelle. It was to the latter, in the November of 615 that Columban returned for the last time, leaving Attala with the charge of the monastery. It is a long walk up the steep hills opposite the monastery to this high valley – at least a day's journey for Columban depending on the state of his health and the weather. The narrow valley where the hermitage still stands has precipitously steep shale banks and abrupt craggy escarpments. The chestnut trees are no longer harvested up the valley and trees lie across the tracks where a previous generation used to find their living.[758]

Did Columban know this was his last journey into the wilderness? We don't know. But we do know what he was thinking on that last long walk away from civilisation. Strabo, in his Life of Gall, tells us that Columban was thinking about his old friend Gall in those last days on earth. The breach had cost them both, and Columban wanted to put it right. In a similar way, the apostle Paul, in his last days, called for John Mark, with whom he had fallen out so tragically with Barnabas. Writing to his protégé Timothy, he says bring John Mark with you when you come, 'for he is useful to me for the work.'[759] In the end it is great love that outlasts timber and masonry.

I remember a friend of mine, dying painfully with cancer aged only 46, wanting to make peace with anyone he might have offended over the years. In a similar way, perhaps Columban could see, now that his labours were finally at an end, the importance of the things that had seemed so secondary earlier. His last order was to have the staff (called a *Cambutta*) which had supported him across so many mountain miles, sent to that other great support; his *anamchara,* Gall. Gall was forgiven and was to receive the staff as comfort and affirmation.[760]

Here, I think we see the dichotomy between Columban's pastoral and pioneer sides. I have wracked my brains throughout this book to find a character similar in our age but have failed. If anyone comes close, I think it is the missionary David Livingstone, whose pioneer drive cost him the deaths of other missionaries, not least his own wife Mary. That is and always has been the true cost of the entrepreneur, the explorer, the pioneer; to kill the thing they love while pursuing their vision. Liv-

ingstone could not make that right in this life, Columban could. His final act of love was forgiveness. It is well for a man to die at peace with
himself and others. He died in the early hours of Sunday morning, on
21st November, 615, and was from there interred in the abbey at Bobbio, where he remains today.[761]

This was only really the beginning of a golden age, of our Anglo-
Irish, intellectual exports to Europe. For even as Columban passed from
this life, others were arising who would one day fill the great halls,
courts, palace schools, and monasteries of the continent. Some we have
mentioned already, and others like Alcuin of York, Marianus Scotus,
and Johannes Scotus Eriugena had a tremendous impact on Carolingian
life and thought, and are reasonably well known already, but the bulk of
these *peregrinatio pro Christo* will only ever be known to the enthusiasts
and the few in those localities where they laboured.

Sedulius Scottus ran the cathedral school in Liege. Kilian worked
in Würzburg. Donatus, the Irish Bishop of Fiesole above Florence in
829-876, was a poet, biographer of St. Brigid, and a man who wrote
a Latin description of his homeland. Another formidable intellect was
Dungal, an Irish scholar who came to St Denis near Paris in 784. After
an eclipse of the sun, in 810, he was invited by Charlemagne to explain
it. Later he became supervisor of education (OFSTED is nothing
new[762]) for northern Italy, rating scholars, inspecting schools, and offering refresher courses. Dungal left his own library to Bobbio (including
a copy of the Bangor Antiphonary).

Another great name was Fursa (or Fursey,) who was inspired by
Columban; and was given land by Erchinaold, Major of the Palace in
Neustria, to found a monastery in Lagny, near Paris in 644. His accounts of visions of the world of the spirits, both good and evil, and of
the fires of hell and joys of the redeemed were one of Dante's sources
for the Divine Comedy. And following Frigidian to Lucca, was Finnian,
son of King Ultach of Ulster, who also had been educated in Irish
monasteries.

A sample below gives a sense of the people and foundations in the
next few centuries following Columban. There was Andrew the Scot of

Fiesole outside Florence, and Fridolin of Säckingen, Konstanz. There was Wendelin of Trier, Kilian, Arbogast, Landelin, Trudpert, Pirmin (who founded Reichenau abbey), Corbinian, Emmeram, and Rupert of Salzburg. There were the three Irishman called Marianus, Iohannus, and Candidus who founded Regensburg which itself was the mother-house for many more, including; the abbeys of St. James at Würzburg (1134), St. Aegidius at Nuremberg (1140), St. James at Constance (1142), Our Blessed Lady at Vienna (1158), St. Nicolas at Memmingen (1168), Holy Cross at Eichstätt (1194), St. James at Erfurt (1036) and the Priory of Kelheim (1231).

There were over 100 other continental monasteries like Honau in Baden (721), Murbach in Upper Alsace (727), Altomünster in Upper Bavaria (749) all founded by the advancing Irish. And they were not just in Western and Eastern Europe either. In the 9th century the Norse settlers found Irish monks already present in Iceland before they got there in 874.[763] And these *Scotti* didn't just *found* new monasteries but also restored fallen ones, like 'St. Michel in Thiérache (940), Walsort near Namur (945), and, at Cologne, the Monasteries of St. Clement (about 953), St. Martin (about 980), St. Symphorian (about 990), and St. Pantaléon (1042).'[764]

Here, is only a tantalising glimpse of the industry and effort that the Irish, along with many other nations, put into saving Europe during their day. So much of that involved the combatting of cultural and religious amnesia. To preserve a living, rooted, intellectual, and spiritual tradition took the combined labours of people of goodwill from all the nations. The Irish happened to have had some *slack* and so provided for Europe's *lack* in a great time of need. And they did so *gratis*.

That is the European and Christian spirit – the evangelic love of one's neighbour. That is the soul of Europe and that is, in the deepest sense, what Schuman, De Gasperi, and Adenauer strove for against all the odds. Not for merely 'Christian ethics' but a living Christianity. Whether Europe can enjoy the fruit of this without the root is a matter under discussion in the epilogue. But now we must take our leave of Columban and the Irish altogether. And in closing let us remember this, that even as some of these stalwart pioneers went out – in fact, even as they laid Columban's weary bones to rest – the seers among them might well have sensed new seeds blowing through the winds of history; some new force awakening that would one day stamp out the Anglo-Irish missionary zeal.

Columban died in 615. That same year, Aethelfrith massacred eleven hundred and fifty Welsh monks at Bangor-is-y-Coed. Also, in that year Mohammed's followers were beginning to grow and migrate. And just over a year after Columban's death, Bangor itself was burnt down. On the Island of Eigg, off the west coast of Scotland, the monks of Donnan's monastery were put to the sword by raiders from the sea. Those Celtic monks who had courted green, then white martyrdom, now found the red martyrdom battering down their doors. That was Easter Sunday morning, in 617AD. The swords and axes fell like the wrath of Satan. And if those sea raiders were indeed Vikings,[765] then it was the red dawn of a new day. Once more, migratory pressures would soon be bringing barbarians into a fragile civilisation – not across the Danube, but the North Sea. It was as if the Irish achievement had flourished, just long enough to produce a cultural engine profound enough to assist their European counterparts in the transformation of Western Civilisation – to save it from what would otherwise have been very Dark Ages indeed.

From my office window, I look out on beautiful mountains and fields, but I know that even these highlands of West Cumbria were once part of a vast slave empire ruled by Viking Dublin. It is a sobering thought. Those raids reached their apogee three hundred years later when the Sea Kings were themselves conquered by the Gospel. But even before then, during those dark days when, as the Anglo-Saxon Chronicle says, 'heathen men miserably devastated God's church,' the embers rekindled by the Irish monks and farsighted pioneers like Benedict and Cassiodorus, were already too much aflame to be quenched. Their job on our behalf was done – their great work had begun.

But it would be wrong to finish this chapter without some more fitting tribute to Columban, and who better to do it than the man who, in 1957, reproduced the best collection of Columban material since Patrick Fleming,[766] in 1667. The historian G. S. M. Walker writes;

'It is the misfortune of commanding characters to arouse consuming hatreds; and Columban, by the outspoken freedom of his language and the tenacious independence of his mind, was plunged into animated quarrels for the greater portion of his life. His integrity was hard and cutting as a diamond. Ruthless to himself, he could be inexorable in his demands on others with a determination that not even a mother's tears were able to soften into compromise. Choosing solitude, he acquired great public influence; teaching humility, he found himself obliged to correct both popes and kings...The real man, in all his simplicity and tenderness, was jealously shielded by an aversion to any display of sentiment; but in rare unguarded moments, he was found playing with a little girl at her father's villa, or sending to one of his monks the kiss, which in the haste of exile he had omitted to bestow. The poor, the sick and the unfortunate were drawn to him by his sharing in their common lot; even criminals, released from their fetters, felt impelled to kneel beside him as he prayed; and rough soldiers asked him for his pardon when they came to take him from Luxeuil...... Except for the more pedantic type of punning, he was devoid of humour; yet the very tenderness of his natural melancholy rendered him attractive to all classes of society, so the noblemen entrusted him with their son's education, and kings and courtiers were ready to welcome his reproof. At home with all men, he rested nowhere; capable of all tasks, he set his heart on self-denial. Scholarship had failed to impress its objective balance on the poetic ardour of his nature, and solitude led him to seek truth on the side of the minority.... Lacking originality, his talents were best suited to the quiet of the cloister, yet sheer determination made him an outstanding leader of his age. A character so complex and so contrary, humble and haughty, harsh and tender, pedantic and impetuous by turns, had as its guiding and unifying pattern the ambition of sainthood. All his activities were subordinate to one end, and with the self-sacrifice that can seem so close to self-assertion, he worked out his soul's salvation by the one sure pathway that he knew. He was a missionary through circumstance, a monk by vocation; a contemplative, too frequently driven to action by the world; a pilgrim, on the road to Paradise.'

728. Paul the Deacon, *History of the Lombards*; translated by William Dudley Foulke, 1907 (Philadelphia: University of Pennsylvania, 1974), pp.148-150

729. The actual date of his conversion is debated. For example, some say Columban was instrumental in it, and George Metlake deduces (from the letter to Pope Boniface IV) that Agiluf was still an Arian Christian in 613. I am not sufficiently proficient in Latin to disagree with any certainty, but a casual reading in the Walker translation seems ambiguous to me.

730. Other churches they built in Lombardy and Tuscany include the first baptistery in Florence.

731. He was not the first of his countrymen to bend his energies to fight Arianism; a half century earlier Fridian (Fridianus) became notable in the fight against the Arians in Lucca (where he accepted the office of bishop). His remains are still interred (reconstituted in wax) at the church that bears his name. (Source: Wikipedia)

732. The 'Three Chapters' were writings by Syrian bishops suspected of Nestorianism, which had been condemned in the fifth century as heresy.

733. Columban later refers to three letters sent to Gregory.

734. According to Wikipedia, an Adonic (Latin: adoneus) is a unit of Aeolic verse, a five-syllable metrical foot consisting of a dactyl followed by a trochee. The last line of a Sapphic stanza is an adonic. The pattern (with "-" a long and "u" a short syllable) is: "- u u - -" when the pattern ends with a spondee (i.e. --) or " -uu -u " if a trochee is intended.

735. Romulus Augustulus (r. 475-476)

736. Diarmaid McCulloch writes generously about Boethius' legacy to the west in *A History of Christianity* (p.320). Boethius, though a Christian, did not write as one, but by shoring up fragments and by producing translations of Aristotle and Plato; and by writing commentaries on them; and preparing manuals of music, mathematics, geometry, and astronomy, he left a valuable legacy for future generations.

737. Dante almost canonises the scholar in *Il Paradiso*, canto X: 'Lo corpo ond'ella fu cacciata giace, giuso in Cieldauro; ed essa da martiro, e da essilio venne a questa pace.' ("The body whence it was chased forth / lieth down below in Cieldauro and itself from martyrdom / and exile came unto this peace."

738. This church 'Saint Peter's with the gold ceiling' gets this name because of the golden background in the roof mosaics of the original wooden church that stood on the site. This gold-painted wooden ceiling of earlier times was also noted by the later Italian humanists Dante, Petrarch, and Boccaccio.

739. This, I think, mainly refers to the books. The library at St Gallen, one of the most important in Europe, was called the 'hospital for souls' as they believed that ignorance and error were maladies of a grievous sort.

740. No record remains of Columban's reactions to Pavia, although he would have been pleased that an Irishmen of a later generation, sent by no less than Charle

magne, laboured here. We know this because an Irish monk at the later monastery of St. Gall was writing a biography of Charlemagne, and in it, he says, two 'Scots of Ireland' who were 'travelling in the company of traders, arrived on the coast of Gaul ....in the moment when Charlemagne had begun to reign as sole king." These were Clement and Ailbe, and they set themselves up in the market as vendors of learning. Word of them reached the ear of Charlemagne, and such was the fame of Irish scholarship in those days, he quickly offered them important academic posts. Clement was put at the head of one of the king's schools for noble and common boys in France, while Ailbe was given the direction of the 'monastery of Saint Augustine' near Pavia (i.e., the Abbey of San Pietro in Ciel d'Oro), 'sometimes named after Saint Augustine, because it contained many of his relics.' The seventh century wooden church was replaced by a grand Romanesque basilica six hundred years later.

741. Jonas of Bobbio, Vita Columbani

742. Also, in Lombardy other towns like San Colombano Belmonte (near Turin) and San Colombano Certénoli, near Genoa take their names from the saint.

743. Victor Davis Hanson

744. Columban in Rome? Padre della Torre suggested that he made two journeys into Italy and that these have been forgotten by Jonas. On the first occasion, della Torre hypothesises, that Columban went to Rome and received from Pope Gregory many sacred relics (Stokes, *Apennines*, p132). If this were true, which I doubt, it would at least explain the traditional spot in St. Peter's, where St. Gregory and St. Columban are supposed to have met (Moran, *Irish Saints in Great Britain*, p105).

745. The spring mentioned in the grant might be the salt spring of Piancascale, which is rich in sodium chloride, bromine and iodine. Salt was an important export of the north of Italy and salt monopolies were a source of contention between the Papal States and the northern city states as late as the sixteenth century.

746. 'Announce, therefore, to Theuderich that he and his children will die within three years, and his entire family will be exterminated by the Lord.' Jonas' *Life of Columbanus*

747. *Bobbio in the Early Middle Ages: The Abiding Legacy of Columbanus.* By Michael Richter. (Dublin: Four Courts Press. Distrib. in the United States by SBS, Portland, OR.2008. Pp.211ISBN 978-1-846-82103-5.)

748. It would cheer him, I think, that one of the oldest churches Bologna, founded in 616 by his disciple Bishop Peter, bears the Irishman's name, and moreover, that it is a few hundred yards from the oldest university in the world. (The Oratory of San Colombano is on Parigi Street, 5, Bologna 40121)

749. More detail from Alexander O'Hara can be found at https://www.academia.edu/20294938/Columbanus_ad_Locum_The_Establishment_of_the_Monastic_Foundations

750. Paul the Deacon, History of the Lombards; translated by William Dudley Foulke, 1907 (Philadelphia: University of Pennsylvania, 1974),

751. From the biography of Bercher of Montier-en-Der

752. During the 7th century, the disciples of Columbanus and other Scottish and Irish missionaries founded several monasteries in what are now France, Germany, Belgium, and Switzerland. The best known are St. Gall in Switzerland, Disibodenberg in the Rhine Palatinate, St. Paul's at Besançon, Lure and Cusance in the Diocese of Besançon, Bèze in the Diocese of Langres, Remiremont Abbey and Moyenmoutier Abbey in the Diocese of Toul, Fosses-la-Ville in the Diocese of Liège, Mont Saint-Quentin at Péronne, Ebersmunster in Lower Alsace, St. Martin's at Cologne, the Scots Monastery, Regensburg, Vienna, Erfurt, and Würzburg. Near Florence, at different times, there was Andrew the Scot of Fiesole and Donatus. Another early Schottenkloster was Säckingen in Baden, founded by the Irish missionary Fridolin of Säckingen, who is said to have founded another at Konstanz. Other Hiberno-Scottish missionaries active at the time, predominantly in Swabia, were Wendelin of Trier, Kilian, Arbogast, Landelin, Trudpert, Corbinian, Emmeram, and Rupert of Salzburg.

753. The sanctuary and the tower are now the oldest parts above ground, and they date to the tenth or eleventh century. The nave and other adjacent buildings date to the fifteenth century.

754. Abbot Coelfrith created a 'Codex Grandior' of the bible, which he had copied at his monasteries at Wearmouth and Jarrow in the northeast of England. He took one of them to Italy in person but died before he could present it to the pope. For many years the Bible (which is so big that a budget airline would not let you have it as cabin baggage) was in the mountain monastery at Amiata, but now it can be viewed at the Laurentian Library in Florence. It is a strange thought that the Geordies who built ships on the Tyne, at another time built bibles for export.

755. This patrician knew more than any the precariousness of the times in which he lived. His father had led a Roman delegation to Attila the Hun. Cassiodorus spent decades in Constantinople and did what he could to mend the titanic rifts all around him. He switched allegiance from Odoacer to Theodoric with characteristic ease and even managed to retire with his head still attached, unlike his predecessor Boethius. His final and greatest act was to preserve learning and moral civility at his Vivarium in southern Italy.

756. Italian for 'Span' perhaps referring to the expansive vista.

757. Nowadays 90% of the world's chestnuts come from China, the young men and women of Italy have moved away from these high villages. When visiting the area, we camped high up near an abandoned hilltop village and cooked the chestnuts we had foraged on an open fire, wondering what the future held for us all. There are so many changes happening so fast.

758. 2 Timothy 4v11

759. The staff was still at St. Galen in the ninth century, though by then St. Nokter had broken it in three places while beating a wild dog that had strayed into the church. (In Nokter's defence, he had assumed the dog was a manifestation of the Devil, and so probably thought he needed something more powerful than an average stick.)

760. His marble sarcophagus, carved by Giovanni di Argennio in 1480 with scenes from his life, is rather fittingly looked upon by a stained-glass window with him, flanked by Patrick (the Pioneer) and Benedict (the greatest monastic founder).

761. The Office for Standards in Education (OFSTED) in the UK is responsible for inspecting a range of educational institutions, including state schools.

762. 'The oldest source mentioning the Papar is the Íslendingabók ("*Book of the Icelanders*"), between 1122 and 1133. Such figures are also mentioned in the Icelandic Landnámabók ("Book of Settlements", possibly going back to the early 12th century) which states that the Norse found Irish priests, with bells and crosiers, at Iceland at the time of their arrival.' https://en.wikipedia.org/wiki/Hiberno-Scottish_mission

763. https://en.wikipedia.org/wiki/Hiberno-Scottish_mission

764. There are accounts that these were in fact the Queen of Moidart's henchmen.

765. In 1623 a Franciscan called Patrick Fleming from County Louth travelled to Bobbio searching out monasteries and libraries for material of Columban interest. His *Collectanea Sacra* published posthumously in 1667, was eventually surpassed in 1957 by Walker's Sancti Columbani Opera. Source: Tomas O'Fiaich, Columbanus in his own worlds, p.71

766. It is interesting to note that French historian Alexis de Tocqueville viewed the rise of democracy in colonial America as a dangerous despotism.

Paul van Zeeland (B), Joseph Bech (L), Joseph Meurice (B), le comte Carlo Sforza (I), Robert Schuman (F), Konrad Adenauer (RFA), Dirk Stikker (PB) et Johannes van den Brink (NL) pose after the signature of the Paris Treaty creating ECSC - CECA

CHAPTER 18

Schuman: The Father of Europe

CHAPTER SUMMARY - 1951-1957, THE THREE-LEGGED STOOL and also NATO (1949), The Treaty of Paris (1951), and the Treaty of Rome (1957). The Schuman Plan in the light of history and the limitations of the Coal and Steel Treaty. 1957, A GOOD DEATH - De Gasperi's death and burial. PAUL HENRI SPAAK, THE 'CHAMPAGNE SOCIALIST' – a warm biographical sketch of Belgium's Prime Minister. TIMELY INTERVENTION - Spaak provides much-needed impetus to a political project in peril. The Treaty of Rome. The deaths and burials of Adenauer, Buchman, and Schuman and the world they left behind. 1967–2020, EUROPE'S UNFACED DILEMMA - The EU's achievements and Schuman's challenge that it cannot survive as solely 'an economic and technical exercise.' Maritain's challenge that 'an anarchy of atoms' (Enlightenment individualism) is an inadequate base to support the edifice of an enduring civilization.

'It's not vast scenery that makes a great landscape

... no, humanity is the thing.'

William McTaggart, artist.

1951-1957, THE THREE-LEGGED STOOL

Picturing, with proportion, the 'vast scenery' of world events during Schuman's lifetime is hard. But I have endeavoured to capture the human stories as a means of comprehending the whole. 'Humanity *is* the thing.' In Walter's Scott's introduction to the Waverley novels (1814), he says that his interest was in *'men not manners'*, i.e. humanity, not their political views. It is something he did very well. But our work here is to glimpse the vast scenery of historical processes through the eyes of some who were present, and moreover, who were key actors in the political movements of which we are heirs. And in these days of cynicism, and declining public faith in the democratic process, these biographical sketches might also serve as a necessary panacea.

We have observed great and worthy lives that achieved much against extraordinary obstacles. Schuman, De Gasperi, and Adenauer believed in 'humanity', the thing that makes democracy possible, but they also believed in the 'fall of humanity', which makes it so necessary.[767] And they also acknowledged that if the political architecture was wrong, then even titanic human effort would be in vain. That is the terrible lesson we learned as the iron curtain fell over Eastern Europe – a curtain that could have come much closer. Further back, that is also the lesson we gleaned from Europe's recovery after the Roman Empire imploded, when the cultural engines of Church, monastery, and university could not function effectively if there was not first a modicum of political stability. Columban needed Theuderic, even as Theuderic had needed Columban. The sacred had needed the secular and vice versa for they are in fact, part of one world and not two.

The medieval poet Dante believed foremost in the 'system' – get political structures right and people will flourish in it. That is why he wrote *De Monarchia*.[768] But the early renaissance poet Petrarch, emphasised instead the greatness of individual human action. That is why he wrote *De Viris Illustribus* ('On Famous Men'). As Schuman proved, it is not either-or, but both-and; that Europeans and European leaders should ensure 'that spiritual progress go hand in hand with the material.' In previous chapters, we witness him, Gasperi, and Adenauer living lives worthy of Petrarch, and in this chapter, we find them forging a political unity worthy of Dante. They would succeed here where others had failed, but they left the final development of their plan to future generations to tease out. In this chapter, I will only give the very barest details about the European project, which after all is a colossal subject. My focus instead will be to round off the human narratives in their historical context. After all, *humanity is the thing*.

In Chapter 16, we left Schuman awaiting the momentous 1951 Treaty of Paris, which would cause his peers to call him 'The Father of Europe.' He was foresighted predicting: the expanding federation, the spreading east, the joining and eventual leaving of Britain – even, the timescale of Brexit! He saw the dangers of an intolerant secularism but did not foresee the divisiveness of a single currency, that would come later. But, at the very start it is difficult for us to comprehend the sheer unlikeliness of this story and its outcome.

Schuman, the man who refused to leave his religion at the door when he went into politics, was asking his fellow Frenchmen, so abused and degraded by two centuries of *La Decadence*, and two world wars, to initiate forgiveness towards their enemies.[769] Not in a vague, sentimental way, but by ceding part of her sovereignty through economic integration. The level of shock and vulnerability can only be compared with something like Russia and America fusing their oil industries in a new multilateral partnership. In fact, I don't even think this adequately expresses the magnitude of the reality, given the deep historical root of the antagonism, and scale of post-war trauma. For the offended and ostensibly secular French to act on the Gospel command[770] that many Christians fail to practice even in their private lives, is still staggering.

The French Prime minister Georges Bidault (who initially called the plan a 'soap bubble' and 'just one more international body') almost resigned over it,[771] but eventually he came around to support it at the 11th hour. Jean Monnet was with Adenauer a few weeks later and explained that the French proposal was 'essentially political. It even has, let's say, a moral aspect. At its core, it sets a very simple goal which our government will try to achieve without worrying, in a first phase, about the technical difficulties.'[772] How much water had passed under the bridge since their last frosty meeting in Bonn only a few months before? But now, Adenauer's face said it all to Monnet. He was full of emotion when he replied to the Frenchman.

> '*I'm not a technician. And I don't speak now as a politician. I see, like you, this great enterprise in its highest aspect: the moral order. It is the moral responsibility we have towards our people, not the technical responsibility, the one we must implement in order to realise a dream of this calibre. The reception has been enthusiastic in Germany. Nor will we dwell on the details. I have been waiting for this initiative for 25 years. By partnering with you, neither my government nor my country hold any ulterior motives, no hegemonic intentions. Since 1933 history has taught us how vain those concerns are. Germany knows that its fate is tied up with the fate of Western Europe.... if I can bring it to fruition, I think I will not have wasted my life.*'

At a meeting with the Parisian correspondents' club the next year Adenauer also remarked, 'It seems that the day is not far off when the European peoples, full of freedom and rights, can come together under the same roof of a.... truly new Europe ...a citadel of western and Christian tradition, a source of spiritual strength and a place of peaceful work.'

Adenauer & De Gasperi, Rome 1953

The Coal and Steel Community became a reality following Schuman's declaration. Monnet went back to the Rue Martignac to work feverishly with a range of experts from different nationalities. No interpreters were allowed. The team would work together, even through language differences, without intermediary and thus become a team worthy of the task ahead. They ate together and shared their war experiences, it was just as Monnet had hoped, even better. One could even say that amongst them sprang up a proto-European community such as they were hoping to articulate in their planning work. This point must be highlighted, they were not looking at each other but common tasks to be tackled, and it was precisely here that we see a microcosm of the European spirit of solidarity.

During the later negotiations, Adenauer was under pressure from his opponents at home; that the ECSC treaty should include the tacit recognition of the Saar's political independence. Schuman could not give this assurance openly at that moment. That could have been an end to the whole thing. But such was the trust and good faith between these men that Adenauer signed the treaty nonetheless on the gentlemen's agreement that Schuman would do all in his power to have the Saarland's independence respected. This gentlemen's agreement would be achieved simply by an exchange of letters.

On 18th April 1951 the Treaty of Paris, as it became known, was signed – at Monnet's insistence – on paper from Holland, printed in France with German ink, in Belgic and Luxembourgish bindings and Italian silk stitching. It happened before the Saar issue caused another crisis and before German rearmament caused an international revolt. From that moment, even as the ink was still drying, the two nations were bound together in a common future.

The ECSC was a success on many fronts (inward investment, modernisation, the abolition of tariffs, expansion, and worker welfare) but it failed to achieve some basic aims set out by the Treaty of Paris. For example, it did not prevent a resurgence of large coal and steel groups.[773] 'In the Cold War trade-offs, the cartels and major companies re-emerged, leading to apparent price fixing... With a democratic supervisory system, the worst aspects of past abuse were avoided with the anti-cartel powers of the Authority, the first international anti-cartel agency in the world.'[774]

Another deficiency in the ECSE was that it did not anticipate – no one did – the titanic changes that were about to turn Europe's energy consumption on its head. At the beginning of the war, 90% of Europe's energy came from coal, but as things stood after the war, there was a massive 58 million tonne shortage. America became the major supplier, but everyone realised that inward investment and political solutions were quickly needed so that Europe could be more self-sufficient for energy.

In 1947, Britain nationalised its 1500 pits and soon France followed suit. German production was still under Allied control at a time when the Ruhr was producing 50% of Europe's coal. The coal paradigm was so strong that no one realised its days of dominance would soon be over. By 1973 – just 20 years after the treaty – 64% of Europe's energy-needs would be met by petroleum. A radical shift like that could not happen without profound social consequences. Even between 1954 and 1960, Europe's petrol consumption doubled, and Britain's would quadruple in the next 15 years after that.

As oil became ubiquitous and cheap, so coal began to look expensive. In the UK each new oil-fired station meant 5 million tons less coal per annum was needed. Each power station converted from coal to oil was another death-knell to the mining industries and mining towns. In the six years after 1954, oil went from 20% to 30% of the UK's energy supply. The change was even greater in Germany where the energy share of coal in the 1950s dropped by over a half, despite ongoing modernisation. The deep French coal seams also proved uncompetitive when even cheaper coal – let alone much cheaper oil – could be shipped so easily from other parts of the world. By 1962, the French made the decision to switch to oil.[775] The understandable anger of the French public during the planned closures would be repeated in the UK twenty years later. Energy security became an obvious headache for European leaders who saw, through four separate incidences before 1992 that instability in Arabia had become a key factor in the prosperity of Europe.[776]

But none of these issues overshadowed the ECSC's political and psychological breakthrough. It modelled a future of supranational unity that few had thought possible. Its preliminary expression was formulated in 1957, at the Treaty of Rome, when the European Economic Community (EEC) was signed by 'The Big Six'; Belgium, France, Italy, Luxembourg, the Netherlands, and West Germany. And from this point, Schuman must take a back seat, at least until the end of this chapter. For now, we must consider other threads and characters that make our story.

The thorny international issue at his time was not the Saar, but German rearmament. The Americans had been pushing for a new German army to act as a deterrent against the increasing menace of Soviet Communism. But Adenauer knew this was too soon for many surrounding countries, who were still getting used to Germany not being the sum total of all their fears. He feared that rearmament too soon would jeopardise the cohesion of the European movement. When the Americans pushed for 50,000 German troops for NATO Adenauer was swift to distance himself from the plan. He had told the media that he would only consider German rearmament within a European army. At another meeting previous to this, Adenauer passed Schuman a note; 'Attention, this leads us to the resurrection of a German national army, and we do not want any part of it.'[777] When the Treaty establishing the European Defence Community went un-ratified in May 1952, by the Big Six, he was heartbroken by the possibility of another future European civil war.

He was not the only one. Alcide De Gasperi, who became president of the ECSC was very ill and one year away from death. It is highly likely that without his mediation between Adenauer and Schuman over the thorny Saar issue, the project might never have found its wings. Italy had been under a totalitarian dictatorship since the 1920s. An entire generation had grown up, politically crippled by Fascism with the equal and opposite errors that always grow under such abnormal circumstances. De Gasperi saw that European integration was the fireproofing that they all needed.

1957-1967, GOOD DEATHS

Having survived twenty years of Mussolini's totalitarianism, De Gasperi emerged from the rubble in many ways 'the best intellectually prepared leader'. He met regularly with Schuman and Adenauer. Looking back over his life, De Gasperi once told a friend, 'I have lived through deadly dangerous times. I felt alone, abandoned by friends, and what kept me going was to know that I was working for peace.'[778]

In 1952 he and Francesca travelled to Germany where, amongst other things, he received the Charlemagne prize in Aachen for his service to European integration. Like her husband, Francesca was a fluent German speaker, and so conversations with their host, Adenauer, had been friendly and natural. During the ceremony in the great medieval town hall, De Gasperi confided to Francesca that this was the most prized award he had ever received. In January 1954, he took the floor at the European Parliamentary Conference, visibly ill, yet defiant. He spoke with passion about the common European heritage, centred in Christian ethics, liberal democracy and social justice, 'none of which prevail in one or another area of our civilisation ...rather these three tendencies must together contribute to building on this idea and to nourishing its free and progressive development.'

By that summer, confined to bed in Valsugana, De Gasperi followed news about the ratification of the European Defence Community with breathless interest. The phone calls with Germany and France went from optimistic to progressively hopeless as French colonial reversals in Indo-China refuelled the nationalist and militaristic fires of De Gaulle's alternative view of a French future. By August 18th, De Gasperi was heartbroken, and having put the phone down, said to his daughter Maria, 'I have done everything I could. My conscience is clean.'

His political garlands were many, but the unrealised dream to abolish national armies in favour of a European Defence Force (EDC) was a bitter disappointment for his final years.[779] 'You can hardly imagine the pain I feel,' he wrote from his sickbed to the secretary of his party, 'particularly as I can no longer raise my voice.' For De Gasperi, it was a failure of half the project, because the French were only extending one hand in peace to the Germans while firmly keeping the other on their swords.[780] Days before his death he had still been on the phone urging his party to stop Mendez-France scuttling the EDC at the French Assembly with the help 'of a hundred Communists.'[781]

But, despite all his dwindling energies, this is exactly what happened just eleven days after De Gasperi's death, and a few years later. De Gaulle, though so often obstructing integration, understood one thing that De Gasperi was passionate about and that many others missed; the need for Europe to be militarily independent of America at some point. (It was De Gaulle who demanded that NATO leave French soil, in 1966.) The mixed success and uncertain future of NATO have its roots here. Unlike Churchill, the 'Atlanticist' view of European integration was resisted by many at the outset. But, even then, it was a fiscal and strategic necessity. Through NATO, Americans would guarantee Europe's military stability, and through Marshall aid, its political stability too. 'There was little glory for France in World War I, and none in World War II. They knew it and deeply resented it.'[782] As Thackeray wrote, 'some men will never forgive a favour.'[783]

For De Gaulle, Europe must possess its own army. It must not become an American satellite.[784] It might have been his wounded pride that caused him to see it, but if there wasn't any saving grace in integration; then nevertheless, France could lead the way, and that the sooner it did, the sooner it could make NATO obsolete. France led the initiative of forgiveness and perhaps they could lead the initiative in security?

This subject will be revisited in the next chapter, but first, we must pay our respects at the death bed of the politician described by Time magazine as 'the man from the mountains'[785]

On the evening of 19 August 1954, De Gasperi felt fatally sick. Francesca sent for the doctor, and then the priest. Surrounded by their three daughters, the mother and father held hands, looking through the window at their beloved mountains. This was Francesca's parents' house. The house where a penniless student had first noticed how much the 21-year-old sister of his friend had grown into an accomplished and cosmopolitan young woman. Now that same woman, his best and unfailing friend led him in a prayer for a peaceful death. At 2 am, he drew his last breath; and the next day, remembering what he had said in Aachen, Francesca placed the Charlemagne award with him in the coffin. That morning he was mourned for at the house, and then in the town. A second funeral was celebrated in Trento, for he was their champion, first and foremost. But he was also the man who had held a heartbroken nation together in its darkest hour. From a personal abyss, forced on him by 20 years of fascist persecution, he led the Italians back from the precipice. And by his tireless campaigning for solidarity on the national frontiers, he ended up straddling the world stage at a critical hour in human history. He was later also given a state funeral in Rome.

'In De Gasperi', Adenauer later said, 'I found the true spirit of European policy.' Adenauer also said that he lived the most beautiful moment of his life when walking and chatting with De Gasperi around the *Piazza del Popolo* in Rome in mid-June 1951. Often during meetings, he had watched the exasperation on the other politicians' faces as the impassioned De Gasperi dominated the floor. He understood the temperament and heart of this Italian, whose imposed 25-year silence had made him impatient to forge a lasting peace while the iron was still hot.

When news of his death reached the north of Europe it was a bitter blow. Paul Henry Spaak, Prime Minister of Belgium cried 'like a child' while Joseph Bech, the Prime Minister of Luxembourg tried in vain to comfort him. When Monnet heard that the EDC proposal would not be ratified by the French, his wife and the girls were out walking and he was alone. He physically collapsed, as if felled by the blow. All of a sudden, the New World optimism that had characterised his extraordinary career deserted him and for the first time in his life, he began to question whether the whole dream of a united Europe was ever achievable. In the moment of this defeat, the project needed a champion to inject fresh impetus. And this time it is the aforementioned Paul Henri Spaak, this politician of deep feeling and humane sensibilities, who rallied Monnet and the others.

PAUL HENRI SPAAK – THE CHAMPAGNE SOCIALIST

And so, before we continue with this thread, let us first meet this rotund Belgian *bon vivant* who formed an essential link in the chain of causation. Paul Henri Spaak stands in this story for the noble humanist who, whilst acknowledging the importance of the Christian underpinnings of Europe, nevertheless did not embrace it with the same personal piety as Schuman, De Gasperi, and Adenauer. There is much to love and admire in Spaak – such as his personal courage and tender feeling. He was, as they say, a well-rounded character – in more ways than one.

Paul Henri Spaak

Spaak's father was professor of French Literature and director of the Royal Theatre *La Monnaie*. His maternal grandfather had been a Liberal MP, his uncle a prime minister, and his mother the first female senator. In mental inclination he was more 'right hemisphere', and hopeless at maths to the despair of his teachers. Spaak had a very close relationship with his politician grandfather and, at 14, never forgot his funeral, when 400,000 workers interrupted their work to pay their respects to the 'father of universal suffrage' in Belgium.

That was 1911, and soon this *Belle Epoque* of his life would be interrupted by World War I. As social tensions took their strain, his mother moved further left from the liberals to the socialist party. In 1916, the Belgian economy plunged. Young Spaak, only 17, wanted to play his part. His parents would not countenance him going to the front, as he was too young. But he disregarded their advice and lied about his age. Belgium was then occupied, and so he planned his escape to the allies, via the Netherlands and England. But he never even got that far, being captured by the Germans near Antwerp and confined to a POW camp. The Germans were fair, the camp tolerable and his letters home downplayed any difficulties he faced.

After the war, he studied law and entered into politics as a liberal. He married Marguerite Malevez in 1922, whose family were industrialists from Namur. His first daughter was born a year later. He admitted that Marguerite's life - as a politician's wife – was not an easy one. He was away a lot, traveling and speaking. But he was always fun to be with when home and tried to make it up to her. They would take a tram into the centre of Brussels just so they could feel like an ordinary couple. On one such occasion, he kissed her passionately for a considerable duration, much to the surprise of Marguerite, and the prim onlookers sitting and standing nearby. But that was nothing compared to their joint amazement when Paul Henri jumped off the tram, shouting impishly, 'my greetings to your husband!'

He spent four weeks in Russia to see first-hand the progress and effects of Communism but quickly saw that Soviet Socialism with its autocratic dictatorship was not the answer. Caught between his mother's socialism and his father's theatre crowd, young Spaak became known by journalists as the *Bolshevik in the Tuxedo*. But like his mother and his grandfather, his heart was for the masses and he worked tirelessly until, while still in his thirties, he was given the position of foreign minister, then transport minister in the Van Zeeland government. At this time also, he was a fan of Astride Briand's speech at the League of Nations promoting a united Europe, and also the *Jeune Europe* magazine of Edouard Didier, which proposed similar options for the future.

A story that illustrates the heart of the man is the personal letter he wrote to the new King Leopold III (then only 35) after the death of his wife in a car crash. Spaak, only two years older, reached out in tender words that transgressed royal protocol, but nevertheless won the king's admiration and friendship. A year later, Spaak became not just the first socialist prime minister of Belgium, but also the youngest. However, during the war, the King went behind Spaak's back, by dealing uni-laterally with the Germans. For Spaak, it was a bitter blow. Spaak and Hubert Pierlot, the then prime minister, escaped via the Pyrenees into Spain and then in a truck across to Portugal. As they got into the van, which had a false compartment to hide just two people, Pierlot asked Spaak if he minded him praying? Spaak certainly did not mind. In that tense twenty-four-hour journey, he called on every deity he could re-member, ancient and modern. For as he said after the event, 'if we need some life insurance, I prefer comprehensive cover.'[786]

A number of happy coincidences (or providences) helped their es-cape succeed, but it was nerve-wracking all the same. When they finally got out of the van in Spain and saw Mrs. Pierlot approaching them, she seemed unusually calm. Spaak was amazed as nobody knew of their es-cape, not even her. He asked her about it and she smiled sweetly, 'this morning in church, when I opened my prayer book, I read the passage that begins with these words, "The prisoner is soon to be set free." So, I was expecting you.' Spaak was flabbergasted, 'it was amazing,' he said, 'so simple and so true.'[787]

From Portugal, they arrived in England and there used the remaining years of the war to run a government in exile, along with their neigh-bours. The time was not wasted and, from their location, remote from the devastated continent, the Belgians, Dutch, and Luxembourgers took stock and spoke of a better future together. Before they left Eng-land after liberation, they announced their plan to integrate their economies. It was a sensible post-war recovery mechanism, but they also knew it could be the beginning of something bigger.

Spaak first met Schuman in the summer of 1948, when the latter had suddenly been made French Foreign Minister after yet another change in government. It is hard to think of two men less alike: one lean as a rake, the other round as a ball, one a conservative and Catholic, the other a socialist and agnostic, one shy and retiring, the other extravagant and theatrical. Spaak noted Schuman's thin, nasal voice that seemed to apologise for each break in the silence. How could such a man be a leader? But the more Spaak listened and observed, the more he understood the power of the simplicity and honesty that undergirded Schuman's words, and also the profundity that held others spellbound.

In the same year, at the UN General Assembly, a cloud was hovering over the meeting. The Russian leader Vichinsky had accused Brussels of forming a defence organisation with the other five countries with the intention of attacking Russia. Spaak stepped into the ring with a stinging response, 'Do you think that my country has the intention of military aggression? ... The Soviet delegation should not look for complex explanations for our policy. Our policy is based on fear. Fear of you! We get together to defend ourselves because we are afraid.'[788] As he returned up the aisle the other members stood and applauded. Two more short stories relating to Spaak are worth recording before we return to the crisis over German rearmament.

The first incident was after reaching a deal with other leaders in Messina in the early hours of 2nd June 1955. It was 4 am, so Spaak decided that he would stay up and serenade the sun as it rose over Mount Etna, from his balcony. To his artistic soul, quite unlike that of the French Minister of Foreign  affairs in the next room, who was trying to sleep, it seemed the most appropriate response to the historic moment. The great orator and hero of European integration opened his lungs with the first birds of that glorious new day to sing *'O sole mio'* - but he was eventually interrupted by Antoine Pinay banging on the walls and telling him to shut up!

Another interesting detail from this conference was the extreme care taken among ministers to eschew even the least hint of the 'gravy-train' accusation that would never be far from people's lips in later years. They had actually been arm twisted by Gaetano Martino to go to Sicily for talks, as it would help him look good for the upcoming local elections. It was a hellish distance to travel for one thing, but the thought of the press interpreting it as a ministers' perk was another. A luxurious seaside resort with a Roman amphitheatre and other remains! They didn't want to let Martino down and got around the embarrassment by announcing that they were returning 'to the Greco-Roman past of Europe to build a common future.'

The other anecdote, which appears in a letter to his mistress Simone, dates from the negotiations in Venice, May 1956. Spaak is again aware of the deep historical currents that were moving around him, but even then, tempers his amazement with mock-grandiose humour. 'If this goes well, my grandchildren will read my biography in the Larousse (encyclopedia) and perhaps even with a portrait. What selfishness in the face of such greatness!'[789]

TIMELY INTERVENTION

So, with those vignettes of Paul Henri Spaak complete, let us now return to the collapse of the initiative for a European army. Spaak, as if he were his theatre-director father, rallied the actors for the next scene. They must bring a united response, it is simple – Germany must re-arm and join NATO. In the Council of Europe's assembly in Strasbourg, Spaak the orator delivered a rousing speech. Though not a practicing Christian, he nevertheless affirmed the essential spiritual roots that ground this international project; 'we share the same civilisation,' he said, 'which is called a Christian civilisation.'[790]

Spaak, the man who called the Russians out and denounced their double talk and double-dealing, was now the man pleading with the other members to make firm the forgiveness that Germany needed. And in a masterstroke, this man with political and theatrical blood in his veins spoke with a quaking voice of his sister-in-law's last days in prison: Suzanne had been a member of the Resistance and she had written a message, with her own blood, on the prison walls in Fresnes, just before her execution by firing squad. She started with Jesus' words from the last book of the Bible, before extrapolating meaning from them for the current situation. 'I have opened a door that no one can close,[791] nothing, no person, no old tradition, no selfish nationalism, no chauvinism.' The message went home; they were honour bound to the dead as well as the living; to find a way, or make one.

The speech and all their joint work eventually paid off when Germany was invited to join NATO on 23rd October 1954. It was not a moment too soon, either. A year later Soviet troops entered Budapest, and of the suffering of Hungary, Poland, Czechoslovakia, and other nations, we have still not heard the depth, even as we have not heard the last.

The Treaty of Paris and Germany's admission to NATO, were both key markers in the success of the fledgling project. Another was the Treaty of Rome on March 25th, 1957, which finalised the treaties for the European Economic Community (EEC) and the European Atomic Energy Community (Euratom). This treaty – whose overarching goal was no less than to substitute civil war with cooperation – was the greatest single political change since the birth of the nation states; of a different species to the Peace of Utrecht, the Treaties of Paris, the Congress of Vienna or even the US Constitution. And it was signed at a moment when the threat to Western European security had moved from the Rhine to the Elbe.

So, let us go now to that wet spring day, on the sacred hill in Rome called the *Campidoglio* where, in former times, the returning legions would offer thanks to Jupiter for their victories. Ministers mounted Michelangelo's famous steps and entered the palazzo. De Gasperi would have loved to have seen this day, but has now been dead three years. A tribute was read early in the proceedings to honour him. Just as the latest miracle of wireless radio had spread propaganda thirty years before, so now the miracle of live television broadcasting sent out the good news that the Big Six were sealing future peace through economic and legal integration. The posters all over Rome read 'Six peoples, one family, for the good of all.'

In the morning, they finalised the EEC treaty and the Euratom treaty. Monnet had been very keen on this. His entrepreneur's eye assumed that if nuclear fusion would produce the energy of the future, then European countries working in cooperation could lead the way. It was an optimistic, though laudable political objective. When amendments and additions were made, the documents – in four languages – came to 157 and 158 pages in total. They had lunch and then travelled to the Basilica of San Lorenzo for mass and to pay tribute to De Gasperi, whose coffin was waiting in the narthex, soon to be re-interred in the Mausoleum. His wife, Francesca, and loving daughters approached the coffin, with the ministers a few paces behind. Even though his country's service took the best years of his life, he had been first of all a husband and father. So, the family laid their flowers ahead of the others. Spaak remembered how distraught he had been at the news three years before. Europe lost a titan in De Gasperi, but they had finally made it through by pulling together. Adenauer was missing Schuman, thinking he should be here. But unlike the Germans, who re-elected Adenauer in successive elections, the French were still changing their governments on a regular basis.

At 6 pm, speeches were given to a large crowd who had gathered in the rain under the statue of the Stoic emperor Marcus Aurelius. After that, the ministers walked up the grand staircase of the Curator's Palace (now the Capitoline Museum) and along the flag-bedecked corridors to the Hall of the Horatii and Curiatii. Around them were the frescoed battle scenes between the Romans and Albanians – a scene that characterised the rise of Rome. But they were here today with a noble resolve to live at peace. Five hundred photographers and journalists were present in the room. A French journalist among them, called Paul

Chalze, wrote, 'it is surprising to see such harmony between Socialists and Christian Democrats.'

The Treaty of Rome 1957 - Spaak, De Gaulle & Adenauer visible (front left)

The fresco included the *Rape of the Sabine Women* and the *Myth of Romulus and Remus*. Before them stood a table upon which they would draw a line under that bloody past. Europe had seen more of this sort of carnage in the last decades than in all human history. Those present had lived their lives on the edge of the abyss and they would ensure their grandchildren would not see what they had seen. The future would be built together, characterised by equality, the rule of law, and cooperation.

Spaak signed first with Adenauer saying out loud, 'he deserves Europe.' The Belgian shaped part of the H of his name into an S so that Simone – his mistress and later wife – could be part of history with him. Adenauer was next, approaching the task with a solemnity worthy of the historic moment. After him the French signed, and then the Italian prime minister Antonio Segni who said,

'We Italians feel the need to give special thanks to two names; Alcide De Gasperi and Carlo Sforza, whose spirits are felt in this room today. We are here to inaugurate a new stage of history of peo-

ples. We must turn our eyes to the future and not the past. It is a new family, a large new family, they will all feel united in a life-long bond, as our Latin ancestors used to say, united in a common destiny.'[792]

His comments might have been seen as comically ironic when considering what his 'Latin ancestors' meant by it, but the seriousness of the event carried the moment as all eyes present were fixed on the signatories.

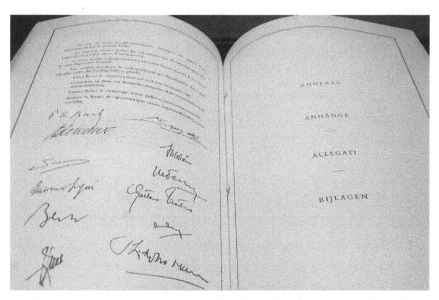

Signatories on The Treaty of Rome, 1957 (Spaak top left with Adenauer underneath)

As we saw in Chapter 1, this was a far cry from the original 'manifest destiny' articulated by former Romans. But all the nations, not just the Romans, had come a long way since then. Others spoke too; 'little Europe' had no enemies, they said, but did have great ambitions to spread north, south, and east. Christian Pineau, the French Foreign Minister added a note of caution. What about the integration of the overseas' territories? What about the British? 'Without them, the construction would be incomplete,' he said.[793] Of course, not all French favoured British participation (De Gaulle would block British membership twice) but this clearly shows an expectation at some level that Britain was a vital component.

By October of that year, the advance in weaponry meant that no place on earth would be more than thirty minutes from a nuclear strike. The world was becoming smaller: Britain would start to feel it, and seek admission a decade later. Back in Rome in 1957, the French Prime Minister Christian Pineau fell silent. He had enough to contend with in the French domestic situation. When a journalist asked him whether the French National Assembly would ratify the treaty; he gave only a politician's answer. He took it before them at the first opportunity, but he knew, as Schuman did at every move, he would be up against the Communists and Gaullists as twin enemies.

Of course, with hindsight, we know they did ratify the treaty eventually, but as the failure of plans for a European Army showed them all, nothing could be taken for granted. For those who waited outside in the rain, the bell ringing at 6.50 pm, signalled the news for which they had been waiting. At that symbolic moment, a new united Europe was born. The youth wing of De Gasperi's Christian Democrat Party released hundreds of paper butterflies from the rooftops, which the rain quickly took to the ground. To an earlier generation of Romans, bound to the pagan deities, this would doubtless have been seen as a terrible omen and dire portent. But nothing was likely to dampen the new generation's spirits that evening. If the Europeans had come far from the dread of occult agencies and attempts to derive their philosophy from elemental nature, then these new Europeans had come just as far in shedding illusions of a demoniacal nationalism or a hegemonic militarism.

The shock of the last decades had been so great, they had banded together against themselves, that is, against the worst inclinations of national selfishness and fear. It took very special conditions for anything so radical to become imaginable, but they had done it.

As they banqueted that evening, at the Villa Madama – a place where Mussolini had entertained Hitler – they had every reason to look back with satisfaction. The mildly thorny issues, about where to place the various EEC institutions, could wait for another day. Tonight, they could walk the terrace at the Medici Palazzo and look out across the *Urbs Aeterna* and feel history smiling on them. They had done it. Against all the insuperable odds, they had actually done it. They had achieved what would become 'the most innovative and successful integration process in the history of humankind.'[794]

When accepting the Charlemagne prize, Konrad Adenauer said that,

> *"the future will not be built through force, nor the desire to conquer, but by the patient application of the democratic method, the constructive spirit of agreement, and by respect for freedom."*

Already in his late seventies, the Chancellor delayed what little retirement he might have expected in order to save Franco-German relations from de Gaulle's nationalism. Adenauer was a complex and subtle politician and a proud man. He was accused of too much leniency toward Nazis after the war, and not enough generosity to their victims. It is beyond our remit to judge on such weighty matters in so brief an account. From the mid-1930s he was almost as much a victim of the Nazis as anyone, and should by rights have died in Buchenwald. But his life was saved by a Marxist, and he lived to save his broken nation.

On 19 April, 1967, aged ninety-one, Adenauer died in his family home at Rhöndorf. One of his daughters, who attended him, said that his last words were *Da jitt et nix zo kriesche!* – Cologne dialect for *'there's nothin' to weep about.'* His state funeral, at the cathedral in Cologne, was attended by many dignitaries from across the world including United States President Lyndon B. Johnson, and Charles de Gaulle. After the service, his remains were taken upstream to Rhöndorf on the Rhine, while thousands stood in silence on both banks of the river. He was interred at the Waldfriedhof ("Forest Cemetery"). In 2003, his countrymen voted him the 'greatest German of all time'.[795] The oldest of the three, Adenauer outlived them all – Schuman by four years, Buchman by five.

In August 1962, Buchman lay dying at the Hotel Waldlust, in the Black Forest. Frank Buchman was no politician or financier, but a praying man of vision and responsibility. America's Marshall aid ran into millions, but Buchman's input may well have been priceless. Prince Richard of Hesse, who attended him, read him Psalm 23. It was amongst Buchman's favourite Bible passages. 'Though I walk through the valley of the shadow of death, I will fear no evil for You are with me. Your rod and staff comfort me....my cup overflows... and may I dwell in the house of the Lord forever.'

Buchman smiled sweetly at the words. Like De Gasperi and Columban his wanderings were over, his pilgrimage done. The final words of this American *peregrinatio pro Christo* are at once striking and profoundly moving. Following the heart attack, his final words on earth took him half an hour to utter, for they were spoken through much pain, *'I want Britain to be governed by men governed by God. I want to see the world governed by men governed by God. Why not let God run the world?'*

That evening, August 7th, 1962, he breathed his last. And thus, prose became poetry, and poetry, prayer.

Schuman died a year later. In many ways the unlikeliest of all French politicians, Schuman had gone from strength to strength for another decade after the founding of the ECSC. He was President of the European Parliamentary Assembly from 1958-1960, and President of the European Movement until 1961. At the end of his term in office at the European Parliament, he was given a standing ovation and the title 'Father of Europe' by his colleagues. He finally retired from political life in 1962, when cerebral arteriosclerosis confined him to his house in Scy-Chazelles. He still cherished a hope that one day Russia and even Britain would join the EU; but this was even as De Gaulle was vetoing the UK from joining the Common Market.

What would a man born in 1886 make of the post war generation? The world had just been to the brink of nuclear catastrophe, during the

Cuban Missile Crisis. As Schuman lay dying, the Beatles were releasing their first album, Bob Dylan his second. The world had moved on, and grown strange. The times, as Bob Dylan observed, were *a'changing*, and Schuman was left, in a bed brought down to the parlour, to fight his last battle.

On the 4th of September, exactly one week after Luther King's 'I have a dream' speech, this unassuming Frenchman passed away at his home, aged 76. He had a dream too, a most unlikely dream. A dream applied to a sphere usually reserved for more proximate solutions. A dream that, strangely enough, came true. Once again, the idealists had become the most practical men of the age.

A Moral Rearmament activist, who had come to know Schuman well, gave a moving eye-witness account of the funeral.

'The hardest thing for him was probably to feel his own mind going during the last moments of his life. There hovered around him the silence of a great solitude. Robert Schuman died as a humble, forgotten man without family. At the funeral in September 1963, the cathedral of Metz was full. All his true friends were there. We looked in the audience to where the official dignitaries were seated. It was made essentially of foreign personalities, who were received by the prefect of service. The deceased did not belong to the party then in power, so it was necessary to be discreet. But the Lorraine crowd expressed the tribute of a nation; impressive floral displays filled the cathedral, according to the wish of Schuman. And then suddenly, like a ray of light, the doors suddenly opened wide and through them came an immense wreath of flowers which were brought along the long central aisle. It was sent by the king of Morocco, an astonishing witness of recognition, emanating from (Morocco's) 'commander of the believers' towards a man who had been above all, only a Christian. My comrade Michel Koechlin and I returned to his home at Scy Chazelles after the ceremony. His secretary watched over the deceased's house now deserted. On opening

the door of the room where he died on the ground floor, his glasses and his watch were still on the bedside table. This room was a picture of his simple lifestyle (depouillement, lit. indigence).[796]

Schuman was later buried near his home village of Scy-Chazelles, outside Metz in the fortified church of Saint Quentin. Today a bronze floor relief marks the spot. The medieval church, which is literally across the lane from his little house, is unusual for it has been fortified against looters (no doubt, looters from across the river), which is perhaps ironic for a man who took away the boundaries and turned the enemies into allies.

Even more symbolic, is the hill of Mont St. Quentin that broods over his village. Its slopes are riven with earthworks for the defence of the area, once so vulnerable to invasion. It is productive farmland now. Again, a fitting metaphor. Cannon, the then weapon of mass destruction, was first used in the siege of Metz, 1324 – but the man from Metz has made the guns silent now for 70 years.

Schuman & Adenauer - the two men who led, but also embodied the Franco-German peace

Just below the hill in Le Ban-Saint-Martin, the Bismarck Tower also still stands as a reminder of German imperial aggression. It is the only one left in France, but unlike the Civil War monuments in America, no one makes a fuss about dismantling it. As Schuman said, 'we do not pretend to adjust history.'[797] Bismarck's tower looks east across the Moselle river to Metz, as Pharaoh's Pyramids must one day have looked down at the imprisoned Hebrew slave, Joseph. On the *Rue Maurice Barres*, Schuman spent seven cold winter months in solitary confinement as a prisoner of the Gestapo. But he emerged, as did Joseph, not just to save his own people, but also to save his enemies.

The French have longed for secular saints since *la Révolution*; it is one of the downsides in such a rapid switch from being so Catholic to being so piously secular. When Jacques Louis David painted his friend Marat after his assassination in 1793, he painted him as a saint and martyr, even when he knew Marat had encouraged the September Massacres.[798] David didn't just airbrush Marat's hideous skin disease out of the frame, but also the truth that he knew – the necessary evils that they both hoped would bring utopia closer, but which never did. Marat is interred in the great Pantheon in Paris, while Schuman lies in the little church opposite his home. It is reward enough, I suppose, to die with a clean conscience, to be laid to rest, as Thomas Gray put it, like 'some Cromwell guiltless of his country's blood.'[799]

But if he cannot be a secular saint, can he be a Catholic one? Apparently not, for once again this *homme de frontières* seems to fall between the lines in the Catholic system of categories. For in the Roman church, a saint must produce two verifiable miracles after their death.[800] You and I might think that rather exacting, but that is the way it goes, and they are very rigorous about the verification process. Having read this book, most people would agree that there are few words as succinct as 'miracle,'[801] by which to describe the post-war Franco-German reconciliation. Posthumous miracles or not, at least no one has been able to cast aspersions on the integrity of his personal conduct. When Schuman's hero Aquinas lay dying, his friend and confessor Reginald came out from the saint's death bed weeping for, he said, 'his sins were only those of a child.' It is extraordinary that in everything I have read, there is only one recorded incidence of Schuman buckling.

It was not under the Gestapo, or Bürckel, who in any case could find no dirt on him, but just before his arrest when he carried the near immense burden, in 1940, as the Under Secretary for the Presidency of the Council for Refugees. He was attempting to shield and help millions of them while his own government was in disarray. His dismay at the crucifixion of his country was intense, as was his distress at his inability to help the millions of refugees fleeing Nazi occupation. And it was during this time that he once lost his temper, throwing a managerial tantrum in front of astonished colleagues. But the measure of his impact on others is shown in their reactions, as they could all see this was completely out of character. He returned fifteen minutes later, saying 'I am truly ashamed of myself'[802] and offering them all dinner in recompense. He was an exemplar of that great truth preached by many religions, that self-governance – what Gandhi called *Swarāj* – was the prerequisite for governing others.

'So, feet of clay after all,' a critic might say, 'and no doubt just the tip of an iceberg of other monkish sins.' But if a detractor is to be even-handed, then he or she must first explain how, with one of those feet so firmly in the past, Schuman could have the other so far in the future. I don't think we can easily understand him, for we are not used to expecting too much from public figures, or even ourselves. He seems ethereal to us, as if he came from another world into Europe for a particular time and purpose. Of course, one might say the same for Adenauer and De Gasperi, but they at least left human footprints as fathers and husbands. Schuman; not so, he is simply *other*. In some ways, we see here a parallel to those Irish monks, who just appeared when we needed them, who did their work and then disappeared again. Schuman was born at the fracture point, inside the very jaws, as it were, of two warring, imperial powers. He died leaving those powers not just at peace, but in almost full cooperation.

'We are but very imperfect instruments of Providence,' he said once, 'which uses us to accomplish great designs that are beyond our comprehension.' The toleration and free movement Columban pleaded for, Schuman *et al* delivered. We cannot calibrate the scale of our debt to either of them because we cannot know what might have been if they had not lived and played their part. The fact that no one seriously put the 'Seventy-years-peace' factor in the balances during the Brexit debate shows how successful the Fathers of Europe have been. For most, war has become unthinkable in Western Europe. In an article written for an educational magazine, Schuman wrote,

'Europe has become for us, men of 1956, the most palpable expression of the solidarity of western nations in their battle for existence before the perils which surround them and before the task which they cannot accomplish other than in common [...] it is not, therefore, an appeal to our generosity or to our charity but to the conviction that we depend upon one another, that we will be able to save ourselves only in a morally united and politically organised Europe. In the last analysis, Europe, thus unified, will be the establishment upon our continent, theatre of incessant discord, of the great principle of human and more specifically Christian fraternity....Reconciliation is a great thing but it does not suffice; it risks being precarious and superficial if it is not anchored in free cooperation in the service of the works of peace, in a climate of renewed confidence and a feeling of solidarity. This is the purpose of the European organisation in which France has taken the initiative and the preponderant responsibility. What we want is not a simple assurance against the risk of war [but]... an association... in which everyone, vanquishers and the vanquished of yesterday, will find their place.'[803]

The last section of this chapter will examine how 'vanquishers and the vanquished of yesterday' found 'their place' in the new Europe.

1967–2020 EUROPE'S UNFACED DILEMMA

Since the Treaty of Rome in 1957, the Union has incorporated a further 22 countries. It now comprises over half a billion people over 4.5 million square kilometres.[804] The EU is just 7.3% of the world's population and yet it generates 22.2% of global nominal GDP and provides more foreign aid than any other economic union. There is so much for which we should be grateful, not least those seventy-five years without war. The level of economic and political cooperation, and the expansion of the union, and the way in which it has lifted so many out of intellectual and economic poverty are all achievements for which we can be justly proud.[805]

We Europeans are still religious too, surprisingly so. 72% still own some form of Christianity (48% Roman Catholic, 12% Protestant, 8% Eastern Orthodox, 4% other Christian), 23% say they are irreligious (about half agnostic and half atheist), 2% are Muslim and 3% are of other faiths.[806] So, as we have said before, 'Europe is still the place where Christianity is the religion to reject. To rebel against religion requires that there be a religion to rebel against.'[807] I have never heard of it being done here, but other countries celebrate Europe Day on 9th May, the date of Schuman's declaration, and sing the European Anthem to Beethoven's *Ode to Joy*. Schiller's lyrics (German Romanticism with a sprinkling of Christianity in the final stanza) have been replaced with others less likely to offend or, for that matter, to inspire.

> *'Europe is united now*
> *United it may remain*
> *Our unity in diversity*
> *May contribute to world peace.*
> *May there forever reign in Europe*
> *Faith and Justice*
> *And freedom for its people*
> *In a bigger motherland.*
> *Citizens, Europe shall flourish*
> *A great task calls on you*
> *Golden stars in the sky are*
> *The symbols that shall unite us.'*

Admittedly they scan better in Latin,[808] but even so, they are not the sort of thing that will put a lump in your throat, or steel your courage charging into battle. *Unity, Justice, and Peace* are obviously what we are all after, but even anecdotally, the anthem strikes an alarmingly lame note on the theme of European identity.

So, in some ways, this was the challenge Schuman gave at the outset of the project. He knew there were many great partners, like Paul Henri Spaak, for whom peace and the rise in living standards was understandably a sufficient target. But could such a vast and innovative political project be sustained merely by a secular vision? Many would argue with an indefatigable affirmative, even as the great ship appears to be tottering. The three founding fathers that we have been studying, would all say, 'no' with insistence, as we will see. And Maritain was already warning Europeans not to succumb to such proximate solutions. He had seen how easily 'the dignity of the person is disregarded, and the human person [would be] sacrificed to the titanism of industry, which is the god of the economic community.'[809] His words are certainly archane and possibly reactionary, but Maritain, who after all was the drafter of the *Universal Declaration of Human Rights,* is not a man one can easily sweep aside. There is something in his polemic writing that cuts sharply through our complacency, even now, or especially now, seventy years later.

> *'In the bourgeois-individualist type of society there is no common work to do, nor is there any form of communion. Each one asks only that the State protect his individual freedom of profit against the possible encroachments of other men's freedoms. .... It is not for an objective purpose that they assemble, but rather for the subjective pleasure of being together, of marching together (zusammenmarschieren). The Germanic notion of community is built on a nostalgic longing to be together, on the emotional need for communion for its own sake—fusion within the community thus becomes a compensation for an abnormal feeling of loneliness and distress....*
>
> *Let us not say that the aim of society is the individual good or the mere aggregate of the individual good of each of the persons who constitute it. Such a formula would dissolve society as such for the*

benefit of its parts and would lead to an "anarchy of atoms". It would amount either to a frankly anarchic conception or to the old disguised anarchic conception of bourgeois materialism, according to which the entire duty of society consists in seeing that the freedom of each one be respected, thereby enabling the strong freely to oppress the weak. The aim of society is its own common good, the good of the social body. But if we fail to grasp the fact that this good of the social body is a common good of human persons, as the social body itself is a whole made up of human persons, this formula would lead in its turn to other errors of a collectivist type—or to a type of state despotism.' [810]

An 'anarchy of atoms' leads to despotism. That is the warning of Maritain and others.[811] To preserve the balance between *freedom and social justice, freedom and security*[812] and to escape alternatives like the 'guided democracy'[813] of Russia, Europeans have to return in some sense *to the rock from which they were hewn.*[814] Schuman wrote that the EEC 'cannot and must not remain an economic and technical enterprise; it needs a soul, a consciousness of its historical affinities and its responsibilities in the present and in the future...'[815] In the epilogue we will explore to what extent this challenge went unheeded.

We started with a painter so let us finish with one. William Turner once strapped himself to the mast of a storm-tossed boat so that he could gaze unstintingly at the raging seas in all their terrible majesty. He painted his masterpiece 'Shipwreck' as a metaphor for Britain's nakedness and vulnerability at the height of the Napoleonic wars – the helpless lifeboat crews at the mercy of insuperable forces. Considering present geopolitical currents, it seems that Europe in general, and Britain in particular is once more at such a juncture in history. The difficulties of Brexit and the financial strain of the COVID pandemic are waves on their own that will rock the ship. It is at times like these when governments and populations select a mast to strap themselves to. Of course, the question we must debate – and be open to debate, indeed to be free to debate – is which one?

Schuman, and indeed the central actors in our story, strapped themselves to a mast from which they not only 'looked on tempests', but from which they also steered a great ship through a very great storm. They were not acting alone, and theirs was not the only 'mast' in use, or indeed, the only mast that held in the storm. I have given biographical sketches of men like Spaak and Monnet for this reason. We must be, as they were, open-handed and open-hearted enough to work together for the temporal common good with others of good will. Schuman, De Gasperi, and Adenauer acted precisely in this way because of their faith. They strapped themselves to a mast that was, in fact, a cross. In that respect, Europeans alive today, whether religious or not, are as much the beneficiaries of Schuman's faith, as they are of Columban's. We stand on giants' shoulders.

Can we imagine what Europe might be today if Schuman, De Gasperi, and Adenauer had been disqualified from office because of their overt religious commitments?[816] Having just studied their lives, is there any non-religious reader who would wish it? I do not believe so. And neither would any religious believer discount the genius of a Spaak or a Monnet despite their lack of dogmatic faith. As it is likely that politically active Christians will remain a minority in positions of influence, we need one another to build the future, and that starts with patient dialogue.

So, in the next chapter I would like to explore one side of that dialogue, and offer it as a base for reflection and perhaps even further discussion. The Christian thought-leaders of the war years, faced the future with a mixture of determination and very deep disquiet. They knew that their religious perspective was a minority one, even then. But their age did boast some of the finest Christian poets, writers, theologians, and public intellectuals in the western Christian tradition. That is why a survey of their literary work, given as it was from the storm-tossed deck of 1943, might prove helpful to many in understanding their grandparents' generation, and perhaps even their own.

767. Dante believed that Europe had gone downhill with the loss of Imperial power. Gibbon blamed the tyrannical new Christian religion.

768. Jurjen A. Zeilstra's dissertation *European Unity in Ecumenical Thinking 1937-1948* (Zoetermeer: Uitgeverij Boekencentrum, 1995) tells this part of the story of international forgiveness in great detail.

769. Luke 6:27-29 "But to you who are listening, I say: Love your enemies, do good to those who hate you, bless those who curse you, pray for those who mistreat you. If someone slaps you on one cheek, turn to them the other also. If someone takes your coat, do not withhold your shirt from them."

770. Bideault thought that he was going to draft the document but by leaving the paper in a desk drawer, he accidentally forgot about it.

771. Monnet, Mémoires p.365–366. "La proposition française est donc, dans son inspiration essentiellement politique. Elle a même un aspect pour ainsi dire moral. Dans son essence, elle vise un objectif très simple que notre gouvernement cherchera à réaliser sans se préoccuper, dans une première phase, des difficultés techniques."

772. Like the Konzerne, which helped Adolf Hitler rise to power

773. https://en.wikipedia.org/wiki/European_Coal_and_Steel_Community

774. Since then, the French have undergone a further revolution in energy consumption: 'Nuclear power accounted for 72.3% of total electricity production in 2016, while renewables and fossil fuels accounted for 17.8% and 8.6%, respectively. France has the largest share of nuclear electricity in the world. The country is also among the world's biggest net exporters of electricity.' https://en.wikipedia.org/wiki/Energy_in_France

775. Statistics are drawn from *The Birth of Europe,* Mike Andrews, BBC Books.

776. This was recorded by Georgette Elgey in *La Republique des Contradictions.* (Fayard, Paris.) The incident was witnessed by the State Secretary of Foreign Affairs who saw Schuman visibly moved during the meeting and so asked him about it afterward. The note was written in French, even though Schuman and Adenauer spoke German when together. Schuman, who apparently collected autographs, told his colleague, 'I guard it preciously. You can imagine the importance that a thing like this has addressed from him to me.'

777. The words of his former secretary and later Prime Minister Giulio Andreotti

778. The Treaty establishing the European Defence Community, was an unratified treaty signed on 27 May 1952 by the 'six inner' countries.

779. With regard to militarism, Schuman wrote in *Pour l'Europe*: 'There is no question of Europe becoming a zone of influence to be used by anyone for political, military or economic domination....it has no aggressive intention, it is not invested with any kind of egotistic or imperialist inclination, neither internally nor with re

gard to other countries.' 'The European Community will not reflect the image of an empire or a holy alliance; it will be based on democratic equality applied to relations between nations. The right of veto is incompatible with such a structure, which implies majority decisions and excludes the dictatorial use of material superiority.'

780. In the wake of the French scuttling the EDC, Anthony Eden played a key role in bringing Mendes-France and Adenauer to an agreement. In fact, after a dinner in England, he invited them into the library and waited outside until 3 o'clock in the morning until they reached an agreement about ending the allied occupation and the return of German sovereignty.

781. George Friedman, *Flashpoints – The, Emerging Crisis in Europe* Doubleday p.85

782. These words are from the mouth of poor, old Mr. Sedley in *Vanity Fair,* Thackeray

783. He was ultimately unsuccessful but when President Trump threatened to withdraw NATO support, it was interesting to see President Macron in 2019 drawing closer to Germany and talking again about the need for a European army. NATO is poised between a double threat. On the one hand, the alliance faces a resurgent Russia who is wooing Turkey, and on the other hand, she must suffer the techno-imperialism of China who is picking off NATO countries with strategic partnerships in their ports, steel, and energy sectors.

784. Time Magazine, 25 May 1953

785. Victoria Martin De La Torre, *Europe, A Leap into the Unknown.*

786. Ibid

787. Ibid

788. Ibid

789. Speaking in 1954, Spaak asked, 'Do you really need me to remind you that if you sometimes think differently, you all pray in the same way? And that it is the same gestures which welcome you to life and the same words which console you, calm you as you reach death. We are members of the same civilisation, known as Christian Civilisation.' Source: https://www.bbc.co.uk/worldservice/theneweurope/wk13.htm

790. Bible, Book of Revelation Ch.3 v8

791. Because the final translations from earlier that morning were not complete, some ministers are actually signing beautifully bound folios of blank paper! (Of course, the pages will be filled before ratification.)

792. Victoria Martin De La Torre, *Europe, A Leap into the Unknown.*

793. Javier Solana (former Secretary General of the Council of the European Union, and High Representative of the Common Foreign and Security Policy) wrote this in his forward to Victoria Martin De La Torre's wonderful book, *Europe, A Leap into the Unknown.*

794. Ref: http://news.bbc.co.uk/1/hi/world/europe/3248516.stm

795. Michel J Sentis, *Eveillers de Conscience.* Caux Books, p.94-95

796. *The Schuman Declaration* – 9 May 1950

797. This was a pre-emptive strike to kill half the prisoners in Paris, just in case they might be freed by an advancing Royalist army. Most were petty criminals.

798. *Elegy Written in a Country Churchyard*, by Thomas Gray

799. Alcide de Gasperi's canonisation is at a similar impasse

800. Divine Providence and Miracles: I was cheered to find that the much-lauded (Cambridge) Regius Professor of History Sir Herbert Butterfield was not 'above' admitting divine providence at work in history. He was a specialist in historicism, and also a devout and life-long Methodist from humble, Yorkshire origins.

801. *Robert Schuman* by Robert de Rochefort (Editions du Cerf, Paris 1968) p.87

802. *Pour une éducation Européene à Bruxelles*, Avril 1956,

803. That is 20% more people than the British Empire in less than a third of the geographical area

804. That is not to gloss over the many bureaucratic failures and instances of corruption, such as those exposed by Paul van Buitenen. (He was the office worker at the European Commissiontale who exposed corruption and cronyism involving Former French Premier, Edith Cresson, which eventually led to the resignation of the Jacques Santer's European Commission in 1999. At great personal cost Van Buitenen battled on until 2009, uncovering many instances of corruption in EU-institutions, which had all been ignored by the EU anti-fraud department OLAF.)

805. The question asked was "Do you consider yourself to be...?" With a card showing the categories above and others like Sikh, Buddhist, Hindu which did not reach the 1% threshold. Discrimination in the EU 2012, p. 233, 2012, archived on 2 December 2012, retrieved 14 August 2013. https://ec.europa.eu/commfrontoffice/publicopinion/archives/ebs/ebs_393_en.pdf

806. George Friedman, *Flashpoints – The Emerging Crisis in Europe*, Doubleday p.227

807. Not actually the official lyrics yet, they were written by Austrian Professor Peter Roland of the Europa Academy in Vienna, who presented them to European Commission President Romano Prodi.

808. From Part II of Maritain's lecture, *What is Man?* Ref: https://maritain.nd.edu/jmc/jm502.htm

809. Jacques Maritain, *Christianity and Democracy and The Rights of Man and Natural Law*

810. T.S Eliot wrote in *"The Idea of a Christian Society"* (1939 Faber and Faber Ltd.) that "... Liberalism may be a tendency towards something very different from itself, is a possibility in its nature. For it is something which tends to release energy rather than accumulate it, to relax rather than to fortify. It is a movement not so much defined by its end, as by its starting point; away from, rather than towards, something definite... Liberalism can prepare the way for that which is its negation: the artificial, mechanised or brutalised control which is a desperate remedy for its chaos." P.15-16

811. Thierry CHOPIN & Lukáš MACEK. European Issues n°479 02nd July 2018. *'In the face of the European Union's political crisis: the vital cultural struggle over values.'* https://www.robert-schuman.eu/en/doc/questions-d-europe/qe-479-en.pdf

812. Cf. Hassner, Pierre (2015), *La transition autocratique en Russie*, in La revanche des passions, Fayard,

813. Like this phrase from Isaiah 51.1, the theme of returning to orthodoxy is a key theme for the Hebrew prophets.

814. Robert Schuman, *Pour l'Europe*

815. Discrimination is not unusual, nor even hid from plain sight. For example, the Italian politician Rocco Buttiglione was explicitly disqualified from being Commissioner of Justice because he was a Christian, even though he had taken pains to stress that he would uphold the current law without prejudice. He could have been almost anything else with regards to gender, sexuality, or political leaning, and never had his integrity questioned. Yet for being a Christian, no number of assurances he might give were admissible.

816. T. S. Eliot, *On Poetry and Poets* p.10

Jean Monnet - international networker and political impresario par excellence

CHAPTER 19

Unexploded Bombs from the Spring of 1943

CHAPTER SUMMARY: Bonhoeffer's letter and challenge. T. S Elliot's *Four Quartets*. Maritain's Yale lectures, *'Education at the Crossroads'*. Auden's lecture, *'Vocation and Society'*. C.S. Lewis' Newcastle lectures and wartime Broadcasts. Simone Weil's life and book, *Enracinement* (Rootedness). Oldam's Moot, UK. Mortimer Adler at Chicago University, and the defence of democracy. Henri de Lubac, *The Drama of Atheist Humanism*. Charles Norris Cochrane's *'Christianity and Culture'* and Auden's response. Eliot's *Christianity and Culture* and *The Social Function of Poetry*. Jacques Ellul, *Présence au monde moderne: Problèmes de la civilisation post-chrétienne*. Auden and the conquest of Apollo. Sartre, Foucault, and Nietzsche's tarantula. The sins of the political left and the right. Caesar's last fear and the final flight of Hegel's Owl of Minerva.

'The dead are invisible, not absent.'

Saint Augustine of Hippo (354-430)

In one of his wartime lectures, T. S. Eliot wrote that if a country cannot 'go on producing great authors, and especially great poets, their culture will deteriorate and perhaps be absorbed by a stronger one.'[817] He had believed that the crucible of wartime was precisely the moment for a culture to hammer out its first principles. War stripped away the enchantments and focused the minds of a complacent society.

All momentous events bring out the deepest reflections from us, exerting pressure on the human spirit and calling for authentic solutions. Simply put, 'great necessity calls out great virtue.'[818] When the luxury of an unreflective life, and passivity, is no longer an option; we cast our intellectual and imaginative eye about us in search of meaning, in search of strength, in search of roots. Using the analogy from the end of the last chapter we might say this, no one ties themselves to a mast, or even thinks too much about the mast, when there is no storm. But when the storm strikes, the search for security and hope is redoubled.

As the great events of the War progressed, and especially as its outcome became increasingly clear, numerous voices could be heard from all sides, each attempting to influence the post-war settlement. In political thought, a crop of enormously influential texts appeared: the UK alone saw the Beveridge Report (November 1942) which led directly to the Welfare State and arguably the Labour victory in 1945. At the other pole, there was Hayek's *The Road to Serfdom* (March 1944) which would become a textbook for neo-liberal economics throughout Europe. But in this chapter, I wish to hone in on the Christian imaginative and intellectual contribution given at this significant moment, with the hopes that it might be a means of inspiration, reflection, and perhaps even further discussion.

In the spring of 1943, by some strange providence, a remarkable number of Christian intellectuals in the west spoke powerfully, even prophetically, to the rising powers of the post-war age, much as Columbanus had spoken to emerging powers which had arisen on the rubble of the post-Roman 'dark age'. This chapter attempts to capture a sample of these currents of Christian thought as embattled Europeans began to look to the future. I am particularly indebted to Baylor's Auden scholar Alan Jacobs for his excellent book *The Year of Our Lord 1943*, for it seems to pinpoint this pivotal moment with particular power and insight.

1943 was the year when Schuman was in hiding, probably somewhere between the abbey of Notre-Dame des Neiges (where he had been reading Shakespeare in English) and the shrine of La Sallette high in the Alps, where he studied Aquinas, in preparation for the real battle; the years of reconstruction that he knew would soon come.

1943 was also the year that De Gasperi was thinking ahead to reconstruction in Italy. For it was in January that he published "Ideas for Reconstruction" (*Idee Ricostruttive*). In secret, he was preparing a new generation of leaders. The Mussolini years had run their desperate course, after nearly a quarter century, and Italy needed to be ready to rebuild.

Over in Berlin on New Year's Day, 1943, Dietrich Bonhoeffer was looking back over a decade of Hitler's rule. 'We have been the silent witnesses to evil deeds,' he writes. 'The great masquerade of evil has played havoc with all our ethical concepts. For evil to appear disguised as light, charity, historical necessity, or social justice is quite bewildering...' Bonhoeffer would have more time to think and write about this when he was arrested later that spring.

And before his own execution two years later, he would ask; 'Who stands fast?' At the end of the day, what sort of person can stand strong against such deceptive evil? That was the big question for his generation, and for all generations. His answer was surprising. 'Only the man whose final standard is not his reason, his principles, his conscience, his freedom, or his virtue, but who is ready to sacrifice all this when, in relation to God alone, he is called to obedient and responsible action.'[819]

Bonhoeffer was engaged on 13th January (a marriage never to be) the day before the Allied powers met in North Africa. The Casablanca Conference (14th – 24th January) was ostensibly to coordinate Allied action for the remainder of the war. It was a watershed, and now the balance of history's greatest conflict had tipped in favour of an allied victory. The

Americans had come. 'So, we will win after all', Churchill said when he got the news that Hitler had declared war on America. But victory gave rise to some obvious questions. If we are not to be overcome by force, and if civilisation is to be given one last reprieve, then what lessons should be learnt from the cultural malaise that led us to war? Indeed, *how should we then live?* How should we educate the next generation, so they don't repeat the errors of their parents and grandparents' generation?

In London at exactly the same time, in January 1943, T. S. Eliot was completing the last of his *Four Quartets* and beginning his January and February essays called *The Definition of Culture*. Eliot felt the need to explore these very questions and, moreover, he correctly understood, they must be done now because, '...we cannot afford to defer our constructive thinking to the conclusion of hostilities – a moment when, as we should know from experience, good counsel is liable to be obscured.'[820]

It was on the opening day of the Casablanca conference, though a few thousand miles away at Yale University, that the French Catholic Philosopher Jacques Maritain was giving the first of his four Terry Lectures, *'Education at the Crossroads.'* The same questions about education that were troubling Eliot, were on his mind. He tells the students gathered, that the beginning and ground of education is an answer to the question, *'What is the nature and the destiny of man?'* It cannot be escaped, he said, and it cannot be a question answered by science, as the modern technocrat would like. For that would lead to a 'spurious metaphysics disguised as science ...in which education loses all human sense or becomes the training of an animal for the utility of the state.'[821]

Like a new de Tocqueville, this émigré Frenchman was only too aware of the big state operating beyond its competence. 'The state would summon education to... compensate for all the deficiencies in civil society' and thus become 'uniquely dependant on the management of the state.' The result of this interference in education would be that 'instead of a genuine personality, sealed with the mysterious face of its creator, there [would appear] ... a mask, that of the conventional man or that of the rubber-stamped conscience, incorporated.'[822] Such a technocratic approach to moral education would leave 'human life with nothing but relationships of force, or at best those of pleasure' and necessarily lead to 'a philosophy of domination. A technocratic society is but a totalitarian one.' And this deep disquiet was not only felt and explored by Christian thinkers, but was also part of a wider self-reflection occurring within European culture. (For example, Adorno and Horkheimer's *Dialectic of Enlightenment*, concluded that 'Enlightenment [itself] is totalitarian.' Like Edmund Burke, they said that the rule of ideas leads to ideology.)

The next day, on 15th January, W. H. Auden, who had only recently returned to Christian faith, delivered a lecture at Swarthmore College on 'Vocation and Society.' The poet was wrestling with similar issues, and attempting to help the students secure meaningful and responsible futures.

At the same time, back across the Atlantic in Oxford, C. S. Lewis was (like Maritain) drafting his notes for similar lectures. These lectures would be given at Newcastle University and eventually become his book, '*The Abolition of Man*'. The analysis of a progressive education cut loose from 'objective value,' and overseen by, what he calls *scientific conditioners of an omnicompetent state*, was damning in the extreme. Lewis traced technological modernity further back than Maritain; and by twinning scientism and technocracy, he sought to show with these four lectures, not just its deep roots, but also its dark end point. Like Maritain, Lewis foresaw the remaking of conscience, the abolition of norms that had held for millennia and then the swift road to tyranny. Again, it was not a uniquely Christian observation. Others, like Aldous Huxley gave warning of a possible dystopia in his 1932 book, 'Brave New World'.

At the same moment in 1943, another extraordinary French émigré called Simone Weil was writing her most famous book *The Need for Roots* (*Enracinement* – Rootedness) in London. It addressed the past and future of France. She painstakingly analysed the spiritual and ethical milieu that led to France's defeat by Germany, and then faced the issues that would arise after the Allied victory. 'If we are only saved by

American money and machines,' she wrote, 'we shall fall back, one way or another, into a servitude like the one which we now suffer.'[823]

Also in England in 1943, a less conspicuous gathering of Christian minds assembled at, what became known as, 'Oldham's Moot.' (They actually met for weekend residential house parties a few times a year between 1938 and 1947) Convened by an ecumenically minded, retired, missionary called J. H. Oldham, this quasi-Christian think-tank also focused on the problem of post-war reconstruction. Regular members included John Baillie, Fred Clarke, T. S. Eliot, Eric Fenn, Herbert Arthur Hodges, Eleonora Iredale, Karl Mannheim, Walter Moberly, John Middleton Murry, Mary Oldham, Gilbert Shaw and Alec Vidler. C. S. Lewis never attended but was called on to send papers for discussion.

All this might strike the modern reader as an almost hysterical outpouring of Christian thought until one realises just how sharply war focuses those issues that had hitherto been obscure. In the preface of her 1943 book *Darkness Over Germany*, Amy Buller wrote that she had deliberately recorded conversations with young Germans to highlight for those involved in post war cultural formation 'the full significance of the tragedy of a whole generation of German youth who, having no faith, made Nazism their religion.' This was exactly what happened to the philosopher Martin Heidegger.

Buller blamed not just the capitulation of ecclesiastical institutions but also the *complicity of universities*. She also acknowledged, as did the historian Christopher Dawson, that the problems facing Europe were hundreds of years in the making. Something had gone culturally awry, which meant that – in the words C. S. Lewis used in his 1941 BBC broadcasts – that 'real progress' at this point of history meant 'doing an about turn and walking back to the right road.'[824] And moreover 'the man who turns back soonest is the most progressive man.' In 1941, Lewis too, acknowledged that the present concerns went deeper than Mussolini, Stalin and Hitler. He described it in terms of a cultural bewitching and that we needed 'the strongest spell that can be found to wake us from the evil enchantment of worldliness which has been laid upon us for nearly a hundred years.'[825] This was indeed, as Mark Greif put in the title of his book, '*The Age of the Crisis of Man.*'

Some years earlier, in September 9-11th, 1940, Judeo-Christian thinkers had gathered at the Jewish Theological Seminary, New York, to give papers in response to the spectre of totalitarianism. The organisers hoped the conference would 'serve as the first step toward a more general project, looking to the integration of Science, Philosophy and Religion.' Maritain told the organisers that they should only really invite people who had a substantial religious viewpoint to ground their work. He was quite certain that democracy without Judeo-Christian underpinnings would collapse under its own weight – it was not self-sustaining.

Two men that emerged from the conference were Mortimer Adler and Robert Maynard Hutchins of Chicago University, and later its President. Adler told the conference that democracy had 'much more to fear from its teachers than the nihilism of Hitler.' For Adler it was the double pincer of *positivism* in the sciences that had rotted the universities; and *pragmatism* beyond the campus that rotted society from the inside out. He believed that both these 'isms' grew in the soils of moral relativism. If absolute moral truth could not be obtained by humanity, then these perversions were the result. Hutchins wrote, 'Is democracy a good form of government? Is it worth dying for? Is the United States a democracy? If we are to prepare to defend democracy, we must be able to answer these questions.' He also wrote, 'Our ability to answer them is more important than the quantity or quality of airplanes, bombs, tanks, flamethrowers and miscellaneous munitions that we can hurl at the enemy.'[826]

Nazism needed a comprehensive opposing system to face it. But not everyone thought Christianity was desirable. Many, for example, after the loss of their faith, opted for a Deweyan pragmatism – an elevation of democracy itself as philosophically self-sustaining and sufficient to meet the threat.[827] But philosophers like Sidney Hook went further, saying that in his view Christianity was even inimical to democracy. But pragmatism itself settles no claim between democracy and totalitarianism. Indeed, as C. S. Lewis would argue, pragmatism would more easily refit human psychology for totalitarianism. For Hutchinson, who had been a law professor, only a rationally defensible moral view of justice and ethics could withstand the totalitarianism engulfing the old world. Dewey accused Hutchins that, through his 'distrust of freedom' and 'appeal to some fixed authority,' he was smuggling in a premodern, undemocratic system. But Hutchins, though the son of a Presbyterian minister, was never explicitly Christian in style or content. Neither was Adler (mentioned above), who was Jewish by birth and only came to Christian conversion decades later.

Back in Europe their argument was echoed and magnified. The French philosopher Paul Ricœur also asserted that anthropogenic humanism – what he called '*the cult of humanity*' – could mount no coherent epistemic defence against Communism or National Socialism. Going one step further the Jesuit theologian Henri de Lubac argued, in *The Drama of Atheist Humanism*, Nazism was actually secular humanism's direct result and logical expression.[828] For Paul Ricœur, a French protestant of the Huguenot stripe, there remained only 'two pure positions; the *pure atheist* position, and the *pure Christian* position.' The 'pure' Christian position for Maritain was, what he termed, an *integral humanism*[829] based on his reading of Aquinas.

Maritain contended that secular humanism had done a great disservice to both God and man by robbing both of their focus and power. In one illustration about medieval art, Maritain wrote that 'man created more beautiful things in those days, and he adored himself less. The blessed humility in which the artist was placed exalted his strength and freedom.' For some neo-Thomists, Aquinas represented the perfect balance between reason and revelation. Other traditions had trumped one over the other; Augustine was over-reliant on revelation, the Averroes were over-reliant on reason, but Aquinas had both in the right degree. This is vastly simplistic, but enough for us here. Schuman, Adenauer, and De Gasperi were nourished to a great extent from this root but it must be noted that this was not the only root available in the Christian tradition.

For example, Simone Weil, who never quite became a Catholic, wrote that humanism *per se* was not something that ought to be reclaimed by Christians at all. Rather it was 'a development of poisons internal to Christianity'[830] and had to be disregarded. For her, any movement that placed human beings at the centre of their own narratives was itself a symptom of the poison and a principal cause of all the madness. Her emphasis, and one that would chime more easily with Frank Buchman's message, was for Christ to 'take possession' of individuals – as she believed had happened to her – and for him to form the interior centre.[831]

Weil was about as morally serious a person as it is possible to be. Even from a very young age she identified with the suffering. Aged five she had refused any more sugar than could be had by the soldiers on the Western Front. Simone de Beauvoir said that she 'envied her for having a heart that could beat right across the world.'[832] André Gide declared her "the most spiritual writer of this century', and Albert Camus called her 'the only great spirit of our times.'[833] She was one of those Jewish French émigrés in London working for the French Resistance and trying to convince Charles de Gaulle (who thought she was mad) and Roosevelt (by petitioning him through Maritain) to form an order of nurses who would serve at the front lines. Her family was Jewish but secular, and she grew to be left-leaning – fighting in the Spanish Civil War – but was never a Marxist. (She once held her own against Trotsky in debate.)

When she did eventually come to Christian faith, she found it hard to embrace the institutional church, indeed any structure that utilised force. And though she kept up a correspondence with a priest called Father Perrin, she was never actually baptised into any denomination. In fact, her internal debate about this issue of church membership led her to reach out further and further until she had formulated an almost fully realised political philosophy. She understood that the church must manifest itself as a social institution, but was equally convinced that, out of love *for the church*, her place should be outside it in a prophetic role.

She says she did this not out of personal aloofness or Olympian virtue, but almost on the contrary. She actually feared that she was too susceptible in social situations, so easily led that she would lose all critical distance and be of no service whatever.[834] This perhaps is what she suspected in Maritain, and why in her opinion, he did not go far enough. In the place of the suffering Messiah, institutional Christianity had embraced worldly power – Jupiter not Jesus. 'The Roman conception of God still exists today, even in such minds as Maritain.' He, like so many, looked back only to the scholastics, and the great era of gothic art. She looked further back, to the heroic age of Christianity as a persecuted faith, caring for the poor and marginal of the Empire.

She saw the era of scholastic philosophy as itself suspect because it marked some of the church's darkest dalliance with force. The early 13th-century Albigensian crusade was an unpardonable war crime, the 'murder' of an entire country in name of – what she called – 'totalitarian spirituality'. It also, in her reading, put an end to the Romanesque era (10-11th centuries) which for her was 'the true Renaissance'. 'The Greek spirit was reborn in the Christian form which is its truth.'[835] The greatest tragedy in Weil's view was that by this 'unconditional subjection of the mind to external authority' a worldly church had rendered 'impossible that mutual penetration of the religious and the profane which would be the essence of Christianity.'[836] The various subsequent humanist movements (the Renaissance, the Enlightenment, and *la Révolution*) were, in her view, the understandable – if misguided – revolts of people trying to escape 'the imposition of belief' by force – to undo the 'spiritual totalitarianism.'[837]

In a like manner, she saw that the force that threatened the church, and the whole of civilisation in her day, was nothing more than the boomerang of historical causality. In the 13th century, the church allied itself with expansionist state power to achieve something useful for each by genocide. France absorbed the Languedoc and the church obliterated the Cathars. It was a devil's bargain, a contract with power, which turned the Bride of Christ into 'the social beast' that 'alone possesses force.' The church had sowed to the winds and now all Europe would reap the whirlwind. Of course, she was no lone prophet crying in the wilderness. Many other Christians were acutely aware of the Gospel critique of power and the difficulties it posed to those involved in education and political action.

W. H. Auden is just one example. A work that shaped Auden's thinking with regards to religion and earthly power was Charles Norris Cochrane's 1940 book *'Christianity and Culture: A Study of Thought and Action from Augustus to Augustine.'* In a review of the book, Auden warned of the dangers of 'a new Constantinism' emerging in the current crisis, evidenced by letters in the press calling for 'religious instruction in schools as a cure for juvenile delinquency.' For Auden, the book's 'terrifying description of the "Christian" empire under Theodosius should discourage such hopes of using Christianity as a spiritual Benzedrine[838] for the earthly city.'

In Cochrane's language, Constantine 'both professed and practiced the religion of success'[839] and his Christianity was in essence little more than a 'talisman' that ensured the renewal of the state – the *Romanitas*. It was a synthesis that failed. Either Yahweh wasn't God after all, or else He wouldn't be co-opted by such a system. Auden understood that any 'programme of Christian social renewal' would face 'its own dangers and temptations – and its own characteristic illusions.' In part of his poem 'For the Time Being' – which marks his return to Christian faith with all its historical and political implications - Auden imagines Herod as a 60-year-old, rationalist technocrat reflecting back on a 20-year career of social reform.

Herod muses over his modest achievements; 'the darkness has been pushed back a few inches,' but, alas, there are still people who believe in witches and there still isn't 'a single town where a good bookshop would pay.' It is satirical, which for Auden usually means he is in earnest. And it reminds one of Dostoyevsky's *Grand Inquisitor*. What does Auden's Herod most fear? Why must this news from Bethlehem be stamped out? It is certainly not because it hails a 'spiritual Benzedrine for the earthly city' but rather because it signals the beginning of the end of the earthly city at its core – the *Romanitas* – altogether. It signals the final demise of everything they call power and order. This is what, after all, the Devil offers Jesus in the wilderness in exchange for worship – and

Jesus flatly refuses. And it is this paradigm shift that Auden presents. Therefore, the God-baby must be killed.

'The child marks the end of the machine, the end of the military-industrial complex, the end of force.'[840]

After 1943, Eliot's literary contribution, and perhaps even his hopes for the sort of change sought, seemed to dissipate. His *Notes toward the Definition of a Christian Culture*, published in that year, was a final literary wave[841] breaking on a cultural shore that would appear less and less what he had imagined it could be.

Education was a key area of concern. Like Lewis, Weil, and Maritain; Eliot believed that one of the purposes of education was to produce the *ordo amoris* – that is, to aid the development of correct emotional responses before looking to the rational faculties. Lewis speaks at length of this in the first chapter of *The Abolition of Man*. He touches on Augustine's *Ordo Amoris*, but also that of Plato and other ancients' emphasis to 'inculcate just sentiment' in the younger generation.

Where Eliot differed from the others is that he insisted that this should be a lifelong training. And he feared that the post-war world would not be able to achieve this. He could already see that a new West was being unified not with the golden threads of Latin, but with the steel of scientism and technocracy. This he feared, as did Lewis, would be the thread that would undo all threads of genuinely rich culture. In *The Man of Letters and the Future of Europe* he described the technocrat as having an 'engineering mind' that could not comprehend what culture is, but is nevertheless in a hurry to tidy it up as efficiently as possible. This is pertinent at the national level, but of course even more so when applied to the international and global order.

True, rich culture, in Eliot's mind, could not flourish in either 'a complete and universal uniformity, nor in an isolated self-sufficiency.' But above all, Eliot wrote, 'uniformity means the obliteration of culture, and self-sufficiency means its death by starvation.'[842] He envisioned a homogenising technocracy that would destroy what it could not understand. For the engineering mind, 'the union of local cultures in a general culture is more difficult to conceive, and more difficult to realise.'

Eliot, often accused of vagueness in his prescriptions for a Christian society, nevertheless had a deep foreboding about the sort of cultural deterioration from which none could recover. 'What I am apprehensive of is death...that the feeling for poetry, the feelings which are the materials of poetry may disappear forever.' C. S. Lewis prophesied something very similar in *The Abolition of Man*. He called the subjects of these social experiments 'Men without Chests,' that is, not fully human in the old sense. This perhaps is the most frightening and penetrating analysis of all, because a culture undergoing this slow dehumanising anaesthesia would not be aware of it. (And, by implication, nor would our own culture if we had been subject to such forces, unless we were armoured with history, philosophy and theology.) Eliot believed that people in such a society would be willing 'to facilitate that unification of the world' which he already knew that 'some people consider desirable for its own sake.'[843] Eliot would be a delegate at the 1948 Congress of The Hague, described in chapter 13, but even back in 1943, he was aware of the difficulties of the pan European movement.

'I have suggested that the cultural health of Europe, including the cultural health of its constituent parts, is incompatible with extreme forms of both nationalism and internationalism. But the cause of that disease, which destroys the very soil in which culture has its roots, is not so much extreme ideas... as the relentless pressure of modern industrialism setting problems which the extreme ideas attempt to solve. ...the effect of industrialism is that we become mechanised in mind, and consequently attempt to provide solutions in terms of *engineering*, for problems which are essentially problems of *life*.'[844]

One can almost hear Eliot's concerns in Auden's words as if it each had foreseen a post-Maastricht Europe:

'That machine has now destroyed
The customs we enjoyed,
Replaced the bonds of blood and nation,
By personal confederation.
To judge our means and plan our ends...'

If Eliot's output and influence in regard to these matters were in decline at the war's close, nothing could have been more different for Maritain, who found himself rocketing to prominence as De Gaulle's ambassador to the Vatican and gaining a major influence in the developing and drafting of the *Universal Declaration of Human Rights*. Into this functional document of European identity, Maritain was able to insert the premises of his Christian *personalism*.[845] It allowed a largely post-Christian society, to enjoy the fruit *if not the root* of Christian suppositions. The coming decades would soon see the benefit of this, but also the growing incongruities. These were anticipated almost prophetically by Simone Weil, who wrote,

'The notions of the obligations come before that of rights, which are subordinate and relative to the former. A right is not effectual by itself, but only in relation to the obligation to which it corresponds, the effective exercise of a right springing not from the individual who possesses it, but from the other men who consider themselves as being under a certain obligation makes it effectual. An obligation that goes unrecognised by anybody loses none of the full force of its existence. A right which goes unrecognised by anybody is not worth very much.' [846]

This idea of the technological society, the new submission to Aristotle's *techne* or technique, was also articulated well by the philosopher Jacques Ellul. In his earlier years Ellul had been a prolific Marxist exegete steeped in French secularism. He described his father as Voltairean – but he himself had undergone, what he described as, 'a very brutal and very sudden conversion' to Christianity, in 1932. Significantly he had been alone in a house translating *Faust* (the man who made a devil's bargain, exchanging power for his own soul) when he experienced a transcendent power which had entered the very centre of his being. It was so profound and shocking that he fled the house on a bike, concluding only later that he had been in the presence of God.[847]

In 1940, Ellul lost his chair as a professor of Roman law at Strasbourg, for denouncing both the Nazis and the Vichy government. He lived hand to mouth in the south of France during the war, working for the Resistance and pastoring a small church. After the war, he became deputy mayor of Bordeaux and began to think deeply about what the Christian presence should be in a post-Christian world. (The title of his 1948 book was *Présence au monde moderne: Problèmes de la civilisation post-chrétienne.*)[848]

Like the other Christian thinkers, Ellul thought deeply about the difficulties of post-war Europe. 'In our technological society, technique is the totality of methods rationally arrived at and having absolute efficiency (for a given stage of development) in every field of human activity.'[849] His concern was that modern technology had and would increasingly 'become a total phenomenon for civilization, the defining force of a new social order in which efficiency is no longer an option but a necessity imposed on all human activity.'[850] And, in a language very similar to Lewis, about the 'scientific conditioners' in *The Abolition of Man*, Ellul wrote that 'not even the moral conversion of the technicians could make a difference. At best, they would cease to be good technicians. In the end, technique has only one principle, efficient ordering.[851]

In a strange way, the two writers form a pair, Ellul emphasising the failure of Christendom that had created a warped binary in modernity, and Lewis emphasising the impotence of an Enlightenment kidnapped by secular ideology. (In his *Pilgrim's Regress,* which is an allegorical journey through Western Philosophy, Lewis takes pains to show how the various streams of Enlightenment expression swelled both the capitalist and socialist ranks. It was published in 1933, just before the election of Hitler, and one cannot read without a shudder, that section where old

Mr. Sensible's servant Drudge throws in his lot with Savage's dwarfs in the northern mountains. Savage represents not just the cruel race theorists – the Nazis, Japanese, or Fascists – but also their enemies the Marxists. Lewis saw them all in the same mountain, not really human in the old sense, and all craving for human blood. It proved to be chillingly prophetic.

But even after these ideologies were stamped out in the main, there remained not just their seeds within European life, but also the techniques they had developed. An example of the barbarians within the frontiers can be seen when Auden confronted his publisher in an incident that has a strangely prescient ring to it. When Random House removed Ezra Pound's poems from their poetry anthology, because he had endorsed fascism, Auden threatened to sever his connection with them. Auden didn't care for Pound's poems or his politics but he objected to the *totalitarian principal* that had led the publisher into this error. In the age of no-platforming and crucifixion-by-twitter, of statue- smashing and building renaming, it has an all too familiar ring. In a letter to the publisher about it, he said,

> *'...the war is not over. The incident is only one sign... that there was more truth than one would like to believe in Huey Long's cynical observation that if fascism came to America it would be called Antifascism. Needless to say, I am not suggesting that you desire any such thing – but I think your very natural abhorrence to Pound's conduct has led you to take the first step which, if not protested now, will be followed by others which will horrify you.'*

Auden feared that the great victory (achieved through the military-industrial complex with all its technocratic excellences) would not be content to be just a temporary saviour, but would itself become a guiding ideal. He cast this as 'the other war' between the sons of Apollo (the rational technocrats) and the 'unpolitical sons of Hermes', whom he describes as the god 'of our dreams.' Auden saw that, following the necessities of war 'that made Apollo welcome to the throne', Apollo's sons would thenceforth never be content to achieve competency merely in their own sphere.

> *'But jealous of our god of dreams,*
> *His common-sense in secret schemes*
> *To rule the heart:*
> *Unable to invent the lyre,*
> *Creates with simulated fire*
> *Official art.'*[852]

Apollo's sons will not outlaw Hermes but will put his sons to work to produce the 'simulated fire' of 'Official art'. Apollo's final conquest, and the death of real mankind, would be 'when he occupies a college,' and 'Truth is replaced by useful Knowledge.' This 'continuing war' was encapsulated in a letter Auden wrote to a friend after meeting James Bryant Conant, the new president of Harvard, and a man with political reach,[853] who embodied the Apollonian position perfectly. Auden remarked that he felt like 'Falstaff the fool' confronting 'the prig Prince Hal.' Conant gave him 'the notion of sheer naked power.' '"This is the real enemy' I thought to myself. And I'm sure he had the same impression about me."

Writing against the tide in 1943: W. H. Auden, Jacques Maritain, and Simone Weil

In 1943, precisely as the tide of war was turning, the historian Christopher Dawson, like Auden, was summing up his deep sense of foreboding: (It is a quote that we have already read in Chapter 15) In his book, *The Year of Our Lord 1943*, Alan Jacobs gives almost a lament for the unheeded Christian philosophers of that generation. His words below will serve as a full-stop for this chapter, and also as a comma for the next, as we travel forward 70 years to the present day and consider how we have fared in the Europe they bequeathed to us.

> *'It is no wonder that having spent the years of the war narrating, dramatizing, and arguing for a richly humane model of personal and cultural formation, they all – save Weil, lying in her grave in Kent – turned to other matters: Maritain to his human rights work and then to aesthetics, Eliot to the theatre, Lewis to the children's books that would win him his greatest and most lasting fame, Auden to his theology of the inarticulate human body and his hopes of becoming 'a minor Atlantic Goethe.' In some ways the opportune time, the kairos moment for Christian cultural renewal, had passed. When the clocks were reset at Stund Null, it was technique that proved adequate to that challenge.... Each of the writers.... Worked with astonishing energy to rescue their world for a deeply thoughtful, culturally rich Christianity, and to rescue that Christianity for their world.'*
>
> *'Their diagnostic powers were great indeed: they saw with uncanny clarity, and exposed with incisive intelligence, the means by which technocracy had arisen and the damage it had inflicted and would continue to inflict, on human persons. Few subsequent critiques of 'the technological society' rival theirs in imagination or moral seriousness. But their prescriptions were never implemented, and could never have been: they came a century too late, after the reign of technocracy had become too complete that none can foresee the end of it while this world lasts.'* [855]

CHAPTER 19
FOOTNOTES & REFERENCES

817. America's second First Lady, the remarkable Abigail Adams.

818. Dietrich Bonhoeffer, *Letters and Papers from Prison*. enl. ed. (New York: Macmillan, 1972)

819. T. S. Eliot, *Christianity and Culture*, p.51

820. Jacques Maritain, Lecture 1 of the Terry Lectures, *Education at the Crossroads*.

821. Maritain, *Education at the Crossroads*, p.51

822. Weil, *A War of Religions, Selected Essays*, p.218

823. C. S. Lewis, *Mere Christianity*

824. C. S. Lewis, *The Weight of Glory*, p.31

825. Hutchins, *What shall we Defend? Are we losing our moral principles?*

826. A slightly later but very influential example of this would be Richard Rorty (1931-2007)

827. De Lubac was demoted and silenced for teaching that Catholic Thomism wasn't really Thomism. His daring challenge to the Vatican was completely vindicated at Vatican II, with subsequent popes honouring him. His was a story of confrontation, suppression, and vindication which chimes well with the heroes in this book.

828. For readers wishing to go further, Dr. Alan Fimister (quoted twice earlier) has recently co-authored a book on the subject *'Integralism - A Manual of Political Philosophy'*. EDITIONES SCHOLASTICAE (30 Mar. 2020)

829. Simone Weil, *Gravity and Grace*. P.163

830. T. S. Eliot, perhaps sensing an ambiguity in term Humanism, effectively abandons its use around the time of his conversion to Christianity. C. S. Lewis, as a scholar of early modern literature, similarly does not use the term.

831. Simone de Beauvoir, *Memoirs of a Dutiful Daughter*, 1958 p.239 (published in French as Mémoires d'une jeune fille rangée, p. 236-7)

832. John Hellman (1983). *Simone Weil: An Introduction to Her Thought*. Wilfrid Laurier University Press. pp. 1–23.

833. Auden was aware of this same weakness. He admitted that while listening to Hitler's speech that it 'was a positive revelation to me how while the speech lasts it is impossible not to waver a little.' After he gave a political speech in 1939 to raise money for refugees of the Spanish Civil War he wrote, 'I suddenly thought I could really do it, that I could make a fighting demagogic speech and have the audience roaring. I just felt covered with dirt afterwards.'" (Auden in Smith, 2004, p. 2).

834. Simone Weil, *Selected Essays, 1934–1943: Historical, Political, and Moral Writings*. P.47

835. Simone Weil, *The Need for Roots: Prelude to a Declaration of Duties Towards Mankind*. P.292

836. During this same period, the Dutch, neo-Calvinist philosopher Herman Dooyeweerd was exploring similar themes in his Roots of Western Culture.

837. It is a curious term he uses and quite apt, for when I looked it up, I found that Benzedrine is the stimulant very much in demand in our own time to counter the epidemics of obesity and ADHD.

838. Charles Norris Cochrane's *'Christianity and Culture: A Study of Thought and Action from Augustus to Augustine.'* 1940 p.235

839. Alan Jacobs *'The Year of Our Lord 1943'* p.85

840. His book *The Idea of a Christian Society,* was in fact a collection of much earlier lectures from 1939.

841. T.S. Eliot, *The Man of Letters and the Future of Europe* Originally appeared in *The Norseman* (July-August 1944) and reprinted in The Sewanee Review, Volume 53, 1945.

842. Russel Kirk, *Eliot and His Age: T.S. Eliot's Moral Imagination in the Twentieth Century,* 2008. P.285

843. T.S. Eliot, *The Man of Letters and the Future of Europe* (1944) in G de Huszar (ed.), The Intellectuals (Illinois 1960) p.258

844. This is covered at length in Samuel Moyn's, *Christian Human Rights, A moral history of the West,* 2015. In it, he mentions how Emanuel Mounier and later, Jacques Maritain articulated a concept of personalism that seemed to lead the West on a path out of the vortex of the totalitarian ideologies and also the slough of Romantic individualism. The manifesto was Maritain's *Integral Humanism.* But it was also present in the *Enracinement* of Weil and the counterpoints offered by Lewis in *The Hideous Strength.*

845. Simone Weil, *The Need for Roots: Prelude to a Declaration of Duties Towards Mankind* p.3

846. Patrick Troude-Chastenet, *On Religion, Technology, Politics: Conversations,* (1998) France, Joan Mendes transl., Scholars Press.

847. The publisher: Geneva: Roulet, 1948. Lausanne: Presses Bibliques Universitaires, 1988.

848. Ellul, Jacques, (1964). *The Technological Society.* New York: Vintage Books. pp. xxv. ISBN 9780394703909.

849. Fasching, Darrell (1981), *The Thought of Jacques Ellul: A Systematic Exposition,* Edwin Mellen Press, p. 17.

850. Ellul 1964, p. 79.

851. W. H. Auden, *Under Which Lyre,* (Phi Beta Kappa Poem, Harvard, 1946)

852. Auden suspected Conant's influence was decisive for Trueman, when America dropped the atomic bombs on the Japanese.

853. Christopher Dawson's *The Judgment of the Nations* (1942)

854. Alan Jacobs, *The Year of Our Lord 1943: Christian Humanism in an Age of Crisis,* p.206

855. Jacques Maritain, *Christianity and Democracy and The Rights of Man and Natural Law*

EPILOGUE - Soul Searching

CHAPTER SUMMARY - INTRODUCTION: THE LOOMING CRISIS - The three legs of European stability under threat. 1. OUR GREAT QUEST FOR THE SOUL OF EUROPE - the historical quest for the soul of Western Europe, and its failure. 2. BECOMING LES PERSONNES DES FRONTIÈRES - The call for Christians to engage constructively in culture *and to* resist the siren call of a pseudo-Christian populism. 3. MAKING LESSING'S DITCH LESS UGLY – Re-issue of Schuman's challenge that European integration could not survive if it was solely 'an economic and technical exercise.' 'Lessing's Ditch' and the failure of the Enlightenment settlement. CONCLUSION – A PERSONAL CHALLENGE - To be actors not audience members in the drama of Western Civilisation.

'If the world has not approached its end, it has reached a major watershed in history, equal in importance to the turn from the Middle Ages to the Renaissance. It will demand of us a spiritual blaze; we shall have to rise to a new height of vision, to a new level of life.'
Alexander Solzhenitsyn

'If our civilization is in the throes of death, this is neither because it has ventured too much, nor because it has proposed too much to men. It is rather because it has not ventured enough and because it has not proposed enough. It will revive, a new civilization will come to life, on condition that men hope and love and strive, truly and heroically, for truth, liberty, and fraternity.' [856]
Jacques Maritain

*'I believe that the choice before us now is between the formation
of a new Christian culture, and the acceptance of a pagan one.
Both involve radical changes; but I believe that the majority of
us, if we could be faced immediately with all the changes which
will only be accomplished in several generations, would prefer
Christianity... a thoroughgoing secularism would be objection-
able, in its consequences, even to those who attach no positive importance to the survival of Christianity for its own sake.'* [857]

T.S. Eliot

INTRODUCTION: THE LOOMING CRISIS

As the quotes above signal, this concluding chapter aims at something more than just a summary. The challenge seems so much more prescient to us because if having had so long to learn, we yet fail to make a humane future for our great-grandchildren, then our failure will have been the most inexcusable in history. The general who burned Carthage quoted Homer, while weeping at the sight. 'I have a terrible foreboding that someday the same doom will be pronounced upon my city.' In this book, we have seen the rise and fall of kingdoms and empires and now we, as beneficiaries of the ages, must consider our own.

In January 2019, a group of 30 highly respected public intellectuals, writers, and historians published a manifesto voicing with alarm what many people of diverse political persuasions were already feeling; Europe was 'falling apart before our eyes.' Even as we in Britain prepared for Brexit, 'populist and nationalist' parties across the continent stood poised to make sweeping gains in elections. The brief manifesto warned moderate and sensible liberals that they must now 'fight for the idea of Europe or perish beneath the waves of populism... resentment, hatred...' It warned that future elections in Europe might soon be 'the most calamitous that we have ever known; victory for the wreckers; disgrace for those who still believe in the legacy of Erasmus, Dante, Goethe, and Comenius; disdain for intelligence and culture; explosions of xenophobia and antisemitism; disaster.'

These fears are not those of demagogues seeking votes but people of good faith and learning. When a Jewish historian (and national treasure) like Simon Schama, and others with a deep historical sensibility tell us that the coming elections might be more disastrous than those of the 1920s and thirties, everyone sits up and takes notice.[858]

But what is the cure? Where is this Holy Grail of moral civility and European solidarity? Whatever it is *or is not*, most now understand that it is at least one vital leg of the three-legged stool which supports Europe's existence – or perhaps even the existence of Western Civilisation in any recognisable form. The other two legs are economic stability (supposedly guaranteed by the EU) and military stability (supposedly guaranteed by NATO). As we have noted elsewhere, both those legs were dealt severe blows in the autumn of 2008 with the financial crisis and the sabre-rattling of Russia, from which they have not yet recovered. But, for the purposes and competencies of this book, they are of secondary importance.

What we have been led to define and secure for future generations, is the source, or sources, of the cultural vitality and meaning that have made Western Europe such a singular mainspring of human flourishing – the third leg of Europe. As the reader will expect by now, I will argue that a large part of this third leg is, or at least was Christianity. I offer this case for the reader's consideration, pulling on as many secular and atheist sources as Christian ones because it is only together that we can tackle the problems that now threaten Europe.

So, I conclude this book with four final sections. The first articulates the missing or damaged 'third leg' of European stability, referred to above. From the founding fathers to current international figures, it is helpful to emphasise how this problem has been framed up until now – and the attempts made to answer it. Essentially, we begin to see a replacement third leg largely made up of a misdirected Enlightenment secularity. This last vestige of the European imperialist impulse, with all it's *a priori* commitments to a reductive materialism, has unsuccessfully attempted to co-opt and develop aspects of the Judeo-Christian heritage. However nobly-intended initially, we now live amidst the moral and ethical wreckage of that failed enterprise, which in essence is the failure of the Religion of Man.

This failure ought to be admitted more openly, even as it is already by some farsighted atheists.

Speaking in the Nietzschean vein, the philosopher John Gray writes that, *'Humanism is not science, but religion - the post-Christian faith that humans can make a world better than any in which they have so far lived. ... Humanism is the transformation of this Christian doctrine of salvation into a project of universal human emancipation. The idea of progress is a secular version of the Christian belief in providence...'* And with a bleakness that would chill the heart of the dourest pessimist among us, he later says that this, 'irrational faith in progress may be the only antidote to nihilism' without which the humanist endeavour, 'could not go on.'[859] I am sure that many secular readers will find Grey's position overstated, but it will be this sort of issue under discussion in section 1.

In section 2 of this epilogue, I will present a challenge to those with a Christian conviction. In Section 3 I will do something similar for the secular reader. The opportunities and challenges are made regarding Europe, but in essence, they are equally applicable more generally to Western civilization. If I might misquote Nietzsche; 'How much must collapse now that this faith [in the Religion of Man in its diverse manifestations] has been undermined.' In the next 30 years alone, Europe will face fiscal, demographic, and geopolitical threats that will call for a quality of leadership at least equal to that shown by the subjects of this book. Whether we like it or not, Europe is already moving into a post-secular age, and if the current structures have become too ossified to absorb this emerging reality, then there will be great trouble – most likely the collapse of the E.U. as a political enterprise, but also the real possibility of bloody conflict on European soil. The final section will attempt a general conclusion and a more personal challenge for all people of good faith to work for greater understanding and beneficial cultural renewal.

I began this book as a journey to understand the historical and cultural consciousness of Western Europe. And now I discover that it has also been the underlying quest of a continent struggling through the mists of amnesia.

I came, like Columban, from the *finibus extremis* of that great landmass, in my case from the mountains of Cumbria where the shepherds still count in old Norse and where there are traces of the yet more ancient Brythonic dialect in local speech and place names. I, like Columban and Schuman, have journeyed around Western Europe only to find that my post-Brexit search – the one I started with at the outset of this book – was for the same key eagerly sought by my European neighbours. Indeed, it was almost like a key we had all lost. In the midst of an almost wilful cultural dementia, we seemed to sense that a key is missing; or, at least that the secret door which could bring cultural renewal and international solidarity had been locked to us.

Perhaps we begin to see that all the talk of economics and higher political action is only so much tinkering with the cogs, while the great ghost in the machine – the mysterious music in the music box – remains a mystery. As Philosopher Alain de Botton reminds us, people with dementia cannot plan for the future, for their recollection of the past is so incomplete and fragmentary. Most tragically of all, to the extent that the condition has taken hold in advanced sufferers, so too does their lack of awareness of it. And yet, even in these cases, remains that seismic, primal fear and panic.

This is what I sense in the cultural discourse of our time. It is not just the growing outrage of social media and identity politics, but also in the bewildering vulgarity of political intercourse. We speak and act as people riddled with fear and doubt – people who cannot remember their own names. Frightened children who have lost their father in a crowd and have forgotten their name and his.

It permeates the popular media and is evident in the statements of the MEPs. It is in their desperate speeches and pleas; if this key is not found soon then the internal forces pulling Europe apart will prevail and there shall be no cultural glue strong enough to resist the forces tearing it apart. Of course, they do not call it cultural glue. Nor does anyone, as I did, call it the 'historical and cultural consciousness of Europe' – they refer to it as 'the soul of Europe.' And I often imagine them stumbling about the halls of power slowly and absently, asking themselves and other bewildered MEPs, 'Have you seen it? Our grandfathers had it or knew someone who had it. But alas we cannot find it. 'Have you seen the key?' They seem to say, 'Do you know where we can find *the soul of Europe?*'

Finding the eponymous 'Soul of Europe'[860] has not just been a subject of scholarly debate, or something mentioned by the founding fathers which is now an irrelevance as we are riding the rails they laid down. It is not a small or insignificant, or even optional thing. It is the third leg of European stability, arguably even the mainspring of Western Civilisation itself: a vital root sustaining the superstructure. In the 1980s the often-reactionary Jacques Delors, then president of the European Commission, challenged European citizens, particularly religious leaders, to redouble their efforts to find 'the soul of Europe'. As a Christian, Delors viewed the neo-secular hegemony within the EU governing elites as something unhealthy and unrepresentative. He argued that if Brussels failed to acknowledge a spiritual heritage then the EU would inevitably fail. His very last official words as president were: 'if in the next ten years we haven't managed to give a soul to Europe, to give it spirituality and meaning, the game will be up.'[861] That was 1995, three years after Maastricht. In 2020, the rhetoric remains, even as the prescriptions appear more anaemic.

In 2015 Frans Timmermans, EU Commissioner Juncker's deputy, warned of a crisis of support for the EU. "What was unimaginable before now becomes imaginable, namely the disintegration of the European project," he told the *Friends of Europe* forum in Brussels. "The European ideals still have very strong support among the population across Europe. What do not have strong support are European politicians and European politics."[862]

On the 13th November 2018, Angela Merkel – the inheritor of Adenauer's mantel in the CDU who has been a titan in German politics for 18 years – warned MEPs at a plenary session in Strasbourg that as the strains of public debt, terrorism, populism and migration increase,[863] they must remember that 'tolerance is the soul of Europe and an essential basic value of the European idea.'[864] Merkel, a Lutheran pastor's daughter who grew up under Soviet Communism, said that Europeans need to learn again to, 'treat the interests and needs of others as [their] own. Solidarity is based on tolerance and this is Europe's strength. It is part of our common European DNA and it means overcoming national egoisms.'[865] She closed with the plea; 'Europe is our best chance for peace, prosperity and a good future. We must not let this chance slide; we owe this to ourselves and to past and future generations. Nationalism and egoism must never have a chance to flourish again in Europe. Tolerance and solidarity are our future. And this future is worth fighting for.'[866]

All three 'legs' are mentioned by Merkel here; the *prosperity* delivered by the EU, the *peace* preserved by a NATO, and the *soul of Europe*, in this instance referred to as *tolerance* – whose roots are usually assumed to be solely the province of Enlightenment secularism. But all three legs are now showing alarming signs of disintegration. The stool's bracing (i.e., the increasingly robust European bureaucratic structures) can exert all the lateral pressure they like, but they cannot, for all their strength, in and of themselves hold up the stool. They are able to exert an important technical function but at the end of the day, they are not legs. Angela Merkel's appeal to tolerance on its own may not prove equal to the task, particularly if we are to remain a determinedly post-Christian continent.

Tolerance is frequently more the fruit of indifference than love, perhaps more akin to the Greek virtue of *apetheia*. I have yet to meet someone from an ethnic minority or the LGBTQ community who is clamouring to be merely tolerated. No one wants to be tolerated *per se*, they want to be loved. To love is to will the good of the other, as *other*. It encompasses tolerance, but it will not settle for the indifference which is more often meant by the term. The same love and respect that binds a family and a community together is the same force that can grow between nations together in solidarity. If this third leg of European stability cannot manufacture that most ineluctable cultural force called *love*, then its tolerance will be worse than hatred. A portion of the blame for this rests historically with an unlived Christianity, as we have already observed, but by no means all of it.

Europe faces a legitimation crisis at the most fundamental level, a crisis of meaning. And yet some still look to the technicians in Brussels for an anti-dote. Jean-Noël Tronc,[867] the Chief Executive Officer of *Sacem*, the world's second largest music society for authors, songwriters, and publishers, has written about it more as a technical-cultural issue, yet he is nonetheless urgent in his call for Europe's elites to find solutions for, what he sees, as an 'existential' crisis. 'Re-conquering Europe with a European policy for culture and European cultural identity has now become an existential issue for the Union.' The *'siliconisation* or *uberisation'* of Europe has been culturally corrosive. America and China have achieved increased 'technological and cultural domination based both on the protection and expansion of their tools and their creations.'[868]

Others place their faith in economics, believing that trade alone will carry Europe. But even the EU's internal trade solidarity is no antidote for the titanic forces now stirring around it. China is expanding its 'Belt and Road' initiative into southern European countries that will act as gateways for a new Silk road. Greece has already done so and in 2019 Italy signed agreements for Trieste and Genoa.[869] The year before, France signed 20 trade deals. China is Germany's all-time biggest trading partner, valued at $230 billion. Each deal looks bilaterally advantageous but, with a foot in the door for China, many commentators are already nervous.

Curiously, the subject of European identity (what we are here calling the Soul of Europe) was much under scrutiny at exactly the time when the UK and Ireland entered the EEC. That is why it was in 1973 that the EEC adopted a *Declaration on European identity* with the hope that a declaration would 'ensure the survival of the civilization which they have in common'.[870] The declaration spoke of a 'diversity of cultures within the framework of a common European civilisation' and 'common values and principles... of representative democracy, the rule of law and social justice, and the respect of Human Rights.' Though taken for granted in Britain, these precious affirmations were a mainspring of hope for Eastern Europeans back then, and still an almost-unimaginable dream for others around the world. But the founding fathers we have observed in earlier chapters did not think these values could ultimately be sustained in a post-Christian continent.

Nearer our own time, the absence of vitality crops up in different places and is picked up by people you would not expect. Tronc, mentioned above, sees the graphic design of the Euro as almost emblematic; 'Bridges on one side, windows and doors on the other, which are supposed to symbolise the "spirit of opening and cooperation of the European Union, as well as the communication between peoples." Every day the European Union's identity vacuum is palpable for millions via their disembodied banknotes.' But Tronc, from a CEO's desk, sees only the technological tsunami flooding into a cultural and legislative vacuum. Others observe the issue from a geopolitical standpoint.

For example, according to analyst George Friedman, there are not one but *four Europes*; the German states, the northern European states, the Mediterranean states, and the states that border with Russia. The fragmentation is real and growing. The fiscal policy gridlock will not change until a spectacular catastrophe overtakes it. The Soviet Union crumbled very slowly, then very fast, and no leading sovietologist was able *to predict the day or the hour*. In the E.U.'s case, there are prophets-a-plenty and it is not hard to see why. The largest economic cog in Europe is Germany. 35-40% of her GDP comes from exports. That is an unusually high percentage for such a major economy.[871] She is extremely dependent on her customers, half of whom are in the EU. If they can't buy her goods, then she has a very big problem. So, keeping Europeans in a position to buy German exports is key to the European Central Bank's policy. That has made Germany very unpopular and it has also made southern Europe almost bankrupt.

Germany has channelled the national psyche into *economism without militarism*, which was partly Adenauer's legacy, and partly American influence. It was necessary then, but since 2008 that older settlement – of letting the USA (through NATO) maintain a *cordon sanitaire* against a resurgent Russia – has been brought into question. As Hannah Arendt wrote, the most dangerous position to hold is to be rich and weak. Germany cannot, as Merkel has rightly hinted, keep allowing America to pick up the tab for European stability. NATO had its 70th birthday in December 2019 and not one of the 29 members was then paying the required 2% contribution. Germany says it planned to get there in 2031. With China ever more looming as Americas' greatest strategic threat, it is little wonder the Americans are getting the 70-year itch. In many ways the timing could not be worse,[872] but then again, times are rarely optimal. The best time to call the dentist is when you first detect the abscess, not a week later when it has burst. To their credit, since 2014, the EU has seen the birth of joint defence initiatives, led by Jean Claude Junker.[873] But even so this does mean that Germany must simultaneously face, not only its past but also its uncertain future.

Quite naturally, Germany fears having to lead Europe (something that Churchill pushed for) and, as George Friedman argues, she also fears that the old Germany has not died but has been sleeping. 'The fundamental question is the relationship between Germany and Russia, and the question will define Europe as a whole.'[874] If the EU fails, some believe that Germany might realign with Russia.[875] Their economies are currently asymmetrical but Merkel's successors may not have her sensibilities or historical affinities. Friedman framed the Euro-German tension as a declining marriage. 'There is little thought of divorce, but the things that bound them together passionately are no longer there. Germany is not seeking redemption. France is not seeking to dominate an integrated Europe. They do, however, have neighbours who are attractive and are flirting.'[876]

The accuracy of Friedman's assessment is open to debate, but even now, people of goodwill and historical sense are looking on aghast as the dream, that Europe could transcend its bloody history, is being shaken. It is evident that reform within the structure of the institutions, the single currency, and EU defence are urgently needed, but our attention must also be focused on the third leg. The current third leg, that dogmatic insistence on a purely secular project, has not delivered meaning or a source of solidarity to hold up the stool when the other two legs were shaken. And this has been compounded by an arrogant group deafness within the power-sharing elites, which in turn has fuelled dangerous counter-forces across the bloc.

Farsighted, Schuman was adamant seventy years ago that 'Peace will not be saved other than by a return to the foundations of our Christian Civilisation.' In another article Schuman stated, 'One would commit an error and fall victim to a dangerous illusion, were one to believe that to create Europe it will suffice to create European institutions. This would be a body without a soul. These institutions must be animated by a European Spirit such as His Holiness Pius XII[877] has defined.'

Exactly what Schuman meant, and the challenge that it poses to people of goodwill, whether religious or secular, is something we will address in the next two sections.

2. BECOMING *LES PERSONNES DES FRONTIÈRES*

This section deals with the challenge and opportunities facing people of faith in general and Christians in particular. Essentially it compasses the challenge to become once again successful frontiersmen and frontierswomen. It has been a recurrent theme in this book. Columban bridged the boundaries by stepping over them. Schuman and De Gasperi had those very boundaries move around them. Columban and his contemporaries became the bridge across an earlier Dark Age; Schuman, Adenauer, and De Gasperi became a bridge in a later one. The generations now living, form a bridge over which the nascent technologies (the internet of things and artificial intelligence, etc.) and the effects of dramatic social change will be transferred to their great-grandchildren. We are that bridge whether we want to be or not, whether we like it or not. Very much is asked of us. Who is equal to such a task?

I cannot speak with authority about other religious traditions, but for the Christian, the frontier is or at least should be an optimal habitat. It is almost a sacred obligation, as with the white martyrdom and peregrinations of the Irish monks. The Christian is called to live between the present and future, heaven and earth, the sacred and the secular, the moral law and the civic law, the eternal and temporal common good. In the words of Paul, the Christian is to be 'in the world but not of it', and consequently 'to use the things of this world, as if not absorbed by them.'

But with this dual citizenship comes a dual temptation; either of retreating miles from the frontier into the hinterlands of cultural accommodation, or crossing in the opposite direction into the enclaves of cultural Christianity or ghettos of sectarian theocracy. The church, in the supranational sense, should be like a lifeboat. It should be in the waters, however turbulent, but should not have the waters in it, if it is to be at all useful.

That prophetic calling means that Christians will almost always be on the wrong side of the prevailing cultural consensus. Think of Frank Buchman. The nearer the frontier, the better the target you represent to both sides. It goes with the call. Christians have to get used to it.

Throughout this book, we have endeavoured to observe some exceptional frontiersmen and women through the long lens of history. Upstream of politics we have observed Columban, and downstream we have observed Schuman. The further downstream Christians work – the nearer the frontier – the greater is the call for nuance and wisdom. If Christians think that they can operate as decisively as Buchman or Schuman without putting in similar groundwork – similar training, dedication, focus, and suffering – then they should consider working further upstream where they will do less damage.

This book has focused on characters whose Christian commitments made them exceptional in their day and generation. But a combative atheist could quite as easily – alas far too easily – choose from a vast array of Christians who have been equally radical but in the wrong way, and complicit with abusive power. There is no shying away from it, Christians particularly must take serious notice of their own history – the many triumphs but also the many sins. And Christians, in particular, should form a bulwark against the siren call of populism that has always proved so disastrous in Europe – especially a pseudo-Christian populism.[878]

Men like Adenauer knew that Christians had to renounce their addiction to that memory of 19th century cultural dominance and embrace true repentance over their past political sins. That is why he let the old Catholic *Zentrum* party die, a very controversial move at the time, and formed a new one on a broader Christian consensus. *He knew what he had to do, but do modern Christians?*

In response to the deep intellectual and spiritual heritage, men like Adenauer, Schuman, De Gasperi, and others were part of a generation that shifted from being the last bastion of the *ancien régime* of Christendom to the vanguard of the new movement of political renewal and social justice. Their example, and that of their contemporaries, should serve as a reassurance to secularists reading this book. The lives of these men should also form a gold standard for religious people seeking to engage in the public sphere.

So here is both challenge and opportunity. As the Christian seeks to re-gain the lost art of cultural persuasion, he or she will be aware of a level of unfairness. Some of this will be dealt with below in the next section, but I want to point out here that the temptation to laziness: to seek shortcuts, to fight fire with fire, to adopt the abuses of identity and victim politics; all these should be avoided at all costs.

It is true that power corrupts, and probably true that absolute power corrupts absolutely, but it is not yet apparent that absolute powerlessness makes anyone pure. Christians have wielded earthly power with very mixed results and now it is our turn to see what it is like when the boot is on the other foot. Certainly, secularism has often been guilty of blind intolerance, but it only rides the rails laid down by its religious counterparts, in the cen-turies before. In Europe, toleration had a long and protracted birth in re-sponse to the awful Wars of Religion. If Christians suffer discrimination in public life now, then they may at least do so humbly remembering that the current settlement was a response to a cultural Christianity corrupted by secular power. Christians often complain that the secularist's talk of '*di-versity and toleration*' is just one more mask for cultural hegemony. Per-haps true, but let them remember that it is more or less exactly what some 19th century state protestant groups meant by *religious liberty*. These are ancestral ghosts come back to haunt us. Now that the boot is on the other foot, Christians must share with humility and repentance, what they have learned.

And what has been learned? It is that those holding power – whether in the EU, the Media, or the Church – all too easily champion diversity in the abstract; but not in the concrete. That is the point. As Tom Paine wrote,

> '*toleration is not the opposite of intoleration but it is the counterfeit of it. Both are despotisms. The one assumes to itself the right of withholding liberty of conscience, and the other of granting it.*'

This quote is worth reading twice, for in it, Paine articulates precisely the growing despotism of our own time. He saw it the first time around when privileged Christian groups were doing it, but now secularists, Paine's hereditary heirs, are 'withholding liberty of conscience' from religious groups seeking to engage in a secular public sphere.

Historically, toleration assumed clear commitments to certain belief structures, with a corresponding commitment to tolerate those who believed something different. This settlement was finally if falteringly, reached in part as recent history had shown them that it was better than the alternative – intolerance, and polarisation in the political and religious sphere. But today, tolerance has evolved to mean intolerance of any fixed beliefs that are deemed judgmental or – strangely enough – intolerant. It is a new dogmatism with a purely progressive component but no eventual destination. The special pleading for tolerance from progressives is all the more alarming when each decade brings a new revelation of the utopian future society. Cultural conservatives must, at the risk of lynching by media, watch the forcible indoctrination of primary school children into untested, social doctrines that are barely as old as the children themselves. Viewpoint diversity in the classroom, on the campus, and in the Commons is fast becoming the unforgivable sin.[879] The extent and speed of this anti-liberal development are hard to exaggerate.

Douglas Murray's '*The Madness of Crowds*' covers this ground very humanely from a secular viewpoint, but Christians who know their own history have seen all this before. From the Manicheans to the Marxians, we have seen it all before. As Milton wrote, 'New Presbyter is but Old Priest writ large.' To our shame, our own sons and daughters have learned all the wrong lessons from us, and are now returned with wrath. Schuman, with more than a hint of foreboding of the future, wrote that an 'anti-Christian democracy would be a caricature which would sink into either tyranny or anarchy.'[880]

This might be the neatest summary of Europe's current position or at least its current trajectory. In a letter dated 31st May 1948, when the tremendous work of material and social reconstruction was underway, Schuman acknowledged the severe limitations of merely political solutions. 'But all these efforts will be insufficient and in vain if they are not built on a solid moral base. The morality [springing from] the individual, of the family, is the true source, and at the same time the guarantee of (international) peace and human flourishing. The democracies, more than any other political regime require such [interior/personal] regulators of freedom (*régulateur de la liberté*).'[881] Secular humanism has posited that it does not need religion to do this. Schuman was sceptical of this claim. Observing our societies 70 years on; we should all be doubly sceptical. He perhaps had been thinking of President John Adam's famous view of the American political settlement. 'Our Constitution was made only for a moral and religious people. It is wholly inadequate to the government of any other.' Adams, not an optimist by temperament, also once wrote that 'there is never a democracy that did not commit suicide.'[882]

A reckless experiment in unlimited moral freedom has definitely not proved to be a glue that in the end binds individuals, marriages, families, societies, or nations together. Leftist philosopher Jurgen Habermas astonished his usual admirers by saying, 'Christianity, and nothing else, is the ultimate foundation of liberty, conscience, human rights and democracy, the benchmarks of western civilisation. To this day, we have no other options. We continue to nourish ourselves from this source. Everything else is postmodern chatter.... Recognizing our Judeo-Christian roots more clearly not only does not impair intercultural understanding, it is what makes it possible.'[883]

So, a Christian who wishes to serve Britain or Europe in the political sphere has nothing personally to feel inadequate about if they enter that sphere with humility, dedication, and love. He or she can expect a stiff climb, but there are solid guides to help and many pioneers who have charted different routes.

Schuman's intellectual father, the philosopher Jacques Maritain, has become a nuanced guide to European Christians thinking about politics. He was adamant that we should shun 'every attempt at a clerical or decoratively Christian state,' such as were attempted in 'the absolutist era.'[884] For Maritain, theocracy was to confuse 'temporal common good...of political society, [with the] supernatural common good...of the kingdom of God, which is supra-political.'[885] To privilege the position of 'one religion, even though it were the true religion...would be to inject into political society a divisive principle and, to that extent, to jeopardize the temporal common good.'[886]

Old lessons had been learned; the cultural privilege of the European state churches had given fuel to secularising fires. But Maritain, aware of all this, still argued for an epistemically 'theist or Christian' society, 'not that it would require every member of society to believe in God and to be Christian,' but that the governing consensus recognised 'in the reality of things' that the Judeo-Christian revelation of God was the guarantor of the 'human person and prime source of natural law.'[887] And not only so but that it was also 'the prime source of political society and authority among men; and in the sense that it recognizes that the currents of liberty and fraternity released by the Gospel, the virtues of justice and friendship sanctioned by it, the practical respect for the human person proclaimed by it, the feeling of responsibility before God required by it, as much from him who exercises the authority as from him who is subject to it, are the internal energy which civilization needs to achieve its fulfilment.'[888]

Maritain's prescription for the 'internal energy which civilisation needs' is controversial, but at least it does sound less bloodless than Merkel's plea for tolerance – which after all is only to say, what each new generation decides is tolerable. Toleration is a fruit, not a root. In Britain, the tradition of Christian democracy has been prevalent – though seldom acknowledged – within existing political structures. Some readers might only think here of Cromwell's Puritan commonwealth (and his ban on plum pudding!) without realising the full impact of Christian activists and politicians working within the existing currents of political life – which has always been the more British way. But this has meant that Christian Democracy in general has not been well understood in Britain (or even the United States), which is a shame.

Michael Fogarty's *Christian Democracy in Western Europe 1820-1953* asserts that some of the most important political movements of the 20th century have been generated directly out of the Christian tradition. Across the channel, there were Christian parties, of various creeds and varying degrees of internal piety, engaged in most democratic elections in Europe from the 1890s onwards. The roots are variously Catholic, Lutheran, Reformed, and Anabaptist and mixes of each, and they naturally have produced varied expressions in Italy, Germany, the Netherlands, Belgium, Switzerland, Sweden, Norway, Eastern Europe, and elsewhere. And so, we should not misunderstand what Schuman meant when he spoke about Christianity as a basis for political action. In 1958 he said,

> '(W)e are called to bethink ourselves of the Christian basis of Europe by forming a democratic model of governance which through reconciliation develops into a community of peoples in freedom, equality, solidarity and peace, which is deeply rooted in Christian basic values.'

Schuman, De Gasperi, and Adenauer urged other Christians to go through that door, and secularists not to close it to them. Shriven of the ambiguous, and often terrible, legacy of cultural Christian hegemony, each of these men argued for functional plurality and freedom for others. But they also saw clearly how a new faith-based religion called secular humanism, claiming to be neutral and representative of the common core, might well, when harnessed by even well-meaning elites, all too easily usurp the majority view and push a continent towards a dangerous place. For them, the nihilistic materialism of the Communists and Nazis, or the softer equivalent among progressive socialists, was very much what they saw as Europe's real enemy – the real barbarians within the frontiers.

Schuman was adamant that 'the European Movement would only be successful if future generations managed to tear themselves away from the temptation of materialism (read 'scientism' or 'atheism') which corrupted society by cutting it off from its spiritual roots.' Their insistence on the recognition of Christianity was not for the church's benefit but as the surest safeguarding of the freedoms they believed had arisen alone from it. Christianity, in that sense, is not under threat. Dogmatic secularists will not ruin sacred things, but they will spoil the secular things for themselves and everyone else, just as 'the Titans did not scale the heavens but laid waste the world.'[889]

So, this is the challenge to Christians, and they must be under no illusions if they feel called to serve in this sphere. As apologist Os Guinness reminds them, those who wish to serve society in politics today must be prepared to suffer a double loss. First, because they must force their faith to be unfairly subservient to hegemonic secular truth claims, and then also, they must endure a loss of independence when trying to find political solutions to pre-political or cultural problems. Of course, if this has given some Christians pause for thought, then that is good. After all, political action has never been the majority focus for Christians as it has been for Marxists. For most people, politics is, and always has been, downstream of where they are called to serve within their culture. As Father John Nehaus wrote, *'the first thing to say about politics is that politics is not the first thing.'*

The Christian sociologist James Davison Hunter writes about the American situation:

> 'Cultural conservatives bet on politics as a strategy and means to respond to the changes in the world, but that politics can only be a losing strategy. What political solution is there to the absence of decency? To the spread of vulgarity? To the lack of compassion? The answer, of course, is none – there are none... and the headlong pursuit of them by conservatives will lead, inevitably to failure.'

He has a profound point. We can pass a law that a French far-right nationalist might not beat an Eritrean refugee, but not even De Gaulle could promulgate a law that would give that same nationalist, sufficient love to adopt an asylum seeker into his or her own family. Europe needs good laws, but it also cries out for saints.

No one is born a saint. Saints – even secular 'saints' – are people who have undergone profound inner change to make them who they are. The Swiss theologian Emil Brunner warned those gathered at St Andrew's University's Gifford Lectures in 1947:

> '...all changes which begin from without are no real changes. For after all it is always man who makes the conditions and not the conditions that make men. Outward revolutions are therefore at bottom fictitious... Of course, the world does not believe this. For the superficial mind, which fails to understand the real relation between centre and periphery, the silent revolutions always are too slow and not radical enough.'[890]

So here is the challenge to Christians. Are they prepared for the cost of this inner change? Have they really counted the cost as Jesus recommended; to be taken apart as their Bible heroes were; Moses, Joseph, David, or as this book's heroes were; De Gasperi, Adenauer, Columbanus, and Schuman? Think carefully how you answer. As we have seen, a life of suffering and self-sacrifice is no small thing. Christians must embrace tectonic personal change before they can be part of a solution. The Bible calls this holiness.

When I visited Schuman's old constituency of Thionville, the octogenarian Charles Danguy told me that, 'if Christians enter politics as servants then maybe there is some hope for them that they will do good. But,' warned the veteran peace activist, who still acts as an unofficial liaison between different groups within the EU Strasbourg Parliament, 'if they do it with ambition, it is all over for them.' The call and challenge of Danguy and Brunner's generation is salient and pressing. Brunner was in hope that the defeat of Hitler and Mussolini would give some 'further breathing space... to build up a new European civilisation on the ruins of the old.' He was not alone and perhaps he was thinking here of Winston Churchill's 1940 *Finest Hour* speech.

> '...the Battle of Britain is about to begin. Upon this battle depends the survival of Christian civilization... The whole fury and might of the

enemy must very soon be turned on us now.... If we can stand up to him (Hitler), all Europe may be free, and the life of the world may move forward into broad, sunlit uplands. But if we fail, then the whole world, including the United States, including all that we have known and cared for, will sink into the abyss of a new Dark Age, made more sinister, and perhaps more protracted, by the lights of perverted science. Let us therefore brace ourselves to our duties, and so bear ourselves that.... men will say, "This was their finest hour."'

Could Churchill have foreseen that equal and greater dangers were waiting in *the broad, sunlit uplands;* where we have built a civilization in which GDP – or the hidden hand of the market – is our final god, to which other considerations are often sacrificed? In those same 1947 lectures, Brunner warned that a culture's 'loss of faith usually means that Mammon becomes God.'[891] And that a 'practical materialism of the Occident is a direct and provable consequence of secularisation.' Since the wars, the GDP of Western Europe has risen exponentially and it has had many beneficial effects, but let us not be naïve; over time our core commitments become formational of our national institutions and character. The Europhile analyst Dominique Giuliani, gave a damning summary of what he thought Britain had become when he asked,

'Where are the brilliant elites who succeeded over the centuries in carrying forward the Kingdom's superior interest? What has become of the UK? An off-shore platform anchored just outside the Single Market, largely managed by non-Europeans, financed by Russian, Asian or Arab billionaires in total breach of its brilliant, glorious past?'

We British, at any rate, cannot escape the possibility, or the challenge that our biggest battle and our finest hour might yet be before us. The next decades for Britain will call forth great virtue and greater sacrifice from its citizens, and it is incumbent on Christians particularly, to serve by example as the times require. Voltaire said that 'when it comes to money, all men are of the same religion.' Christians should be the people that prove Voltaire wrong. Jesus explicitly commands it. But as we know that has not always been the case. And beyond the churches' primary obligation to worship God and preach the gospel, the coming decades also present an opportunity for Christian investors, entrepreneurs, and business people to sacrificially invest capital in wealth-creating businesses that are ethical and beneficial. Somewhere between the Stoical Capitalism of Adam Smith, and the chivalric capitalism of John Ruskin[892] (and other great Christian thinkers), there is adequate ground for new models of business that could make Britain an inspirational economy.[893]

Serving their country in political action, must also be the concern now of Christians, as they view the coming decades. Into the breach of polarised political factions, the mature and humane Christian voice must find its place. In Britain, there are few now who do not desire the root-and-branch renewal of the two main political parties. This book was written to give examples of how this sort of political work can be done, and why it should be done. It is the work of the many and the few; the *few* who have been taken apart by God in the wilderness and put back together for his work, and the *many* who must pray for them.

Beyond political renewal, Christians with political vocations must also anticipate what the inevitable rise of an Islamic voting block will mean in various European cities and nations in the next 30 years. This is almost impossible to write without being misunderstood, but I believe a moderating Christian presence within future Islamic political movements[894] might save Europe much pain.[895] Europe needs new Schumans and De Gasperis to straddle this difficult frontier in the coming decades. For various reasons, I think this is a role best suited to Christians of serious conviction and integrity.

Slightly upstream of politics, Christian renewal in the media and the academy (education) remains a real obligation. And in the third sector also, the call for entrepreneurs will become ever more pressing in the next 30 years as the demographic decline takes full effect. The migration of social services from an over-stretched public sector is already underway.[896] Elderly care, mental health and family support, food security, education, and even medical care must all be reappraised in the next 30 years. Christians are in familiar historical territory here, for it was in the very soil of Roman cultural exhaustion that the church first grew. From the later 19th century onwards, multi-faceted, organic social services in Britain were transferred (often forcibly so) from churches to the state. It is a complex and controversial story, covered well by Dr. Frank Prochaska in *Christianity and Social Service in Modern Britain*.[897] Many saw dire portents of state overreach, (education was bitterly contested) but others welcomed the regulation and professionalism.

Whatever the case, the historical situation that made this transfer possible, and sometimes desirable, is no longer with us. Social entrepreneurs must rise to the challenge once more, just as men like Basil and Benedict did in their generation.[898] There came a day, during World War I when Schuman shed his frontiersman's indifference. That day is upon European Christians who, although a minority voice, may yet be a stabilising and innovative one during the rocky times ahead.

As George MacDonald said, to obey obligation before it becomes a necessity, isn't necessarily a virtue. At the end of the day, we are all still very poor creatures and unprofitable servants. Simone Weil was correct when she said that the virtue required by the modern age was not merely the negation of vice. 'Whoever is only incapable of being as brutal, violent and inhuman as the adversary, yet without exercising the opposite virtues, is inferior to the adversary in both inner strength and prestige; he will not hold his own against him.'[899] The 'prince of preachers' Charles Spurgeon called-out Victorian Christians for possessing no more vital holiness than a washed corpse on a mortuary slab. In the same way, our age calls forth, as Solzhenitsyn says, 'a spiritual blaze.' European Christians live in the flickering twilight of Columban's Irish mission, which rekindled the fires of faith, learning, and civility that became the Europe in which we are privileged to have our part.[900]

Remembering the moral seriousness of those opposed to religious views, the most prescient challenge to those who bear Christ's name is that they incarnate his selfless life and humility in perfect accord. Way back in 1871 George Dawson preached a sermon called '*The Folly of Abuse*' which laid out the Christian path as more ethos than agenda.

'We must do what we can to prevent any being driven to atheism by our theism. In the presence of justice, rebellion grows unholy. In the presence of tyranny, it is a virtue ...Let it be ours not to get angry with such as are so unhappy as to have lost their faith... Let us strive when we use the name of God to keep it righteous, and to force no man into doubt by the unloveliness of our faith.' [901]

Only Christians who have submitted to the process of holiness, as Columban, De Gasperi, and Schuman did, will be of any use to their fellow citizens. The well they must dig is deep. The need for freshwater is critical. The fields for work, diverse. Schuman firmly believed that lasting reconstruction was only possible in a Europe 'deeply rooted in Christian basic values.' He was not alone. In a letter very early on, Adenauer told Schuman that he too was 'filled with the desire to build the new edifice of Europe on Christian foundations' and that it was 'not only a political and economic aim worth striving for but as a real Christian, obligation.' For European Christians, this obligation remains – at the personal, local, national, and even international level. We must simultaneously resist the siren call of pseudo-Christian populism in the public realm, while also refusing the sectarian echo-chambers of ecclesiastical irrelevance.

In *Lord of the Rings* parlance, some Hobbits must leave the Shire if there is to be any Shire left. And Hobbit-help must be welcomed by the 'secular' elites in Rohan and Gondor if there is to be any Edoras and Minas Tirith left standing. The greatness of Frodo and Sam is their willingness to go. The greatness of Aragorn and Faramir was in not preventing them. If we are to face our modern Mordors and 21st-century Saurons, then we too will need both. If Christians feel increasingly alienated and shaken by the times in which they live, then they should remember that they are not the first to feel so. 'So do all who live to see such times,' Gandalf reminds Frodo, 'but that is not for them to decide. All we have to decide is what to do with the time that is given us." It is wise advice. Writing in the wake of World War II's devastation, the Cambridge professor of history Herbert Butterfield sought to answer the question; could history provide future generations with anything solid enough to build on with hope? His surprising answer, which is the answer of both a leading expert in historiography and a devout Methodist, would have been much approved by the lead characters in this book:

"I have nothing to say at the finish except that if one wants a permanent rock in life and goes deep enough for it, it is difficult for historical events to shake it. There are times when we can never meet the future with sufficient elasticity of mind, especially if we are locked in the contemporary systems of thought. We can do worse than remember a principle which both gives us a firm Rock and leaves us the maximum elasticity for our minds: the principle: Hold to Christ, and for the rest be totally uncommitted."[902]

3. MAKING LESSING'S DITCH LESS UGLY

For the more secular reader who has reached this far, I have nothing but respect and thanks. It will have taken an almost superhuman sense of self-control on occasions to keep reading, but I hope at many points it has also been worth it. In a recent debate between atheist Sam Harris and theist psychologist Jordan B. Peterson, the interviewer asked each of them to 'steel-man' the other's arguments as an introduction. To 'steel-man' an argument is the opposite of the more disingenuous foible of 'straw-manning' the position of someone with whom you disagree. It is laudable and something I have doubtlessly failed to do in this book. My stated intent, given in the introduction, was to establish a bridgehead for further dialogue, and yet doubtless I will often have appeared reactionary and dogmatic. Please forgive me these offenses and my other shortcomings as a historian as you endure these final two sections.

In the introduction, we began with the analogy of walking a ridge together and now we end this book by turning that ridge into a ditch, to be precise, Lessing's 'ugly wide ditch'. The German philosopher Gotthold Lessing (1729 - 1781) articulated the gap – or the "ugly wide ditch" (*der garstige breite Graben*) between the claims of historical truth – that Lessing claimed could not be demonstrated – and the *necessary truths* of reason, which can. In short: Reason was in, religion was out. Reason would give us 'necessary truth'; religion could authenticate itself only by 'inner truth' and perhaps even genuine Christian love.

Lessing's brilliance was that he so perfectly forecasted, not the Enlightenment's whole trajectory (for much of it had strong Christian elements) but certainly where we are now; benighted Christians on one side of the ditch (offering 'moral' truth and allowed to run Foodbanks and Aid programmes), and the Champions of Reason on the other side, giving 'necessary' truth and running the education, government, and science. That broadly is *Lessing's Ditch*, and it is an ugly parody of a healthy society. Lessing's ditch has, to the rejoicing of many, grown wider over the decades, and it has been the unpleasant task of scholars to autopsy the corpse of Western history in order to measure the increasing length.

One such generational study, already mentioned in the previous chapter, is *The Year of Our Lord 1943: Christian Humanism in an Age of Crisis*.[903] Back in 2016, the same author published an essay in Harpers, asking why the late 20th and early 21st century seemed to lack the same calibre of Christian public intellectuals[904] present in the early and mid-20th century. Why, for example, does it appear that Christian intellectuals had retreated ever more into the ecosystems of the already-converted?

Auden, like his contemporaries, understood that World War II was a manifestation of modernity's wider dehumanization. A civilisation encamped on one side of Lessing's ditch was looking increasingly untenable – an inhuman, refugee camp, 'highly condensed and functional and all under the cover of plastic.' Their diagnosis was succinct. They saw a technocratic society reduced to impersonal forces, grounded in Lessing's *essential truths* and now in collusion with technological power – what Lewis termed '*That Hideous Strength*'. Lessing's *essential truths* had disenchanted the world of all superstition – bad fairies as well as good ones. Psychoanalysis had explained away all guilt and every sin. Monsters, demons, and sins were relegated to the other side of the ditch.

But, warned Auden, the monsters only grow more powerful by our not believing in them. The monsters know that there is, in actual fact, no ditch at all. German-Jewish philosopher Ernst Cassirer had once believed in 'man's progressive self-liberation,' that was, until the Holocaust.

'We could hardly be prevailed upon to take them (Nazi racial myths) seriously, but by the end of the war, however, it had become clear that to all of us that this was a great mistake.... The mythical monsters were not entirely destroyed. They were used for the creation of a new universe...'[905]

Lessing's Ditch had been erected to save nations from the irrationality of the wars of religion. But it turned out that human evil was equally as capable of generating war from the rationalist side of the ditch. The terrible irony of the 20th century was that hundreds of millions of lives were taken by those who had believed that religion was the cause of all evil. This was happening even as Auden was challenging the West to recover a sense of evil, sin, and, even wonder. But he was also aware that, even in his day, how little leverage the Judeo-Christian consensus actually had. When he wrote his poem on *September 1, 1939*, he spoke with pathos of the 'just' as 'ironic points of light' in the vast darkness of a 'haunted wood' where 'children afraid of the night... have never been happy or good.' It is bleak, but not without a flicker of hope.

In concluding his book *The Year of Our Lord 1943*, Alan Jacobs' analysis, like Auden's, is realistic about the legacy of Christian intellectuals within post-war western culture. They were, to use our Tolkien metaphor again, just so many Hobbits wandering the vast plains of Middle Earth. Maritain was the only one who really bridged the gap into political life, and we have traced his influence already on the Catholic founders of the EEC, and the drafting of the Universal Declaration of Human Rights. Yet, even Maritain remains little known outside specialist circles. Even Lewis and Eliot, who were given rare access to British and continental audiences through radio, found themselves after the war in the sort of secular welfare state that they had worried about. In a later Harper's article,[906] Jacobs admits that even in what looked like a golden age of Christian intellectual production – when the turmoil of a great international crisis made it seem that civilization itself was ready for a reset – the Christian voice was still very much a distant, if comforting, voice from the cultural margins, the far side of Lessing's ditch.

Many secularists would not have it otherwise, and some would go further. The new atheists, like Richard Dawkins, are all too keen to dig a deeper ditch – to class Sunday School as child abuse. But this fringe of atheism is not representative of all others who have (understandable) reservations about giving the religious voice a share in a civil public square. They want an assurance that separation of powers between church and state, of what belongs to Caesar and what belongs to God. That is as it should be. For one thing, Christ taught it.

In Britain, it should be Christians, particularly Anglicans, calling for the disestablishment of the Church of England. It has 'no right to speak on behalf of British Protestants, let alone British Christians',[907] and yet the trappings of the *ancien régime* still persist, as if through sheer inertia. Prussia and America addressed this issue 200 years ago,[908] and even in Britain, many Anglicans have been calling to be released from the shackles imposed on it by Henry VIII and given their freedom from being the plaything of 'godless political machinery.'[909] In Britain, the renegotiation around Lessing's Ditch must be worked at seriously from both ends. By studying the lives and thought of men like Schuman, De Gasperi, Adenauer, Kuyper, and Dooyeweerd; voices on both sides of the ditch should be assured of being heard. And the more willing the ears, the less need there will be to shout.

Christians should not seek a sacral public square, but neither must secular humanists continue to insist on, what Richard John Neuhaus called a *naked public square* – where their own viewpoint is privileged. If we are all to live together, and if we are to seek solutions to the very specific problems facing Europe, then we must admit that Lessing's Ditch was a human solution to a historical situation. The entrenchments on either side of Lessing's Ditch must be gradually deconstructed within the next half century if Europe wishes to escape from calamity. That calls for secular Spaaks and Monnets and also religious Schumans to reach across the chasm.

In '*The Strange Death of Europe*' the journalist Douglas Murray articulates the double bind that a doggedly secular Europe has found itself in. "'Reason' and 'Rationalism' had led men to do the most unreasonable and irrational things. It had been just another system used by men to control other men. Belief in the autonomy of man had been destroyed by men."[910] In Murray's view, Europe had pursued rational autonomy and nearly destroyed itself in the process. Before that, it had tried giving what was Caesar's to God, or at least to the church, and that had also been deeply problematic. For many, the premodern church-state synthesis had been deadly, but not as deadly as when, in the 20th century, Caesar also took what was God's, by which point Europe had invented and tried almost every political system known to humanity.

In her 1996 book *Le Souci Contemporain,* the French philosopher-novelist Chantal Delsol compares the West to a new Icarus who, having flown too close to the sun, plummeted to earth, and yet survived the fall to look back with a pathos mingled with confusion. And the pathos must be keenly felt. Philosopher, Jurgen Habermas' 2007 lecture '*An Awareness of What is Missing'* highlighted the expanding vacuum at the centre of the post-secular age. The twentieth and twenty-first century will surely appear to history as a struggle between competing totalitarian visions for a world that had abandoned its religious underpinnings.

The Enlightenment quest to have the icing without the cake, ethics and rights without the 'mumbo jumbo' - Atlee's phrase – has seen mixed results, generally in a downward direction. Ludwig Feuerbach and Wagner hoped that the arts could, as Wagner said, 'save the spirit of religion'. This has been the earnest endeavour of many sincere, good-hearted people; people with whom we stand shoulder to shoulder in the maintenance of a richly humane society. But to imbue the arts with such a salvific role, to burden it with such responsibility, will surely cripple it and leave many disillusioned.[911]

The much-decorated, German legal scholar and judge Ernst-Wolfgang Böckenförde (who died in 2019) wrote as far back as 1960: 'Does a free, secularised state exist on the basis of normative presuppositions that it itself cannot guarantee?' That question has been receiving a fairer hearing at the popular level in the past decade – not just from the lips and pens of religionists either. This is partly arisen from the external pressures of migration, but partly also due to the weaknesses in neo-secular claims whose expiry date recedes further into the past.

But even before the migration pressures became acute, the warnings of the philosophers and theologians had begun to reach the popular culture. The "undisputed star, and *enfant terrible*, of modern French literature,"[912] Michel Houellebecq achieved acclaim and booming sales with his 1998 novel *Atomised*, which depicts a Europe in existential despair. One of his ennui-stricken characters remains in bed for two full weeks staring at the radiator, asking, 'How long could Western Civilisation continue without religion?' It is perhaps indicative that by 2016 the author became even more controversial in his book *Submission,* because it imagines France politically submitting to Islam in the mid-2020's through a mixture of political ineptitude and stealth. He is controversial, but also 'France's biggest literary export and, some say, greatest living writer,'[913] which means he is a disquieting litmus.

It is easy to dismiss alarmist literature, less so the slow mill of demography that has been and is grinding all our pretensions fine as dust. Demography is not destiny, but it usually becomes so for want of farsighted leadership. There are no simple solutions for something as big as the European Union; but some radical renewal of the governing political structures is an obvious technical measure. I have no doubt that the founders would also be aghast and wish to reform, not just the gravy train in Brussels, but also some of the less accountable power structures that have grown up around it.

These matters are now for other European countries to consider seriously, but it remains a concern for the British too. Our destiny is still tied to Europe by a myriad of strands, although we will never again be the sort of ally we were in the Napoleonic and German wars. Our star has passed in that regard, yet there still exists great solidarity between us and our continental cousins. From this, there may yet spring some unexpected help in troubled times. So, we watch and wait, and hope.

I don't think anyone seriously questions the utility of a limited European integration, as espoused by the founding fathers. A peaceful Europe made of sovereign states working in cooperation and solidarity is, as we have seen, the most successful piece of political integration since the League of Delos. But where the founding fathers (leaving Monnet out for a moment) would go further is to insist that at the social level, we cannot function outside a coherent hierarchy of values with solid epistemic roots.

The founding fathers' roots were in the Judeo-Christian revelation; their successors have chosen their roots in a purely secular reading of the Enlightenment. As conservative Michael Novak observed, 'a very large part of the "European Crisis" is the crisis of the Enlightenment. On that ground, a civilisation cannot be built, a civilisation can only burn down to the last waxed threads of its wick.'[914] That reading, and therefore that imposition on the political possibilities bequeathed to us by the founding fathers, is now a large part of the forces destroying the E.U.

The question is whether there is enough flexibility within the secular mind, and enlightenment-based secular-liberal institutions to respond to reality before catastrophe overtakes us all.[915] Europe probably already is, to use leftist philosopher Jürgen Habermas' phrase, *post-secular*[916] but, even if it isn't, the data exists to show that the seeds of that reality are already evident in her demography. French sociologist Yves Lambert argues that we should be seeking a *pluralist secularisation* model in which religion 'should not hold sway over social life, but it can play its full role as a spiritual, ethical, cultural or even political resource in the broadest sense of the term, while respecting individual autonomy and democratic pluralism'[917]

His compatriot Bérengère Massignon identifies this as the 'second phase of secularisation' – the first phase being the emergence of the omni-competent state which confused – with a mix of fear and hubris – what belonged to Caesar with what belonged to God. The first phase lasted only 200 years, and in some places in Europe only half that. This is not long by a sociological measure, and perhaps post-secular currents will gain traction in considered and helpful ways within the current century.

Schuman was well aware that 'the creation of European institutions' would never itself be enough. In 1953 he wrote:

> *'In this construction of a new world we are aware that political technique left to itself will not be enough without the spirit which must orient it. For this reason, in everything that we attempt together, be it at the United Nations or in the regional organisations such as NATO or the Council of Europe, we place the accent upon spiritual and cultural tasks. The primacy of the spiritual affirms itself here as elsewhere.'*[918]

The great epistemic difficulty facing the secular claim, and one which must be tacitly acknowledged, is that it still pretends that Human Rights[919] can be defended without the Judeo-Christian doctrine of human exceptionalism - the *Imageo Dei* doctrine we discussed in relation to Patrick. Even Atheist Professor John Gray, in his book *Straw Dogs*, demolishes that claim – calling Humanism 'Christianity in disguise.' Once you take God out of the picture, he posits, there is no basis for talking about the dignity of man or human exceptionalism.[920]

The atheist theologian Don Cupitt writes that 'Nobody in the West can be wholly non-Christian. You may call yourself non-Christian, but the dreams you dream are still Christian dreams.' Further, Cupitt carries forward the point that 'the modern Western secular world is itself a Christian creation.' The journalist Douglas Murray, again not religious, makes the point that 'the post war culture of human rights that insists upon itself and is talked of by its devotees as though it were a faith does itself appear to be an attempt to implement a secular version of the Christian conscience. It may be partially successful in doing so. But it is a religion that must necessarily be ill at ease with itself because it is uncertain of its moorings.'[921]

In *After Virtue*, Alasdair Macintyre goes deeper, claiming that the concept of a man as a man (qua man) *with inalienable rights* is itself a modern construct. His research showed that there is not even a word approaching this concept until the High Middle Ages. Apparently, it lacks content when viewed in the light of Hebrew, Greek, Latin, and Arabic thought until 1400 AD. (And not in Japan before the mid nineteenth century.) Furthermore, he says, all efforts to give good reasons for believing such rights exist have failed.

To say that human exceptionalism is a self-evident truth will not do either, for that is to derive what ought to be from what is. There are no self-evident truths.[922] The mantra, oft-repeated and thus culturally embedded has had undoubted value but, as Macintyre (himself, a Christian convert from atheism) argues, when human rights are balanced against utility or traditional justice, there is often found to be no way of prioritizing. In the end, 'moral incommensurability is itself the product of a particular historical injunction.... the concepts of rights and utilities are a matching pair of incommensurable fictions. .... the mock rationality of the debate conceals the arbitrariness of the will to power at work in its resolution.' No wonder, as one person's rights are infringed by another's utility, Macintyre says that, 'protest becomes the predominant moral feature of the modern age and why indignation, the predominant modern emotion.'

Perhaps we are just too close to see this. Professor Gray's claim that Humanism is 'Christianity in disguise,' is essentially what Nietzsche was saying 150 years ago; railing against what he called an 'English inconsistency'[923] of 'petty females' (he was referring to George Eliot) who thought they could keep Christian ethics without the credal assent. Nietzsche knew this would ultimately fail, but that the inconsistent English were not thorough enough to accept the logical conclusion. On the contrary, he observed with scorn, 'In England, one must rehabilitate oneself after every little emancipation from theology by showing, in a veritably awe-inspiring manner, what a moral fanatic one is. That is the price they pay there.' It is the price we still pay, and at one level we can be thankful, for at least this illusion meant we didn't fall for something worse, like the race-based morality espoused by the Nazis, Italians, and Japanese, or the utopia of the Soviet, Chinese or Korean Communists.

As we have noted in an earlier chapter, a major solvent of late 19th and 20th century British Christianity was, ironically, a secularised Christian conscience; a moral seriousness attempting to maintain the high call of Christian ethics without the 'barbarities' of atonement theology. Essentially, Jesus' teaching without Jesus' blood. A Christ without a cross. Easter morning without Good Friday. It was gradual but no less thorough for all that. In Chapter 29 of *Thus Spake Zarathustra*, Nietzsche attacked the hypocrisy at the centre of those new 'preachers of equality' in his day for accepting Christian suppositions into their movements, and using them to mask a 'will to power.' The Communist Manifesto had already been in circulation for over three decades when Nietzsche wrote:

'Lo, this is the tarantula's den! Would'st thou see the tarantula itself? Here hangeth its web: touch this, so that it may tremble. There cometh the tarantula ... and I know also what is in thy soul. Revenge is in thy soul: wherever thou bitest, there ariseth black scab; with revenge, thy poison maketh the soul giddy!

Thus, do I speak unto you in parable, ye who make the soul giddy, ye preachers of equality! Tarantulas are ye unto me, and secretly revengeful ones! ...Otherwise, however, would the tarantulas have it. "Let it be very justice for the world to become full of the storms of our vengeance"— thus do they talk to one another. "Vengeance will we use, and insult, against all who are not like us"— thus do the tarantula-hearts pledge themselves.

"And 'Will to Equality'— that itself shall henceforth be the name of virtue; and against all that hath power will we raise an outcry!" Ye preachers of equality, the tyrant-frenzy of impotence crieth thus in you for "equality": your most secret tyrant-longings disguise themselves thus in virtue-words! ...Fretted conceit and suppressed envy—perhaps your fathers' conceit and envy: in you break they forth as flame and frenzy of vengeance. ...In all their lamentations soundeth vengeance, in all their eulogies is maleficence; and being judge seemeth to them bliss. But thus, do I counsel you, my friends: distrust all in whom the impulse to punish is powerful! ...And when they call themselves "the good and just," forget not, that for them to be Pharisees, nothing is lacking but — power! .... Thus, spake Zarathustra.'[924]

Fortunately, as the decades have rolled on and given some critical distance, secular historians have found the courage and the market to say so. Tom Holland's Times-best-selling *Dominion – How Christianity made the Western Mind*, is an obvious example. But so too are works by Kyle Harper of Oklahoma University on sexual consent, and Brian Tierny of Cornell University, in the field of Human Rights. Holland writes, 'If secular humanism derives not from reason or from science, but from the distinctive course of Christianity's evolution—a course that, in the opinion of growing numbers in Europe and America, has left God dead—then how are its values anything more than the shadow of a corpse? What are the foundations of its morality, if not a myth?'

To be fair to my secular readers, Holland's book *Dominion* makes uncomfortable reading for Christians too, as he highlights the many failings of Christians to live up to Jesus' teaching. We stand in the dock together, but please note the all-important point, that the church's failure – great as it is – is not epistemic. As an atheist, Harvard's George Sciallabba shows great courage in voicing his own self-doubt, when reviewing Charles Taylor's *A Secular Age*:

'Repeatedly, whether crashing through the canals of Tenochtitlan, or settling the estuaries of Massachusetts, or trekking deep into the Transvaal,
the confidence that had enabled Europeans to believe themselves superior to those they were displacing was derived from Christianity. Repeatedly, though . . . it was Christianity that . . . provided the colonized and
the enslaved with the surest voice. The paradox was profound. No other
conquerors, carving out empires for themselves, had done so as the servants of a man tortured to death on the orders of a colonial official. No
other conquerors . . . had installed . . . an emblem of power so deeply ambivalent as to render problematic the very notion of power.'

But Sciallabba's admission is certainly not the norm in academia or the
mainstream. 'No doubt there are many reasons for this state of affairs,'
writes the atheist philosopher, John Gray, 'but I suspect it is the repression
of the religious impulse that explains the obsessive rigidity of secular
thought. Liberal humanists repress religious experience – in themselves
and others – in much the same way that sexuality was repressed in strait-
laced societies.... In secular cultures, religion is buried in the unconscious,
only to reappear – as sex did among the Victorians – in grotesque and illicit
forms.'[925]

Judaism and Christianity gave the West freedom of conscience based on
a conception of human dignity so revolutionary, that it would not be tolerated in many countries even today. The paradox of this freedom, touched
on by Professor Butterfield in his 1951 Riddell Lectures, is that freedom of
choice is necessarily a double-edged sword:

> '...precisely because the medieval church did its job so well, it was
> bound to promote a kind of world that would be liable to rebel against
> its authority. A Christian civilisation by its nature has to develop to
> what its most faithful servants feel to be its own undoing. Once civilisa-
> tion has so far advanced, freedom of conscience becomes the first requi-
> site for a Christian order of things, even if the result is a kind of world
> in which it is harder to be a Christian and even if religion loses its mo-
> nopoly in society.'

In the same lectures, Butterfield pinpointed the mayhem of Rome's collapse as a moment that gave the new religion 'maximum opportunity; for directing a Europe that had become young and malleable again...' The patrician elites who had not converted, and had been the last bastion of the Ancien Régime, (see chapter 1) were soon to be replaced by Goths and Vandals who needed teachers, scribes and social services. Butterfield did not think that such a historical conjunction was 'repeatable in any or every age of history....except after a catastrophe (that had)... overwhelmed civilisation.' Columban laboured in the aftermath of such a catastrophe, Schuman and Buchman et al did so in a less severe situation. And if our civilisation does go down, as it was in Augustine's day, there will be plenty for us all to do as it goes, and even more to do in the aftermath.

Ardent secularists should welcome the Christian perspective into the public square for their own sake, not the churches' sake. The church will survive in any case, indeed if history is any measure, it will thrive best in the rubble of collapse. The apologist Os Guinness was approached by a very earnest dean of one of China's most prestigious universities. 'What am I missing?' He asked, 'we in China are fascinated by the Christian roots of the western past, in order to see what we can learn for China's future. But you in the West are cutting yourself off from those roots. What am I missing?'

On the sixtieth anniversary of the EU, the French chairman of the convention took pains not to mention Judeo-Christian values in the proposed EU constitution. Valery Giscard d'Estaing, claimed that any reference to God and Christianity would be a 'violation of freedom of conscience.' D'Estaing said, 'Europeans live in a purely secular political system, where religion does not play an important role.' From across the pond an aghast George Weigel called it a 'self-inflicted amnesia.' And for others, like the Irish Prime minister John Bruton, D'Estaing's comments seemed to perpetuate a form 'of secular intolerance in Europe that is every bit as strong as religious intolerance was in the past.'[926] But we might also say when viewing the lives and work of Schuman, Adenauer, and De Gasperi, that the very best of the Christian tradition finds its optimal expression in political life precisely when it secularizes itself and works non-hegemonically within the secular system - and is allowed to do so. In 1979, a more conciliatory

Louise Weiss, who chaired the opening assembly of the European Parliament, said, 'Let us not forget that we are the heirs of an essential spirituality and the witnesses to this spirituality for the well-being of generations to come.'

Dutch philosopher Evert-Jan Ouweneel has made his own analysis of the four specific values Schuman identifies as distinctly European; that of *freedom, equality, solidarity and peace* – and then examines what happens to each of these values when cut off from their Judeo-Christian roots. His conclusion, in line with Schuman and Delors, is that Europe's core problems stem from *the loss of roots*, and that the Christian faith might once again make its vital contribution to European society through the recovery of these roots, and thus these values. 'No-one wants to return to the old days of cultural Christianity in Europe,' he concludes, 'but there is no reason for us to be timid about the Christian roots of Europe's most respected values.'[927]

And what might be said to assure secularists? As a person of faith, I really shrink from taking splinters from the eyes of others when everything I read and see usually only reveals the roof timbers (Jesus' actual words) in my own, and particularly when misunderstanding is so easy on these often-irreducible issues. But then I remember that we have just been observing the diplomatic miracle of the last century – a swift, deep and lasting Franco-German reconciliation. That political settlement was only achieved by a risky acceptance of goodwill between former antagonists.

In fact, there came a most critical moment, as we have seen, when Adenauer had to ratify the Treaty of Paris with nothing more than the gentleman's agreement from Schuman that the Saar issue would be dealt with sometime in the future. My clumsy point here is: we cannot move forward into a more human future if we are not prepared to extend good faith to our former, cultural nemeses. You cannot do this without real risk and misunderstandings: it is the nature of the beast. The sanguine De Gasperi; the choleric Adenauer; the melancholic Monnet; and the phlegmatic Schuman only achieved a solution in so far as they were able to listen, build trust and compromise with the others.

I think that we are culturally mature enough now to acknowledge that well-meaning secularists have often been philosophically inconsistent, whether out of genuine concern for the alternatives or merely to protect their own hegemony. Irresponsible religionists have their share of the blame in this, a great share maybe, but let us acknowledge this inequity. Progressives have claimed that secularism is not a faith like others, while at the same time espousing a progressive liberalism that should be privileged as the coming single faith of an enlightened humanity.[228] But their secularism clearly is, and has always covertly been, a naturalistic faith, and their liberalism too has been religious in substance and style.[229]

They are often, as sociologist, Rodney Stark observed, 'the worst current offenders of norms of civility.' It may be unintentional but secular humanists have demeaned human personhood when they have invited people into the public square .... only on the condition they leave their faith – the foundation of their core beliefs and commitments – at home, on the other side of Lessing's ditch. It is reminiscent of how the Jews were treated after the French Revolution.[230] Thus, dominant parties the world over have recreated the terms of engagement and dismissal. What makes it doubly unjust in Europe, is that it is so obvious to everyone (apart from secular European elites) that the Judeo-Christian heritage is the mainspring, of so much that formed and underpins its uniqueness.

Part of that group blindness was caused by the Lessing's Ditch, Enlightenment settlement. But that cultural settlement was not uniform in extent or character. In fact, there have been three Enlightenments (French, British, and American) that have led to three different constitutional settlements between religion and public life.[231] Gertrude Himmelfarb's *The Roads to Modernity* sets the British and American Enlightenments against the French. Himmelfarb praises the British 'age of benevolence' over the French 'age of reason' and champions even the British Sunday School Movement over against the French *Encyclopédie*. The British Enlightenment, she says, is misrepresented and misunderstood partly because – and here perhaps is a clue – the actual word 'Enlightenment' only entered the English language in the early 20th century. (She assigns its origins to Lord Shaftesbury's *Inquiry Concerning Virtue or Merit* in the early 18th century.) And along with Adam Smith, she rehabilitates Edmund Burke, insisting his love of religion was an essential component to his love of liberty.[232]

But all three settlements have been upset recently: the Americans by a resurgent right; the French by immigrant Muslims who refuse to have a privatised faith; and the English by similar processes, but also by a century of her established church's waning influence in politics and education.[933] For all three, the rise of Islamism as a binary of Western Imperialism has been a litmus.[934] A degraded, secular, self-righteous west has 'fashioned' Islamism almost as much, perhaps more than, the Koran. The West's inability to see this is more than evenly matched by their governments' inabilities to confront it.

Ideologies may be resisted with guns but cannot be fought with guns. The secular ideology will not be found a compelling bulwark against Islamism, in the same way, that it was not against Communism in Schuman's day. The arrogance of secularism, as an 'ism', is that it assumed religion would evaporate under the explanatory powers of science. That giant hubris has come back to haunt it and will one day be its epitaph.

Of course, the EU has not tried to abolish religion but it has marginalised it as a source for valid norms of thought and behaviour in public life. That has been a mistake – understandable given Europe's history – but nevertheless a terrible mistake. Where are these virtues that were supposedly discovered and unleashed by the enlightenments? We have all been educated in them, relentlessly so, but where are they now when Europe needs them most? They have largely evaporated under pressures far less extreme than our grandparents faced. *That is a massive wake up call.* How bad does it have to get before we give up on plasters and call in a doctor? If there is no fruit, we had better re-examine the root. We had better, also identify where, if anywhere, the fabled European Spirit is still actually growing.

The secular view of religion in the UK is five parts irrelevance, four parts obscurantism, and one-part sectarian hatred. But is this reality or a wish-fulfilment projection? What do the facts say about this minuscule percentage of the population who many assume should be, if they are not already, extinct? In England and Wales, research done in 2016 by the (non-religious) consultancy group New Philanthropy Capital (NPC) found that 'faith-based charities make up 49% of all overseas-aid charities and 45% of human-rights charities. The faith-based sector also accounts for 39% of all anti-poverty charities.'[935] That is staggering when one considers how few 'people of faith' England and Wales now have. While some special advocacy groups are good at punching above their weight in the halls of power (a Marxian trait), it seems that religious people are quietly doing something equivalent in the third sector, which after all is crudely worth a massive £23.1 Billion in Britain.

Evangelical Christians – usually the most maligned sector of the Christian community – are three times as likely to volunteer compared to the national average.[936] And the more seriously Christians take their faith the more hours they volunteer. That is not to disparage the work of other groups (I am the trustee of a Christian Foodbank where many of the 160 plus volunteers claim no religious affiliation) but merely to highlight in very simplistic terms that secular people need not necessarily fear conceding a measure of the public square to fellow citizens who think differently from them on key issues and yet also are working for a just and equitable society.

We must all face the monsters under the rug before they get too big. It is not secularism *per se,* but a hegemonic neo-secularism that has embedded itself into the gateways of power, to eventually bring down the West in its attempts to maintain it in its own image. As I pointed out in an earlier chapter, brute demography predicts that Europe will become more religious in the next half century. From Jacques Delors' 1990's viewpoint, there are only two possible outcomes. Either the governing elites acknowledge their inability to generate civility without significant ballast from the Judeo-Christian epistemic base, or 'the whole thing blows.'

The geopolitical consequences of a fragmented Europe, at this moment in history, are barely worth thinking about. The EU elites should take Odon Vallet's advice: 'If you are the type of person who buys stocks and bonds, I'd buy Christianity. The price is now very low... it has to go up.' As the Burgundians encouraged those Irish monks, so the EU should be allowing the Christian viewpoint to compete with the secular-liberal viewpoint on equal terms in a civil public square. Frankly, as Theudeuric or Guntrum could easily tell them: 'Yes, certain Christians can be troublesome, but on balance and if regulated correctly, they have in their religious DNA all the right impulses to build what you're after and hold it together. And, well, frankly, they are cheap too, when you consider the alternatives.'

Europeans urgently need to make some admission of this ideological failure. A leading English political journalist wrote that the lack of reflection within E.U. leadership, between 2016-2019, was akin to the directors in denial about any shared responsibility for insolvency of their company. 'Trapped in the sterility of the status quo, its leaders are like members of the *ancien régime*, oblivious to legitimate complaint,' and by so doing 'risk their own undoing.'[937] Let us hope not. What I argue for here is a new ideological pluralism as articulated in the 'Sphere Sovereignty' of Abraham Kuyper, the early 20th century Dutch Prime Minister. (See the text and footnote in Chapter 8) But that will require repentance.

The word *repentance* in Greek literally means to 'change one's mind'. And along with a tacit renegotiation of the religious (faith-based) nature of secularism, one would hope also that its myth of *the common core* would be laid to rest. Patient and determined dialogue is to be applauded and is not without its garlands. But this can only go so far. This is where tolerance is key; for in the public sphere, there is no real common core, no course to which history will progress, no universal civilisation of mankind yet to be uncovered by political science; no pure humanity or irreducible unity beyond the complexity and diversity we already see.

In saying this I am saying little more than John Stuart Mill in *On Liberty* or Isaiah Berlin in *Four Essays on Liberty*. A utopian belief that the global free market will smooth the world's diversity is perhaps more dangerous than the blooded sword of Charlemagne or the phalanxes of Alexander the Great – who attempted and failed in producing a similar homogeneity. 'At some point, differences will always be 'religiously irreducible, philosophically incommensurable and politically intractable.'[938] And if the core has proved a myth, then so too that neo-secular liberalism was its great protector. In its place, we all need (both secular and religious voices) to seek for peaceful means of existing with our deepest differences, rather than trying to find a rational all-inclusive identity that will never come.

Pierre Hassner is clear that the power of the EU is in its mass only so far as it is a unified mass. But here too is the EU's problem; the 'imperfect, even ambiguous and shaky nature of its unity.'[939] Euroscepticism and Europhobia took the greatest hold exactly as the Euro was introduced when we could have expected the greatest solidarity. What could be more unifying than forms of fiscal integration? Quite a lot, it seems. Was the ensuing fallout the result of Schuman's challenge gone unheeded? Partially perhaps. But if national populations are merely told the soul of Europe is peace and personal affluence, might they withdraw support when that promise proves inadequate? Is this not, at least partially, behind the rise of populist movements and even populist governments within the EU bloc?

But if instead, we say it was, rather, mass migration pressures, then the obvious counter argument would be that surely the pressure of increased migration has only highlighted the existing and underlying weakness. The sharp increase in pressure on an abscess will tell you soon enough that something rotten has been growing in your gums hitherto unknown. Migration is the pressure; Europe without a soul is the abscess.

'At present, we are witnessing a wave that is challenging the base of these values across all European societies. Political forces, which are highly critical, hostile or even disdainful of these values, and which aim to change the system, are gathering strength, sometimes in a spectacular manner and they are even entering office, at both local and national level.'[940]

The USSR collapsed because it was a top-down political system too rigid for change, at least until it was too late. When it fell, it did so with a speed that took everyone by surprise. Many are warning that the rigidity of the Euro itself is at the heart of schismatic forces within the EU. To mark its 20th anniversary in January 2019 the EU Commissioner Jean Claude Juncker hailed the single currency as a 'symbol of unity' and as delivering 'prosperity' – a claim that is quite extraordinary when one considers the rather obvious political divisions and unsustainable credit it has created. Economist Paul Krugman wrote that the 'real story behind Europe's troubles lies not in the deficit but in the policy elites, who pushed the Continent into adopting a single currency well before it was ready for such an experiment.'

Italy and Greece are a case in point. More than most geographically vulnerable, to migration from Africa, they were badly let down by the EU who did not do enough to help when help was definitely needed. In May 2018, the EU was shocked when the Italians voted-in a bizarre coalition of right-wing and left-wing populist parties[941] that not only threatened to deport half a million illegal immigrants, and hold a referendum on continued EU membership, but also to flout the EU budget deficit rules. As the fourth largest EU economy, an irresponsibly spendthrift Italian government would not only make Greece and Brexit look like a fleabite, but would also have jeopardised the entire Eurozone. As one British newspaper put it, 'if Italy blows, the whole thing will blow.'[942] Brussels ultimately made the Italians bend as they did Greece, but it will not be the end of the story.

The Italian capitulation meant the breaking of a cornerstone of an election pledge. When an electorate can't even trust a populist government to deliver, what is the world coming to![943] The tragic spiral of populism is well known: unhappy voters, irresponsible promises, bad outcomes; even unhappier voters; and still more irresponsible promises, and worse outcomes.'[944] You can almost hear De Gasperi turning in his grave.

And Italy is no isolated case. France has flouted its budgetary commitments year on year. And even in Germany, it is not so unthinkable that the alternative wing (AfD) and the ultra-left-wing party could one day come to power. The leftist economist Yanis Varoufakis,[945] is outspoken in his criticism of the inflexible architecture of the Euro, but also of the hubris of cynical elites in Brussels whom he dealt with as finance minister of a bankrupted Greece – elites, he claims, who place their political hegemony over and above sensible economic policies.[946]

Pierre Hassner delivered a grim challenge to the EU in the final paragraph of his article for the Schuman Foundation in 2018; 'Faced with the evidence of impotence and the risk of catastrophe, only a rebound in solidarity, simultaneously political, social and European, overcoming at the same time individual selfishness and the absolute power of the markets, can give Europe any chance of regaining a sense of its vocation and its power.'

On 4th March 2019, President Macron issued a letter asking all citizens of Europe for 'renewal together around three ambitions: freedom, protection, and progress.' Still recovering from the yellow-vested unrest in France, Macron voiced what we have seen above; that this is a critical moment when we risk losing the gains of the founding fathers of Europe to populists with anger but few solutions. He gives various sensible prescriptions, one of them is to have a multidisciplinary 'conference.... with citizens' panels' which can 'hear academics, business and labour representatives, and religious and spiritual leaders.' Macron hopes that such a direct approach would:

> '...define a roadmap for the European Union that translates these key priorities into concrete actions. There will be disagreement, but is it better to have a static Europe or a Europe that advances, sometimes at different paces, and that is open to all?
>
> In this Europe, the peoples will really take back control of their future. In this Europe, the United Kingdom, I am sure, will find its true place. Citizens of Europe, the Brexit impasse is a lesson for us all. We need to escape this trap and make the upcoming elections and our project meaningful. It is for you to decide whether Europe and the values of progress that it embodies are to be more than just a passing episode in history. This is the choice I propose: to chart together the road to European renewal.[947]

This all sounds laudable and Macron should be applauded. He would certainly be cheered on by Churchill, who would approve of the French showing such leadership. Let us hope he receives the support of key partners and this becomes more than just another talking shop. In a fit of enthusiasm, I wrote to him asking him to consider having the conference at The Hague in order to honour the extraordinary Congress there in 1948. There is no reason why this could not be similarly formative in resolving the issues we have mentioned in this and other chapters.

But, all that aside, I stress again that a challenge of this magnitude cannot be addressed solely downstream in politics. And neither can it be addressed if those power structures are systemically antithetical to democratic change. If Macron only seeks solutions that confirm existing Brussels group-think, then his call for a new movement will be worse than pointless. History's verdict is almost unanimous: when you have the power, and *you know that you are right*, then you (or your tribe, caste, party, religion) are usually the most dangerous element in the commonweal. Religious people have proved that, and so now neo-secularists are proving it in their turn. If there is, or will be, a happier ending to this story, it will be through the people who build bridges across Lessing's Ditch – psychological bridges, personal friendships, community initiatives, political structures, and international networks.

The surprise of this book for me is just how few people that actually takes. As I look back on the drama in this book, there are certain things that will always stay with me; like the roomful of European idealists toasting Churchill with water at The Hague in 1948 because there was no wine; or Frank Buchman wading through the mire of German ecclesiastical politics in the thirties to offer opportunities of gospel-transformation to a fallen Nazi-bishop and demoniacal Reichsführer; or the embryonic prototype of post-fascist Italy flowering among the 800 dissidents hiding in St John Lateran; or Monnet's tiny, multinational team working without interpreters on the ECSC drafts; or Schuman and Adenauer working through the almost insurmountable problems of the Saar; or Giuseppe Saragat risking the coalition with Christian Democrats. There are small details, like Spaak's inconsolable grief at the news of De Gasperi's death, weeping like a child while the Luxembourg prime minister tries to comfort him. And then there are things too large to comprehend; the Holocaust and the depths of human evil; the sacrifice of the Russians on the eastern front, and of Britain as they bankrupted themselves for their allies, or the American sacrifice when they voluntarily taxed themselves to ensure Europe's physical and social reconstruction.

How can an individual, a country, a continent live in the light of such great sacrifice? How can we be worthy of such men and women? And how can we interpret this history without an invitation to dialogue across Lessing's Ditch? Let this epilogue, crude as it is, serve as an entrée for further discussion and change on both sides.

CONCLUSION – A PERSONAL CHALLENGE

Columban, Schuman, Adenauer, and De Gasperi (amongst others) have reissued to us Petrarch's challenge to become *Viris Illustribus* –

that is, great men and women of purpose and action in our day, not just in politics but in the many other culture-shaping activities upstream of it. Thomas Carlyle wrote that 'a man lives by believing something; not by debating and arguing about many things.'

I have endeavoured to put flesh and bones on that amorphous word, 'spirituality'. Frankly, the world needs more Schumans and Columbans, more 'saints in suits', or 'imperfect instruments of providence', as Schuman would phrase it. More De Gasperis to stand astride the frontiers between nation and nation, and more Buchmans to stand across the frontiers between man and man, upholding repentance and forgiveness. And yes, we need more Monnets and Spaaks too. Flexible networkers of good faith, not afraid of new solutions – or even old ones. Out of the box, straddling the ditch, open hands and open hearts. If we are to rise to Solzhenitsyn's 'spiritual blaze' for the renewal our age demands, then we must face down every polarizing element as an enemy at least as serious as every other. The level of solidarity between nations following World War II looks, from our end of history, like the miraculous conjunction of planetary forces and persons of almost mythic virtue. Our faith for similar alignments and equally heroic leaders in the future may be small but small faith is not no faith. We need not despair.

In 2007 Alasdair MacIntyre was asked to explain the closing lines of *After Virtue*, 'we're not waiting for Godot, but for another—doubtless very different—St. Benedict.' He wrote in the new edition,

> 'It was my intention to suggest......that ours too is a time of waiting for new and unpredictable possibilities of renewal. It is also a time of resisting as prudently and courageously and justly and temperately as possible the dominant social, economic, and political order of advanced modernity.'[948]

Perhaps we can close with the observation that it is not the place of actors in a play to instruct the writer, or the director, or even to know the lines and actions of other players. We are actors, and we are placed on earth to act the best part we may with the lines and the stage-time we are given. I have been thrilled and enriched by studying these great personalities. It has affirmed for me the wonderful truth that it is not always faceless bureaucrats and nameless syndicates, but often human beings and human friendships that move the hour hand of history in positive ways. But I know too, that I must not fool myself by just leaving the matter there, for that would leave me only as an audience member and not an actor. We have tried to glimpse from the outside something we are very much within, and for which we have responsibilities. Schuman *et al* left a vision of international cooperation that was open-ended. Their heirs have taken it in a direction and to an extent that many find problematic. But this does not mean the course of history is set.

In the 20th century, we British have had to learn that our stability is not to hold the balance of power in Europe after all, nor even that our strength is in the weakness of other nations. In the 21st century Americans too will have to adjust to being second place in the league of global economies as China soars ahead.[949] To repeat Bunyan's words in *Pilgrim's Progress*, 'it is hard to go down to the valley of humiliation without catching a slip by the way.' It has been hard for Britain and still is, and it will be so for America. On the international scene, the next century will bring drastic realignment of powers, and between those powers will be individuals who will shape the future in unpredictable ways. That is one of the more constant lessons in this great drama of history, where we are all called upon to play, rarely a brilliant hand, but usually a bad hand as best we may.

Churchill gave, what many consider, his best speech at a recruiting meeting in London, not during World War II but in the hell of World War I. The 'home by Christmas' motif was long gone but Churchill nevertheless found grounds for hope among his countrymen as they faced German industrial militarism. 'They think we cannot beat them. It will not be easy. It will be a long job; it will be a terrible war, but in the end, we shall march through terror to triumph.' Churchill's Sceptred Isle has produced many surprises and many solutions. The islands' bovine inability to embrace extremism, except in tea drinking, has caused us to resist many harmful political innovations, but has also paradoxically led us to make unexpected contributions to many spheres of modern life. Churchill's speech, far from echoing the disillusion of other soldiers like Sassoon, takes on an almost biblical fervour when he considers how the challenge and sacrifice of the international crisis was bringing the best out of the British:

Churchill and De Gasperi in London seeking to win the peace after World War II

'There is something infinitely greater and more enduring which is emerging already out of this conflict – a new patriotism, richer, nobler... I see among all classes, high and low, shedding themselves of selfishness, a new recognition that the honour of the country does not depend merely on the maintenance of its glory in the stricken field, but also in protecting its homes from distress. It is bringing a new outlook for all classes. The great flood of luxury and sloth which has submerged the land is receding and a new Britain is appearing.'

The inevitable hardship that Britain expects in the next decade, and the difficulties faced by our continent which we have enumerated above, may yet all call forth some greatness of soul among us. We may yet be a blessing. The history books are still open. MacIntyre's mention of 'unpredictable possibilities of renewal' sounds more hopeful and less reactionary than 'resisting......the dominant order.... of advanced modernity,' but either way there is plenty here for the optimist and pessimist alike. What we must escape is the fatalism that causes inertia, so characteristic of late antiquity.

In the famous film, Lawrence of Arabia emerges from the Nefud desert, having gone back to rescue the Arab Gasim. The sheik, played by Omar Sharif, had initially considered it impossible. Lawrence should just accept it was Gasim's fate to die. 'It is written,' he tells him. But now Lawrence has returned having rescued Gasim and he says, after a long and meaningful stare, 'Nothing is written.' It is a pregnant moment, and many viewers' favourite line of the film. Determinism is a philosophical black hole from which any culture would be glad to escape. It may be almost certain that the European Union will break apart,[950] *but nothing is written.* History, as ever, hangs on more slender threads than some scholars are ever willing to admit. MacIntyre's 'unexpected possibilities of renewal' may even come from just one reader of this book. As Omar Sharif's character says later, 'truly for some men nothing is written unless they write it.'

Escaping the inertia of fatalism: Sharif and O'Toole in the 1962 film 'Lawrence of Arabia.'

The men and women we have studied in this book certainly did that. Maritain, who spurred Schuman, Adenauer and De Gasperi on to so much, speaks powerfully across time to us all:

'The more difficult this immense task appears, the more it should tempt men. Peoples are set in motion only for difficult things. In all the nations today.... the leading classes have gone morally bankrupt. The failure of our world is their failure. The time has come to call upon the moral and spiritual reserves of the people, of common humanity—the last reserves of civilization—indissolubly in support of victory and reconstruction. And these moral and spiritual reserves are not a tool in the hands of those with authority; *they are the very power*, and the source of initiative, of men cognizant of their personal dignity and their responsibility.... The essential problem of reconstruction is not a problem of plans, it is a problem of men, the problem of the new leadership to come. ... Everything depends on the new leaders. The world has desperate need of them. But the task to which we are summoned, the task we have to pursue with all the more courage and hope because at each moment it will be betrayed by human weakness, this task will have to have for its objective... a world of free men imbued in its secular substance by a genuine and living Christianity, a world in which the inspiration of the Gospel will orient common life toward an heroic humanism.' [951]

'Above all, throughout our history it has been of the first importance that.... the Church stands as a perpetual centre from which the whole process can be forever starting over again. Those who preach the Gospel, nurse the pieties, spread New Testament Love, and affirm the spiritual nature of man are guarding the very source, and keeping open the very spring from which new things will still arise. .... The continually renascent power of our religion seems to consist in this unlimited opportunity to return to the original spring, the original simplicities of the faith.'

Prof H. Butterfield, *Christianity in European History,* 1951

THE FOUNDING FATHERS LOOKING ON AT THE EUROPE WE WILL MAKE.
(Author filming with the director of the Schuman house museum in Oct 2018)

856. T.S. Eliot *"The Idea of a Christian Society"*, 1939 p13 & p25

857. As of December 2018, even Spain, whose suffering under Franco had seemingly immunised them to far-right populism, elected an almost unknown far-right group (called Vox) to 12 seats in the Andalusia regional parliament. One more set of symptoms masquerading as a cure? Germany's possible leader in waiting is vocal in her opposition to further EU integration in defence and environmental projects. An active Catholic, Annegret Kramp-Karrenbauer appears to favour turning back the clocks to a community based on economic cooperation. A reconstituted E.U. on those lines would be more palatable to the English and would cut the rug from radical political elements across the bloc.

858. John Gray, *Straw Dogs: Thoughts on Humans and Other Animals*

859. *"Recapturing the SOUL OF EUROPE*: Interview with P. Hassner, « Tout l'art de la politique est de combiner passion et modération », As Pierre Hassner said, "Liberal democracy which won the Second World War and the Cold War is under attack from all sides. Some explain this by the fact that the liberals do not really believe their own ideas and that they are not prepared to sacrifice themselves for them.' Centre de Recherches Internationales (CERI) de Sciences Po, 17 December 2015 http://www.sciencespo.fr/ceri/fr/ content/tout-l-art-de-la-politiqueest-decombiner-passion-etmoderation See also A. Shulsky, « La démocratie libérale : victorieuse et assaillie », Commentaire n°148, Winter 2014-2015, pp. 725-732.

860. This speech was given in Brussels, on the 14 April, 1992. And Delors wasn't a lone Christian voice in the 1990s. The president of the Evangelical Alliance in the UK, Sir Fred Catherwood, also held the position as vice-president of the European Parliament (1989-1992). His case for Christian engagement in shaping the European Union can be found in his book; *Pro-Europe?*

861. Telegraph: Matthew Holehouse, in Brussels, 6:35PM BST 22 Oct 2015

862. I note in passing that as a key contributor to EU funds, Britain's exit will produce heightened fiscal bickering within the remaining member states. Along with the demographic, migratory, and geopolitical issues outlined in this book, it could be one more nail in the coffin for the most ambitious political project since the league of Delos.

863. http://www.europarl.europa.eu/news/en/press-room/20181106IPR18316/ merkel-nationalism-and-egoism-must-never-have-a-chanceagain-in-europe

864. In Merkel's view, the timing had never been more crucial 'because the times where we could rely unreservedly on others are over.' She was referring here to the American's wavering commitment to NATO. Her partial solution to this dilemma, and also one that ensured that Europe is 'heard in a globalised world' was to resurrect proposals for a European army – what De Gasperi always saw as a necessary leg of the stool. In Merkel's words, an EU defence force 'would show the world that there will never be war again between European countries.'

865. Ibid

866. Jean-Noël Tronc, And what if we started over, beginning with culture? How can Europe win back its sovereignty from the American, Russian and Chinese blocks? https://www.robert-schuman.eu/en/doc/questions-d-europe/qe-507-en.pdf

867. A study, undertaken by Harris Interactive, in 7 of the Union's Member States, found that two thirds of Europeans believe that the 'technological giants are now more powerful than the Union's institutions.' Indeed, nearly the same figure (61%) thinks that the very same giants 'are affecting the functioning of democracy.'

868. During the Covid crisis, China targeted countries aggrieved by Brussels, like Greece and Serbia, with medical aid. Beijing hopes to rehabilitate its reputation as the rising benevolent superpower. The markets watch hopefully for Chinese economic recovery as a bellwether global salvation. The 500 billion Euro recovery fund that EU leaders agreed by June 2020 was a necessary start, but not the 'Hamiltonian Moment' that some had hoped for. (The US founding father Alexander Hamilton got the federal authorities to assume the debts of individual states) The EU was criticised by almost all the press for its slowness to act, as COVID exposed the existing tensions discussed in this chapter.

869. Paragraph 1 of the *Document on The European Identity* published by the Nine Foreign Ministers on 14 December, 1973, in Copenhagen. https://www.cvce.eu/content/publication/1999/1/1/02798dc9-9c69-4b7d-b2c9-f03a8db7da32/publishable_en.pdf

870. China is 30% but the USA is only 10%

871. East-West relations are precarious. After repeated Russian violations of the Open Skies Treaty in 2019, the USA pulled out in 2020. As Putin positioned himself to be Russia's leader almost permanently in 2020, China created even great waves elsewhere. Friction in Hong Kong and on the Indian border is one concern, but so too is Chinese imperial overreach in the South China Sea in defiance of international law. If ever there was an oven-ready US-China naval conflict, it is here.

872. President Juncker announced the creation of a European Defence Fund in his 2016 State of the Union address. The Commission was already paving the way under the EU budget period which ended in 2020. For the first time in European history, the EU was incentivising European defence cooperation with a budget envelope of €590 million (€90 million for research over 2017-2019 and €500 million for developing equipment and technology during 2019-2020). On the basis of these two "pilot" programmes, and scaling up initial funding, the Commission proposed in June 2018 a fully-fledged European Defence Fund worth €13 billion under the next EU long-term budget to cover both the research and capability strands. The European Defence Fund will complement other EU programmes proposed by the Commission, in particular, the €6.5 billion earmarked for the Connecting Europe Facility to enhance the EU's strategic transport

infrastructures to make them fit for military mobility, and the proposal for a new €100 billion research and innovation programme Horizon Europe. Source: http://europa.eu/rapid/pressrelease_IP-19-1269_en.htm

873. George Friedman, *Flashpoints – The Emerging Crisis in Europe,* Doubleday p.185

874. Ibid p.254. We must remember that in 2018 Russia's GDP was little over a third of Germany's and as Friedman goes on to explain, 'Russia is trying to rebuild its buffers to the west. The Europeans and Americans would like to deny them those buffers so they can reshape Russian behaviour. But the lack of European military power makes it an uneven game.... just as Russian power moves westwards, securing its buffer, the question for these countries is how far will Russians go.'

875. Ibid, p.254.

876. Pius XII has been labelled 'Hitler's Pope' by his detractors for not taking a more vocal stand against Hitler's treatment of the Jews. His supporters claim that his behind-the-scenes work saved many lives and that it was not cowardice but wisdom that led him to avoid direct confrontation with Hitler. In March 2020, Historians were finally given access to the Vatican archives to settle the question. As one journalist in a German newspaper commented, 'the archives provide many explanations, but no redemption.'

877. Have European Christians forgotten Hitler? During the 1930's malaise of growing permissiveness, easy divorce, abortion, and decadence, reactionary German Christians were easy prey for Hitler who pledged that the 'national government will make its first and foremost duty to restore the unity and spirit of our people. I will preserve and defend the foundations upon which the power of our nation rests. It will take Christianity, as the basis of our collective morality, and the family as the nucleus of our people and state, under its protection.' It was thus easy for him to buy the allegiance of, what he called 'this clerical gang' who he knew he could make 'go the way we want quite easily.'

878. Perhaps the most miserable facets of the new woke religion is that it bears all the appearances of the worst excesses of Calvinist predestination theology with none of the positive points. Select groups of 'the chosen' – who infight quite as viciously as any fanatical religious group has ever done – are predestined to inherit earthly righteousness. But for others (most notably heterosexual, Caucasian males, no matter how virtuous, apologetic or low-born) there is no salvation – no place in the 'hierarchy of grievances.'

879. Robert Schuman, *Pour L'Europe*

880. Strong words indeed. The brackets are mine. Michel J Sentis, *Eveillers de Conscience.* Caux Books, p.82

881. John Adams to John Taylor, 17 December 1814.'Remember Democracy never lasts long. It soon wastes, exhausts and murders itself. There never was a Democracy yet, that did not commit suicide. It is in vain to say that Democracy is less vain, less proud, less selfish, less ambitious, or less avaricious than Aristocracy or Monarchy. It is not true in Fact and nowhere appears in history. Those

Passions are the same in all Men under all forms of Simple Government, and when unchecked, produce the same Effects of Fraud Violence and Cruelty.'

882. Jürgen Habermas, *Time of Transitions* (Polity Pres, 2006) and also Michael Burliegh, 'Godless Europeans Turn to Cultural Christianity,' Daily Telegraph, 31st July, 2006

883. Jacques Maritain, *Christianity and Democracy: The Rights of Man and Natural Law*

884. Jacques Maritain, *Man and the State.* Page 175

885. Jacques Maritain, *Christianity and Democracy: The Rights of Man and Natural Law*

886. Ibid. P.78

887. Ibid

888. G. K. Chesterton, *Orthodoxy*

889. Emil Brunner, *Christianity and Civilisation: Foundations and Specific Problems* p.198

890. Summarised pithily; 'I shop therefore I am', or in Latin: *Tesco Ergo Sum!*

891. An accessible introduction to Ruskin's works on Political economy can be found in *Unto This Last*. I have also done a rough summary in my 2012 paper, John Ruskin & the Economics of Inequality, retrievable here: https://1drv.ms/b/s!Anbjq9cpZ1JDjb0zjnRuxH8RdFEXKw?e=flB793

892. The British do not have to look back far in their history to find inspirational examples of this. George Cadbury is one, and so is Catherine Booth, who on her death bed made her husband (General Booth of the Salvation Army) promise to build, not a chapel, but a just match factory. This he did to good effect. In the new factory, the labourers were paid double what Bryant & May offered. Nor were employees forced to use the dangerous yellow phosphorus – an example that their competitors were eventually forced to follow too.

893. The idea that forms of Islamism could be totalitarian is not a new or controversial observation after ISIS' caliphate. Bassam Tibi's book *Islam and Islamism* has a chapter on totalitarianism, stating 'Political Islam is a totalitarian ideology that presents itself as ... a kind of magic answer for all of the problems – global and local, socioeconomic or value-related – in the crisis-ridden world of Islam.' For Tibi, the totalitarianism of Islamism is ultimately found at the ideological level.

894. I noted recently that Jordan allots a minimum of 7% of parliamentary seats to Christians, even though they only comprise 4% of the population. Jordan also has experienced high levels of Islamic immigration in recent decades but has managed a far more successful integration of the migrant populations than Europe. There may be much we can learn from Jordan about the future of Europe.

895. At the time of writing, my own family is involved with 3 excellent Christian charities that have arisen in the last decade to address these needs. The Trussel Trust Foodbanks are well known for addressing food security. Safe Families and Linking Lives (which mentor vulnerable families, and tackle loneliness) have also both been greeted with open arms by Doctors and Social Services, who struggle to deal with,

what is in many cases, the fallout from the breakdown of the nuclear family and increase in social problems which represent the wider story of late modernity's existential issues.

896. See Dr. Frank Prochaska in *Christianity and Social Service in Modern Britain: The Disinherited Spirit.* Oxford University Press (16 Feb. 2006)

897. The silver tsunami alone will call forth either societal renewal in a deep way or else a catastrophe of increasing neglect and euthanasia.

898. Simone Petrement, from *The Six Pillars of Peace*, May 31st, 1943 issue of Christianity and Crisis

899. When Jeff Fountain (Director of the Schuman Centre for European Studies and former European director of YWAM) was asked by evangelical Christians whether or not the European Union might become the apocalyptic vehicle for the Beast of Revelation (in the Bible), he replied, 'definitely: if Christians who are commissioned to be light and salt in the world remain disengaged on the side-lines and only active in their own church circles.' In his book *Deeply Rooted* about Schuman and the birth of the European integration, Fountain also wrote that 'if Europe becomes a greedy, godless, selfish Beast, it is not because God has destined that or willed that, but because His people have been disobedient and ineffective, sniping from the side-lines.' For Fountain, it is the compromised, worldly-wise church that needs radical change first. Although, perhaps even that is too general for someone like Frank Buchman, who felt that the correct level of analysis was the individual. He, like Christ, addressed his appeal, not to the mass but the person – 'whosoever will hear me and do the will of my Father...' This most interior of challenges must be restated for each generation.

900. George Dawson, *The Folly of Abuse*, from The Birmingham Pulpit, 22nd July 1871, p.3

901. Herbert Butterfield, *Christianity and History* (London: Bell, 1949) 88-89, 130. There have been reprints and revisions in 1950, 1954, 1957, 1960, 1964, 1967, and 2009.

902. *The Year of Our Lord 1943: Christian Humanism in an Age of Crisis*, by Alan Jacobs, Oxford University Press

903. "*The Watchmen*," Harper's, September 2016

904. Quoted from Delblanco's '*The Death of Satan*' p.89

905. https://harpers.org/archive/2016/09/the-watchmen/

906. 'It's bishops were appointed by the Crown on the advice of Prime Ministers who did not need to be English or Christians, let alone Anglicans. The legislation of its General Synod was still subject to parliament, even though the majority of parliamentarians became non-believers. Yet the Anglican hierarchy had no special authority in the kingdom as a whole... The Archbishop of Canterbury... had no right to speak on behalf of British Protestants, let alone British Christians.' Norman Davies, *The Isles*, p. 913 (Macmillan, 1999)

907. It is very interesting to see the same issues addressed from the 19th century Russian orthodox perspective through the mouths of monks and laymen in Dostoyevsky's *The Brothers Karamazov*. Chapter 5, p61-63

908. C. O. Ogilvie, *Cut the Connection: disestablishment and the Church of England* (London 1994)

909. Douglas Murray, *The Strange Death of Europe.'* Bloomsbury

910. I have a particular memory of sitting in a secondary school staff room talking to two English literature teachers who had invited me to do an author day at their school. Just like in the wonderful film 'Dead Poets' Society', they had hoped that beautiful literature could 'save' the children they taught. Their despondency was palpable, and worst of all, their own love of literature had suffered a fatal blow too.

911. A selection of France's best contemporary writers | DW | 11.10.2017". Deutsche Welle. 11 October 2017.

912. Angelique Chrisafis, Michel Houellebecq: "Am I Islamophobic? Probably, yes." 20 October 2017 at the Wayback Machine, The Guardian, September 2015

913. Michael Novak, *The Myth of Romantic Love and Other Essays* p.125

914. The Enlightenment was a decisive departure from the classical and medieval view. For example, Aristotle gave four causes in understanding any phenomena: material causes, formal causes, final causes and efficient causes. In the Lessing's Ditch analysis, the formal and final causes have almost entirely been trodden into the mud and buried from view. This is evident in our arts and our ethics. We are fast losing what Aquinas called recto ratio factabilium (right reason in regard to making things) in the arts, and also recta ratio agibilium, (right reason applied to practice) in ethics and the juridical sphere. Without formal causality, art can become detached from reality and little more than an expression of the artists' intent. (Marcel de Champ famously said, 'what the artist spits is art') And without final causality in law; truth and justice can become expressive merely of subjective desires. Sartre's expression; existence perceives essence, means 'what I desire I will be', and it is the direct outworking of the Nietzschean position in *Beyond Good and Evil*.

915. Jürgen Habermas, *Time of Transitions*, Polity Press, 2006

916. Jean-Paul Willaime, *Europe et religions*, Fayard, 2004

917. *L'Avenir de la France repose sur sa culture*. Montréal, 2nd October 1949 [34J23]

918. No wonder MacIntyre says, in *After Virtue*, 'protest becomes the predominant moral feature of the modern age and why indignation the predominant modern emotion.' Protest is now usually a negative form of engagement because my rights are infringed by someone else's utility. The aggravated unreasonable tone in modern political discourse is often precisely because the two claims are incommensurable. And so, under these conditions, neither can win nor lose the argument in any logical forum.

919. *Straw Dogs;* the book's title comes from a traditional Chinese festival in which straw dogs are created and worshipped for a day, then burnt. Since there is no Creator God, Gray contends, humans have no special significance in the big order of things, yet we esteem ourselves irrationally before, like the straw dogs, we meet a final, meaningless extinction. Therefore, humanism, claiming to be a rational response to irrational religion, is itself irrational! (source Wikipedia)

920. Douglas Murray, *The Strange Death of Europe*, Bloomsbury

921. In fairness, as Ronald Dworkin points out, we cannot prove that these rights do not exist either, but nor can we do it vice versa.

922. *The Twilight of the Idols*, 1888

923. Nietzsche, *Thus Spake Zarathustra*, Ch. 29. The Tarantulas

924. John Gray, *Heresies: Against Progress and Other Illusions*

925. Bruton's accusation is not without some basis. As many test cases over the last decades have shown, nations within the EU have divided civil and religious liberty and elevated one above the other. They have made conscience-based differences into matters of discrimination and so embarked down a dangerous and slippery slope. All disagreements are not discrimination. Hate speech legislation, which assumes a knowledge of intimate motives, has become another clumsy weapon marshalled in the fight against prejudice. Hate, sometimes existing solely in the eye of the beholder, has been instrumentalised by small interest groups to the point where it threatens the rights of other minorities, particularly those groups like Christians whose opinions are out of favour. The softer, though no less devastating, extension of this crude logic easily spills into many other aspects of public life. For example, in 2017, the British were treated to the appalling spectacle of the leader of the Liberal Democrat party being tried by media and resigning his position. Tim Farron, an evangelical Christian was hounded by the press to say whether he believed homosexuality was a sin.

926. From an article entitled *Back to the Roots*, retrieved 2020 https://www.schumancentre.eu/2020/06/back-to-the-roots-brussels-may-9-2010

927. John Gray, *The Seven Types of Atheism* (2018) has been a helpful critique on the religious aspects of atheism – not least because he is an atheist, and therefore brings his challenge from the inside.

928. Anglo-European diplomat Robert Cooper said that if the United States constitutes liberal imperialism, the European Union could be seen as an imperial liberalism.

929. Comte de Clermont-Tonnerre set the terms for all Jews in France by saying, 'the Jews should be denied everything as a nation, but granted everything as individuals... If they do not want this, they must inform us, and we shall then be compelled to expel them.'

930. The French settlement was the most openly atheistic. Mirabeau observed in 1792 'the declaration of the rights of man has become a political Gospel and the French constitution, a religion for which people are prepared to die.' And within a few years this overtly political religion had morphed into overtly religious politics. Burke even wrote of 'Atheism by establishment.'

931. Gertrude Himmelfarb, *The Roads to Modernity: The British, French, and American Enlightenments*. Knopf Doubleday Publishing Group, 18 Dec 2007

932. Os Guinness, *The Case for Civility* p.67

933. Os Guinness, *The Case for Civility* p.96 Guinness also makes an interesting point that Islamic extremism (Islamism as an 'ism') is a truly modern reaction to the modern world, not a medieval one. Islamism's belief in a revolutionary vanguard and 'the power of violence to remake humanity, are highly modern ideas and closer to the views of nineteenth century anarchists and nihilists'.

934. Retrieved Nov 2020: https://www.thinknpc.org/resource-hub/what-a-difference-a-faith-makes/

935. Article in Guardian, 17th March 2011. '81% of evangelical Christians do some kind of voluntary work at least once a month. This compares with a much lower figure of 26% for the population at large, obtained in citizenship surveys by the Department for Communities and Local Government, and is consistent with comparable differences identified by researchers in North America... The level of community engagement is influenced not only by faith, but by how seriously faith is taken. So, their research also showed that those who consider their faith to be the most important thing in their life undertake an average of two hours' volunteering each week, compared with an average of one hour 15 minutes by those who do not consider their faith to be the most important thing in their life. Eighty-six per cent of evangelicals voted in the last general election, compared with 65% in the population at large.' https://www.theguardian.com/commentisfree/belief/2011/mar/17/christians-bigsociety-voluntary-work

936. Jeremy Warner, The Daily Telegraph 27th September 2019 https://www.telegraph.co.uk/politics/2019/09/27/ancien-regime-may-laughingbrexit-britain-just-cutting-edge/

937. Os Guinness, *The Case for Civility*.

938. The geopolitical theorist Pierre Hassner was former research fellow at the CERI-Sciences, and passed away 26th May, 2018 while the first draft of this manuscript was being completed. This extract is from his article What European 'Power'? Source: https://www.robertschuman.eu/en/doc/questions-d-europe/qe-475-en.pdf

939. Thierry CHOPIN & Lukáš MACEK. European Issues n°479 02nd July, 2018. 'In the face of the European Union's political crisis: the vital cultural struggle over values.' https://www.robert-schuman.eu/en/doc/questions-d-europe/qe-479-en.pdf

940. It was referred to at the time as the 'most unconventional and inexperienced government to rule a Western Democracy' since the EU's treaty of Rome in 1957. (The Financial Times)

941. Jeremy Warner in The Telegraph, May, 2018.

942. The Italians, so contemptuous of government generally, have had 20 years re-sisting the structural reforms prescribed by the EU after Brussels bent the rules to allow Italy to join the Eurozone in 1999. (They are doing the same in 2020 with regard to Albania which is so politically corrupt that a gallop poll found the 56% of the population wanted to emigrate something that would be easy within EU membership.) Since the introduction of the Euro, Italy has suffered 20 years of financial stagnation, with a lower GNP per capita today than when it joined. Youth unemployment currently runs at 30%. Under such pressure is easy to see why post-modern people, who have been raised to believe that the highest goal is the happiness of the individual, would choose a populist government, regardless of the consequences for their own nation long term, or the countries of the Eurozone. Apres moi le deluge.

943. Martin Wolf in a Financial Times article about the result of the Italian elections, May 2018

944. Varoufakis calls himself an 'erratic Marxist'.

945. He is part of the leftist DieM25 pan-European political movement which aims to bring the political renewal needed to the EU.

946. https://www.elysee.fr/emmanuel-macron/2019/03/04/for-european-renewal.en

947. Alasdair MacIntyre, *After Virtue*. Prologue xvii

948. They were surpassed by China in 2015

949. Those who still think this impossible should remember that not one leading Sovietologist predicted the failure of the USSR until it happened. The disease is perhaps obvious, and so too the inability of the patient to deal with it, but the extent to which it has taken hold and the timing of death always remain a mystery. The first symptom of British Imperial decline was actually trouble in Ireland, which happened while the empire was outwardly still in the ascendant. Brexit should ring some same bells of alarm in Brussels and Strasbourg.

950. Jacques Maritain, *Christianity and Democracy and The Rights of Man and Natural Law*

951. Lane Fox, *Pagans and Christians* p.141

Appendix 1 – How this Story found the Author

I first heard of Robert Schuman at the Vrije (Free) University in Amsterdam. It was a three-day economics conference in the spring of 2012 and I, interloping as ever as a 'blue-collar scholar', was giving a paper on John Ruskin's economic writings. I am not an economist, far less a Ruskin scholar. In fact, I can't exactly remember how I got onto the speaker's list. It confirmed my existing opinion that the Dutch are far too tolerant as a nation! The place was crawling with academics and public economists from across Europe, North America and Canada. It was the first time I'd heard of Robert Schuman – in fact it was the first time I had heard a lot of things. I was quite over my head and frankly in heaven. (I spent an extra couple of days studying the Impressionist and Industrial design at the Hermitage and the Stedelijk museum, and the Rijks, and dreamily walking the streets listening with earphones to art history lectures by Hans Rookmaaker, a post-war lecturer from the Vrije University. It was bliss.)

But it was through that initial mention of Schuman that I also attended the *State of Europe Forum* a few months later in Dublin, a conference run by the Schuman Centre for European Studies. And it was there that I first heard a summary of Schuman's actual story. (It was also there that I talked with the Czech economist Tomáš Sedláček whose bestselling book *The Economics of Good and Evil* influenced my own writing and histography.) It was also at this Dublin Conference – and this really is a strange link in the chain of causation – that I heard from Sociologist, Os Guinness of those intrepid Irish monks who travelled from their homeland to relight the lamp of learning throughout Europe. Here perhaps was the first twinning of these two men who would form the subject of this book. Anyway, I was thrilled. This was all magnificent stuff. Schuman, the Celtic monks, what an inspiration! Yet somewhere between the island of 'Saints and Scholars' and Liverpool Airport, Ryanair squeezed any thoughts of inspiration right from my mind. And so that knowledge, like the Ring of Power from *Lord of the Rings*, lay dormant for some years until it was ready to find me again.

It happened on the last day of a house-swap holiday on Lake Constance in 2015. We had been there for a month, working on a new edition of a novel, in between camping, hiking, and kayaking trips to the Austrian and Swiss Alps. For our last day I took my wife and one of the younger children to the monastic island of Reichenau, which sits on a bend in the Rhine a few kilometres west of the Swiss city of Konstanz. It was a calm, bright day as we drove the half hour to the causeway, passing vineyards, orchards and glancing wistfully toward the distant Swiss Alps where we had been only a few days before. The 4-kilometre-long island, mainly given over to fruit growing, was designated a UNESCO World Heritage site in 2000 because of the monastery and other churches. One church has 10th century frescoes, a very rare survival. And the abbey itself is of that very simple Romanesque style that I have always preferred to almost any other form of ecclesiastical architecture. Rough-hewn sandstone and limestone polychrome banded arches; monumental, local, honest. Outside, the bailiff's house, partially stone with timber extensions is one of the oldest timber-frame buildings in south Germany. The whole place had once been a hive of scholarship, art, science, and music during the Carolingian renaissance. The great names of Walafrid Strabo and Herman the Lame alone will ensure the island's undying fame.

We visited the museum and learned that the monastery had been founded by a Celtic monk called Pirmin. That was the first surprise. And then I began to remember the conference in Dublin and the peregrinations of the Irish monks. After viewing and photographing the exhibits, we had lunch in the museum café, which doubled as a bookshop. It was a rare moment of decadence, something that the parents of a large family seldom experience. Afterwards, at the bookstall, I saw a graphic art hardback book that caught my eye. It was written in German which I could not read, but I understood it was not about Pirmin, but two other Irish monks who had come before. Columbanus was mentioned. The pictures showed a band of monks building huts in the wilderness. I turned a page and saw a monk was breaking down a pagan shrine, which I guessed was what passed for cultural appropriation in his day. A few pages on some monks had been set upon and slain. I couldn't tell if it was Columban who died, and I didn't bother to buy the book as none of my children were learning German.

So, once again the knowledge of these things remained dormant until twelve months later, during the Brexit vote that I began to casually thumb a copy of Thomas Cahill's popular history 'How the Irish Saved Civilisation'. But at that time, I was up to my eyes writing two large Renaissance novels and had no plans to make the European debate a subject of serious study. As a dyslexic, I am not so proficient as Benjamin Disraeli who said, 'When I want to read a book, I write one.' I am a Landscape Architect-turned-property developer-turned-novelist with six home-schooled children. My only recourse is to hide with my books in a laundry room so small that even the mice are hunchbacks. Furthermore, I am not even someone of deep political convictions, especially about the Brexit debate where the shrill demagogy – more heat than light – was only matched by the absence of meaningful data upon which the electorate were supposed to make so momentous a decision.

But when I finally finished the Renaissance novels that I had been working on for three years, and was walking around Brussels, Liege and Antwerp in July 2017, the idea came back to me with force. It involves two areas of history with which I am only on nodding terms, and which I have never previously seriously studied or written about – which for me was a bonus, as I love new subjects. It took me a few weeks of further reading and pouring over maps to convince myself that I could bring anything like a coherent structure to bear on such a sprawling subject. But when that was done, I began more and more to see how a split biographical work of this manner, could form one ideal set of binoculars with which to observe the drama of Western Civilisation. After that, a further four years went very quickly! The rest, as they say, is history.

Appendix 2 - Key Dates & Context for Columban

211 – 4th Feb Septimus Severus dies in Eboracum, York. The Antonine or Severan Wall dies with him.

306 – Constantine declared emperor in York

313 – Toleration of Christians

367 – The great barbarian conspiracy is launched against roman Britain by coordinated attacks of Picts, Irish, Saxons and rebellious frontier troops.

378 – Eastern Empire defeated at Hadrianopolis and emperor Valens killed by Gothic army

383 – Roman troops in Britain call Magnus Maximus Emperor. He crosses over to the continent and makes Trier his capital.

391 – Emperor Theodosius issues laws against pagan sacrifice

401 – Goths led by Alaric enter Italy, only to be driven out by Stilicho a year later

405 – A Germanic army led by Radagaisus, is defeated at Fiesole, near Florence

406 – Rhine freezes, and on the last day of the year Vandals, Sueves and Alans pour enmass into Gaul and ravage it

407 – Last roman emperor in Britain, Constantine III (a usurper) leaves for the continent

408 – The Goths under Alaric re-enter Italy, but this time General Stilicho has been murdered with the connivance of Emperor Honorius.

409 – The Vandals cross into Spain

410 – Roman administration dissolves in Britain. Alaric sacks a surprised Rome (28th August). Not quite recovered from the shock, Emperor Honorius replies to the groans of the Britons with the immortal words; 'look to your own defences.'

418 – The Anglo-Saxon chronicle describes Romans hiding their treasure and fleeing overseas to Gaul.

429 – The Vandals cross into Africa. Germanus of Auxerre comes to Britain in order to fight the British Heresy of Pelagianism.

430 - Augustine, dying, listening to barbarians battering at the gates of Thargaste, having just finished writing *Civitas Dei*, blaming the pagans and not the Christians for the collapse of the empire.

431 – Pope Celestine sends Palladius (Patrick?) to establish bishoprics in Hibernia.

432 – Justinian's plague, 100 million die, perhaps half the population (he survived it but became even more tyrannical

447 – 'Days as dark as night' - *Annales Cambriae*

457 – 'Patrick goes to the Lord' - *Annales Cambriae*

453 – Attila dies and his empire dissolves

476 – The last Western Roman emperor Romulus Augustus is deposed by Odoacer.

486 – Pagan Clovis defeats last Roman prefect in Gaul at the battle of Soissons and so becomes king of Franks. He converts to Christianity 10 years later and then dies in 511.

489 – Theodoric deposes Odoacer

496 – Clovis and army become Christians, Clovis conversion, almost chosen people

533 – The Vandals are defeated in North Africa and those lands were incorporated in Byzantium.

535 – The Byzantine armies begin a twenty-year war against Ostrogothic Italy.

537 – *Annales Cambriae* records that the Dux Brittonum called Arthur dies in the strife of Camlann.

541 – Bubonic plague spreads from Egypt to Europe

543 – Columban born, and disastrous earthquakes shake other parts of the world.

544 – Cassiodorus founded his learning monastery called the Vivarium.

546 – Totilla enters Rome and would have raised it to the ground if not for the pleading of Belisarius. Audoin founds the new Lombard kingdom beyond the Save river.

547 – King Ida accedes to throne of Bernicia. San Vitale (Ravenna) and Bamburgh castle are being built. A plague described by Gildas reaches Britain. The *Annales Cambriae* record that Maelgwyn of Gwynedd dies in plague.

549 – Finnian of Clonard dies. The Sassanid dynasty of the neo-Persian empire are cultivating music, chess and dance.

550 – Columban's co-worker Gall is born. Totilla conquers Rome a second time, while Procopius is writing up a history of the Gothic and, Vandal and Persian wars. Draw looms in Egypt are weaving patterned silk and the Indians are playing chess. St David is active in Wales

552 – Emperor Shotoko Taishi introduces Buddhism into Japan. Justinian sends missionaries to China and Ceylon to smuggle out silk worms, thus beginning the European silk industry.

553 – Ostrogoths finally defeated and ruled by the Byzantine Empire

555 – Monastery at Bangor (Ireland) established

557 – Justinian reconquered the West and inadvertently destroyed it, ushering in the Dark Ages.

558 – Clovis' son Clothar I, reunites the kingdom of the Franks only to be divided among his 4 sons three years later

560 – The great abbey of Bangor in Wales is founded by Deniol. The Irish monk Fridian (who had been bishop of Lucca) dies 588. (His relics are in his church in a glass coffin.)

563 – Columbkille leaves for Iona. 20-year-old Columbanus will certainly have heard of it, and is maybe itching for white martyrdom too. Christendom's largest church *Hagia Sopia* in Constantinople is consecrated.

568 – The Lombards invade and occupy northern Italy.

565 – Justinian succeeded by his nephew and the Lombards drive the Byzantines to Ravenna.

570 – Mohamed born

573 – Clothar's sons fighting. One of them Sigibert will die three years later leaving his widowed queen Brunhilda to reign as regent.

583 – Cassiodorus dies aged 93

584 – Clothar II (son of Chilperic who fought his brother Sigibert) becomes king of Neustria (proves a helper to Columban 20 years later)

585 – Columban arrives in Brittany aged 42. Leovigild conquers all of Spain. Horyu-ji temple built in Nara, Japan.

589 – Council of Toledo, when Spain is reconciled from Arianism to Rome.

590 – Columban given Luxeuil. Gregory is made Pope. There is a plague in Rome. Gregory of Tours mentions window glass in church, and completes his history of the Franks 4 years later.

592 – Guntram dies

594 – Ends nearly 50 years of plague that has halved the European population.

596 – Chilbert dies

597 – Augustine arrives in England, a year later the first school is founded. It becomes the oldest continuous school in world. Columbkille dies, 9th June, in Iona

600 – Barbarian incursions in Western Europe cease. Fortunatus Ventantius, bishop of Poitiers, author and poet dies. In Rome, currency and monetary system collapses and is replaced by barter. Gregory the Great works to peaceably covert the Jews. He produces a picture book to teach the scriptures to illiterates, and a manual for the use of clergy. In the same year the lyric poetry of the T'ang dynasty is helping spread the Chin language. Isidore of Seville is collecting Greek and Roman manuscripts. Construction of Arles Cathedral begins. Development in the goldsmith's craft that allows flowering of the Merovingian jewellery.

601 – Comgall dies

603 – Frankish bishops sit in judgement of Columban, who refuses to attend but sends a letter. History records the first mention of London and the founding of St Paul's church. All the Lombards convert to Nicaean Christianity. This is the year Augustine alienates the indigenous British church. It will take another 65 years before the equally strident Wilfred will bring the British church more fully under the Latin system.

604 – Pope Gregory dies and Columban writes to Boniface, and the first bell rings in Rome. The Shotoko code in Japan demands veneration of Bhudda, his priests and codes.

607 – Completion of Horyuji Temple and hospital, oldest surviving wooden building in the world

610 – Columban refuses the king access to the cloister and, at the age of 67, is sent into exile. Mohamed's vision in Arabia signals the beginning of Islam. Phocas, the

usurper of eastern empire (having killed Maurice 8 years earlier) is killed by Heraclius, who will reign for the next 31 years.

611 – Columbanus left Neustria for the court of King Theudebert II of Austrasia, in the north-eastern part of the Kingdom of the Merovingian Franks

612 – Columban arrives in Milan and Gall founds a monastery in Saint Gallen. Theodoric is killed by his brother. Arnulf, counsellor to Clothar II, becomes bishop of Metz and his wife enters a convent. His daughter marries the Mayor of the Palace Pepin of Landen. This joining of their two houses would eventually lead to the great Carolingian dynasty.

614 – Columban founds Bobbio. In France the *Edictum Clothacharii* defines rights of king, nobles and church.

615 – Columban dies, and in Britain, Aethelfrith massacres Bangor-is-y-Coed monks.

633 – Muslim armies begin to conquer the Levant.

640 – Muslim armies extend their power in the Aegean and Africa.

646 – Muslims control all Egypt.

674 – Muslim armies blockade Constantinople.

711 – Muslim Armies enter Spain and begin their successful conquest of the peninsula.

732 – Muslim raids in Francia, but are defeated by Charles Martel at Poitiers.

768 – Accession of Martel's grandson Charlemagne

800 – Charlemagne crowned in Rome as the first western emperor in 300 years.

From the front piece of the Annals of Cambriae

Appendix 3 - Key Dates and Context for Robert Schuman

1886 – 9 June: Birth of Robert Schuman, in Clausen, a suburb of Luxembourg. (same year as Rerum Novarum, a seminal papal encyclical about the conditions of the working classes, and Catholic social teaching is published.)

1900 – Schuman's Father, Jean-Pierre Schuman dies.

1896 – Secondary education at the Athénée – Luxembourg.

1903 – The French and English sign the Entente Cordiale. In London the Russian Social Democrats split – the new Bolshevik faction is led by Lenin and Trotsky.

1904 – Schuman receives his Baccalauréat at the Lycée Impérial - Metz.

1904 -1910 – Schuman reads law at the Universities of Berlin, Munich, Bonn and Strasbourg, Portuguesel revolution and republic, China abolishes slavery, Japan annexes Korea

1911 – Schuman's mother dies.

1912 – Schuman's final examination in Strasbourg, called to the bar in Alsace Lorraine. He opens his own legal office in Metz.

1913 – Schuman attends the German Catholic Congress (Katholikentag) in Metz.

1914 – Schuman called up for service in an auxiliary service of the German army - Metz. WWI

1915 – Schuman seconded to the Civil Service in Boulay.

1917 – The Russian revolution

1919 – Schuman elected MP for Moselle, appointed to the Consultative Council of Alsace Lorraine (President of the Council for General Affairs linked to administration, legislation and security). First League of Nations meeting for the peace conference opens at Versailles. German fleet scuppered at Scapa flow and peace treaty signed. Allied peace treaty with Austria signed in St. Germain, and the Hapsburgs exiled. Mussolini founds the Fascist party

1920 – Schuman nominated for the Consultative Council of Alsace Lorraine in Strasbourg (President of the Council in charge of general issues linked to administration, legislation and security). Conference in San Remo to discuss German reparations even as Hitler announces 25-point program at the Hofbrauhuas in Munich. The year following Mussolini will march on Rome and form a Fascist government and dissolves all non-fascist parties.

1924 – Schuman re-elected as MP for Moselle. The year before Hitler's coup d'état in Munich fails and the US withdraws from the Rhineland, Germany declares a policy of passive resistance, French army occupy Karlsruhe, Darmstadt and Mannheim. Lenin dies. Hitler sentenced to 5 years in prison but then released after 8 months. Fascist elections show 65% favour Mussolini.

1928 – Schuman elected MP for the constituency of Thionville East. Allied Military control of Germany ends. The German economy crashes on Black Friday. Gottfried Feber publishes 'The program for the NSDAP'. Hitler's Nazi party in Germany has been a member of the League of Nations for two years. Dr. Joseph Goebbels named Nazi Gauleiter in Berlin. German ministers have already been in office in Czechoslovakia for two years.

1929 – Schuman becomes a member of the Finance Commission (until 1939, Secretary of this Commission from 1932-36). Himmler appointed by Hitler as Reichsfuhrer S.S.

1930 – Last allied troops leave the Rhineland and Saar region.

1932 – Schuman re-elected MP for the constituency of Thionville East. There is mass famine in the USSR as Stalin rolls out his second, five-year plan.

1933 – Reichstag fire, Goebbels is appointed minister of propaganda. Herman Goering named Prussian Prime minister, Hitler is granted dictatorial powers even as he suppresses as all other political parties. Boycotts of Jews begin in Germany. German labour unions suppressed. 92% of German electorate vote for the Nazis at Danzig elections. The start of 60,000 emigrations of artists and performers from Germany. The first concentration camps are built into which 8-11 million people will enter over the next 12 years, half never to leave alive.

1936 – Schuman elected General Councillor for the Cattenom region. Germany had just repudiated the treaty of Versailles, and introduced compulsory military service. Nuremburg laws against the Jew. There are now German troops occupying the Rhineland, and Hitler, with a 99% vote publishes his 4-year plan. Spanish civil war begins. The Frank and Lira are both devalued. Mussolini and Hitler form the Berlin Axis. Mussolini invades Abyssinia.

1940 – Schuman nominated Under Secretary for the Presidency of the Council for Refugees under the Raynaud and Pétain governments (March to July). On 14th September Schuman is arrested by the Gestapo.

1941 – 13th April Schuman confined to house arrest in Neustadt (Palatinate).

1942 – 1st August: Schuman escapes from Neustadt and crosses the Vosges Mountains into Free France taking vital data for the resistance and the first qualified news of the Holocaust. In November, he goes underground for two years (aged 56).

1944 – In September, Schuman returns to Moselle, where he is elected MP.

1945 – Schuman re-elected MP for the Moselle, and also becomes a member of the Finance Commission (November 1945- May 1946). The Nuremburg trials begin and Petain, Laval and Quisling are sentenced to death. (Petain's death sentence commuted) Hitler commits suicide and Mussolini is killed by Italian partisans.

1946 – Schuman is re-elected MP for the Moselle(Member of the Finance Commission). East German democrats merge with communists, Gaspari becomes Head of

State. Another peace conference held in Paris attended by 21 nations. Nuremburg trials sentence ten Nazis to death.

1947 – Schuman becomes Finance Minister under the Ramadier Government (January to November) President of the Council (24th November to 19th July 1948). Year of the Marshall Plan for European reconstruction and recovery. More peace treaties signed in Paris and the Benelux agreement ratified.

1948 – Schuman appointed Foreign Minister. Churchill chairs the Hague Congress on European unity. USSR stops road and rail link between East and West Berlin. Communist coup in Czechlosavakia, and China.

1949 – In August, Schuman undertakes an inspection visit to the Rhineland as French foreign minister where he finally meets Adenauer at his home at Zennigsweg, Rhöndorf. NATO signed in Washington. US grants $5.43 billion loan to Europe. Most European currencies are devalued.

1951 – Schuman re-elected MP for Moselle, and delivers his famous speech (The Schuman Declaration) in May. Petain dies aged 94.

1952 – Schuman involved in crisis over Saar administration

1955 – Schuman elected President of the European Movement (1955-1961).

1956 – Schuman re-elected MP for Moselle.

1958 – Schuman made President of the European Parliamentary Assembly in Strasbourg (1958-1960).

1960 – At the end of his term in office at the European Parliament, Schuman is awarded the title "Father of Europe".

1962 – Retirement from political life.

1963 – 4th September: Robert Schuman dies in Scy-Chazelles

Schuman's grave in the Eglise Saint-Quentin opposite his home

Appendix 4 – A Post-War European Integration & Brexit Timeline

1945 – The end of World War II

1948 – Congress of The Hague

1951 – Treaty of Paris creates Coal and Steel Community

1957 – Treaty of Rome creates the European Economic Community (by "The Six": Belgium, France, Italy, Luxembourg, the Netherlands, and West Germany)

1963 – Ankara Agreement initiated a three-step process toward creating a Customs Union which would help secure Turkey's full membership in the EEC.

1963 – Charles de Gaulle vetoes UK entry

1967 – ECSC, EEC, and Euratom merged

1973 – Accession of Denmark, Ireland, and the UK

1979 – First direct elections to Parliament

1981 – Accession of Greece

1985 – Delors Commission, Greenland leaves Community.

1986 – Single European Act; Accession of Portugal and Spain; flag adopted

1989 – The fall of the Iron Curtain in Eastern Europe

1992 – Maastricht Treaty formally called the Treaty on European Union - The European Union is born and Euro was introduced as the fellow currency - Denmark and the UK are not included in the EMU (European Monetary Union).

1993 – Copenhagen criteria defined

1995 – Accession of Austria, Finland, and Sweden

1999 – Fraud in the Commission results in resignation

2002 – The euro replaces twelve national currencies

2004 – Accession of ten countries (Cyprus, Czech Republic, Estonia, Hungary, Latvia, Lithuania, Malta, Poland, Slovakia, Slovenia); signing of Constitution

2005 – France and the Netherlands reject the Constitution after their own internal referendums (for France it was a binding one only)

2007 – Accession of Bulgaria and Romania

2009 – Lisbon Treaty abolishes the three pillars of the European Union

2013 – Accession of Croatia

2016 – UK holds a Membership Referendum and votes to leave the European Union

2017 – Negotiations between UK and the EU officially started in June 2017

2017 – Start of Brexit: On 29 March 2017, the Government of the United Kingdom invoked Article 50 of the Treaty on European Union. The UK was due to leave the EU on 29 March 2019 at 11 p.m. GMT, when the period for negotiating a withdrawal agreement was set to end

2020 – UK leaves the EU after the Brexit withdrawal agreement takes effect on 31 January 2020 at 11 p.m. GMT

OTHER WORKS BY THIS AUTHOR :

SAVING EUROPE DOCUMENTARY: (Youtube channel)
- Pravda Media, 2021. www.savingeurope.com

THE RENAISSANCE TRILOGY: (Historical Fiction)

- THE HERETIC: Tudor thriller/novel of ideas. First published by Lion Fiction (19 Sept. 2014) N.B. This book, which is chronologically the 3rd of the trilogy, will be republished by Pravda Press in 2021-2022.
- ABSOLUTION: Italian Renaissance thriller & novel of ideas (Pravda Press 2021)
- THE SHADOW OF CAIN: Italian Renaissance thriller & novel of ideas (Pravda Press 2021)

THE WILL HOUSTON MYSTERIES: (Young Adult Fiction)

- ON THE SHOULDERS OF GIANTS: Piquant Fiction (25 Feb. 2011) with accompanying Music album (CD/Download)
- THE OLD SCHOOL SECRETS: Piquant Editions (25 Feb. 2016)
- THE CRADLE SNATCHERS: Piquant Editions; Illustrated edition (8 Jun. 2017)

THE LINE: (Apologetics/Devotional)
- Pravda Press (1 July 2011)
- accompanying music album (CD/Download)

JOHN MARK: (Historical Fiction)
- Pravda Press 2022